Clinical Psychology

I dedicate this book to my children, Benjamin and Daniel.
I love you and I'm proud of you every day!

Clinical Psychology

Science, Practice, and Culture

Third Edition

DSM-5 Update

Andrew M. Pomerantz

Southern Illinois University Edwardsville

Los Angeles | London | New Delhi
Singapore | Washington DC

Los Angeles | London | New Delhi
Singapore | Washington DC

FOR INFORMATION:

SAGE Publications, Inc.
2455 Teller Road
Thousand Oaks, California 91320
E-mail: order@sagepub.com

SAGE Publications Ltd.
1 Oliver's Yard
55 City Road
London EC1Y 1SP
United Kingdom

SAGE Publications India Pvt. Ltd.
B 1/I 1 Mohan Cooperative Industrial Area
Mathura Road, New Delhi 110 044
India

SAGE Publications Asia-Pacific Pte. Ltd.
3 Church Street
#10-04 Samsung Hub
Singapore 049483

Copyright © 2014 by SAGE Publications, Inc.

Printed in the United States of America

A catalog record of this book is available from the Library of Congress.

ISBN 978-1-4833-4504-8

This book is printed on acid-free paper.

Acquisitions Editor: Kassie Graves
Editorial Assistant: Elizabeth Luizzi
Digital Content Editor: Megan Koraly
Production Editor: Laura Barrett
Typesetter: C&M Digitals (P) Ltd.
Proofreader: Eleni Georgiou
Indexer: Sylvia Coates
Cover Designer: Candice Harman
Marketing Manager: Shari Countryman

13 14 15 16 17 10 9 8 7 6 5 4 3 2 1

Brief Contents

Detailed Contents

PART 3: PSYCHOTHERAPY   261

11. General Issues in Psychotherapy   263

Preface

Clinical psychology is an increasingly expansive field. This book effectively introduces its students to the vast range of issues it encompasses. My rationale for creating this textbook was multifaceted:

- *To provide a balanced approach to clinical psychology.* There is no shortage of healthy debates within clinical psychology, and I believe that the ideal way to introduce students to the spectrum of opinions represented by clinical psychologists is to maximize the even-handedness of the text.
- *To promote cultural competence.* Clinical psychologists must appreciate cultural factors in all their professional activities, and as students familiarize themselves with the field, cultural sensitivity should be woven into their lessons.
- *To offer many illustrative examples,* including clinical applications for clinically relevant topics.
- *To write in a professional yet clear and accessible style and include up-to-date information on all topics.* Also, the text covers a distinctly broad range of topics while maintaining an adequate degree of depth.

The first and second editions of this text were enthusiastically received by both instructors and students. We were pleased to learn that they found numerous components of the book—its emphasis on issues of culture, its unique pedagogical features, its scholarly yet readable style, its many clinical examples, its balanced approach, and its ancillary package, among others—beneficial to student learning.

What's the Same in the Third Edition

This edition retains all the strengths of the previous edition of the book:

- *Considering Culture* boxes appear in almost every chapter. These boxes highlight multicultural aspects of the various topics covered throughout the book. Along with the discussions of culture integrated throughout the text, these boxes encourage the student to appreciate culturally relevant issues surrounding research, psychotherapy, assessment, and other topics.
- Chapter 4, "Cultural Issues in Clinical Psychology," is entirely devoted to topics related to multiculturalism.
- Interviews with nine renowned experts in multicultural clinical work appear in Chapter 4 and on the companion website. These experts—Melba Vasquez, Frederick Leong, Richard Williams, Monica McGoldrick, Joseph Trimble, Nadya Faoud, Kathleen Bieschke, Karen Haboush, and Lewis Schlosser—each discuss cultural competence with a specific cultural group based on ethnicity, religion, gender, or sexual orientation.

- *Metaphorically Speaking* boxes appear in almost every chapter. These boxes use metaphors to teach students about novel concepts by drawing parallels to concepts with which they are already familiar.

- *Denise in _____ Psychotherapy* boxes appear in all the chapters relevant to psychotherapy. "Denise" is a fictional therapy client created exclusively for this textbook. She is introduced at the end of Chapter 11, and the *Denise* boxes that appear at the end of each of the subsequent chapters illustrate how she would be treated according to psychodynamic, humanistic, behavioral, cognitive, and group approaches.

- Chapter 3, "Current Controversies in Clinical Psychology," is devoted entirely to contemporary issues such as prescription privileges, evidence-based practice, and technological advances.

- Chapter 5, "Ethical Issues in Clinical Psychology," is devoted entirely to ethical issues in clinical psychology.

- Chapters 12 through 16 are each devoted entirely to a particular approach or modality of psychotherapy (i.e., psychodynamic, humanistic, behavioral, cognitive, and group/family), and each contains coverage of the most current versions of these therapies, including mindfulness-based therapies, motivational interviewing, and behavioral activation.

What's New in the Third Edition

This edition includes numerous important enhancements and updates:

- More than 350 new references, including more than 250 published since 2010, ensuring extremely current coverage across all chapters

- Icons (three to five per chapter) in the margin referring students to web-based resources (e.g., videos, websites, articles), accessible through the student study site, that have been carefully selected to enhance learning of key concepts

- Mobile tags (QR codes) at the end of each chapter linking the student via smartphone to brief videos of the author offering clinical examples from his own practice, chapter summaries, or commentary to enhance learning of chapter concepts

- Expanded coverage of graduate training, including application suggestions, in Chapter 1 ("Clinical Psychology: Definition and Training")

- Expanded coverage of cybertherapy in Chapter 3 ("Current Controversies in Clinical Psychology")

- Expanded coverage of evidence-based practice, including issues related to dissemination and culture-based adaptation, in Chapter 3 ("Current Controversies in Clinical Psychology") and Chapter 4 ("Cultural Issues in Clinical Psychology")

- Enhanced and updated chapters on psychotherapy, incorporating new material on positive interventions and strength-based counseling, stages of change, psychotherapy relationships that work, empirical evidence for specific components of psychodynamic and humanistic therapies, and more
- Enhanced and updated chapters on assessment, incorporating new material on possible changes in the upcoming revision of the *Diagnostic and Statistical Manual of Mental Disorders*; new coverage of the Wechsler Memory Scale; and new editions of tests such as the WIAT-III, MMPI-2-RF, and others
- Coverage of new trends in health psychology (Chapter 18), including values affirmation and patient-centered medical homes

What's New in the DSM-5 Update

The publication of *DSM-5* in May 2013 represents a major event in the field of clinical psychology. Students deserve current coverage of the changes the DSM-5 introduced, as well as the process that led to its publication and the consequences it may have for our field. Thus, this *DSM-5* Update includes:

- Detailed descriptions of what changed in *DSM-5*, including:
  - new features (e.g., Arabic rather than Roman numeral system to facilitate the transition to a "living document"),
  - new disorders (e.g., disruptive mood dysregulation disorder, mild neurocognitive disorder, binge eating disorder),
  - and adjusted criteria for existing disorders (e.g., autism spectrum disorder encompassing autism and Asperger disorder, revision of the bereavement exclusion criteria for major depressive episodes, more inclusive criteria for bulimia nervosa and attention-deficit/hyperactivity disorder)
- Coverage of what didn't change in *DSM-5* (changes that were considered but rejected)
- Coverage of how *DSM-5* was made, including:
  - Steps in the revision process
  - Controversies that arose during the process
  - Criticisms by prominent authors about the process
  - Forces that may have influenced the process
- Possible consequences of *DSM-5*, including
  - Continued broadening of the scope of mental illness
  - Treatment issues (e.g., insurance coverage, psychotherapy, drug treatment)
  - Other implications (e.g., legal issues, disability claims)

A Chapter-by-Chapter Overview

The textbook begins with a definition of clinical psychology, a consideration of how clinical psychologists are trained, and a survey of the professional activities and settings of clinical psychologists (Chapter 1). Chapter 2 considers the rich history of clinical psychology, and Chapter 3 highlights the current controversies that characterize the field. Chapter 4 discusses the cultural issues relevant to clinical psychology. Chapter 5 offers detailed analysis of some of the most important ethical issues for clinical psychologists, including confidentiality and multiple relationships, among others. Chapter 6 focuses on research and describes both "how" and "why" clinical psychologists conduct it.

Chapter 7 marks the beginning of the Assessment section of the textbook, and it focuses on issues of diagnosis and classification of disorders, with special attention paid to the recent publication of DSM-5. Chapter 8 spotlights the clinical interview. Chapter 9 outlines intellectual and neuropsychological assessment, while Chapter 10 focuses on personality and behavioral assessment.

The section on psychotherapy begins with Chapter 11, which provides an overview of general psychotherapy issues such as efficacy, effectiveness, and the commonality of various psychotherapy approaches. Chapters 12 through 15 each focus on a single approach to individual psychotherapy: psychodynamic (Chapter 12), humanistic (Chapter 13), behavioral (Chapter 14), and cognitive (Chapter 15). Chapter 16 is separated into two parts, one covering group therapy and the other family therapy.

Special topics are featured in the last three chapters. Chapter 17 discusses clinical child and adolescent psychology, including assessment and psychotherapy topics. The final two chapters cover growing specialty areas among clinical psychologists: health psychology (Chapter 18) and forensic psychology (Chapter 19).

Supplements for Students and Instructors

Student Study Site: www.sagepub.com/pomerantz3eupdate

This open access student study site provides a variety of additional resources to build on students' understanding of the book content and extend their learning beyond the classroom. Students will have access to the following resources:

- Each chapter in the text is accompanied by **self-quizzes**, which includes 10-15 true/false and multiple-choice questions for students to independently assess their progress in learning course material.

- **eFlashcards** reinforce student understanding and learning of key terms and concepts that are outlined in the book.

- Fictional vignettes in the form of **Sample Case Studies** allow students the opportunity to apply therapeutic principles introduced in key chapters.
- **Culture Expert Interviews** with renowned experts in multicultural issues discuss psychotherapy, assessment, and training regarding specific cultural groups, including some based on ethnicity, religion, gender, and sexual orientation.
- **SAGE Journal Articles** provide access to recent, relevant full-text articles from SAGE's leading research journals. Each article includes discussion questions to focus and guide student interpretation.
- Carefully selected **web resources** feature relevant content for use in independent and classroom-based exploration of key topics.
- **Mock Assessment Data** provides realistic assessment profiles to invite in-depth consideration of fictional clients.

Instructor Teaching Site: www.sagepub.com/pomerantz3eupdate

A password-protected instructor teaching site offers the following resources for each chapter:

- An updated **test bank** available in Microsoft Word offers a diverse set of test questions and answers to aid instructors in assessing students' progress and understanding.
- **PowerPoint presentations** designed to assist with lecture and review highlight essential content, features, and artwork from the book.
- **Classroom Activities and discussion questions** are provided to reinforce active learning.

End of Chapter QR codes

QR codes at the end of each chapter link to chapter summary videos by the author. Visit http://gettag.mobi using your smartphone browser to download the free Microsoft Tag app. Once installed, scan the tags to go directly to these brief videos.

Margin icons

Icons appearing in the margin of the text will direct you to corresponding links on the open-access study site. This additional media includes video, audio and web links which elaborate on key concepts within the chapter.

Acknowledgments

This book was undoubtedly a team effort. Many, many people facilitated or contributed to it in meaningful ways. For what they offered before or during the process of this book's creation, I am immeasurably appreciative. I wish to sincerely thank:

- my wife, Melissa Lynn Pomerantz—your love, support, confidence, understanding, belief, and patience made this book possible;

- my parents, Carol and Bill Pomerantz, for a lifetime of love and support;

- my colleagues and chapter coauthors, Laura Pawlow and Bryce Sullivan— I greatly appreciate your expertise and collaborative spirit;

- my teammates at SAGE: Kassie Graves, Reid Hester, Diane McDaniel, Eve Oettinger, Lisa Sheldon Brown, MaryAnn Vail, Sarah Quesenberry, Sarita Sarak, Megan Granger, Laura Barrett, Jennifer Barron, Candice Harman, Lauren Habib, and many more—your receptiveness, patience, support, and input have proven that the value of the "working alliance" is as great in publishing as it is in psychotherapy;

- Mary Ellen Lepionka—you have been a crucial source of publishing expertise, wisdom, and advice, and I am truly grateful for your interest and willingness to listen;

- the reviewers—M. Colleen Byrne, University of Maryland; Krista Fritson, University of Nebraska at Kearney; Robert Hard, Albertus Magnus College-New Haven; Cindy Lou Matyi, Ohio University, Chillicothe Campus; Jill Panuzio, VA Boston Healthcare System; Llewellyn E. Piper, Campbell University; Erica Seemann, The University of Alabama at Huntsville; and Shirley Thomas, University of Nottingham.

- my undergrad professors at Washington University, who sparked my interest in clinical psychology and provided a strong foundation of knowledge;

- my graduate professors at Saint Louis University, whose trust, patience, and attention facilitated my competence and confidence;

- my clients and my students, who have taught me immeasurably;

- the staff at my various library "hangouts," who provided essential resources: SIUE, WUSTL, SLU, St. Louis County Library (Midcounty), Missouri Institute of Mental Health, University City Public Library, and St. Louis Public Library; and, finally,

- the musicians who inhabit my iPod, frequent companions during my researching and writing process.

About the Author

Andrew M. Pomerantz, PhD, is a professor of psychology and director of the Clinical Adult Psychology Graduate Program at Southern Illinois University Edwardsville. He teaches a variety of undergraduate and graduate courses related to clinical psychology. He also maintains a part-time private practice of clinical psychology in St. Louis, MO. He earned his BA in psychology from Washington University in St. Louis and his MA and PhD in clinical psychology from Saint Louis University. He completed his predoctoral internship at Indiana University School of Medicine Psychology Training Consortium. He has served on the editorial boards of the *Journal of Clinical Psychology, Ethics & Behavior,* and the *Journal of Contemporary Psychotherapy,* and has published articles in numerous professional journals, including *Professional Psychology: Research and Practice, Teaching of Psychology, Ethics & Behavior,* and *Training and Education in Professional Psychology.* He also coauthored *Psychological Assessment and Report Writing* with Karen Goldfinger. His primary research interests include psychotherapy and ethical/professional issues in clinical psychology. He served two terms as president of Psychotherapy Saint Louis and is a member of the American Psychological Association.

Introducing
Clinical Psychology

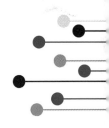

Clinical Psychology
Definition and Training

Welcome to clinical psychology! Throughout this book, you'll learn quite a bit about this field: history and current controversies, interviewing and psychological assessment methods, and psychotherapy approaches. Let's start by defining it.

What Is Clinical Psychology?

Original Definition

The term **clinical psychology** was first used in print by **Lightner Witmer** in 1907. Witmer was also the first to operate a psychological clinic (Benjamin, 1996, 2005). More about Witmer's pioneering contributions will appear in Chapter 2, but for now, let's consider how he chose to define his emerging field. Witmer envisioned clinical psychology as a discipline with similarities to a variety of other fields, specifically medicine, education, and sociology. A clinical psychologist, therefore, was a person whose work with others involved aspects of treatment, education, and interpersonal issues. At his clinic, the first clients were children with behavioral or educational problems. However, even in his earliest writings, Witmer (1907) foresaw clinical psychology as applicable to people of all ages and with a variety of presenting problems.

More Recent Definitions

Defining clinical psychology is a greater challenge today than it was in Witmer's time. The field has witnessed such tremendous growth in a wide variety of directions that most simple, concise definitions fall short of capturing the field in its entirety. As a group, contemporary clinical psychologists do *many* different things, with *many* different goals, for *many* different people.

Some in recent years have tried to offer "quick" definitions of clinical psychology to provide a snapshot of what our field entails. For example, according to various introductory psychology textbooks and dictionaries of psychology, clinical psychology is essentially the branch of psychology that studies, assesses, and treats people with psychological problems or disorders (e.g., Myers, 2013, VandenBos, 2007). Such a definition sounds reasonable enough, but it is not without its shortcomings. It doesn't portray all that clinical psychologists do, how they do it, or who they do it for.

An accurate, comprehensive, contemporary definition of clinical psychology would need to be more inclusive and descriptive. The **Division of Clinical Psychology (Division 12)** of the **American Psychological Association (APA)** defines clinical psychology as follows:

> The field of Clinical Psychology integrates science, theory, and practice to understand, predict, and alleviate maladjustment, disability, and discomfort as well as to promote human adaptation, adjustment, and personal development. Clinical Psychology focuses on the intellectual, emotional, biological, psychological, social, and behavioral aspects of human functioning across the life span, in varying cultures, and at all socioeconomic levels. (APA, 2012a)

The sheer breadth of this definition reflects the rich and varied growth that the field has seen in the century since Witmer originally identified it. (As Norcross and Sayette, 2012, put it, "Perhaps the safest observation about clinical psychology is that both the field and its practitioners continue to outgrow the classic definitions" [p. 1].) Certainly, its authors do not intend to suggest that each clinical psychologist spends equal time on each component of that definition. But, collectively, the work of clinical psychologists does indeed encompass such a wide range. For the purposes of this textbook, a similarly broad but somewhat more succinct definition will suffice: Clinical psychology involves rigorous study and applied practice directed toward understanding and improving the psychological facets of the human experience, including but not limited to issues or problems of behavior, emotions, or intellect.

⊕ **Web Link 1.1**
APA Division 12

Education and Training in Clinical Psychology

In addition to explicit definitions such as those listed above, we can infer what clinical psychology is by learning how clinical psychologists are educated and trained. The basic components of clinical psychology training are common across programs and are well established (Vaughn, 2006). The aspiring clinical psychologist must obtain a doctoral degree in clinical psychology, about 2,800 of which are awarded each year (Norcross & Sayette, 2012). Most students enter a doctoral program with only a bachelor's degree, but some enter with a master's degree. For those entering with a bachelor's degree, training typically consists of at least 4 years of intensive, full-time coursework, followed by a 1-year, full-time predoctoral internship. Required coursework includes courses on psychotherapy, assessment, statistics, research design and methodology, biological bases of behavior, cognitive-affective bases of behavior, social bases of behavior, individual differences, and other areas. A master's thesis and doctoral dissertation are also commonly required, as is a practicum in which students start to accumulate supervised experience doing clinical work. When the on-campus course responsibilities are complete, students move on to the predoctoral internship, in which they take on greater clinical responsibilities and obtain supervised experience on a full-time basis. This predoctoral internship, along with the postdoctoral internship that occurs after the degree is obtained, is described in more detail below.

Beyond these basic requirements, especially in recent decades, there is no single way by which someone becomes a clinical psychologist. Instead, there are many paths to the profession. One indication of these many paths is the multitude of specialty tracks within clinical psychology doctoral programs. Indeed, more than half of APA-accredited doctoral programs in clinical psychology offer (but may not require) training within a specialty track. The most common specialty areas are clinical child, clinical health, forensic, family, and clinical neuropsychology (Perry & Boccaccini, 2009). (Each of these specialty areas receives attention in a later chapter of this book.) Another indication of the many paths to the profession of clinical psychology is the coexistence of three distinct models of training currently used by various graduate programs: the scientist-practitioner (Boulder) model, the practitioner-scholar (Vail) model, and the clinical scientist model. Let's consider each of these in detail.

Balancing Practice and Science: The Scientist-Practitioner (Boulder) Model

In 1949, the first conference on graduate training in clinical psychology was held in Boulder, Colorado. At this conference, training directors from around the country reached an important consensus: Training in clinical psychology should jointly emphasize both practice and research. In other words, to become a clinical psychologist, graduate students would need to receive training and display competence in the application of clinical methods (assessment, psychotherapy, etc.) *and* the research methods necessary to study and evaluate the field scientifically (Klonoff, 2011). Those at the conference also agreed that coursework should reflect this dual emphasis, with classes in statistics and research methods as well as classes in psychotherapy and assessment. Likewise, expectations for the more independent aspects of graduate training would also reflect the dual emphasis: Graduate students would (under supervision) conduct both clinical work and their own empirical research (thesis and dissertation). These graduate programs would continue to be housed in departments of psychology at universities, and graduates would be awarded the PhD degree. The term **scientist-practitioner model** was used to label this two-pronged approach to training (McFall, 2006; Norcross & Sayette, 2012).

For decades, the scientist-practitioner—or the **Boulder model**—approach to clinical psychology training unquestionably dominated the field (Klonoff, 2011). In fact, more programs still subscribe to the Boulder model than to any other. However, as time passed, developments took place that produced a wider range of options in clinical psychology training. The pendulum did not remain stationary at its midpoint between practice and research; instead, it swung toward one extreme and then toward the other.

Leaning Toward Practice: The Practitioner-Scholar (Vail) Model

In 1973, another conference on clinical psychology training was held in Colorado—this time, in the city of Vail. In the years preceding this conference, some discontent had arisen regarding the Boulder or scientist-practitioner model of training. In effect, many current and aspiring clinical psychologists had been asking, "Why do I need such extensive training as a scientist when my goal is simply to practice?" After all, only a minority of clinical psychologists were entering academia or otherwise conducting research as a primary professional task. Clinical practice was the more popular career choice (Boneau & Cuca, 1974; McConnell, 1984; Stricker, 2011), and many would-be clinical psychologists sought a doctoral-level degree with less extensive training in research and more extensive training in the development of applied clinical skills. So the **practitioner-scholar model** of training was born, along with a new type of doctoral degree, the **PsyD**. Since the 1970s, graduate programs offering the PsyD degree have proliferated. In fact, in the 1988 to 2001 time period alone, the number of PsyD degrees awarded increased by more than 160% (McFall, 2006). Compared with PhD programs, these programs typically offer more coursework directly related to practice and fewer related to research and statistics (Norcross et al., 2008). See Box 1.1 for a point-by-point comparison of PhD and PsyD models of training.

The growth of the PsyD (or practitioner-scholar or **Vail model**) approach to training in clinical psychology has influenced the field tremendously. Of course, before the emergence of the PsyD, the PhD was the only doctoral degree for clinical psychology. But, currently, more than half the doctoral degrees being awarded in the field are PsyD degrees (Norcross, Kohout, & Wicherski, 2005). The number of PsyD programs is actually quite small in comparison with the number of PhD programs—about 80 versus about 250—but the typical PsyD program accepts and graduates a much larger number of students than does the typical PhD program, so the number of people graduating with each degree is about the same (roughly 1,400 each) (Klonoff, 2011; Norcross & Sayette, 2012; Stricker, 2011).

● ● ● BOX 1.1 ● ● ●

Comparing PhD Programs With PsyD Programs

Quite a bit of variation exists between PhD programs, just as it does between PsyD programs. However, a few overall trends distinguish one degree from the other. *In general, compared with PhD programs, PsyD programs tend to*

- place less emphasis on research-related aspects of training and more emphasis on clinically relevant aspects of training;
- accept and enroll a much larger percentage and number of applicants;
- be housed in free-standing, independent (or university-affiliated) "professional schools," as opposed to departments of psychology in universities;
- accept students with lower Graduate Record Examination (GRE) scores and undergraduate grade point averages (GPAs);
- offer significantly less funding to enrolled students in the form of graduate assistantships, fellowships, tuition remission, and so on;

(Continued)

(Continued)

- accept and enroll a higher percentage of students who have already earned a master's degree;
- have lower rates of success placing their students in APA-accredited predoctoral internships;
- produce graduates who score lower on the national licensing exam (EPPP);
- graduate students in a briefer time period (about 1.5 years sooner);
- graduate students who pursue practice-related careers rather than academic or research-related careers; and
- have at least a slightly higher percentage of faculty members who subscribe to psychodynamic approaches, as opposed to cognitive-behavioral approaches.

Sources: From Gaddy, Charlot-Swilley, Nelson, and Reich (1995); Klonoff (2011); Mayne, Norcross, and Sayette (1994); McFall (2006); Norcross and Castle (2002); Norcross and Sayette (2012); Norcross, Sayette, Mayne, Karg, and Turkson (1998).

Table 1.1, which features data from a large-scale survey of graduate programs (Graham & Kim, 2011), offers more detailed findings regarding the general trends listed above.

Table 1.1 Comparison of PsyD and PhD Programs in Clinical Psychology

Variable	PsyD	PhD
Mean GRE (Verbal + Quantitative) score of admitted students	1116	1256
Mean undergraduate GPA	3.4	3.6
Percentage of students receiving at least partial tuition remission or assistantship	13.9	78.4
Number of students in incoming class	37.4	9.7
Percentage of applicants attending	26.3	7.4
Percentage successfully placed in APA-accredited predoctoral internships	66.0	92.8

Source: Graham, J. M., & Kim, Y.-H. (2011). Predictors of doctoral student success in professional psychology: characteristics of students, programs, and universities. *Journal of Clinical Psychology, 67,* 340–354.

Leaning Toward Science:
The Clinical Scientist Model

After the advent of the balanced Boulder model in the late 1940s and the subsequent emergence of the practice-focused Vail model in the 1970s, the more empirically minded members of the clinical psychology profession began a campaign for a strongly research-oriented model of training.

Indeed, in the 1990s, a movement toward increased empiricism took place among numerous graduate programs and prominent individuals involved in clinical psychology training. In essence, the leaders of this movement argued that science should be the bedrock of clinical psychology. They sought and created a model of training—the **clinical scientist model**—that stressed the scientific side of clinical psychology more strongly than did the Boulder model (McFall, 2006). Unlike those who created the Vail model in the 1970s, the leaders of the clinical scientist movement have not suggested that graduates of their program should receive an entirely different degree—they still award the PhD, just as Boulder model graduate programs do. However, a PhD from a clinical scientist program implies a very strong emphasis on the scientific method and evidence-based clinical methods.

⊕ **Web Link 1.2**

Manifesto for a Science of Clinical Psychology

Two defining events highlight the initial steps of this movement. In 1991, **Richard McFall**, at the time a professor of psychology at Indiana University, published an article that served as a rallying call for the clinical scientist movement. In this "Manifesto for a Science of Clinical Psychology," McFall (1991) argued that "scientific clinical psychology is the only legitimate and acceptable form of clinical psychology . . . after all, what is the alternative? . . . Does anyone seriously believe that a reliance on intuition and other unscientific methods is going to hasten advances in knowledge?" (pp. 76–77).

A few years later, a conference of prominent leaders of select clinical psychology graduate programs took place at Indiana University. The purpose of the conference was to unite in an effort to promote clinical science. From this conference, the **Academy of Psychological Clinical Science** was founded. McFall served as its president for the first several years of its existence, and as time has passed, an increasing number of graduate programs have become members. The programs in this academy still represent a minority of all graduate programs in clinical psychology, but among the members are many prominent and influential programs and individuals (Academy of Psychological Clinical Science, 2009).

⊕ **Web Link 1.3**

Academy of Psychological Clinical Science

Considering the discrepancies between the three models of training available today—the traditional, middle-of-the-road Boulder model; the Vail model, emphasizing clinical skills; and the clinical scientist model, emphasizing empiricism—the experience of clinical psychology graduate students varies widely from one program to the next. In fact, it's no surprise that in the *Insider's Guide to Graduate Programs in Clinical and Counseling Psychology* (Norcross & Sayette, 2012), a valuable resource used by many applicants to learn about specific graduate programs in clinical psychology, the first pieces of information listed about each program is that program's self-rating on a 7-point scale from "practice oriented" to "research oriented." Moreover, it's no surprise that applicants can find programs at both extremes and everywhere in between. Table 1.2 includes examples of specific graduate programs representing each of the three primary training models (scientist-practitioner, practitioner-scholar, and clinical scientist), including quotes from the programs' own websites that reflect their approach to training.

Just as training in clinical psychology has changed dramatically throughout its history, it continues to change today and promises to change further in the future (Grus, 2011). Undoubtedly, technology is increasingly influential in the training of clinical psychologists. For an increasing number of students, learning psychotherapy or assessment techniques involves the use of webcams and other computer-based methods that allow supervisors to view, either live or recorded, students trying to apply what they have learned in class (Barnett, 2011; Manring, Greenberg, Gregory, & Gallinger, 2011; Wolf, 2011). Another growing emphasis in training is specific *competencies*, or skills the students must be able to demonstrate. Emphasizing competencies ensures that the students who graduate from clinical psychology programs not only will have earned good grades on exams, papers, and other academic tasks but also will be able to apply what they have learned. Specific competencies that may be required of students could center on intervention (therapy), assessment, relationship, research, consultation/education, management, and diversity (Barlow & Carl, 2011; Peterson, Peterson, Abrams, Stricker, & Ducheny, 2010).

Getting In: What Do Graduate Programs Prefer?

The *Insider's Guide* mentioned above (Norcross & Sayette, 2012) is one of several resources to educate and advise aspiring clinical psychology graduate students. Others include *Graduate Study in Psychology* (APA, 2012b) and *Getting In: A Step-by-Step Plan for Gaining Admission to Graduate School in Psychology* (APA, 2007). Getting into a graduate program in clinical psychology is no easy task: Admission rates are competitive, and the application process is demanding. (On average, PhD programs in clinical psychology receive 270 applications and admit only 6% of them; Norcross & Sayette, 2012). Knowing how to prepare, especially early in the process, can provide an applicant with significant advantages. Among the suggestions offered by resources such as those listed above are the following:

- *Know your professional options.* Numerous roads lead to the clinical psychologist title; moreover, numerous professions overlap with clinical psychology in terms of professional

Table 1.2 Sample Information Regarding Specific Graduate Programs in Clinical Psychology

Graduate Program	Training Model	Degree Awarded	Clinical/ Research Rating	Self-Description on Program Website
Indiana University	Clinical scientist	PhD	7	"Indiana University's Clinical Training Program is designed with a special mission in mind: To train first-rate clinical scientists. . . . Applicants with primary interests in pursuing careers as service providers are not likely to thrive here."
Northwestern University	Clinical scientist	PhD	7	"The Clinical Psychology Program . . . is designed to train students for primary careers in research and teaching in clinical psychology. . . . The major emphasis of the program is clinical research and research methods."
University of California, Los Angeles	Clinical scientist	PhD	7	"The curriculum is designed to produce clinical scientists: clinically well-trained psychologists devoted to the continuous development of an empirical knowledge base in clinical psychology, with a particular emphasis on preparing graduates for employment in academic and research settings."
Yale University	Clinical scientist	PhD	7	"The Clinical Psychology area is dedicated to research and training in clinical science. Unlike many scientist-practitioner programs, the main training objective at Yale is to cultivate the development of scholars through exposure to a rich and multidisciplinary array of research opportunities. . . . The clinical program at Yale is not a match for students primarily interested in clinical practice."

Table 1.2 (Continued)

Graduate Program	Training Model	Degree Awarded	Clinical/ Research Rating	Self-Description on Program Website
American University	Boulder/ scientist-practitioner	PhD	4	"[Our doctoral program offers] rigorous training in both research and applied clinical work . . . [and] reflects the scientist-practitioner model of training. We provide students with the skills to pursue careers in academics, research, and clinical practice."
University of Alabama	Boulder/ scientist-practitioner	PhD	4	"Graduates function in a variety of settings as teachers, researchers, and providers of clinical services. . . . The program emphasizes the integration of scientific knowledge and the professional skills and attitudes needed to function as a clinical psychologist in academic, research, or applied settings."
Saint Louis University	Boulder/ scientist-practitioner	PhD	4	"The mission of the clinical psychology graduate program is to educate and train students broadly in the science and the practice of clinical psychology."
DePaul University	Boulder/ scientist-practitioner	PhD	4	"The clinical program prepares graduate students to work in applied and academic settings."
University of Denver	Vail/ practitioner-scholar	PsyD	2	"[Our] mission is to provide an innovative educational environment that promotes the application of psychological theory, knowledge, skills, and attitudes/values to professional practice. . . . The mission of the PsyD program is to train competent doctoral level practitioners/scholars."

Graduate Program	Training Model	Degree Awarded	Clinical/ Research Rating	Self-Description on Program Website
Chicago School of Professional Psychology	Vail/ practitioner-scholar	PsyD	2	"As a professional school, our focus is not strictly on research and theory but on preparing students to become outstanding practitioners, providing direct service to help individuals and organizations thrive."
Alliant University, San Diego	Vail/ practitioner-scholar	PsyD	2	"[Ours is] a Practitioner-Scholar model program . . . emphasizing the applications of theory and research to clinical practice. The program develops competent professional clinical psychologists . . . who have acquired the skills necessary to deliver a variety of clinical services to people from diverse backgrounds within many types of settings and institutions."
Argosy University, Washington, D.C.	Vail/ practitioner-scholar	PsyD	1	"The PsyD in Clinical Psychology degree program at Argosy University's Washington, D.C., campus emphasizes the development of knowledge, skills, and attitudes essential in the formation of professional psychologists who are committed to the ethical provision of quality services."

Sources: Indiana University, http://psych.indiana.edu/clinic/ClinicalHandbook.pdf; Northwestern University, www.wcas.northwestern .edu/psych/program_areas/clinical/; University of California, Los Angeles, www.psych.ucla.edu/graduate/areas-of-study-1/clinical-psychology; Yale University, http://psychology.yale .edu/research_area/clinical-psychology; American University, http://www.american .edu/cas/psychology/clinical/index.cfm; University of Alabama, http://psychology.ua.edu/academics/graduate/clinical/clinical .html; St. Louis University, www.slu.edu/x13071.xml; DePaul University, www.depaul.edu/admission/types_of_admission/graduate/psychology/ clinical.asp; University of Denver, http://www.du.edu/gssp/degree-programs/clinical-psychology/overview/; Chicago School of Professional Psychology, www.thechicagoschool .edu/content.cfm/about; Alliant University, San Diego, http://catalog.alliant.acalog.com/preview_program .php?catoid=19&poid=1815&returnto=655; Argosy University, www.argosy.edu/Colleges/ProgramDetail .aspx?id=887.

Note: Clinical/research ratings by directors of each graduate program, as reported in Norcross and Sayette (2012). Ratings range from 1 ("practice oriented") to 7 ("research oriented"), with 4 representing "equal emphasis."

activities. Researching these options will allow for more informed decisions and better matches between applicants and graduate programs.

- *Take, and earn high grades in, the appropriate undergraduate courses.* Graduate programs want trainees whose undergraduate programs maximize their chances of succeeding at the graduate level. Among the most commonly required or recommended courses are statistics, research/experimental methods, psychopathology, biopsychology, and personality (Norcross & Sayette, 2012). Choose electives carefully, too—classes that have direct clinical relevance, including field studies or internships, are often seen favorably (Mayne et al., 1994).

- *Get to know your professors.* Letters of recommendation are among the most important factors in clinical psychology graduate admissions decisions (Norcross, Hanych, & Terranova, 1996). Professors (and, to some extent, supervisors in clinical or research positions) can be ideal writers of such letters—assuming the professor actually knows the student. The better you know the professor, the more substantial your professor's letter can be. For example, a professor may be able to write a brief, vaguely complimentary letter for a quiet student who earned an A in a large lecture course. But the professor would be able to write a much more meaningful, persuasive, and effective letter for the same student if the two of them had developed a strong working relationship through research, advising, or other professional activities.

- *Get research experience.* Your experience in a research methods class is valuable, but it won't distinguish you from most other applicants. Conducting research with a professor affords you additional experience with the empirical process, as well as a chance to learn about a specialized body of knowledge and develop a working relationship with the professor (as described above). If your contribution is significant enough, this research experience could also yield a publication or presentation on which you are listed as an author, which will further enhance your application file. In some cases, professors seek assistants for ongoing projects they have designed. In others, the undergraduate student may approach the faculty member with an original idea for an independent study. Regardless of the arrangement, conducting research at the undergraduate level improves an applicant's chances of getting into and succeeding in a graduate program.

- *Get clinically relevant experience.* For undergraduates, the options for direct clinical experience (therapy, counseling, interviewing, testing, etc.) are understandably limited. Even for those who have earned a bachelor's degree and are considering returning to school at the graduate level, clinical positions may be hard to find. However, quite a few settings may offer exposure to the kinds of clients, professionals, and issues that are central to clinical psychology. These settings include community mental health centers, inpatient psychiatric centers, crisis hotlines, alternative schools, camps for children with behavioral or emotional issues, and others. Whether the clinical experience takes the form of an internship or practicum (for which course credit is earned), a paid job, or a volunteer position, it can provide firsthand knowledge about selected aspects of the field, and it demonstrates to admissions committees that you are serious and well informed about clinical psychology.

- *Maximize your GRE score.* Along with undergraduate GPA, scores on the GRE are key determinants of admission to graduate programs. Appropriately preparing for this test—by learning what scores your preferred programs seek, studying for the test either informally or through a review course, taking practice exams, and retaking it as necessary—can boost your odds of admission.

- *Select graduate programs wisely.* Getting in is certainly important, but getting into a program that proves to be a bad match benefits neither the student nor the program. It is best to learn as much as possible about potential programs: What is the model of training (Boulder, Vail, or clinical scientist)? To what clinical orientations does the faculty subscribe? What areas of specialization do the faculty members represent? What clinical opportunities are available? Of course, your own preferences or constraints—geography, finances, family—deserve consideration as well.

- *Write effective personal statements.* In addition to the many other items in your application file, graduate programs will require you to write a personal statement (or goal statement). This is your opportunity to discuss career aspirations, as well as your research and clinical interests—all of which should fit well with the program to which you are applying. It is also a chance to explain in more detail information that may have appeared only briefly on a resume or vita, such as clinical experiences or research with an undergraduate professor. Make sure your writing ability appears strong and that you don't make the statement overly personal or revealing.

- *Prepare well for admissions interviews.* Most doctoral programs invite high-ranking applicants for an in-person interview. These interviews are a wonderful opportunity for professors in the program to get to know you and for you to get to know the program. Arrive (professionally dressed, of course) with a strong understanding of the program and your interest in it. The more specific, the better: Interest in particular professors' research concentrations, for example, makes a better impression than the fact that the program has a strong reputation. Box 1.2 lists some of the questions you should be prepared to answer. And don't forget to develop a list of your own questions—good questions can solicit more detailed information than you were able to find on the program's website and can impress interviewers in the process.

Interview Questions to Anticipate

There is no formula for the kinds of questions that interviewers might ask an applicant to a clinical psychology program, but these questions are especially common. Whether they ask these particular questions or not, you enhance your chances of finding a graduate program that truly fits your interests by giving them serious consideration.

- Why do you want to be a clinical psychologist?
- What attracts you to our graduate program specifically?
- What are your research interests?
- What approach(es) to psychotherapy do you prefer?
- Which of our faculty members would you like to work with?
- What are your long-term career goals? If you were a student in our program, what would you like to do after you graduated?

Source: Adapted from Norcross and Sayette (2012).

- *Consider your long-term goals.* Down the road, do you see yourself as a clinician or a researcher? Have you firmly determined your own theoretical orientation already, or do you seek a program that will expose you to a variety? What specific areas of clinical or scientific work are most interesting to you? How much financial debt are you willing to incur? Thinking ahead about these and other questions can increase the likelihood that you will find yourself at a graduate program at which you thrive and that sets you up for a fulfilling career.

Internships: Predoc and Postdoc

All clinical psychology doctoral programs culminate in the **predoctoral internship** (Kaslow & Webb, 2011). Typically, this internship consists of a full year of supervised clinical experience in an applied setting—a psychiatric hospital, a Veterans Affairs medical center, a university counseling center, a community mental health center, a medical school, or another agency where clinical psychologists work (Baker & Pickren, 2011). As implied by the term *predoctoral*, this internship year takes place before the PhD or the PsyD is awarded. (Along with completion of the dissertation, it is likely to be one of the final hurdles.) It is generally considered a year of transition, a sort of advanced apprenticeship in which the individual begins to outgrow the role of "student" and grow into the role of "professional." In some settings, it is also an opportunity to gain more specialized training than may have been available in graduate school so far. Many internships are accredited by the APA; those that are not may be looked on less favorably by state licensing boards.

The process of applying for a predoctoral internship can feel a lot like the process of applying to graduate school some years earlier. It often involves researching various internships, applying to many, traveling for interviews, ranking preferences, anxiously awaiting feedback, and relocating to a new geographic area. Some students apply to 20 or more internship sites (Keilin, 2000), but 10 to 15 may be more reasonable and equally effective (Keilin & Constantine, 2001). Adding stress to the situation is the fact that in some years, the number of graduate students seeking predoctoral internships has either approached or exceeded the number of available slots (Kaslow & Webb, 2011; Keilin, Thorn, Rodolfa, Constantine, & Kaslow, 2000). In fact, the shortage worsened considerably from 2002 to 2012, as the number of students who applied but were not successfully placed at an internship more than doubled (Dingfelder, 2012). The internship application process can certainly generate stress and feel a bit like a game of musical chairs, but numerous strategies to improve the current situation are under way, and applicants are generally successful in finding an internship position—especially if they don't overly restrict themselves in terms of the number of applications or geographic range.

Beyond the predoctoral internship and the doctoral degree that follows, most states require a **postdoctoral internship** (or postdoc) for licensure as a psychologist. The postdoc typically lasts 1 to 2 years (Vaughn, 2006), and it is essentially a step up from the predoctoral internship. Postdocs take on more responsibilities than they did as predoctoral interns, but they remain under supervision. Like the predoctoral internship, the postdoc often provides an opportunity for specialized training. After postdoctoral interns accumulate the required number of supervised hours (and pass the applicable licensing exams), they can become licensed to practice independently. Some clinical psychologists obtain postdoc positions that are explicitly designed from the start to meet licensing requirements for a particular state; sometimes, such positions are continuations of predoctoral internship experiences. Other clinical psychologists may obtain an entry-level position with an agency and tailor it to meet postdoctoral requirements for licensure.

Getting Licensed

Once all the training requirements are met— graduate coursework, predoctoral internship, postdoctoral internship—**licensure** appears on the horizon. Becoming licensed gives a professional the right to identify as a member of the profession—to present oneself as a psychologist (or clinical psychologist—the terminology, as well as

⊕ **Web Link 1.4**

Association of State and Provincial Psychology Boards

Photos 1.1, 1.2, and 1.3 Clinical psychologists work in a variety of settings, including private offices, universities, and hospitals.

licensing requirements in general, differs from state to state). It also authorizes the psychologist to practice independently (APA, 2007; Schaffer, DeMers, & Rodolfa, 2011).

But you won't be handed a license when you get your doctoral degree or when you finish your postdoc. Becoming licensed also requires passing licensure exams—typically, the **Examination for Professional Practice in Psychology (EPPP)** and a state-specific exam on laws and ethics. The EPPP is a standardized multiple-choice exam on a broad range of psychology topics; all U.S. states and most provinces of Canada establish a minimum score for licensure (Rehm & Lipkins, 2006; Schaffer et al., 2011). The state exams vary, of course, according to state regulations but tend to center on legal issues relevant to the practice of psychology in the state in question. The state exams may be written or oral.

Once licensed, clinical psychologists in many states must accumulate **continuing education units (CEUs)** to renew the license from year to year (Neimeyer & Taylor, 2011). In various states, psychologists can meet these ongoing requirements in a number of ways—by attending workshops, taking courses, undergoing additional specialized training, passing exams on selected professional reading material, and the like. The purpose of requiring CEUs is to ensure that clinical psychologists stay up to date on developments in the field, with the intention of maintaining or improving the standard of care they can provide to clients.

Professional Activities and Employment Settings

Where Do Clinical Psychologists Work?

The short answer is that clinical psychologists work in a wide variety of settings but that private practice is the most common. In fact, this answer applies not only according to a survey of clinical psychologists conducted in the 2000s but also according to similar surveys in the 1980s and 1990s (Norcross & Karpiak, 2012).

Since the 1980s, private practice has been the primary employment site of 30% to 41% of clinical psychologists. The second-place finisher in each survey during that time has been the university psychology department, but that number has not exceeded 19%. Between 2% and 9% of clinical psychologists have listed each of the following as their primary work setting: psychiatric hospitals, general hospitals, community mental health centers, medical schools, and Veterans Affairs medical centers. Interestingly, the third-place finisher (after private practice and university psychology department) in each survey since the 1980s has been the "other" category; for example, in 2003, 15% of psychologists listed "other," writing in diverse settings such as government agency, public schools, substance abuse center, corporation, and university counseling center. It is clear that although private practice remains a common destination, clinical psychologists are finding employment across an expanding range of settings (Norcross & Karpiak, 2012; Norcross, Karpiak, & Santoro, 2005).

What Do Clinical Psychologists Do?

Again, the short answer first: Clinical psychologists are engaged in an enormous range of professional activities, but psychotherapy is foremost. As with employment settings, this finding is true today and has been for decades—at least since the 1970s (Norcross & Karpiak, 2012).

Since 1973, the number of clinical psychologists reporting that they are involved in psychotherapy has always outranked that of any other professional activity and has ranged from 76% to 87%. Moreover, when asked what percentage of their time they spend in each activity, clinical psychologists have reported that they spend between 31% and 37% of their time conducting psychotherapy—a percentage more than double that of any other activity. Of those who practice psychotherapy, individual

Photos 1.4, 1.5, and 1.6 Clinical psychologists' professional activities include psychotherapy, assessment, and education.

therapy occupies the largest percentage of their therapy time (76%), with group, family, and couples therapy far behind (6% to 9% each) (Norcross & Karpiak, 2012).

Of course, a sizable number of psychologists—more than half—have also reported that they are at least somewhat involved in each of the following activities: diagnosis/assessment, teaching, supervision, research/writing, consultation, and administration. Of these, diagnosis and assessment generally occupy more of clinical psychologists' time than do the others. Overall, it is evident that "clinical psychologists are involved in multiple professional pursuits across varied employment sites" (Norcross, Karpiak, & Santoro, 2005, p. 1474). In fact, more than half of clinical psychologists hold at least two professional positions (Norcross & Sayette, 2012). Figure 1.1 illustrates the professional self-views of clinical psychologists.

How Are Clinical Psychologists Different From . . .

Counseling Psychologists

There may have been a time when counseling psychology and clinical psychology were quite distinct, but today, there is significant overlap between these two professions. Historically, they have differed primarily in terms of their clients' characteristics: Clinical psychologists were more likely to work with seriously disturbed individuals, whereas **counseling psychologists** were more likely to work with ("counsel") less pathological clients. But today, many clinical and counseling psychologists see the same types of clients, sometimes as colleagues working side by side. These two fields are also similar in that their graduate students occupy the same internship sites, often earn the same degree (the PhD), and obtain the same licensure status (Norcross, 2000). In fact, the two professions share so much common ground that it is entirely possible for a client who seeks the services of a psychologist with "PhD" behind his or her name never to know whether the PhD is in clinical or counseling psychology.

A few meaningful differences, however, remain between clinical and counseling psychologists. Compared with counseling psychologists, clinical psychologists still tend to work with more seriously disturbed populations and, correspondingly, tend to work more often in settings such as hospitals and inpatient psychiatric units. And compared with clinical psychologists, counseling psychologists still tend to work with less seriously disturbed populations and, correspondingly, tend to work more often in university counseling centers (Gaddy et al., 1995). Some differences in theoretical orientation are also evident: Both fields endorse the eclectic orientation more than any other, but clinical psychologists tend to endorse behaviorism more strongly, and counseling psychologists tend

FIGURE 1.1 **Professional Self-Views of Clinical Psychologists**

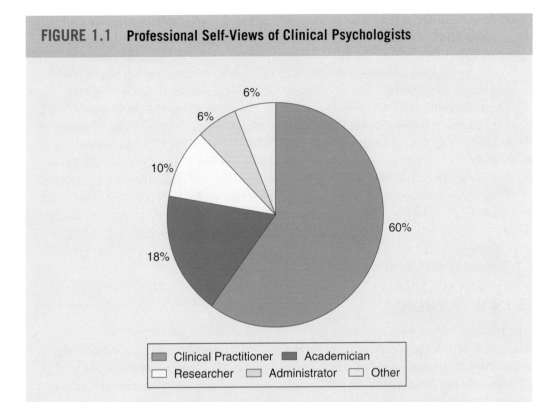

Source: Norcross, J. C., Karpiak, C. P., & Santoro, S. O. (2005). Clinical psychologists across the years: The division of clinical psychology from 1960 to 2003. *Journal of Clinical Psychology, 61,* 1467–1483, published by Wiley, pp. 1473. (Figure 3).

to endorse humanistic/client-centered approaches more strongly. Additionally, counseling psychologists tend to be more interested in vocational testing and career counseling, whereas clinical psychologists tend to be more interested in applications of psychology to medical settings (Norcross & Sayette, 2012).

Psychiatrists

Unlike clinical (or counseling) psychologists, **psychiatrists** go to medical school and are licensed as physicians. (In fact, their specialized training in psychiatry doesn't begin until well into their training; the first several years are often identical to that of other types of physicians.) As physicians, they are allowed to prescribe medication. Until recently, psychologists could not prescribe medication, but as described in Chapter 3, psychologists have rallied in recent years to obtain prescription privileges and have earned important victories in a small number of states.

The difference between psychiatrists and clinical psychologists is more than just medication. The two professions fundamentally differ in their understanding of and approach to behavioral or emotional problems. Clinical psychologists are certainly trained to appreciate the biological aspects of their clients' problems, but psychiatrists' training emphasizes biology to such an extent that disorders—depression, anxiety disorders, attention-deficit/hyperactivity disorder (ADHD), borderline personality disorder, and so on—are viewed first and foremost as physiological abnormalities of the brain. So, to fix the problem, psychiatrists tend to fix the brain by prescribing medication. This is not to imply that psychiatrists don't respect "talking cures" such as psychotherapy or counseling, but they favor medication more than they used to (Harris, 2011; Manninen, 2006). For clinical psychologists, the biological aspects of clients' problems may not be their defining characteristic; nor is pharmacology the first line of defense. Instead, clinical psychologists view clients' problems as behavioral, cognitive, emotional—still stemming from brain activity, of course, but amenable to change via nonpharmacological methods.

Social Workers

Traditionally, **social workers** have focused their work on the interaction between an individual and the components of society that may contribute to or alleviate the individual's problems. They saw many of their clients' problems as products of social ills—racism, oppressive gender roles, poverty, abuse, and so on. They also helped their clients by connecting them with social services, such as welfare agencies, disability offices, or job-training sites. More than their counterparts in psychology or psychiatry, they were likely to get into the "nitty-gritty" of their clients' worlds by visiting their homes or workplaces, or by making contacts on their behalf with organizations that might prove beneficial. When they worked together with psychologists and psychiatrists (e.g., in institutions), they usually focused on issues such as arranging for clients to transition successfully to the community after leaving an inpatient unit by making sure that needs such as housing, employment, and outpatient mental health services were in place.

In more recent years, the social work profession has grown to encompass a wider range of activities, and the similarity of some social workers (especially those conducting therapy) to clinical psychologists has increased (Wittenberg, 1997). The training of social workers, however, remains quite different from the training of clinical psychologists. They typically earn a master's degree rather than a doctorate, and although their training includes a strong emphasis on supervised fieldwork, it includes very little on research methods, psychological testing, or physiological psychology. Their theories of psychopathology and therapy continue to emphasize social and environmental factors.

School Psychologists

As the name implies, **school psychologists** usually work in schools, but some may work in other settings such as day-care centers or correctional facilities. Their primary function is to enhance the intellectual, emotional, social, and developmental lives of students. They frequently conduct psychological testing (especially intelligence and achievement tests) used to determine diagnoses such as learning disabilities and ADHD. They use or develop programs designed to meet the educational and emotional needs of students. They also consult with adults involved in students' lives—teachers, school administrators, school staff, parents—and are involved to a limited degree in direct counseling with students.

Professional Counselors

Professional counselors earn a master's (rather than a doctoral) degree and often complete their training within 2 years. They attend graduate programs in counseling or professional counseling, which should not be confused with doctoral programs in counseling psychology. These programs typically have rather high acceptance rates compared with programs in many similar professions. Professional counselors' work generally involves counseling, with very little emphasis on psychological testing or conducting research. Correspondingly, their training programs include few if any courses on these topics, focusing instead on providing services to clients. Increasingly, professional counselors are among the clinicians who serve wide varieties of clients in community agencies (Norcross & Sayette, 2012), and they often enter private practice as well. They often specialize in such areas as career, school, addiction, couple/family, or college counseling.

CHAPTER SUMMARY

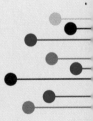

The scope of clinical psychology has expanded greatly since the inception of the field by Lightner Witmer near the turn of the 20th century. Currently, there are multiple paths to the profession, including three distinct approaches to training: the scientist-practitioner (Boulder) approach, with roughly equal emphasis on empiricism and practice; the practitioner-scholar (Vail) approach, with stronger emphasis on practice; and the clinical scientist approach, with stronger emphasis on empiricism. Gaining admission to a training program is a competitive endeavor. Knowledge of the professional training options, successful completion of the appropriate undergraduate courses, research experience, and clinical experience are among the factors that can distinguish an applicant and enhance chances for admission. The final steps of the training process for clinical psychologists are the predoctoral and postdoctoral internships, in which the trainee practices under supervision to transition into the full-fledged professional role. Licensure, which requires a passing grade on the

EPPP as well as state-specific requirements, allows clinical psychologists to practice independently. The most common work setting for clinical psychologists is private practice, but university psychology departments and hospitals of various types are also somewhat frequent. The most common professional activity for clinical psychologists is psychotherapy, but they also spend significant amounts of time in assessment, teaching, research, and supervision activities. The professional roles of counseling psychologists, psychiatrists, social workers, and school psychologists each overlap somewhat with that of clinical psychologists, yet clinical psychology has always retained its own unique professional identity.

KEY TERMS AND NAMES

Academy of Psychological Clinical Science 9

American Psychological Association (APA) 4

Boulder model 6

clinical psychology 4

clinical scientist model 9

continuing education units (CEUs) 18

counseling psychologists 20

Division of Clinical Psychology (Division 12) 4

Examination for Professional Practice in Psychology (EPPP) 18

licensure 17

Richard McFall 9

postdoctoral internship 17

practitioner-scholar model 6

predoctoral internship 16

professional counselors 23

psychiatrists 21

PsyD 7

school psychologists 23

scientist-practitioner model 6

social workers 22

Vail model 7

Lightner Witmer 4

CRITICAL THINKING QUESTIONS

1. Lightner Witmer originally defined clinical psychology as a discipline with similarities to medicine, education, and sociology. In your opinion, to what extent does contemporary clinical psychology remain similar to these fields?

2. Considering the trends in graduate training models observed recently, how popular do you expect the scientist-practitioner, practitioner-scholar, and clinical scientist models of training to be 10 years from now? What about 50 years from now?

3. What specific types of research or clinical experience do you think would be most valuable for an undergraduate who hopes to become a clinical psychologist?

4. In your opinion, to what extent should graduate programs use the GRE as an admission criterion for graduate school in clinical psychology?

5. In your opinion, how much continuing education should licensed clinical psychologists be required to undergo? What forms should this continuing education take (workshops, courses, readings, etc.)?

STUDENT STUDY SITE RESOURCES

Visit the study site at www.sagepub.com/pomerantz3eupdate for these additional learning tools:

- Self-quizzes
- eFlashcards
- Culture Expert Interviews
- Chapter Summary Video

- Full-text SAGE journal articles
- Additional web resources
- Mock Assessment Data

CHAPTER SUMMARY VIDEO

 QR codes at the end of each chapter link to chapter background videos by the author. Visit http://gettag.mobi using your smartphone browser to download the free Microsoft Tag app. Once installed, scan the tags to go directly to these brief videos. In this video, the author explores the implications of the fact that clinical psychology's history is only about a century long.

CHAPTER 2

Evolution of Clinical Psychology

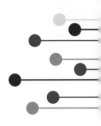

Origins of the Field

Psychology, as we know, has a long, rich history, with roots winding back to some of the great thinkers of prior millennia, such as Socrates, Plato, and Aristotle (Benjamin, 2007; Ehrenwald, 1991). The history of *clinical* psychology is certainly rich as well, but it's also shorter than some might expect. Of course, in recent decades, the clinical specialization has enjoyed great popularity and notoriety among psychology professionals and the general public; in fact, today, when many people hear of a "psychologist," they immediately think of a "clinical psychologist" practicing psychotherapy or assessment. This assumption regarding psychology is inaccurate until at least the early 1900s. The discipline of clinical psychology simply didn't exist until around the turn of the 20th century, and it didn't rise to prominence for decades after that.

Early Pioneers

Even before "clinical psychology" per se had been created, numerous influential individuals in various parts of the world were working to make positive changes in the lives of the mentally ill. Collectively, their accomplishments created a climate from which clinical psychology could emerge. Specifically, in the 1700s and 1800s, the mentally ill were generally viewed and treated much more unfavorably than they are today. In many parts of the world, including much of the Western Hemisphere, they were understood to be possessed by evil spirits. Or they were seen as deserving of their symptoms as a consequence of some reprehensible action or characteristic. They were frequently shunned by society and were "treated" in institutions that resembled prisons more than they did hospitals (Reisman, 1991).

During this time, numerous individuals of various professional backgrounds from Europe and North America assumed the challenge of improving the way people with psychological problems were regarded and treated. Through their efforts, the Western world eventually adopted a new, more humane, approach to the mentally ill, foretelling the emergence of clinical psychology as a formal discipline. The accomplishments of several of these pioneers are described below.

William Tuke (1732–1822)

In his homeland of England, **William Tuke** heard about the deplorable conditions in which the mentally ill lived. He visited asylums to get a firsthand look, and he was appalled by what he saw. Tuke devoted much of his life to improving these conditions. He raised funds to open the **York Retreat,** a residential treatment center where the mentally ill would always be cared for with kindness, dignity, and decency. (The simple act of labeling his facility a "retreat" suggests a fundamentally different approach to the mentally ill compared with the dominant approach at the time.) Patients received good food, frequent exercise, and friendly interactions with staff. The York Retreat became an example of humane treatment, and soon similar institutions opened throughout Europe and the United States. Long after his death, Tuke's family members continued to be involved in the York Retreat and the movement to improve treatment of mentally ill individuals (Reisman, 1991).

⊕ **Web Link 2.1**
William Tuke

Philippe Pinel (1745–1826)

What William Tuke was to England, **Philippe Pinel** was to France—a liberator of the mentally ill. Like Tuke, Pinel worked successfully to move mentally ill individuals out of dungeons in Paris, where they were held as inmates rather than treated as patients (Cautin, 2011; Ehrenwald, 1991). He went to great lengths to convince his contemporaries and those with power in France that the mentally ill were not possessed by devils and that they deserved compassion and hope rather than maltreatment and scorn. He created new institutions in which patients were not kept in chains or beaten but, rather, were given healthy food and benevolent treatment. Particularly noteworthy, Pinel advocated for the staff to include in their treatment of each patient a case history, ongoing treatment notes, and an illness classification of some kind—components of care that suggested he was genuinely interested in improving these individuals rather than locking them away (Reisman, 1991). From Pinel's *Treatise on Insanity* in 1806, we get a sense of his goal of empathy rather than cruelty for the mentally ill: "To rule [the mentally ill] with a rod of iron, as if to shorten the term of an existence considered miserable, is a system of superintendence, more distinguished for its convenience than for its humanity or success" (as quoted in Ehrenwald, 1991, p. 217). As Frances (2013a) describes Pinel, "our field couldn't possibly have a better father and role model…Pinel liked his patients as people and treated them as if they were simply human. When given the choice of joining Napoleon as a personal physician or staying with his patients, he turned down Napoleon" (p. 57).

In Europe in the late 18th and early 19th centuries, society's views toward the mentally ill were undergoing significant change and "the voices of Pinel and Tuke were part of a growing chorus that sang of individual rights and social responsibility" (Reisman, 1991, p. 9).

Eli Todd (1762–1832)

Eli Todd made sure that the chorus of voices for humane treatment of the mentally ill was also heard on the other side of the Atlantic Ocean. Todd was a physician in Connecticut in 1800, a time when only three states had hospitals for the mentally ill. The burden for treating the mentally ill typically fell on their families, who often hid their mentally ill relatives out of shame and embarrassment. Todd had learned about Pinel's efforts in France, and he spread the word among his own medical colleagues in the United States. They supported Todd's ideals both ideologically and financially, such that Todd was able to raise funds to open **The Retreat** in Hartford, Connecticut, in 1824. Todd ensured that patients at the Retreat were always treated in a humane and dignified way. He and his staff emphasized patients' strengths rather than weaknesses, and they allowed patients to have significant input in their own treatment decisions. Similar institutions were soon opened in other U.S. states as leaders elsewhere learned of Todd's successful treatment of the mentally ill (Reisman, 1991).

⊕ Web Link 2.2
Eli Todd

Dorothea Dix (1802–1887)

Despite Todd's efforts, there were simply not enough hospitals in the United States to treat the mentally ill, and as a result, these individuals were too often sent to prisons or jails in an attempt to find any social institution that could house them. In 1841, **Dorothea Dix** was working as a Sunday school teacher in a jail in Boston, where she saw firsthand that many of the inmates were there as a result of mental illness or retardation rather than crime. Dix devoted the rest of her life to improving the lives and treatment of the mentally ill. Typically, she would travel to a city, collect data on its treatment of the mentally ill, present her data to local community leaders, and persuade them to treat the mentally ill more humanely and adequately. She repeated this pattern again and again, in city after city, with remarkable success. Her efforts resulted in the establishment of more than 30 state institutions for the mentally ill throughout the United States (and even more in Europe and Asia), providing more decent, compassionate treatment for the mentally ill than they might have otherwise received (Reisman, 1991).

🌐 **Web Link 2.3**

Dorothea Dix
Tuke, Pinel, Todd, and Dix did not create clinical psychology. Their efforts do, however, represent a movement prevalent through much of the Western world in the 1700s and 1800s that promoted the fundamental message that people with mental illness deserve respect, understanding, and help rather than contempt, fear, and punishment. As this message gained power and acceptance, it created fertile ground in which someone—Lightner Witmer, most would argue—could plant the seed that would grow into clinical psychology (Cautin, 2011).

Lightner Witmer and the Creation of Clinical Psychology

Lightner Witmer (1867–1956) received his doctorate in psychology in 1892 in Germany under Wilhelm Wundt, who many view as the founder of experimental psychology. He also studied under James McKeen Cattell, another pioneer of experimental psychology (Reisman, 1991). At the time Witmer received his doctorate, psychology was essentially an academic discipline, a field of research. It had almost none of the applied functions that characterize the field today. In short, in the late 1800s, psychologists didn't *practice* psychology, they *studied* it.

🌐 **Web Link 2.4**

Lightner Witmer
A major historical shift took place 4 years after Witmer received his doctoral degree when, in 1896, he founded the first psychological clinic at the University of Pennsylvania (Routh, 1996). Although it may be difficult to imagine from our contemporary perspective of the field, this was the first time that the science of psychology was systematically and intentionally applied to people's problems. At the 1896 convention of the American Psychological Association, Witmer (1897) spoke to his colleagues and fellow members about his clinic and encouraged them to open their own—to "throw light upon the problems that confront humanity" (p. 116)—but they were largely unenthusiastic (Reisman, 1991). Decades later, though, clinical settings would certainly proliferate. By 1914, there were about 20 psychological clinics in the United States, most of which were modeled on

Witmer's (Schultz & Schultz, 2011). By 1935, the number had soared to more than 150, and an issue of Witmer's journal from that year was dedicated to a survey of activities taking place in these clinics, as well as some specific suggestions for the training of clinical psychologists (Brown, 1935).

In his clinic, Witmer and his associates worked with children whose problems arose in school settings and were related to learning or behavior (Benjamin, 2007). They were referred by their schools, parents, physicians, or community authorities (McReynolds, 1997). Witmer (1907) emphasized that clinical psychology could be applied to adults as well as children, or to problems that had nothing to do with school: "Indeed, the clinical method is applicable even to the so-called normal child. . . . Whether the subject be a child or an adult, the examination and treatment may be conducted and their results expressed in the terms of the clinical method" (p. 9).

In addition to establishing his clinic, Witmer also founded the first scholarly journal in the field (called *The Psychological Clinic*) in 1907 (Benjamin, 2007). Witmer authored the first article, titled "Clinical Psychology," in the first issue. This article included the first known publication of the term *clinical psychology*, as well as a definition of the term and an explanation of the need for its existence and growth. The article began with a description of Witmer's (1907) innovation: "During the last ten years the laboratory of psychology at the University of Pennsylvania has conducted, under my direction, what I have called a 'psychological clinic'" (p. 1).

Photo 2.1 Lightner Witmer (1867–1956), who created the term *clinical psychology* and founded the first psychological clinic. How has the field changed since Witmer's era?

⊕ **Web Link 2.5**

First "Clinical Psychology" Article

We discussed Witmer's original definition of clinical psychology in Chapter 1, but a consideration in this chapter of Witmer's historical significance gives us an opportunity to examine it further. First, it is worth noting that Witmer defined clinical psychology as related to medicine, education, and social work but stated that physicians, teachers, or social workers would not be qualified to practice clinical psychology. Instead, this new field represented a hybrid of these and other influences, requiring a specially trained professional who, of course, would work collaboratively with members of related fields. It is also interesting that Witmer's definition of clinical psychology is basically uninfluenced by Freud, whose ideas appeared throughout many fields at the time, and that psychotherapy, as it would come to be known, was not explicitly discussed at all. Finally, the treatments that Witmer does discuss in his original definition aren't accompanied by any mention of a plan for empirically evaluating their effectiveness, which is a bit surprising given Witmer's graduate training as an experimental researcher (Routh, 1996; Witmer, 1907).

So by the late 1800s, the work of Tuke, Pinel, Todd, Dix, and others had set the stage for the birth of clinical psychology. Witmer proudly announced its arrival, and although it would thrive in later years, "clinical psychology in the 1890s was a glimmer, a baby just catching its first breath, drawing its life from the new science of psychology" (Reisman, 1991, p. 44).

Assessment

Diagnostic Issues

Categorizing mental illness has been an issue central to clinical psychology since Witmer defined the field. Actually, the debate began long before Witmer entered the picture.

With so many mental disorders tossed around as common terminology today, it can be difficult to imagine a time when such labels didn't exist at all, at least not in any formal sense. In the 1800s in Europe, labeling systems for mental illness began to take shape in a very rudimentary way. Specifically, mental illnesses were often placed in one of two very broad categories: **neurosis** and **psychosis.** Neurotic individuals were thought to suffer from some psychiatric symptoms (including what we would now call anxiety and depression) but to maintain an intact grasp on reality. Psychotic individuals, on the other hand, demonstrated a break from reality in the form of hallucinations, delusions, or grossly disorganized thinking (Reisman, 1991).

Emil Kraepelin (1855–1926), considered the "father of descriptive psychiatry" (Reisman, 1991, p. 30), offered a different two-category system of mental illness. Kraepelin differentiated **exogenous disorders** (caused by external factors) from **endogenous disorders** (caused by internal factors) and suggested that exogenous disorders were the far more treatable type. Kraepelin also assigned names to specific examples of disorders in the broad exogenous or endogenous categories. For example, Kraepelin put forth the term **dementia praecox** to describe one endogenous disorder similar to what is now known as schizophrenia. Later, he also proposed terms such as *paranoia, manic depressive psychosis, involutional melancholia, cyclothymic personality,* and *autistic personality*—terms that had not yet been coined (Millon & Simonsen, 2010). Most of Kraepelin's specific terms have long since been replaced, but by offering such specific terminology, he set a precedent for the creation of diagnostic terms that eventually led to the *Diagnostic and Statistical Manual of Mental Disorders (DSM)* (Widiger & Mullins-Sweatt, 2008).

In the United States, long before the appearance of the first *DSM,* the original reason for categorizing mental disorders was to collect statistics on the population. In 1840, the U.S. Census Bureau included a single category—"idiocy/insanity"—for this purpose. In 1880, there were seven such categories, and soon the American Medical Association and the U.S. Army each made preliminary attempts at classifying mental illness (American Psychiatric Association, 2000).

The original *DSM* was published by the American Psychiatric Association in 1952, representing a more sophisticated attempt to define and organize mental diagnoses. A revision (*DSM-II*) followed in 1968, but it was not considered to be significantly different from the original. However, the next revision—*DSM-III*, which arrived in 1980—signified an entirely new way of thinking about mental disorders (Decker, 2013). Where *DSM* and *DSM-II* included somewhat vague descriptions of each disorder, *DSM-III* provided specific **diagnostic criteria**—lists indicating exactly what symptoms constitute each disorder. *DSM-III* also introduced a **multiaxial system**, a way of cataloguing problems of different kinds on different axes, which remained for multiple editions before being taken out of the most recent. The *DSM* has been revised several more times, with *DSM-III-R*, *DSM-IV*, and *DSM-IV-TR* appearing in 1987, 1994, and 2000, respectively. The current edition is *DSM-5*, which was published in May 2013 after significant anticipation and controversy. (DSM-5 will be covered in more detail elsewhere, especially in Chapter 7.) Each edition varies from its predecessor to some extent, but the most drastic change occurred with the publication of *DSM-III* in 1980 (Lilienfeld & Landfield, 2008; Widiger & Mullins-Sweatt, 2008).

Sheer size is certainly among the most notable differences between *DSM-II* and *DSM-III*. In fact, new *DSM*s typically include more disorders than the editions they replace, with the jump between *DSM-II* and *DSM-III* being the largest. In the time between the original *DSM* (in 1952) and *DSM-IV* (in 1994), the number of disorders increased by more than 300% to a total of 368 distinct diagnoses covering an increasing scope of human behavior (Houts, 2002). The first two editions of the DSM were brief, spiral-bound books; the current DSM is 947 pages long.

What are the reasons for such an increase? On one hand, it is possible that in a relatively brief period of time, psychological science is accurately recognizing disorders that went unrecognized (or at least unlabeled) for centuries before, an explanation called "scientific discovery." On the other hand, it is also possible that psychology is making disorders out of some aspects of human experience that had previously been considered normal, an explanation called "social invention" (Houts, 2002). Ongoing debates have arisen regarding the relative truth of both of these explanations. Debates also continue regarding the expanding range of the *DSM*, in general, and the inclusion and exclusion of some specific disorders as well. Some of these debates call into question the extent to which factors other than empirical data drive the decision making of *DSM* authors, and the histories of certain disorders—some of which appear in the *DSM*, and some of which do not—have been offered as evidence (Caplan, 1995; Eriksen, 2005; Kutchins & Kirk, 1997). Box 2.1 illustrates some of the decisions represented in *DSM* revisions. Regardless of the outcomes or current status of diagnostic debates, recent *DSM* revisions represent important chapters of a long history of diagnostic labeling that characterizes clinical psychology.

● ● ● BOX 2.1 ● ● ●

Is It a *DSM* Disorder? Decisions to Include or Exclude Potential Disorders

Before each edition of the *DSM* is published, its authors oversee an extensive process during which they must, among other important tasks, decide whether or not to include certain experiences or sets of symptoms as official diagnoses. The implications of these classification decisions are quite significant for many people, including clients who may be assigned the diagnosis, mental health professionals who may treat them, health insurance companies who may pay for the treatment, and researchers who may investigate the issue.

Sometimes, *DSM* authors have decided to add an entirely new disorder to a revised edition. For example, borderline personality disorder, narcissistic personality disorder, and social phobia each appeared for the first time in *DSM-III* in 1980. At other times, *DSM* authors have, after serious consideration, decided not to include a proposed set of symptoms as an official disorder. For years prior to the publication of *DSM-IV*, *DSM* authors contemplated adding disorders tentatively named sadistic personality disorder and self-defeating personality disorder, among others, but ultimately decided against it. On occasion, the *DSM* authors reverse a previous decision to include a disorder. Homosexuality was listed as a disorder in *DSM-I* and *DSM-II* but was excluded from *DSM-III* (and subsequent editions) after extensive controversy. *DSM-III* also omitted inadequate personality disorder and asthenic personality disorder, which were included in previous editions.

A section of the current edition of the *DSM* (*DSM-5*) lists numerous proposed disorders that were considered for inclusion but rejected by *DSM* authors. They are included as unofficial "proposed criteria sets" with the hope that additional research will inform future decisions to include or exclude them as official disorders. Included among these proposed disorders are the following (American Psychiatric Association, 2013):

- *Internet gaming disorder,* in which the person's Internet game-playing behavior causes clinically significant impairment or stress. The person is preoccupied with gaming, can't control his or her gaming behavior, experiences withdrawal when access is taken away, experiences relationship problems due to gaming, or has similar symptoms.

Photo 2.2 What distinguishes sadness, or other common but undesirable experiences, from mental illness?

- *Attenuated psychosis syndrome,* in which the person experiences mild or brief delusions, hallucinations, or other psychotic phenomena. These are the same kinds of symptoms experienced by people with schizophrenia, but in attenuated psychosis syndrome, the symptoms would be more fleeting, less intense, and the person's perception of reality would remain largely intact. ("Attenuated" means reduced or lessened.)

- *Persistent complex bereavement,* in which the person experiences the death of a loved one and continues to be preoccupied with, yearn for, and feel intense sorrow about the person (among other symptoms) for over 12 months (or 6 months for children).

- *Nonsuicidal self-injury,* which can involve cutting, burning, or otherwise intentionally hurting one's own body without the intent to kill oneself, on 5 or more days in the last year. This behavior has long been recognized as a symptom of other disorders (especially borderline personality disorder), but with this proposed disorder, nonsuicidal self-injury would be a full-fledged disorder of its own.

There is no doubt that many individuals experience the phenomena described in these "proposed criteria sets." The question is whether these experiences should be categorized as forms of mental illness or understood to be part of the range of normal human experience. Whether these experiences will be classified as official disorders in a future edition of *DSM* depends, ultimately, on decisions made by the *DSM* authors.

Assessment of Intelligence

The emergence of the field of clinical psychology around the turn of the 20th century coincided with a dispute among psychology's pioneers about the nature of intelligence.

Edward Lee Thorndike was among those who promoted the idea that each person possesses separate, independent intelligences, whereas **Charles Spearman** led a group of theorists who argued for the existence of "g," a general intelligence thought to overlap with many particular abilities (Reisman, 1991). The outcome of this dispute would profoundly influence how clinical psychologists assessed intellectual abilities, an activity that, more than psychotherapy or any other, characterized clinical psychology as a profession in the early years of the profession (Benjamin, 2007).

An important development in the history of intelligence testing arose in the early 1900s, when the French government sought help in determining which public school students should qualify for special services. In response to this request, **Alfred Binet** (along with Theodore Simon) created the first Binet-Simon scale in 1905. This test yielded a single overall score, endorsing the concept of "g." It was the first to incorporate a comparison of mental age to chronological age as a measure of intelligence. This comparison, when expressed as a division problem, yielded the "intelligence quotient," or IQ. Binet's test grew in popularity and was eventually revised by Lewis Terman in 1937. Terman's revision was called the **Stanford-Binet Intelligence Scales**, the name by which the test is currently known (Goldstein, 2008; Reisman, 1991).

The standardization sample and the age range of test takers improved with each new version of Binet's test, but even after Terman revised it in 1937, it was still a child-focused measure of IQ. In 1939, **David Wechsler** filled the need for a test of intelligence designed specifically for adults with the publication of his **Wechsler-Bellevue** test. It quickly became popular among psychologists working with adults, and its more recent revisions remain popular today. Since its creation, Wechsler's adult intelligence scale has been revised and restandardized numerous times: the **Wechsler Adult Intelligence Scale (WAIS)** in 1955, the WAIS-R in 1981, and the WAIS-III in 1997 (Goldstein, 2008; Reisman, 1991).

In 1949, Wechsler released a children's version of his intelligence test (a more direct competitor for the Stanford-Binet), which he called the **Wechsler Intelligence Scale for Children (WISC)**. The WISC distinguished itself from the Stanford-Binet by the inclusion of specific subtests as well as verbal and performance scales (in addition to overall IQ). The WISC has been revised and restandardized several times: the WISC-R in 1974, the WISC-III in 1991, and the WISC-IV in 2003. In 1967, Wechsler added an intelligence test designed for very young children called the **Wechsler Preschool and Primary Scale of Intelligence (WPPSI)**. The WPPSI was revised in 1989 (WPPSI-R) and again in 2002 (WPPSI-III).

Many other measures of child and adult intelligence have appeared during the time of the Stanford-Binet and the Wechsler tests, but more than any others, these two have established themselves as standards in the field. They have also established themselves as competitors in the marketplace of psychological assessment, and recent revisions in one have at times represented responses to successful strides made by the other.

Assessment of Personality

The term *mental test* was first used by James McKeen Cattell in 1890 in an article titled "Mental Tests and Measurements." At that time, the term was used to refer to basic tests of abilities such as reaction time, memory, and sensation/perception. Soon, though, the term encompassed a wider range of measures, including not only the intelligence tests described above but also tests of personality characteristics (Butcher, 2010).

The first two decades of the 20th century witnessed some of the earliest attempts to measure personality attributes empirically, but few had significant impact. In 1921, however, **Hermann Rorschach** published a test that had significant impact for many years to come. Rorschach, a Swiss psychiatrist, released his now-famous set of 10 inkblots, which rose quickly in popularity (despite the fact that in the early years, several different competing Rorschach scoring systems existed). As a **projective personality test,** the **Rorschach Inkblot Method** was based on the assumption that people will "project" their personalities onto ambiguous or vague stimuli; hence, the way individuals perceive and make sense of the blots corresponds to the way they perceive and make sense of the world around them. Psychodynamic practitioners, who dominated during the early and mid-1900s, found such tests especially compatible with their clinical approach to clients.

The success of Rorschach's test was followed by a number of other projective techniques (Reisman, 1991). For example, **Christiana Morgan** and **Henry Murray** published the **Thematic Apperception Test (TAT)** in 1935. The TAT was similar to the Rorschach in that the test taker responded to cards featuring ambiguous stimuli. However, instead of inkblots, the TAT cards depicted people in scenes or situations that could be interpreted in a wide variety of ways. Instead of identifying objects in the card (as they might with Rorschach's inkblots), clients were asked to tell stories to go along with the interpersonal situations presented in the TAT cards. Again, their responses were thought to reflect personality characteristics. Other projective techniques that appeared in the aftermath of the Rorschach included the Draw-a-Person test, in which psychologists infer personality characteristics from clients' drawings of human figures, and Julian Rotter's Incomplete Sentence Blank (Rotter & Rafferty, 1950), in which psychologists assess personality by examining the ways clients finish sentence stems. Like the Rorschach, these and other projective personality tests have certainly enjoyed some degree of popularity, but their popularity has declined in recent decades as questions about their reliability and validity have accumulated.

Objective personality tests appeared soon after projectives, offering a very different (and, in many cases, more scientifically sound) method of assessing personality. Typically, these tests were pencil-and-paper instruments for which clients answered multiple-choice or true–false questions about themselves, their experiences, or their preferences. Scoring and interpretation were typically more straightforward than for projective tests. Some objective tests focused on specific aspects of personality, whereas others aimed to provide a more comprehensive overview of an individual's personality. The **Minnesota Multiphasic Personality Inventory (MMPI)**, written by **Starke Hathaway** and **J. C. McKinley,** is perhaps the best example of a comprehensive personality measure. When it was originally published in 1943, it consisted of 550 true–false statements. Test takers' patterns of responses were compared with those of groups in the standardization sample who represented many diagnostic categories. Not only could this test help a psychologist categorize a client through use of its clinical scales, it also used validity scales to assess the test taker's approach to the test. In other words, the MMPI had a built-in system to detect random responding or intentionally misleading responses. The MMPI became very popular, and by 1959, there were more than 200 separate scales consisting of combinations of MMPI items (Reisman, 1991).

In 1989, the **Minnesota Multiphasic Personality Inventory-2 (MMPI-2)** was released. Its norms were more appropriate than those of the original MMPI, especially in terms of including minorities and individuals from various regions of the country in the standardization sample. It also eliminated some of the outdated or confusing language from the original test. An adolescent version of the test (the **Minnesota Multiphasic Personality Inventory-Adolescent [MMPI-A]**) followed in 1992. All versions of the MMPI have featured hallmarks of high-quality objective personality tests: easy administration and scoring, demonstrable reliability and validity, and clinical utility.

Other objective tests have come and gone but none with the lasting impact or research base of the MMPI. The NEO Personality Inventory (NEO-PI), for example, and its successor, the NEO-PI-R, have risen to some degree of prominence in more recent decades as a personality measure less geared toward psychopathology than is the MMPI (Costa & McCrae, 1985, 1992). Rather than diagnostic categories, its scales are based on universal personality characteristics common to all individuals. Instruments measuring more specific states or traits have also appeared, including the Beck Depression Inventory (now in its second edition) and the Beck Anxiety Inventory (Beck & Steer, 1993; Beck, Steer, & Brown, 1996).

In recent decades, personality assessment tools have been used for an increasingly wider range of purposes, including job screenings and forensic purposes (e.g., child custody evaluations; Butcher, 2010). These uses have often generated significant controversy and highlight the importance of validity and reliability in such tests—topics we cover in more detail in Chapter 6.

Psychotherapy

Psychotherapy is the primary activity of clinical psychologists today, but that hasn't always been the case. In fact, in 1930—more than a quarter century after Witmer founded the field—almost every clinical psychologist worked in academia (rather than as a therapist), and it wasn't until the 1940s or 1950s that psychotherapy played a significant role in the history of clinical psychology (Benjamin, 2005; Humphreys, 1996; McFall, 2006; Wertheimer, 2000). In fact, in the first half of the 1900s, psychological testing was familiar territory for clinical psychologists, "but it was important that they knew their place in a field dominated by medical practitioners . . . a strategy for treatment, and treatment—those were in the job description of the physician, not the psychologist" (Benjamin, 2007, p. 163). Without the demand created by psychological consequences of World War II on U.S. soldiers, psychotherapy might have remained an uncommon activity of clinical psychologists even longer (Benjamin, 2007). (See Box 2.2 for further exploration of the impact of war on the history of clinical psychology.)

● ● ● BOX 2.2 ● ● ●

The Influence of War on Clinical Psychology

It is difficult to overestimate the influence of war and its aftermath on the development of clinical psychology as a profession. Therapy, assessment, and training have all been shaped by the attempts of various governments and individuals to select soldiers and treat them after they have served their countries (Baker & Pickren, 2011; Benjamin, 2007; Tryon, 2008). Numerous critical incidents in the history of clinical psychology can be directly tied to military factors:

- Robert Yerkes chaired the Committee on the Psychological Examination of Recruits that created the Army Alpha and Beta intelligence tests during World War I. These tests, which were used to measure the intelligence of recruits and soldiers, are considered precursors to today's most widely used measures of intelligence (McGuire, 1994).
- David Wechsler's creation of the Wechsler-Bellevue, his first intelligence test, stemmed from his clinical experiences during World War I measuring intellectual capacities of military personnel. This test led to the WAIS, and ultimately the WISC and WPPSI, the revisions of which are currently the most widely used measures of adult and child intelligence in the United States (Boake, 2002; Reisman, 1991).

Photo 2.3 War has influenced the field of clinical psychology in numerous ways. For soldiers involved in direct combat, how might clinical psychologists be most helpful?

- In the aftermath of World War II, many U.S. veterans returned home with "shell shock," as it was called at the time, and other psychological effects of battle (Benjamin, 2005; Miller, 1946). (*Posttraumatic stress disorder* later replaced *shell shock* as the accepted diagnostic label.) The U.S. government (specifically, the Veterans Administration—now the Department of Veterans Affairs) responded by requesting that the American Psychological Association formalize the training of clinical psychologists and provided significant funding to ensure the availability of such training opportunities. These efforts led to accreditation of clinical psychology doctoral training programs and ultimately to the scientist-practitioner (i.e., Boulder) model of training. This training model continues to dominate the field, and the strong relationship between Veterans Affairs and clinical psychology training, including a large number of internships at various levels, continues as well (Baker & Pickren, 2011; Humphreys, 1996; Kutchins & Kirk, 1997).

- The Nazi presence in Eastern Europe in the 1930s forced many influential figures in clinical psychology—most notably, Sigmund Freud and other Jewish psychodynamic leaders—to flee their home countries. This forced relocation facilitated the spread of their theories and clinical approaches to England and, ultimately, to the United States (Reisman, 1991).

- Recent U.S. military events, including efforts in Iraq and Afghanistan, have illustrated the crucial role that clinical psychologists continue to play for soldiers and veterans (Lorber & Garcia, 2010; Maguen et al., 2010). In fact, Veterans Affairs is one of the country's largest providers of mental health services, with almost 1 million veterans receiving such services within a recent 1-year period (Hunt & Rosenheck, 2011).

Consider the most recent missions carried out by U.S. military personnel. How will the profession of clinical psychology be shaped by these activities? What needs will clinical psychologists be challenged to meet, and how do these needs compare to those stemming from early war-related activities? Besides military personnel themselves, who might benefit from the services of clinical psychologists in relation to these activities?

In the middle of the 20th century, when psychotherapy rose to a more prominent place in clinical psychology, the **psychodynamic** approach to therapy dominated (Routh, 1996). With time, challengers to the psychodynamic approach emerged (Engel, 2008; Hollon & DiGiuseppe, 2011; Routh, 2011). In the 1950s and 1960s, for example, behaviorism surfaced as a fundamentally different approach to human beings and their behavioral or emotional problems. The **behavioral** approach emphasizes an empirical method, with problems and progress measured in observable, quantifiable terms. This emphasis was in part a reaction to the lack of empiricism evident in psychodynamic psychotherapy. **Humanistic** (or "client-centered") therapy also flourished in the 1960s, as Carl Rogers's relationship- and growth-oriented approach to therapy offered an alternative to both psychodynamic and behavioral approaches that many therapists and clients found attractive. The **family therapy** revolution took root in the 1950s, and as the 1960s and 1970s arrived, understanding mentally ill individuals as symptomatic of a flawed system had become a legitimate—and, by some clinicians, the preferred—therapeutic perspective.

Most recently, interest in **cognitive** therapy, with its emphasis on logical thinking as the foundation of psychological wellness, has intensified to the point that it has become the most popular singular orientation among clinical psychologists (excluding eclectic or integrative approaches) (Engel, 2008; Norcross & Karpiak, 2012; O'Donohue, 2009). Apart from the rise of cognitive therapy, the most striking feature of the current therapy marketplace is the utter range of therapy approaches. To illustrate, modern graduate textbooks for psychotherapy courses typically include at least a dozen chapters on distinct approaches (e.g., Corey, 2009; Prochaska & Norcross, 2010), with each chapter representing a full spectrum of more specific variations.

In addition to the sequential rise of these therapy approaches, recent decades have witnessed a movement toward combining them, in either eclectic or integrative ways (Goldfried, Glass, & Arnkoff, 2011), as well as the tremendous influence of cultural competence on any and all such approaches (Comas-Díaz, 2011).

Many of these therapy approaches are covered in detail elsewhere in this book, but for now, the important point is that the plethora of therapy options currently available to clinical psychologists did not always exist. Rather, these methods have evolved over the history of the discipline, with each new therapy approach emerging from the context of—and often as a reaction against—the therapies that came before it.

Development of the Profession

Just as clinical psychology's primary activities, such as psychotherapy and assessment, have evolved, the profession itself has progressed since its inception. Even in the earliest years, significant steps were evident. For example, in 1917, the American Association of

Clinical Psychologists was founded, and in 1919 it transitioned into Clinical Section of the American Psychological Association. In 1921, the Psychological Corporation was founded, foreshadowing the big business that was to become of psychological tests and measures of intelligence and personality.

In the 1940s, education and training in clinical psychology became more widespread and more standardized. The number of training sites increased dramatically, and the American Psychological Association began accrediting graduate programs that offered appropriate training experiences in therapy, assessment, and research. Veterans Affairs hospitals began their long-standing relationship with clinical psychology by funding graduate training and internships. And in 1949, the historic **Boulder conference** took place, at which training directors from around the country agreed that both practice and research were essential facets of PhD clinical psychology training (Cautin, 2011).

The 1950s produced more evidence that clinical psychology was a burgeoning profession. Therapy approaches proliferated, with new behavioral and humanistic/existential approaches rivaling established psychodynamic techniques. The extent to which psychotherapy did or didn't work also received increased attention, kick-started by Eysenck's (1952) critical analysis. The American Psychological Association also published the first edition of its ethical code in 1953, with significant discussion of clinical activities, reflecting a new level of professional establishment for clinical psychology (McFall, 2006; Tryon, 2008).

In the 1960s and 1970s, the profession of clinical psychology continued to diversify, successfully recruiting more females and minorities into the field. Clinical approaches continued to diversify as well, as behaviorism, humanism, and dozens of other approaches garnered large followings. The first PsyD programs appeared, offering graduate training options that emphasized applied clinical skills over research expertise. And signifying that psychotherapy was becoming a recognized part of American health care, insurance companies began to authorize payment for clinical psychologists' services just as they did for the services of many medical specialists.

In the 1980s, clinical psychologists enjoyed increased respect from the medical establishment as they gained hospital admitting privileges and Medicare payment privileges. Larger numbers of graduate training institutions continued to train larger numbers of new clinical psychologists, and the number of American Psychological Association members who were clinicians approached 50%. Psychotherapy burgeoned, especially in private practice settings, but intelligence and personality testing decreased (Reisman, 1991). The growth of the profession continued through the 1990s and 2000s, as did the trend toward diversity in gender and ethnicity of those joining it (DeLeon, Kenkel, Garcia-Shelton, & Vandenbos, 2011).

The size and scope of the field continues to grow, largely to meet the demand for psychotherapy services. In the late 1950s, only 14% of the U.S. population had ever received any kind of psychological treatment; by 2010, that number had climbed to 50%. Professional training options continue to multiply as well. Today's aspiring clinical psychologists have more choices than ever: the science/clinical balance of traditional PhD programs, PsyD programs emphasizing clinical skills, and more selected PhD programs that endorse the clinical scientist model of training and lean heavily toward the empirical side of the science/clinical continuum (Klonoff, 2011; McFall, 1991; Stricker, 2011). Numerous specializations, including forensic psychology and health psychology (illustrated by the inclusion of increasing numbers of clinical psychologists on primary health care teams), are flourishing (Goodheart & Rozensky, 2011). Empirical support of clinical techniques, prescription privileges, and new technologies (as described in Chapter 3) are among the other major professional developments in recent years.

To summarize the events described in this chapter, Box 2.3 presents a timeline of important events in the history of clinical psychology.

● ● ● BOX 2.3 ● ● ●

Timeline of Key Historical Events in Clinical Psychology

Year	Event
1796	William Tuke opens York Retreat in England
1801	Philippe Pinel publishes book on humane treatment of mentally ill (*Medico-Philosophical Treatise on Mental Alienation or Mania*)
1824	Eli Todd opens The Retreat in Hartford, Connecticut
1840	U.S. Census Bureau lists one category of mental disorder ("idiocy/insanity")
1841	Dorothea Dix encounters mentally ill in Boston prison, prompting extensive efforts for better treatment
1880	U.S. Census Bureau lists seven categories of mental disorders
1890	"Mental test" is used in print for the first time by Cattell

(Continued)

(Continued)

Year	Event
1892	Lightner Witmer earns his doctoral degree
1893	Emil Kraepelin proposes the early diagnostic category "dementia praecox"
1896	Lightner Witmer opens the first psychological clinic at the University of Pennsylvania
1905	Binet-Simon intelligence test is published in France
1907	Lightner Witmer founds the first professional journal of clinical psychology, *The Psychological Clinic*
1914	Psychology clinics proliferate; about 20 in operation
1916	Stanford-Binet Intelligence Test (as translated by Terman) is published in the United States
1917	American Association of Clinical Psychologists is founded
1921	Psychological Corporation is founded
1921	Rorschach inkblot technique published
1930s to 1950s	Psychoanalysis dominates psychotherapy
1935	Thematic Apperception Test published
1935	Psychology clinics proliferate further; more than 150 in operation
1939	Wechsler-Bellevue Intelligence Test published; first designed for adults
1943	Minnesota Multiphasic Personality Inventory (MMPI) published
1949	Wechsler Intelligence Test for Children (WISC) published
1949	Boulder conference held; yields scientist-practitioner training model
1950s to 1970s	Alternatives to psychoanalytic psychotherapy emerge (e.g., behaviorism, humanism, family/systems)
1952	Hans Eysenck publishes early, critical review of psychotherapy outcome
1952	*Diagnostic and Statistical Manual of Mental Disorders* (*DSM*) published
1953	American Psychological Association publishes first ethical code

Year	Event
1955	Wechsler Adult Intelligence Scale (WAIS) published
1967	Wechsler Preschool and Primary Scale of Intelligence (WPPSI) published
1968	*DSM-II* published
1973	Vail conference held; yields PsyD and practitioner-scholar training model
1974	WISC-R published
1980s to 2000s	Cognitive psychotherapy rises in prominence
1980	*DSM-III* published; specific diagnostic criteria and multiple axes appear
1981	WAIS-R published
1985	NEO Personality Inventory (NEO-PI) published
1987	*DSM-III-R* published
1989	MMPI-2 published
1989	WPPSI-R published
1991	Richard McFall publishes "manifesto"; yields "clinical scientist" training model
1991	WISC-III published
1992	MMPI-A published
1994	*DSM-IV* published
1997	WAIS-III published
1999	NEO-PI-R published
2000	*DSM-IV-R* published
2002	WPPSI-III published
2003	WISC-IV published
2008	WAIS-IV published
2008	MMPI-2-RF published
2013	*DSM-5* published

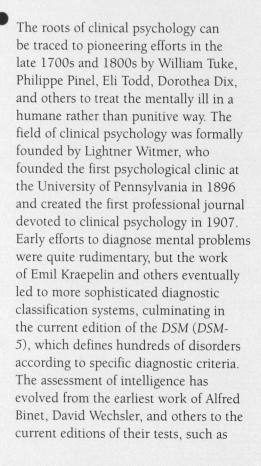

CHAPTER SUMMARY

The roots of clinical psychology can be traced to pioneering efforts in the late 1700s and 1800s by William Tuke, Philippe Pinel, Eli Todd, Dorothea Dix, and others to treat the mentally ill in a humane rather than punitive way. The field of clinical psychology was formally founded by Lightner Witmer, who founded the first psychological clinic at the University of Pennsylvania in 1896 and created the first professional journal devoted to clinical psychology in 1907. Early efforts to diagnose mental problems were quite rudimentary, but the work of Emil Kraepelin and others eventually led to more sophisticated diagnostic classification systems, culminating in the current edition of the *DSM* (*DSM-5*), which defines hundreds of disorders according to specific diagnostic criteria. The assessment of intelligence has evolved from the earliest work of Alfred Binet, David Wechsler, and others to the current editions of their tests, such as the Stanford-Binet and the WAIS, WISC, and WPPSI. Early attempts to assess personality were primarily projective tests, such as the Rorschach inkblot method and the TAT. Those tests were soon followed by objective personality tests such as the MMPI, many of which have achieved high levels of reliability and validity. Although psychotherapy is currently the dominant professional activity of clinical psychologists, it was relatively uncommon until the 1940s and 1950s. At that time, the psychodynamic approach to therapy prevailed, but behaviorism and humanism rose to popularity in the decades that followed. Currently, the cognitive approach is the most popular single-school therapy approach, and the number of distinct approaches to therapy continues to proliferate. As a profession, clinical psychology continues to evolve in many ways, including a diversification of its members and its graduate training options.

KEY TERMS AND NAMES

CRITICAL THINKING QUESTIONS

1. How essential were the contributions of William Tuke, Philippe Pinel, Eli Todd, and Dorothea Dix to the creation of the field of clinical psychology? Would the field exist today without their work?

2. Psychotherapy was not even mentioned in Lightner Witmer's original definition of clinical psychology, but in recent decades, psychotherapy has been the most common activity of clinical psychologists. In your opinion, what factors might have contributed to the rise in prominence of psychotherapy?

3. In your opinion, why has the number of disorders defined by successive editions of the *DSM* continued to increase?

4. In your opinion, which of the current proposed disorders (e.g., premenstrual dysphoric disorder, minor depressive disorder, recurrent brief depressive disorder, binge eating disorder, as listed in Box 2.1) should be included as official disorders in the next edition of the *DSM*? On what do you base your opinion?

5. To what extent would you expect a graduate program's model of training (e.g., scientist-practitioner, practitioner-scholar, or clinical scientist) to influence the types of personality assessment tools (e.g., projective or objective) it trains its students to use?

STUDENT STUDY SITE RESOURCES

Visit the study site at www.sagepub.com/pomerantz3eupdate for these additional learning tools:

- Self-quizzes
- eFlashcards
- Culture Expert Interviews

- Full-text SAGE journal articles
- Additional web resources
- Mock Assessment Data

CHAPTER SUMMARY VIDEO

 QR codes at the end of each chapter link to chapter background videos by the author. Visit http://gettag.mobi using your smartphone browser to download the free Microsoft Tag app. Once installed, scan the tags to go directly to these brief videos. In this video, the author discusses the impact that the changes to the *DSM* can have on what all of us consider normal and abnormal.

Current Controversies in Clinical Psychology

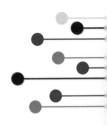

Chapter 2 illustrated that at any given point in the history of clinical psychology, the field is defined by a few topical issues, challenges, and controversies. The present is certainly no exception. The issues facing the field today have an undeniable influence on clinical psychologists and those with whom they work, and the way these issues are resolved will shape the field for decades to come.

Prescription Privileges

⊕ **Web Link 3.1**

Video of group
advocating
prescription
privileges

Historically, the ability to prescribe medication has been one of the primary distinctions between psychiatrists and psychologists. In fact, in the eyes of the general public, it is a defining difference between the professions (Balon, Martini, & Singareddy, 2004). However, in recent years, some clinical psychologists have actively pursued **prescription privileges** (Burns, Rey, & Burns, 2008; DeLeon, Kenkel, Gray, & Sammons, 2011; McGrath, 2010; Tryon, 2008). The roots of the movement were established in the 1980s, but in the 1990s and 2000s, it rose to the level of a high-profile, high-stakes debate. The American Psychological Association published numerous articles endorsing prescription privileges (e.g., American Psychological Association, 1996a) and offering suggestions for training of psychologists to become proficient in the knowledge necessary to prescribe safely and effectively (American Psychological Association, 1996b). In addition, several outspoken and prominent individuals have also promoted the movement toward prescribing, including **Patrick H. DeLeon,** a former president of the American Psychological Association (DeLeon & Wiggins, 1996); **Morgan T. Sammons,** a widely recognized expert on psychopharmacology and 1 of 10 psychologists who took part in the first experimental pilot program of psychologists prescribing medication (Dittman, 2003); and **Robert McGrath,** training director of the Psychopharmacology Postdoctoral Training Program in the School of Psychology at Fairleigh Dickinson University and president of the **American Society for the Advancement of Pharmacotherapy (American Psychological Association, Division 55).**

⊕ **Web Link 3.2**

Prescription
privileges in New
Mexico

The prescription privilege movement scored notable victories when two states—New Mexico and Louisiana—granted prescription privileges to appropriately trained psychologists in 2002 and 2004, respectively. Many other states have given serious consideration to similar legislation in recent years. Other significant steps in the movement toward prescription privileges include the creation of the aforementioned APA Division 55 in 2000, as well as the psychopharmacology training programs available for psychologists in the U.S. military (Sammons, 2011). Nonetheless, the issue remains hotly debated, with significant numbers of clinical psychologists and worthy arguments on both sides (e.g., DeLeon, Dunivin, & Newman, 2002; Heiby, 2002).

Why Clinical Psychologists Should Prescribe

- *Shortage of psychiatrists.* In some parts of the country, there simply aren't enough psychiatrists to serve the population adequately. Especially in some rural areas, there is a strikingly low ratio of professionals with the training and ability to prescribe psychoactive medications to the number of people who need them. In fact, when clinical psychologists successfully lobbied for prescription privileges in New Mexico and Louisiana, a cornerstone of their argument was the low number of psychiatrists per capita in many parts of these two states (Long, 2005). Underserved segments of society would benefit from a higher ratio of prescribers to patients.

- *Clinical psychologists are more expert than primary care physicians.* Although psychiatrists have specialized training in mental health issues, they aren't the only ones prescribing psychoactive medications. In fact, by some estimates, more than 80% of the prescriptions written for psychoactive medications come from primary care physicians (e.g., Cummings, 2007). When it comes to expertise in mental health problems, clinical psychologists' training is more extensive and specialized than physicians'; therefore, clinical psychologists could be better able to diagnose problems correctly and select effective medications.

- *Other nonphysician professionals already have prescription privileges.* Dentists, podiatrists, optometrists, and advanced practice nurses are among the professionals who are not physicians but have some rights to prescribe medication to their patients. Their success in this activity sets a precedent for specially trained clinical psychologists to do the same. Especially when we consider that general practitioner physicians—whose specific training in psychological issues is limited— currently prescribe a high proportion of psychoactive medication, it seems reasonable to allow clinical psychologists to use their specialized expertise for the purpose of prescribing.

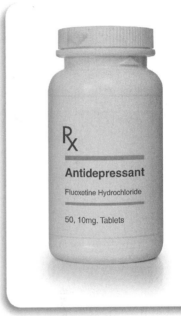

Photo 3.1 In your opinion, should clinical psychologists have prescription privileges? Why or why not?

- *Convenience for clients.* Antonio is a 9-year-old boy with attention-deficit/ hyperactivity disorder (ADHD). Angela is a 38-year-old woman with major depression. Antonio and Angela could benefit from both nonpharmacological interventions (psychotherapy, counseling, etc.) and prescription medications. Without prescription privileges, clinical psychologists can provide the therapy, but they cannot provide the medication. The result is that Antonio (and his parents) and Angela will both need to be referred to a physician, such as a psychiatrist, to be evaluated for medication. Of course, this increases the time and money that these clients must spend on appointments. In addition, it requires the two busy mental health professionals to communicate consistently with each other about their shared clients, and a misunderstanding between the two could result in complications for the clients. With prescription privileges, Antonio and Angela could get both their therapy and their medication from the same source—the clinical psychologist. From the client's perspective, treatment is streamlined, saving both time and money. And the risk of problems due to miscommunication between professionals is eliminated.

- *Professional autonomy.* With prescription privileges, clinical psychologists can feel capable of independently providing a wider range of services to their clients. Without them, they may feel restricted in what they can accomplish for their clients. Of course, clinical psychologists should always strive to work collaboratively with other professionals involved in their clients' treatment. But at the same time, with prescription privileges, their ability to treat the physical and psychological aspects of their clients' difficulties autonomously, without relying on psychiatrists or other physicians, is greatly increased.

- *Professional identification.* In the eyes of the general public, psychologists may be difficult to distinguish from other nonprescribing therapists or counselors such as licensed professional counselors, social workers, and the like. The ability to prescribe immediately sets psychologists apart from—and, many would argue, above—these other professions.

- *Evolution of the profession.* Clinical psychology has undergone many significant changes in its brief history. It has incorporated many treatment techniques (e.g., therapy approaches) that were initially unfamiliar, and in the process, the profession has thrived. Embracing prescription privileges is seen by many as the next logical step in the progression. To stand in its way, some argue, is to impede the evolution of the field (DeLeon et al., 2002). Prescriptive authority could open multiple doors to professional opportunity for clinical psychologists, from direct pharmaceutical treatment of clients to consultation with physicians about psychoactive medications for their patients (Burns et al., 2008).

- *Revenue for the profession.* The profession and its members stand to benefit financially from prescription privileges as well (Cummings, 2007). The potential for increased income as a result of prescription practices may offset some of the salary decreases reported by psychologists in recent decades, including those occurring as a result of the impact of managed care (as reported by Murphy, DeBernardo, & Shoemaker, 1998). In fact, strong opposition to the prescription privilege movement has emerged from psychiatrist organizations, whose members stand to lose business if psychologists gain the ability to prescribe. And the scope of this business should not be underestimated: During the 1990s, the percentage of people in treatment for depression who received an antidepressant drug doubled, from 37% to 74%, and in 2007, antidepressants were the most commonly prescribed category of drug in the United States (Sammons, 2011).

Why Clinical Psychologists Should Not Prescribe

- *Training issues.* What kind of education should clinical psychologists receive before they are licensed to prescribe? What should it cover? Who should teach them? When should it take place? (Early in graduate school? During the predoctoral internship? As specialized training after the doctoral degree?) All these questions complicate the pursuit of prescription privileges. Some have argued that for a comprehensive understanding of everything involved in a prescription decision, the prescriber needs something close to full-fledged medical school training. Only in this way could they appreciate the potential impact of a drug on the multiple systems of the body, the possibility of drug interactions, and all other medical factors (Griffiths, 2001; Robiner et al., 2002). Others have argued that with far less training, clinical psychologists could gain a basic competence in psychopharmacology (Resnick & Norcross, 2002; Sammons, Sexton, & Meredith, 1996). Most proposals fall somewhere between these two extremes, but the scope of pharmacology training for clinical psychologists is not entirely resolved. In fact, debates about current training standards are ongoing, with some arguing that pharmacologically trained psychologists are better trained in psychoactive medications than are the physicians and nurses who prescribe them (Muse & McGrath, 2010) and others strongly disagreeing, labeling psychologists' training substandard (Heiby, 2010). Some have even promoted the notion that clinical psychologists should receive some training in psychopharmacology even if they don't plan to prescribe, because without such training, they are unable to communicate effectively with medical professionals with whom they share clients (Julien, 2011). Moreover, the pragmatics of pharmacological training remain uncertain. If such training were added to existing graduate programs, it might extend them by many semesters. And many graduate programs in clinical psychology currently lack faculty with the expertise to teach these courses.

- *Threats to psychotherapy.* If clinical psychologists can prescribe, what will become of psychotherapy? Some have wondered if we will see a drift within the profession from "talk therapy" to pharmacological intervention. Clients may come to expect medication from clinical psychologists, and clinical psychologists may discover that prescribing is more profitable than therapy. The way psychologists understand and intervene with their clients may fundamentally shift from an appreciation of behavioral, cognitive, or emotional processes to symptom reduction via pharmacology. Some have pointed out that the profession of psychiatry has witnessed a drift of this sort and that clinical psychology could lose something of its essence if it does the same (McGrath, 2004; McGrath et al., 2004). As Cummings (2007) put it,

> Undoubtedly, the acquisition of prescription authority . . . would significantly expand the economic base of psychological practice. When that day comes, it remains to be seen, however, whether they abandon the hard work of psychotherapy for the expediency of the prescription pad. (p. 175)

- *Identity confusion.* Until all active psychologists prescribe (which, if it occurs at all, is certainly decades away), an identity crisis could emerge within the clinical psychology profession. Some clinical psychologists will prescribe, whereas others won't. Some may have been trained during graduate school; others may have returned for specialized training long after they gained their doctoral degrees. Without an effective effort to keep the public educated about our profession, a client referred to a particular clinical psychologist may feel justifiably puzzled about whether prescription medication might be part of the treatment program.

Web Link 3.3

Psychiatry turns to drug therapy

• *The potential influence of the pharmaceutical industry.* Reports of drug companies' attempts to increase profit—by offering gifts to prescribers, funding research, and controlling the publication of research results—have become widespread (e.g., Healy, 2004; Lane, 2007). Some opponents of the prescription movement have expressed concern that if psychologists prescribe, they will inevitably find themselves targeted by the pharmaceutical industry and will be pressured to consider factors other than client welfare when making prescription decisions. Some psychologists have gone so far as to call for formal professional guidelines to address how psychologists should interact with drug companies (McGrath et al., 2004).

● ● ● BOX 3.1 ● ● ●

Prescription Privileges: What if You Were the Client?

If you were the client, would you prefer that your clinical psychologist have the ability to prescribe medication? Does your answer depend on the amount or type of training the clinical psychologist has received? Or on the availability of other qualified prescribers (primary care physicians, psychiatrists, etc.)? Which of the pros and cons listed in the text have the greatest influence on your answer?

Evidence-Based Practice/Manualized Therapy

Like the prescription privilege movement, the movement in favor of **evidence-based practice** and **manualized therapy** has intensified in recent decades, as has the reaction to it. In fact, "few topics in mental health are as incendiary, consequential, and timely as evidence-based practices" (Norcross, Beutler, & Levant, 2006, p. 3; see also, Ollendick & King, 2012). Before we consider both sides of the argument, let's consider a brief history of the factors that have led to the debate.

For many decades, researchers in the field of psychotherapy have sought to answer questions about its benefits, or how well therapy "works." Hans Eysenck's (1952) bold statement that therapy had no proof of positive outcome sparked much research on the topic, and this early wave of research basically proved Eysenck wrong—psychotherapy was found to be quite efficacious (Smith & Glass, 1977; Smith, Glass, & Miller, 1980). However, much of this research was specific neither to any particular type of psychotherapy nor to any particular disorder; it simply supported the idea that therapy of any kind was more helpful than no therapy for people with any disorder. Subsequent steps in this line of research addressed more specific, targeted questions. Rather than asking broadly, "Does therapy work?" researchers began asking more specifically, "Which forms of therapy work best for which disorders?"

⊕ **Web Link 3.4**
Evidence-based practice

Take an insider's perspective on the methodological differences between the more general and more specific types of therapy outcome studies. Imagine that you are one of the therapists involved in an early study on psychotherapy efficacy, perhaps in the 1970s. You and the other therapists are each assigned a certain number of clients and are instructed simply to provide therapy to them. The instructions are no more specific or detailed than that. As a result, the therapy done in this study varies widely from one client to the next and from one therapist to the next. This lack of uniformity between therapies is not a problem, though, because the aim of the study is simply to compare those receiving therapy of any kind with similar individuals not receiving therapy (the control group).

But this lack of uniformity between therapies would be a major problem in the type of therapy outcome study more common in recent years, such as a more targeted study on the effects of a specific form of therapy. In fact, if you designed this type of study, you would want to make absolutely sure that the therapy was somewhat uniform across all clients, even if different therapists provided it. After all, defining the therapy in exact terms is a prerequisite to demonstrating how effective that particular type of therapy is and offering a description of it to others. So rather than broadly instructing the study's therapists to practice therapy, or providing a vague description of the category of therapy to practice, you would provide much more detailed instructions. In short, you would provide a **therapy manual.** One purpose of this manual is to keep variability between therapists to a minimum, such that if the technique proves effective, it can be shared with others in exact, unambiguous terms.

Since the 1980s, publications of this type of outcome research—how well a manualized therapy works on a particular disorder—have proliferated. As examples, researchers have tested **exposure plus response prevention**, a specific form of behavior therapy, for the treatment of obsessive-compulsive disorder; **dialectical behavior therapy** for the treatment of borderline personality disorder; and specific cognitive therapy techniques for the treatment of depression (Woody & Sanderson, 1998). In each of these cases, the specific therapy proved effective in the treatment of the target disorder, and the authors published their results in professional journals. As such published reports accumulated, Division 12 (Clinical Psychology) of the American Psychological Association created a task force to compile them into a list to serve as a reference for therapists who sought the most proven therapies for particular disorders. The therapies on this list were originally called "empirically validated" treatments, but the terminology soon changed to "empirically supported" treatments and eventually to "evidence-based" practice (e.g., Kazdin & Weisz, 2003; La Roche & Christopher, 2009). This change in terminology is important because the current term, *evidence-based practice*, incorporates not only the particular treatment itself but also factors related to the people providing and receiving it. More specifically, evidence-based practice is defined as "the integration of the best available research with clinical expertise in the context of patient characteristics, culture, and preferences" (APA Presidential Task Force on Evidence-Based Practice, 2006, p. 273). So research (often in the form of clinical trials of manualized therapies) is just a piece of the puzzle; the other pieces focus on the clinician's knowledge and capability regarding the treatment and the qualities of the client (including culture and personal preferences) that could influence how effective the treatment will be (Norcross, Freedheim, & VandenBos, 2011; Spring & Neville, 2011).

The first list of empirically validated treatments was published in 1995, and updates appeared in 1996 and 1998 (Chambless et al., 1996, 1998; Task Force on Promotion and Dissemination of Psychological Procedures, 1995). A landmark book titled *A Guide to Treatments That Work* was also published around this time, with more detailed information about these therapies (Nathan & Gorman, 1998). In the years that have followed, numerous books of this type, offering chapter-by-chapter guides to "what works" for which disorders, have emerged (e.g., Carr, 2008; Roth & Fonagy, 2005).

Such lists of "therapies that work" have been celebrated by some as a major step forward for clinical psychology, legitimizing it as a scientific enterprise. Others have voiced concern or disapproval of the implications of evidence-based, manualized therapy.

● ● ● BOX 3.2 ● ● ●

Metaphorically Speaking: Evidence-Based Treatment Manuals and Teaching Manuals

Think about your high school chemistry teacher. Specifically, think about the way that teacher taught chemistry—the general style or approach he or she had, the lectures, discussions, lab experiments, homework, exams, and so on. The material was basically the same for all of us, but we can be sure that our teachers' presentation styles varied widely.

Which of their methods works best? With so many different techniques in practice, it seems reasonable to wonder which particular way of teaching high school chemistry is most effective. To begin to answer this question empirically, we would need to define a few things up front. For example, we'd have to define the teaching techniques very specifically. We couldn't simply compare, say, a "lecture-based" style with a "discussion-based" style, or a "laid-back" approach with a "high-pressure" approach—these descriptions are too vague. Instead, we would need to instruct chemistry teachers *exactly* how to teach—in other words, give them a manual with detailed instructions—to determine exactly what works and what doesn't.

We'd also have to define up front the outcomes, or the results, of the teaching methods we're examining. From our empirical point of view, objective and measurable results would be best. Scores on standardized chemistry exams might work well, for example. We certainly would want to avoid more subjective outcome measures such as, say, students' level of interest in chemistry or the degree to which the course inspired a general passion for learning—these are simply too hard to measure reliably and validly.

Once we have our methods and outcome measures defined, we could run our "chemistry teaching experiment." If the results demonstrate that a particular approach to teaching high school chemistry was in fact effective (especially if these results were obtained in multiple studies), we could share our results with high school chemistry teachers around the world. They, in turn, might adopt our "proven" method rather than use their own personal or idiosyncratic methods, which lack any such empirical support. Eventually, it is possible that all high school chemistry teachers would teach chemistry the same way, using the one method that has the most empirical evidence.

Like teachers, psychologists each have their own unique methods when practicing psychotherapy. But which methods are best for which disorders? Hundreds of empirical studies by clinical psychology researchers have addressed this question, using an approach similar to the one we considered above for teaching high school chemistry. First, the researchers defined the therapy in specific terms in a therapy manual and instructed therapists to follow it closely. They also defined therapy outcome in measurable, objective terms. Then they tested their manualized therapy with clients diagnosed with a particular disorder—for example, depression. When the results were positive, the researchers shared their results with other psychologists in journal articles, book chapters, or conference presentations. These psychologists, in turn, have the option of adopting this "proven" method with their own clients, rather than using their own personal or idiosyncratic methods, which

(Continued)

(Continued)

lack any such empirical support. Eventually, it is possible that all psychologists would treat depressed clients the same way, using the one method that has the most empirical support.

Champions of evidence-based treatment manuals see this movement as a significant step forward for the science of clinical psychology. In fact, some have argued that psychologists should use only therapies that have demonstrated empirical support and that to shun these approaches in favor of other approaches that lack empirical support is professionally irresponsible (e.g., Lilienfeld, Lynn, Ruscio, & Beyerstein, 2010; Lohr, Fowler, & Lilienfeld, 2002). On the other hand, some psychologists feel strongly that the push toward evidence-based treatments and policies that require their use overly restricts psychologists from customizing/personalizing treatments for particular individuals or is based on flawed scientific methods (e.g., Rosenfeld, 2009; Silverman, 1996), or that the problems clients bring to therapists are too idiosyncratic and span too wide a range to ever be captured by a catalogue of treatment manuals (e.g., Zedlow, 2009).

Again, think about your high school chemistry teacher and the thousands of others who teach the same material. If a single, manualized method of teaching high school chemistry had more empirical support than any other, should all high school chemistry teachers use it? If your chemistry teacher had taught "by the manual" in this way, how would your experience as a chemistry student have changed? Those of us whose chemistry teachers were incompetent may have learned more, but those of us whose chemistry teachers were uniquely innovative and effective may have learned less. The same questions, certainly, apply to the issue of evidence-based practice/manualized psychotherapies.

Advantages of Evidence-Based Practice/Manualized Therapy

• *Scientific legitimacy.* Before the emergence of manualized therapies with empirical support, clinical psychology might have been described by empirically minded critics as a "cottage industry" of sorts. In other words, each psychologist provided his or her own unique, "homespun" form of psychotherapy for a particular disorder. A depressed client who saw Dr. A might have received Dr. A's idiosyncratic brand of therapy, but the same client might receive an entirely different brand of therapy from Dr. B, with the differences in treatment stemming from differences in training or the psychologist's professional preference. Such inconsistency hardly seems appropriate for a discipline that calls itself a science. A more scientific, empirical approach to the treatment of depression, or any other disorder, requires that the discipline of clinical psychology determine a beneficial treatment for the disorder and that members of the discipline uniformly practice that treatment. We expect such standards of treatment from medical doctors treating physical diseases, and if clinical psychology subscribes to the medical model of diagnosis and treatment, the same expectation should apply to our field as well.

- *Establishing minimal levels of competence.* Inevitably, if all clinical psychologists are allowed to practice their own unique brands of therapy, a few of them will be ineffective or even harmful to clients. However, as manualized, evidence-based treatments are disseminated and used by clinical psychologists, their presence ensures that a potentially incompetent or detrimental therapist will be educated in treatments with demonstrated effectiveness. Moreover, as these treatments evolve into professional standards, psychologists will be obligated to follow them to some degree. As a result, the public will receive a more consistent, proven brand of treatment for each disorder, and psychologists can be held to a greater standard of accountability (Sanderson, 2003).

- *Training improvements.* Just as therapy in a "cottage industry" can vary widely among psychologists, the training that psychologists receive can also fluctuate widely among graduate programs. As the list of manualized, evidence-based therapies grows, they can be incorporated into graduate programs. In fact, when the American Psychological Association makes accreditation decisions about graduate training programs, it does consider criteria related to training in evidence-based treatments (Lyddon & Chatkoff, 2001). The result is that upcoming generations of psychologists will have been educated in the therapies that have empirical data supporting their success with particular disorders. Some programs may emphasize evidence-based treatments more than others (Hebert, 2002), but all programs can benefit to some extent from their inclusion.

- *Decreased reliance on clinical judgment.* Clinical judgment can be susceptible to bias and, as a result, quite flawed (Dawes, Faust, & Meehl, 1989; Garb, 2005). When subjective, personal judgment of this type is applied to therapy decisions, the outcome of therapy can be compromised. Vrieze and Grove (2009) surveyed clinical psychologists about the way they make decisions in their practices and found that they did, in fact, rely much more often on their own clinical judgment rather than mechanical or actuarial judgment based on empirical evidence. To the extent that manualized therapies lessen the reliance on clinical judgment and replace these components of therapy with evidence-based techniques, outcome may be enhanced (Lilienfeld et al., 2010).

Disadvantages of Evidence-Based Practice/Manualized Therapy

- *Threats to the psychotherapy relationship.* Although some of "what works" in therapy is attributable to specific techniques that therapists employ, a greater proportion of therapy's success is due to the quality of the therapeutic relationship (or "alliance") between the therapist and the client (Norcross & Wampold, 2011a; Rosenfeld, 2009; Wampold, 2001). Therapy manuals typically don't emphasize this relationship; instead, they tend to emphasize technique. In other words, they generally overlook "how" therapists relate to their clients in favor of "what" therapists do with (or to) their clients. A therapist who operates as a technician carrying out mechanical, predetermined methods can do a disservice to clients who seek a meaningful human connection (Sommers-Flanagan & Sommers-Flanagan, 2009). Soon after proponents of the manualized treatment movement published their landmark book *A Guide to Treatments That Work* (Nathan & Gorman, 1998), a group of highly esteemed psychologists responded with contrasting viewpoints in a book fittingly titled *Psychotherapy Relationships That Work* (Norcross, 2002), insisting that the therapist–client relationship should not be neglected but should be recognized and studied as a focal point of what makes therapy work.

- *Diagnostic complications.* Each evidence-based treatment manual targets a particular disorder or issue. Such specificity is at the heart of testing specific treatments for specific disorders. In fact, when manualized treatments are tested in clinical trials, the clients who are allowed into the study are those with the target problem—for example, panic disorder—and without other complicating factors. In other words, researchers typically strive to test their manualized therapies on clients with "textbook cases" of a disorder. But that's not necessarily how clients present themselves in the real world of clinical psychology. In a private practice, a community mental health center, or a hospital, a client with panic disorder might also have something else—another anxiety disorder, a mood disorder, a personality disorder, or cognitive limitations, perhaps. This comorbidity means that the therapy that worked on clients with "clean" (i.e., uncomplicated) disorders in a treatment outcome study may not work as well on clients with more "messy" diagnostic features who commonly seek therapy from clinical psychologists in real-world settings (Angold, Costello, & Erkanli, 1999; Kessler, 1994; Zedlow, 2009).

- *Restrictions on practice.* To some, the evidence-based practice/manualized therapy movement has suggested that the only therapies worth practicing are those with empirical support (Lohr et al., 2002). In other words, if a therapy is not on the list of evidence-based treatments, it is unfounded and should be avoided. That is, "narrowly interpreted, evidence-based practice has become a rationale for mandating particular treatments" (Wampold, 2009, p. ix). In fact, some psychologists have used the term *malpractice* in reference to the act of using a therapy that lacks empirical support (Nathan & Gorman, 1998). In the "advantages" section above, a decreased reliance on personal, clinical judgment was praised, but if empirical support trumps personal decision making completely, the therapist's role may include little more than the routine application of prescribed techniques. Such a job description may prove unsatisfying for many psychologists who seek autonomy and who rely on clinical creativity to customize their treatments, and it may not justify the extensive training they have obtained (Beutler, Kim, Davison, & Karno, 1996; Lebow, 2006; Rosenfeld, 2009). Also, because many treatment manuals emphasize brief (inexpensive) treatments, managed-care and health insurance companies can use empirical support to argue that psychologists should practice them exclusively, further limiting psychologists' autonomy (Seligman & Levant, 1998). Proponents of manualized therapy often respond that manuals get a "bad rap" of sorts:

> We believe that manuals are mischaracterized when they are described as rigid . . . specifying the components of the therapy does not have to deprive a therapy of its lifeblood. At best, it can help everyone involved come to understand what that lifeblood actually is. (Spokas, Rodebaugh, & Heimburg, 2008, p. 322)

Indeed, within the larger debate over manualized therapy, the debate regarding the extent to which strict adherence to manuals produces better outcomes also rages (Norcross et al., 2006). Some studies have actually found that, compared with therapists who follow manuals rigidly, therapists who demonstrate flexibility while using manuals are more successful in terms of engaging clients in therapy and ultimately producing better outcomes (e.g., Chu & Kendall, 2009). The option of flexibility, as opposed to required, rigid adherence, also helps the clinicians themselves accept manualized therapies as a means of practice (Forehand, Dorsey, Jones, Long, & McMahon, 2010). Curry (2009) offered an intriguing metaphor for this balance between rigidity and flexibility regarding therapy manuals by referring to training in musical instruments: It requires the learning of standard techniques but also allows for (or even encourages) improvisation.

- *Debatable criteria for empirical evidence.* What should it take for a manualized therapy to make the "empirically supported" or "evidence-based" list? Some have argued that the current criteria are questionable or do not account for failed trials of a treatment (Garfield, 1996). Others have argued that the criteria are biased in favor of more empirically oriented therapies (e.g., behavioral and cognitive), while therapies that produce less easily quantifiable results (e.g., psychodynamic or humanistic) are shut out (Lebow, 2006). Behavioral and cognitive therapies do dominate the lists of evidence-based therapies, although other orientations are also represented to a more limited extent (Norcross et al., 2006). In any case, the debate over what constitutes empirical evidence will significantly affect which therapies make the list and, in turn, how clinical psychologists treat their clients.

Since evidence-based practice and therapy manuals have risen to a place of prominence in the field, many experts have begun to focus on the issue of *disseminating* these techniques (Beidas & Kendall, 2010; Godley, Garner, Smith, Meyers, & Godley, 2011; McCloskey, 2011). In other words, it's one thing to develop treatments that work but another to educate therapists about them and persuade therapists to use them. Numerous strategies have been employed, with varying results. Stewart and Chambless (2010), for example, found that psychologists in private practice find case studies (i.e., detailed descriptions of a single client successfully treated) more persuasive than research reviews (i.e., presentations of data indicating that the treatment works). Stewart, Chambless, and Baron (2012) found that psychologists in private practice were more willing to undergo training in an empirically supported treatment if the training was brief (i.e., 3 hours) and inexpensive, as opposed to lengthy (i.e., 1 to 3 days) and expensive. Jensen-Doss, Hawley, Lopez, and Osterberg (2009) found that an organization that forces its clinicians to use evidence-based treatments, especially without any attempt to get clinicians "onboard" first, can encounter significant resistance and resentment. Even clinicians who are themselves psychotherapy researchers don't always rank empirical research at the top of their list of factors by which to make clinical decisions (Safran, Abreu, Ogilvie, & DeMaria, 2011).

Despite the ongoing heated debate, evidence-based practice needs not be an "either/or" issue. Messer (2004) argues, "As practitioners, we cannot manage without nomothetic *and* idiographic data, findings based on quantitative *and* qualitative method, and a mixture of scientific *and* humanistic outlooks, which are psychology's dual heritage" (p. 586).

• • • BOX 3.3 • • •

Evidence-Based Practice/Manualized Therapy: What if You Were the Client?

If you were the client, would you prefer that your clinical psychologist adhere to an evidence-based, manualized form of therapy? Or would you prefer that the clinical psychologist ignore such techniques and allow nonempirical factors, including his or her own clinical judgment, to guide your treatment? Which of the advantages and disadvantages listed in the text influence your decision the most? To what extent would you welcome a compromise between the two positions? How would a clinical psychologist create such a compromise?

Overexpansion of Mental Disorders

As we discussed in Chapter 2 (and will discuss further in Chapter 7), the size and scope of the *Diagnostic and Statistical Manual (DSM)* has vastly increased since its inception in the 1950s. Correspondingly, the number of people with mental disorders has climbed: half of the US population is diagnosable at some point in their lifetime, and 11% of the population is currently taking antidepressant medication (Paris, 2013a). This climb in mental disorder rates goes by many names: overdiagnosis, diagnostic expansion, diagnostic inflation, diagnostic creep, medicalization of everyday problems, false positives, and in severe cases, false epidemics (Pierre, 2013; Frances, 2013a).

The authors of the *DSM*, including the current *DSM-5* published in 2013, spend significant time and energy considering every proposed disorder. They review relevant research and solicit feedback from practicing professionals and the public before they decide to include any new disorder or change the criteria for an existing disorder. Among other concerns, they want to minimize the chances that people struggling with mental illness fall through the cracks, so they want to create a diagnostic manual that captures all of them. Obviously, they believe that any disorder that "makes the cut" to appear on the pages of the *DSM* truly deserves to be there. But their decisions have caused significant controversy among those who believe that many of today's disorders actually describe normal life experiences—unfortunate or unpleasant experiences, certainly, but nothing that warrants a label of mental disorder. This was particularly true with *DSM-5*, which introduced numerous new disorders and which changed the criteria for some existing disorders in such a way that they would include more people (to be covered in more detail in Chapter 7) (Paris, 2013b). Among the criticisms about overdiagnosis that were offered about *DSM-5* were these:

- "There has been no real epidemic of mental illness, just a much looser definition of sickness, making it harder for people to be considered well. The people remain the same; the diagnostic labels have changed and are too elastic. Problems that used to be an expected and tolerated part of life are now diagnosed and treated as mental disorder." (Frances, 2013a, p. 82)
- "The danger of DSM-5 ideology is that it extends the scope of mental disorder to a point where almost anyone can be diagnosed with one." (Paris, 2013a, p. 41)
- "The more that psychiatric diagnoses appear to encroach on the boundaries of normal behavior, the more psychiatry opens itself to criticisms that there is no validity to the concept of mental disorders (e.g., there's no such thing as mental illness—it's a 'myth')" (Pierre, 2013, p. 109)

Concerns about the expanding definition of mental illness were around long before *DSM-5* (Dobbs, 2013; Frances, 2013b; Horwitz & Wakefield, 2007). For example, excessive shyness that interfered with a person's life was once considered an unfortunate personality characteristic, but since 1980, it has been included in the DSM as social anxiety disorder (Barber, 2008; Horwitz & Wakefield, 2012). But with each edition of the *DSM*, the scope of mental illness has expanded, along with the controversy surrounding it.

New Disorders and New Definitions of Old Disorders

This expansion of the scope of mental disorders happens in at least two ways: introduction of new disorders to capture experiences once considered normal, and "lowering the bar" for existing disorders such that more people meet the criteria. As examples of new disorders, critics might point to premenstrual dysphoric disorder (a more disabling version of the symptoms of premenstrual syndrome) or binge eating disorder (out-of-control overeating at least once per week), both of which appear for the first time in *DSM-5* and which have the potential to describe large numbers of people. As examples of "lowering the bar," critics might point to changing the age by which symptoms of attention-deficit/hyperactivity disorder must appear from 7 to 12, or changing the required frequency of binges in bulimia nervosa from twice per week to once per week, both of which are also *DSM-5* innovations.

Whether the risk of overdiagnosis comes from a new disorder or a new definition of an old disorder, the consequences can be very real. A diagnosis can help some people with problems get treatment they need, but a diagnosis can also help some people with problems get treatment they *don't* need—medications that have harmful side effects, or unnecessary therapy that undermines a person's ability to use their own coping skills and could have been offered to someone else. A mental illness diagnosis can have many other effects as well: it can affect a person's self-image via the stigma that some people attach to mental illness ("I'm mentally ill") and subsequently their self-efficacy and overall wellness; it can influence how health insurance companies consider the person as a potential enrollee; and it can affect how a court of law views the person in terms of guilt regarding a crime or suitability for child custody (Caplan, 2012, Frances, 2013a, 2013c).

Of course, our discussion of the controversy surrounding overdiagnosis must include not only the diagnoses themselves, but the way they are used in the real world. In other words, it hardly matters what the *DSM* authors label as a mental disorder, or how they define them, if those who diagnose and treat clients ignore such information. There is at least some truth to the notion that practicing clinicians make diagnoses without detailed consideration of the precise definition of a mental disorder, and in some cases, they offer treatments whether or not a diagnosis has been made at all (Greenberg, 2013; Paris, 2013b). For example, 72% of people who receive a prescription for an antidepressant medication do not receive any mental health diagnosis (Mojtabai & Olfson, 2011). Other surveys of mental health professionals indicate that many rely more on professional experience, intuition, and "gut feelings" than symptom checklists to guide diagnostic decisions (Mishara & Schwartz, 2013). In these cases, overdiagnosis is as likely to stem from decisions made by the mental health professional who sees the client as from the mental health professionals who wrote the diagnostic manual.

The Influence of the Pharmaceutical Industry?

Increasingly, the overexpansion of mental health diagnoses has been connected, at least by some experts in the field, to the possible influence of the pharmaceutical industry. To be sure, big drug companies have a stake in the way mental disorders are defined, and to them, the broader the better. The more disorders there are, and the more they overlap with the unfortunate experiences of normal life, the more potential customers these companies have to target their advertising toward (Sadler, 2013; Barber, 2008; Paris, 2013b; Pierre, 2013; Frances, 2013a).

As such, pharmaceutical companies might be pleased if those who write the *DSM*—the prominent research psychiatrists and other professionals who decide what's a mental disorder and what's not—were on their payrolls. A series of recent studies by Lisa Cosgrove and her colleagues found that a majority of them are. Specifically, Cosgrove et al. (2006) found that of the 170 panel members of DSM-IV, 95 of them, or 57%, had financial ties to the major pharmaceutical companies. Interestingly, on the Work Groups for mood disorders (e.g., major depressive disorder, bipolar disorder) and psychotic disorders (e.g., schizophrenia), disorders for which medication is extremely common, the number was 100%. The percentages were also high for other Work Groups in which medication is common, such as anxiety disorders (81%), eating disorders (83%), and childhood disorders (62%), but lower for Work Groups in which medication is uncommon, such as substance related disorders (17%). The most frequent types of financial ties were research funding, consultant fees, and speaking fees.

In 2012, Cosgrove and Krimsky repeated their research for those working on *DSM-5*. The results indicated that the relationship between industry and authors remained. Overall, the percentage with financial ties to the pharmaceutical companies was 69%. In terms of specific Work Groups, psychotic disorders was 83%, mood disorders was 67%, anxiety disorders was 57%, eating disorders was 50%, and ADHD and disruptive behavior disorders (which covered much of the same ground as childhood disorders in *DSM-IV*) was 78%. Cosgrove and Wheeler (2013) have since argued that the pharmaceutical industry is trying to "colonize" psychiatry—that is, attempting to control the mental health field, beginning with a deep connection between its core diagnostic manual and their financial interests.

Do financial connections with drug companies really influence mental health professionals? Couldn't the *DSM* authors make whatever decisions they thought were right, with no regard for any payment they may have received or may soon receive from a particular drug company? One study suggests that the power of such a financial arrangement can be remarkable. Carey and Harris (2008) studied the prescribing habits of psychiatrists in Minnesota and found that those who had received at least $5000 from pharmaceutical companies had written three times as many prescriptions for antipsychotic medication than doctors who had received none. Of course, clinical psychologists are not going to be affected in a major way by prescription rates; as explained earlier in this chapter, only a small minority have the ability to prescribe at all at this point. But clinical psychologists (and most other mental health professionals) use the *DSM*, and the notion that its disorders were defined by people under the influence of financial relationships with pharmaceutical companies whose profits may depend on their decisions is troubling to many.

It is important to note that those in charge of *DSM-5* did place some limits on its authors' financial links to drug companies, in terms of the amount of companies' stock they could own, and the amount of payment they received from the companies; however, neither of these was required to be zero (Greenberg, 2013).

In Chapter 7, we will explore possible reasons for overexpansion of mental disorders and other issues involving the *DSM-5* in greater detail.

Payment Methods: Third-Party Payment vs. Self-Payment

In the earliest days of psychotherapy, clients paid directly out of pocket. With time (and significant effort by professional psychologist organizations), health insurance companies increasingly recognized the worth of clinical psychologists' practices and included them in their coverage. So today, although some clients still pay for therapy on their own, many use their **health insurance/managed care** benefits to pay for therapy at least partially. The presence of this **third-party payer** in the therapy relationship has numerous consequences (Reich & Kolbasovsky, 2006). Certainly, managed-care and insurance benefits bring therapy to many individuals who might not otherwise be able to pay for it. However, the companies who control these benefits are concerned about their financial bottom line as well as the health of their members, and at times, their priorities can strongly affect the work of clinical psychologists.

Effect on Therapy

It would be ideal if clients received the same treatment from psychologists regardless of how they pay, but a growing body of research suggests that this may not be true. Instead, it appears that managed care exerts quite an influence on the day-to-day practices of clinical psychologists. According to a survey by Murphy et al. (1998), psychologists in private practice describe managed care as having a negative impact on their practices and, more specifically, on the quality of therapy they provide. Most of these psychologists reported that their practices were affected by managed care, and, in general, they portrayed managed-care companies as exercising too much control over clinical decisions. Furthermore, their responses indicated that the managed-care companies' emphasis on financial concerns often made it difficult for them to provide appropriate, ethical psychological services.

Confidentiality was specifically noted as an ethical concern. Psychologists can control firsthand the confidentiality of their own private files but not the clinical information they have been required to share with the insurance company. Additional surveys of psychologists have similarly concluded that most psychologists are affected by managed care and that the influences on their practices are generally negative (Rothbaum, Bernstein, Haller, Phelps, & Kohout, 1998; Rothstein, Haller, & Bernstein, 2000). From the psychologists' point of view, the downside of working with managed-care companies can have many facets: lower pay than from clients who pay directly; taking time away from direct clinical work to spend on paperwork, phone calls, and other interaction with the managed-care company; denial of care that the psychologist believes is necessary; and numerous other frustrations (Reich & Kolbasovsky, 2006).

Should clients be informed about the negative influence of managed care? Put yourself in the client's role: If you were seeking therapy and were considering using your insurance benefits or possibly paying out of pocket, would you want to know how your method of payment might influence your treatment? Of course, psychologists are required by the ethical code (American Psychological Association, 2002) to inform therapy clients about the therapy process as early as possible in the process, but the guidelines are vague about exactly what information they should include. An empirical study on the topic indicated that when they learned about psychologists' negative reactions to managed care, many individuals thought more negatively about therapy than they had before. These individuals also felt entitled to know this information before beginning therapy (Pomerantz, 2000).

Of course, paying for psychotherapy without using insurance or managed-care benefits has its own drawbacks. First and foremost, many individuals would struggle to pay for therapy out of pocket, at least without reduced fees or services from low-cost community clinics. For a large segment of the population, self-pay is simply an unaffordable option (and the health insurance/managed-care option is what makes therapy attainable). For those who can afford it, self-pay therapy does allow the therapist and client to make important decisions—such as establishing the goals of therapy, agreeing on a treatment method, and determining when therapy should end—without the intervention of a third party with a financial interest.

Effect on Diagnosis

Although it should not, how clients pay for therapy not only influences therapy but also influences the diagnostic process. It is worth noting first that most health insurance and managed-care companies require a *Diagnostic and Statistical Manual of Mental Disorders* diagnosis for treatment (Ackley, 1997; Chambliss, 2000; Kutchins & Kirk, 1997). Typically, they will not pay for the treatment of issues that a client brings to therapy if those issues do not qualify for a diagnosis. Thus, clients whose symptoms are not severe enough to be diagnosable may find that treatment will not be covered.

A few recent surveys have suggested that psychologists diagnose clients differently depending on how the clients pay for therapy. When psychologists considered clients with mild symptoms of depression or anxiety, they were much more likely to assign a diagnosis when these clients paid via managed care rather than out of pocket. The specific choice of diagnosis depended somewhat on payment method as well (Kielbasa, Pomerantz, Krohn, & Sullivan, 2004). Additional studies have suggested that for a wider range of problems, including symptoms of inattention/hyperactivity and social phobia (Lowe, Pomerantz, & Pettibone, 2007) or for symptoms that are clearly below diagnosable levels (Pomerantz & Segrist, 2006), psychologists' diagnostic decisions depend on whether the client or the client's insurance company pays for therapy.

The Influence of Technology: Cybertherapy and More

Like many other professions, especially in the health care field, clinical psychology has been significantly affected by technological advances in recent years (Dimeff, Paves, Skutch, & Woodcock, 2011; Kraus, Zack, & Stricker, 2004; Marks & Cavanagh, 2009). Particularly groundbreaking—and controversial—is the use of technological tools in the direct delivery of psychological services. Contemporary clinical psychologists can perform assessments and treatments via computer or smartphone as a supplement to, or instead of, traditional in-person meetings with clients (Eonta et al., 2011). This use of technology, and particularly the Internet, by clinical psychologists often goes by the name **cybertherapy** but is also called telehealth and telemental health, among other labels (Mohr, 2009; Yuen, Goetter, Herbert, & Forman, 2012). Cybertherapy and other recent applications of technology in clinical psychology and related professions have generated both enthusiasm and skepticism (e.g., Baker & Ray, 2011). Let's explore various facets of this issue, including specific uses of technology, how well it works, and professional issues surrounding it.

Applications of Technology in Clinical Psychology

Today, technologically savvy clinical psychologists can use

- videoconferencing (such as Skype) to interview or treat a client;
- e-mail or text (in chat-room or one-on-one formats) to provide psychotherapy to a client;
- interactive Internet sites to educate the public by responding to questions about mental health concerns;

- online psychotherapy programs to diagnose and treat specific diagnoses, such as www.fearfighter.com for individuals with panic disorder or specific phobias;

- virtual reality techniques in which clients undergo therapeutic experiences, such as virtual exposure to feared objects;

- computer-based self-instructional programs designed as specific components of a treatment that is otherwise face-to-face; and

- hand-held devices (e.g., cell phones, iPhones, Blackberries, Droids) to monitor clients and interact with them on a regular or random basis between meetings with the psychologist (as described in Dimeff et al., 2011; Hsiung, 2002; Marks & Cavanagh, 2009; Yuen et al., 2012).

Photo 3.2 Increasingly, clinical psychologists are using the Internet and other forms of technology to conduct clinical activities. In your opinion, what are the potential advantages and disadvantages of this increase?

The applications of emerging technologies represent an exciting new horizon to many clinical psychologists. They promise to provide services to populations that have been underserved by clinical psychologists, including people living in poverty, in rural areas, or in war-torn/violent regions (Kraus, 2004; Nelson & Bui, 2010; Reger & Gahm, 2009). Maheu, Pulier, Wilhelm, McMenamin, and Brown-Connolly (2005) summarize the benefits of these technologies as "accessibility, affordability, anonymity, acceptability, and adaptability" (p. 10).

⊕ **Web Link 3.5**
Psychotherapy via Skype

How Well Do Cybertherapy and Other Applications of Technology Work?

Because cybertherapy and other applications of technology are recent developments, the amount of data on their benefits to clients is quite small, and the methodology used to collect the data may be imperfect to some extent (Richardson, Frueh, Grubaugh, Egede, & Elhai, 2009). But the data we have are promising: Cybertherapy appears to work as well as more traditional, in-person forms of psychotherapy for a variety of disorders. Some studies have reached this conclusion regarding particular treatments for particular disorders. For example, Reger and Gahm (2009) found that cognitive-behavioral treatment of anxiety disorders was equally effective whether the treatment was delivered in person or via computer. Similarly, Spence et al. (2011) found that online delivery of cognitive-behavioral therapy to adolescents with anxiety disorders was as effective as face-to-face delivery. Numerous cybertherapy interventions focusing on health psychology are available (Castelnuovo & Simpson, 2011), and a review of the benefits of cybertherapies in this area found that effectiveness of interventions targeting pain and headache were comparable to that of in-person interventions, but some other health psychology interventions were not as effective when implemented via computer as when implemented in person. Other researchers have come to broader conclusions about the relative equality of computer-based and in-person treatments of a wide range of disorders (e.g., Emmelkamp, 2011; Kraus, 2011).

Emerging Professional Issues

As clinical psychologists embrace new technologies and incorporate them into their practices, professional issues—including both the ethical and the practical—continue to arise (Koocher, 2009). In response, the profession is making efforts to ensure that the services provided are safe, effective, and ethical (Baker & Bufka, 2011). The American Psychological Association (2002) ethical code includes several updates designed to address the increasing use of new technological tools. Some experts in the field have also proposed ethical guidelines for psychologists practicing online, via videoconferencing, or through other similar means (e.g., Hsiung, 2002; Ragusea & VandeCreek, 2003).

Like the technologies themselves, guidelines regarding their use are continuously in the works. Some of these guidelines are simply extensions of the guidelines that govern traditional, face-to-face practice, whereas others are quite distinct. As the technology-based practice of clinical psychology evolves, those providing it should follow some fundamental suggestions (adapted from Barnett & Scheetz, 2003; Ragusea, 2012; Rummell & Joyce, 2010):

- Obtain informed consent from clients about the services they may receive, the technologies that may be used to provide them, and the confidentiality of the communication.

- Know and follow any applicable laws on telehealth and telemedicine.

- Know and follow the most recent version of the American Psychological Association ethical code, especially the portions that address technological issues.

- Ensure client confidentiality as much as possible by using encryption or similar methods. Keep updated on ways clinical information could be accessed by "hackers" and techniques for stopping them.

- Appreciate how issues of culture may be involved. As technological tools replace face-to-face meetings, psychologists may need to make special efforts to assess the cultural backgrounds of the clients they serve.

- Do not practice outside the scope of your expertise. Merely having a license may not be enough. Advanced training—either clinical or technological—may be necessary to use a particular technique.

- Be knowledgeable about emergency resources in any community from which your clients may seek services. A crisis related to suicide or psychosis, for example, may require an immediate face-to-face intervention that the psychologist is simply too far away to provide.
- Stay abreast of changes to the laws, ethical codes, or technology relevant to your practice.

As this list suggests, numerous specific ethical issues have arisen as the use of technology in clinical psychology has expanded (Fisher & Fried, 2003; Koocher, 2009; Kraus, 2004; Naglieri et al., 2004; Rummell & Joyce, 2010). These issues begin even before the assessment or therapy does, as the very identity of the client may be questionable. That is, how can the psychologist be sure that the client is in fact the person agreeing to the informed consent statement, responding to assessment items, or providing comments during online therapy? Even if identity is confirmed, the psychologist must be concerned with confidentiality across electronic transmission, making appropriate interpretations in the absence of ability to observe nonverbal cues that would be present face-to-face, and remaining competent regarding not only clinical but technical skills.

In spite of these ethical and pragmatic hurdles and a very short history, evidence is beginning to indicate that cybertherapy can be quite successful, and it is certainly becoming more widespread. However, it is important to remember that the effectiveness of a cybertherapy treatment can depend on a number of factors (adapted from Marks & Cavanagh, 2009):

- Which cybertherapy is being used for which disorder?
- On what device and via what means is the cybertherapy delivered? Computer, cell phone, smartphone, e-mail, text, videoconference, or something else?
- In what setting is the cybertherapy being delivered? Home, clinic, school, public setting (library, café, etc.), or somewhere else?
- How did clients find the cybertherapy? Did they receive a specific referral from a knowledgeable source or stumble across it on the Internet?
- Does the cybertherapy have live human support, and is that support monitored for quality?

Although many therapists remain wary of it and do not utilize it at all (McMinn, Bearse, Heyne, Smithberger, & Erb, 2011), the practice of technologically based therapy and diagnosis is undeniably on the rise and will probably remain so as technology improves and becomes more widespread. As it progresses, the current body of research on cybertherapy's effectiveness will certainly grow as well (Maheu et al., 2005), and the guidelines and training for its use will strengthen. Among the more interesting questions to be addressed will be the effect of technological tools on the client–therapist alliance (Rummell & Joyce, 2010). As we will see in later chapters, a strong professional relationship between client and therapist is crucial to any successful therapy. To the extent that therapy via e-mail, text, website, or videoconference can maintain or enhance that relationship, it stands to benefit the client.

CHAPTER SUMMARY

Several current issues and controversies dominate the contemporary field of clinical psychology. As a primary example, the issue of prescription privileges for clinical psychologists has emerged as a significant development in the profession. Those in favor of prescription privileges cite numerous justifications, including the shortage of psychiatrists in many geographic areas, other nonphysician professions that have obtained prescription privileges, convenience for clients, and autonomy for clinical psychologists. Opponents of prescription privileges cite difficulties related to training, medication as a threat to the practice of psychotherapy, identity confusion with the profession of clinical psychology, and the potentially negative influence of the pharmaceutical industry. The issue of evidence-based practice/manualized therapy has also stirred debate in recent years. Proponents point out that these treatments enhance the scientific legitimacy of psychotherapy, help establish standards of competence, and decrease reliance on therapists' clinical judgment. Those who oppose evidence-based practice/manualized therapy emphasize that these therapies

can threaten the therapeutic relationship, can overly restrict practice options, and may be based on empirical standards or specifically selected client populations that limit applicability to the broad field of psychotherapy. Overdiagnosis—also known as diagnostic inflation or the medicalization of everyday problems—has stirred significant controversy with each new edition of the *DSM*, especially *DSM-5*. Although the DSM authors follow a thorough process when deciding whether to label an experience as a mental disorder, critics argue that too often, they have included experiences that are unfortunate parts of normal life or have used criteria that set the bar so low that too many people qualify for the disorder. Consequences of an overly broad or loose definition of mental illness can include unnecessary treatment, stigma, and legal implications. How a client pays for psychotherapy—specifically, whether a managed-care/health insurance company pays the bill or the client pays independently—appears to have an impact on clinical psychologists and their work with clients. Especially in the private practice field, psychologists report that their practices have been negatively affected by the increased involvement of managed-care companies. Evidence suggests that psychologists' diagnostic decisions about clients can be significantly influenced by the presence or absence of a health insurance/managed-care company paying the bill. Recent technological innovations have expanded the range of tools that clinical psychologists can use to treat clients. Cybertherapy of various kinds, including videoconferencing, online therapies, e-mail–based therapeutic interventions, virtual-reality technology, and other forms of computer-aided treatment have all been successfully used. Initial outcome data are promising, but outcome may depend on a wide variety of factors related to the intervention, the delivery mode, and the setting in which it is used. Along with these new technologies have come corresponding ethical and professional issues, including informed consent, laws and ethics, confidentiality, and effectively managing client emergencies from a distance.

KEY TERMS AND NAMES

American Society for the Advancement of Pharmacotherapy (American Psychological Association, Division 55) 50

cybertherapy 68

Patrick H. DeLeon 50

dialectical behavior therapy 55

evidence-based practice 54

exposure plus response prevention 55

health insurance/ managed care 66

manualized therapy 54

Robert McGrath 50

prescription privileges 50

Morgan T. Sammons 50

therapy manual 55

third-party payer 66

CRITICAL THINKING QUESTIONS

1. In your opinion, should clinical psychologists have prescription privileges? Why or why not?

2. In your opinion, is mental illness currently overdiagnosed?

3. In your opinion, to what extent should the use of evidence-based practice be required for clinical psychologists?

4. In your opinion, how much should clinical psychologists tell new clients about the impact that payment method (e.g., managed care/health insurance vs. out of pocket) might have on their diagnosis or treatment?

5. In your opinion, what are the most important advantages and disadvantages of recent forms of technology on the practice of clinical psychology?

STUDENT STUDY SITE RESOURCES

Visit the study site at www.sagepub.com/pomerantz3eupdate for these additional learning tools:

- Self-quizzes
- eFlashcards
- Culture Expert Interviews

- Full-text SAGE journal articles
- Additional web resources
- Mock Assessment Data

CHAPTER SUMMARY VIDEO

QR codes at the end of each chapter link to chapter background videos by the author. Visit http://gettag.mobi using your smartphone browser to download the free Microsoft Tag app. Once installed, scan the tags to go directly to these brief videos. In this video, the author explores the issue of prescription privileges, particularly from the perspective of clients.

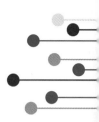

CHAPTER 4

Cultural Issues in Clinical Psychology

The Rise of Multiculturalism in Clinical Psychology

The Diversification of the U.S. Population

🌐 **Web Link 4.1**
Cultural diversity in the U.S.

Cultural diversity has historically been a hallmark of the U.S. population, but in recent years, the country has become *much* more diverse. The number of people of minority ethnicities, as well as the proportion of the U.S. population they represent, has increased dramatically. For example, in a single decade (1990–2000), the Asian American/Pacific Islander population and the Latino/Latina/Hispanic population each grew by about 50% (U.S. Census Bureau, 2001). Also, in 2000, there were 28 million first-generation immigrants in the United States, representing about 10% of the entire U.S. population (Martinez, 2004). One in five U.S. schoolchildren speaks a language other than English at home (Roberts, 2004). And by 2050, about half the country's population will identify at least partially as African American, American Indian, Asian American, or Latino/Latina (U.S. Census Bureau, 2008).

In certain parts of the United States, the increasing diversity is especially pronounced. In Miami, for example, Latino/Latina/Hispanic residents represent the majority of the population (U.S. Census Bureau, 2006c). In San Francisco, individuals of Asian descent represent almost one third of the population (U.S. Census Bureau, 2006d). And more than 55% of the populations of Detroit and Washington, D.C., are African American (U.S. Census Bureau, 2006a, 2006b).

Clinical psychologists have recognized that the people who might seek their professional services represent a growing variety of cultural backgrounds. As individuals and as a profession, clinical psychologists are making efforts to address issues of culture sensitively and competently (Comas-Díaz, 2011, 2012). As stated by McGoldrick, Giordano, and Garcia-Preto (2005b), "We must incorporate cultural acknowledgment into our theories and into our therapies, so that clients not of the dominant culture will not have to feel lost, displaced, or mystified" (p. 4).

Photo 4.1 Cultural diversity is a hallmark of the U.S. population, especially in certain geographical areas. How has the profession of clinical psychology emphasized the importance of cultural diversity in recent years?

Multiculturalism as the "Fourth Force"

The impact of cultural issues on mental health professionals in recent years has been so extensive that some authors have identified **multiculturalism** as a defining issue of the current era of psychology. For example, Pedersen (1990, 1999, 2008) has put forth the argument that in the evolution of the clinical/counseling field, multiculturalism represents the "fourth force." With this label, multiculturalism is ranked with the three previous movements that have been broadly recognized as dominant paradigms in their respective eras: psychoanalysis as the first force, behaviorism as the second force, and humanism/person-centered psychology as the third force (Bugental, 1964). Multiculturalism, then, stands as a major pervasive influence on the work of contemporary clinical psychologists (Gelso, 2011). It represents a fundamental change of emphasis but one unlike the previous three in terms of its method of impact. Whereas behaviorism and humanism emerged as challenges to the incumbent first force of psychoanalysis, multiculturalism does not necessarily aim to dethrone any of the first three forces. Instead, it enhances and strengthens existing models by infusing them with sensitivity and awareness of how they can be best applied to individuals of various cultural backgrounds (Mio, Barker-Hackett, & Tumambing, 2006).

One reason culture is such a powerful force in the clinical and counseling fields is that it shapes the way the client understands the very problem for which he or she is seeking help. This understanding—this worldview, applied to psychological problems—is what the therapist should appreciate as he or she devises an approach to helping the client. Comas-Díaz (2011) encourages therapists to directly assess clients' understanding of their own psychological problem by asking them these questions:

- What do you call your problem (or illness or distress)?
- What do you think your problem does to you?
- What do you think the natural cause of your problem is?
- Why do you think this problem has occurred?
- How do you think this problem should be treated?
- How do you want me to help you?
- Who else (e.g., family, friends, religious leader) do you turn to for help?
- Who (e.g., family, friends, religious leader) should be involved in decision making about this problem? (Adapted from p. 875).

Recent Professional Efforts to Emphasize Issues of Culture

Clinical psychology and related professions have addressed the issue of cultural diversity in many tangible ways. In the 1970s, efforts toward educating therapists and therapists-in-training on the importance of race and ethnicity were in their early stages. These efforts expanded through the 1980s and by the 1990s were much more widespread and comprehensive in terms of the variables, beyond ethnicity and race, around which culture might be defined (J. E. Harris, 2012). In recent years, a plethora of efforts reflects the increasing importance of culture within clinical psychology.

Journals and Books

Numerous publications on cultural issues in mental health have appeared in recent years. Scholarly journals in clinical psychology have increasingly included articles on cultural topics, and some psychology journals are devoted entirely to issues of culture. (See Table 4.1 for examples.) In addition, a wide variety of books now offer education and guidance to psychologists working with culturally diverse populations. Some of these books focus on a single population, such as *Working With Asian Americans* (Lee, 1997), *Psychotherapy With Women* (Mirkin, Suyemoto, & Okun, 2005), or *Counseling Muslims* (Ahmed & Amer, 2012), whereas others compile chapters on many different populations, such as *Ethnicity and Family Therapy* (McGoldrick, Giordano, & Garcia-Preto, 2005a) or *Counseling Diverse Populations* (Atkinson & Hackett, 2003). Collectively,

Table 4.1 Scholarly Journals Relevant to Multicultural Issues in Clinical Psychology

Among others, these journals focus on issues of culture and commonly include articles of clinical relevance:

Cultural Diversity and Ethnic Minority Psychology	*Journal of Gender, Culture, and Health*
Hispanic Journal of Behavioral Sciences	*Journal of Multicultural Counseling and Development*
Journal of Black Psychology	*Psychoanalysis, Culture, and Society*
Journal of Cross-Cultural Psychology	*Psychology of Men and Masculinity*
Journal of Cultural Diversity	*Asian American Journal of Psychology*

Among others, these journals focus on clinically relevant issues and commonly feature articles emphasizing culture or diversity:

Clinical Psychology: Science and Practice	*Journal of Marital and Family Therapy*
Counseling Psychologist	*Journal of Mental Health Counseling*
Journal of Abnormal Psychology	*Professional Psychology: Research and Practice*
Journal of Clinical Psychology	*Psychotherapy: Theory, Research, Practice, Training*
Journal of Counseling Psychology	*Journal of Consulting and Clinical Psychology*

these publications represent a wealth of cultural knowledge for contemporary clinical psychologists, and their increasing presence acknowledges the importance of the topic.

Emergence of American Psychological Association Divisions

Within the American Psychological Association, new divisions arise when a subset of members recognizes a need to study or examine a specific topic in depth. Among the divisions created most recently, many have focused on cultural issues, including the following:

⊕ **Web Link 4.2**

Cultural Diversity & Ethnic Minority Psychology

- Division 35—Society for the Psychology of Women
- Division 36—Psychology of Religion
- Division 44—Society for the Psychological Study of Lesbian, Gay, and Bisexual Issues
- Division 45—Society for the Study of Ethnic Minority Issues
- Division 51—Society for the Psychological Study of Men and Masculinity

American Psychological Association Ethical Code

Numerous specific standards and principles in the most recent edition of the American Psychological Association (2002) ethical code compel psychologists to work with cultural sensitivity and competence. Their inclusion as standards makes it clear that awareness of diversity issues is a requirement rather than merely an aspiration for ethical psychologists. See Table 4.2 for a list of specific ethical standards and principles that relate to multiculturalism.

Table 4.2 Selected Excerpts From the American Psychological Association's (2002) "Ethical Principles of Psychologists and Code of Conduct" Relating to Multiculturalism

- Principle E: Respect for People's Rights and Dignity

  Psychologists respect the dignity and worth of all people, and the rights of individuals to privacy, confidentiality, and self-determination. Psychologists are aware that special safeguards may be necessary to protect the rights and welfare of persons or communities whose vulnerabilities impair autonomous decision making. Psychologists are aware of and respect cultural, individual, and role differences, including those based on age, gender, gender identity, race, ethnicity, culture, national origin, religion, sexual orientation, disability, language, and socioeconomic status and consider these factors when working with members of such groups. Psychologists try to eliminate the effect on their work of biases based on those factors, and they do not knowingly participate in or condone activities of others based on such prejudices.

  (Continued)

Table 4.2 (Continued)

- Standard 2.01 Boundaries of Competence

  (b) Where scientific or professional knowledge in the discipline of psychology establishes that an understanding of factors associated with age, gender, gender identity, race, ethnicity, culture, national origin, religion, sexual orientation, disability, language, or socioeconomic status is essential for effective implementation of their services or research, psychologists have or obtain the training, experience, consultation, or supervision necessary to ensure the competence of their services, or they make appropriate referrals, except as provided in Standard 2.02, Providing Services in Emergencies.

- Standard 3.01 Unfair Discrimination

  In their work-related activities, psychologists do not engage in unfair discrimination based on age, gender, gender identity, race, ethnicity, culture, national origin, religion, sexual orientation, disability, socioeconomic status, or any basis proscribed by law.

- Standard 9.06 Interpreting Assessment Results

  When interpreting assessment results, including automated interpretations, psychologists take into account the purpose of the assessment as well as the various test factors, test-taking abilities, and other characteristics of the person being assessed, such as situational, personal, linguistic, and cultural differences, that might affect psychologists' judgments or reduce the accuracy of their interpretations. They indicate any significant limitations of their interpretations. (See also Standards 2.01b and c, Boundaries of Competence, and 3.01, Unfair Discrimination.)

Source: American Psychological Association (2002). Ethical principles of psychologists and code of conduct. *American Psychologist, 57,* 1060–1073.

American Psychological Association Accreditation Standards

When the American Psychological Association decides whether to give its "seal of approval"—in other words, accreditation—to a graduate program in psychology, multiculturalism is a primary focus. In the most recent edition of the American Psychological Association (2005) standards of accreditation, "Cultural and Individual Differences and Diversity" is one of the eight domains that an educational program must address adequately to be accredited. This requirement applies to doctoral programs, predoctoral internships, and postdoctoral internships seeking accreditation. Specifically, the accreditation standards for doctoral programs list criteria such as (1) including people of diverse backgrounds among students and faculty and (2) educating students about the role of culture in the science and practice of professional psychology.

DSM Efforts Toward Multiculturalism

The authors of the fifth edition of the *Diagnostic and Statistical Manual of Mental Disorders* (*DSM-5*) state in the Introduction that "key aspects of culture relevant to diagnostic classification and assessment have been considered in the development of *DSM-5*" (American Psychiatric Association, 2013, p. 14). In addition to information on cultural variation embedded in the descriptions of specific disorders, it provides more general guidance for clinicians to help with overall cultural competence. For example, it offers an "Outline for Cultural Formulation," which instructs clinicians in various aspects of culture to assess in clients, such as cultural identity, cultural conceptualization of distress, and cultural features of the relationship with the mental health professional. It also offers a "Cultural Formulation Interview," a series of 16 specific questions that can guide a clinician toward a culturally informed interview. All of these efforts support the growing body of research suggesting that culture influences the experience or expression of a variety of psychological problems, including anxiety disorders, eating disorders, substance use, and many others (e.g., Chentsova_Dutton & Tsai, 2007).

Another effort toward cultural awareness incorporated into *DSM-5* is a glossary listing **cultural concepts of distress** (many of which were called "culture-bound syndromes" in *DSM-IV*). The glossary of cultural concepts of distress includes nine terms that represent psychological problems observed in groups from various parts of the world. Some are described as similar to a *DSM-5* disorder, but others bear little resemblance. Examples include *taijin kyofusho*, in which a person anxiously avoids interpersonal situations because he or she believes that his or her appearance, actions, or odor will offend other people (found in Japanese and some other cultures); *sutso*, in which a frightening event is thought to cause the soul to leave the body, resulting in depressive symptoms (found in some Latino/ Latina/Hispanic cultures); and *maladi moun*, in which one person can "send" psychological problems like depression and psychosis to another, usually as a result of envy or hatred toward the other person's success (found in some Haitian communities; similar experiences called the "evil eye" are more common in other parts of the world). Although some authors (McGoldrick et al., 2005b) have pointed out that a few of the official disorders included in *DSM* might in fact be better described as culturally bound to U.S. or North American cultures (e.g., eating disorders, as discussed in Chapter 7), the list of culture-bound syndromes in the *DSM* nonetheless signifies an increase in the profession's recognition of multicultural issues.

Revisions of Prominent Assessment Methods

Several prominent assessment tools used by clinical psychologists have been revised in recent years with the specific intent of making them more culturally appropriate and serviceable. The Minnesota Multiphasic Personality Inventory (MMPI), an especially popular and well-respected personality test, underwent a major overhaul in the 1980s, resulting in the publication of the MMPI-2 in 1989. Compared with the original MMPI, the normative scores for the MMPI-2 were based on population samples much more representative of the cultural diversity of the U.S. population (Nichols, 2001). (Chapter 10 includes much more information on the MMPI and MMPI-2.) Other examples include the adult and child versions of the Wechsler tests of intelligence (e.g., Wechsler Adult Intelligence Scale, Wechsler Intelligence Scale for Children), which are among the most widely used and highly esteemed in their respective categories. As these tests have been revised in recent years, their authors have made efforts to create instruments that minimize cultural bias and maximize cultural inclusion (Flanagan & Kaufman, 2009). (Chapter 9 includes much more information on the Wechsler tests.)

Cultural Competence

What Is Cultural Competence?

Clinical psychologists should strive for **cultural competence** (Vasquez, 2010). Indeed, when clients perceive their therapists as culturally competent, they are more likely to form strong working relationships with them, which leads to better therapy outcome (Owen, Tao, Leach, & Rodolfa, 2011). But what exactly does cultural competence involve? According to Sue and Sue (2008),

⊕ **Web Link 4.3**

National Center for Cultural Competence

> Multicultural counseling competence is defined as the counselor's acquisition of awareness, knowledge, and skills needed to function effectively in a pluralistic democratic society . . . and on an organizational/societal level, advocating effectively to develop new theories, practices, policies, and organizational structures that are more responsive to all groups. (p. 46)

A key phrase in the definition above is "awareness, knowledge, and skills." As described by Sue and Sue (2008), these are the three primary components to multicultural competence as applied to clinical/counseling work. Let's examine each one in detail.

Cultural Self-Awareness

Cultural competence begins with learning about one's own culture—not only the basic facts such as where one's parents or ancestors came from but also the values, assumptions, and biases that one has developed as a result of all cultural influences (J. E. Harris, 2012). When a clinical psychologist attains **cultural self-awareness**—that is, comes to understand that his or her viewpoint is (like everyone's) unique and idiosyncratic—several conclusions are within reach (Fouad & Arredondo, 2007). For example, the psychologist may adopt a viewpoint toward clients that is less egocentric and more appreciative of the varying experiences of life. Also, the psychologist may come to recognize that differences between people are not necessarily deficiencies, especially if the difference demonstrated by the client is common or valued in his or her own cultural group. Rather than glossing over differences between themselves and their clients, psychologists should explore their own personal reactions to these differences and address any discomfort they may initially feel about them (Greene, 2007).

⊕ Web Link 4.4
Cultural
Competence &
Cultural Self-
Awareness

Of course, the process of cultural self-awareness can be difficult or unpleasant for psychologists, because it may require admitting and coming to terms with some undesirable "isms"—racism, sexism, heterosexism, classism, ethnocentrism, or similar prejudicial or discriminatory belief systems that we'd rather pretend we don't have. But by examining them and exposing them to ourselves, we can take steps toward minimizing them and the negative impact they might have on our clients (Vasquez, 2010).

Cultural self-awareness is important regardless of the psychologist's own cultural background. Whether a member of a majority or minority, the psychologist will inevitably encounter clients whose cultural backgrounds differ— sometimes slightly, sometimes considerably—from his or her own. Thankfully, scholars in our field are paying increasing attention to the cultural status of the therapist (e.g., Gelso, 2010; Mirsalimi, 2010; Nezu, 2010).

Photo 4.2 Cultural self-awareness, or an appreciation of the clinical psychologist's own unique cultural viewpoint, is a key element of cultural competence.

● ● ● BOX 4.1 ● ● ●

Considering Culture

Interviews With Multicultural Experts: Cultural Competence With Clients From Specific Cultures

Knowledge of diverse cultures is one of the core elements of cultural competence. Here, we ask nine highly respected experts in multicultural mental health to provide their thoughts

(Continued)

(Continued)

about what clinical psychologists should know about particular cultural groups. The cultural groups they discuss span ethnicity, gender, religion, and sexual orientation.

This box is just a start! It contains brief excerpts of the experts' responses, but this textbook's companion website (www.sagepub.com/pomerantz3eupdate) contains the experts' full biographies as well as their full-length responses to these five questions about clinical work with their cultural groups:

1. In general, why is it important for clinical psychologists to be culturally competent when working with members of this culture?
2. What can clinical psychologists (or students in training) do to enhance their cultural competence with members of this culture?
3. What specific considerations should clinical psychologists keep in mind when conducting assessment (interviewing, intelligence testing, personality testing, etc.) and diagnosis with members of this culture?
4. What specific considerations should clinical psychologists keep in mind when conducting psychotherapy with members of this culture?
5. Any other thoughts about culturally competent practice with members of this culture?

Latino/Latina Clients

Dr. Melba Vasquez is the cofounder of the Society for the Psychological Study of Ethnic Minority Issues (American Psychological Association Division 45), the first Latina member-at-large on the board of directors of the American Psychological Association, and 2011 president of the American Psychological Association.

- "Latino/a cultural factors for assessment may include relevant generational history (e.g., number of generations in the country, manner of coming to the country); citizenship or residency status (e.g., number of years in the country, parental history of migration, refugee flight, or immigration); fluency in 'standard' English or other language; extent of family support or disintegration of family; availability of community resources; level of education; change in social status as a result of coming to this country (for immigrant or refugee); work history; and level of stress related to acculturation and/or oppression."
- "The demographic changes in the world and in this country have significant implications for counseling and clinical psychologists. Although Latinos/Latinas typically

present with similar problems, relative to other clients, variations in conceptualizations and interventions may be important in providing effective services."

Asian and Asian American Clients

Dr. Frederick Leong is a professor of psychology at Michigan State University, director of the Center for Multicultural Psychology Research, and founding editor of the *Asian American Journal of Psychology.*

- "Intra-group heterogeneity is particularly important to recognize when it comes to a group such as Asian Americans given that this population comprises approximately 43 different ethnic groups with over 100 languages and dialects represented."

- "For many Asian Americans, constancy and equilibrium, duty, obligation and appearance of harmonious relations are important in their family relations. In addition, Asian families tend to emphasize connectedness of the family, while European Americans tend to prioritize separateness and clear boundaries in relationships due to the two groups' value differences. It has become well known that Asian Americans tend to be more collectivistic in cultural orientation while European Americans tend to be individualistic."

American Indian/Alaska Native Clients

Dr. Joseph E. Trimble is a Distinguished University Professor and member of the Department of Psychology and a research associate in the Center for Cross-Cultural Research at Western Washington University. In 1994, he received a Lifetime Distinguished Career Award from American Psychological Association Division 45 for his research and dedication to cross-cultural and ethnic psychology.

- "Providers of traditional helping services in Indian communities most likely exemplify empathy, genuineness, availability, respect, warmth, congruence, and concreteness, characteristics that are likely to be effective in any therapeutic treatment setting, regardless of the provider's theoretical orientation or counseling style. Effective counseling with Indians begins when a counselor carefully internalizes and uses these basic characteristics in counseling settings."

- "A constant theme occurs repeatedly in the Indian and Native counseling literature— counselors of Indian and Native clients must be adaptive and flexible in their personal orientations and in their use of conventional counseling techniques."

(Continued)

(Continued)

African American Clients

Dr. Robert L. Williams was a founding member of the National Association of Black Psychologists in 1968. From 1970 to 1992, he served as Full Professor of Psychology and African and African-American Studies at Washington University in St. Louis.

- "The first step in gaining cultural competence is self-knowledge. Psychologists need to become aware of their own racial scripts and beliefs, and how these might affect the way they conduct therapy. Racial scripts are programmed messages from parents to children about African Americans of which the children, even when they have become adults, are not fully aware. They can have a powerful influence, so it's important for psychologists to recognize their own racial scripts and alter them to meet the reality of the African American community."

- "Perhaps most importantly, psychologists working with clients of diverse backgrounds, including African American clients, need to know and accept that a *cultural difference is not a deficiency.* In other words, differences between the cultures exist, but they need not suggest that one is better or worse than the other."

Irish American Clients

Dr. Monica McGoldrick is the director of the Multicultural Family Institute of New Jersey and an adjunct associate professor of clinical psychiatry at UMDNJ-Robert Wood Johnson Medical School. Her many books include *Ethnicity and Family Therapy* (McGoldrick et al., 2005a).

- "Traditionally (and I'm overgeneralizing a bit to make the point) the Irish, although they were big talkers, were not big talkers about emotional issues. In fact, they seemed afraid of emotional issues. So, if you asked them the kinds of questions that would, say, come from a Freudian perspective (which is still very strong in psychology), they would probably look much more pathological than they really are, because they would be extremely uncomfortable with questions about their inner feelings, especially negative feelings or sexual feelings."

- "The Irish have a long history in which they learned how to keep their emotional process under wraps, and often the church encouraged certain attitudes which led them to feel guilty about some feelings that wouldn't even be an issue in other cultural groups."

Female Clients

Dr. Nadya A. Fouad is a Distinguished Professor in the Department of Educational Psychology at the University of Wisconsin–Milwaukee. She served as co-chair of the writing team for the American Psychological Association's *Multicultural Guidelines on Education, Training, Practice, Research and Organizational Change.*

- "It's important to understand how a client's gender is interwoven in his or her culture or ethnicity. For example, a traditional Hispanic woman facing a decision like moving across the country to go to college and moving away from her family might experience that decision in a unique way, and differently from a man in the same situation. If a client senses that the psychologist isn't taking these kinds of issues into account, the client might not return at all."

- "Be aware of your own biases with regard to gender. For example, do you have a bias toward women being in a particular role, either traditional or nontraditional? Do you have a bias toward one type of relationship in which women should be?"

Middle Eastern Clients

Dr. Karen Haboush is a visiting associate professor, Applied Visiting Faculty at the Graduate School of Applied and Professional Psychology at Rutgers University. She has published articles and chapters on culturally competent practice with children and families of Middle Eastern descent.

- "Because the popular media often presents predominantly negative images of Middle Easterners (i.e., terrorists, religious extremists), psychologists may unwittingly internalize these images which subsequently influences their clinical work. As with all ethnic groups, the first step in developing cultural competence is for psychologists to examine their own attitudes and knowledge."

- "In Middle Eastern culture, the welfare of the family has much greater significance than individual autonomy and independence. . . . This makes Middle Eastern culture quite different from the prevailing emphasis on individual achievement which is more characteristic of North American and European countries. Of course, great variability exists across cultures and countries, but generally speaking, a collectivist emphasis on the well-being of the family tends to characterize the Middle East."

Lesbian/Gay/Bisexual/Transgender (LGBT) Clients

Dr. Kathleen J. Bieschke is a professor of counseling psychology at Pennsylvania State University. Dr. Bieschke has written extensively about the delivery of affirmative counseling and psychotherapy to LGBT clients. Dr. Bieschke is a coeditor of the *Handbook of*

(Continued)

(Continued)

Counseling and Psychotherapy With Lesbian, Gay, Bisexual, and Transgender Clients
(Bieschke, Perez, & DeBord, 2007).

- "Attention must be paid to the development of a productive therapeutic relationship. This is particularly true when working with sexual minority clients, as LGBT individuals have learned to carefully assess the extent to which therapists are affirmative. There are myriad ways in which therapists can convey affirmation to clients. For example, having a symbol in one's office indicating knowledge of the LGBT community (e.g., a small pink triangle) or using language that is inclusive (e.g., not using gender-specific pronouns when referring to sexual partners) can provide LGBT clients with concrete evidence of a therapist's openness to sexual minorities."
- "A particularly fruitful strategy is getting to know someone who identifies as a sexual minority or as a strong ally; relationships such as these can shatter stereotypes and assumptions."

Jewish American Clients

Dr. Lewis Z. Schlosser is an associate professor of counseling psychology at Seton Hall University. His research focuses on multicultural counseling and development, specifically the intersection of race, religion, and ethnicity; anti-Semitism; and Jewish identity development.

- "Being Jewish is largely an invisible minority status. Psychologists might never know that they have a Jewish client in front of them unless the client discloses her or his identity. Because Jews have endured a long history of oppression, many American Jews will assess the safety of the current environment prior to disclosing their identity. A culturally competent psychologist will strive to foster an environment of safety so that the American Jewish client would feel comfortable disclosing her or his Jewish identity."
- "It is important to note that cultural competence is not assured simply by being Jewish. That is, we can't assume that Jews are going to be culturally competent with Jewish clients, as internalized anti-Semitism or other factors might be operating."

Knowledge of Diverse Cultures

To know one's own culture is a good first step, but it won't amount to much unless the psychologist also possesses information about the client's cultural groups. Simply put, the psychologist should know the client's culture. Efforts in this direction should be continual—learning through reading, direct experiences, relationships with people in various cultures, and other means. Of course, therapists can't know everything about every culture that might be represented by a client in a country as diverse as the United States. In fact, acknowledging cultural differences with clients is typically a good idea, and asking a client to explain the meaning or importance of a particular experience from his or her point of view can ensure a more culturally sensitive understanding. But clients shouldn't bear too much of the burden of educating the psychologist; instead, the psychologist should aim to enter each session with sufficient knowledge of the client's cultural background.

Cultural knowledge should include not only the current lifestyle of the members of the culture but also the group's history, especially regarding major social and political issues. For example, the history of African Americans—including slavery, cruelty, exploitation, and overt and covert racism—can understandably affect the formation of a trusting relationship with a psychologist or with the mental health system more generally (Constantine, Redington, & Graham, 2009; Terrell, Taylor, Menzise, & Barett, 2009). A clinical psychologist who fails to recognize these historical realities and their potential impact on clients may form expectations or make interpretations that are culturally insensitive and jeopardize the therapeutic relationship (Shorter-Gooden, 2009).

Of course, the psychologist should not assume that every individual is typical of his or her cultural group. In other words, although a cultural group may have a collective tendency, its individual members may vary greatly from that tendency. To assume that a member of a cultural group will exhibit all the characteristics common to that group is to prejudge. The individual would be better served by a psychologist who appreciates the cultural group norms but also appreciates the **heterogeneity** inherent in every culture. See Box 4.2 for further discussion of heterogeneity within a culture.

Some of the heterogeneity within a culture stems from differences in **acculturation** (Organista, Marin, & Chun, 2010; Rivera, 2010). That is, when people find themselves in a new cultural environment, they may respond in a variety of ways, especially with regard to adopting elements of the new culture or retaining elements of their original culture. Four separate acculturation strategies have been identified (Berry, 2003; Rivera, 2008): *assimilation,* in which the individual adopts much of the new culture and abandons much of the original; *separation,* in which the individual rejects much of the new culture and retains much of the original; *marginalization,* in which the individual rejects both the new and the original culture; and *integration,* in which the individual adopts much of the new culture and retains much of the original. As these four strategies illustrate, individuals can combine an appreciation of their new and original cultures in many ways, resulting in remarkable diversity within any cultural group. So simply knowing that Hajra immigrated to the United States from Bosnia 15 years ago leaves much unknown about her cultural identity. To what extent has she embraced mainstream U.S. culture? To what extent has she carried on her Bosnian cultural beliefs and traditions? Culturally competent clinical psychologists strive to learn their clients' acculturation strategies in an effort to understand more completely their unique ways of life (Shin & Munoz, 2009).

Metaphorically Speaking

If You've Seen Yao Ming, You Understand Heterogeneity Within a Culture

The average height of a Chinese man is about 5 ft. 7 in.—about 2 to 3 in. shorter than the average height of men from the United States. So if you are a clinical psychologist and you know that the new client in your waiting room is a Chinese man, you might expect to see someone around 5 ft. 7 in. tall. But when you open the waiting room door and Yao Ming stands up—all 7 ft. 6 in. of him—you understand right away that your client is a huge exception to the rule.

Yao Ming is a Chinese man and was a star basketball player in the NBA until his retirement in 2011. His height illustrates a powerful lesson about cultural competence: Although members of a culture *as a group* may tend toward certain norms, any *individual* within that group may fall far from that norm. Clinical psychologists should aspire to understand the norms of the cultures with which they work, but if they rigidly assume that every person in that culture fits those norms, they are guilty of unfair and often inaccurate prejudice. To some extent, generalizing is inevitable when discussing cultural groups (McGoldrick et al., 2005a), but our generalizations should be "guidelines for our behaviors, to be tentatively applied in new situations, and they should be open to change and challenge. It is exactly at this stage that generalizations remain generalizations or become stereotypes" (Sue & Sue, 2008, p. 154).

Photo 4.3 Yao Ming's extraordinary height illustrates that the characteristics of an individual do not necessarily follow cultural trends. Regarding their clients' psychological characteristics, culturally competent clinical psychologists appreciate the exceptions as well as the rules.

Actually, your statistics course probably included some basic concepts that can help illustrate this point: measures of central tendency, such as the mean, and measures of variability, such as range or standard deviation. Any group of numbers will yield a mean, but a quick glance at the scatterplot shows that there is some variation around that mean, and in some cases the outliers are quite extreme. The client in the psychologist's office represents one of those points on the scatterplot, and although it is important to appreciate the important central tendencies of that group, it is equally important to recall that the client might be an outlier.

Consider another central tendency of Chinese and many other Asian cultures—the emphasis on collectivism over individualism. In contrast to the tendencies in European American cultures, members of Asian cultures tend to value the welfare of the family or group over their own welfare as individuals. Numerous authors on the subject have indicated that members of Asian cultures assign great significance to harmony, interdependence, respect, and loyalty in close relationships, and they will often forgo individual self-directed accomplishments as a result (e.g., Dana, 1993; Lee & Mock, 2005; Shibusawa, 2005). It is important for a clinical psychologist to be aware of this tendency toward collectivism among Asians, but any particular client may be an exception to the rule, and the clinical psychologist must be open to this possibility as well. Just as Yao Ming stands almost 2 ft. higher than the average Chinese man, the Chinese client in the waiting room may hold very individualistic—rather than collectivistic—values. Although this client's status as a cultural outlier is less obviously visible than Yao Ming's height, it is nonetheless the responsibility of the clinical psychologist to be perceptive and responsive to the existence of such atypical cultural members.

Culturally Appropriate Clinical Skills

Once the psychologist has attained cultural knowledge of self and clients, the next step is to develop suitable strategies for assessment and treatment. In other words, the approaches and techniques that a psychologist uses to improve a client's life should be consistent with the values and life experience of that client (Hall, Hong, Zane, & Meyer, 2011; Hwang, 2011; Toporek, 2012). "Talk therapy" may work well for many, but for some cultural groups, it may be a bad fit. Similarly, clients from some cultures may place great value on "insight" into their psychological problems obtained over many months, but clients from other cultures may respond much more positively to action-oriented therapies with a short-term focus. Other common features of traditional psychotherapy, including verbal self-disclosure of personal problems and 50-minute sessions in an office building, may not be entirely compatible with clients from certain cultural backgrounds (Comas-Díaz, 2012).

One essential culturally appropriate clinical skill that is receiving more attention in recent years involves **microaggressions.** Microaggressions are comments or actions made in a cross-cultural context that convey prejudicial, negative, or stereotypical beliefs and may suggest dominance or superiority of one group over another (Fouad & Arredondo, 2007; Sue, 2010; Sue et al., 2007). Often, they are "little things" that one person may say to another without any intention of hostility or any

⊕ **Web Link 4.5**
Microaggressions

awareness that the comments might be invalidating or insulting—but, in fact, they are. Microaggressions often center on ethnicity or race (e.g., Franklin, 2007; Sue, Capodilupo, & Holder, 2008) but can involve any number of differences between people, such as age, gender, socioeconomic status, religion/spirituality, or sexual orientation. As an example, consider a psychologist who, during an initial interview with a 19-year-old male college student, asks, "Do you have a girlfriend?" The "girlfriend" question might communicate an assumption on the psychologist's part that heterosexual relationships are the norm or what is expected or "right." Especially if the client is gay or bisexual, such a question might have negative consequences in terms of forming a therapeutic relationship in which the client feels valued and accepted. Or if a psychologist meets with a 7-year-old therapy client on December 27 and asks, "So what did Santa bring you?" the child may feel devalued if he or she is a Muslim, Jew, Buddhist, or otherwise doesn't celebrate Christmas. The best way for psychologists to avoid microaggressions is to examine the thoughts and beliefs that underlie them, which can result in greater humility and self-awareness for the psychologist (Vasquez, 2010).

Recent efforts toward the attainment of culturally appropriate clinical skills have emphasized the notion of *cultural adaptation* of treatments with empirical evidence to support them (Bernal, Jiménez-Chafey, & Rodríguez, 2009; Smith, Rodríguez, & Bernal, 2011). In other words, now that clinical psychology has generated lists of treatments that work, an important subsequent step is to determine how those treatments might need to be adapted for members of diverse cultures (Castro, Barrera, & Steiker, 2010; Mulvaney-Day, Earl, Diaz-Linhart, & Alegría, 2011). (After all, many of the studies that generated the empirical support for evidence-based treatments were conducted on clients whose collective cultural range was very narrow.) For example, La Roche, Batista, and D'Angelo (2011) examined a large number of guided-imagery scripts—the instructions that psychologists read or record for their clients when they are trying to induce relaxation. Often, these scripts include statements such as, "Imagine yourself alone on a calm beach" or "Picture yourself in a beautiful meadow." Such situations are remarkably "solo"—in other words, the idyllic setting involves the client alone. In many ethnicities, scenes that invoke feelings of togetherness or connectedness with other people might better capture relaxation or happiness—something along the lines of, "Imagine yourself amongst people who are positive and make you feel good about yourself." La Roche et al. found that guided imagery scripts emphasize a "solo" (or idiocentric) orientation rather than a "together" (or allocentric) orientation, which could prove inconsistent with the cultural values of many clients. They recommend that clinicians who use such techniques develop a variety of guided-imagery scripts, including some that are allocentric, rather than imposing idiocentric scripts on all clients. This kind of adaptation—in which clinicians consider how diverse clients might respond differently to the standard (often evidence-based) treatment, versus one that has been customized for them—is on the rise (Gelso, 2011; Hwang, 2011).

Are We All Alike? Or All Different?

The discussion of cultural issues brings up some important, fundamental questions about human beings that are applicable to psychologists and the clients they see. To what extent are all people—and the experiences and problems they bring to therapy—similar? And to what extent might they differ from one another?

Etic Versus Emic Perspective

Dana (1993) describes two distinct perspectives that psychologists have used during the history of the profession. The first, known as the **etic** perspective, emphasizes the similarities between all people. It assumes universality among all people and generally does not attach importance to differences between cultural groups. This perspective was more dominant in the early days of psychology, when most of the people teaching and practicing psychology were male, of European descent, and of middle-class or higher socioeconomic standing. Generally, their viewpoint was put forth as the normative viewpoint on issues such as defining psychological health, identifying and labeling psychological disorders, and developing therapy approaches.

The **emic** perspective differs from the etic perspective in that it recognizes and emphasizes culture-specific norms. A psychologist employing the emic perspective—which has grown in prominence along with the rise in multiculturalism—considers a client's behaviors, thoughts, and feelings within the context of the client's own culture rather than imposing norms of another culture on the client. Compared with the etic perspective, the emic perspective allows psychologists more opportunity to appreciate and understand how the client might be viewed by members of his or her own cultural group. In short, the emic approach stresses that individuals from various cultural groups "must be understood on their own terms" (Dana, 1993, p. 21).

As a side note, Dana (1993) mentions that the terms *etic* and *emic* were derived from the field of linguistics and, specifically, from the terms *phonetic* and *phonemic*. Historically, linguists have used the term *phonetics* for sounds that are common to all languages and the term *phonemics* for sounds that are specific to a particular language (Dana, 1993; Pike, 1967). The distinction between the two terms—*universality* versus *culture specificity*—remains in the way the terms *etic* and *emic* are currently used in psychology.

Tripartite Model of Personal Identity

If the etic and emic perspectives represent two opposite viewpoints, perhaps it would be beneficial to consider a continuum that includes not only these two extremes but also some middle ground. Sue and Sue (2008) offer a three-level model called the **tripartite model of personal identity** in which all levels hold some degree of importance.

One level in this model is the **individual level.** Here, the premise is that "all individuals are, in some respects, like no other individuals." A second level is the **group level,** where the premise is that "all individuals are, in some respects, like some other individuals." The final level is the **universal level,** based on the premise that "all individuals are, in some respects, like all other individuals" (Sue & Sue, 2008, pp. 38–39). A psychologist who can appreciate a client on all three levels will be able to recognize characteristics that are entirely unique to the client, others that are common within the client's cultural group, and still others that are common to everyone. Sue and Sue (2008) argue that appreciation of all three levels is indeed the goal but that the group level has been overlooked traditionally in psychology, especially when the group is a minority culture, so psychologists may need to make more deliberate efforts in that direction. See Figure 4.1 for a visual representation of the tripartite model of personal identity.

What Constitutes a Culture?

When someone inquires about your own cultural background, which of your characteristics come to mind? Many would list their race and ethnicity, and others would include a multitude of additional characteristics. If clinical psychologists are to function in a culturally competent and sensitive way, it makes sense to consider what exactly we refer to when we say "culture."

Narrow Versus Broad Definitions

Those who argue for a more narrow definition of culture typically point to ethnicity and race as the defining cultural characteristics. Indeed, many books and articles on the topic of culture focus exclusively on issues of race or ethnicity. According to some who endorse this perspective, the inclusion of other variables as "cultural" would unfairly deemphasize the socially, politically, and personally important characteristics of race and ethnicity (Mio et al., 2006).

On the other hand, some argue that culture can be defined by a much broader range of variables, including "any and all potentially salient ethnographic, demographic, status, or affiliation identities" (Pedersen, 1999, p. 3), or that culture can be composed of "any group that shares a theme or issues(s)" (Sue, Ivey, & Pedersen, 1996, p. 16). Others have stated that ethnicity may be the primary determinant of culture but not the only one: Further factors can include socioeconomic status, gender, geography/region, age, sexual orientation, religion/spirituality, disability/ability status, and political affiliation (Artman & Daniels, 2010; Lyons, Bieschke, Dendy, Worthington, & Georgemiller, 2010; McGoldrick et al., 2005a; McKitrick & Li, 2008; Robinson-Wood, 2009; Sewell, 2009).

Whether or not the characteristics beyond race and ethnicity are universally accepted as components of culture per se, quite a few books, chapters, and articles have been

FIGURE 4.1 Tripartite Model of Personal Identity

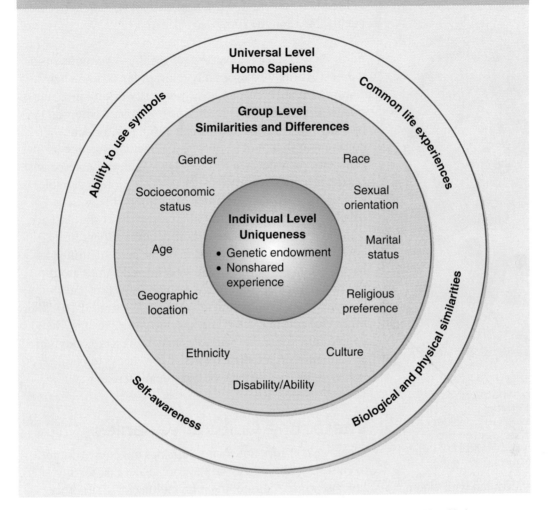

Source: Sue, D. W. & Sue, D. (2008). *Counseling the Culturally Diverse* (5th ed.). New York: Wiley, p. 12.

written with the intent of making psychotherapists and counselors more sensitive to these characteristics. For example, therapists can educate themselves about LGBT clients (Bieschke et al., 2007; Diamond, Butterworth, & Savin-Williams, 2011); disabled clients (Kosciulek, 2003); elderly clients (Qualls, 2003); rural clients (Rainer, 2010; Smalley et al., 2010); low-income clients (Acosta, Yamamoto, & Evans, 1982); Appalachian clients (Harper, 1996); Orthodox Jewish clients (Mirkin & Okun, 2005); and many, many other specific groups whose defining characteristic is neither race nor ethnicity.

Photo 4.4 In your opinion, what variables should clinical psychologists consider when they appreciate their clients' cultural backgrounds?

Indeed, as time goes by, the range of variables that clinical psychologists include when they consider culture continues to broaden (Brown, 2011; Green, Callands, Radcliffe, Luebbe, & Klonoff, 2009).

Additionally, some subsections of society— **subcultures,** if you will—may be especially relevant for certain clients. As an example, consider a psychologist working in a prison setting or with a former prison inmate who was recently released. If there is such a thing as "prison culture"—a shared lifestyle with its own unique norms, expectations, values, and so on—it would probably be wise for the psychologist to consider it in addition to variables such as race, ethnicity, gender, and others. Likewise, a psychologist working with military personnel should have some appreciation of how military culture differs from civilian culture. Even adolescents have been identified as having a culture of their own, with shared values around the importance of technology, peer relationships, and independence from parents (Nelson & Nelson, 2010). Many other "subcultures" based on specific work settings, living communities, or other variables may represent enough of an influence on the life experiences of clients to justify tailoring the treatment to best fit them (Arredondo et al., 1996; Truscott, 2010).

Interacting Cultural Variables

When we consider how many variables might contribute to culture, it's hard to avoid the conclusion that for any individual with whom a psychologist works, culture might be multifactorial. In other words, lots of cultural variables may interact in unique ways to shape the life experience of a client. Of course, ethnicity and race may be most important for certain clients. But other variables might play significant roles as well.

Consider, for example, Esteban and Maria, two clients who share similar Latino/Latina/ Hispanic ethnic backgrounds. In the spirit of cultural competence, their respective therapists should appreciate their ethnicity, but perhaps the cultural considerations should incorporate other factors as well. If Esteban is a 28-year-old gay man living an upper-middle-class life in Los Angeles, while Maria is a 66-year-old heterosexual woman living a lower-class life in a small town in rural West Virginia, the cultures of their day-to-day lives are probably quite different in spite of similar ethnic heritage. Indeed, if they visited each other's homes, they might find themselves living in very different worlds. Culturally competent therapists would certainly appreciate their ethnicity, but such therapists would also consider the way that other variables in their lives interact with their ethnicity to create a unique set of cultural circumstances (Arredondo et al., 1996; Truscott, 2010).

Training Psychologists in Cultural Issues

With the increasing emphasis on multiculturalism in clinical psychology has come an increased responsibility to train psychologists to become culturally sensitive and competent. Graduate program directors, professors, and providers of continuing education share this challenge.

Educational Alternatives

What are the best methods for training clinical psychologists in multicultural issues? Graduate programs have tried a variety of approaches. Often, graduate programs include one or more courses specifically designed to address culture. In addition, some graduate programs may weave cultural training into all the educational experiences of the graduate student. Courses in psychotherapy, assessment, and research, as well as practicum training, can be designed to incorporate issues of culture. This way, issues of culture are not considered a specialized topic to be examined in isolation but a factor relevant to all professional activities of the clinical psychologist.

Another less traditional approach to training in cultural issues emphasizes real-world experience with individuals of diverse cultures. Supporters of this approach contend that reading about a different culture in a book, or discussing a different culture in class, is no substitute for immersing oneself in that culture to some extent. Thus, through experiences that are professional (such as clinical work or research projects incorporating diverse clients, participants, colleagues, or supervisors) or personal in nature, some training programs promote learning about cultural groups by interacting directly with their members (Center for Multicultural Human Services, 2006; Magyar-Moe et al., 2005).

No single "best method" or consensus has emerged for training psychologists to be culturally competent. However, leaders in this field have begun to identify essential components for graduate training programs. For example, Fouad and Arredondo (2006, as cited in Fouad, 2006) identify seven specific "critical elements of a multiculturally infused psychology curriculum" that they believe will improve psychologists working as practitioners, teachers, or researchers. According to these authors, graduate training programs should

1. explicitly state a commitment to diversity;
2. actively make an effort to recruit graduate students from diverse populations;
3. actively make an effort to recruit and retain a diverse faculty;
4. make efforts to make the admissions process fair and equitable;
5. ensure that students gain awareness of their own cultural values and biases, knowledge of other groups, and skills to work with diverse populations;
6. examine all courses for an infusion of a culture-centered approach throughout the curriculum; and
7. evaluate students on their cultural competence on a regular basis. (Adapted from Fouad, 2006, pp. 7–9)

Regardless of the methods used to train clinical psychologists to be culturally competent, an essential ingredient is that the psychologist (or trainee) reaches a deeper appreciation of his or her own cultural identity. Hardy and Laszloffy (1992) describe numerous ways in which self-knowledge can be examined during training, such as in-class discussions, in-class presentations, self-guided assignments, and assigned discussions with one's own family of origin. In the end, the ability to relate to clients of diverse cultures may depend not only on information obtained through courses and assignments but also on an attitude of "respect, curiosity, and especially humility" (McGoldrick et al., 2005b, p. 6).

Measuring the Outcome of Culture-Based Training Efforts

Let us not forget that psychology is a science, and as such we take a keen interest in measuring the outcome of our efforts to increase cultural sensitivity and competence of psychologists. But consider some of the difficult methodological questions:

- How should we reliably and validly measure the outcome of culture-based training efforts?
- How can we reliably and validly establish a baseline for the level of cultural competence of a psychologist or trainee before the training takes place?
- When we assess the cultural competence component of psychotherapy, whose opinion should we seek? The client's? The psychologist's? The supervisor's? Another interested party's?
- How can we make a causal connection between particular culture-based training efforts and particular outcomes? How can we be sure that confounding or unexamined variables aren't responsible for the outcomes we observe?

At the moment, measuring the outcome of culture-based efforts is at a very early stage of empirical investigation, as researchers grapple with issues such as those suggested by the questions above. There is some evidence to suggest that psychologists are learning the ideals of cultural competence but are not always implementing them as often or as comprehensively as they know they should. In other words, there may be a gap between what psychologists "practice" and what they "preach" regarding multicultural competence (Hansen et al., 2006).

On a more positive note, efforts promoting multiculturalism are clearly resulting in some needed improvements related to clinical and research activities of clinical psychologists. In 2003, Sue and Sue lamented the fact that evidence-based treatments very rarely incorporate significant numbers of minority clients in their research trials, so despite the growing number of evidence-based treatments, these treatments may not be applicable to diverse populations. Only 2 years later, however, Munoz and Mendelson (2005) provided one of the first reports of a study attempting to establish empirical evidence for a treatment with a specific minority population. This report outlined the development and empirical evaluation of prevention and treatment manuals for depression and other mental health problems designed for San Francisco's low-income ethnic minority populations at San Francisco General Hospital. The authors noted many promising evaluations of these culture-specific manuals and concluded that "certain psychological theories describe universal aspects of human behavior and can thus profitably inform core therapeutic strategies. However, the effective clinical application of such strategies requires group-specific knowledge and cultural adaptation to increase the likelihood of positive outcomes" (p. 797). Additional research (e.g., Barrera & Castro, 2006; Lau, 2006) has significantly advanced the efforts to adapt evidence-based practices for specific cultural groups.

An Example of Culture Influencing the Clinical Context: The Parent–Child Relationship

Let's consider the cultural issues related to a specific aspect of clients' lives that might be involved in the assessment or treatment of a wide variety of individuals and families: the relationship between parents and their children. Perhaps the first thing that the psychologist should recall is that his or her own expectations regarding parent–child relationships are probably influenced by his or her own culture and that those expectations don't hold true for everyone. For example, in some cultures (e.g., British), parenting that produces a child who grows up, moves out, and lives an independent life is usually considered successful. But families of other cultural backgrounds (e.g., Italians) usually prefer that their children stay geographically and emotionally close even

after they reach adulthood. Some cultures (e.g., Chinese) tend to insist that children obey parental authority without discussion or negotiation. But families of other cultural backgrounds (e.g., Jewish) tend to create a home life in which open discussion of feelings, including children disagreeing or arguing with parents, is tolerated or even encouraged (McGoldrick et al., 2005a).

It is essential that the clinical psychologist seeing an individual or family such as those described above attain the multicultural competence to consider these varying norms and implement a form of treatment that is consistent with them. Especially in the United States, where diversity is extensive and on the rise, clinical psychologists are likely to work with clients from a wide variety of backgrounds. And as in this example, the cultural issue may serve as a backdrop to any number of presenting problems, including mood disorders, disruptive behavior disorders, relationship

Photo 4.5 Norms or expectations for the parent–child relationship can differ across cultures. How is this fact important to clinical psychologists who work with adults, children, or families?

problems, and many others. A culturally sensitive appreciation of the Italian family, for example, might include exploration of parents' depressive feelings about a 25-year-old daughter whose successful career has served to separate her from them. But if the family were British, an exploration of depressive feelings in the parents might strike the clients as off the mark. Similarly, if an 11-year-old boy had a heated argument with his parents because he didn't want to take the piano lessons they had arranged, a culturally sentient response might depend on whether the family were Chinese, Jewish, or of another cultural background.

CHAPTER SUMMARY

As the U.S. population has become increasingly diverse, multiculturalism has risen to prominence in clinical psychology. Evidence of its growing influence includes books and articles on multiculturalism; revisions to the *DSM,* including the inclusion of cultural concepts of distress; the creation of culturally relevant American Psychological Association

divisions; and the addition of ethical standards directly related to culture. Cultural competence, for which all clinical psychologists should strive, involves cultural self-awareness, knowledge of diverse cultures, and culturally appropriate clinical skills. Knowledge of cultural norms should be accompanied by an appreciation of the heterogeneity of that culture and the likelihood that an individual may vary from some cultural norms, especially when acculturation strategies are considered. The tripartite model of personal identity suggests that an individual can be understood as an entirely unique person, similar to members of a cultural group, or similar to all human beings. Cultures are often defined by ethnicity or race, but numerous other variables may also constitute culture, such as gender, religion/spirituality, disability status, socioeconomic status, age, and sexual orientation. Training efforts intended to increase cultural sensitivity and competence among clinical psychologists and trainees include traditional coursework as well as direct interaction with members of diverse cultures.

KEY TERMS AND NAMES

acculturation 89

cultural competence 82

cultural concepts of distress 81

cultural diversity 76

cultural self-awareness 82

emic 93

etic 93

group level 94

heterogeneity 89

individual level 94

microaggressions 91

multiculturalism 76

subcultures 96

tripartite model of personal identity 93

universal level 94

CRITICAL THINKING QUESTIONS

1. In your opinion, how important is the issue of cultural self-awareness to clinical psychologists? What is the best way to increase cultural self-awareness among current members of the profession?

2. In your opinion, which level of the tripartite model of personal identity (individual level, group level, or universal level) is most important in the conceptualization of clients?

3. What are the pros and cons of defining culture in a narrow versus broad way?

4. If you were a client, how important would it be to you that your clinical psychologist had received training in cultural issues? Which methods of training would you expect to contribute most to your clinical psychologist's cultural competence?

5. Considering the discussion in Box 4.2 about heterogeneity within a culture, can you think of a cultural group to which you belong but within which you represent an exception to a cultural tendency?

STUDENT STUDY SITE RESOURCES

Visit the study site at www.sagepub.com/pomerantz3eupdate for these additional learning tools:

- Self-quizzes
- eFlashcards
- Culture Expert Interviews

- Full-text SAGE journal articles
- Additional web resources
- Mock Assessment Data

CHAPTER SUMMARY VIDEO

 QR codes at the end of each chapter link to chapter background videos by the author. Visit http://gettag.mobi using your smartphone browser to download the free Microsoft Tag app. Once installed, scan the tags to go directly to these brief videos. In this video, the author discusses the clinical implications of the fact that many important cultural variables are not immediately obvious.

CHAPTER 5

Ethical Issues in Clinical Psychology

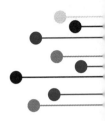

Clinical psychologists are obligated to behave ethically in all their professional activities (Pope & Vasquez, 2011). As such, discussion of ethical issues occurs at numerous points in this textbook. For example, among our considerations of culture, we discuss a subset of ethical standards most relevant to cultural sensitivity and competence. In another chapter, we discuss the ethical standards most relevant to research. In this chapter, we focus entirely on ethical issues as they apply to the wide spectrum of clinical psychology.

American Psychological Association Code of Ethics

⊕ **Web Link 5.1**

Code of Ethics

The **American Psychological Association** published its first **code of ethics** in 1953. The appearance of the initial code corresponded with the rise of professional psychology around that time period. Subsequently, nine revised editions of the ethical code have been published, including the most recent edition published in 2002 (Behnke & Jones, 2012). (Two amendments were added in 2010, emphasizing the fact that psychologists cannot use particular ethical standards to justify or defend the violation of human rights; C. B. Fisher, 2012.) Since its inception, the code has applied not only to clinical psychologists but also to psychologists of all specialties. Some of its guidelines are especially relevant to the most common professional activities of clinical psychologists, such as therapy, assessment, research, and teaching.

⊕ **Web Link 5.2**

Comparison of 1992 & 2002 Ethical Codes

Aspirational and Enforceable

The current American Psychological Association (2002) ethical code features two distinct sections: General Principles and Ethical Standards. Each of these sections steers psychologists toward ethical behavior in a different way. The items in the **General Principles** section are **aspirational**. In other words, they describe an ideal level of ethical functioning or how psychologists should strive to conduct themselves. They don't include specific definitions of ethical violations; instead, they offer more broad descriptions of exemplary ethical behavior. There are five general principles, and in Table 5.1, each appears alongside a selected sentence cited from the lengthier description included in the ethical code.

In contrast to the General Principles section, the **Ethical Standards** section of the ethical code includes **enforceable** rules of conduct. Thus, if a psychologist is found guilty of an ethical violation, it is a standard (not a principle) that has been violated. These standards are written broadly enough to cover the great range of activities in which psychologists engage, but they are nonetheless more specific than the general principles. Although each general principle could apply to almost any task a psychologist performs, each ethical standard typically applies to a more targeted aspect of professional activity. The ethical

Table 5.1 American Psychological Association General Ethical Principles

Ethical Principle	Sample Sentence From Description in Ethical Code
A. Beneficence and Nonmaleficence	"Psychologists strive to benefit those with whom they work and take care to do no harm."
B. Fidelity and Responsibility	"Psychologists establish relationships of trust with those with whom they work. They are aware of their professional and scientific responsibilities to society and to the specific communities in which they work."
C. Integrity	"Psychologists seek to promote accuracy, honesty, and truthfulness in the science, teaching, and practice of psychology."
D. Justice	"Psychologists recognize that fairness and justice entitle all persons to access and benefit from the contributions of psychology and to equal quality in the processes, procedures, and services being conducted by psychologists."
E. Respect for People's Rights and Dignity	"Psychologists respect the dignity and worth of all people, and the rights of individuals to privacy, confidentiality, and self-determination."

Source: American Psychological Association (2002). Ethical principles of psychologists and code of conduct. *American Psychologist, 57,* 1060–1073.

standards are divided into 10 categories (listed in Table 5.2), and, collectively, these 10 categories include 89 individual standards.

In this chapter, we zoom in on some of the standards most relevant to clinical psychologists. Throughout our discussion, it's important to remember that the ethical code should be understood not only as a list of rules to follow and mistakes to avoid but also as a source of inspiration for ethical behavior of the highest order. Knapp and VandeCreek (2006) describe these two approaches to ethics as "remedial" and "positive" ethics, respectively. A remedial approach to ethics would involve doing just enough to avoid any trouble that might come from a violation of ethical standards, but a positive approach to ethics would involve making every effort to ensure that one's professional behavior was as consistent with ethical principles as possible. As an example, Knapp and VandeCreek consider the ethical obligation

Table 5.2 Categories of American Psychological Association Ethical Standards

1. Resolving Ethical Issues
2. Competence
3. Human Relations
4. Privacy and Confidentiality
5. Advertising and Other Public Statements
6. Record Keeping and Fees
7. Education and Training
8. Research and Publication
9. Assessment
10. Therapy

Source: American Psychological Association (2002). Ethical principles of psychologists and code of conduct. *American Psychologist, 57,* 1060–1073.

of competence (which we discuss in more detail later in this chapter). Psychologists with a remedial approach to ethics might do the bare minimum to make themselves competent for a particular activity (e.g., taking courses, getting supervision), but psychologists with a positive approach to ethics will strive to become as competent as possible (e.g., additional courses, extra supervision, self-study, self-care).

Ethical Decision Making

When any ethical issue arises, a clinical psychologist should be equipped with a process by which to make the most ethical decision possible. The American Psychological Association's (2002) ethical code does not offer any such decision-making models per se, but such models have been recommended by a number of experts in the field (e.g., Knapp & VandeCreek, 2006; Koocher & Keith-Spiegel, 2008; Pope, 2011; Treppa, 1998). One such expert is **Celia Fisher,** who served as chair of the American Psychological Association's Ethics Code Task Force, the committee responsible for creating the 2002 revision of the ethical code. In her book *Decoding the Ethics Code,* Fisher (2012) proposes an eight-step model for **ethical decision making.** In slightly adapted language, that model is presented here:

1. Prior to any ethical dilemma arising, make a commitment to doing what is ethically appropriate.
2. Become familiar with the American Psychological Association ethical code.

3. Consult any law or professional guidelines relevant to the situation at hand.

4. Try to understand the perspectives of various parties affected by the actions you may take. Consult with colleagues (always protecting confidentiality) for additional input and discussion.

5. Generate and evaluate your alternatives.

6. Select and implement the course of action that seems most ethically appropriate.

7. Monitor and evaluate the effectiveness of your course of action.

8. Modify and continue to evaluate the ethical plan as necessary.

Before turning to any step-by-step ethical decision-making model, psychologists best prepare themselves to deal with ethical dilemmas by becoming generally ethical people with sound values. In other words, functioning as an ethical psychologist should not be a rote exercise in which a predetermined model for decision making is the sole guide. While such models can certainly enhance the psychologist's chances of making the most ethical decision, they work best when utilized by a person who has already examined his or her own values and aligned them with the ethics of the profession (Tjeltveit & Gottlieb, 2010).

Psychologists' Ethical Beliefs

The American Psychological Association's (2002) ethical code may instruct psychologists on how to conduct themselves ethically, but what do psychologists actually believe about the ethicality of various behaviors they might perform? In other words, as a group, what ethical beliefs do psychologists hold? This question, especially as it applies to psychotherapy-related behaviors, was addressed in a large-scale survey of American Psychological Association members (Pope, Tabachnick, & Keith-Spiegel, 1987). In this study, more than 450 members of Division 29 (Psychotherapy) of the American Psychological Association rated the ethicality of 83 separate behaviors that a psychologist might perform toward, with, or in response to a client. Results indicated that a few behaviors—for example, sex with clients or former clients, socializing with current clients, and disclosing confidential information without cause or permission—are viewed as blatantly unethical. In contrast, a few other behaviors—for example, shaking hands with clients, addressing clients by first name, and breaking confidentiality if clients are suicidal or homicidal—are viewed as unquestionably ethical. But most of the 83 behaviors fell in the gray area between ethical and unethical, illustrating both the challenges that psychologists face in making wise judgments regarding ethical issues and the importance of a sound model of ethical decision making (Cottone, 2012).

In the years since the 1987 study by Pope et al., other researchers have used similar methodologies to further examine the ethical beliefs of psychologists. One study found that psychologists' ethical beliefs may vary according to the point in time or the region of the country in which they are collected (Tubbs & Pomerantz, 2001), whereas others found that psychologists' ethical beliefs may vary according to the gender or age of the clients toward whom the behaviors may be directed (Pomerantz, 2012a; Pomerantz & Pettibone, 2005). Thus, although the American Psychological Association's (2002) ethical code serves as a guiding force, the beliefs psychologists actually hold, which correspond strongly with the behaviors they act out (Pope et al., 1987), may be subject to other influences.

Confidentiality

One of the characteristics most closely associated with the ethical practice of clinical psychology is **confidentiality** (M. A. Fisher, 2012). In fact, confidentiality is specifically mentioned among the general principles (in Principle E: Respect for People's Rights and Dignity) and in numerous specific ethical standards—including Standard 4.01, "Maintaining Confidentiality," which begins, "Psychologists have a primary obligation and take reasonable precautions to protect confidential information" (American Psychological Association, 2002, p. 1066).

There is good reason for the emphasis on confidentiality in the profession of psychology: Our profession is entrusted by the public to provide professional services without sharing the private, personal details offered in the process. However, the public may be unaware of the fact that confidentiality is not absolute. Although most people outside of the mental health profession may assume that psychologists hold all information confidential (Miller & Thelen, 1986), the truth is that situations arise in which psychologists are obligated to break confidentiality. Many such situations have been defined by court cases, including the well-known case involving the death of Tatiana Tarasoff.

Tarasoff and the Duty to Warn

In 1969, Prosenjit Poddar was a student at the University of California at Berkeley. He became romantically interested in Tatiana Tarasoff, and when their relationship did not advance as he would have preferred, his mental state worsened and he sought psychotherapy at the university counseling center from a psychologist, Dr. Lawrence Moore. During a session in August 1969, Poddar told Dr. Moore that he intended to kill Tarasoff. Dr. Moore believed that Poddar's comment was credible, so he broke therapist–client confidentiality and contacted campus police. The campus police interviewed Poddar but did not hold him, because he promised to avoid Tarasoff and seemed rational at the time of the interview. Poddar never returned to therapy. On October 27, 1969, Poddar killed Tarasoff by stabbing and shooting her. Tarasoff's parents later sued Dr. Moore and the others involved in the case for wrongful death. The court found that the psychologist was liable for failure to warn Tarasoff of the danger (Knapp & VandeCreek, 2006). In other words, although Dr. Moore broke confidentiality and contacted campus police, the court decided that his actions were insufficient—he should have made efforts to contact Tarasoff directly to warn her that she was in harm's way.

From the *Tarasoff* **case,** the **duty to warn** was born. That is, since the *Tarasoff* case set the legal precedent, clinical psychologists (and other therapists) have understood that there are limits to their confidentiality agreements with clients and that they have a duty to warn people toward whom their clients make credible, serious threats. As stated in the *Tarasoff* ruling, "The confidential character of patient-psychotherapist communications must yield to the extent to which disclosure is essential to avert danger to others. The protective privilege ends where the public peril begins" (*Tarasoff v. The Regents of the University of California*, 1974, p. 561, as cited in Tribbensee & Claiborn, 2003, p. 287).

⊕ **Web Link 5.3**

Tarasoff Case

Certainly, the rationale behind the duty to warn is clear: In the Tarasoff situation, a young woman's life could have been spared if a warning had been issued. And if we consider more recent tragedies—the Virginia Tech killings or the September 11 terrorist attacks, for example—we can see how, if the perpetrators had disclosed their homicidal plans to therapists, the duty to warn could have prevented large-scale "public peril" (Pope, 2011). In its application, however, the duty-to-warn issue is fraught with difficult questions for the clinical psychologists expected to uphold it. For example, how accurately can clinical psychologists assess the credibility of their clients' threatening statements, or their intent to follow through with them? What kinds of threats merit warnings—only blatant life-or-death threats or other kinds of harm, such as drunk driving or intimate partner violence, as well (Guedj, Sastre, Mullet, & Sorum, 2009; Welfel, Werth, & Benjamin, 2012)? At what point in therapy and to what extent should psychologists prioritize the protection of potential victims over the treatment of their clients? (See Bersoff, 1976; Knapp & VandeCreek, 2006; Tribbensee & Claiborn, 2003.)

In recent decades, clinical psychologists have faced a version of the duty-to-warn decision regarding clients with HIV/AIDS (Chenneville, 2000; Peter, 1998). To exemplify this dilemma, imagine that Paul, a 30-year-old, single, HIV-positive client, is seeing Dr. Reed, a clinical psychologist, for depressive symptoms. During the course of their conversations, Paul mentions to Dr. Reed that he is sexually active, that he doesn't always follow safe-sex practices, and that he has withheld from his partners that he is HIV positive. Dr. Reed immediately faces numerous challenging questions: Does Paul's behavior constitute a threat worthy of a warning to the potential victims? How does it compare with Poddar's threat to kill Tarasoff? If Dr. Reed breaks confidentiality to warn potential victims, what effect will that have on the therapeutic alliance with Paul and, ultimately, on Paul's well-being? To whom does Dr. Reed have a primary obligation—Paul or those whom Paul might endanger? Unfortunately for clinical psychologists, there are no easy answers to questions of this type.

When the Client Is a Child or Adolescent

More confidentiality-related challenges arise when clinical psychologists provide services to minors. One particular challenge centers on the fact that for many children and adolescents, the establishment of a close, trusting relationship with a clinical psychologist depends on the extent to which the psychologist reveals details of one-on-one conversations with the child's parents (Knapp & VandeCreek, 2006; Richards, 2003; Tribbensee & Claiborn, 2003). Simply put, kids might choose to withhold rather than discuss important personal issues if they know that their psychologists will subsequently share the information with the kids' parents. Of course, as legal guardians, parents are ultimately entitled to be informed about their children's progress in therapy; moreover, it's effective clinical practice to keep parents actively engaged in a child's therapy.

Sometimes, clinical psychologists can discuss this confidentiality dilemma openly with child clients and their parents, and a mutually agreeable arrangement can be reached (Knapp & VandeCreek, 2006; Richards, 2003). In other words, "therapists working with minor clients often negotiate an arrangement with their clients and their parents whereby the parents will not expect to be informed of what the client discloses in therapy except under specified conditions" (Tribbensee & Claiborn, 2003, p. 297). Those specified conditions should, at the very least, include any situation in which children might be harmed by the behavior of others or themselves, as well as general information about the child's psychological condition or progress in therapy. Even if the clinical psychologist offers the rationale that such an agreement would benefit the child's well-being, parents may refuse it, and the acceptability of such an arrangement may depend on cultural variables involving parent–child relationships. Koocher and Daniel (2012) offer this script as a prototype of what the psychologist may say to an adolescent client and his or her parent(s) together at the outset of therapy:

> Psychotherapy works best when people have confidence in the privacy of their conversations. At the same time, parents do want to feel confident about their child's well-being and safety. Since parents were once teenagers, you certainly know that an adolescent may want to use therapy to talk about sex, alcohol, smoking, or other activities that parents may not approve of. Let's talk about how we can assure your child of confidentiality so s/he can talk openly about what's on her/his mind and at the same time assure your parents about your safety. (p. 12)

When parents do accept such an arrangement, they place quite a bit of trust in the psychologist's judgment. Consider some of the behaviors in which minor clients might engage: smoking, drinking, sex, drug use, crime, and "cutting" (self-mutilation), to name a few. At what point or under what conditions do these behaviors constitute harm that merits the psychologist's informing the child's parents? To what extent is the child's age a factor?

As a clinical example, consider Danica, a 17-year-old girl seeing Dr. Terry, a clinical psychologist. Danica's parents believe that Danica deserves some confidentiality with Dr. Terry, and they agree that Dr. Terry need not repeat the full contents of their sessions; however, they understandably insist that they be informed of any harm or danger that Danica may experience. As the sessions progress, the therapeutic relationship strengthens, and Danica begins to reveal to Dr. Terry details of her life about which Danica's parents are unaware. These details include the fact that Danica drinks alcohol about once a week (but does not get drunk), that she intentionally cut her forearm with a razor blade once a few months ago, and that one night she was a passenger in a car driven by a friend who may have been stoned. Do any of these behaviors or situations call for Dr. Terry to inform Danica's parents? If not, how much would the behaviors have to intensify before they did? What consequences might Dr. Terry be able to expect if she did or did not tell Danica's parents? Would the answers differ if Danica was 14, or 11, or 8 years old?

● ● ● BOX 5.1 ● ● ●

Considering Culture

Confidentiality, Ethnicity, and Family

Clients from diverse cultural groups, along with their relatives, may have very different beliefs regarding confidentiality in mental health (e.g., McGoldrick, Giordano, & Garcia-Preto, 2005b). An informative book on this topic, *Ethics, Culture, and Psychiatry* (Okasha, Arboleda-Florez, & Sartorius, 2000), focuses on such cultural differences regarding confidentiality and other ethical issues. It includes separate chapters on many specific groups, including African, Indian, Japanese, Latin American, German, West Mediterranean, and Chinese cultures. When directly compared with each other, two of these chapters—on Arab and Scandinavian culture—illustrate quite a contrast in beliefs regarding confidentiality. Regarding Arab culture, Okasha (2000) states the following:

- "In Arab culture, issues of illness are dealt with as family matters. Whether a patient is hospitalized, for example . . . is dependent not on what the patient wants himself or herself but on the estimation, need, or wish of the extended family." (pp. 24–25)
- "In the Arab region, a person may actually change doctors . . . if the doctor persists in considering the patient the only decision maker." (p. 26)
- "In Arab culture, the norm is to convey the [diagnostic] information to the family first and then leave it up almost entirely to the family to decide whether to inform the patient." (p. 27)

(Continued)

(Continued)

Photos 5.1 and 5.2
Assumptions about
confidentiality may vary
between cultural groups.
In your opinion, how should
clinical psychologists address
these assumptions?

Regarding Scandinavian culture, Kastrup (2000) offers these descriptions:

- "The key role of patient autonomy has been increasingly emphasized in recent years. A patient has the right to make decisions about his or her treatment without interference from family." (p. 79)
- "Emphasis on autonomy is part of Scandinavian culture, and . . . lack of autonomy is considered the greatest unhappiness of the modern person. . . . The ideal is to be able . . . to live independently, without the need for support from others." (p. 79)

It is clear that Arab clients and Scandinavian clients—and possibly their family members as well—may enter into a working relationship with a clinical psychologist holding very different assumptions about confidentiality. In one culture, it is assumed that family members will be included, whereas in the other, it is assumed that family members will be excluded. Other cultures will certainly have their own unique assumptions about confidentiality as well.

In culturally diverse countries such as the United States, a clinical psychologist could see both Arab clients and Scandinavian clients. Even if these clients have similar diagnoses, clinical psychologists may find themselves working in dissimilar ways, especially in terms of the involvement of family members. To be ethical, of course, clinical psychologists must adhere to the American Psychological Association's (2002) code of ethics, yet to be culturally competent, they must also recognize that clients of various cultures will bring their own ethical values as well. If you were a clinical psychologist, how would you handle apparent conflicts between the ethical code and clients' cultural norms? Besides confidentiality, in what other areas of ethics might culture play a role in clients' expectations about clinical psychologists' behavior?

A separate confidentiality issue for clients who are minors involves **child abuse.** Every state has laws requiring mental health professionals to break confidentiality to report known or suspected child abuse (Knapp & VandeCreek, 2006; Koocher & Daniel, 2012; Tribbensee & Claiborn, 2003). (Many states have similar laws pertaining to abuse of vulnerable adults as well.) The rationale behind such laws is similar to the rationale behind the *Tarasoff* ruling; namely, some situations demand that the clinical psychologist's primary responsibility shift to the immediate prevention of harm. And, like duty-to-warn situations, child abuse situations often require the clinical psychologist to make difficult judgment calls. It can be exceedingly challenging to determine with confidence whether child abuse is likely to have taken place, especially with children who may not be entirely forthcoming, who may exaggerate claims against their parents, or whose communication skills may be limited. The clinical psychologist's overarching goal of treatment may remain simple— the well-being of the child—but in cases in which child abuse is suspected, determining the means to attain this goal can become complex.

Photo 5.3 In your opinion, to what extent should clinical psychologists share the content of a child's sessions with the child's parent(s)?

As a final note on confidentiality, it is important to note the difference between legal standards and ethical standards. Although they may differ in rare situations, the directives for clinical psychologists listed in this section—duty to warn in *Tarasoff*-like situations and required reporting of suspected child abuse—often represent both legal standards and ethical standards. That is, state law typically requires such behavior by clinical psychologists, and the American Psychological Association's (2002) ethical code includes standards that are consistent with these laws. In fact, one ethical standard (4.02, "Discussing the Limits of Confidentiality") specifically instructs clinical psychologists to "discuss . . . the relevant limits of confidentiality" with clients (p. 1066). Such a discussion is a key component of the informed consent process to which we now turn our attention.

Informed Consent

You may have been exposed to the notion of **informed consent** through psychological research. If you have participated in a psychological study, you probably received written information about the study first, and only after you provided consent by signing your name did the research begin. Research is certainly an important application of the ethical standards involving informed consent, but it is not the only one. Assessment and therapy also require informed consent according to the ethical code (American Psychological Association, 2002). Actually, in any professional activity conducted by psychologists, informed consent is an essential process. It assures the person with whom the psychologist is working the opportunity to become knowledgeable about the activities in which they may participate, and it facilitates an educated decision. Moreover, it affords individuals the opportunity to refuse to consent if they so choose.

Regarding research, Standard 8.02 ("Informed Consent to Research") of the American Psychological Association's (2002) ethical code instructs psychologists to inform prospective participants about numerous aspects of the study, including its purpose, procedures, and length of time it may require; any predictable risks or adverse effects; incentives for participation; and the right to decline or withdraw from participation. If the study is an investigation of a treatment method, psychologists should also inform clients that the treatment is experimental in nature, that some clients may be assigned to groups that receive no treatment (control groups), and of available alternative treatments outside the scope of the current study.

It is also necessary to obtain informed consent for psychological assessments. According to Standard 9.03 ("Informed Consent in Assessments"; American Psychological Association, 2002), psychologists should offer information about the nature and purpose of the assessment; any relevant fees; the involvement of other parties, if any; and limits of confidentiality (e.g., duty-to-warn or child abuse situations).

Psychotherapy requires an informed consent process as well. Ethical Standard 10.01 ("Informed Consent to Therapy") explains that

> psychologists inform clients/patients as early as is feasible in the therapeutic relationship about the nature and anticipated course of therapy, fees, involvement of third parties, and limits of confidentiality and provide sufficient opportunity for the client/patient to ask questions and receive answers. (American Psychological Association, 2002, p. 1072)

Several phrases of this ethical standard highlight the fact that therapy stands apart from other professional activities of clinical psychologists. For one, the phrase "as early as is feasible" suggests that there may be different points at which information could be presented to clients. In fact, a survey of psychologists providing therapy found that in general, they are comfortable providing some generic information, such as payment and confidentiality policies, at the outset of therapy, but more specific information, such as the length, goals, and substance of psychotherapy, requires more time for therapists to get to know their clients. As a result, informed consent to therapy—unlike informed consent to research or assessment—may be best understood as an ongoing process rather than a one-time event

(Pomerantz, 2005). Another noteworthy phrase in Standard 10.01 is "the involvement of third parties"; indeed, it has been a subject of debate exactly what or how much to tell clients about managed care's influence on the therapy process (e.g., Cohen, Marecek, & Gillham, 2006; Huber, 1997; Pomerantz, 2000). Finally, the phrase "provide sufficient opportunity for the client/patient to ask questions and receive answers" has been addressed by the publication of lists of questions that psychologists could offer to clients at the outset of therapy or at any other relevant point (e.g., Pomerantz & Handelsman, 2004). From this list, clients could choose the questions in which they have interest, some of which may not have occurred to them on their own.

Especially in psychotherapy, the informed consent process presents the clinical psychologist the chance to begin to establish a collaborative relationship with the client (Pomerantz, 2012b). As we examine in more detail in later chapters, this kind of relationship is central to the success of psychotherapy of all kinds. Thus, it can be beneficial for clinical psychologists to invite clients to participate actively in the informed consent process and genuinely to join in the decision-making process regarding their treatment plan (Knapp & VandeCreek, 2006; Pomerantz & Handelsman, 2004).

Boundaries and Multiple Relationships

In general, it can be problematic for clinical psychologists to know someone professionally—as, say, a therapy client or student—and also to know that person in another way—as, say, a friend, business partner, or romantic partner. The term used to describe such situations is **multiple relationships** (although the term *dual relationships* has also been used). It would be nice to state that psychologists never engage in such relationships, but such a claim would be false (Borys & Pope, 1989); in fact, a significant portion of complaints to the American Psychological Association Ethics Committee in recent years involve "incidents of blurred boundaries" (Schank, Slater, Banerjee-Stevens, & Skovholt, 2003, p. 182).

Web Link 5.4

Multiple relationships

Defining Multiple Relationships

Ethical Standard 3.05a (American Psychological Association, 2002) states that a multiple relationship

> occurs when a psychologist is in a professional role with a person and (1) at the same time is in another role with the same person, (2) at the same time is in a relationship with a person closely associated with or related to the person with whom the psychologist has the professional relationship, or (3) promises to enter into another relationship in the future with the person or a person closely associated with or related to the person. (p. 1065)

So multiple relationships can form not only when a psychologist knows one person both professionally and nonprofessionally but also when a psychologist has a relationship with someone "closely associated with or related to" someone the psychologist knows professionally. As an example, if Monique, a 36-year-old woman, is the therapy client of Dr. Davis, a clinical psychologist, Dr. Davis would be forming a multiple relationship if she became Monique's friend, business partner, or romantic partner. Additionally, Dr. Davis would be forming a multiple relationship if she became similarly involved with Monique's romantic partner, sibling, or close friend. For clinical psychologists considering this ethical standard, defining "closely associated or related" can be a challenge, especially considering the "six degrees of separation" nature of our cities and communities. For example, would Dr. Davis be forming a multiple relationship if she dated Monique's second cousin, went into business with Monique's neighbor, or became a friend of Monique's coworker?

As indicated by the examples above, multiple relationships can take many forms (Sommers-Flanagan, 2012). Perhaps the most blatant and damaging are **sexual multiple relationships,** in which the clinical psychologist becomes a sexual partner of the client. The American Psychological Association's (2002) code of ethics offers a direct and inflexible standard about such behavior: "Psychologists do not engage in sexual intimacies with current therapy clients/patients" (Standard 10.05, p. 1073). Such behavior represents a fundamental breach of the healthy therapist/client relationship and often results in significant psychological or emotional damage for the client (Pope, 1994; Sonne, 2012).

The nonprofessional involvement between client and clinical psychologist need not be sexual to constitute a multiple relationship or to cause the client harm. Indeed, psychologists may have opportunities to engage in a wide variety of **nonsexual multiple relationships:** friendships, business or financial relationships, coworker or supervisory relationships, affiliations through religious activities, and many others (Anderson & Kitchener, 1996; Zur, 2007). An essential task for clinical psychologists is to appropriately recognize the overlapping nature of these relationships as well as their potential to cause problems for the client.

What Makes Multiple Relationships Unethical?

Not every multiple relationship is, by definition, unethical. To help identify the specific elements of multiple relationships that characterize them as unethical, we again turn to Ethical Standard 3.05a:

> A psychologist refrains from entering into a multiple relationship if the multiple relationship could reasonably be expected to impair the psychologist's objectivity, competence, or effectiveness in performing his or her functions as a psychologist, or otherwise risks exploitation or harm

to the person with whom the professional relationship exists. Multiple relationships that would not reasonably be expected to cause impairment or risk exploitation or harm are not unethical. (American Psychological Association, 2002, p. 1065)

As this standard indicates, there are essentially two criteria for impropriety in a multiple relationship. The first involves impairment in the psychologist; if the dual role with the client makes it difficult for the psychologist to remain objective, competent, or effective, then it should be avoided. The second involves exploitation or harm to the client. Psychologists must always remember that the therapist–client relationship is characterized by unequal power, such that the therapist's role involves more authority and the client's role involves more vulnerability, especially as a consequence of some clients' presenting problems (Pope, 1994; Schank et al., 2003). Thus, ethical psychologists remain vigilant about exploiting or harming clients by clouding or crossing the boundary between professional and nonprofessional relationships. Above all, the client's well-being, not the psychologist's own needs, must remain the overriding concern.

As the last line of the standard above indicates, it is possible to engage in a multiple relationship that is neither impairing to the psychologist nor exploitive or harmful to the client. (And in some settings, such as small communities, such multiple relationships may be difficult to avoid. We discuss this in more detail later in this chapter.) However, multiple relationships can be ethically treacherous territory, and clinical psychologists owe it to their clients and themselves to ponder such relationships with caution and foresight. Sometimes, major violations of the ethical standard of multiple relationships are preceded by "a slow process of boundary erosion" (Schank et al., 2003, p. 183). That is, a clinical psychologist may engage in some seemingly harmless, innocuous behavior that doesn't exactly fall within the professional relationship—labeled by some as a "boundary crossing" (Gabbard, 2009b; Zur, 2007)—and although this behavior is not itself grossly unethical, it can set the stage for future behavior that is. These harmful behaviors are often called "boundary violations" and can cause serious harm to clients, regardless of their initial intentions (Gutheil & Brodsky, 2008; Zur, 2009).

As an example of an ethical "slippery slope" of this type, consider Dr. Greene, a clinical psychologist in private practice. Dr. Greene finishes a therapy session with Annie, a 20-year-old college student, and soon after the session, Dr. Greene walks to his car in the parking lot. On the way, he sees Annie unsuccessfully trying to start her car. He offers her a ride to class, and she accepts. As they drive and chat, Annie realizes that she left her backpack in her car, so Dr. Greene lends her some paper and pens from his briefcase so she will be able to take notes in class. Dr. Greene drops off Annie and doesn't give his actions a second thought; after all, he was merely being helpful. However, his actions set a precedent with Annie that a certain amount of nonprofessional interaction is acceptable. Soon, their out-of-therapy relationship may involve socializing or dating, which would undoubtedly constitute an unethical circumstance in which Annie could eventually be exploited or harmed. Although such "boundary erosion" is not inevitable (Gottlieb & Younggren, 2009), minor boundary infractions can foster the process. As such, clinical psychologists should give careful thought to certain actions—receiving or giving gifts, sharing food or drink, self-disclosing one's own thoughts and feelings, borrowing or lending objects, hugging—that may be expected and normal within most interpersonal relationships but may prove detrimental in the clinical relationship (Gabbard, 2009b; Gutheil & Brodsky, 2008; Zur, 2009).

Competence

The American Psychological Association's (2002) code of ethics devotes an entire section of ethical standards to the topic of **competence.** In general, competent clinical psychologists are those who are sufficiently capable, skilled, experienced, and expert to adequately complete the professional tasks they undertake (Nagy, 2012).

One specific ethical standard in the section on competence (2.01a) addresses the **boundaries of competence:** "Psychologists provide services, teach, and conduct research with populations and in areas only within the boundaries of their competence, based on their education, training, supervised experience, consultation, study, or professional experience" (American Psychological Association, 2002, p. 1063).

An important implication of this standard is that having a doctoral degree or a license in psychology does not automatically make a psychologist competent for all professional activities. Instead, the psychologist must be specifically competent for the task at hand. As an example, consider Dr. Kumar, a clinical psychologist who attended a doctoral training program in which she specialized in child clinical psychology. All her graduate coursework in psychological testing focused on tests appropriate for children, and in her practice, she commonly uses such tests. Dr. Kumar receives a call from Rick, an adult seeking an intelligence test for himself. Although Dr. Kumar has extensive training and experience with children's intelligence tests, she lacks training and experience with the adult versions of these tests. Rather than reasoning, "I'm a licensed clinical psychologist, and clinical psychologists give these kinds of tests, so this is within the scope of my practice," Dr. Kumar takes a more responsible, ethical approach. She understands that she has two options: become adequately competent (through courses, readings, supervision, etc.) before testing adults such as Rick, or refer adults to another clinical psychologist with more suitable competence.

Psychologists not only need to become competent, but they must also remain competent: "Psychologists undertake ongoing efforts to develop and maintain their competence" (Standard 2.03, American Psychological Association, 2002, p. 1064). This standard is consistent with the **continuing education** regulations of many state licensing boards. That is, to be eligible to renew their licenses, psychologists in many states must attend lectures, participate in workshops, complete readings, or demonstrate in some other way that they are sharpening their professional skills and keeping their knowledge of the field current.

Among the many aspects of competence that clinical psychologists must demonstrate is **cultural competence** (as discussed extensively in the previous chapter). Ethical Standard 2.01b (American Psychological Association, 2002) states that when

> an understanding of factors associated with age, gender, gender identity, race, ethnicity, culture, national origin, religion, sexual orientation, disability, language, or socioeconomic status is essential for effective implementation of their services or research, psychologists have or obtain the training, experience, consultation, or supervision necessary to ensure the competence of their services. (pp. 1063–1064)

Ethical psychologists do not assume a "one-size-fits-all" approach to their professional work. Instead, they realize that clients differ in important ways, and they ensure that they have the competence to choose or customize services to suit culturally and demographically diverse clients (Salter & Salter, 2012). Such competence can be obtained in many ways, including through coursework, direct experience, and efforts to increase one's own self-awareness. Readings sponsored by the American Psychological Association, such as the "Guidelines for Psychotherapy With Lesbian, Gay, and Bisexual Clients" (Division 44, 2000) and "Guidelines for Providers of Psychological Services to Ethnic, Linguistic, and Culturally Diverse Populations" (American Psychological Association, 1993) can also be important contributors to cultural competence for clinical psychologists.

It is important to note that ethical violations involving cultural incompetence (e.g., actions reflecting racism or sexism) are viewed just as negatively by nonprofessionals as other kinds of ethical violations, such as confidentiality violations and multiple relationships (Brown & Pomerantz, 2011). In other words, cultural competence is not only a wise clinical strategy; it is an essential component of the ethical practice of clinical psychology that can lead to detrimental consequences for clients when violated (Gallardo, Johnson, Parham, & Carter, 2009).

The American Psychological Association's (2002) code of ethics also recognizes that psychologists' own personal problems can lessen their competence: "When psychologists become aware of personal problems that may interfere with their performing work-related duties adequately, they take appropriate measures, such as

Web Link 5.5

Burnout among therapists

obtaining professional consultation or assistance, and determine whether they should limit, suspend, or terminate their work-related duties" (Standard 2.06, p. 1064). Of course, personal problems that impede psychologists' performance can stem from any aspect of their personal or professional lives (Barnett, 2008). On the professional side, the phenomenon of burnout among clinical psychologists has been recognized in recent decades (e.g., Grosch & Olsen, 1995; Morrissette, 2004). **Burnout** refers to a state of exhaustion that relates to engaging continually in emotionally demanding work that exceeds the normal stresses or psychological "wear and tear" of the job (Pines & Aronson, 1988). Due to the nature of the work they often perform, clinical psychologists can find themselves quite vulnerable to burnout. In one study of more than 500 licensed psychologists practicing therapy (Ackerley, Burnell, Holder, & Kurdek, 1988), more than one third reported that they had experienced high levels of some aspects of burnout, especially emotional exhaustion. In this study, the factors that increased a psychologist's susceptibility to burnout included feeling overcommitted to clients, having a low sense of control over the therapy, and earning a relatively low salary. A more recent study confirmed that over involvement with clients correlates strongly with burnout, particularly in the form of emotional exhaustion (Lee, Lim, Yang, & Lee, 2011).

Burnout and other factors can contribute to a level of impairment—in the form of depression, substance use, or other manifestations—that directly interferes with clinical work (Tamura, 2012; Williams, Pomerantz, Pettibone, & Segrist, 2010). As the ethical standard suggests, psychologists should take action to prevent or minimize their own impairment, including professional burnout. Such actions can include varying one's work responsibilities, keeping one's expectations reasonable, consulting with other professionals, maintaining a balanced and healthy personal life, or seeking psychotherapy as necessary (Barnett, 2008; Grosch & Olsen, 1995; Smith & Moss, 2009). At the same time, it is important for psychologists to remain alert to signs that they are experiencing impairment—which, to some extent, is a universal experience for those who stay in the profession—and take appropriate action when such situations arise (Good, Khairallah, & Mintz, 2009). Collective efforts can also be helpful; that is, not only can each psychologist look out for herself or himself, but clinical psychologists can look out for one another, both informally (e.g., among colleagues) and formally via efforts by professional organizations to promote self-care among their members (Barnett & Cooper, 2009).

Photo 5.4 Burnout can have a negative influence on a clinical psychologist's competence. If you were a clinical psychologist, what steps would you take to avoid burnout?

Ethics in Clinical Assessment

Many of the principles and standards discussed so far in this chapter relate to all clinical activities, but there are some that address assessment specifically. For example, the American Psychological Association's (2002) code of ethics obligates psychologists to select tests that are appropriate for the purpose of the assessment and the population being tested. **Test selection** should entail a number of factors, including the psychologist's competence; the client's culture, language, and age; and the test's reliability and validity. Additionally, psychologists must not select tests that have become obsolete or have been replaced by revised editions that are better suited to the assessment questions being addressed. Sometimes, psychologists find themselves in a position of constructing a new test rather than selecting from existing tests. Psychologists involved in test construction should do their best to establish adequate reliability and validity, minimize test bias, and accompany the test with a coherent, user-friendly test manual (Pomerantz & Sullivan, 2006).

Test security represents another specific area of focus of the American Psychological Association's (2002) ethical code. Psychologists should make efforts to protect the security and integrity of the test materials they use. In other words, psychologists should prevent the questions, items, and other stimuli included in psychological tests from entering the public domain (Bersoff, Dematteo, & Foster, 2012). When psychologists allow test materials to be taken home by clients, photocopied, or posted on Internet sites, not only might they be violating copyright laws, but they might also be allowing prospective test takers inappropriate access to tests. This could lead to preparation or coaching for psychological tests, which could, in turn, produce invalid test results. As described by Knapp and VandeCreek (2006), depending on the test in question, such invalid test results could place a nongifted student in a school's gifted program, a psychologically unstable police officer on the streets, or a child in the custody of an emotionally unfit parent.

Although psychologists should keep test materials secure, the American Psychological Association's (2002) ethical code explains that they are generally obligated to release test data to clients on request. **Test data** refers to the raw data the client provided during the assessment—responses, answers, and other notes the psychologist may have made. Although previous editions of the ethical code instructed psychologists not to release test data to clients, the current edition instructs psychologists to release test data unless there is reason to believe that the data will be misused or will harm the client. This revision reflects the more global shift toward patient autonomy in the health care field (C. B. Fisher, 2012).

Ethics in Clinical Research

The American Psychological Association's code of ethics includes numerous standards that apply to research of all kinds, including clinical research. So, just like psychologists from other specialty areas, clinical psychologists who conduct research are ethically obligated to minimize harm to participants, steer clear of plagiarism, and avoid fabrication of data, among other things (Fisher & Vacanti-Shova, 2012). Here, we will focus our discussion on one issue particularly relevant to an essential area of clinical research: **efficacy** of psychotherapy.

When clinical psychologists conduct empirical studies to measure how well a particular therapy works, they typically conduct the therapy in question with one group of participants, whereas a second group does not receive this therapy. What should the second group receive? This is a question with important ethical implications (Imber et al., 1986; Lindsey, 1984; Saks, Jeste, Granholm, Palmer, & Schneiderman, 2002). Although studies of this type may ultimately benefit many clients via the identification of evidence-based treatments, psychologists should be careful not to mistreat or harm some of our clients/research participants in the process.

Most commonly, the participants in therapy efficacy studies who don't receive the treatment being studied are placed in one of three conditions: no treatment (often called a "wait-list control" group), a placebo treatment (some kind of interpersonal interaction with a professional but with presumably therapeutic techniques deliberately omitted), or an alternate treatment (the efficacy of which may be unknown) (Bjornsson, 2011). Is it ethical to provide any of these options to people who have psychological problems and have chosen, presumably with the hope of improvement, to participate in a study on its treatment? Of course, it is essential to inform participants before they consent to the study that some of them may not receive the treatment being studied or any treatment at all. Even if participants agree to this arrangement, the ethicality of the treatment they receive throughout a study of this type has been questioned (e.g., Arean & Alvidrez, 2002; Street & Luoma, 2002). Indeed, it is a significant ethical challenge for clinical psychologists to determine empirically the efficacy of their therapies without unduly exploiting or failing to help some of the participants while doing so (Saks et al., 2002).

Contemporary Ethical Issues

Managed Care and Ethics

As we discuss in another chapter, managed care exerts a strong influence on the current practice of clinical psychology. Among the new challenges it has presented are numerous ethical issues.

To begin, managed-care companies can put clinical psychologists in a position of divided loyalty. Although psychologists are ethically committed to "strive to benefit" and "safeguard the welfare" of their clients (American Psychological Association, 2002, p. 1062), they may be professionally pressured to minimize the services they provide to limit the cost of mental health care. In other words, clinical psychologists may find themselves in a tug-of-war between the managed-care companies' profits and their clients' psychological well-being (Alcaron, 2000; Wilcoxon, Remley, Gladding, & Huber, 2007). Moreover, to the extent that clients can perceive that the clinical psychologist has divided loyalties, the therapeutic relationship may suffer (Haas & Cummings, 1991).

Actually, the clinical psychologist could tell the client about loyalties to managed-care companies—and much more about managed care for that matter—during the informed consent process. Indeed, there are many aspects of managed mental health care that could be included in the informed consent process. For example, managed-care plans typically require that a *Diagnostic and Statistical Manual of Mental Disorders* (*DSM*) diagnosis be assigned to a client to qualify for payment (Ackley, 1997; Chambliss, 2000). Also, managed-care companies typically require that the clinical psychologist share at least some clinical information about the problem or its treatment with the company. To what extent should clinical psychologists discuss this and other facts of managed-care therapy with clients at the outset of therapy? Although the question is important, the answer is unclear (Acuff et al., 1999). Little empirical research has been conducted on the question, but some studies have suggested that information on managed care does strongly impact attitudes toward therapy (e.g., Pomerantz, 2000).

The aforementioned requirement that clients must be diagnosed with a *DSM* disorder for their managed-care companies to pay for treatment can present another ethical dilemma for clinical psychologists. If a client is struggling with a problem that does not meet the criteria for any *DSM* disorder, or if a family or couple has problems that don't stem directly from an identifiable disorder in one person, the psychologist can face pressure to falsely assign a diagnosis to ensure that the managed-care company will pay the bill (Kielbasa, Pomerantz, Krohn, & Sullivan, 2004; Pomerantz & Segrist, 2006; Wilcoxon et al., 2007). Or the psychologist may be tempted to "upcode," or assign a more serious diagnosis than the client's symptoms actually merit, to increase the amount of sessions or money the managed-care company will devote to treatment (C. B. Fisher, 2012; Parry, Furber, & Allison, 2009). Even if the psychologist's motivation is the client's welfare, such actions are unethical and can constitute the illegal act of insurance fraud as well (Miranda & Marx, 2003).

Technology and Ethics

Along with managed care, technological advances have led to changes in the practice of clinical psychology in recent years, and new ethical challenges have also arisen. For example, a quick Internet search will yield a wide array of so-called "psychological tests" of one kind or another, claiming to measure intelligence, personality, and other variables. Many of these tests have questionable validity or reliability, and the feedback they provide may be inaccurate and distressing to clients. Any clinical psychologist who creates or uses unscientifically sound tests of this type may be engaging in unethical practice (Buchanan, 2002). And online assessment raises many more ethical questions (e.g., Knapp & VandeCreek, 2006; Naglieri et al., 2004): As the client is taking the test, are the testing conditions standardized? Will the client keep the test materials secure? Is the client distracted by other tasks? Is the client actually the person completing the test? Are there important behavioral observations the psychologist might be missing because of the remote nature of the assessment?

Some of these concerns apply to online therapy practices as well (e.g., Shapiro & Schulman, 1996). When therapy is done via computer, the clinical psychologist and client may not be able to fully appreciate all aspects of communication (e.g., nonverbals). Moreover, online therapy gives rise to concerns about confidentiality and client identity that don't exist when the clinical psychologist works with the client in person (Fisher & Fried, 2003; Kraus, 2004).

Ethics in Small Communities

Although they have become increasingly acknowledged and researched in recent decades, the ethical challenges unique to small communities are certainly not a recent development. Clinical psychologists who work and live in small communities have always experienced these challenges (Werth, Hastings, & Riding-Malon, 2010). Rural areas and small towns may be the most obvious examples of small communities, but there are many others as well. Even within large cities, clinical psychologists can find themselves living and working in small communities defined by ethnicity, religion, or sexual orientation, or on military bases, at small colleges, or in similar settings (Hargrove, 1986; Schank, Helbok, Haldeman, & Gallardo, 2010; Schank & Skovholt, 1997, 2006; Schank et al., 2003).

Multiple relationships are perhaps the most distinctively difficult ethical issue for clinical psychologists in small communities. In fact, "nonsexual overlapping relationships are not a matter of *if* as much as *when* in the daily lives of many small- and contained-community psychologists" (Schank et al., 2003, p. 191). Unlike clinical psychologists in larger communities, those in small communities may not be able to live in one population and practice in another, so keeping personal and professional aspects of their lives entirely separate may prove impossible. Consider Dr. Peters, the only clinical psychologist in a remote town with a population of 1,500. Any of Dr. Peters's activities—shopping at the grocery store, working out at the gym, visiting a dentist—might require her to interact with a client or former client. And when we recall that multiple relationships can involve those close to clients (e.g., family, friends) in addition to clients themselves, the likelihood of such interactions increases tremendously. Dr. Peters may be the only qualified mental health professional in the community, so for her, referring clients to others may not be a viable option.

For clinical psychologists such as Dr. Peters, it is wise to discuss multiple relationships with clients at the outset of psychological services as part of the informed consent process. Although multiple relationships may be somewhat inevitable, educating clients about the complications they can cause, as well as the psychologist's ethical obligations, can clarify boundaries and prevent misunderstandings. In addition, clinical psychologists in small communities should do their best to live a healthy, well-balanced personal life to ensure that they don't find themselves inappropriately leaning on clients to meet their own personal needs. And even if some degree of overlap is inevitable, clinical psychologists in small communities must nonetheless make every effort to avoid the impaired judgment and client exploitation that can make multiple relationships unethical and harmful (Curtin & Hargrove, 2010).

● ● ● BOX 5.2 ● ● ●

Metaphorically Speaking

If You've Played the "Six Degrees of Kevin Bacon" Game, You Understand Multiple Relationships in Small Communities

It's hard to find a Hollywood actor or actress without a connection to Kevin Bacon. Hundreds have direct connections, meaning that they have costarred in films with him. Thousands more are indirectly connected to him, often through a surprisingly small number of links. Take Keira Knightley, for example. She's just two links away from Kevin Bacon—she appeared in *Love Actually* with an actress who appeared in *Wild Things* with Kevin Bacon. Lindsay Lohan? Shia LaBeouf? Spike Lee? Seth Rogen? Meryl Streep?—all just a couple of steps away from Kevin Bacon. (Check www.oracleofbacon.org for more Kevin Bacon connections.)

The experience of clinical psychologists living and working in small communities might be a bit like Kevin Bacon's experience at a Hollywood party. For Bacon, everyone at the party could be a friend or the friend of a friend; for the clinical psychologist, everyone in the community could be a client or a client's friend, partner, brother, sister, parent, child, and so on. There are a few differences, however. For one, Kevin Bacon can skip the party if he chooses to avoid seeing people to whom he is connected, but it's not so easy for the clinical psychologist, whose personal life requires regular contact with community members. Also, Kevin Bacon doesn't need to be wary of ethical pitfalls as the clinical psychologist does; if

(Continued)

(Continued)

he blurs relationship boundaries at the party, it might be called "networking," but if a clinical psychologist does so in the small community, it might result in confusion, reduced objectivity, or even exploitation.

In larger communities, clinical psychologists may have more options to avoid multiple-relationship predicaments. They might be able to find accountants, physicians, yoga instructors, or basketball coaches for their kids who have no connections to their clients. But in smaller communities, the degrees of separation are far fewer, so multiple relationships can be unavoidable. It is possible to manage this situation successfully, however, and the American Psychological Association's (2002) ethical code explicitly states that multiple relationships need not be unethical. An essential strategy for clinical psychologists in small communities includes communication with clients early in the professional relationship about the "ground rules" regarding multiple relationships, and always steering clear of the most toxic elements of multiple relationships, such as exploitation and harm of clients.

CHAPTER SUMMARY

The American Psychological Association's code of ethics was originally created in 1953 and was most recently fully revised in 2002. The current code includes both aspirational principles and enforceable standards. In addition to a thorough knowledge of the code, a psychologist's ethical decision-making process should include a thoughtful consideration of the perspectives of all parties involved in the situation, consultation with trusted colleagues, and careful evaluation of all alternatives. Confidentiality is a particularly significant ethical issue for clinical psychologists. Although some clients may mistakenly believe that confidentiality is absolute, some situations necessitate a breach of confidentiality. For example, the ruling in the *Tarasoff* case assigns psychologists the duty to warn potential victims of harm, and state laws require psychologists to report ongoing child abuse. Policies regarding confidentiality and other aspects of psychological services should be addressed in the informed consent process. Unlike informed consent for research, which is typically a single event at the outset, informed consent for psychotherapy may be better understood as a process that continues over time as the psychologist is increasingly able to provide information specific to each client. Multiple relationships, in which a psychologist knows a client both professionally and nonprofessionally (or has a relationship with someone close to the client), can constitute ethical violations when they impair the psychologist's objectivity, competence, or effectiveness, or when they exploit or harm the client.

Not all multiple relationships are unethical, however, and in small communities, some degree of overlapping relationships may be unavoidable. Regarding competence, psychologists should (1) ensure that their professional activities match their training and expertise, (2) make efforts to avoid any negative impact of burnout or personal problems on their work, and (3) attain cultural competence for a diverse range of clients. Some contemporary developments have created additional ethical concerns for psychologists, including diagnostic and informed consent issues related to managed care and numerous ethical issues related to online assessment and therapy.

KEY TERMS AND NAMES

American Psychological Association 104

aspirational 104

boundaries of competence 118

burnout 120

child abuse 113

code of ethics 104

competence 118

confidentiality 108

continuing education 119

cultural competence 119

duty to warn 109

efficacy 122

enforceable 104

ethical decision making 106

Ethical Standards 104

Celia Fisher 106

General Principles 104

informed consent 113

multiple relationships 115

nonsexual multiple relationships 116

sexual multiple relationships 116

Tarasoff case 109

test data 121

test security 121

test selection 121

CRITICAL THINKING QUESTIONS

1. What is the primary difference between the aspirational and enforceable sections of the American Psychological Association's (2002) code of ethics? Which would you expect to have the most direct influence on the professional behavior of a clinical psychologist?

2. What conclusions do you draw from the research findings that psychologists' ethical beliefs may vary across time, client gender, client age, or other variables?

3. Provide separate lists of examples of client threats that, in your opinion, do and do not invoke the "duty to warn" as established by the *Tarasoff* case.

4. In your opinion, what information is most essential to informed consent for psychotherapy?

5. If you were a clinical psychologist, what efforts would you make to ensure that you did not experience personal problems or burnout that impaired your work?

STUDENT STUDY SITE RESOURCES

Visit the study site at www.sagepub.com/pomerantz3eupdate for these additional learning tools:

- Self-quizzes
- eFlashcards
- Culture Expert Interviews

- Full-text SAGE journal articles
- Additional web resources
- Mock Assessment Data

CHAPTER SUMMARY VIDEO

 QR codes at the end of each chapter link to chapter background videos by the author. Visit http://gettag.mobi using your smartphone browser to download the free Microsoft Tag app. Once installed, scan the tags to go directly to these brief videos. In this video, the author describes a couple of his own clients whose comments made him consider breaking their confidentiality.

CHAPTER 6

Conducting Research in Clinical Psychology

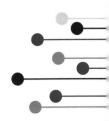

Like the other specialty areas in psychology, clinical psychology addresses its fundamental questions via scientific study and empirical research. Of course, many of the research methods used by clinical psychologists overlap with those used by other psychologists and scientists (and with those that may have been covered in other courses you have taken by this point). The goal of this chapter is to place emphasis on how *clinical* psychologists conduct research, which involves the introduction of some research-related concepts as well as the reconsideration of others in this specialized context.

Why Do Clinical Psychologists Do Research?

Treatment Outcome

A primary reason clinical psychologists have conducted research is to determine how well their therapies work (Spokas, Rodebaugh, & Heimburg, 2008). Research on **treatment outcome** has a rather extensive history, with Hans Eysenck's (1952) unfavorable review of psychotherapy outcome serving as a landmark study and a catalyst for additional investigations on the subject. In the decades subsequent to Eysenck's review, researchers established that psychotherapy is indeed effective and ultimately moved on to exploring which particular therapies are most successful at treating which particular disorders (a topic covered in more detail in Chapter 11). Today, professional journals such as *Professional Psychology: Research & Practice*; *Psychotherapy: Theory, Research, Practice, Training*; and *Clinical Psychology: Science and Practice* frequently feature treatment outcome studies.

● ● ● BOX 6.1 ● ● ●

Measuring Therapy Outcome: Essential Questions

Clinical psychologists who investigate therapy outcome face many fundamental questions when designing their studies. The choices they make can have a profound influence on the data they collect and the conclusions they draw.

How should psychotherapy outcome be measured?

Questionnaires are an efficient, convenient way to evaluate therapy outcome. In fact, some of the most commonly used and widely accepted measures of therapy outcome are written surveys of some type. However, other possibilities certainly exist, including interviews and direct observation of the client in or out of therapy sessions. If questionnaires are the chosen method, more specific "how" questions arise, such as the length and format of the questionnaire.

What should be measured when assessing psychotherapy outcome?

Specifically, what aspects of a client do we hope to change via psychotherapy? Given the enormous breadth of problems for which people seek psychotherapy and the vast array of therapy techniques and approaches available, the answer can vary greatly: observable behavior, thought patterns or cognitive processes, emotional responses, interpersonal tendencies, awareness of internal mental processes, and academic or professional outcomes, among others. Researchers who conduct empirical inquiries about therapy outcome must consider which of these outcomes is most important for the purpose of their particular study and design their outcome measure accordingly.

When should psychotherapy outcome be measured?

The possible answers to this question vary widely as well. If the emphasis is evaluative (i.e., determining after the fact how well the therapy worked), measurements could occur immediately after therapy ends or as "follow-up" efforts after a week, a month, a year, or any other chosen time period has elapsed. If the emphasis is formative (i.e., determining how therapy is working while it is still happening, with the intent of making immediate adjustments), measurements could take place at each session or on a less frequent basis throughout the course of therapy. Of course, researchers could combine these approaches as well.

Who should rate psychotherapy outcome?

There are numerous parties who may have an interest and some knowledge regarding how psychotherapy turns out for a particular client. The client is an obvious source of information, but the reliability and validity of clients' opinions of their own therapy can be questionable as a result of their biases, expectations, and in some cases the very psychological issues that prompted the therapy. (For example, a depressed client who consistently focuses on the negative aspects of his life while ignoring the positive aspects may apply this negative bias toward the question of therapy outcome as well.) Moreover, if therapy involves multiple individuals (as in couples therapy or family therapy), different people may have very different opinions. Psychotherapists can provide their own perspectives, but these are subject to biases and other threats to objectivity as well. In addition to the client and the therapist, other parties can have a justified interest in therapy outcome, including spouses, family members, employers, law enforcement and judicial institutions, managed-care/insurance companies, and society as a whole (Strupp, 1996; Strupp & Hadley, 1977).

Efficacy Versus Effectiveness

It is important to distinguish studies of psychotherapy outcome into studies that measure efficacy and those that measure effectiveness (Spokas et al., 2008; Truax & Thomas, 2003). **Efficacy** refers to the success of a particular therapy in a controlled study conducted with clients who were chosen according to particular study criteria. In short, the efficacy of a form of therapy is how well it works "in the lab," where it is practiced according to manualized methods and where outcome for treated individuals is compared via clinical trial with outcome for individuals who receive alternate or no treatment (Chambless et al., 1998; Garske & Anderson, 2003). Participants are often selected on the basis of meeting strict (e.g., diagnostic) criteria and are randomly assigned to either a treatment group or a control group (Durand & Wang, 2011). (In many cases, more than half of those interested in being participants are excluded. Those who are included are typically less severe, more likely to have comorbid diagnoses, and less likely to be from minority populations than are comparable clients in actual clinical settings; Rosqvist, Thomas, & Truax, 2011.) As an example, cognitive behavior therapy has been listed as a treatment with demonstrated efficacy for panic disorder (Chambless et al., 1998) as a result of efficacy studies conducted with carefully selected clients in a controlled, quasi-experimental setting (e.g., Barlow, Craske, Cerny, & Klosko, 1989; Clark et al., 1994).

⊕ **Web Link 6.1**
Article about
Consumer
Reports
effectiveness
study

Effectiveness, on the other hand, refers to the success of a therapy in actual clinical settings in which client problems span a wider range and are not chosen as a result of meeting certain diagnostic criteria. In short, the effectiveness of psychotherapy is how well it works "in the real world," or how well it translates from the lab to the clinics, agencies, hospitals, private practices, and other settings where clinical psychologists conduct therapy (Chambless et al., 1998; Garske & Anderson, 2003). For example, the November 1995 issue of *Consumer Reports* magazine featured a survey of its readers who had received psychotherapy in the early 1990s (Seligman, 1995). Overall, they provided a positive view of their psychotherapy experiences: More than 90% reported that therapy was beneficial; the type of therapy, the profession of the licensed provider, and the presence of medication were generally unimportant; and longer therapy tended to produce greater benefit. Additional findings were reported as well, but the essential point here is that this study provides data on the effectiveness, not the efficacy, of psychotherapy. This was not a study that was designed and controlled by researchers from the outset. An experimental or quasi-experimental design was not used, nor was an untreated control group included. Although we can be sure that these results are valid in the "real world," the lack of scientific rigor leaves us unsure that the therapy is undoubtedly the factor that produced the outcome. Issues of effectiveness and efficacy are considered further in Chapter 11.

When measuring the outcome of therapy in either an efficacy or an effectiveness study, researchers must be careful to distinguish *statistical significance* from *clinical significance* when interpreting their results. Simply put, statistical tests can, at times, indicate that a significant difference exists between two groups (e.g., those who received the treatment and those who did not). But a statistically significant difference doesn't necessarily mean that the two groups differ much in real-world terms. For example, consider a study in which the two groups both start therapy with average ratings of 80 on a 100-point depression scale—in other words, both groups are markedly depressed. After one group receives Therapy A, that group's average drops to 75, while the control group's average stays at 80. Especially if the number of participants in each group is high, that 5-point difference could turn up as significant according to a statistical test. But is that jump—a mere 5 points on a 100-point scale—clinically significant? Does it make a meaningful difference in the quality of the participants' lives? Probably not. For this reason, both statistical significance, which is assessed quantitatively, and clinical (or real-world) significance, which is measured more qualitatively, should be taken into account when interpreting the results of a therapy outcome study (Conner, 2010).

Internal Versus External Validity

The distinction between efficacy and effectiveness exemplifies how the fundamental research concepts of internal and external validity are applicable to clinical psychology. **Internal validity** refers to the extent to which the change in the dependent variable is due solely to the change in the independent variable. On the other hand, **external validity** refers to the generalizability of the result—to what extent is the same finding valid for different settings and populations?

When psychotherapy outcome researchers design an efficacy study, they aim to minimize any element of the study that may bring into question the causal connection between the treatment and the outcome (such as variability in client diagnosis or in therapist methods). This bolsters the study's internal validity. However, even in the most internally valid study, the extent to which its results are replicable in other settings with other clients—in other words, the generalizability or external validity—is not guaranteed. In fact, the more "controlled" and internally valid an efficacy study is, the more dissimilar it can become from therapy in the "real world," thus undermining external validity. Efficacy studies are often respected for their internal validity but discounted for their external validity, whereas the opposite is often true for effectiveness studies (Scotti, Morris, Stacom, & Cohen, 2011; Spokas et al., 2008).

● ● ● BOX 6.2 ● ● ●

Considering Culture

Treatments That Work, but for Whom?

When researchers investigate the efficacy of a particular form of therapy, they select clients who meet the criteria of interest for that study. For example, if the treatment

(Continued)

(Continued)

Photo 6.1 When clinical psychologists conduct research on therapy outcome, how can they ensure that their results will apply to diverse clients?

targets generalized anxiety disorder (GAD), the researchers will select clients who meet the official diagnostic criteria of GAD and whose diagnostic profiles are free of other complicating factors or comorbidities.

What if the resulting population of selected clients is culturally limited? To what extent can the study's results be generalized to individuals from a broader range of cultures? Some have argued that the outcome studies that have formed the empirical basis of "what works" in psychotherapy lack minority participants and, moreover, that their conclusions regarding efficacy are not necessarily applicable to those who differ from the studies' participants in terms of ethnicity, gender, or other variables (e.g., Bernal & Scharro-del-Rio, 2001; Miranda, Azocar, Organista, Munoz, & Lieberman, 1996; Sue, Cheng, & Sue, 2011; Sue & Sue, 2008). Munoz and Mendelson (2005) stated: "Clinical trials have seldom included adequate samples of people of color. . . . Indeed, most empirically supported therapies were evaluated with samples drawn primarily from a White, middle class, English-speaking, female population" (p. 790).

It is encouraging that numerous investigations of evidence-based treatments have found that many do, in fact, work as well with ethnic minority clients as with the majority culture. For example, Miranda et al. (2005) found that Latino/Latina clients and African American clients who have received evidence-based therapy for major depression have experienced results similar to those of white clients. However, studies of this type are limited, particularly for certain ethnic groups such as Asian American and American Indian populations. If additional research establishes more firmly that "what works" works for all—or if it determines that such equality requires certain adaptations for certain populations—the related problem of cultural disparities in access to care can receive more attention. That is, ethnic minorities simply receive less psychotherapy than those in the majority (Snowden & Yamada, 2005). So clinical psychologists should not only ensure that they provide members of various cultures therapy that works for them specifically but, more fundamentally, that these clients have access to their services in the first place.

Imagine that you are a clinical psychologist and you learned that the GAD study described above, as well as others examining the same form of therapy, concluded that this therapy was efficacious. If the sample in these studies was predominantly white, middle class, English speaking, and female, how confident would you be in its potential for success with your clients who don't match these characteristics? If you were a client who did not match these characteristics, how would you feel about a clinical psychologist choosing this form of therapy for you?

Assessment Methods

Clinical psychologists conduct research to evaluate and improve the assessment methods they use with clients. Such studies may involve the development, validation, or expanded use of new instruments; the establishment of normative data for specific populations on an assessment tool; a comparison of multiple assessment tools to one another; or other research questions. Numerous professional journals, including *Assessment, Psychological Assessment,* and *Journal of Personality Assessment,* are dedicated primarily to empirical studies of assessment issues in clinical psychology.

A few recent studies provide examples from the spectrum of research being conducted in this area.

- Can an Internet-based, self-administered version of a clinical interview match an in-person interview with a live clinician in terms of diagnosing attention-deficit/hyperactivity disorder (ADHD) in children? Researchers examined a new instrument of this type, the Diagnostic Interview Schedule for Children-Version 4 (DISC-IV), and found that, indeed, the correspondence between the two types of interviews (conducted with parents of the child in question) was extremely high (Steenhuis, Serra, Minderaa, & Hartman, 2009). The researchers acknowledge that further research is necessary, but this study is a promising first step toward establishing a potentially cost-effective, efficient, and convenient form of assessment.

- Speaking of ADHD, another group of researchers published a study in which they reported the development and validation of a new ADHD scale for young adults (Caterino, Gómez-Benito, Balluerka, Amador-Campos, & Stock, 2009). Young adults often seek assessment for ADHD-related symptoms; this instrument is intended to assess these problems in a manner that fits this population specifically, rather than overextending other instruments designed primarily to be used with children. Results indicated strong evidence for the validity of the scale, suggesting that with additional research, it could be a clinically useful assessment tool.

- Researchers conducted a study to compare English and Spanish versions of a commonly used written self-report measure of depression (Wiebe & Penley, 2005). Titled "A Psychometric Comparison of the Beck Depression Inventory-II in English and Spanish," the study concluded that the reliability and validity of the Spanish version of the test was comparable to that of the original English version.

- The Minnesota Multiphasic Personality Inventory-2 (MMPI-2) is the most widely used and psychometrically sound objective personality test, and one of its strengths is its ability to detect "faking" by the test taker. Hahn (2005) conducted a study to examine whether the scales that detect faking in North American, English-speaking clients are also effective in the translation of the MMPI-2 for Korean clients. Results indicated that the scales that identify "fake-good" and "fake-bad" test takers were equally adequate in the North American and Korean versions of the test.

Diagnostic Issues

Clinical psychologists conduct research to explore issues of diagnosis and categorization regarding psychological problems. Such studies may examine the validity or reliability of existing or proposed diagnostic constructs, the relationships between disorders, the prevalence or course of disorders, or numerous related topics. Such studies often appear in *Clinical Psychology: Research and Practice, Journal of Abnormal Psychology, Journal of Consulting and Clinical Psychology,* and other journals. A few recent examples include the following:

- Paranoid personality disorder is a commonly diagnosed personality disorder, but is paranoid personality best understood as a categorical or a dimensional characteristic? In other words, is paranoid personality something an individual "has" or "doesn't have," or is it something we all have to varying degrees? Edens, Marcus, and Morey (2009) empirically examined this question by reviewing hundreds of structured interviews and self-report questionnaires of individuals assessed for personality disorder characteristics. Their primary finding was that paranoid personality has a dimensional, rather than categorical, underlying structure. Research of this type can have an influence on the way psychological disorders are defined in future editions of the *Diagnostic and Statistical Manual of Mental Disorders (DSM)*.

- When clinical psychologists assess children for ADHD or oppositional defiant disorder (ODD), should they use gender-specific norms? In other words, should girls be compared only with girls and boys be compared only with boys? Researchers recently examined this question using teacher ratings of about 1,500 elementary school students (Waschbusch & King, 2006). Results indicated that when gender-specific norms were used, a small group of girls were identified who had significantly elevated ADHD and ODD levels but were not diagnosable by standard *DSM* criteria.

- Lilenfeld, Wonderlich, Riso, Crosby, and Mitchell (2006) conducted a review of empirical studies on the relationship between eating disorders and personality disorders. Among other conclusions, the authors found that anorexia nervosa overlaps significantly with obsessive-compulsive personality disorder and that individuals predisposed to one of these may be similarly predisposed toward the other.

- Personality disorders are often assumed to be stable over time. Researchers recently tested this assumption by assessing personality disorder characteristics in the same clients five times over a 10-year period (Durbin & Klein, 2006). According to this longitudinal study, stability of personality disorder traits was not as strong as often assumed and was comparable with some Axis I disorders, such as anxiety disorders.

Professional Issues

Clinical psychologists also examine elements of their own profession through empirical research. They study clinical psychologists' activities, beliefs, and practices, among other aspects of their professional lives. *Professional Psychology: Research & Practice; Psychotherapy: Theory, Research, Practice, Training;* and *Journal of Clinical Psychology* are among the journals that feature such research. Some recent studies of this type include the following:

- Do the ethical dilemmas and problems psychologists encounter depend on whether they work in rural or urban communities? Helbok, Marinelli, and Walls (2006) conducted a survey to explore this question and discovered some significant differences. Among other findings, results suggested that small-town/rural psychologists were more likely than their urban counterparts to encounter multiple relationships with clients (i.e., to find themselves interacting with clients in another context besides the clinical work), and small-town/rural psychologists were also less likely to have access to professional resources such as medication prescribers and specialized services.

- Maxie, Arnold, and Stephenson (2006) surveyed licensed psychologists to assess the extent to which they discuss ethnic and racial differences directly with psychotherapy clients. The researchers found that while most psychologists have had such discussions with some clients in the past, they don't happen as consistently as might be expected or hoped. The psychologists reported that when they took place, these discussions facilitated the therapy process.

Photo 6.2
Professional issues—
for example, the
frequency and effect
of discussing cultural
differences directly
with clients—are
common topics of
research within clinical
psychology.

- Stevanovic and Rupert (2009) empirically investigated a simple question: "How do the professional lives of psychologists influence their personal and family lives?" (p. 62). They surveyed almost 500 psychologists and found evidence for both positive and negative "spillover." That is, psychologists reported that their work lives provided both enhancement and stress to their personal lives. Good news: positive spillover, which often stemmed from a sense of accomplishment at work, was more common than negative spillover, which often stemmed from work-related emotional exhaustion.

- What attitudes do contemporary psychologists hold toward gay, lesbian, and bisexual lifestyles? Kilgore, Sideman, Amin, Baca, and Bohanske (2005) examined this question via a survey of psychologists. They found that compared to similar studies in the past, psychologists are more likely to view such lifestyles as acceptable and nonpathological. They also found that compared with male psychologists, female psychologists held more positive beliefs about gay, lesbian, and bisexual lifestyles and gay-affirmative therapy.

Teaching and Training Issues

Clinical psychologists also pursue research questions related to how to educate those entering the profession. Training philosophies, specific coursework, opportunities for specialized training, and the outcome of particular training efforts all represent areas of study. *Training and Education in Professional Psychology, Teaching of Psychology,* and *Journal of Clinical Psychology* are among the journals that often publish articles of this type. A small sample of recent articles in this area includes the following:

- When training graduate students in assessment, teaching them to write effective reports can be particularly challenging, with a variety of different styles of report writing available for the instructor to emphasize. Pelco, Ward, Coleman, and Young (2009) conducted an interesting study in which sample reports of various types were provided to elementary school teachers (who often receive such reports about their students), and the teachers were asked to compare the effectiveness of the reports. Results indicated that teachers preferred a report in which the results of different psychological tests were organized by theme, rather than one in which the results were reported test by test. They also gave higher ratings to the most "readable" report, as opposed to reports with higher-level professional terminology. Results of studies such as this can guide graduate programs in providing instruction regarding psychological report writing for particular audiences.

- To what extent do graduate programs in clinical psychology train students to manage potentially violent clients? Researchers examined this question by surveying graduate students regarding their exposure to violent clients and the training they had received in dealing with them (Gately & Stabb, 2005). Results indicated that in general, graduate students encountered violent clients infrequently and that they felt their training to handle such clients was lacking. The researchers noted a correlation between trainees' perception of training to manage violent clients and their confidence level in handling such situations.

- Both clinical psychology and counseling psychology graduate students complete predoctoral internships. How is the placement process—applying and obtaining the internship—similar and different between these two types of training programs? Neimeyer, Rice, and Keilin (2009) studied thousands of placement experiences of graduate students and found that each type of program "matched" at higher rates with certain types of internship sites. Specifically, clinical psychologist students had a higher match rate with medical facilities, while counseling psychology students had a higher match rate with college counseling centers.

How Do Clinical Psychologists Do Research?

The Experimental Method

Like other psychologists (and more generally, scientists), clinical psychologists adhere to the **experimental method** whenever possible in their research efforts. In general, this method involves a number of discrete, sequential steps. It begins with an observation of events. Second, the clinical psychologist develops a hypothesis to explain the observed events. Included in this hypothesis development is the definition of independent and dependent variables. **Independent variables** are those variables in the study that are manipulated by the experimenter, whereas **dependent variables** are those variables that are expected to change as a result of changes in the independent variables. In short, it is hypothesized that the dependent variables "depend" on the independent variables. After the hypothesis is developed, the third step, empirical testing of the hypothesis, ensues. The fourth step takes place after this testing has been completed and involves altering the hypothesis to match the results and interpretations obtained during empirical testing (Greenhoot, 2003; Moyer & Gross, 2011).

Quasi-Experiments

Research in clinical psychology often involves variables that the researcher is not entirely able to control. Ethical, practical, or other constraints often limit the researcher's ability to assign people randomly to certain conditions, make particular manipulations, or otherwise experimentally test certain hypotheses. In such cases, clinical psychologists may use a **quasi-experimental design** rather than a true experimental design. Quasi-experimental designs are less scientifically sound than experimental designs; nonetheless, they are frequently used in clinical psychology and have often yielded very meaningful and important results (Greenhoot, 2003; Moyer & Gross, 2011).

As an example, consider a group of clinical psychology researchers who are interested in examining the outcome of a particular therapy for specific phobias. If the researchers were designing a true experiment, they would need to take identical individuals, induce in them identical fears, and then assign them to different conditions (perhaps treatment vs. no treatment, or treatment vs. alternate treatment) to measure the influence of the treatment. Obviously, such a method is implausible and unjustifiable for both practical and ethical reasons. Instead, the researchers may choose to use a quasi-experimental design, acknowledging that the individuals in the two comparison groups will necessarily have phobias of different objects and different intensities and that they will differ in many other ways as well (age, personality characteristics, ethnicity, etc.) even if the researchers make attempts to "match" the groups as much as possible. Such a study may not be as internally valid as a true experiment, but especially when many such studies converge on the same conclusions, they can provide important data.

Between-Group Versus Within-Group Designs

When clinical psychologists conduct a study with a **between-group design,** participants in different conditions receive entirely different treatments. Often, such studies involve two conditions or groups, one of which (the **experimental condition**) receives the treatment, whereas the other (the **control group**) receives no treatment (Moyer & Gross, 2011). As an example, consider a clinical psychology researcher who examines the relationship between physical exercise and depression. After taking a baseline measure of depression of all participants at the outset of the study, the researcher might assign some participants to Condition A, in which they follow an exercise regimen over 8 weeks, and other participants to Condition B, in which they do not follow the exercise regimen. The crucial question is whether changes in depression levels from pre- to post-test depended on whether a participant was assigned to Condition A or Condition B.

By contrast, a **within-group design** involves comparisons of participants in a single condition to themselves at various points in time. Essentially, all participants experience the same condition or conditions (Moyer & Gross, 2011). For example, the same empirical issue—the relationship between physical exercise and depression—could be examined via a within-group design if the researcher introduced to all participants an exercise regimen lasting 8 weeks. The researcher could compare depression levels each week from start to finish. The crucial question is whether changes in depression levels depend on the point in time when depression was assessed.

At times, clinical psychology researchers will combine aspects of between-group and within-group designs, creating a **mixed-group design** (Moyer & Gross, 2011). As an example, researchers could merge the approaches to studying exercise and depression described in the two previous paragraphs by assigning participants to two conditions (exercise regimen vs. no exercise regimen) *and* by measuring changes of all participants on a weekly basis. This way, at the end of the study, the researchers would be able to compare the two groups with each other, and they would also be able to compare each group with itself at various points in time.

Analogue Designs

When clinical psychologists seek to study clinical populations or situations but are unable to access them adequately, they may conduct a study with an **analogue design**. A study of this type involves an approximation of the target client or situation as a substitute for the "real thing." At times, it can involve asking participants to remember or imagine themselves in a certain situation.

Photo 6.3 A clinical psychologist conducting research on any topic—for example, the relationship between physical exercise and depression—makes numerous important choices regarding the design of the study.

Consider again the physical exercise/depression research topic. If the researchers were primarily interested in the relationship of physical exercise on severely depressed individuals but could not access this population in sufficient numbers, they might access a more available population, such as undergraduates at their university whose depression levels are mild to moderate according to a self-report depression questionnaire. Of course, if the researchers conduct the study with this analogue population and find that mood improved as exercise increased, they should not definitively state that this result is similarly applicable to the severely depressed.

Correlational Methods

Clinical psychology researchers often conduct a correlational study, especially when neither an experiment nor a quasi-experiment is plausible. Studies utilizing **correlational methods** examine the relationship that exists between two or more variables (Goldstein, 2011). Unlike experiments and quasi-experiments, correlational studies do not identify variables as either independent or dependent. Similarly, causality is not implied by the results of correlational studies. In other words, although a correlational study can conclude that one variable predicts or associates with another, it cannot conclude that one variable causes changes in another. Sometimes, correlational studies constitute important early steps in an evolution of research on a particular topic, leading eventually to more experimental or quasi-experimental studies.

Again, consider the research topic of the relationship between physical exercise and depression. If a correlational study produces results that include a negative correlation between these two variables (increased exercise is associated with decreased depression), numerous causal questions arise. Does increased exercise cause mood to improve? Does an improvement in mood cause exercise to increase? Do both of these changes—increased exercise and improved mood—cause each other in a reciprocal manner? Could both of these observed changes be byproducts of some other cause that was outside the scope of this study? Although the link between the variables can be determined, none of these questions can be answered definitively by a study with a correlational design.

Statistically, correlations between two variables can range from +1 to −1. Correlations approaching +1 are positive correlations, suggesting that the two variables vary together—as A increases, B increases; as A decreases, B decreases. Correlations approaching −1 are negative correlations, suggesting that the two variables vary in an inverse way—as A increases, B decreases; as A decreases, B increases. Correlations near 0 are neither strongly positive nor negative and suggest that the two variables vary independently of each other.

Case Studies

Unlike the methods described thus far that involve larger numbers of participants, **case studies** involve a thorough and detailed examination of one person or situation. Typically, they include descriptive observations of an individual's behavior and an attempt by the researcher to interpret it. The researcher may speculate about how explanations of the target individual may also apply to others who are similar in some way. Also, case studies can stimulate more systematic research, and together, these forms of research can converge on important findings (Davison & Lazarus, 2007; Kazdin, 2011). In clinical psychology, case studies can be used to examine the outcome of a treatment or the course of a disorder, among other phenomena.

⊕ **Web Link 6.2**

Debate Between the Idiographic and Nomothetic Approaches

Case studies tend to be held in high regard by researchers who prefer the **idiographic approach**—emphasizing or revealing the unique qualities of each person—to the **nomothetic approach**—determining similarities or common qualities among people. Sometimes, case studies are qualitative in nature, such as Freud's descriptions of "rat man" and "wolf man" (as cited in Gay, 1995), Watson's descriptions of Little Albert (Watson & Rayner, 1920), and many other classic studies in clinical psychology.

Although case studies are not experiments, they can feature some experimental qualities. For example, a single-subject design study focuses on one person at various points in time under changing conditions. It is similar to the within-group design discussed previously, but the "group" consists of only one person. Commonly, such studies use a particular method known as an **ABAB design** (or some variation thereof), in which a treatment is alternately applied and removed (with "A" and "B" each representing the presence or absence of the treatment). Although case studies such as these may have limited generalizability on their own, they can be a relatively inexpensive and convenient way to do research with direct clinical relevance (Freeman & Eagle, 2011; Photos, Michel, & Nock, 2008).

Meta-Analysis

Among the most powerful tools used by clinical psychology researchers is the **meta-analysis.** A meta-analysis is a statistical method of combining results of separate studies (translated into effect sizes) to create a summation (or, statistically, an overall effect size) of the findings. As its label implies, a meta-analysis is a study of studies, a quantitative analysis in which the full results of previous studies each represent a small part of a larger pool of data (Durlak, 2003; Thomas & Michael, 2011). So, although it is informative to read the results of a single study on, say, the benefits of psychotherapy, it can be far more enlightening to read a meta-analysis on the topic that encompasses many comparable studies (e.g., Smith, Glass, & Miller, 1980; Wampold et al., 1997).

⊕ **Web Link 6.3**

History of Meta-Analysis In Psychotherapy

Meta-analysis is a sophisticated statistical technique, and meta-analysts must ensure that their method is scientifically sound. According to Durlak (2003), meta-analyses in clinical psychology should incorporate the following five steps:

1. Formulate the research question, including reasonable, important, testable hypotheses.

2. Obtain a representative study sample. Determine and explain the criteria by which individual studies will be included or excluded. Consider unpublished reports as well as those that have been published.

3. Obtain information from individual studies. Take into account the specific methodology of each individual study and ensure that reliability is adequate when coding previous findings.

4. Conduct appropriate analyses. When combining effect sizes from individual studies, assign appropriate weights to each, such that larger-scale studies "count" more than smaller-scale studies.

5. Reach conclusions and offer suggestions for future research.

Box 6.3 offers further discussion of meta-analysis in clinical psychology.

• • • BOX 6.3 • • •

Metaphorically Speaking

If You Read Movie Reviews, You Understand Meta-Analysis

A bad review of a new movie will make you think twice about seeing it. But 10 bad reviews of the same movie, especially if they come from different sources, will definitely keep you away from it. We can't put too much trust in any single review, but when multiple reviews agree (or disagree) about a movie, we feel more confident in allowing our impression to be influenced by their collective opinions. In an informal way, we combine the separate impressions of the various reviewers into a single, overall impression. Stated another way, as we read each new review, we meld the "effect" the movie had on each reviewer into an overall, cumulative "effect."

Meta-analyses are a conceptually similar but methodologically more rigorous way of combining effects. In clinical psychology, meta-analysts do the melding quantitatively rather than qualitatively. They collect studies that have investigated a similar topic and convert the results of each into an effect size, which provides a common numerical language to make the findings comparable and compatible, and then statistically merge them to form one overall effect size to encapsulate the multitude of findings.

In the popular magazine *Entertainment Weekly,* the movie section of each issue contains a feature called "Critical Mass." It's a chart that lists 10 popular new movies and the ratings

FIGURE 6.1   Meta-movie Review

	Reviewer A	Reviewer B	Reviewer C	Reviewer D	Reviewer E	Reviewer F	Reviewer G	Reviewer H	Meta-review Score
The Avengers	10	8	9	7	10	8	9	9	8.8
Hunger Games	7	6	5	8	7	7	6	7	6.6
The Amazing Spider Man	1	3	0	1	4	1	3	1	1.8
The Artist	9	10	10	7	8	8	10	9	8.9
Hugo	7	6	5	7	8	6	5	7	6.5

(letter grades A through F) of each according to about a dozen reviewers, as well as a "critic's average" that they calculate much like students calculate their GPAs. This way, readers can learn not only what a particular reviewer thought about a movie but what many other reviewers thought of it as well. Sometimes there is consistency (almost every reviewer gives the movie a B); sometimes there is variability (grades ranging from A to F for the same movie). The same is true in clinical psychology research: Sometimes studies on a topic converge on the same finding, whereas at other times they produce discrepant results. In evaluating the "effects" of movies or psychology research, rather than relying on a single study (or review), it is more scientifically sound to rely on the meta-analysis, which provides an overview of the "effect size" of a treatment (or movie) across multiple research settings (or movie reviewers).

Cross-Sectional Versus Longitudinal Designs

Cross-sectional designs assess or compare a participant or group of participants at one particular point in time. By contrast, **longitudinal designs** emphasize changes across time, often making within-group comparisons from one point in time to another. Cross-sectional designs tend to be easier and more efficient, whereas longitudinal designs require much longer periods of time. However, cross-sectional studies may not provide valid approximations for changes that take place or evolve over time, whereas longitudinal studies may have a unique ability to do so.

Reconsider the research topic of the relationship between physical exercise and depression. A longitudinal study of this topic might be quite different from any variation we have considered previously. For example, rather than focusing on an 8-week time period, the researchers could extend the scope of the study to 10 years. They could follow the participants to determine whether the relationship of the two variables remains the same or changes over that time. They could consider such issues as long-term adherence to the exercise regimen, the effect of physical injury and aging, lifestyle changes, spontaneous remission of depression, recurrence of depression, and other issues that would have little opportunity to arise in a cross-sectional study.

Actual longitudinal studies are often much longer than 10 years. For example, Kamen, Cosgrove, McKellar, Cronkite, and Moos (2011) followed individuals for 23 years to assess the relationship between family support and depression, and found that those with higher family support at the beginning (and throughout) predicted lower levels of depressive symptoms. In a 15-year study, Lönnqvist, Verkasalo, Mäkinen, and Henriksson (2009) found that neuroticism among 20-year-olds predicted the likelihood of mental disorders and low self-esteem among the same individuals at age 35. Such results would simply be unattainable by any method other than longitudinal research.

Ethical Issues in Research in Clinical Psychology

Of course, clinical psychology researchers must adhere to ethical standards when conducting research. In the ethics chapter of this textbook, we discuss in detail the ethical issues involved in psychotherapy outcome studies in which some of the participants are withheld therapy (e.g., Saks, Jeste, Granholm, Palmer, & Schneiderman, 2002; Street & Luoma, 2002). The American Psychological Association's (2002) code of ethics includes many specific standards that apply to clinical psychologists conducting research (Miller & Williams, 2011). Box 6.4 offers some of the most relevant of these standards, additional discussion of which appears in Chapter 5.

● ● ● BOX 6.4 ● ● ●

Key American Psychological Association Ethical Standards Related to Research in Clinical Psychology

- Researchers should obtain informed consent from prospective participants. The information they present should include the purpose and duration of participation as well as the participants' right to decline or withdraw. (Standard 8.02)

- Researchers should not coerce participation by offering excessive or inappropriate rewards (financial or otherwise). (Standard 8.06)

- Researchers should avoid using deception in their studies unless the prospective value of the research justifies its use and nondeceptive methods are not feasible. If deception is used, the researcher should explain it fully to participants as soon as possible and allow them to withdraw their data if they choose. (Standard 8.07)

- If researchers discover that research procedures have harmed a participant, they should take reasonable steps to minimize the harm. (Standard 8.08)

- Researchers should never fabricate or falsify data. (Standard 8.10)

- Researchers should list themselves as authors of a study only when their contributions are justifiably substantial and the order of authorship reflects the relative contributions of the individuals involved. (Standard 8.12)

- Researchers should share their data with other competent researchers who intend to reanalyze it for verification. (Standard 8.14)

Source: Adapted from the American Psychological Association's (2002) Code of Ethics.

CHAPTER SUMMARY

Clinical psychologists conduct empirical research for a number of purposes. For example, empirical studies examine the outcome of treatment, both in terms of efficacy (how well a therapy works under controlled conditions with selected clients) and effectiveness (how well a therapy works in "real-world" clinical settings with a wider variety of clients). Clinical psychologists similarly conduct empirical research to study assessment methods, diagnostic issues, professional issues, and training issues. Often, this research follows the experimental or quasi-experimental method, in which the impact of an independent variable on a dependent variable is measured. In other cases, a correlational design is employed to establish a noncausal link between two variables. Between-group designs typically involve a comparison of a control (or no-treatment, or placebo) group to an experimental group, whereas within-group designs typically involve a comparison of the same group to itself at different points in time. Case studies have limited generalizability but can provide important clinical information or lead to more large-scale research. When it is impractical to study a clinical phenomenon as it happens, researchers can conduct an analogue study, in which the situation is simulated in the lab. Meta-analyses enable researchers to statistically combine the results of individual studies regarding the same research question, producing a single overall estimate of effect size.

KEY TERMS AND NAMES

CRITICAL THINKING QUESTIONS

1. What is the difference between efficacy and effectiveness? Why is this distinction important to clinical psychologists involved in research and practice?

2. What can clinical psychologists do to maximize the generalizability of an analogue study to a broader population?

3. In your opinion, how important should case studies be in the establishment of a treatment method as valid?

4. Considering the questions raised in Box 6.1, when, in your opinion, should the outcome of psychotherapy be measured?

5. Considering the questions raised in Box 6.1, who, in your opinion, should rate the outcome of psychotherapy?

STUDENT STUDY SITE RESOURCES

Visit the study site at www.sagepub.com/pomerantz3eupdate for these additional learning tools:

- Self-quizzes
- eFlashcards
- Culture Expert Interviews

- Full-text SAGE journal articles
- Additional web resources
- Mock Assessment Data

CHAPTER SUMMARY VIDEO

QR codes at the end of each chapter link to chapter background videos by the author. Visit http://gettag.mobi using your smartphone browser to download the free Microsoft Tag app. Once installed, scan the tags to go directly to these brief videos. In this video, the author discusses the perspectives of his clinical psychology colleagues—some full-time clinicians, some full-time researchers—on either side of the efficacy/effectiveness divide.

Assessment

Diagnosis and Classification Issues: *DSM-5* and More

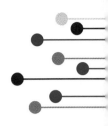

Defining Normality and Abnormality

Much of the practice and research conducted by clinical psychologists focuses on **abnormality**, also known as mental disorders, psychiatric diagnoses, or, more broadly, psychopathology. Through their training and their professional activities, clinical psychologists become very familiar with the definitions of various forms of abnormal behavior and the ways it differs from normal behavior. But before these diagnostic categories are put to use by clinicians and scholars, they must be defined.

What Defines Abnormality?

Over time, mental health professionals have put forth a variety of answers to the question of what makes behavior abnormal. These answers have included criteria such as personal distress to the individual (as in severe depression or panic disorder), deviance from cultural norms (as in many cases of schizophrenia), statistical infrequency (as in rarer disorders such as dissociative identity disorder), and impaired social functioning (as in social phobia and, in a more dangerous way, antisocial personality disorder).

In the 1990s, **Jerome Wakefield,** a renowned scholar in the field of abnormal psychology, offered a theory that put forth a more simplified (in comparison with the multifaceted criteria above) definition of mental disorders (Wakefield, 1992, 1999). His theory has generated enough support to become quite prominent in recent years. Wakefield (1992) explains his **harmful dysfunction theory** of mental disorders in the following way:

> I argue that a disorder is a harmful dysfunction, wherein harmful is a value term based on social norms, and dysfunction is a scientific term referring to the failure of a mental mechanism to perform a natural function for which it was designed by evolution. Thus, the concept of disorder combines value and scientific components. (p. 373)

The harmful dysfunction theory proposes that in our efforts to determine what is abnormal, we consider both scientific (e.g., evolutionary) data and the social values in the context of which the behavior takes place. As such, it can account for a wide range of behavior that clinical psychologists have traditionally labeled as psychopathological according to the multiple criteria listed above.

● ● ● BOX 7.1 ● ● ●

Considering Culture

Typical but Abnormal?

At one time or another, many of us have used the "everybody else is doing it" explanation to rationalize our aberrant behavior. Drivers who speed, kids who steal candy, partiers who drink too much, citizens who cheat on their taxes: Any of them might argue, "I'm not the only one," and they'd be right. Should the commonality of a behavior affect the way we evaluate that behavior? If we tweak the question to consider abnormal (but not necessarily unlawful or unruly) behavior, does behavior become normal—and possibly, by extension, healthy or acceptable—if lots of people engage in it? Or is it possible that abnormal is abnormal—and possibly, by extension, unhealthy or unacceptable—no matter how many people do it?

These questions are particularly relevant to the definition of mental illness, especially when we take cultural variables into account. Recently, Thomas A. Widiger and Stephanie Mullins-Sweatt (2008) considered the issue and came to this conclusion: "Simply because a behavior pattern is valued, accepted, encouraged, or even statistically normative within a particular culture does not necessarily mean it is conducive to healthy psychological functioning" (p. 360). This statement suggests that it is possible for a behavior to be quite common, even conventional, within a culture yet pathological at the same time. They question whether numerous behavior patterns—extensive and meticulous rituals among some religious groups, patterns of interpersonal submission in some Asian cultures, and the practice of remaining house-bound among some Muslim women in certain parts of the world—might actually represent disordered behavior (obsessive-compulsive disorder, dependent personality disorder, and agoraphobia, respectively) despite their prevalence within the culture.

Do you agree with the idea that a behavior can be pathological within a particular culture even if it is common or typical within that culture? Why or why not? If so, can you think of examples in other cultures and in your own culture as well? And, importantly, who should determine the definitions of universal psychological wellness or disorder?

Who Defines Abnormality?

Wakefield's definition of abnormality, along with other definitions, continues to be debated by academics and researchers in the field (e.g., Lilienfeld & Marino, 1999; Wakefield, 2010). However, clinical psychologists have certainly not waited for a resolution of this scholarly debate before assigning, treating, and studying disorders. They use disorders—as defined by the *Diagnostic and Statistical Manual of Mental Disorders* (*DSM*), the prevailing diagnostic guide for mental health professionals—every day as they perform assessments, conduct therapy, and design and execute research studies.

In the introductory pages of the latest versions of the *DSM* (*DSM-5*; American Psychiatric Association, 2013), its authors offer a broad definition of mental disorder. It is not entirely dissimilar to Wakefield's harmful dysfunction theory (Spitzer, 1999), yet it also incorporates aspects of the other criteria discussed above.

In *DSM-5*, mental disorder is defined as a "clinically significant disturbance" in "cognition, emotion regulation, or behavior" that indicates a "dysfunction" in "mental functioning"

Photo 7.1 Distinguishing normality from abnormality has been the focus of many theories offered throughout the history of clinical psychology. In your opinion, what are the most important distinguishing factors?

that is "usually associated with significant distress or disability" in work, relationships, or other areas of functioning (American Psychiatric Association, 2013, p. 20). In addition, the definition states that expectable reactions to common stressors are not mental disorders.

Who created this definition, as well as the specific diagnostic categories that fill *DSM?* Many people played significant roles, but the most significant were those on the Task Force for each edition of *DSM* (American Psychiatric Association, 2013). This group consisted largely of leading researchers in various specialty areas within psychopathology who were selected for their scholarship and expertise in their respective fields. It is noteworthy that this task force consisted primarily of psychiatrists, and a relatively small number of psychologists and other mental health professionals were included.

Moreover, the *DSM-5* and all previous editions of the *DSM* have been published by the American *Psychiatric* Association (as opposed to the American *Psychological* Association). Thus, although the *DSM* has been used extensively by clinical psychologists and a wide range of other nonmedical mental health professionals (social workers, counselors, etc.), the authors who have had the most significant impact on its contents are medical doctors. So it should come as no surprise that the *DSM* reflects a **medical model of psychopathology** in which each disorder is an entity defined categorically and features a list of specific symptoms. (We discuss these aspects of *DSM* disorders in more detail later in this chapter.)

Besides their profession, what else do we know about the primary authors of the *DSM?* The first edition of the *DSM,* published in 1952, was created by the foremost mental health experts of the time, who were almost exclusively white, male, trained in psychiatry, at least middle age, and at least middle class. Especially with the most recent revisions of the *DSM,* deliberate efforts have been made to include more diversity among the contributors. In spite of this forward progress, some have remained critical: "The designers of the *DSM-III* and *DSM-III-R* (and to a lesser extent the fourth edition and the text revision) were still predominantly senior White male psychiatrists who embedded the document with their biases" (Malik & Beutler, 2002, pp. 5–6). As we will explore later in this chapter, the culture and values of those who define mental disorders can play an influential role in the definitions they produce.

Why Is the Definition of Abnormality Important?

The process by which disorders are defined is much more than an academic exercise for scholars to debate. Instead, this process and the definitions it yields have very real consequences for professionals and nonprofessionals alike (Kinghorn, 2013; Widiger & Mullins-Sweatt, 2008).

As an example, consider attenuated psychosis syndrome. Currently, attenuated psychosis syndrome is not an official diagnostic category. Instead, it is listed as a **proposed criteria set** in the "Emerging Measures and Models" section of *DSM-5* (American Psychiatric Association, 2013). This section describes conditions that DSM authors decided to leave out of the list of "official" disorders, at least for now, but to list as "unofficial" conditions for the purpose of inspiring clinicians and researchers to study them more. Attenuated psychosis syndrome (as described earlier in this chapter) is a bit like a "light" version of schizophrenia ("attenuated" means reduced or lessened). Its symptoms include delusions, hallucinations, and disorganized speech that are not severe or long-lasting. Its description also mentions that the person's "reality testing"—their ability to stay in touch with the same reality that the rest of us experience—remains relatively intact. The symptoms must only be present once per week within the last month, but must be distressing or disabling.

Importance for Professionals

By listing attenuated psychosis syndrome as a proposed criteria set, the *DSM* authors have facilitated the study of attenuated psychosis syndrome by researchers and its consideration by clinicians. If attenuated psychosis syndrome becomes an official diagnosis, we will undoubtedly see an increase in both these activities. Additionally, if attenuated psychosis syndrome becomes official, people will be diagnosed with it and will be conceptualized (by professionals and themselves) as having this form of mental illness. On the other hand, if attenuated psychosis syndrome had never appeared in any form in any edition of *DSM*, it is less likely that researchers would study it or clinicians would add it to their professional vocabulary. And the same people who would have received the diagnosis would be viewed as slightly odd or eccentric, but not mentally ill. Thus, the presence or absence of a diagnostic label for a particular human experience has a powerful impact on the attention it receives from clinical psychologists.

Importance for Clients

For clients, future decisions by *DSM* authors about the status of attenuated psychosis syndrome may carry special significance. Some clients could experience beneficial consequences of being diagnosed with attenuated psychosis syndrome. Consider Lucinda, a woman whose experience over the past few months meets the criteria for attenuated psychosis syndrome. If this disorder was available as an official label, the label could help Lucinda identify and demystify an otherwise nameless experience; feel as though she shares a recognized problem with others (rather than feeling like the only one with the problem); acknowledge the significance of her experience with family, friends, and employers; and gain access to treatment that might have been unavailable without a diagnosis (especially if she uses health insurance to pay; Eriksen & Kress, 2005; Langenbucher & Nathan, 2006). On the other hand, Lucinda could also experience harmful consequences from being diagnosed with attenuated psychosis syndrome. The label could carry a stigma that damages her self-image; lead to stereotyping by individuals who know her or work with her; and even have an effect on the outcome of legal issues she may encounter, such as child custody cases, sentencing decisions, and fitness-to-stand-trial decisions (Butcher, Mineka, & Hooley, 2007; Eriksen & Kress, 2005).

Thus, the decisions *DSM* authors make when defining abnormality, both as a broad concept and as specific diagnostic categories, profoundly influence many aspects of clients' lives.

Diagnosis and Classification of Mental Disorders: A Brief History

Before the *DSM*

Abnormal behavior garnered attention long, long before the first version of the *DSM* appeared. Discussion of abnormal behavior appears in the writings of ancient Chinese, Hebrew, Egyptian, Greek, and Roman societies (Butcher et al., 2007; Millon & Simonsen, 2010). Hippocrates (460–377 BCE) wrote extensively about abnormality, but unlike most of his predecessors, he did not offer supernatural explanations such as possession by demons or gods. Instead, his theories of abnormality emphasized natural causes. Specifically, he pointed to an imbalance of bodily fluids (blood, phlegm, black bile, and yellow bile) as the underlying reason for various forms of mental illness (Blashfield, 1991; Butcher et al., 2007). Although his specific theory is viewed by contemporary mental health experts as outdated, Hippocrates' accent on natural causes of psychopathology was a significant early step toward more current definitions.

If we fast-forward from Hippocrates to the 19th century, we find an era when many cities in Europe and the United States were establishing asylums for the treatment of the mentally ill (as opposed to the imprisonment or abuse they might have suffered previously). In these inpatient treatment settings, mental health professionals had the opportunity to observe individuals with mental disorders for extended periods of time. In many such settings, a byproduct of this extended care was a list of categories into which clients could be organized. One example occurred in France, where Philippe Pinel (discussed in more detail in Chapter 2) proposed specific categories such as melancholia, mania, and dementia, among others. Eventually, the staff of some of these institutions shared their idiosyncratic diagnostic systems with one another, and more common terminology evolved (Langenbucher & Nathan, 2006).

Around 1900, more important steps were taken toward the eventual *DSM* system that we currently use (Widiger & Mullins-Sweatt, 2008). **Emil Kraepelin** (also discussed in Chapter 2) labeled specific categories such as manic-depressive psychosis and dementia praecox (roughly equivalent to bipolar disorder and schizophrenia, respectively) (Millon & Simonsen, 2010). These and other contributions by Kraepelin have resulted in his reputation as a founding father of the current diagnostic system (Langenbucher & Nathan, 2006). During the late 1800s and early 1900s, the primary purpose of diagnostic categories was the collection of statistical and census data. Later, in the mid-1900s, the U.S. Army and Veterans Administration (now Veterans Affairs) developed their own early categorization system in an effort to facilitate the diagnosis and treatment of soldiers returning from World War II (American Psychiatric Association, 2000; Office of the Surgeon General, Army Service Forces, 1946). This military categorization system was quite different from the most recent editions of the *DSM,* but it actually had significant influence on the creation of the first edition of the *DSM,* which appeared less than a decade later (Langenbucher & Nathan, 2006).

DSM—Earlier Editions (I and II)

DSM-I was published by the American Psychiatric Association in 1952. *DSM-II* followed as a revision in 1968. These two editions of the *DSM* were actually quite similar to each other, but as a pair, they were quite different from all the *DSM* editions subsequently published (Lilienfeld & Landfield, 2008). *DSM-I* and *DSM-II* contained only three broad categories of disorders: psychoses (which would contain today's schizophrenia), neuroses (which would contain today's major depression, bipolar disorder, and anxiety disorders), and character disorders (which would contain today's personality disorders) (Blashfield, Flanagan, & Raley, 2010).

It is particularly noteworthy that the definitions of disorders in *DSM-I* and *DSM-II* were not scientifically or empirically based. Instead, they represented "the accumulated clinical wisdom of the small number of senior academic psychiatrists who staffed the *DSM* task forces" (Langenbucher & Nathan, 2006, p. 5). Most of these psychiatrists were psychoanalytic in orientation, and the language of the first two *DSM* editions reflected the psychoanalytic approach to understanding people and their problems. Additionally, the descriptions of individual disorders in *DSM-I* and *DSM-II* were not lists of specific symptoms or criteria; instead, they were simply prose, typically one paragraph per disorder, offering relatively vague descriptions of clinical conditions. As a result, the diagnostic categories in

DSM-I and *DSM-II* had very limited generalizability or utility for clinicians in practice at the time (Woo & Keatinge, 2008).

DSM—More Recent Editions (III, III-R, IV, and IV-TR)

DSM-III, published in 1980, was very dissimilar from *DSM-I* and *DSM-II* (Widiger & Mullins-Sweatt, 2008; Widiger & Trull, 2007). In comparison to *DSM-I* and *DSM-II*, it reflected an approach to defining mental disorders that differed substantially in some important ways (Decker, 2013; Whooley & Horwitz, 2013; Blashfield et al., 2010):

- It relied to a much greater extent on empirical data to determine which disorders to include and how to define them.
- It used specific diagnostic criteria to define disorders. Whereas the *DSM-III* retained some descriptive paragraphs (and in fact augmented them for most disorders), these paragraphs were followed by specific criteria—checklists, basically—that delineated in much greater detail the symptoms that must be present for an individual to qualify for a diagnosis.
- It dropped any allegiance to a particular theory of therapy or psychopathology. As a result, the psychoanalytic language of previous editions was replaced by terminology that reflected no single school of thought.
- It introduced the **multiaxial assessment** system that remained in *DSM* through the next several editions but was dropped in *DSM-5*. When multiaxial assessment was in place, the psychiatric problems were described on each of five distinct axes. Axis I included disorders thought to be more episodic (likely to have beginning and ending points), and Axis II included disorders thought to be more stable or long-lasting. Axes III and IV offered clinicians a place to list medical conditions and psychosocial/environmental problems, respectively, relevant to the mental health issues at hand. And Axis V, known as the Global Assessment of Functioning (GAF) Scale, provided clinicians an opportunity to place the client on a 100-point continuum describing the overall level of functioning.

An immediately noticeable feature of *DSM-III* was its size: it was a significantly longer, more expansive diagnostic manual than its predecessors. For the disorders that had appeared in earlier editions, *DSM-III* offered extended descriptions and added lists of specific criteria. In addition, it included many new disorders—265 disorders in total, as compared with 182 in *DSM-II* and 106 in *DSM-I*. As a result of all these factors, *DSM-III* contained more than three times as many pages as *DSM-II* (Houts, 2002). Subsequent revisions to the *DSM—DSM-III-R* (American Psychiatric Association, 1987), **DSM-IV** (American Psychiatric Association, 1994), and **DSM-IV-TR** (American Psychiatric Association, 2000)— retained the major quantitative and qualitative changes instituted by *DSM-III* in 1980. *DSM-5* retained many of these changes as well, although it also features some significant changes of its own (to be discussed in detail later in this chapter).

Table 7.1 offers an example of a specific disorder—generalized anxiety disorder, or "anxiety neurosis," as it was previously described—defined at an early stage of *DSM* history (*DSM-II*; American Psychiatric Association, 1968) and at the most recent stage (*DSM-5*; American Psychiatric Association, 2013). In contrast to the current definition, several features of the *DSM-II* definition are noteworthy, including the psychoanalytically derived term *neurosis* in the title of the disorder and the use of a brief descriptive paragraph rather than the more detailed checklist of specific criteria.

Table 7.1 Anxiety Neurosis/Generalized Anxiety Disorder as Defined in *DSM-II* and *DSM-5*

DSM-II (American Psychiatric Association, 1968): 300.0 Anxiety Neurosis	DSM-5 (American Psychiatric Association, 2013): 300.02 Generalized Anxiety Disorder
This neurosis is characterized by anxious over-concern extending to panic and frequently association with somatic symptoms. Unlike Phobic neurosis, anxiety may occur under any circumstances and is not restricted to specific situations or objects. This disorder must be distinguished from normal apprehension or fear, which occurs in realistically dangerous situations	A. Excessive anxiety and worry (apprehensive expectation), occurring more days than not for at least 6 months, about a number of events or activities (such as work or school performance) B. The person finds it difficult to control the worry C. The anxiety and worry are associated with three (or more) of the following six symptoms (with at least some symptoms present for more days than not for the past 6 months). Note: Only one item is required in children 1. restlessness or feeling keyed up or on edge 2. being easily fatigued 3. difficulty concentrating or mind going blank 4. irritability 5. muscle tension 6. sleep disturbance (difficulty falling or staying asleep, or restless unsatisfying sleep) D. The anxiety, worry, or physical symptoms cause clinically significant distress or impairment in social, occupational, or other important areas of functioning.

(Continued)

Table 7.1 (Continued)

DSM-II (American Psychiatric Association, 1968): 300.0 Anxiety Neurosis	DSM-5 (American Psychiatric Association, 2013): 300.02 Generalized Anxiety Disorder
	E. The disturbance is not attributable to the physiological effects of a substance (e.g., a drug of abuse, a medication) or another medical condition (e.g., hyperthyroidism).
	F. The disturbance is not better explained by another mental disorder (e.g., anxiety or worry about having panic attacks in panic disorder, negative evaluation in social anxiety disorder [social phobia], contamination or other obsessions in obsessive-compulsive disorder, separation from attachment figures in separation anxiety disorder, reminders of traumatic events in posttraumatic stress disorder, gaining weight in anorexia nervosa, physical complaints in somatic symptom disorder, perceived appearance flaws in body dysmorphic disorder, having a serious illness in illness anxiety disorder, or the content of delusional beliefs in schizophrenia or delusional disorder).

DSM-5: The Current Edition

In May 2013, *DSM-5* was published. It was the first substantial revision of the manual in about 20 years, and it was a massive effort. Led by two prominent mental health researchers, David Kupfer and Darrel Regier, it involved hundreds of experts from over a dozen countries contributing their time and expertise over a 12-year period that was particularly intensive in the last half-dozen years before its release (American Psychiatric Association, 2013; Kupfer et al., 2013; Regier, Kuhl, et al., 2013; Paris, 2013b, 2013c).

Many steps were involved in this huge undertaking. Early on, a Task Force—essentially, a committee of prominent researchers in various areas of mental disorders—was created. The members of this Task Force then led Work Groups, each of which focused on a particular area of mental disorders (e.g., the Eating Disorders Work Group, the

Psychotic Disorders Work Group). These Work Groups reviewed the disorders listed in the previous DSM and considered proposals for revision, including ideas for adding, eliminating, combining, splitting, or revising the definitions of disorders. The leaders also created a Scientific Review Committee of experts separate from the Work Groups whose job was to make sure that there was sufficient scientific evidence to support the changes proposed by the Work Groups (Kendler, in press). Later in the process, they conducted field trials for their proposed changes—in other words, they asked practicing clinicians to try using them with clients, with the intention of determining how reliable and clinically useful they were (Clarke et al, 2013; Regier, Narrow, et al., 2013; American Psychiatric Association, 2013).

Beginning in 2010, the *DSM-5* authors maintained a website (dsm5.org) on which they communicated to the public about their progress, including posts of the drafts of proposed changes. The website also solicited comments from interested parties, whether professionals, clients, mental health advocacy groups, or any member of the public. And they received plenty—over 13,000 comments through the website, plus another 12,000 in other forms such as email and letters (Jeste et al., 2012; Porter, 2013; American Psychiatric Association, 2013).

Throughout the process, the *DSM-5* authors tried to coordinate their efforts with those of the World Health Organization (WHO), which publishes the *International Classification of Diseases (ICD)*. *ICD*, currently on its 10th edition with an 11th expected soon, is the primary way that diseases—both mental disorders and all other health-related problems—are coded and categorized in many countries outside the U.S. Greater consistency between DSM and ICD will allow better communication between countries and improved research design (Frances, 2013a, Regier, Kuhl, et al., 2013, Paris, 2013c; Frances & Nardo, 2013; American Psychiatric Association, 2013). (China also has its own system of classifying mental disorders, the *Chinese Classification of Mental Disorders*).

Changes *DSM-5* Didn't Make

The authors of *DSM-5* made plenty of changes, but before we review them, let's review the changes they considered but ultimately did *not* make. These are important because they illustrate decision-making processes used by the DSM-5 authors, the fact that not every proposal is adopted, and changes that may be reconsidered for future editions of the manual.

- Initially, the authors of *DSM-5* considered significantly overhauling the manual to emphasize neuropsychology, or the biological roots of mental disorders. This would have been a significant paradigm shift in which the fundamental way we define mental disorders changes from descriptions of behavioral symptoms to biological evidence—in much the same way that many areas of medicine use blood tests, biopsies, x-rays, PET scans, gene analyses, or other lab results to determine whether a person has a disease. However, it became evident to the *DSM* authors that mental health lags behind many other specialties in this regard. In other words, although there are many mental disorders that involve biological factors, those disorders lack definitive, reliable "biological markers"—the kinds of things that indicate that a person "tests positive" or "tests negative" in a conclusive way. Such biological markers may become known in time as neuroscience advances, but for now, research has simply not yet uncovered them clearly enough to use them as diagnostic tools (Paris, 2013b, 2013c; Pierre, 2013; Stringaris, 2013). As one author put it, "*DSM-5* has been written for 2013, not for 2063 or 2113," at which time the connections between mental disorders and their neurological or biological underpinnings may be sufficiently strong (Paris, 2013a, p. 41).

- Another across-the-board change that the *DSM-5* authors considered was a shift toward a dimensional definition of mental disorders. This issue is discussed in more detail later in the chapter, but essentially, it involves viewing disorders not strictly in a categorical or "yes or no" way, but along a continuum. In other words, rather than describing a client only as either "having" or "not having" major depressive disorder, the clinician could rate the client's depression symptoms (or another underlying characteristic) on a scale (e.g., a range of 1-10) (Whooley & Horwitz, 2013). Ultimately, this idea was rejected as too premature and overly complicated to justify such a comprehensive renovation of the manual, but the *DSM-5* authors suggest that it may be seriously considered for future editions (De Fruyt et al., 2013; Phillips, 2013; Gore & Widiger, 2013; American Psychiatric Association, 2013).

- A dimensional approach was also seriously considered for a particular subset of mental disorders: personality disorders. As described later in this chapter, a significant body of research has accumulated to suggest that personality disorders fit best with the idea of dimensional, as opposed to strictly categorical, conceptualization. The *DSM-5* authors proposed a specific way of understanding personality disorders dimensionally, but the proposal was rejected as being too complex and not clinically useful enough. Although it is not in effect, that proposal is included in a later section of *DSM-5* called "Emerging Measures and Models" with the hope that researchers will study and possibly revise it for future consideration (Hopwood et al., 2013; Skodol et al., 2013; Black, 2013; American Psychiatric Association, 2013).

- Speaking of personality disorders, the *DSM-5* authors considered removing 5 of the 10 personality disorders previously included in that section, a change that would have significantly reshaped that category. The five that were on the chopping block at one point were paranoid, schizoid, histrionic, dependent, and narcissistic personality disorders. The *DSM-5* authors ultimately decided to retain all of them (Pull, 2013).

- There were numerous proposals for specific new disorders that were considered but rejected. Many of these appear in the "Emerging Measures and Models" section as "proposed criteria sets" to enable researchers to conduct studies that will help determine whether they "make the cut" for future editions of *DSM*. Among them:

o *Attenuated psychosis syndrome*, which features the hallucinations, delusions, and disorganized speech characteristic of schizophrenia but in much less intense and more fleeting forms, and in which the person doesn't lose touch with reality in a pervasive way (American Psychiatric Association, 2013; Frances, 2013a, Wakefield, 2013a; Tsuang et al., in press)

o *Mixed anxiety-depressive disorder*, which features some symptoms of anxiety, some symptoms of depression, but not enough of either to qualify for any existing disorder (such as generalized anxiety disorder or major depressive disorder) (American Psychiatric Association, 2013; Frances, 2012a)

o *Internet gaming disorder*, which features excessive and disruptive Internet game-playing behavior. To a lesser extent, the *DSM-5* authors also considered other disorders based on various non-substance addictive-related behaviors such as shopping, exercise, work, and sex (American Psychiatric Association, 2013; Wakefield, 2013a; Frances, 2013a; Greenberg, 2013; Kafka, 2013; King & Delfabbro, 2013; Petry & O'Brien, 2013)

New Features in *DSM-5*

Some of the most significant changes in *DSM-5* do not focus on specific disorders, but on the way the entire manual is organized or presented. Among them:

• The title of the manual is not *DSM-V*, but *DSM-5*. That is, the authors deliberately shifted away from the traditional Roman numerals used in previous editions (e.g., *DSM-II*, *DSM-III*, *DSM-IV*) and toward Arabic numerals instead. The reason for this shift is to enable more frequent minor updates that will be named just as changes to computer operating systems and applications are often named: *DSM-5.1*, *DSM-5.2*, etc. Thus, this naming change is not merely superficial. It suggests that *DSM* is a "living document" that, in the future, will be more quick to respond to new research that improves our understanding of mental disorders. No longer will we have to stick with a single, static version of *DSM* for a decade or two until the time arrives for a major revamp; instead, smaller-scale changes can be made more continuously. The "Emerging Measures and Models" section of the manual (mentioned above) goes hand-in-hand with this notion of a living document, as it prompts researchers and clinicians to consider conditions that have not yet been officially included in *DSM* but may, after more attention, be included in future editions (Whooley & Horwitz, 2013; Kraemer, 2013; Moran, 2013a; Paris, 2013b, 2013c; Wakefield, 2013a; Stringaris, 2013).

• The multiaxial assessment system—a central feature of *DSM* since its introduction in *DSM-III* in 1980—was dropped altogether from *DSM-5*. This removal brings a number of important changes to the way clinicians diagnose clients. For example, the tradition of separate axes for disorders that tend to persist long-term (such as developmental disorders and personality disorders, formerly on Axis II) from disorders that tend to be more short-term or episodic (such as major depression, formerly on Axis I) is now gone. This could result in different conceptualizations of these disorders by researchers, clinicians, clients, or third-party-payers in the future. Also, Axis V, the Global Assessment of Functioning (GAF) scale, is now eliminated, so there is no longer a single numeric scale on which clinicians can describe their clients' level of functioning across all disorders (although a questionnaire that clients complete themselves that the World Health Organization has created is included for future consideration in the "Emerging Measures and Models" section) (American Psychiatric Association, 2013; Kupfer et al., 2013; Paris 2013c, Wakefield, 2013a).

New Disorders in *DSM-5*

DSM-5 introduced a number of new disorders—not merely revisions or regroupings of existing disorders (as we'll see in the next section), but disorders that at least to some extent cover problems that were not covered by any disorders in the previous edition of the manual. Among them:

- *Premenstrual dysphoric disorder* (PMDD; discussed in more detail in a box later in this chapter), which is essentially a severe version of premenstrual syndrome (PMS) including a combination of at least 5 emotional and physical symptoms occurring in most menstrual cycles during the last year that cause clinically significant distress or interfere with work, school, social life, or relationships with others (American Psychiatric Association, 2013; Paris, 2013b, Wakefield, 2013a; Regier, Kuhl, et al., 2013).

- *Disruptive mood dysregulation disorder* (DMDD), which is essentially frequent temper tantrums in children 6-18 years old (at least 3 tantrums per week over the course of a year) that are clearly below the expected level of maturity and occur in at least two settings (e.g., home, school, or with friends) along with irritable or angry mood between the temper tantrums. The creation of this new diagnosis was prompted by the drastic increase in the diagnosis (and possible overdiagnosis and overmedication) of bipolar disorder in children in recent decades (American Psychiatric Association, 2013; Pierre, 2013; Copeland et al., 2013, Frances & Bastra, 2013).

- *Binge eating disorder* (BED), which resembles the part of bulimia nervosa in which the person overindulges on food but lacks the part in which the person tries to subtract the calories through compensatory behaviors like excessive exercise. Binges must take place at least once per week for three months and be accompanied by a lack of control over the eating as well as other symptoms like rapid eating, eating until overly full, eating alone to avoid embarrassment, and feelings of guilt or depression afterward (American Psychiatric Association, 2013; Ornstein et al., 2013; Moran, 2013b, Stice et al., 2013).

- *Mild Neurocognitive Disorder* (mild NCD), which is essentially a less intense version of major neurocognitive problems like dementia and amnesia. It requires modest decline in such cognitive functions as memory, language use, attention, or executive function, but nothing serious enough that it interferes with the ability to live independently (American Psychiatric Association, 2013; Blazer, 2013; Frances, 2013a).

- *Somatic symptom disorder* (SSD), which involves a combination of at least one significantly disruptive bodily (somatic) symptom with excessive focus on that symptom (or symptoms) that involves perceiving it as more serious than it really is, experiencing high anxiety about it, or devoting excessive time and energy to it (American Psychiatric Association, 2013; Frances & Chapman, 2013; Frances, 2012; 2013d).

- *Hoarding disorder*, in which the person has continuing difficulty discarding possessions no matter how objectively worthless they are, and as a result lives in a congested or cluttered home and experiences impairment in important areas such as work, socialization, or safety. In past *DSMs*, the diagnosis of obsessive-compulsive disorder may have been considered for hoarders, but their behavior often matched OCD criteria imperfectly, and with *DSM-5*, the criteria for hoarding are now distinct (American Psychiatric Association, 2013; Regier, Kuhl, et al., 2013; Greenberg, 2013).

Revised Disorders in *DSM-5*

In some cases, changes in *DSM-5* involved established disorders being revised in some way—diagnostic criteria were modified, disorders were combined, or age limits were adjusted. Among the revisions:

- The so-called "bereavement exclusion" formerly included in the diagnostic criteria for major depressive episode was dropped. To explain, previous editions of *DSM* featured a statement that major depression could not be diagnosed in a person who was mourning (or bereaving) the death of a loved one during the first two months following the death. The rationale for the exclusion was that the sadness that commonly comes with such loss should not be confused with the mental disorder of major depression. The decision to drop this statement in *DSM-5* means that now the diagnosis *can* be given to people who lost a loved one within the last two months, but only if the clinician determines that the symptoms (sadness, changes in sleeping and eating, etc.) exceed expectations based on the person's own history and culture. The rationale for dropping the exclusion was to make sure that people in mourning who are indeed experiencing abnormal levels of depressive symptoms will be recognized, diagnosed, and promptly treated before things get even more dire (American Psychiatric Association, 2013; Fox & Jones, 2013; Parker, 2013; Porter et al., 2013; Wakefield, 2013; in press).

- The *DSM-IV* diagnoses of autistic disorder, Asperger's disorder, and related developmental disorders were combined into a single *DSM-5* diagnosis: *autism spectrum disorder*. The reason for consolidating these disorders is that, according to *DSM-5* authors, they represent various points on the same spectrum of impairment, defined by social communication problems and restrictive or repetitive behaviors and interests (American Psychiatric Association, 2013; Kupfer, Kuhl, et al., 2013; Regier et al., 2013; Mayes et al., 2013; Kent et al., 2013; Pina-Camacho et al., 2013). In other words, they now seem as mild, moderate, or severe versions of the same problem.

- In the criteria for attention-deficit/hyperactivity disorder (ADHD), the age at which symptoms must first appear was changed from 7 to 12 years old, and the number of symptoms required for the diagnosis to apply to adults was specified as 5 (as opposed to 6 for kids) (American Psychiatric Association, 2013; Paris, 2013a; Wakefield, 2013a; Frances, 2013a).

- In the criteria for bulimia nervosa, the frequency of binge eating required for the disorder was dropped from twice per week to once per week. In the diagnosis of anorexia nervosa, the requirement that menstrual periods stop has been omitted, and the definition of low body weight has been changed from a numeric definition (less than 85% of expected body weight) to a less specific description that takes into account age, sex, development, and physical health (American Psychiatric Association, 2013; Ornstein et al., 2013; Moran, 2013b).

- The two separate *DSM-IV* diagnoses of substance abuse and substance dependence have been combined into a single diagnosis: *substance use disorder*. Tolerance and withdrawal, which had been solely linked to substance dependence in *DSM-IV* (and confused with addiction), were not in fact solely experienced by those with substance dependence but also by people who use substances in various capacities (American Psychiatric Association, 2013; Hasin et al., 2013; Compton et al., in press).

- Mental retardation was renamed *intellectual disability (intellectual development disorder)*, and learning disabilities in reading, math, and writing were combined into a single diagnosis with a new name: *specific learning disorder* (American Psychiatric Association, 2013).

Controversy Surrounding *DSM-5*

DSM-5 arrived in May 2013 amidst controversy that had already been swirling for many months (Cooper, 2013). The controversy extended well beyond academic journals and professional conferences into popular media such as magazines, newspapers, books, television, and websites geared toward the general public. Coverage of controversy extended well past the US into Europe, Australia, Asia, and South America (Frances, 2013e). Members of multiple Work Groups quit in the middle of the revision, publicly casting doubt on the process used to create the *DSM-5* (Frances, 2012c; Greenberg, 2013). Letters of protest came from leaders of multiple mental health organizations, including Division 32 (Society of Humanistic Psychology) of the American Psychological Association, the American Counseling Association, and the British Psychological Society (Whooley & Horwitz, 2013; Greenberg, 2013). Numerous mental health professionals called for a boycott of *DSM-5* (Caccavale, 2013; Frances, 2013g).

Almost all of the commentary surrounding *DSM-5* was critical, and the most vocal critic was Allen Frances (Frances 2012a, 2012b, 2013a, 2013b, 2013c, 2013d, 2013e, 2013f, 2013g). It is important to recognize that Frances was the Chair of the Task Force for *DSM-IV*—in other words, he led the previous revision of the manual that published in 1994, and as such he has direct experience with the enormous challenge and consequences of producing a new *DSM*. Frances had actually been retired for almost a decade, with no intention of being involved in *DSM-5* at all, until he found himself at a cocktail party at the annual meeting of the American Psychiatric Association in 2009 and was pulled into the debate about *DSM-5* by colleagues who informed him about the revision process (Frances, 2013a). Since that time, Frances has put forth a steady stream of articles, blog posts, radio and TV appearances, and even a full book on the flaws and failings of *DSM-5*. His tone has been consistently critical and condemning, and in many cases, he has been remarkably outspoken. For example:

- "This is the saddest moment in my 45-year career of studying, practicing, and teaching psychiatry. The Board of Trustees of the American Psychiatric Association has given its final approval to a deeply flawed *DSM-5* containing many changes that seem clearly unsafe and scientifically unsound…Our patients deserve better, society deserves better, and the mental health professions deserve better." (Frances, 2012b).

- "With the *DSM-5*, patients worried about having a medical illness will often be diagnosed with somatic symptom disorder, normal grief will be misidentified as major depressive disorder, the forgetfulness of old age will be confused with mild neurocognitive disorder, temper tantrums will be labeled disruptive mood dysregulation disorder, overeating will become binge eating disorder, and the already overused diagnosis of attention-deficit disorder will be even easier to apply" (Frances, 2013i)

- "[I have offered many] warnings about the risks that DSM-5 will mislabel normal people, promote diagnostic inflation, and encourage inappropriate medication use…Many other individuals, mental health organizations, professional journals, and the press have loudly sounded the very same alarm. We have had some positive impact…but overall we failed. *DSM-5* pushes psychiatric diagnosis in the wrong direction…" (Frances, 2013a, p. x,iii).

- "My advice…is to ignore *DSM-5*…It is not well done. It is not safe. Don't buy it. Don't use it. Don't teach it." (Frances, 2013f)

Frances is certainly not alone. Although few were quite so blunt, many others offered harsh criticism of many aspects of *DSM-5* (e.g., Greenberg, 2013; Paris, 2013a, 2013c). What, specifically, did they criticize?

- *Diagnostic overexpansion.* The primary criticism of *DSM-5*, which is a continuation of a complaint of recent *DSMs*, is that its diagnoses cover too much of normal life —in other words, too often it takes difficult or inopportune life experiences and labels them as mental illnesses (Wakefield, 2013a). (The history of this criticism is covered later in this chapter, and the current version of the controversy is covered in more detail in Chapter 3.) These critics argue that prior to *DSM-5*, a woman with severe PMS, an aging adult whose memory isn't quite what it used to be, an adult who binges on food once a week and feels guilty about it, and a child who throws temper tantrums were experiencing normal life struggles, but with the publication of *DSM-5*, they run the risk of being labeled mentally ill, with premenstrual dysphoric disorder, mild neurocognitive disorder, binge eating disorder and disruptive mood regulation disorder, respectively. These critics also point out that the addition of these disorders in *DSM-5* was often done in spite of questionable research evidence (Wakefield, 2013a, Frances, 2013a). They further emphasize the likelihood that the revisions in diagnostic criteria to existing disorders—the removal of the bereavement exception for major depressive episode, the older age by which ADHD symptoms may now start, the lower frequency requirement for binge eating for bulimia—will result in higher rates of these disorders (Wakefield, 2013b, in press; Fox & Jones, 2013; Parker, 2013). The only change likely to go against this trend is the consolidation of autistic disorder, Asperger's disorder, and similar developmental disorders into the single autism spectrum disorder (Frances, 2012b; Mayes et al., 2013; Dobbs, 2013). A possible factor in this overexpansion—the pharmaceutical industry—is discussed in more detail in Chapter 3.

- *Transparency of the revision process.* Although the *DSM-5* authors maintained a website on which they shared information throughout the revision process, including proposals for changes to the manual, some critics argued that they were vague and selective about what they shared, that too many of their ideas and decisions were eventually made behind closed doors, and that the members of the Work Groups were required to sign confidentiality agreements to keep their processes out of public awareness (Frances, 2012c; Paris, 2013a; Cosgrove & Wheeler, 2013).

- *Membership of the Work Groups.* The decisions made by *DSM* authors depends, at least to some extent, on who those authors are. Those who were invited into the *DSM-5* revision process were, predominantly, researchers. Undoubtedly, they understand the disorders in their area of expertise in terms of designing and conducting empirical studies, but some of them do not practice at all, and those who do may only do so minimally, so their ability to assess the impact of *DSM* changes on full-time clinicians practicing in real-world clinics, hospitals, and private practices may have been lacking (Paris, 2013a, 2013c; Whooley & Horwitz, 2013). That is, the clinical utility of *DSM-5* may suffer from a lack of clinical practice experience among its authors. On the other hand, *DSM-5* also received criticism from the director of the National Institute of Mental Health (NIMH), a leading funding agency for mental health research, in which he announced that NIMH will be developing its own "Research Domain Criteria" (RDoC) by which to define mental health problems for research purposes. In the meantime, NIMH will show preference to research proposals that consider mental health issues across *DSM-5* categories, rather than within them (Insel, 2013). Also related to the membership of the Work Groups is the fact that some of these members have "pet" diagnostic proposals of their own, and a Work Group member who promotes his or her pet proposal consistently and effectively had a better chance of a successful negotiation, resulting in *DSM-5* change, than someone who wasn't invited into the Work Group in the first place (Shorter, 2013; Frances, 2013a).

- *Field trial problems.* As mentioned earlier, the authors of DSM-5 ran field trials in which they tested the reliability of their new diagnoses with clinicians in real-world clinical settings. The problem, according to critics, is that some of the reliability ratings that these field tests produced were too low. In other words, these changes didn't yield sufficiently consistent diagnoses across clinicians. A second stage of field trials, in which some of these issues could have been corrected, was cancelled (Frances, 2012d, 2013a).

- *Price.* The list price for DSM-5 is $199 hardback, $149 paperback, and $149 ebook. By comparison, when DSM-IV was released in 1994, it cost $65 (Frances, 2013h). Some critics view this as a steep price for a book considered an essential reference for all mental health professionals, all students of clinical psychology, psychiatry, and related fields, and many health professionals more broadly. (It is worth noting that

Photo 7.2 The definitions of mental disorders, including the anxiety-based disorders, have changed as the DSM has been revised. In your opinion, what are the pros and cons of the changes?

ICD, the manual of mental disorders used in other parts of the world outside the US, is available for free on the internet.) In fact, since the success of DSM-III in the 1980s, DSM proceeds have provided significant funding to its publisher, the American Psychiatric Association. Sadler (2013) reports that according to American Psychiatric Association treasurer reports, DSM-IV brought in between 5 and 6 million dollars per year between 2005 and 2011—years well after its initial publication, when sales might be even higher. These critics and others have questioned the extent to which profits might influence the price point of the book as well as the decisions made in the process of creating it.

● ● ● BOX 7.2 ● ● ●

Considering Culture

Are Eating Disorders Culturally Specific?

DSM-5 (American Psychiatric Association, 2013) includes a Glossary of Cultural Concepts of Distress, which lists syndromes and experiences that are relatively unique to particular cultures. Do anorexia and bulimia belong on this list?

(Continued)

(Continued)

Currently, of course, anorexia and bulimia are included among the official *DSM* disorders rather than among the cultural concepts of distress, most of which originate outside the United States. But there is reason to question whether these disorders are culturally specific—after all, they are far more prevalent among females in industrialized, Western societies, especially the United States, than in other cultures and locations. Pamela K. Keel and Kelly L. Klump (2003) conducted an extensive study of this question, examining the incidence rates of anorexia and bulimia in Western and non-Western parts of the world, as well as the history of these two disorders before they were officially defined and labeled. In their review of previous studies on the subject, Keel and Klump stated that some researchers had put forth the argument that these eating disorders were limited to Western culture and were therefore culture-bound. Other researchers emphasized that factors besides culture, including genetics, were the primary causes of these disorders. Ultimately, Keel and Klump concluded that although anorexia did not meet their definition of a culture-bound condition, bulimia did. Among the evidence they cited was a study of eating disorders in Fiji where bulimic behaviors (especially self-induced vomiting and other compensatory behaviors) were virtually nonexistent until immediately following the introduction of television—which glamorizes Hollywood's thinness-based definitions of female ideal body image — at which point these behaviors increased suddenly and dramatically (Becker, Burwell, Gilman, Herzog, & Hamburg, 2002).

The questions raised by Keel and Klump's (2003) study are certainly important to clinical psychology. What separates a local, indigenous, "folk" syndrome from a bona fide, official disorder? Culture can certainly shape psychological problems, but can each culture create entirely unique disorders that are unrelated to disorders elsewhere? And, ultimately, to what extent should a clinical psychologist's treatment of a client depend on whether the client's problem is defined as culturally bound or more universal?

Criticisms of the *DSM*

The most recent editions of *DSM* have been widely used by all mental health professions, and they undeniably represent improvements over their predecessors in some important ways. Strengths of recent editions include their emphasis on empirical research, the use of explicit diagnostic criteria, interclinician reliability, and atheoretical language (e.g., Klerman, 1984; Malik & Beutler, 2002; Matarazzo, 1983). Additionally, the *DSM* has facilitated communication between researchers and clinicians by providing a common professional language that has become very widely accepted (Lilienfeld & Landfield, 2008; Wilson, 1993). However, the recent *DSMs* have received significant criticism as well. We touched on some of this criticism in our discussion of *DSM-5* above; here, we consider those topics in more detail and other topics as well.

⊕ **Web Link 7.1**

Open letter of concern about proposed *DSM* changes

Breadth of Coverage

Recent editions of the *DSM* include many more disorders than editions published a relatively short time earlier. Some have argued that this expansion has been too rapid and that the result is a list of mental disorders including some experiences that should not be categorized as forms of mental illness (e.g., Burr & Butt, 2000; Langenbucher & Nathan, 2006; Pilgrim & Bentall, 1999). Houts (2002) points out that many of the newer disorders are not entirely "mental" disorders, including some disorders with physical factors such as the sexual disorders, substance-related disorders, and sleep disorders. Kutchins and Kirk (1997) and Caplan (1995) make the case that the *DSM* includes an increasing number of disorders that are better understood as problems in day-to-day life than as diagnosable mental illnesses—an argument not dissimilar to the one made decades ago by Thomas Szasz (1961, 1970), when the diagnostic manual was nowhere near as wide ranging. A potential risk of expanding the range of pathology this way is that greater numbers of people may face stigma associated with a diagnostic label, either from others or as self-stigma. Or the concept of mental illness may be spread too thin, which would solve the stigmatization problem but could result in the trivialization of any form of mental illness, such that they are not taken as seriously as they should be (Hinshaw & Stier, 2008). In addition, as psychological diagnoses multiply, the chances that they will overlap with one another increase, leading to a likelihood of comorbidity (diagnosis of more than one disorder) that some argue is excessively high (e.g., Kendall & Drabick, 2010).

Controversial Cutoffs

⊕ **Web Link 7.2**

DSM criticism

One of the essential differences between earlier and later editions of *DSM* is the presence of lists of specific symptoms and, moreover, specific cutoffs regarding those lists of symptoms. For example, the current diagnostic criteria for major depressive disorder include nine specific symptoms, at least five of which must be present for at least a 2-week period. Why a minimum of five symptoms rather than three, seven, or some other number? And why 2 weeks rather than 1 week, 1 month, or some other duration? Some have argued that these cutoffs have been arbitrarily or subjectively chosen by *DSM* authors and that, historically, the consensus of the *DSM* authors (as opposed to empirical data) has played a significant role in these cutoff decisions (Barlow & Durand, 2005; Widiger & Mullins-Sweatt, 2008). Similarly, many *DSM* diagnoses include criteria intended to establish a level of severity that must be met in order for the diagnosis to be assigned— statements that the symptoms must cause significant distress or impairment in various areas of the client's life, including interpersonal relationships or functioning at work/school. What, exactly, constitutes significant distress or impairment? And how are mental health professionals trained to make such a judgment? Such questions remain problematic in the controversy over cutoffs that separate normal from abnormal functioning (Narrow & Kuhl, 2011; Spitzer & Wakefield, 1999).

Cultural Issues

When *DSM-IV* arrived in 1994, it signaled important advances in the consideration of cultural issues regarding mental disorders. *DSM-5* continues many of those advances. As described in Chapter 4, *DSM-5* includes an Outline for Cultural Formulation and the accompanying Cultural Formulation Interview designed to help clinicians assess in a culturally competent way. It also includes a glossary of cultural concepts of distress, or terms used by various cultural groups to describe specific psychological conditions. In addition, for many disorders, the text describing the disorder now includes comments on cultural variations, such as the way a disorder may be expressed differently in different cultures. For example, in the paragraphs describing schizophrenia, *DSM-5* contains several paragraphs on cultural issues, including such statements as "Ideas that appear to be delusional in one culture (e.g., witchcraft) may be commonly held in another" (American Psychiatric Association, 2013, p. 103).

Despite this considerable progress toward improving cultural sensitivity, the recent editions of *DSM* have received pointed criticism for shortcomings related to culture (e.g., Mezzich, Kleinman, Fabrega, & Parron, 1996). For example, although more ethnic minorities and women were included among the authors of recent *DSM*s than earlier editions, these authors weren't creating a new *DSM* from scratch. Instead, they were revising an established manual that was originally created by a group of authors that was overwhelmingly white and male. So although their input was valued and incorporated, its impact was limited to revisions of previously confirmed *DSM* decisions rather than a more substantive renovation (Velasquez, Johnson, & Brown-Cheatham, 1993).

Also, although the recent revisions of the *DSM* have been praised for basing decisions on empirical data, critics have questioned the extent to which culturally diverse populations are included among the participants in those empirical studies. In fact, some detractors of the *DSM* have stated that very few of the empirical studies considered by the authors of the current *DSM* have focused sufficiently on ethnic minorities, which suggests that the *DSM* still may not reflect minority experiences (e.g., Markus & Kitayama, 1991; Mezzich et al., 1996). The implicit values of Western culture have been the focus of some *DSM* critics as well. They argue that these values are embedded in the *DSM* and that they don't encompass the values of many people from non-Western societies. Specifically, Eriksen and Kress (2005) explain that in comparison with the traditional Western view, the majority of the world's population believes that the boundaries between an individual and the people or environment surrounding him or her are more permeable and that interdependence between individuals, rather than striving for independence and self-sufficiency, is highly valued.

The *DSM* conceptualizations of some disorders (such as some psychotic disorders, some personality disorders, and a number of others) may presume a Western worldview (Lewis-Fernandez & Kleinman, 1994).

Gender Bias

Some disorders are diagnosed far more often in males: alcohol use disorder, conduct disorder, ADHD, and antisocial personality disorder, to name a few. Other disorders are diagnosed far more often in females: major depression, many anxiety disorders, eating disorders, borderline personality disorder, histrionic personality disorder, and others (American Psychiatric Association, 2013; Cosgrove & Riddle, 2004). Critics of the current *DSM* have argued that some diagnostic categories are biased toward pathologizing one gender more than the other. Specifically, these diagnoses may represent exaggerations of socially encouraged gender roles, suggesting that society, rather than or in addition to the individual, plays a prominent role in their emergence (e.g., Caplan & Cosgrove, 2004; Kutchins & Kirk, 1997; Yonkers & Clarke, 2011). Some empirical studies have found that clinicians define mental health differently for males and females (e.g., Broverman, Broverman, Clarkson, Rosenkrantz, & Vogel, 1970; Ritchie, 1994; Sherman, 1980) and that clients of different genders with identical symptoms often receive different diagnoses from clinicians (Becker & Lamb, 1994). The controversy over **premenstrual dysphoric disorder (PMDD)**, which had been rejected from previous editions of *DSM* but is now included as a disorder in *DSM-5*, has renewed this criticism of *DSM* authors. See Box 7.3 for more on PMDD.

⏺ Web Link 7.3
Premenstrual Dysphoric Disorder

● ● ● BOX 7.3 ● ● ●

Premenstrual Dysphoric Disorder

One of the most notable new disorders listed in *DSM-5* is premenstrual dysphoric disorder (PMDD). It falls within the "Depressive Disorders" category, along with major depressive disorder and other disorders that center around sad or irritable mood. According to its description, PMDD should not be equated with premenstrual syndrome, or PMS, which is more common and less severe than PMDD. Instead, PMDD requires either "clinically significant distress" or "interference with work, school, usual social activities, or relationships with others" (American Psychiatric Association, 2013, p. 172). The diagnosis of PMDD requires at least 5 symptoms from a list of 11 occurring in most menstrual cycles of the past year during the week before the menstrual period, at least one of which is mood-related (e.g., mood swings, irritability, sadness) and at least one of which is behavioral or physical

(Continued)

(Continued)

(e.g., trouble concentrating, lack of energy, changes in eating or sleeping, breast tenderness or swelling, or pain in joints or muscles).

There is no question that some women experience severe premenstrual symptoms that meaningfully influence their lives. There is a question, however, as to whether that experience should be labeled a mental illness. Some benefits could certainly accompany the diagnosis of PMDD: It could legitimize the severity of the experience for women who receive the diagnosis, provide an explanation for their symptoms, elicit compassion from others, prevent misdiagnosis under another category, and enable treatment (Gallant & Hamilton, 1988). However, there may also be some drawbacks to the diagnosis of PMDD. Specifically, for a woman who has received the diagnostic label of PMDD and shared it with others, it may pose a significant challenge to convince other people (e.g., employers, friends, family) that she is not psychologically abnormal (Caplan, 1992). Moreover, the presence of a PMDD diagnosis in a woman's medical record could have an effect on legal cases in which she is involved. For example, in a custody dispute, a woman with a PMDD diagnosis may be at a distinct disadvantage compared with a woman with identical symptoms for which no diagnostic category exists (Caplan, 1992; Eriksen & Kress, 2005).

The idea of a PMDD diagnosis has generated controversy since it was first proposed in the 1980s (under the name "Late Luteal Phase Dysphoric Disorder" at the time). It was considered for inclusion in previous editions of *DSM*, and listed in an appendix of conditions to be considered for the future in *DSM-IV* in 1994, but it became a full-fledged disorder in 2013 with the publication of *DSM-5*. Feminist groups in particular have opposed its inclusion as an official disorder in the *DSM*. They have emphasized that it represents a form of gender bias likely to overpathologize women, especially since there is no parallel diagnosis for men despite the fact that men also experience some degree of hormonal fluctuations. Additionally, they have pointed out that although premenstrual symptoms can be problematic, they are better understood as physical or gynecological problems rather than a form of mental illness, especially since they last a short time and subside on their own without treatment. Opponents of the proposed PMDD diagnosis have also criticized the quality and quantity of the research on PMDD, concluding that it does not substantiate PMDD as a distinct form of mental illness (Caplan, 1992, 1995; Caplan & Cosgrove, 2004; Eriksen & Kress, 2005).

Many questions relevant to contemporary clinical psychologists arise from the PMDD debate. Where should we draw the line between diagnosable mental illness and the unpleasant or problematic aspects of normal life? What quantity and quality of empirical research should be necessary to support the inclusion of a new disorder in the *DSM*?

Looking ahead, these questions apply not only to the new disorders included in *DSM-5*, but to its "proposed criteria sets" as well—in other words, the non-official conditions that are being considered for official status in a future edition of DSM. These conditions include Internet Gaming Disorder (based on excessive use of Internet games leading to distress or impairment), Nonsuicidal Self-Injury (based on "cutting" or otherwise harming the surface of one's own body), Persistent Complex Bereavement Disorder (based on prolonged severe grief after the loss of a loved one), and Attenuated Psychosis Syndrome (based on relatively mild and infrequent experiences of hallucinations, delusions, and disorganized speech).

Nonempirical Influences

Authors of recent editions of the *DSM* have increasingly used empirical evidence to determine the diagnostic categories, and the manual is certainly more reliable as a result. However, nonempirical influences have intruded on the process to some extent, according to various commentators on the *DSM* process (e.g., Blashfield, 1991; Caplan, 1995; Kutchins & Kirk, 1997). At times, political wrangling and public opinion may have pressured *DSM* authors to make certain decisions. For example, once-proposed disorders such as masochistic personality disorder have been strongly and publicly opposed by political organizations, and decisions not to include them officially in the *DSM* may stem in part from this opposition. The changing status of homosexuality— which was an official disorder in *DSM-I* and *DSM-II,* was a disorder only if "ego-dystonic" (in other words, if it caused distress) in *DSM-III,* and has been absent from the manual since *DSM-III-R*—also may reflect efforts during the 1970s and 1980s by organized groups to influence the mental health establishment as well as changing values in *DSM* authors and society more generally.

In addition to politics and public opinion, financial concerns may have played a role in some *DSM* decisions, according to some (e.g., Blashfield, 1991; Cosgrove, Krimsky, Vijayaraghavan, & Schneider, 2006; Kirmayer & Minas, 2000). As increasing numbers of therapy clients paid via health insurance in the last several decades of the 1900s, clinicians found that, typically, the health insurance companies required a diagnosis for payment. As it happens, the number of *DSM* diagnoses expanded substantially around that time. Also, pharmaceutical companies sponsor a substantial number of research projects on various forms of psychopathology, including those that are proposed and under consideration for future inclusion in the *DSM*. As mentioned earlier in this chapter, quite a few *DSM* authors have financial ties to these companies (Cosgrove et al., 2006; Cosgrove & Krimsky, 2012). Of course, drug companies stand to boost profits when new diagnostic categories, and the new client "markets" that come along with them, are created.

⊕ **Web Link 7.4**

DSM author ties to pharmaceutical companies

Limitations on Objectivity

No matter how much the *DSM* authors emphasize empiricism in the process of defining mental disorders, there is a limit to their objectivity. In fact, the leading authors of the *DSM-IV* and *DSM-IV-TR* stated themselves that "although based on empirical data, *DSM-IV* decisions were the results of expert consensus on how best to interpret the data" (Frances, First, & Pincus, 1995, p. 34). To some extent, the opinions of these experts can be influenced by changes in our society: "Throughout the manufacture of the *DSM*, people are making decisions and judgments in a social context. Whether or not a new set of behaviors warrants a diagnostic label depends on culturally varying judgments about what is clinically significant" (Houts, 2002, p. 53).

Alternative Directions in Diagnosis and Classification

Photo 7.3 Homosexuality was considered a disorder in earlier editions of the *DSM* but has not been considered a disorder in more recent editions.

DSM has always offered a **categorical approach** to diagnosis. The word *categorical* refers to the basic view that an individual "has" or "does not have" the disorder—that is, they can be placed definitively in the "yes" or "no" category regarding a particular form of psychopathology. Popular and professional language reflects this categorical approach: "Does my child *have* ADHD?"; "Some of my clients *have* bipolar disorder"; "Michael *has* obsessive-compulsive disorder."

In recent years, and especially regarding some disorders (e.g., personality disorders), noncategorical approaches to psychopathology have received significant attention and empirical support. Specifically, the **dimensional approach** has been proposed by a number of researchers and clinicians (e.g., Blashfield, 1991; Costa & Widiger, 2001; Trull & Durrett, 2005; Widiger & Trull, 2007). According to a dimensional approach, the issue isn't the presence or absence of a disorder; instead, the issue is where on a continuum (or "dimension") a client's symptoms fall. As an example, consider Robert, a client with a strong tendency to avoid social situations because he fears criticism and rejection from others. A categorical system would require Robert's psychologist to determine whether Robert has a particular disorder—perhaps social phobia or avoidant personality disorder. A dimensional system wouldn't require a yes or no answer to the question. In place of this dichotomous decision, Robert's psychologist would be asked to rate Robert on a continuum of anxious avoidance of social situations. In other words, rather than a "black-or-white" type of decision, Robert's psychologist would determine which "shade of gray" best describes Robert's symptoms.

The dimensions of psychological disorders may not be defined by traditional *DSM* categories. Instead, proponents of the dimensional approach to abnormality suggest that all of us—the normal and the abnormal—share the same fundamental characteristics but that we differ in the amounts of these characteristics that we each possess. What makes some of us abnormal is an unusually high or low level of one or more of these characteristics.

⊕ **Web Link 7.5**
Dimensional approach

But what are these fundamental shared characteristics? The **five-factor model of personality** (also known as the "Big Five" model) is the leading candidate, at least for the personality disorders, and perhaps more broadly (Costa & Widiger, 2001; Widiger & Mullins-Sweatt, 2009; Widiger & Trull, 2007). In other words, according to the dimensional approach to abnormality, each of our personalities contains the same five basic factors—neuroticism, extraversion, openness to experience, agreeableness, and conscientiousness. These five factors, rather than the disorders listed in the *DSM,* could constitute the dimensions on which clinical psychologists could describe clients with personality problems. Thus, in the case of Robert described above, instead of giving him a high rating on a dimension called "avoidant personality disorder" or "social phobia," the clinician would give the client a low rating on the dimension of extraversion. (As mentioned earlier in this chapter, the authors of *DSM-5* seriously considered a dimensional make-over of the personality disorders, but ultimately decided against it, at least for now.)

Conceptualizing people's psychological problems the way *DSM* always has—categorically—certainly has many advantages. In fact, some have argued that categorical thinking is unavoidable and essential to our understanding and communication about mental disorders: "Just as water is basic to human existence, classification is fundamental to human cognition. As human beings, we are hardwired to think in categorical terms. Human cognition without categorization is unimaginable" (Blashfield & Burgess, 2007, p. 113). Perhaps most important, categories of mental illness facilitate efficient communication between professionals as well as nonprofessionals. If we instead conceptualized people's psychological problems dimensionally, communication would necessarily become more cumbersome. Moreover, generations of mental health professionals have been trained to understand psychopathology categorically, so it has become firmly established as the preferred model (Lilienfeld & Landfield, 2008), and accumulating evidence suggests that some specific disorders, such as the psychotic disorders, may indeed exist categorically rather than dimensionally (Linscott & van Os, 2010). However, the dimensional model offers some interesting advantages as well. It allows for a more thorough description of clients. Also, rather than arbitrarily dividing a dimension into two categories, it allows for more detailed placement on that dimension. Although clinical psychologists currently work within the categorical *DSM* system, a growing body of research supports the possible incorporation of a dimensional model of psychopathology, perhaps in some kind of combination with categorical approaches and at least with the personality disorders (Achenbach, 2009; Costa & Widiger, 2001; Maser et al., 2009; Simonsen, 2010; Skodol, 2010; Widiger & Trull, 2007). While this dimensional model was not used to revamp the personality disorders section of *DSM-5*, it may appear in some form in a future edition of the manual.

Metaphorically Speaking

If You've Eaten Chocolate Chip Cookies, You Understand the Dimensional Model of Psychopathology

Chocolate chip cookies are usually made from the same short list of ingredients: flour, sugar, chocolate chips, butter, eggs, baking soda, vanilla. If you bite into a chocolate chip cookie and it tastes unusual, atypical, or even "abnormal," what's the reason? Perhaps it contains the same ingredients as other chocolate chip cookies but simply in different amounts—more sugar, less butter, fewer chocolate chips—than "normal" cookies. In other words, the difference between "abnormal" and "normal" cookies could be quantitative. Or maybe the "abnormal" cookie contains some entirely different ingredients that "normal" cookies simply don't contain—nutmeg, cinnamon, pepper, garlic, or something else. In this case, the difference is qualitative.

The proponents of the dimensional model of psychopathology believe that the same question of qualitative versus quantitative differences between normality and abnormality applies to people as well as to chocolate chip cookies. They believe that all our personalities are made of the same short list of "ingredients," or traits. In the past few decades, they have increasingly pointed to the Big Five—neuroticism, extraversion, openness, conscientiousness, and agreeableness—as characteristics that are common to all of us, including normal and abnormal individuals. According to the dimensional model, what is abnormal about abnormal people is the amount of one of these basic ingredients—extremely high neuroticism, extremely low extraversion, or extremely high openness, for example. In other words, abnormal people have the same "ingredients" as normal people but in significantly different amounts—a quantitative difference. In contrast, supporters of the categorical approach to psychopathology tend to believe that the difference between abnormal and normal people is more qualitative, suggesting that abnormal people have an "ingredient" that normal people simply don't have.

Certain forms of psychopathology tend to lend themselves to the dimensional model more than do others. Specifically, a growing body of research suggests that the personality disorders can be conceptualized quite well using the dimensional approach based on the Big Five personality factors (e.g., Widiger & Mullins-Sweatt, 2009; Widiger & Trull, 2007). This makes some intuitive sense: If human personality essentially consists of these five factors and we have a category of disorders called "personality disorders," it stands to reason that the personality disorders we have identified should map onto the five factors of personality we have recognized. Empirical support for this theory has suggested several specific links: Paranoid personality disorder is characterized by very low agreeableness; histrionic personality disorder is characterized by very high extraversion; obsessive-compulsive personality disorder is characterized by very high conscientiousness; borderline personality disorder is characterized by very high neuroticism. Evidence linking the Big Five to other disorders, however, is less impressive (Costa & Widiger, 2001).

The debate regarding the dimensional and categorical models of psychopathology evokes important questions for clinical psychologists. Are people, in fact, all made of the same psychological "ingredients"? If so, should we understand the differences between abnormal and normal people as quantitative? Or are we made of entirely different "ingredients," and would it be more advantageous to understand our differences as qualitative? How might the answers to these questions influence the assessment and treatment that clinical psychologists conduct?

CHAPTER SUMMARY

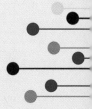

Diagnosis is a primary task of clinical psychologists, but the process of defining mental disorders, and abnormality more generally, has been the subject of some debate. The DSM is generally considered the authoritative source of definitions for mental disorders, and it is widely accepted and used among mental health professionals. The DSM has been revised several times since its original publication by the American Psychiatric Association in 1952. The most recent edition, DSM-5, was published in 2013 and offers numerous new features, new disorders, and revised definitions of previously included disorders, many of which have elicited controversy and criticism. The *DSM* has always employed a medical model of psychopathology characterized by a categorical approach that describes disorders as either present or absent. An alternative, dimensional approach has been promoted in recent years, especially for the personality disorders, which would describe the extent to which clients have particular universal characteristics rather than whether or not they have a disorder. The *DSM* has become increasingly empirical and reliable as it has been revised, but it has also received criticism for pathologizing aspects of normal life, using arbitrary cutoffs regarding some diagnostic criteria, paying insufficient attention to issues of culture and gender, and allowing nonempirical factors too much influence.

KEY TERMS AND NAMES

CRITICAL THINKING QUESTIONS

1. In your opinion, what factors are most important in distinguishing abnormal from normal behavior?

2. In your opinion, who should define normal versus abnormal behavior?

3. How might the changes in the *DSM-5* influence both clinical psychologists and the clients they treat?

4. Of the criticisms of the current *DSM* described in this chapter, which seem most and least legitimate?

5. In your opinion, what are the strengths and weaknesses of the categorical and dimensional approaches to diagnosis?

STUDENT STUDY SITE RESOURCES

Visit the study site at www.sagepub.com/pomerantz3eupdate for these additional learning tools:

- Self-quizzes
- eFlashcards
- Culture Expert Interviews

- Full-text SAGE journal articles
- Additional web resources
- Mock Assessment Data

CHAPTER SUMMARY VIDEO

 QR codes at the end of each chapter link to chapter background videos by the author. Visit http://gettag.mobi using your smartphone browser to download the free Microsoft Tag app. Once installed, scan the tags to go directly to these brief videos. In this video, the author tells the story of two clients who received the same diagnosis but reacted very differently.

CHAPTER 8

The Clinical Interview

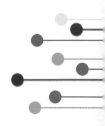

Web Link 8.1
Psychological
Assessment
& Assessment
Journals

This chapter focuses on the **clinical interview**, and it is the first of the series of chapters on **assessment**. Assessment is closely and uniquely associated with the identity of clinical psychology. None of the other mental health professionals—psychiatrists, social workers, professional counselors, nonclinical psychologists—incorporate assessment into their training and their work to the extent clinical psychologists do.

Any assessment technique used by a clinical psychologist should possess the qualities of validity, reliability, and clinical utility (Wood, Garb, & Nezworski, 2007). An assessment technique has **validity** to the extent that it measures what it claims to measure. If you've taken certain "intelligence" or "personality" tests, perhaps on the Internet or in popular magazines, and wondered, "Does this really measure what it says it measures?" you were wondering about validity. The technique has **reliability** to the extent that it yields consistent, repeatable results. If its results depend on when, where, or how the technique was administered, its reliability might be questionable. Finally, assuming the technique is used in clinical settings, it should provide **clinical utility** as well. Even the most valid and reliable test ever created wouldn't be helpful to a clinical psychologist if it didn't benefit the clinician and ultimately the client in some meaningful way. These terms, as well as subtypes of validity and reliability, are explained further in Table 8.1.

Photo 8.1 The clinical interview is a core element of most assessments conducted by clinical psychologists. In your opinion, what are the most important skills and behaviors of the interviewer?

An element common to all kinds of psychological assessment is *feedback*. In other words, clinical psychologists provide their clients with the results of tests or interviews that have been conducted (American Psychological Association, 2002). This feedback can come in the form of a face-to-face meeting, a written report, or other forms. Psychologists learn to provide feedback during graduate training, but postgraduate internships and professional experience also shape the way they provide feedback to clients (Curry & Hanson, 2010). Most psychologists believe that clients find their feedback to be helpful and positive, even before any type of intervention (e.g., psychotherapy) is implemented (Smith, Wiggins, & Gorske, 2007).

Clinical psychologists conducting assessments can employ a wide variety of methods, including intelligence tests, achievement tests, neuropsychological tests, personality tests, and specialized measures for targeted variables. In fact, psychological testing, which we cover in the next chapters, has been called "one of the brightest jewels in the crown of clinical psychology" (Wood et al., 2007, p. 77). However, of all the

Table 8.1 Defining Validity, Reliability, and Clinical Utility for Assessment Methods

Validity	is the extent to which the assessment technique . . .	measures what it claims to measure.
Content validity	is the extent to which the assessment technique . . .	has content appropriate for what is being measured.
Convergent validity	is the extent to which the assessment technique . . .	correlates with other techniques that measure the same thing.
Discriminant validity	is the extent to which the assessment technique . . .	does not correlate with techniques that measure something else.
Reliability	is the extent to which the assessment technique . . .	yields consistent, repeatable results.
Test-retest reliability	is the extent to which the assessment technique . . .	yields similar results across multiple administrations at different times.
Interrater reliability	is the extent to which the assessment technique . . .	yields similar results across different administrators.
Internal reliability (e.g., split-half reliability)	is the extent to which the assessment technique . . .	consists of items that are consistent with one another.
Clinical utility	is the extent to which the assessment technique . . .	improves delivery of services or client outcome.

Source: Wood, J. M., Garb, H. N. & Nezworski, M. T. (2007). Psychometrics: Better measurements makes better clinicians. In S. O. Lilienfeld & W. T. O'Donohue (Eds.), *The great ideas of clinical science: 17 principles that every mental health professional should understand*, pp. 77–92. New York: Routledge.

available procedures, clinical psychologists rely most frequently on the clinical interview. The vast majority of clinical psychologists use interviews, and few assessments are conducted without an interview of some kind (Norcross, Hedges, & Castle, 2002; Watkins, Campbell, Nieberding, & Hallmark, 1995).

The Interviewer

The most pivotal element of a clinical interview is the person who conducts it. A skilled interviewer is not only a master of the technical and practical aspects of the interview but also demonstrates broad-based wisdom about the human interaction it entails.

General Skills

Before leaping into any interview, the interviewer should have acquired some general skills to serve as a foundation for interviewing in any context. These general skills focus on the interviewer's own frame of mind rather than any particular set of techniques. Sommers-Flanagan and Sommers-Flanagan (2009) describe several such requirements: quieting yourself, being self-aware, and developing positive working relationships.

The term **quieting yourself** does not simply mean that the interviewer shouldn't talk much during the interview (although rambling by the interviewer is usually not a good idea). Rather than the interviewer's speech, what should be quieted is the interviewer's internal, self-directed thinking pattern. To the extent that interviewers are preoccupied by their own thoughts, they will struggle in the fundamental task of listening to their clients. Simply put, the voice in the interviewer's own mind should not interrupt or drown out the voice of the client.

As an example, consider Joseph, a second-year graduate student in a clinical psychology program. Joseph has just begun his supervised practicum work in an outpatient mental health clinic, and clinical interviews are among his frequent activities at the site. As a novice interviewer, Joseph may find a number of self-directed questions repeatedly running though his mind while an interview takes place: "Was that a good question? Should I have asked something else? What does this client think of me? Do I come across as competent? Am I competent? What should I ask next?" A certain amount of self-reflection and thoughtfulness about the ongoing process of an interview is beneficial, but Joseph's extensive self-questioning may distract him from his client. As Joseph gains more experience and confidence through graduate school and later as a professional, his listening capacity may increase as he is increasingly able to quiet such internal questions.

Being self-aware is another important skill for the clinical interviewer. This self-awareness should not be confused with the excessive self-consciousness exemplified by Joseph in the above example, which should be minimized. The type of self-awareness that should be maximized is the interviewer's ability to know how he or she tends to affect others interpersonally and how others tend to relate to him or her. To illustrate this point, imagine yourself as a new client in a clinical psychologist's waiting room for the first time. When the psychologist comes out to greet you, he looks and speaks exactly like Albert Einstein. Would his appearance and demeanor influence the way you responded to him during the interview? What if the psychologist resembled Kim Kardashian? Or LeBron James? Or Betty White? Every interviewer has a distinct combination of idiosyncratic qualities—looks, voice, mannerisms, body language, accents, and so on—that may evoke certain responses from clients. Skilled interviewers are cognizant of their unique traits, including their cultural assumptions as well as more superficial characteristics, and consider their effect on the interview process (Sommers-Flanagan & Sommers-Flanagan, 2009).

In addition to quieting themselves and knowing themselves, good interviewers appreciate the importance of **developing positive working relationships** with clients. In many clinical settings, an interview client is likely to become a psychotherapy client, so a good start to the working relationship benefits both parties. There is no formula for developing positive working relationships during an interview; however, attentive listening, appropriate empathy, genuine respect, and cultural sensitivity play significant roles. Positive working relationships are always a function of the interviewer's attitude as well as the interviewer's actions (Sommers-Flanagan & Sommers-Flanagan, 2009).

Specific Behaviors

When interviewers succeed in quieting themselves, knowing themselves, and developing good working relationships, they have laid the groundwork for conducting successful interviews. The next task is to master the tools of the trade, the specific behaviors characteristic of effective interviewers.

As mentioned above, a primary task of the interviewer is to listen. **Listening** may seem like a simple enough task, but it can be broken down into even more fundamental building blocks of **attending behaviors** (many described in Ivey, Ivey, & Zalaquett, 2010).

Eye Contact

Perhaps it's an obvious point, but interviewers must realize the connection between attentive listening and eye contact. Eye contact not only facilitates listening, but it also communicates listening. That is, when the client notices the interviewer's continuous, appropriate eye contact, the client feels heard. Of course, culture plays a significant role in the meaning of eye contact. In some cultures, eye contact that lasts too long or is too intense may communicate threat, seduction, or other messages that an interviewer would be wise to avoid. On the other hand, scarce, inconsistent eye contact may be viewed by some clients as inattentive or insulting. Like so many other aspects of the clinical interview, eye contact is a specific behavior that requires cultural knowledge and sensitivity on the part of the interviewer, both as the sender and receiver of eye contact.

Body Language

As with eye contact, culture can shape the connotations of **body language**. There are a few general rules for the interviewer: face the client, appear attentive, minimize restlessness, display appropriate facial expressions, and so on. But even these basic rules are subject to cultural interpretation, and a client may not feel understood if an interviewer unknowingly communicates disinterest through body language. Furthermore, the client's body language can be misinterpreted by an interviewer whose knowledge of the client's cultural background is deficient.

Vocal Qualities

Skilled interviewers have mastered the subtleties of the **vocal qualities** of language—not just the words but how those words sound to the client's ears. They use pitch, tone, volume, and fluctuation in their own voices to let clients know that their words and feelings are deeply appreciated. And these interviewers also attend closely to the vocal qualities of their clients.

Verbal Tracking

Effective interviewers are able to repeat key words and phrases back to their clients to assure the clients that they have been accurately heard. Interviewers don't do this in a mechanical way; instead, they weave the clients' language into their own. In addition, interviewers skilled at **verbal tracking** monitor the train of thought implied by clients' patterns of statements and are thus able to shift topics smoothly rather than abruptly.

Referring to the Client by the Proper Name

It sounds simple enough, but using the client's name correctly is essential (Fontes, 2008). Inappropriately using nicknames or shortening names (e.g., calling Benjamin "Benji"), omitting a "middle" name that is in fact an essential part of the first name (e.g., calling John Paul "John"), or addressing a client by first name rather than a title followed by surname (e.g., addressing Ms. Washington as "Latrice") are presumptuous mistakes that can jeopardize the client's sense of comfort with the interviewer. Especially with clients of certain ethnicities or ages, the misuse of names in this way may be disrespectful and may be received as a microaggression (discussed in Chapter 4; Sue, Capodilupo, & Holder, 2008; Sue et al., 2007). The initial interview is an ideal opportunity to ask clients how they would prefer to be addressed and to confirm that it is being done correctly. This gesture in itself can be interpreted by clients as a sign of consideration.

The interviewer should carry out all these attending behaviors naturally and authentically (Ivey et al., 2010). Beginners may need to make deliberate attempts to incorporate such behaviors, but with experience, they should occur more effortlessly. As they do, clients will respond more positively.

Specific examples of the importance of cultural variables to listening during the clinical interview may help illustrate the points above. Compared with traditional Western culture, Chinese culture tends to feature far less eye contact, especially between members of the opposite sex. Eye contact that falls within the normal range among Western individuals may communicate rudeness or sexual desire among Chinese people. Norms for physical touch also differ from one culture to another, with Asian cultures typically incorporating less than European Americans. Thus, a touch on the shoulder, intended and received as innocuous from one European American to another, might be received as inappropriate by an Asian individual. People from diverse cultures have also developed measurable differences in the physical distance or "personal space" they maintain. Individuals of Middle East and Latino/Latina cultures tend to stand or sit closer together, whereas North American and British people tend to maintain more space between themselves. Tendencies such as these represent essential knowledge for the culturally competent interviewer (Ivey et al., 2010; Sue & Sue, 2008).

Components of the Interview

Although interviews may vary drastically according to the setting, purpose, and other factors, several components are universal to interviews: rapport, technique, and conclusions.

Rapport

Rapport refers to a positive, comfortable relationship between interviewer and client. When clients feel a strong sense of rapport with interviewers, they feel that the interviewers have "connected" with them and that the interviewers empathize with their issues. In this situation, clients tend to disclose more information and invest themselves further in the interview process than they might have otherwise.

How can an interviewer establish good rapport with clients? No foolproof technique exists, especially across the culturally, demographically, and diagnostically wide range of clients with whom a clinical psychologist might work. And if the goal is to make the client feel connected and sympathized with, there is no substitute for genuinely connecting and sympathizing with the client. However, there are some specific efforts interviewers can make to enhance the client's experience of rapport.

First, interviewers should make an effort to put the client at ease, especially early in the interview session. For some clients, the first visit to a clinical psychologist can be daunting. They may be fearful about the interview or may be under a misperception of what the session will entail. Engaging in small talk about innocuous topics ("Did you have any trouble finding the office?" or "I haven't been outside in a while—is it still cold out?") for a minute or two at the beginning of the interview can make an initially nervous client feel more comfortable (Othmer & Othmer, 1994). Of course, this small talk should not be excessive, nor should it distract from the purposes of the interview.

Second, interviewers can acknowledge the unique, unusual situation of the clinical interview. From the client's perspective, the interview experience is unlike any other interaction: They are expected to discuss private, difficult, often emotionally charged issues with a person they just met and know very little about. Letting clients know that you recognize their position and appreciate their willingness to participate communicates empathy and enhances rapport. Along the same lines, inviting clients to ask questions about the interview process provides them with a sense of knowledge and control, which can also improve their comfort level (Sommers-Flanagan & Sommers-Flanagan, 2009).

Third, interviewers can enhance rapport by noticing how the client uses language and then following the client's lead. Interviewers should pick up on the client's vocabulary and, as much as possible, speak in similar terms (Othmer & Othmer, 1994). For example, if a client frequently uses visual imagery ("I can't see the forest for the trees," "That's a blind spot for me," etc.), interviewers should make an effort to use visual terminology as well. If they use more tactile, "touch" words ("It feels like everything's slipping through my fingers," "I'm losing my grip," etc.), interviewers should respond accordingly. When a client uses a metaphor, the interviewer can extend it. For example, consider Ian, a full-time undergraduate student with a demanding job, several extracurricular activities, and numerous family obligations. When he describes his anxiety and stress by saying, "It's like I'm juggling, and I can't keep all the balls in the air," the interviewer would establish better rapport by asking, "What if one of the balls fell?" than "What would happen if you failed in one of your responsibilities?" Clients whose interviewers literally "speak their language" tend to feel relaxed and understood.

Technique

If rapport is *how* an interviewer *is* with clients, **technique** is *what* an interviewer *does* with clients. These are the tools in the interviewer's toolbox, including questions, responses, and other specific actions.

● ● ● BOX 8.1 ● ● ●

Considering Culture

Communication Across Cultures

Members of some cultures tend to exhibit identifiably distinct communication behaviors. Interviewers should accept this concept generally, but they should also be aware of as many of these distinct communication tendencies as possible.

Sue and Sue (2008) identify some of these variables in communication style and describe how they differ across ethnicities. In terms of speaking volume, Asian Americans and

Hispanic Americans tend to speak more softly than whites. Whites, in turn, tend to speak more quickly than some other cultural groups, such as Native Americans. African Americans tend to maintain more direct eye contact when speaking than when listening, whereas the opposite is true for whites. Native Americans often display an indirect gaze during conversation, whereas Asian Americans are inclined to avoid eye contact when speaking to people of higher status (including, possibly, the interviewer). And when we consider the amount of time before responding, African Americans and whites are likely to respond rather quickly, whereas Native Americans, Asian Americans, and Hispanic Americans may demonstrate a mild delay.

But ethnicity is not the only characteristic on which communication differences may center. Mio, Barker-Hackett, and Tumambing (2009) and Wood (1994, 1999) highlight the observable and common differences in speaking style between men and women. Men tend to use talk to assert themselves, promote their ideas, and achieve goals, whereas women are more likely to use talk to build rapport and sustain relationships. Women are apt to value self-disclosure for the closeness it brings; men are apt to believe that self-disclosure increases vulnerability. When men use speech to help others, the help is likely to take the form of advice or problem solving. In contrast, when women use speech to help others, the help is likely to take the form of empathy or understanding of emotions.

Any or all of these differences could be among the cultural factors of interest to the clinical interviewer. Imagine, for example, that Dr. Ryan, a clinical psychologist, was to conduct clinical interviews of five clients: a Hispanic American woman, an African American man, an Asian American woman, a Native American man, and a white woman. How crucial is it for Dr. Ryan to have some appreciation of ethnicity- and gender-related communication tendencies? As each interview ends, how might Dr. Ryan's conclusions depend on this appreciation of communication tendencies?

Directive Versus Nondirective Styles

Interviewers who use a **directive** style get exactly the information they need by asking clients specifically for it. Directive questions tend to be targeted toward specific pieces of information, and client responses are typically brief, sometimes as short as a single word (e.g., "yes" or "no"). On the other hand, interviewers who use a **nondirective** style allow the client to determine the course of the interview. Without direction from the interviewer, a client may choose to spend a lot of time on some topics and none on others.

Certainly, both directive and nondirective approaches play an important role in interviewing. Direct questioning can provide crucial data that clients may not otherwise choose to discuss:

important historical information ("How often have you attempted suicide in the past?"; "Is there a history of schizophrenia in your family?"), the presence or absence of a particular symptom of a disorder ("How many hours per day do you typically sleep?"), frequency of behaviors ("How often have you had panic attacks?"), and duration of a problem ("How long has your son had problems with hyperactivity?"), among other information. For example, imagine Dr. Molina interviewing Raymond, a client whose presenting problem is depressive in nature. If Dr. Molina directly inquires about symptoms and duration—"When did you first notice these feelings of sadness? Has your weight changed during that time? Do you feel fatigued? Do you have trouble concentrating?"—Dr. Molina will be sure to gather information essential for diagnosis.

Indirect questioning, conversely, can provide crucial information that interviewers may not otherwise know to inquire about. If, instead of the direct questions listed above, Dr. Molina asks Raymond, "Can you tell me more about your feelings of sadness?" Raymond's response may not specifically mention how long the symptoms have been present or refer to each individual criterion for major depression, dysthymia, or other related disorders. However, Dr. Molina's indirect question does allow Raymond to expand on anything he believes is essential, including symptoms, duration, background data, or other elements that may prove to be extremely relevant (Morrison, 2008).

Both directive and nondirective approaches have shortcomings as well, especially when an interviewer relies too heavily on either one. Sometimes, directive approaches can sacrifice rapport in favor of information. In other words, interviewers who are overly directive may leave clients feeling as though they didn't have a chance to express themselves or explain what they thought was important. Although nondirective interviewing can facilitate rapport, it can fall short in terms of gathering specific information. Interviewers who are overly nondirective may finish an interview without specific data that is necessary for a valid diagnosis, conceptualization, or recommendation.

Perhaps the best strategy regarding directive and nondirective interviewing is one that involves balance and versatility (Morrison, 2008). At the outset of the interview, it may be wise to allow clients to speak freely to communicate what they think is most important. Even without direction from the interviewer, most clients will nonetheless address a number of direct questions that the interviewer might have asked. Later in the session, the interviewer can become more directive, asking the remaining targeted questions and soliciting more limited answers (e.g., yes/no, specific factual information) from clients.

Specific Interviewer Responses

Ultimately, interviewing technique consists of what the interviewer chooses to say. The interviewer's questions and comments can span a wide range and serve many purposes. There are numerous common categories of interviewer responses: open- and closed-ended questions, clarification, confrontation, paraphrasing, reflection of feeling, and summarizing (Othmer & Othmer, 1994; Sommers-Flanagan & Sommers-Flanagan, 2009).

Open- and Closed-Ended Questions

Whether a question is open- or closed-ended can have great impact on the information a client provides an interviewer. For example, consider a clinical psychologist interviewing Brianna, a 24-year-old outpatient client who mentioned in her initial phone call that she thinks she may be bulimic. An **open-ended question,** such as, "Can you please tell me more about the eating problems you mentioned on the phone?" may take the interview in a different direction than a **closed-ended question,** such as, "How many times per week do you binge and purge?" "Which purging methods do you use—vomiting, exercise, nausea?" or "Have you been diagnosed with an eating disorder in the past?" Open-ended questions allow for individualized and spontaneous responses from clients. These responses tend to be relatively long, and although they may include a lot of information relevant to the client, they may lack details that are important to the clinical psychologist. Closed-ended questions allow for far less elaboration and self-expression by the client but yield quick and precise answers. Indeed, open-ended questions are the building blocks of the nondirective interviewing style described above, whereas the directive interviewing style typically consists of closed-ended questions.

● ● ● BOX 8.2 ● ● ●

Metaphorically Speaking

If You've Taken Multiple Choice, True/False, and Essay Exams, You Understand Open- and Closed-Ended Interview Questions

As you are surely well aware by this point in your academic career, there is a big difference between multiple choice/true-false (MC/TF) exams and essay exams. MC/TF questions usually target a specific piece of information, and students' responses are restricted (in most cases, to a single word or letter). There are usually more items on an MC/TF exam than on an essay exam, because each MC/TF question is brief and of limited scope. As a student, when you take an MC/TF exam, you are providing your teacher with the units of knowledge that the teacher has deemed important.

Essay exams are different in that they allow you to "show what you know" in a more unrestricted way. Although you may or may not provide the specific information that the teacher is looking

(Continued)

(Continued)

for, you nonetheless choose what you think is most important in responding to the questions. The number of essay questions is typically small, since they allow for longer, more expansive answers. The scope of essay questions is typically more broad than that of MC/TF questions.

Closed-ended interview questions are quite similar to MC/TF questions, whereas open-ended interview questions are quite similar to essay exam questions. Closed-ended questions (and the structured interviews in which they are prominently featured) are more targeted; elicit brief, pointed responses; and allow for less elaboration. They usually appear in long series, and they reflect the specific topics that the interviewer considers most relevant. Open-ended questions (and the unstructured interviews in which they tend to appear) are less focused and allow for more free-form responses. Clients determine the content of these responses according to the topics they believe are most relevant. There are usually a relatively small number of open-ended questions, since they can elicit lengthy responses.

One important point about this metaphor is that as the interviewer, your position is parallel to that of the teacher, not the student. In other words, as students, you are accustomed to answering test questions, but as interviewers, your task is to design test questions. In your opinion, what are the advantages and disadvantages from the teacher's perspective of MC/TF and essay exams? If you were the teacher, would one type of exam question (MC/TF or essay) tend to produce more valid assessments of your students' knowledge than the other? If you were an interviewer, would one type of interview question (open- or closed-ended) tend to produce more valid assessments of your clients than the other? What about combining the two types of questions?

Clarification

The purpose of a **clarification** question is to make sure the interviewer has an accurate understanding of the client's comments. Clarification questions not only enhance the interviewer's ability to "get it," they also communicate to the client that the interviewer is actively listening and processing what the client says. For example, with Brianna (the client with bulimic symptoms described above), the interviewer may at one point say, "You mentioned that a few months ago you started exercising excessively after eating large amounts of food but that you've never made yourself vomit—do I have that right?" or "I want to make sure I'm understanding this correctly—did you mention that you've been struggling with eating-related issues for about 6 months?" Either of these questions would allow Brianna to confirm or correct the interviewer so that ultimately the client is correctly understood.

Confrontation

Interviewers use **confrontation** when they notice discrepancies or inconsistencies in a client's comments. Confrontations can be similar to clarifications, but they focus on apparently contradictory information provided by clients. For example, an interviewer might say to Brianna, "Earlier, you mentioned that you had been happy with your body and weight as a teenager, but then a few minutes ago you mentioned that during high school you felt fat in comparison with many of your friends. I'm a bit confused."

Paraphrasing

Unlike clarifying or confronting, paraphrasing is not prompted by the interviewer's need to resolve or clarify what a client has said. Instead, **paraphrasing** is used simply to assure clients that they are being accurately heard. When interviewers paraphrase, they typically restate the content of clients' comments, using similar language. So if Brianna mentions, "I only binge when I'm alone," the interviewer might immediately respond with a statement such as, "You only binge when no one else is around." A paraphrase usually doesn't break new ground; instead, it maintains the conversation by assuring the client that the interviewer is paying attention and comprehending.

Reflection of Feeling

Whereas a paraphrase echoes the client's words, a **reflection of feeling** echoes the client's emotions. Reflections of feeling are intended to make clients feel that their emotions are recognized, even if their comments did not explicitly include labels of their feelings. For example, if Brianna's comment above ("I only binge when I'm alone") was delivered with a tone and body language that communicated shame—her hand covering her face, her voice quivering, and her eyes looking downward—the interviewer might respond with a statement like, "You don't want anyone to see you binging—do you feel embarrassed about it?" Unlike paraphrasing, reflecting a client's feelings often involves an inference by the interviewer about the emotions underlying the client's words.

Summarizing

At certain points during the interview—most often at the end—the interviewer may choose to summarize the client's comments. **Summarizing** usually involves tying together various topics that may have been discussed, connecting statements that may have been made at different points, and identifying themes that have recurred during the interview. Like many of the other responses described above, summarizing lets clients know that they have been understood but in a more comprehensive, integrative way than, say, paraphrasing single statements. After a full interview with Brianna, an interviewer may summarize by offering statements along the lines of, "It seems as though you are acknowledging that your binging and purging have become significant problems in recent months, and while you've kept it to yourself and you may feel ashamed about it, you're willing to discuss it here with me and you want to work toward improving it." An accurate summarization conveys to the client that the interviewer has a good grasp on the "big picture."

Conclusions

Typically, clinical interviews involve a **conclusion** of some kind made by the interviewer. The conclusion can take a number of different forms, depending on the type of interview, the client's problem, the setting, or other factors. In some cases, the conclusion can be essentially similar to a summarization, as described above. Or the interviewer might be able to go a step further by providing an initial conceptualization of the client's problem that incorporates a greater degree of detail than a brief summarization statement. In some situations, the conclusion of the interview may consist of a specific diagnosis made by the interviewer on the basis of the client's response to questions about specific criteria. Or the conclusion may involve recommendations. These recommendations might include outpatient or inpatient treatment, further evaluation (by another psychologist, psychiatrist, or health professional), or any number of other options.

Pragmatics of the Interview

Web Link 8.2
Effects of note-taking on clients

The interviewer encounters quite a few decisions long before the client arrives for the interview. Many of these decisions involve the setting in which the interview will take place and the professional behaviors the interviewer plans to use during the interview itself.

Note Taking

Should an interviewer take notes during an interview? There is little consensus about note taking among clinical psychologists. Some write profusely during interviews, filling pages with observations of their clients and selected snippets of the conversation. Others choose to take no notes at all during the session, although they may write what they recall soon after the interview ends (Greenson & Jaffe, 2004; Hickling, Hickling, Sison, & Radetsky, 1984).

There are good reasons for taking notes. Written notes are certainly more reliable than the interviewer's memory. Many clients will expect the interviewer to take notes and may feel as though their words will soon be forgotten if the interviewer is not taking notes. On the other hand, there are also drawbacks to taking notes. The process of note taking can be a distraction, both for the interviewer, who may fail to notice important client behaviors while looking down to write, and for the client, who may feel that the interviewer's notebook is an obstacle to rapport. Some interviewers aim for a middle ground between no notes and excessive notes, such that they jot down the most essential highlights of an interview but prevent the note-taking process from disrupting the conversation or their attention toward the client. In some clinical situations, interviewers may be wise to explain their note-taking behavior to clients. In particular, a client-centered rationale for the note-taking behavior—"I'm taking notes because I want to make sure I have a good record of what you have told me" or "I don't take notes during interviews because I don't want anything to distract either of us from our conversation"—may enhance rapport between interviewer and client (Fontes, 2008; Sommers-Flanagan & Sommers-Flanagan, 2009).

Photo 8.2 In your opinion, what are the most important reasons for and against note taking during clinical interviews?

Audio and Video Recordings

Written notes are not the only way of documenting an interview. Clinical psychologists may prefer to audio- or video-record the session. Unlike note taking, recording a client's interview requires that the interviewer obtain written permission from the client. While obviously providing a full record of the entire session, recordings can, with some clients, hinder openness and willingness to disclose information. As with note taking, an explanation of the rationale for the recording, as well as its intended use (e.g., review by the interviewer or a supervisor) and a date by which it will be erased or destroyed, is typically appreciated by the client.

The Interview Room

What should the interview room look like? In truth, there is tremendous variability between the rooms in which clinical psychologists conduct interviews. The size of the room, its furnishings, and its decor are among the features that may differ. As a general rule, "when choosing a room [for interviews], it is useful to strike a balance between professional formality and casual comfort" (Sommers-Flanagan & Sommers-Flanagan, 2009, p. 31). That is, the interview room should subtly convey the message to the client that the clinical interview is a professional activity but one in which warmth and comfort are high priorities.

As a specific example, consider seating arrangements, one of the many features of interview rooms that may vary. There are quite a few options: the traditional (and increasingly rare) psychoanalytic arrangement in which the client lies on a couch while the interviewer sits in a chair, interviewer and client sitting face-to-face, interviewer and client in chairs at an angle between 90° and 180°, and others. A table or desk may be positioned between the chairs, small side tables may accompany each chair, or the chairs may have no furniture between

Photo 8.3 The interview room itself—its decor, furnishings, style, size, etc.—can influence the client's level of comfort and ultimately the success of the interview. If you were a clinical psychologist, what priorities would you have regarding the design of your office?

them at all. And depending on the setting, the chairs themselves may run the gamut of anything available at office- or home-furniture stores. As long as the interview room facilitates the fundamental goals of the interview, such as gathering information and building rapport in a private setting free of interruptions, its purpose is well served (Sommers-Flanagan & Sommers-Flanagan, 2009).

Devlin and Nasar (2012; see also Nasar & Devlin, 2011) have surveyed both therapists and nonprofessionals regarding the impressions that clinicians' offices can make on clients. They showed participants 30 different photographs of actual clinicians' offices—the rooms where interviews (and psychotherapy) take place—and asked them to rate the rooms in a variety of ways. Results indicated that the most preferred offices were the ones that were orderly rather than messy and "soft" (with comfortable seats, decorative rugs, muted lighting, art, and plants) rather than "hard" (sparsely furnished, institutional, or overly modern). Additionally, more spacious, uncluttered offices were rated more positively than offices that were cramped and featured disordered piles of papers and tangles of electric cords. Although individual responses may certainly differ between clients, such studies indicate that decisions clinicians make about the rooms where they conduct interviews and other clinical services can be quite important.

When making decisions related to the decor of an office, clinical psychologists usually steer clear of overtly personal items such as family photos, souvenirs, and memorabilia. Such items might be inconsistent with the professional ambiance that the interview room should exude, and, perhaps more important, they can influence the content of the interview in some cases. For example, consider Rochelle and Javon, a married couple seeking help from Dr. Warner for relationship problems due to infertility. A prominent photo of Dr. Warner's own infant son or daughter may evoke feelings in this couple that would alter the course of the interview. Rochelle or Javon may experience envy or resentment or assume that Dr. Warner may be unable to empathize fully with their difficulties, and these feelings may impair the interview process.

Confidentiality

When clients enter the interview room, they may have inaccurate assumptions about the **confidentiality** of the ensuing discussion. Many people incorrectly assume that any session with a psychologist is absolutely confidential (Miller & Thelen, 1986), when in fact there are some situations that require the psychologist to break confidentiality. These situations are typically defined by state law and often involve the psychologist discovering during a session that the client intends to seriously harm someone (self or others) or that ongoing child abuse is occurring. (These exceptions to confidentiality are discussed in greater detail in Chapter 5, "Ethical Issues in Clinical Psychology.") Some clients may make the opposite mistake, wrongly assuming that their relatives, supervisors, or others will have access to their interview records, and as a result may choose to disclose very little about their problems.

To inform their clients about confidentiality, and especially to correct any misconceptions such as those described above, interviewers should routinely explain policies regarding confidentiality as early as possible. Such explanations should be consistent with state law and professional ethics and provided in writing, with ample opportunity for oral discussion offered as well. Psychologists who discuss confidentiality and its limits with interview clients demonstrate competent and ethical practice (American Psychological Association, 2002).

Types of Interviews

Clinical interviews take on different forms according to the demands of the situation, which may depend on the setting, the client's presenting problem, and the issues the interview is intended to address. In actual practice, there are countless unique, idiosyncratic varieties of interviews, but most fall into a few broad categories: intake interviews, diagnostic interviews, mental status exams, and crisis interviews.

Intake Interviews

The purpose of the **intake interview** is essentially to determine whether to "intake" the client to the setting where the interview is taking place. In other words, the intake interview determines whether the client needs treatment; if so, what form of treatment is needed (inpatient, outpatient, specialized provider, etc.); and whether the current facility can provide that treatment or the client should be referred to a more suitable facility.

Intake interviews typically involve detailed questioning about the presenting complaint. For example, consider Julia, a 45-year-old client who arrives for an intake interview at an outpatient community mental health center and describes "hearing voices." Dr. Epps, the clinical psychologist conducting the intake interview, is likely to ask questions about the frequency, intensity, and duration of Julia's psychotic symptoms, as well as symptoms of other conditions that Julia may exhibit. Dr. Epps would also closely observe Julia during the interview and note any relevant behaviors. Questions about Julia's personal history, especially the previous existence of this or other psychological or psychiatric problems, would also be an important part of the intake interview. At the conclusion of the interview, Dr. Epps would use all information solicited to decide whether Julia's problems would be best treated at this community mental health center and, if so, recommend a particular mode or frequency of treatment. If not, Dr. Epps would provide Julia with referrals to other treatment providers, including inpatient or outpatient settings as appropriate.

Diagnostic Interviews

As the name indicates, the purpose of the **diagnostic interview** is to diagnose. At the end of a well-conducted diagnostic interview, the interviewer is able to confidently and accurately assign *Diagnostic and Statistical Manual of Mental Disorders* (DSM) diagnoses to the client's problems. When an interview yields a valid, specific diagnosis, the effectiveness of the recommendations and subsequent treatment may be increased.

If the purpose of the diagnostic interview is to produce a diagnosis, it would make sense for the diagnostic interview to include questions that relate to the criteria of *DSM* disorders. How directly should the questions reflect the diagnostic criteria? Some clinical psychologists believe that the questions should essentially replicate the *DSM* criteria; after all, if our profession follows a diagnostic manual with disorders defined by meticulous lists of symptoms, what better way to reach a diagnosis than to ask directly about each symptom? Other clinical psychologists believe that every question in a diagnostic interview need not be coupled with a specific *DSM* diagnostic criterion. These clinical psychologists prefer a more flexible interview style in which they choose or create questions as they move through the interview, and they use inference rather than absolute fact to make diagnostic decisions. In other words, some clinical psychologists prefer structured interviews, while others prefer unstructured interviews.

Structured Interviews Versus Unstructured Interviews

A **structured interview** is a predetermined, planned sequence of questions that an interviewer asks a client. Structured interviews are constructed for particular purposes, usually diagnostic. An **unstructured interview**, in contrast, involves no predetermined or planned questions. In unstructured interviews, interviewers improvise: They determine their questions on the spot, seeking information that they decide is relevant during the course of the interview (Maruish, 2008; O'Brien & Tabaczynski, 2007).

Structured interviews possess a number of advantages over unstructured interviews, particularly from a scientific or empirical perspective (Sommers-Flanagan & Sommers-Flanagan, 2009; Villa & Reitman, 2007):

- Structured interviews produce a diagnosis based explicitly on *DSM* criteria, reducing reliance on subjective factors such as the interviewer's clinical judgment and inference, which can be biased or otherwise flawed.

- Structured interviews tend to be highly reliable, in that two interviewers using the same structured interview will come to the same diagnostic conclusions far more often than two interviewers using unstructured interviews. Overall, they are more empirically sound than unstructured interviews.
- Structured interviews are standardized and typically uncomplicated in terms of administration.

On the other hand, structured interviews have numerous disadvantages as well:

- The format of structured interviews is usually rigid, which can inhibit rapport and the client's opportunity to elaborate or explain as he or she wishes.
- Structured interviews typically don't allow for inquiries into important topics that may not be directly related to *DSM* criteria, such as relationship issues, personal history, and problems that fall below or between *DSM* diagnostic categories.
- Structured interviews often require a more comprehensive list of questions than is clinically necessary, which lengthens the interview.

⊕ **Web Link 8.3**

SCID

In the early days of clinical psychology, structured interviews were uncommon, but in recent years they have become more accepted and in many settings preferred. There are a number of published structured interviews that focus on specific diagnostic issues, such as the Anxiety Disorders Interview Schedule-Revised (Di Nardo & Barlow, 1988), the Acute Stress Disorder Interview (Bryant, Harvey, Dang, & Sackville, 1998), and the Asperger Syndrome Diagnostic Interview (Gillberg, Gillberg, Rastam, & Wentz, 2001). However, especially in recent years, the most prominent structured interview has been the more wide-ranging **Structured Clinical Interview for *DSM-IV* Disorders (SCID)** (soon to be revised for *DSM-5*) (First, Gibbon, Spitzer, Williams, & Benjamin, 1997; First, Spitzer, Gibbon, & Williams, 1997a, 1997c).

The SCID was created by some of the leading authors of recent editions of the *DSM,* and it is essentially a comprehensive list of questions that directly ask about the specific symptoms of the many disorders included in the *DSM-IV.* For the most part, each question in the SCID has a one-to-one correspondence with a specific criterion of a *DSM-IV* diagnosis. In fact, the SCID administration booklet is structured in a two-column format such that each *DSM* symptom appears parallel to a question specifically about it. As an example, one of the specific *DSM-IV* criteria for obsessive-compulsive disorder is "recurrent and intrusive distressing recollections of the event, including images, thoughts, or perceptions"; the SCID, next to this criteria, includes the question, "Did you think about [TRAUMA] when you did not want to or did thoughts about [TRAUMA] come to you suddenly when you didn't want them to?" (First, Spitzer, Gibbon, & Williams, 1997b, p. 74). Like this one, most SCID questions are designed to elicit "yes" or "no" answers, and clients can be asked to elaborate briefly when they say "yes."

The SCID is modular, which means that interviewers can choose only those modules (or sections) of the SCID that are relevant for a particular clinical case and omit the other modules. For example, imagine that Dr. Rodriguez is interviewing Ethan, an adult client in an outpatient clinic. In an initial phone call to the clinic and on a brief waiting-room screening form, Ethan has indicated that his problem involves a severe phobia of dogs. Dr. Rodriguez may choose to administer the anxiety module of the SCID but to omit the modules that are irrelevant to Ethan's problems, such as the module on psychotic disorders. One benefit of this modular design is a reduction in the time needed to complete the SCID. Of course, if an interviewer prefers to administer the entire SCID, no module omission is required.

Whereas some clinical psychologists—namely, researchers and those clinicians who emphasize the empirical foundations of clinical psychology—use structured interviews such as the SCID regularly, others use unstructured interviews regularly. In actual practice, quite a few clinical psychologists blend these approaches to conduct an interview that may be labeled as a partially structured or **semistructured interview** (Maruish, 2008; Nock, Holmberg, Photos, & Michel, 2007). Such interviews may include unstructured segments, typically at the beginning of the interview, which allow clients to describe in their own words the current problem and any relevant history. (The SCID, actually, includes an "overview" section at the outset that is intended to fulfill this purpose.) After this unstructured segment, an interviewer may ask a succession of targeted questions to address specific diagnostic criteria.

Photo 8.4 The mental status exam is commonly used in hospitals and medical centers to quickly estimate a client's current level of functioning.

Mental Status Exam

The **mental status exam** is employed most often in medical settings. Its primary purpose is to quickly assess how the client is functioning at the time of the evaluation. The mental status exam does not delve into the client's personal history, nor is it designed to determine a *DSM* diagnosis definitively. Instead, its yield is usually a brief paragraph that captures the psychological and cognitive processes of an individual "right now"—like a psychological snapshot (Lukas, 1993; Morrison, 2008; Sommers-Flanagan & Sommers-Flanagan, 2009; Strub & Black, 1977).

The format of the mental status exam is not completely standardized, so it may be administered differently by various health professionals. (Psychiatrists, in addition to clinical psychologists and other mental health professionals, often use the mental status exam.) Although specific questions and techniques may vary, the following main categories are typically covered:

- Appearance
- Behavior/psychomotor activity
- Attitude toward examiner
- Affect and mood
- Speech and thought
- Perceptual disturbances
- Orientation to person, place, and time
- Memory and intelligence
- Reliability, judgment, and insight

Because of its lack of standardization, two interviewers who use the mental status exam may ask different questions within the same category. For example, in the "memory and intelligence" category, the interviewer may assess memory by asking the client about schools attended or age differences with siblings and assess intelligence by asking the client to count backward by 7 from 100, to recall a brief series of numbers or words, or to indicate the direction traveled between two cities. The mental status exam is not intended as a meticulous, comprehensive diagnostic tool. Instead, it is intended for brief, flexible administration, primarily in hospitals and medical centers, requiring no manual or other accompanying materials.

Photo 8.5 Crisis interviews are unique among clinical interviews because they typically involve not only assessment of the client's problems but immediate intervention as well.

Crisis Interviews

The **crisis interview** is a special type of clinical interview and can be uniquely challenging for the interviewer. Crisis interviews have purposes that extend beyond mere assessment. They are designed not only to assess a problem demanding urgent attention (most often, clients actively considering suicide or another act of harm toward self or others) but also to provide immediate and effective intervention for that problem. Crisis interviews can be conducted in person but also take place often on the telephone via suicide hotlines, crisis lines, and similar services.

Quickly establishing rapport and expressing empathy for a client in crisis, especially a suicidal client, are key components of the interview. Providing an immediate, legitimate alternative to suicide can enable the client to endure this period of very high distress and reach a later point in time when problems may feel less severe or solutions may be more viable. Sometimes, interviewers in these situations ask clients to sign or verbally agree to suicide prevention contracts. These contracts essentially require the client to contact the interviewer before committing any act of self-harm.

When interviewing an actively suicidal person, five specific issues should be assessed (adapted from Sommers-Flanagan & Sommers-Flanagan, 2009):

- *How depressed is the client?* Unrelenting, long-term depression and a lack of hope for the future indicate high risk.
- *Does the client have suicidal thoughts?* If such thoughts have occurred, it is important to inquire about their frequency and intensity.
- *Does the client have a suicide plan?* Some clients may have suicidal thoughts but no specific plan. If the client does have a plan, its feasibility (the client's access to the means of self-harm, such as a gun, pills, etc.), its lethality, and the presence of others (family, friends) who might prevent it are crucial factors.
- *How much self-control does the client currently appear to have?* Questions about similarly stressful periods in the client's past, or about moments when self-harm was previously contemplated, can provide indirect information about the client's self-control in moments of crisis.
- *Does the client have definite suicidal intentions?* Direct questions may be informative, but other indications such as giving away one's possessions, putting one's affairs in order, and notifying friends and family about suicide plans can also imply the client's intentions.

Cultural Components

Appreciating the Cultural Context

All human behaviors, including the words and actions of a client during a clinical interview, take place in a cultural context. It is imperative that the interviewer retain this perspective when observing and listening to the client. Interviewers should possess sufficient knowledge about culture—their own as well as their clients'—to understand the meaning of interview material within the appropriate cultural context. Behaviors, thoughts, or emotions that might be viewed as abnormal or pathological by some cultural standards may in fact be normal according to others, and interviewers should be careful not to overpathologize by imposing their own cultural values. Clinical psychologists should make efforts, in interviews and other interactions with clients, to appreciate clients from a perspective that takes into account the clients' own cultures.

As an example, consider Paula, a 60-year-old Jewish mother of two grown children, who is being interviewed by Dr. McMillan, a clinical psychologist whose own religious background is Catholic. Paula explains her anxiety and depression as partially stemming from her son's recent announcement that his own 10-year-old son (Paula's grandson), unlike the generations before him, will not study Hebrew and become a bar mitzvah. Although the bar mitzvah (a traditional Jewish ritual symbolizing entry into adulthood that culminates in reading Hebrew from the Torah at age 13—or at age 12 for girls, for whom it is called a bat mitzvah) may not be a milestone for Dr. McMillan personally, it is vital that Dr. McMillan recognize its significance within Jewish culture and to Paula in particular. If Dr. McMillan fails to appreciate the significance of the bar or bat mitzvah in the Jewish community, Paula's problems may be misinterpreted or underestimated. And as a result, during her interview, Paula may feel misunderstood and rapport may be damaged.

Of course, the culturally competent interviewer should not assume that every person from a culture holds identical values. As a group, members of a culture may tend to act, believe, or feel a certain way, but tremendous variability often exists among individuals within that cultural group. Thus, in the above example, Dr. McMillan should have some idea of the meaning that Jews attach to the bar or bat mitzvah but not rigidly assume that Paula's individual views are necessarily prototypical.

Religion, of course, is just one of many components of culture that may be important to a particular client (Grieger, 2008). Box 8.3 provides a broad list of questions interviewers can use to inquire about clients' cultural backgrounds (Fontes, 2008).

● ● ● BOX 8.3 ● ● ●

Interview Questions to Consider When Inquiring About the Cultural Backgrounds of Clients

1. Where were you born?
2. Who do you consider family?
3. What was the first language you learned to speak?
4. Tell me about the other language(s) you speak.
5. What language or languages are spoken in your home?
6. What is your religion? How observant are you in regard to practicing that religion?

(Continued)

(Continued)

    7. What activities do you enjoy when you are not working?

    8. How do you identify yourself culturally?

    9. What aspects of [client's self-reported cultural background] are most important to you?

    10. How would you describe your home and neighborhood?

    11. Who do you usually turn to for help when facing a problem?

    12. What are your goals for this interview today?

Source: Fontes (2008, p. 31).

Acknowledging Cultural Differences

When cultural differences exist between interviewer and client—which happens quite frequently, especially if we define culture by ethnicity, gender, religion, age, or a number of other variables—it is often wise for the interviewer to acknowledge these differences openly. Open, respectful discussion of cultural variables can enhance rapport, increase the client's willingness to share information, and help the interviewer gain a more accurate understanding of the client's issues (Sommers-Flanagan & Sommers-Flanagan, 2009). Without it, the interview process—and the assessment process more broadly—can prove invalid and can lead to culturally insensitive treatment (Ridley, Tracy, Pruitt-Stephens, Wimsatt, & Beard, 2008).

In many cases, it is appropriate for the interviewer to inquire directly about cultural background to become more informed about the client's perspective. Of course, such questions (as listed in Box 8.3) should be asked sensitively rather than callously. Clients can be an enlightening source of information about their own cultural backgrounds; however, the interviewer should not lean on them too strongly. The purpose of the interview, after all, is not for the client to educate the interviewer. Interviewers should continually seek other sources of information about specific cultures—written, experiential, or otherwise—to increase their cultural awareness. In the example of Paula (above), it would be preferable if Dr. McMillan came into the interview already having a sense of what a bar mitzvah is and what it typically means to Jewish people. If he made it clear to Paula that he had this basic knowledge but asked her about some of the finer points or some of her specific feelings about it, she might admire his efforts. On the other hand, if he entered the interview completely ignorant and insisted that Paula explain the basics to him—what a bar mitzvah is, when it takes place, what it means—she may perceive his questions as burdensome, and the interview may suffer as a result.

CHAPTER SUMMARY

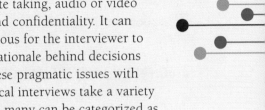

Like any assessment technique, the clinical interview should be reliable, valid, and clinically useful. The clinical interview is a core element of psychological assessment. Skillful interviewers are adept at quieting their internal self-talk to enhance attentiveness; being self-aware, particularly regarding the responses they tend to elicit from others; and developing positive working relationships. They establish rapport via a respectful, caring attitude and attend to subtle aspects of communication such as body language and vocal qualities in their clients. Skillful interviewers are also proficient with specific interviewing techniques, including open- and closed-ended questions, clarifications, confrontations, paraphrasing, reflection of feeling, summarizing, and forming conclusions. There are numerous pragmatic issues relevant to the clinical interview, including note taking, audio or video recording, and confidentiality. It can be advantageous for the interviewer to discuss the rationale behind decisions regarding these pragmatic issues with clients. Clinical interviews take a variety of forms, but many can be categorized as intake interviews, diagnostic interviews, mental status exams, or crisis interviews. Structured clinical interviews such as the SCID tend to have strong reliability and validity but may sacrifice rapport; unstructured clinical interviews are more client directed and may facilitate rapport, but their reliability and validity are weaker. Semistructured interviews strike a balance between structured and unstructured approaches. Appreciation of and acknowledgment of multicultural issues enhance any clinical interview and should be a primary goal for all interviewers.

KEY TERMS

CRITICAL THINKING QUESTIONS

1. This chapter describes an interviewer's self-awareness as an important general skill. What steps should clinical psychologists take to become more self-aware?

2. Describe two different client–therapist pairings in which issues of culture might influence the meaning of eye contact or body language in different ways.

3. Considering the wide range of clinical problems that clients might bring to an interview, for which, in your opinion, would direct versus indirect questioning be best suited?

4. If you were a clinical psychologist, would you take notes during a clinical interview? Why or why not?

5. If you were a clinical psychologist, in what situations would you openly acknowledge cultural differences between yourself and an interview client?

STUDENT STUDY SITE RESOURCES

Visit the study site at www.sagepub.com/pomerantz3eupdate for these additional learning tools:

- Self-quizzes
- eFlashcards
- Culture Expert Interviews

- Full-text SAGE journal articles
- Additional web resources
- Mock Assessment Data

CHAPTER SUMMARY VIDEO

QR codes at the end of each chapter link to chapter background videos by the author. Visit http://gettag.mobi using your smartphone browser to download the free Microsoft Tag app. Once installed, scan the tags to go directly to these brief videos. In this video, the author describes his clients' own reaction to his note-taking habits.

CHAPTER
9

Intellectual and Neuropsychological Assessment

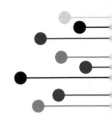

Measuring cognitive performance has been a hallmark of clinical psychology since its origin (Wood, Garb, & Nezworski, 2007). Knowledge of a client's level of cognitive functioning, including both strengths and deficits, can help a clinical psychologist with diagnosis and treatment of many presenting problems. Some assessments, such as those for specific learning disorder (formerly known as learning disabilities), intellectual disability (also known as intellectual developmental disorder, and formerly known as mental retardation), or giftedness, focus on cognitive issues from the start. In other assessments, such as those focusing on mood disorders or disruptive behavior, cognitive tests can provide important contextual information.

This chapter focuses on three types of tests, each related to cognitive functioning in some way but each with a distinct purpose. **Intelligence tests** measure a client's intellectual abilities. **Achievement tests**, in contrast, measure what a client has accomplished with those intellectual abilities. **Neuropsychological tests** focus on issues of cognitive or brain dysfunction, including the effects of brain injuries and illnesses.

Intelligence Testing

Classic Theories of Intelligence

The specific intelligence tests used by contemporary clinical psychologists are rooted in contrasting theories of intelligence. Each of these theories puts forth a different answer to the essential question: What is **intelligence?** Actually, clinical psychologists have never reached a consensus regarding the definition of intelligence. Experts in this area of clinical psychology have emphasized many abilities as central to intelligence: speed of mental processing, sensory capacity, abstract thinking, imagination, adaptability, capacity to learn through experience, memory, reasoning, and inhibition of instinct, to name a few (as summarized by Sternberg, 2000; Sternberg & Grigorenko, 2008; and Wasserman & Tulsky, 2005). In the debate about defining intelligence, perhaps no specific issue has received as much attention as the singular versus plural nature of intelligence. In other words, is intelligence one thing or many things?

Charles Spearman: Intelligence Is One Thing

In the early 1900s, **Charles Spearman** proposed a theory: Intelligence is a singular characteristic. Spearman labeled this characteristic "**g**" for general intelligence and argued that it represented a person's global, overall intellectual ability. His theory was based on research in which he measured many different, specific capabilities of his participants, including academic abilities and sensory-discrimination tasks. The primary finding was a strong correlation between this wide range of abilities, suggesting that a single factor underlies them all. Spearman did acknowledge that more specific abilities ("s") existed, but he argued that they played a relatively minor role in intelligence. Essentially, according to Spearman, intelligence was one thing (Brody, 2000).

Photo 9.1 Clinical psychologists use tests of intelligence, achievement, and neuropsychological functioning for many purposes, such as the assessment of a child exhibiting academic problems.

Louis Thurstone: Intelligence Is Many Things

Louis Thurstone was among the first and the strongest opponents to Spearman's singular theory of intelligence. According to Thurstone, intelligence should not be understood as a single, unified ability but as numerous distinct abilities that have little relationship to one another. Among his other contributions in the first half of the 1900s, Thurstone was a pioneer of the statistical procedure called multiple factor analysis, which enabled him to identify underlying factors in a large data set. When he performed these statistical analyses on examinations of various intellectual abilities, he could have found one dominant factor underlying all abilities. Instead, he found several independent factors. These factors were given labels such as verbal comprehension, numerical ability, spatial reasoning, and memory. The specific names and number of the factors are less important, however, than Thurstone's fundamental point: Intelligence is not one thing; it is many things (Brody, 2000). Thus, according to Thurstone, if you know how capable someone is regarding, say, mathematics, you cannot predict with confidence how capable that person is regarding, say, verbal skills.

Eventually, Spearman and Thurstone each acknowledged the validity of the other's arguments and came to somewhat of a compromise. They settled on a **hierarchical model of intelligence** in which specific abilities ("s") existed and were important, but they were all at least somewhat related to one another and to a global, overall, general intelligence ("g").

More Contemporary Theories of Intelligence

Other theories of intelligence have emerged since the debates between Spearman and Thurstone, most of which provide a fresh perspective on the singular versus plural issue (Brody, 2000; Davidson & Downing, 2000; Nisbett et al., 2012). For example, in the latter half of the 1900s, **James Cattell** proposed two separate intelligences: **fluid intelligence**—the ability to reason when faced with novel problems—and **crystallized intelligence**—the body of knowledge one has accumulated as a result of life experiences. With exactly two very broad categories of intelligence, Cattell's theory falls somewhere between Spearman's theory of a singular intelligence and Thurstone's theory of many intelligences. More recently, new hierarchical models of intelligence have emerged as well, including **John Carroll's (2005) three-stratum theory of intelligence**, in which intelligence operates at three levels: a single "g" at the top, 8 broad factors immediately beneath "g," and more than 60 highly specific abilities beneath these broad factors. This model, like most contemporary models of intelligence, not only acknowledges "g" but also recognizes that more specific abilities exist as well (Wasserman & Tulsky, 2005). As we see in this chapter, most contemporary intelligence tests mirror this view by producing a single overall score—one number to represent how intelligent a person is—in addition to a number of other scores representing more specific abilities. The Wechsler intelligence tests are among these.

⊕ **Web Link 9.1**
John Carroll

••• BOX 9.1 •••

Metaphorically Speaking

If You've Watched Michael Jordan, Then You Understand the Challenges of Defining and Assessing Intelligence

Michael Jordan is undoubtedly one of the greatest basketball players of all time. His five MVP awards and six NBA championships offer indisputable proof. But if we broaden the question—is Michael Jordan a great *athlete?*—we can begin to appreciate some of the challenges in defining ability, whether athletic or intellectual.

In 1993, after 9 extremely successful years in the NBA, Jordan decided (to the surprise of many) to leave basketball and focus on baseball. He signed on with the Birmingham Barons, a Double-A level minor league team, and struggled. His prowess did not easily transfer from the basketball court to the baseball diamond. Instead of the familiar highlights of acrobatic dunks and picturesque jump shots, sports fans saw Jordan flailing at curve balls and misjudging fly balls. His hitting and fielding improved slightly but not enough to advance any closer to the major leagues.

Should we expect that a person who excels at one sport will similarly excel at others? If so, perhaps each of us possesses a general athletic ability that influences our performance at any sport—a lot like Spearman's concept of a general intelligence ("g"). If not, perhaps each of us has a number of specific athletic abilities that are unrelated to one another—a lot like Thurstone's theory of specific ("s"), multiple intelligences.

Which theory does the example of Michael Jordan support? On the one hand, the contrast between Jordan's basketball excellence and baseball mediocrity supports the idea that our abilities are independent. Indeed, in the history of athletics, there have been very few people (e.g., Jim Thorpe, Bo Jackson) who have reached the highest level of multiple sports. On the other hand, despite focusing exclusively on basketball for many years, Jordan was able to, with minimal preparation, step onto a minor league baseball team and at least hold his own. He may not have excelled, but he did achieve some success at a level of baseball—a minor league team just two steps away from the majors—that far exceeds the talents of the vast majority of players. This would suggest that he possesses some fundamental, general athletic ability that applies, to some extent, to any sport. Perhaps Michael Jordan's experiences best support the hierarchical models of ability, which acknowledge a general, across-the-board ability (of athletics or intelligence) as well as more specific talents (basketball vs. baseball, math vs. verbal skills) that are influenced by the general ability but may be somewhat independent as well.

In your personal experience, does athletic ability seem to be one thing or many things? Consider the athletic abilities of people you have known (or perhaps played with or against). Are the best at one sport typically among the best at other sports? What about intellectual ability? Among your friends and family, do people seem to have a singular, general intelligence that influences all their abilities or many distinct intelligences that operate independently?

Wechsler Intelligence Tests

Since **David Wechsler's** earliest attempts to measure intelligence in the early 1900s, the tests that bear his name have risen to prominence among clinical psychologists (Coalson, Raiford, Saklofske, & Weiss, 2010; Goldstein, 2008; Lichtenberger & Kaufman, 2009). There are three separate Wechsler intelligence tests, each the most highly respected and popular among clinical psychologists for its respective age range. The names and current editions of the Wechsler intelligence tests are as follows:

Web Link 9.2
David Wechsler

- Wechsler Adult Intelligence Scale—Fourth Edition (WAIS-IV)
- Wechsler Intelligence Scale for Children—Fourth Edition (WISC-IV)
- Wechsler Preschool and Primary Scale of Intelligence—Third Edition (WPPSI-III)

Web Link 9.3
Site for WAIS-IV

Table 9.1 provides a brief description for each of these Wechsler intelligence tests, as well as the other intelligence, achievement, and neuropsychological tests covered in detail in this chapter.

Collectively, the three Wechsler intelligence tests cover virtually the entire life span. They vary slightly from one another, as necessitated by the demands of measuring intelligence at different ages. And in practical terms, they are indeed separate tests rather than slight variants of one another. (They are purchased as separate kits with separate manuals, answer sheets, materials, etc.) However, the three Wechsler intelligence tests share many fundamental characteristics:

- They yield a single **full-scale intelligence score**, four **index scores**, and about a dozen (give or take a few, depending on optional subtests chosen) specific **subtest scores**. Together, this collection of scores indicates that the Wechsler tests employ a hierarchical model of intelligence (as discussed above), in which the full-scale intelligence score reflects a general, global level of intelligence ("g"), and the index/factor scores and subtest scores represent increasingly specific areas of ability ("s"). These scores allow clinical psychologists to focus broadly or narrowly when making interpretations regarding intellectual ability.

Table 9.1 At-a-Glance Information About the Tests Detailed in This Chapter

	Most Recent Edition	Year Published	Age Range (Years)
Intelligence Tests			
Wechsler Adult Intelligence Scale (WAIS)	IV	2008	16 to 90
Wechsler Intelligence Scale for Children (WISC)	IV	2003	6 to 16
Wechsler Preschool and Primary Scale of Intelligence (WPPSI)	III	2002	2 years and 6 months to 7 years and 3 months
Stanford-Binet Intelligence Scales	V	2003	2 to 85+
Universal Nonverbal Intelligence Test (UNIT)	I	1996	5 to 17
Achievement Tests			
Wechsler Individual Achievement Test (WIAT)	III	2009	4 to 50
Neuropsychological Tests			
Halstead-Reitan Neuropsychological Test Battery (HRB)	I	Varies by test	15+
Bender Visual-Motor Gestalt Test	II	2003	4+

- They are administered one-on-one and face-to-face. In other words, the Wechsler tests cannot be administered to a group of examinees at the same time, nor are they entirely pencil-and-paper tests (e.g., multiple choice, true/false, essay) that examinees simply administer to themselves. Administration of the Wechsler intelligence tests is a structured interpersonal interaction requiring extensive training, typically received during graduate programs in clinical psychology (Raiford, Coalson, Saklofske, & Weiss, 2010).

- Each subtest is brief (lasting about 2–10 minutes) and consists of items that increase in difficulty as the subtest progresses. Most often, the subtests are designed such that examinees continue until they fail a predetermined number of consecutive items (or "max out," to state it informally). The nature of the tasks performed varies widely across the dozen or so subtests but includes both verbal and nonverbal tasks. (More detailed descriptions of the subtests follow.)

- Although each of the three Wechsler tests has a small number of unique subtests, most subtests appear in all three tests and form the core of the Wechsler battery. These common subtests are described in detail in Table 9.2.

- Originally, the Wechsler tests were designed with two categories of subtests: verbal and performance. ("Performance" was essentially equivalent to "nonverbal.") In more recent years, statistical tests including factor analyses have concluded that the subtests don't, in fact, cluster together into those two groups. Instead, they cluster together in four, rather than two, factors. Thus, the original verbal/performance split has been replaced by four factors, each receiving contributions from several subtests (Groth-Marnat, 2009; Weiss, Saklofske, Coalson, & Raiford, 2010). These four factors form the names of the four index scores common to all Wechsler intelligence tests:

  o **Verbal Comprehension Index**—a measure of verbal concept formation and verbal reasoning
  o **Perceptual Reasoning Index** (called Perceptual Organization Index in the WAIS)—a measure of fluid reasoning, spatial processing, and visual-motor integration
  o **Working Memory Index**—a measure of the capacity to store, transform, and recall incoming information and data in short-term memory
  o **Processing Speed Index**—a measure of the ability to process simple or rote information rapidly and accurately

- They feature large, carefully collected sets of **normative data.** That is, the manual for each Wechsler test includes norms collected from about 2,000 people (to be exact, 2,200 for the WAIS-IV, 2,200 for the WISC-IV, and 1,700 for the WPPSI-III). These normative groups closely match recent U.S. Census data in terms of gender, age, race/ethnicity, and geographic region, among other variables (Zhu & Weiss, 2005). So when an examinee takes a Wechsler intelligence test, the examinee's performance is compared with the performance of a large, same-age sample of individuals representing a wide-scale national population.

- The full-scale and index scores generated by the Wechsler tests are "IQ" scores, meaning that they reflect an intelligence "quotient." This quotient is the result of a division problem in which the examinees' raw scores are compared with age-based expectations. For all Wechsler tests, mean IQ scores (full-scale and index) are 100, with a standard deviation of 15. For each subtest, a score of 10 is average, with a standard deviation of 3.

- The Wechsler intelligence tests share a general approach to interpretation of scores. Assessors are instructed to first consider the full-scale IQ score. Next, they move on to

Table 9.2 Subtests Common to Wechsler Tests of Intelligence

Subtest Name	Description of Examinee's Task	Simulated Item(s)
Vocabulary	Orally explain the meaning of a word	• What does "consistent" mean? • What is an "intersection?"
Similarities	Orally explain how two things or concepts are alike	• How are a door and a window alike? • How are success and failure alike?
Information	Orally answer questions focusing on specific items of general knowledge	• On what continent is Spain? • How many cents is a quarter worth?
Comprehension	Orally answer questions about general social principles and social situations	• Why is it important for people to show identification before being allowed to vote? • What are some advantages of using only the minimal amount of water necessary in our homes?
Block Design	Re-create a specific pattern or design of colored blocks	
Picture Completion	View picture of a simple object or scene and identify the important part that is missing	
Matrix Reasoning	View an incomplete matrix and select the missing portion from multiple choices provided	

Subtest Name	Description of Examinee's Task	Simulated Item(s)
Coding	Using pencil and paper, repeatedly copy simple shapes/symbols in appropriate spaces according to a key provided	Key: 1 2 3 4 5 6 7 8 9 with corresponding symbols. Rows: 5 7 3 1 4 2 5 4 1 / 2 4 3 7 5 4 1 6 8 / 7 5 9 1 8 6 3 2 4 (with blank boxes to fill in)
Symbol Search	Scan a group of visual shapes/symbols to determine if target shape(s)/symbol(s) appear in group	Rows of target symbols followed by groups of symbols, each with YES / NO response boxes

interpret each index score in relation to the others and then the pattern of subtest scores. Finally, they note more detailed aspects of the testing, such as observable patterns of behavior that may have contributed to scores or inconsistent performance within a single subtest. Essentially, these successive steps allow the assessor to grasp the "big picture" of the intellectual profile before delving into increasingly detailed levels of analysis (Groth-Marnat, 2009).

- The Wechsler intelligence tests are all backed by very impressive psychometric data. That is, a large number of empirical studies suggest that these tests have the characteristics that clinical psychologists should seek in any test: strong reliability and validity. They measure what they intend to measure, and they do so consistently (Canivez & Watkins, 2010; Groth-Marnat, 2009; Lichtenberger & Kaufman, 2004; Zhu & Weiss, 2005).

- The Wechsler intelligence tests—and most other intelligence tests, for that matter— are used for a wide range of clinical applications, including evaluations that focus on issues of intellectual disability (intellectual developmental disorder), developmental delays, giftedness, educational and vocational planning, school placement and qualification, and other targeted assessment questions (Zhu & Weiss, 2005). They can also be used to provide general intelligence information in broader contexts, including a comprehensive assessment of a client whose presenting problems are more neuropsychological (e.g., Alzheimer's disease), emotional (e.g., mood disorders), or behavioral (e.g., attention-deficit/ hyperactivity disorder [ADHD]).

- Generally, the Wechsler intelligence tests have a number of notable strengths: They have impressive reliability and validity; they feature comprehensive and recent normative data; they cover an extremely wide age range; they provide full-scale, index, and subtest scores that have great clinical utility; and at this point in their history, they are very familiar to most clinical psychologists. On the other hand, these tests have received criticism for some limitations: Some subtests may be culturally loaded or biased, the connection between the tests and day-to-day life (ecological validity) may be limited, and scoring can be complex or subjective on some subtests (Groth-Marnat, 2009; Zhu & Weiss, 2005). On the whole, however, the Wechsler tests are held in high esteem by clinical psychologists.

Stanford-Binet Intelligence Scales—Fifth Edition

The Stanford-Binet intelligence tests have a rich history in clinical psychology. The first editions of the Stanford-Binet intelligence test dominated the field in the early 1900s until Wechsler's tests began to provide competition. Although Wechsler's tests have taken a leading role in recent decades, the Stanford-Binet remains highly respected and offers an approach to assessing intelligence that is both similar to and different from that of Wechsler's tests (Goldstein, 2008).

⊕ Web Link 9.4

Site for SB5

The most recent revision of the Stanford-Binet, the **Stanford-Binet Intelligence Scales—Fifth Edition (SB5)**, is like the Wechsler tests in many ways. It is administered face-to-face and one-on-one. It employs a hierarchical model of intelligence and therefore yields a singular measure of full-scale IQ (or "g"), five factor scores, and many more specific subtest scores. It features the same means (100) and standard deviations (15) as the Wechsler intelligence tests for its full-scale and factor scores. Its psychometric data, including reliability and validity, are similarly strong.

The SB5 differs from the Wechsler tests in some important ways, however. Rather than three separate tests for three different age ranges, the SB5 covers the entire life span (ages 2–85+) as a single test. The normative sample is like those of Wechsler tests in that it matches recent U.S. Census data on important variables, but it additionally includes normative data from individuals with specific relevant diagnoses, including learning problems, intellectual disability (intellectual developmental disorder), and ADHD. Its subtests include extensions at the low and high ends—in other words, a greater number of very easy and very difficult items—as an effort to more accurately assess people at the extremes, including those who may be profoundly mentally retarded or highly gifted (Kamphaus & Kroncke, 2004).

Perhaps the most important difference between the SB5 and the Wechsler tests involves their specific factors and subtests. Whereas the Wechsler tests feature four factors, each of which yields an index score, the SB5 features five, described briefly here:

- **Fluid Reasoning**—the ability to solve novel problems
- **Knowledge**—general information accumulated over time via personal experiences, including education, home, and environment
- **Quantitative Reasoning**—the ability to solve numerical problems
- **Visual-Spatial Processing**—the ability to analyze visually presented information, including relationships between objects, spatial orientation, assembling pieces to make a whole, and detecting visual patterns
- **Working Memory**—the ability to hold and transform information in short-term memory

Each of these five factors is measured both verbally and nonverbally, a deliberate innovation that is new to the SB5 and to IQ tests more generally. Each of these 10 areas (five factors, each measured both verbally and nonverbally) is assessed by one to three specific types of items (Kamphaus & Kroncke, 2004).

Overall, current editions of the Wechsler tests may have become more widely used than the current edition of the Stanford-Binet, but the SB5 continues to hold a similar position of respect and, in some settings, popularity as it has for the past century.

Additional Tests of Intelligence: Addressing Cultural Fairness

Especially in recent years, one of the primary criticisms of the Wechsler tests, the SB5, and other renowned IQ tests has centered on issues of **cultural fairness**. Specifically, these tests have been described as featuring numerous subtests, especially those relying on verbal skills, that place individuals from minority cultural groups at a disadvantage. In other words, to the extent that an intelligence test is based on culture-specific concepts, it may unfairly assess the intelligence of people of other cultures. Certainly, the authors of prominent tests, including the Wechsler tests and the SB5, have made significant efforts to make recent editions of their tests less culturally biased or loaded. But entirely new tests have also emerged, with the explicit purpose of measuring IQ in a more culturally fair way.

A leading example of such a test is the **Universal Nonverbal Intelligence Test (UNIT)** (Bracken & McCallum, 2009; McCallum & Bracken, 2005). Originally published in 1996, the UNIT is a completely language-free test of intelligence. It requires no speaking or shared understanding of language between the person administering the test and the person taking it. Like the Wechsler and Stanford-Binet intelligence tests, the UNIT is administered one-on-one and face-to-face, but rather than using verbal instructions, the examiner presents instructions via eight specific hand gestures taught in the test manual and demonstrated in an accompanying video. Additionally, the responses of the examinee all consist of either pointing with fingers or minor manipulation of objects with hands or fingers.

Web Link 9.5
Site for UNIT

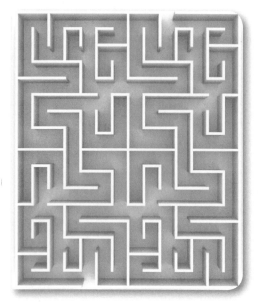

Photo 9.2 The Universal Nonverbal Intelligence Test (UNIT) attempts to maximize cultural fairness by using tasks, such as mazes, that require no language skills. In your opinion, what are the strengths and weaknesses of language-free tests of intelligence?

The UNIT is appropriate for children aged 5 to 17 years and was normed on 2,100 children who match recent U.S. Census data in terms of age, sex, race, parent education, community size, geographic region, and ethnicity. A small body of psychometric data on the UNIT has been published and suggests generally acceptable reliability and validity.

The UNIT consists of six subtests organized into a two-tiered model of intelligence. The two tiers are identified as Memory and Reasoning. The three subtests contributing to the memory tier are

- Object Memory, in which the examinee views a visual assortment of common objects for 5 seconds and then views a larger array and identifies the objects from the first array;
- Spatial Memory, in which the examinee recalls the placement of colored chips on a three-by-three or four-by-four grid; and
- Symbolic Memory, in which the examinee recalls and recreates sequences of visually presented symbols.

The three subtests contributing to the reasoning tier are

- Cube Design, in which the examinee arranges colored blocks in a specific three-dimensional design;
- Mazes, in which the examinee completes traditional maze puzzles; and
- Analogic Reasoning, in which the examinee solves analogy problems that are presented visually rather than verbally.

The UNIT is not without its shortcomings. It assesses a more limited range of abilities than more traditional IQ tests, it is appropriate only for school-age children (no preschool or adult version has yet been developed), and its psychometric data, although encouraging, is limited in quantity. Additionally, as a relative newcomer to the intelligence test field, it is nowhere near as well established or popular as the Wechsler or Stanford-Binet tests, so the structure and format of the UNIT remain unfamiliar to many clinical psychologists. Such limitations are common to nonverbal or "culture-free" tests more generally (Ortiz & Dynda, 2005). However, the development and increasing acceptance of the UNIT and similar tests represent a significant step forward in the culturally sensitive practice of intelligence assessment. Considering the large numbers of non-English-speaking people in the United

States—nearly 47 million and on the rise (U.S. Census Bureau, 2003)—clinical psychologists will increasingly require intelligence tests that are applicable and fair to clients of a broad cultural and linguistic range (Pieterse & Miller, 2010).

Achievement Testing

Achievement Versus Intelligence

Clinical psychologists assess clients' intelligence, but with separate tests they also assess clients' achievement. What's the difference between intelligence and achievement? As we have discussed, intelligence refers to a person's cognitive capacity. In short, intelligence is what a person *can* accomplish intellectually. In contrast, **achievement** is what a person *has* accomplished, especially in the kinds of subjects that people learn in school, such as reading, spelling, writing, or math. Achievement tests typically produce age- or grade-equivalency scores as well as standard scores.

Prior to *DSM-5*, the comparison of intelligence and achievement was a key factor in determining learning disabilities. In *DSM-5*, the terminology changed ("learning disability" are now called **specific learning disorder**), and the definition has changed as well, such that the primary comparison is between the person's achievement (as measured by achievement tests and performance at school or work) and expected levels of achievement for people of the same age (American Psychiatric Association, 2013).

● ● ● BOX 9.2 ● ● ●

Considering Culture

Defining Intelligence Around the World

What is intelligence? It depends on the cultural values of those we ask. When we direct the question to people outside traditional Western culture, the answer sometimes features characteristics that are quite different from definitions that Spearman, Thurstone, Cattell, or Carroll have proposed (as summarized by Sternberg, 2000, and Sternberg & Grigorenko, 2008):

- In some societies in Africa (e.g., Zambia, Mali, and Kenya), intelligence consists largely of skills that preserve harmony in interpersonal relationships, both between and within

(Continued)

(Continued)

Photo 9.3 In various cultures around the world, intelligence is defined in different ways. In your opinion, are any aspects of intelligence universal?

groups. Interviews with some residents of Zambia, for example, suggest that cooperation, deference, respect for elders, and acceptance of social responsibilities characterize intelligent people.

- In Zimbabwe, the word for intelligence—*ngware*—literally translates into a prudent and cautious approach to life and especially to social relationships.

- In some Asian cultures, the definition of intelligence also involves heavy doses of social responsibility and benevolence. More specifically, Taoist conceptions of intelligence highlight humility, independent (rather than conventional) standards of judgment, and thorough knowledge of self.

- The emphasis on social duties as central to intelligence appears in some Hispanic cultures as well. In fact, in a study of parents of schoolchildren in San Jose, California, in the 1990s, parents of Hispanic descent rated social competence as more closely related to intelligence than did parents of European descent (Okagaki & Sternberg, 1993).

- The Western emphasis on speed of mental processing is not shared by all ethnic groups. In fact, some ethnic groups may value depth of thought more highly than speed of thought and may look unfavorably or doubtfully on work performed very quickly.

This variety of defining characteristics of intelligence raises a number of important questions. Is the definition of intelligence completely dependent on cultural context, or are some aspects of intelligence universal? To what extent should intelligence tests reflect the alternate definitions of intelligence held around the world or around the United States? Where should we draw the line between personality traits and intelligence? And, as Spearman and Thurstone debated many years ago, is intelligence one thing or many things?

When clinical psychologists conduct tests of intelligence or achievement (or any other kind of assessment), they typically explain their findings in a written psychological report. Psychological reports are the formal means by which they communicate their findings to others. Depending on the case, these "others" can represent a wide range of individuals: clients, parents of child clients, teachers, lawyers, judges, physicians, or other mental health professionals, just to name a few. It is important that clinical psychologists not only write intelligible, accurate reports that address the reason for referral but that they also "know their audience" in order to customize their reports in terms of readability, selection of relevant information, and recommendations (Blais & Smith, 2008; Goldfinger & Pomerantz, 2010).

Achievement tests come in many varieties. Some measure a single area of achievement in detail, such as the KeyMath or the Gray Oral Reading achievement tests. Others are more comprehensive, featuring a wide range of subtests. Examples of these include the Woodcock Johnson Tests of Achievement, the Wide Range Achievement Test, and the Wechsler Individual Achievement Test, the latter of which we consider below in more detail.

Wechsler Individual Achievement Test—Third Edition

The **Wechsler Individual Achievement Test—Third Edition (WIAT-III)** is a comprehensive achievement test for clients aged 4 to 50 years. Like the Wechsler intelligence tests, the WIAT-III is administered face-to-face and one-on-one.

The WIAT-III measures achievement in four broad areas: reading, math, written language, and oral language. Each of these broad areas is assessed by two to four subtests. The Oral Language Composite derives from two subtests: Listening Comprehension (paying attention to orally presented information and answering questions about it) and Oral Expression (using speech to repeat spoken material, create stories about presented pictures, provide directions, etc.). The Reading Composite derives from scores on such subtests as Word Reading (reading isolated words), Pseudoword Decoding (using phonetic skills to sound out nonsense words, such as *plore* or *tharch*), and Reading Comprehension (reading sentences or passages and answering questions about their content). The Mathematics Composite derives subtests such as Numerical Operations (written math problems) and Math Problem Solving (word problems, numerical patterns, statistics and probability questions, etc.). The Written Language Composite derives subtests such as Spelling (increasingly difficult words) and Sentence Composition, Essay Composition (constructing sentences, paragraphs, or essays as instructed) (Lichtenberger & Breaux, 2010).

The WIAT-III yields standard scores on the same scale as most intelligence tests: a mean of 100 and a standard deviation of 15. It also yields age and grade equivalencies for each subtest. The test was standardized on 3,000 people who were chosen to match recent U.S. Census data in terms of sex, age, race/ethnicity, geographic region, and parent education level. Many of the individuals in the standardization sample also took the age-appropriate Wechsler intelligence scale, so the WIAT-III is "linked" to the Wechsler IQ tests, which enhances the validity of comparisons between these two types of tests. Overall, the reliability and validity data supporting the WIAT-III are quite strong (Lichtenberger & Breaux, 2010).

Neuropsychological Testing

Neuropsychological testing represents a specialized area of assessment within clinical psychology. The intent of neuropsychological tests is to measure cognitive functioning or impairment of the brain and its specific components or structures. Medical procedures such as computed tomography (CT), magnetic resonance imaging (MRI), and positron emission tomography (PET) scans can show that part of the brain looks abnormal, but neuropsychological tests show how that part of the brain is actually functioning. Such tests are especially useful for targeted assessment of problems that might result from a head injury, prolonged alcohol or drug use, or a degenerative brain illness. They can also be used to make a prognosis for improvement, plan rehabilitation, determine eligibility for accommodations at school or work, and establish a baseline of neuropsychological abilities to be used as a comparison at a later time (Golden, 2008; Hebben & Milberg, 2009; McCaffrey, Lynch, & Westervelt, 2011).

Some neuropsychological testing procedures are lengthy, comprehensive batteries that include a broad array of subtests. The patterns of scores on these subtests can go a long way toward pinpointing specific cognitive weaknesses. Other neuropsychological tests are much briefer and are typically used as screens for neuropsychological impairment rather than as full-fledged neuropsychological assessment tools. Let's consider two of the batteries—the Halstead-Reitan and the Luria-Nebraska—and several of the briefer neuropsychological measures in more detail.

Full Neuropsychological Batteries

The **Halstead-Reitan Neuropsychological Battery (HRB)** is a battery of eight standardized neuropsychological tests. It is suitable for clients of age 15 years and above, but alternate versions are available for younger clients. The HRB is administered only as a whole battery; its components are not to be administered separately. Thus, it is a thorough (and rather lengthy) neuropsychological battery. Essentially, its primary purpose is to identify people with brain damage and, to the extent possible, provide detailed information or hypotheses about any brain damage identified, including specific cognitive impairments or physiological regions of the brain that may be deficient. The findings of the HRB can help in diagnosis and treatment of problems related to brain malfunction (Broshek & Barth, 2000).

Some of the eight tests in the HRB involve sight, whereas others involve hearing, touch, motor skills, and pencil-and-paper tasks. An example of one of the tests of the HRB is the Trail Making Test, which resembles the familiar "dot-to-dot" puzzles that children complete, but this test is timed, contains both numbers and letters, and produces a rather haphazard line instead of an identifiable figure or shape. A second example is the Category Test, in which a client sees a pattern of shapes and designs on a screen and presses the number key

(1–4) that is suggested by the pattern. Clients hear a bell when correct and a buzzer when wrong, and their successes and failures are noted by the examiner. The Finger Tapping (or Finger Oscillation) Test is a third example; in this test, clients tap a single typewriter key as rapidly as they can with the index finger for 10-second intervals. The number of taps they can produce, averaged across multiple attempts with each hand, estimates motor speed (Goldstein & Sanders, 2004; Reitan & Wolfson, 2004).

The examiner using the HRB compares a client's test scores to published norms to assess overall performance and also to each other to determine the client's own relative strengths and weaknesses. Interpretation of results can include detailed inferences about specific neuropsychological pathologies and the localization of problems in cognitive functioning (e.g., a particular lobe or hemisphere of the brain).

In the decades since it was introduced, the HRB has been evaluated more than any other comprehensive neuropsychological test. These studies suggest strongly that the HRB and each of its tests have been established as reliable and valid. Additional strengths of the HRB include its comprehensiveness and clinical usefulness. Drawbacks of the HRB include its length (and corresponding expense), inflexibility (as a fixed battery), and a limited overlap with real-life, day-to-day tasks (Broshek & Barth, 2000; Hebben & Milberg, 2009).

The HRB may be the most commonly administered comprehensive neuropsychological battery (Guilmette & Faust, 1991), but a respected and popular alternative is the **Luria-Nebraska Neuropsychological Battery (LNNB).** The LNNB is similar to the HRB in that it is a wide-ranging test of neuropsychological functioning. It consists of 12 scales, with a similar range to that of the HRB. A primary difference is the LNNB's emphasis on qualitative data in addition to quantitative data. In other words, to a greater extent than the HRB, the LNNB relies on qualitative written comments from the examiner about the testing process. These comments describe what the examiner observed about the client, such as problems comprehending the test (e.g., confusion, poor attention); how or why the client is missing items (e.g., slow movement, sight or hearing problems, speech flaws); or unusual behaviors (e.g., inappropriate emotional reactions, hyperactivity, distraction). Another difference between the HRB and the LNNB is that the LNNB tends to be slightly briefer. As for the HRB, a strong body of psychometric data supports the LNNB's reliability and validity (Golden, 2004; Golden, Freshwater, & Vayalakkara, 2000; Hebben & Milberg, 2009).

Brief Neuropsychological Measures

The Bender-Gestalt test, originally published in 1938 and currently available as the **Bender Visual-Motor Gestalt Test—Second Edition (Bender-Gestalt-II),** is the most commonly used neuropsychological screen among clinical psychologists (Watkins, Campbell, Nieberding, & Hallmark, 1995). The test is a straightforward copying task: The client is given a pencil, blank paper, and nine simple geometric designs (primarily made of combinations of circles, dots, lines, angles, and basic shapes) and is asked to copy each design as accurately as possible. It measures visuoconstructive abilities, which are also commonly known as perceptual-motor or visual-spatial skills (Lacks, 2000). The current edition is quite similar to the original Bender-Gestalt, but it offers memory tasks and additional stimuli.

This test is remarkably brief—on average, it takes only 6 minutes to administer (Lacks, 2000). It is appropriate for clients of any age above 3 years. For these reasons, clinical psychologists frequently include it as a quick "check" for neuropsychological problems. In other words, if it is already established that the client being evaluated has or is strongly suspected to have a neuropsychological problem, it is likely that the clinical psychologist will select a more comprehensive battery, such as the HRB or the LNNB, rather than the Bender-Gestalt. However, when the evaluation is for another purpose and the clinical psychologist simply wants a rapid appraisal of overall neuropsychological functioning, the Bender-Gestalt can be a good choice. Its results cannot specify locations of brain damage, but poor performance on the Bender-Gestalt can suggest brain damage in a diffuse way. As such, it can alert the clinical psychologist to the general presence of neuropsychological problems, and more thorough testing can subsequently be conducted. Poor performance on the Bender-Gestalt is indicated by a variety of errors that clients may make in copying the figures, including figures in which details are missing or notably inexact; figures that collide with each other on the page; inability to accurately "close" shapes such as circles or squares; disproportionate size of a figure or part of a figure; and angles in copied figures that do not match the angles in the originals (Lacks, 1999).

Another common neurological screen among clinical psychologists is the **Rey-Osterrieth Complex Figure Test,** originally published in 1941. This test is also a brief pencil-and-paper drawing task, but it involves only a single, more complex figure. The Rey-Osterrieth also features the use of pencils of different colors at various points in the test; this way, the examiner can trace the client's sequential approach to this complex copying task. It also includes a memory component, in which clients are asked 3 to 60 minutes after copying the form to reproduce it again from memory (Helmes, 2000; Lacks, 2000).

The **Repeatable Battery for the Assessment of Neuropsychological Status (RBANS;** Randolph, 1998) is a neuropsychological screen that focuses on a broader range of abilities than does either the Bender-Gestalt or the Rey-Osterrieth. The RBANS tests not only visuomotor abilities but also verbal skills, attention, and visual memory. It takes 20 to 30 minutes to complete and includes 12 subtests in 5 categories. The subtests involve such tasks as learning a list of 10 words presented orally, naming pictures of various objects, recalling an orally presented list of numbers, recalling a story told 20 minutes earlier, and (like the Bender-Gestalt and Rey-Osterrieth) copying of visual figures. The RBANS yields a total score as well as scores for each of the 12 subtests and 5 indices into which they are organized (Groth-Marnat, 2009).

Although it is used for a variety of other purposes as well, the **Wechsler Memory Scale—Fourth Edition (WMS-IV**; Wechsler, 2009a, 2009b) is frequently utilized for neuropsychological purposes. The WMS-IV is a memory test often used to assess individuals aged 16 to 90 who are suspected of having memory problems due to brain injury, dementia, substance abuse, or other factors. It assesses both visual and auditory memory across its seven subtests. It also assesses both immediate and delayed recall. One of the WMS-IV subtests, Logical Memory, involves the client hearing a story read aloud and then trying to recall the story both immediately and after a 20- to 30-minute delay. Another subtest, Visual Reproduction, involves presenting abstract visual figures to the client and asking him or her to reproduce them after they have been removed. For adults over 65 years of age, the WMS-IV offers a version that is shorter in duration, therefore minimizing the impact of fatigue on test results (Drozdick, Holdnack, & Hilsabeck, 2011; Holdnack & Drozdick, 2010).

A final note about neuropsychological testing: As with any other kind of assessment, it is essential for clinical psychologists to develop and use cultural competence when selecting, administering, scoring, and interpreting neuropsychological tests. Many neuropsychological instruments were standardized (either originally or currently) on European Americans, and their form or structure can emphasize European American values. When working with diverse clients, it is important to caution against overpathologizing and to consider (or consider developing) culture-specific norms whenever possible (Horton, 2008).

CHAPTER SUMMARY

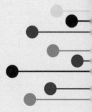

Clinical psychologists use intelligence tests, achievement tests, and neuropsychological tests to assess various intellectual capacities of their clients. The most widely accepted intelligence tests endorse a hierarchical model of intelligence, as indicated by the fact that they yield a single overall intelligence score as well as more specific index, factor, or subtest scores. The Wechsler intelligence tests, including the WAIS-IV for adults, the WISC-IV for school-age children, and the WPSSI-III for preschoolers, rank among the most commonly used and psychometrically sound measures of intelligence. Each Wechsler test features about a dozen subtests grouped into four factors, each of which contributes to the full-scale IQ. The Stanford-Binet intelligence test, which covers the entire age range in a single version, is also frequently used, especially among clinical psychologists who may be testing clients at the extremes of the intelligence range. Concerns about the cultural fairness of prominent intelligence tests has fostered the development of less culturally dependent tests such as the UNIT, which does not depend on linguistic compatibility between examiner and client. Whereas intelligence tests measure abilities, achievement tests such as the WIAT-III measure accomplishments, particularly in core academic areas such as math and reading. Achievement tests are commonly used when assessing for specific learning disorder.

Neuropsychological tests are intended to measure cognitive function and dysfunction and in some cases to localize impairment to a particular region of the brain. Some neuropsychological measures are lengthy and comprehensive, such as the HRB and LNNB; others, such as the Bender-Gestalt-II, Rey-Osterrieth Complex Figure Test, and RBANS, are briefer screens for neuropsychological problems.

KEY TERMS AND NAMES

CRITICAL THINKING QUESTIONS

1. In your opinion, what aspects of intelligence do contemporary intelligence tests overemphasize?

2. In your opinion, what aspects of intelligence do contemporary intelligence tests overlook?

3. To what extent do you agree with the idea that intelligence is a single ability ("g"), as opposed to separate unrelated abilities ("s")?

4. Which subtests of the Wechsler intelligence tests seem most culturally fair? Which seem most potentially culturally unfair?

5. Why is it important for clinical psychologists who do not specialize in neuropsychology to be competent in the use of brief neuropsychological screens?

STUDENT STUDY SITE RESOURCES

Visit the study site at www.sagepub.com/pomerantz3eupdate for these additional learning tools:

- Self-quizzes
- eFlashcards
- Culture Expert Interviews
- Full-text SAGE journal articles
- Additional web resources
- Mock Assessment Data

CHAPTER SUMMARY VIDEO

 QR codes at the end of each chapter link to chapter background videos by the author. Visit http://gettag.mobi using your smartphone browser to download the free Microsoft Tag app. Once installed, scan the tags to go directly to these brief videos. In this video, the author raises questions about the definition of intelligence and the extent to which traditional IQ tests cover all of its components.

CHAPTER 10

Personality Assessment and Behavioral Assessment

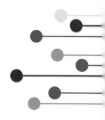

Clinical psychologists have developed many different approaches to assessing clients' personality and behavior. But before we examine any specific tests or methods, there are three important, overarching themes to emphasize: multimethod assessment, evidence-based assessment, and culturally competent assessment.

Multimethod Assessment

No measure of personality or behavior is perfect. Some have excellent reliability, validity, and clinical utility, but even these have their limitations. For that reason, it is important for clinical psychologists not to rely exclusively on any single assessment method. Instead, personality is best assessed by using multiple methods, including tests of different types, interview data, observations, or other sources. Each method offers a unique perspective on the client, and often they converge on similar conclusions. To the extent that these conclusions are supported by multiple tests rather than only one, the clinical psychologist can assert them with confidence.

Photo 10.1 Personality is best assessed by using multiple methods, including tests of different types, interview data, observations, or other sources.

The advantages of **multimethod assessment** hold true even in less formal and professional settings. Consider a situation in which you are getting to know someone, such as in a new dating relationship. Your initial "assessment" of your partner's personality may take place on the first date—at a restaurant and a movie, perhaps. As the relationship continues, you'll have a chance to "assess" your partner's personality using other "methods"—you'll see his or her personality and behavior with family, with friends, at parties, at home, at work, at school, and so on. You may get a strong first impression on the first date, but you probably won't feel that you genuinely know and understand your partner's personality until you've "assessed" him or her in a variety of contexts, because each situation will reveal a different aspect of personality. In a more professional sense, the same applies to clinical psychologists "getting to know" a client via personality tests: Each method offers a unique perspective, and although some may be more enlightening than others, it is the integration of multiple methods that ultimately proves most informative.

Evidence-Based Assessment

In an earlier chapter, we discussed the recent advancement toward evidence-based treatments, or "treatments that work." The movement toward **evidence-based assessment,** resting on the same principle of "what works" empirically, isn't far behind. Clinical psychologists who practice evidence-based assessment select only those methods that have strong psychometrics, including reliability, validity, and clinical utility (each defined in Chapter 8). Moreover, they select tests that have sufficient normative data and are sensitive to issues of diversity such as age, gender, race, and ethnicity. They typically target their assessment strategies toward a particular diagnosis or problem, such that "what works" for assessing attention-deficit/hyperactivity disorder might be a different set of assessment tools than "what works" for assessing panic disorder, schizophrenia, bulimia, or any other clinical issue (Hunsley & Mash, 2008b). For example, two methods—the Structured Clinical Interview for *DSM-IV* (SCID; soon to be updated for *DSM-5*, and described in Chapter 8) and the Beck Depression Inventory-II (described later in this chapter)—are specifically identified as "highly recommended" instruments for diagnosing depression in adults (Persons & Fresco, 2008).

How do researchers determine "what works" when assessing particular clinical problems? In other words, what criteria should distinguish evidence-based assessment methods from those lacking evidence? This is one of the great challenges in the early development of evidence-based assessment (Hunsley & Mash, 2008b). Of course, some of the strengths or weaknesses of an assessment method can be expressed quantitatively. For example, test-retest reliability, which measures the extent to which the method yields similar results at different points in time, is expressed as a correlation coefficient ranging from −1 to +1. In a landmark book on evidence-based assessment—*A Guide to Assessments That Work*—its editors define "adequate" test-retest reliability this way: "Preponderance of evidence indicates test-retest correlations of at least .70 over a period of several days to several weeks" (Hunsley & Mash, 2008a, p. 8). They go on to define "good" test-retest reliability as the same .70 level "over a period of several months" and "excellent" test-retest reliability as the same .70 level "over a period of a year or longer" (p. 8). These definitions seem reasonable enough, but they also point out that any criteria designed to delineate levels of evidence for assessment tools will incorporate some subjective decision making (e.g., why .70 rather than .60 or .80? Why those specific time periods rather than shorter or longer periods?), along with objective data.

Evidence-based assessment has gained quite a bit of momentum within the context of evidence-based practices in health care more broadly. Some of its advocates hope it will not only influence current graduate students in clinical psychology but also experienced psychologists "who use assessment instruments because they learned them in graduate school, rather than because there is strong evidence that they work. Now, a different and better standard is available" (Nathan, 2008, p. xvii). There are those who remind us that not every decision within a clinical assessment should be predetermined by the instructions of guidebooks or manuals. For example, in a discussion of clinical interviewing, Sommers-Flanagan and Sommers-Flanagan (2009) state that these manuals cannot address nuances in human interaction—nuances that sometimes elicit anger or tears—and these manuals cannot adequately guide clinicians on when to self-disclose, when to just listen, how to respond to client questions, or effective methods for establishing rapport with a living, breathing, culturally unique individual whom they want to help. (p. xi)

Undoubtedly, relying on assessment methods with demonstrable reliability, validity, and clinical utility for particular clinical problems is a professional step forward, especially if the other alternative involves choosing methods on the basis of familiarity, popularity, or similarly unempirical factors. Contemporary clinical psychologists now face the challenge of integrating "what works" empirically with their own clinical judgment and their clients' needs as they make decisions about assessment.

Culturally Competent Assessment

Cultural competence is essential across all activities of clinical psychologists, especially personality assessment. Simply put, every culture has its own perception of "normal" and its own variations of "abnormal" as well. A personality assessment conducted without knowledge or sensitivity to these cultural specifics can be a dangerous thing; in fact, it has been labeled "cultural malpractice" by some (e.g., Dana, 2005). A primary danger lies in the possibility of **overpathologizing**—that is, viewing as abnormal that which is culturally normal. In other words, the clinical psychologist must appreciate the meaning of a behavior, thought, or feeling within the context of the client's culture, which may differ from the context of the psychologist's own culture.

As an example of overpathologizing, consider Duron, a 45-year-old African American client who was urged by his wife and children to seek psychotherapy. On the intake form Duron completed in the waiting room of Dr. Platt, a white clinical psychologist, he indicated that he was struggling with symptoms of depression and excessive alcohol use. But as Duron and Dr. Platt spoke during the initial session, Dr. Platt was struck by what he considered excessive suspiciousness. He noticed that Duron was somewhat reluctant to reveal details about himself, posed numerous questions about confidentiality, and asked, "Why do you need to know that?" several times in response to interview questions. Duron did not schedule a second appointment when the first appointment ended, and Dr. Platt interpreted this as a sign of distrust. By the end of the session, Dr. Platt was convinced that Duron's primary problem was not depression or alcohol abuse but paranoia. He subsequently administered personality tests to Duron and interpreted the results to support his hypothesis that Duron was paranoid. Of course, Dr. Platt's mistake throughout this assessment process was his lack of knowledge of

African American cultural norms, especially as they relate to seeking psychological services from white therapists. In this situation, African Americans often exhibit a guardedness justified by many years of formal and informal racial prejudice, oppression, and betrayal (Boyd-Franklin, 1989; Hines & Boyd-Franklin, 2005; Maultsby, 1982). Through Dr. Platt's cultural insensitivity and ethnocentrism, he wrongly judged Duron's behavior as pathologically paranoid when, in fact, Duron's behavior was reasonable based on his cultural background.

In Duron's case, the source of the cultural bias was the clinician himself. During personality assessment, the bias can actually stem from a number of other sources as well, including the test and the service delivery method (Dana, 2005). For example, a test can be biased if it features language or structure that is culture specific rather than universally applicable. The test may also include norms that are not adequately culturally inclusive, resulting in a comparison of the client's scores with the scores of an inappropriate reference group (see Box 10.1). Additionally, the service delivery method (essentially, the way the clinician uses the test) can be biased by including interpersonal interaction or an approach to time and task that is inconsistent with some cultures. Whether the bias stems from the clinician, the test, or the service delivery method, the clinical psychologist is responsible for recognizing and minimizing it in order to conduct culturally competent assessments.

● ● ● BOX 10.1 ● ● ●

Considering Culture

Culture-Specific Norms for Personality Tests

Claudia is a Cuban American woman who has just completed the Minnesota Multiphasic Personality Inventory-2 (MMPI-2), a popular multiple-choice, pencil-and-paper personality test for adults (covered later in this chapter). The MMPI-2 yields a wide variety of scores on variables such as depression, anxiety, paranoia, schizophrenia, mania, and others. To score Claudia's test, her clinical psychologist will compare her responses with those of a "normative" group of people who took the test prior to its publication and whose scores form the basis of the norms tables in the MMPI-2 manual. What cultural characteristics should the people in the normative group have? In other words, with whose scores, specifically, should Claudia's scores be compared?

(Continued)

(Continued)

Photo 10.2 Should a client's scores on a personality test be compared with scores of the population as a whole or with scores of others who are culturally similar?

The possibilities range from very broad groups to very specific groups. Most broadly, the normative group could be a cultural mix representative of the U.S. population, and Claudia's scores could be compared with those of the entire group as a whole. On the other hand, a more narrowly defined normative group could be used, such as Cuban Americans or females. In fact, we could combine these variables and consider an even more culturally specific group: Cuban American females.

There would be advantages to ignoring the culture-specific norms and instead comparing Claudia's scores with those of the entire normative sample (which, for the MMPI-2, consists of 2,600 adults). The full normative sample is, by definition, larger than any cultural subset. Only a small fraction of those 2,600 adults were Cuban American females, and such a small group may not be statistically representative of Cuban American females more generally. Test developers and researchers could make efforts to establish sufficiently large normative groups specific to each culture, but this could prove excessively costly and time-consuming, especially if many cultural variables are considered in combination (Cuban American females of Claudia's age range and religion, for example).

On the other hand, there would be advantages to comparing Claudia's scores with culture-specific norms. By doing so, we could ensure that Claudia's responses are being evaluated in a culturally sensitive manner. We could reduce the chances of overpathologizing her scores, a risk involved in comparing them with norms that do not reflect her own cultural background and values. Comparing Claudia's scores only with the scores of others like her prevents an ethnocentric judgment of Claudia's mental health according to standards established by others culturally unlike her (Wood, Garb, & Nezworski, 2007).

In actual practice, clinical psychologists compare client test data with both broad, heterogeneous normative groups and more specific, homogeneous normative groups. The MMPI-2 manual, for example, does not include ethnicity-specific norms, but it does include gender-specific norms, and in the years since the MMPI-2 was published, numerous researchers have established and published more culturally specific normative information for clinical psychologists to use (e.g., Butcher, Cheung, & Lim, 2003; Dana, 1995; Garrido & Velasquez, 2006; Kwan & Maestas, 2008; McNulty, Graham, Ben-Porath, & Stein, 1997; Velasquez, Garrido, Castellanos, & Burton, 2004). Even cultural groups as specific as the Old Order Amish have their own set of MMPI-2 norms (Knabb, Vogt, & Newgren, 2011). One solution to this quandary is to consider both broad and culture-specific normative data. Both can provide meaningful comparisons for a client's responses to a personality test.

Objective Personality Tests

Generally speaking, personality tests can be placed in one of two categories: objective and projective. **Objective personality tests** include unambiguous test items, offer clients a limited range of responses, and are objectively scored. Most often, the objective personality tests that clinical psychologists use are questionnaires that clients complete with pencil and paper (or in some cases, on a computer). They typically involve a series of direct, brief statements or questions and either true/false or multiple-choice response options in which clients indicate the extent to which the statement or question applies to them (Morey & Hopwood, 2008). By contrast, *projective* personality tests feature ambiguous stimuli and an open-ended range of client responses. They are based on the assumption that clients reveal their personalities by the way they make sense of vaguely defined objects or situations (Smith & Archer, 2008). Projective personality tests will be covered in more detail in a later section. For now, let's consider some of the most commonly used and reputable objective personality tests.

Minnesota Multiphasic Personality Inventory-2

The **Minnesota Multiphasic Personality Inventory-2 (MMPI-2)** is both the most popular and the most psychometrically sound objective personality test used by clinical psychologists (Butcher & Beutler, 2003; Camara, Nathan, & Puente, 2000; Frauenhoffer, Ross, Gfeller, Searight, & Piotrowski, 1998). It is used in many countries and cultures around the world and has been translated into dozens of languages (Butcher, Mosch, Tsai, & Nezami, 2006; Graham, 2012). The format of the MMPI-2 is simple: The client reads 567 self-descriptive sentences and, using a pencil-and-paper answer sheet, marks each sentence as either true or false as it applies to him or her. The items span a wide range of behavior, feelings, and attitudes. A few simulated MMPI-2 items appear in Box 10.2.

⊕ **Web Link 10.1**
MMPI-2 Site

• • • BOX 10.2 • • •

Simulated MMPI-2 Items

- I feel like I am low on energy much of the time.
- I often find myself in conflicts with people in authority.
- During times of stress, I usually experience an upset stomach.
- Most of the people I know have plans to hurt me in some way.
- I have visions of things that aren't real and that other people can't see.
- I enjoy going to social events with dozens of people.
- I often can't stop worrying about things even when there is no reason for the worry.

The MMPI-2 is a revision of the original MMPI, which was published in 1943. When **Starke Hathaway** and **J. C. McKinley**, the authors of the original MMPI, began their work in the 1930s, they sought an objective way to measure psychopathology. Numerous questionnaires of this type were available at that time, but none were based on a solid empirical foundation as the MMPI would be. When creating a personality test, it is relatively easy for an author to create a list of items that should, *theoretically,* elicit different responses from "normal" and "abnormal" people of various categories. Hathaway and McKinley chose to take on a greater challenge: to create a list of items that *empirically* elicits different responses from people in these normal and abnormal groups (Ben-Porath & Archer, 2008; Graham, 2012).

Hathaway and McKinley succeeded in creating such a list of items by using a method of test construction called **empirical criterion keying**. Essentially, this method involves identifying distinct groups of people, asking them all to respond to the same test items, and comparing responses between groups. If an item elicits different responses from one group than from another, it's a worthy item and should be included on the final version of the test. If the groups answer an item similarly, the item is discarded because it does not help categorize a client in one group or the other. When empirical criterion keying is used, it doesn't matter whether an item should, in theory, differentiate two groups; it matters only whether an item does, in actuality, differentiate two groups. As an example, consider the simulated item, "I have visions of things that aren't real and that other people can't see." In theory, we may expect schizophrenics to endorse this item far more often than would nonschizophrenics. According to the empirical criterion keying method, this theoretical expectation is not enough. It must be supported by evidence that schizophrenics do, in fact, endorse this item far more often than do nonschizophrenics. According to the empirical criterion keying method, only if the two groups actually respond differently to the item should it be included on the final version of the test.

Metaphorically Speaking

If You've Shopped on Amazon.com, You Understand Empirical Criterion Keying

How do the people at Amazon.com (or most other online shopping sites) decide which items to suggest to customers? Actually, they use a strategy similar to empirical criterion keying. As you read through the description of an item on Amazon.com, the listing always includes the section, "Customers who bought this item also bought . . . ." The site uses its sales statistics to link certain items together: People who downloaded Adele's *21* also downloaded Kelly Clarkson's *Stronger*, people who bought *Star Wars* DVDs also bought *Lord of the Rings* DVDs, and people who bought John Irving's latest novel also bought Barbara Kingsolver's.

The important point is that these suggestions are based on empirical data—not theory, common sense, logic, or any other nonempirical criteria. In other words, the people at Amazon.com could, if they chose, recommend to fans of *Star Wars* other DVDs that would seem, theoretically, to make sense. Rather than stating, "Customers who bought this item also bought . . . ," they could tell us, "Customers who like this item might also like . . . ." The "might also like" list would include DVDs similar in some way to *Star Wars*—other movies set in outer space, other movies directed by George Lucas, other movies featuring Harrison Ford, etc.

Instead, the suggestions from Amazon.com are based entirely on connections between movies according to empirical sales data. Perhaps your intuition wouldn't have told you that customers who bought *Star Wars* DVDs also bought *Back to the Future* or *The Muppets,* but according to sales data, they did. None of these "also bought" movies is especially similar to *Star Wars,* but the sales figures nonetheless demonstrate empirically that they sell to the same audience. Appearance on the list of suggestions has nothing to do with a connection between movies in terms of actors, subject matter, or any other criteria besides empirical sales data.

In a similar way, the creators of the MMPI were blindly empirical when they constructed their tests. Previous designers of personality tests had primarily relied on items they believed would separate abnormal people from normal people. The MMPI's creators instead insisted that an item would be included in their test only if it demonstrated empirically that it produced different responses from people in different groups. It didn't

(Continued)

(Continued)

matter whether the item *should* distinguish the groups according to intuition, logic, common sense, or clinical wisdom; what mattered was whether the empirical data showed that the item *did* in fact distinguish between groups. As a hypothetical example, if the item, "I cry a lot," did not separate depressed people from nondepressed people, it would be eliminated from the test, even if in theory it seems like an obvious distinction between the two groups. And if a seemingly unrelated item such as, say, "I prefer apples to oranges," did separate depressed people from nondepressed people, it would be kept, despite no conceptual connection to depression.

What do you think of the "Customers who bought this item also bought . . ." suggestion lists on websites such as Amazon.com? What are the benefits and drawbacks to using an empirical criterion keying approach to create such suggestion lists? Similarly, how do you evaluate the empirical criterion keying approach to personality test construction? What are its benefits and drawbacks?

For Hathaway and McKinley, the distinct groups on which potential items were evaluated consisted of people who had been diagnosed with particular mental disorders (e.g., depressed, paranoid, schizophrenic, anxious, sociopathic, and hypochondriacal groups) and a group of "normals" who did not have a mental health diagnosis at all. Although they began the process with more than 1,000 potential items, only 550 were retained after the empirical criterion keying method was complete. The items appeared in the test in random order, but for scoring purposes, they were organized into groups related to 10 specific pathologies. Each of those 10 groups of items represented a **clinical scale**, and the higher a client scored on a particular scale, the greater the likelihood that he or she demonstrated that form of psychopathology. The 10 clinical scales remain the same in the MMPI-2 and are described in Table 10.1 below (Ben-Porath & Archer, 2008).

Some of the names of the clinical scales described in Table 10.1 may seem unfamiliar, but they actually refer to very familiar and common clinical issues. The unfamiliar terms were commonly used when the MMPI was originally created, and they were retained in the MMPI-2 to maintain continuity even though some have become outdated. For example, Scale 4, "Psychopathic Deviate," would probably be labeled "Antisocial" today. And the name for Scale 7, "Psychasthenia," is an obsolete word roughly equivalent to "Anxiety."

Another important feature introduced by the MMPI (and retained in the MMPI-2) was a way to assess clients' **test-taking attitudes**. Hathaway and McKinley realized that self-report instruments are vulnerable to insincere efforts by the client. Some clients may intentionally

Table 10.1 Clinical Scales of the MMPI, MMPI-2, and MMPI-A

Scale Number	Scale Name	Abbreviation	Description of High Scale Scores
1	Hypochondriasis	Hs	Somatic problems, excessive bodily concern, weakness, ailments, complaining and whining
2	Depression	D	Depressed, unhappy, low confidence, pessimistic
3	Hysteria	Hy	Vague medical reactions to stress, somatic symptoms, denial of conflict and anger
4	Psychopathic Deviate	Pd	Antisocial, rebellious, blaming others, poor consideration of consequences of actions
5	Masculinity-Femininity	Mf	Rejection of traditional gender roles, effeminate men, masculine women
6	Paranoia	Pa	Suspicious, guarded, hypersensitive, belief that others intend to harm
7	Psychasthenia	Pt	Anxious, nervous, tense, worrisome, obsessive
8	Schizophrenia	Sc	Psychotic, disorganized, or bizarre thought process, unconventional, hallucinations, delusions, alienated
9	Mania	Ma	Manic, elevated mood, energetic, overactive, accelerated movement and speech, flight of ideas
10	Social Introversion	Si	Introverted, shy, reserved, more comfortable alone than with others

Sources: Archer (1997) and Butcher (2011).

exaggerate their symptoms ("fake bad") to appear more impaired than they really are; others may intentionally minimize their symptoms ("fake good") to appear healthier than they really are. Still other clients may respond randomly without paying much attention to items at all. The MMPI and MMPI-2 include a number of items designed to "catch" these test-taking attitudes. When responses to these items are grouped together, they constitute the test's **validity scales.** These validity scales inform the clinical psychologist about the client's approach to the test and allow the psychologist to determine whether the test is valid and what kinds of adjustments might be appropriate during the process of interpreting the clinical scales. The MMPI and MMPI-2 contain three specific validity scales: L (*Lying*, suggesting "faking good"), K (*Defensiveness*, also suggesting "faking good"), and F (*Infrequency*, suggesting "faking bad").

As an example of the importance of validity scales, consider Tammy, a 24-year-old woman on trial for armed robbery. Her attorney has argued that Tammy is seriously mentally ill and that, as a result, she should be found not guilty by reason of insanity and placed in a psychiatric treatment center rather than imprisoned. The judge in Tammy's case orders Tammy to undergo a psychological examination, and Dr. Reed, the clinical psychologist in the case, uses the MMPI-2, among other tests. Dr. Reed finds that many of Tammy's MMPI-2 clinical scales, especially scales 2 (Depression) and 8 (Schizophrenia), are extremely high. Alone, this information would suggest that Tammy is experiencing significant psychopathology. However, Tammy's MMPI-2 validity scales (especially her F scale) strongly suggest that she "faked bad" on the test; that is, she exaggerated her symptoms in an attempt to look more pathological than she truly is. (Clinical psychologists often use the term *malingering* to describe this type of deliberate behavior.) With this information, Dr. Reed may determine that Tammy's MMPI-2 results are altogether invalid or may interpret the clinical scales with the knowledge that Tammy tended to overstate her problems.

The MMPI grew tremendously in popularity from the 1940s to the 1980s and was eventually replaced by the MMPI-2 in 1989. The revision process addressed several weaknesses that had become increasingly problematic for the original MMPI. Foremost among these weaknesses was the inadequate normative sample of the original MMPI. The "normal" group with which the clinical groups were compared consisted of 724 individuals from Minnesota in the 1940s. (To be specific, they were visitors to the University of Minnesota Hospital.) This group was overwhelmingly rural and white, and as such, they were not at all an adequate microcosm of the U.S. population. So for the MMPI-2, normative data was solicited from a much larger and demographically diverse group. In all, the MMPI-2 normative group includes 2,600 people from seven states who closely matched U.S. Census data from the 1980s regarding age, ethnicity, and marital status (Butcher, 2011; Greene & Clopton, 2004). Other improvements included the removal or revision of some test items with outdated or awkward wording. Otherwise, the authors of the MMPI-2 sought to keep the revised version as similar as possible to the original MMPI to take advantage of the familiarity of the test to many clinical psychologists and the enormous body of literature that had accumulated regarding the MMPI.

Soon after the MMPI-2 was published, an alternate version of the MMPI was created for younger clients. Whereas the MMPI-2 is appropriate only for adults (18 years and older), the **Minnesota Multiphasic Personality Inventory-Adolescent (MMPI-A)** was designed for clients aged 14 to 18 years. It was published in 1992 and is very similar in administration, format, scoring, and interpretation to the MMPI-2. It is a true/false, pencil-and-paper test consisting of 478 items. Some of its items are shared with the MMPI-2, and some are original items targeting common teen issues such as school, family, substance use, and peer relations. It yields the same validity scales and clinical scales as the MMPI-2. It was normed on 2,500 adolescents chosen to match 1980 U.S. Census data on many important demographic variables (Archer, 1997; Baer & Rinaldo, 2004; Ben-Porath & Archer, 2008).

The MMPI-2 and MMPI-A yield the same 10 clinical scale scores that the original MMPI yielded. After considering the validity scores, clinical psychologists interpret the MMPI-2 or MMPI-A by considering the clinical scale scores most elevated above normal levels. In some cases, a single clinical scale score will stand out; in others, two or three clinical scale scores may be elevated. As shorthand, clinical psychologists often use the elevated scale numbers ("code-types") to refer to a client's profile, as in, "her MMPI-A profile is a 3/6" or "his MMPI-2 is a 2/4/8." Once these high clinical scales are identified, clinical psychologists turn to the empirical literature describing clients with that pattern of elevations. Numerous books and computer programs, many of which were authored by individuals involved in the creation of the MMPI, MMPI-2, or MMPI-A, supply psychologists with this interpretive information. In addition to the 10 clinical scales, a number of additional scales—known as **supplemental scales** and **content scales**—have been developed to measure other, often more specific aspects of personality and pathology (Butcher, 2011; Butcher & Beutler, 2003).

The MMPI-2 is extremely well supported by research on its psychometric characteristics. Thousands of studies examine some aspect of reliability or validity regarding the MMPI tests, and the results have been consistently positive. In short, the MMPI-2 is established as a reliable and valid test of personality and psychopathology, justifying its extensive use by clinical psychologists (Greene & Clopton, 2004). Although the research base is not as extensive, similar conclusions have been reached for the MMPI-A (Archer, 1997; Baer & Rinaldo, 2004).

In late 2008, a new, shorter version of the MMPI-2 was released. The **MMPI-2 Restructured Form** (**MMPI-2-RF;** Ben-Porath & Tellegen, 2008) contains only 388 of the 567 items on the MMPI-2. Its clinical scales, called the Restructured Clinical scales, are close to the 10 clinical scales in the other forms of the MMPI but different in important ways. Each scale includes fewer items, and each is more homogeneous or "tighter." In other words, each scale overlaps less with the others due to the removal of items that overlapped between the scales. Much of this overlap stemmed from items that tap into the concept of demoralization, which developers of the MMPI-2-RF believed to be pervasive across many forms of psychopathology. So, demoralization gets a scale of its own in the MMPI-2-RF, and the remaining clinical scales are a bit more streamlined and distinctive from one another. (Two of the original 10 clinical scales, Scale 5 [Masculinity-Femininity] and Scale 0 [Social Introversion], are omitted from the MMPI-2-RF.) The MMPI-2-RF also includes the new Higher-Order scales, which correspond with common two-point codes from the MMPI-2 but are measured as single scales, and the new PSY-5 scales, which are related to personality disorders (Ben-Porath & Archer, 2008; Groth-Marnat, 2009). It is too early to know how it will be embraced by clinical psychologists—and in fact, the MMPI-2-RF has a number of detractors (Butcher, 2010, 2011; Butcher & Williams, 2009)—but the introduction of the MMPI-2-RF certainly presents an intriguing alternative.

The MMPI-2 and MMPI-A are currently used for a wide variety of purposes in a wide variety of settings. They are considered comprehensive tests of personality characteristics and psychopathology, and they can be helpful in forming *Diagnostic and Statistical Manual of Mental Disorders* (*DSM*) diagnoses and suggesting placement (e.g., inpatient vs. outpatient) and treatment. They are also used in numerous specialty areas of psychology, including forensic settings and personnel testing (Butcher, 2011).

An unusual but interesting use of the MMPI-2 has been described by Stephen Finn and his colleagues: *Therapeutic Assessment* (TA). As the name implies, TA involves the use of psychological testing—including feedback about the results—as a brief therapeutic intervention. Early in his career, Finn noticed that his assessment clients often seemed to benefit from the feedback session in which he explained the results of their testing. Despite the fact that the effect was unintended, Finn pursued specific methods by which to maximize it. He has focused on the MMPI-2 specifically and emphasizes a feedback session that is interactive discussion between client and clinician rather than a unidirectional lecture. TA works most effectively when the assessment is voluntary (rather than required) and when the client can pose specific questions for the clinician to address during feedback (Finn & Kamphus, 2006; Finn & Tonsager, 1992; Newman & Greenway, 1997). More broadly, the notion of psychological assessment as a therapeutic tool in and of itself has accumulated significant empirical support (Hanson & Poston, 2011; Poston & Hanson, 2010) and has even been extended to assessments conducted via computer or smartphone (R. E. Smith et al., 2011).

The MMPI-2 and MMPI-A tests are not without limitations. They have been criticized for being too lengthy, requiring reading ability and prolonged attention beyond the capability of some clients, and being susceptible to "faking" by sophisticated clients who can outwit the validity scales. A final criticism of the MMPI tests focuses on their emphasis on forms of psychopathology as the factors that make up personality. That is, the clinical scales of the MMPI tests describe a client's personality by describing the extent to which they have various pathologies (depression, schizophrenia, etc.) as opposed to emphasizing other aspects of personality, such as normal traits or strengths.

Clinical psychologists use numerous other objective personality tests similar to the MMPI tests in some ways yet different in some important ways as well. Examples include the Millon Clinical Multiaxial Inventory-III, which emphasizes personality disorders; the NEO Personality Inventory-Revised, which emphasizes normal personality traits; and the California Psychological Inventory-III, which emphasizes positive aspects of personality.

Millon Clinical Multiaxial Inventory-III

The **Millon Clinical Multiaxial Inventory-III (MCMI-III)** is like the MMPI-2 in many ways: It is a comprehensive personality test in a self-report, pencil-and-paper, true/false format. The primary difference between the tests is the MCMI-III's emphasis on personality disorders. Although it does feature scales for many clinical syndromes related to other disorders such as depression, anxiety, and posttraumatic stress, the MCMI-III is notable for its many scales related to the personality disorders in *DSM*. In fact, the MCMI-III features separate clinical scales corresponding to each of the 10 current personality disorders (e.g., antisocial, borderline, narcissistic, paranoid). It also includes clinical scales for other forms of personality pathology that have been considered for inclusion as disorders in *DSM* but are currently omitted (e.g., self-defeating personality, negativistic/passive-aggressive personality, depressive personality; Craig, 2008; Retzlaff & Dunn, 2003).

The MCMI was originally created in 1977 by **Theodore Millon,** a widely recognized scholar on personality disorders. The current version, MCMI-III, was published in 1994 to correspond with the publication of *DSM-IV.* The MCMI-III consists of 175 true/false items. In addition to its clinical scales, it includes "modifier indices," which function similarly to the validity scales of the MMPI tests by assessing the test-taking attitude of the client. Reliability and validity data for the MCMI-III are strong, suggesting it is a wise choice for clinical psychologists who seek a broad assessment of personality with an emphasis on personality disorders (Craig, 2008; Meagher, Grossman, & Millon, 2004).

⊕ **Web Link 10.2**
Theodore Millon

⊕ **Web Link 10.3**
NEO-PI-R Site

NEO Personality Inventory-Revised

As stated above, the MMPI emphasizes the pathological aspects of personality by producing scores that indicate the extent to which the client is symptomatic of various disorders. The authors of the **NEO Personality Inventory-Revised (NEO-PI-R), Paul Costa** and

Robert McCrae, sought to create a personality measure that assesses "normal" personality characteristics. The five characteristics measured by their test emerge from decades of research on normal personality, much of which was factor analytic in nature. In short, the authors of the NEO-PI-R (who also put forth the corresponding **five-factor model of personality** or "Big Five") argue that the many words our language offers for describing personality traits "cluster" into five fundamental traits of personality that characterize everyone in varying degrees. These traits—Neuroticism, Extraversion, Openness, Agreeableness, and Conscientiousness—are the five primary scales yielded by the NEO-PI-R and are described in Table 10.2. The NEO-PI-R also produces 30 "facet" scores (6 facets within each of the 5 domains) to offer more specific descriptions of components within each trait (Costa & McCrae, 1992, 2008).

In terms of format, the NEO-PI-R is comparable to the other objective personality tests described in this chapter. It is a 240-item, pencil-and-paper, self-report questionnaire. The

Table 10.2 Normal Personality Traits Assessed by the NEO-PI-R

Trait/Scale	Description of High Score	Description of Low Score
Neuroticism	Prone to emotional distress, negative affect, anxiety, sadness	Emotionally stable, even tempered, secure even under stressful conditions
Extraversion	Sociable, talkative, outgoing, prefer to be with others	Introverted, reserved, shy, prefer to be alone
Openness	Curious about novel ideas and values, imaginative, unconventional	Conventional, conservative, traditional, prefer familiar ideas and values
Agreeableness	Sympathetic, cooperative, accommodating, prefer to avoid conflict	Hardheaded, competitive, egocentric, uncooperative, unsympathetic
Conscientiousness	Organized, purposeful, disciplined, methodical, tend to make and carry out plans	Easygoing, spontaneous, disorganized, spur-of-the-moment, laid-back

Sources: Costa and McCrae (1992) and Costa and Widiger (2001).

items are short statements with multiple-choice responses ranging from "strongly agree" to "strongly disagree." The original NEO Personality Inventory was published in 1985, with the current edition, NEO-PI-R, arriving in 1992. A short form of this test (with 60 items), the **NEO Five Factor Inventory (NEO-FFI),** is also available but produces a less detailed profile. Psychometric data on the NEO-PI-R suggests that it has very strong reliability and validity (Costa & McCrae, 1992).

The NEO-PI-R has been criticized for its lack of validity scales. Unlike the MMPI tests and the MCMI-III, the NEO-PI-R lacks any substantive measurement of the test taker's approach to the test, leaving it rather vulnerable to "faking" or inattention by clients. Clinicians have also commented on the test's limited clinical utility, especially regarding diagnosis. Although the NEO-PI-R can indicate that an individual is extremely high or low in any of the five fundamental personality traits, such extreme scores do not readily translate into specific, diagnosable mental disorders. However, recent research suggests that some disorders, especially personality disorders, correlate strongly with particular combinations of high scores on NEO-PI-R scales, which bolsters the clinical utility of the NEO-PI-R for many psychologists (Costa & McCrae, 2008; Costa & Widiger, 2001).

California Psychological Inventory-III

The **California Psychological Inventory-III (CPI-III)** goes a step further than the NEO-PI-R in deemphasizing pathology as the defining characteristic of personality. Whereas the MMPI tests emphasize pathology and the NEO-PI-R emphasizes normal traits, the CPI-III emphasizes the positive attributes of personality. The CPI-III, published in 1996, was designed to assess the strengths, assets, and internal resources of clients (Donnay & Elliott, 2003). The CPI-III is a pencil-and-paper, self-report questionnaire including 434 true/false items. (The CPI-III also goes by the name CPI-434, referring to the total number of items. There is also a shorter version, called the CPI-260.) It yields scores on 20 scales, the names of which reflect the positive nature of this test: Independence, Self-Acceptance, Empathy, Tolerance, Responsibility, and Flexibility, among others. Because it emphasizes strengths rather than deficiencies, the CPI-III is regarded negatively by clinicians looking to diagnose disorders but positively by those looking to understand a broad range of their clients' abilities and talents.

The CPI-III is consistent with the recent, growing movement within the mental health field toward **positive psychology,** which accentuates the strong and healthy rather than the pathological aspects of human behavior (Donnay & Elliott, 2003; Seligman & Csikszentmihalyi, 2000). In the assessment field, positive psychology often takes the form of *strength-based assessment,* in which the clinician seeks a comprehensive view of his or her client that will include "what's strong" in addition to "what's wrong" (Rashid & Ostermann, 2009, p. 490). As with the names of the CPI-III scales, the names of the other strength-based assessment tools reflect the positive attributes on which they focus: Satisfaction With Life Scale, Love Attitudes Scale, Heartland Forgiveness Scale, Authentic Happiness Questionnaire, General Happiness Questionnaire, Gratitude Questionnaire, and, perhaps the most widely used, the Values in Action Inventory of Strengths (Peterson & Seligman, 2004).

Beck Depression Inventory-II

⊕ **Web Link 10.4**

BDI-II Site

Comprehensive objective personality tests—such as the MMPI tests, the MCMI-III, the NEO-PI-R, and the CPI-III—provide clinical psychologists with a broad overview of personality and provide scores on a broad range of variables.

But sometimes, clinical psychologists prefer more targeted, noncomprehensive objective measures. These tests are typically briefer and focus exclusively on one characteristic, such as depression, anxiety, or eating disorders. The **Beck Depression Inventory-II (BDI-II)** is a widely respected and used example of this type of test. (It appears in this section about objective personality tests even though it assesses only one characteristic, rather than personality more fully.)

The BDI-II is a self-report, pencil-and-paper test that assesses depressive symptoms in adults and adolescents. The original BDI was created by **Aaron Beck**, a leader in cognitive therapy of depression and other disorders, in the 1960s; the current revision was published in 1996. The BDI-II is brief—only 21 items, usually requiring a total of 5 to 10 minutes to complete. Each item is a set of four statements regarding a particular symptom of depression, listed in order of increasing severity. The clients choose the one sentence in each set that best describes their personal experience during the previous 2 weeks (a time period chosen to match *DSM* criteria). The 21 item scores are summed to produce a total score, which reflects the client's overall level of depression (Brantley, Dutton, & Wood, 2004; Quilty, Zhang, & Bagby, 2010). As a simulated sample BDI-II item, consider the following set of statements, of which the client would choose one:

- I never think about dying. (0 points)
- I occasionally think about dying. (1 point)
- I frequently think about dying. (2 points)
- I constantly think about dying. (3 points)

The BDI-II lacks validity scales, and of course its scope is much more limited than those of the other objective tests discussed in this chapter. However, its reliability and validity are strongly established (Brantley et al., 2004), and it is a frequent choice of psychologists seeking a quick, empirically sound answer to a specific assessment question regarding depression.

Projective Personality Tests

Objective personality tests are based on the assumption that personality is best assessed by directly asking people to describe themselves. **Projective personality tests** are based on a fundamentally different assumption: People will "project" their personalities if presented with unstructured, ambiguous stimuli and an unrestricted opportunity to respond. Imagine a group of people lying on the ground, looking up at the same series of vaguely shaped clouds in the sky. The way each person makes sense of the series of clouds implies something about that person's personality, according to supporters of projective personality tests. To extend this analogy, projective personality tests are similar to a series of "clouds" that psychologists display to clients. Clients are given freedom to make sense of these stimuli in any way they choose—they are not restricted to multiple-choice or true/ false options. Clients' responses may be compared with those of others in a normative group, and psychologists will ultimately form hypotheses about the clients' personalities based on their responses.

The lack of objectivity, especially in scoring and interpreting, highlights the most frequently cited shortcoming of projective personality tests. Critics of projective tests stress that they are far too inferential to be empirically sound; that is, they rely too heavily on a psychologist's unique way of scoring and interpreting a client's responses (Hunsley, Lee, & Wood, 2003). In an objective test in which a client's responses consist of "true" or "false," scoring is standardized and consistent. But in a projective test in which each client produces unique responses, scoring may vary across psychologists. Additionally, once items are scored, the process of assigning meaning to them is, according to many, less systematic and more idiosyncratic in projective tests. Indeed, the standing of projective tests has undoubtedly declined in popularity in recent decades, to the satisfaction of critics who claim that their reliability and validity are insufficient to justify psychologists using them or graduate programs teaching them (e.g., Lilienfeld, Wood, & Garb, 2000).

However, other experts in the field of projective personality testing have argued vigorously in favor of their use (Meyer & Viglione, 2008). They point to unique assets of projective tests, such as the fact that they aren't as "fake-able" as objective tests: "Given the research on the human capacity to create a façade of mental health, personality assessment using [projective] methods affords the clinical psychologist the means to bring to light a person's true emotional troubles" (Fowler & Groat, 2008, p. 491). They also point to empirical data, such as a review of 184 meta-analytic studies of the psychometric characteristics of personality tests that found the reliability and validity of common projectives such as the Rorschach Inkblot Method and the Thematic Apperception Test (TAT), when scored systematically and accurately, roughly equal to those of commonly used objective personality tests (Meyer, 2004). However, critics cast serious doubt on

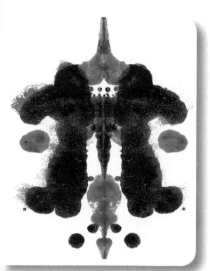

Photo 10.3 This inkblot closely resembles those used in the Rorschach Inkblot Method. In your opinion, how well can responses to inkblots reveal personality characteristics?

the methods and data used to support these conclusions. So the controversy continues. Although projective personality tests may not be as popular as they once were and some detractors decry their continued use, surveys of psychologists suggest that some, including the Rorschach, the TAT, and sentence-completion tests, remain very much a part of contemporary clinical psychology (e.g., Watkins, Campbell, Nieberding, & Hallmark, 1995).

Rorschach Inkblot Method

In 1921, **Hermann Rorschach** created the **Rorschach Inkblot Method.** Rorschach was a Swiss psychiatrist who, as a child, played a game in which participants looked at vague blots of ink and said what they saw in the blots. As an adult, he decided to apply a similar method to his patients, with the hypothesis that their responses would reveal their personality characteristics (Weiner, 2004).

For his test, Rorschach created 10 inkblots, 5 with only black ink and the other 5 with multiple colors. Administration occurs in two phases. In the "response" or "free association" phase, the psychologist presents one inkblot card at a time, asks, "What might this be?" and writes down the client's responses verbatim. After the client has responded to all 10 cards, the "inquiry" phase begins, in which the psychologist reads the client's responses aloud and asks the client to describe exactly where in the inkblot each response was located and what features of the inkblot caused the client to offer that response. A simulated Rorschach inkblot appears in Photo 10.3.

⊕ **Web Link 10.5**

Hermann Rorschach Archives and Museum

When Rorschach published his inkblots in 1921, they were not accompanied by a scoring method. Rorschach died about a year later, and in his absence, numerous scoring systems were independently created and used in the United States and Europe. Ultimately, **John Exner** combined aspects of many scoring systems to create the **Comprehensive System,** which has become the most common method of scoring the Rorschach (Exner, 1986; Wood, Nezworski, Lilienfeld, & Garb, 2003). Exner's Comprehensive System includes normative data collected from thousands of children and adults; thus, the Rorschach can be used with clients across almost the entire life span.

When a clinical psychologist uses Exner's Comprehensive System, each Rorschach response is coded in many ways. The scoring of a Rorschach response has as much to do with the process by which the client made sense of the blot as the content of the client's perceptions.

In other words, *how* the client perceives the blot is no less important than *what* the client sees. A small sample of the many variables examined by the Comprehensive System includes the following:

- *Location.* Does the response involve the whole inkblot, a large portion of it, or a small detail?
- *Determinants.* What aspect of the inkblot—its form, color, shading, etc.—caused the client to make a particular response?
- *Form Quality.* Is the response easily identifiable and conventional? Or is it unique or distorted?
- *Popular.* Each card has a response or two that occurs relatively frequently. How often does the client offer these popular responses?
- *Content.* What kinds of objects appear with unusual frequency in the client's responses? People, animals, food, clothing, explosions, body parts, nature, or other categories of items?

After each response is scored, the scores are combined into a variety of indices, and the scores and indices are then interpreted. Although interpretive strategies vary somewhat and some may be more empirically based than others, a rule of thumb is that the way the client makes sense of the inkblots parallels the way the client makes sense of the world. Consider, for example, the Form Quality variable described above. Clients who consistently offer distorted, atypical perceptions of inkblots are thought to do similar things in life—misperceive situations, use distorted judgment, or make sense of things in an unconventional manner. Or consider the Location variable. A client whose responses almost always incorporate the whole inkblot may tend to focus on the "big picture" of life rather than "breaking it down" into smaller pieces or attending to details, whereas a client whose responses always involve very small parts of the inkblot may tend to focus excessively on details and overlook the "big picture" in day-to-day life.

Together, the multitude of variables yielded by the Comprehensive System shed light on many aspects of personality. However, the psychometric foundation underlying the Rorschach has, for some, cast doubt on the clinical conclusions it can offer. Supporters of the Rorschach point out that the reliability data regarding scoring, especially test-retest reliability, is quite strong according to some studies and that validity for the Rorschach has been measured at a comparable level to that of the MMPI tests (e.g., Meyer, 2004; Rose, Kaser-Boyd, & Maloney, 2001). However, many critics of the Rorschach have pointed out some serious shortcomings: Numerous studies have found weak reliability and validity data; scoring and interpretation guidelines are complex, and psychologists do not always follow them as closely as they should; results can't often distinguish those who have a particular disorder from those who don't; moreover, norms for the Rorschach may be inadequate for some populations (as summarized by Wood et al., 2003; see also Wood et al., 2010). Controversy regarding the scientific status of the Rorschach has raged in recent years, and although it remains widely used and respected by many clinical psychologists today, the long-term future of the Rorschach depends largely on how that controversy is resolved.

Thematic Apperception Test

The **Thematic Apperception Test (TAT)**, published by **Henry Murray** and **Christiana Morgan**, is similar to the Rorschach in that it involves presenting the client with a series of cards, each featuring an ambiguous stimulus (Morgan & Murray, 1935; Murray, 1943). Unlike the Rorschach cards, however, the TAT cards feature interpersonal scenes rather than inkblots. The client's task is to create a story to go along with each scene (Gieser & Stein, 1999; Morgan, 1999). They are asked to consider not only what is happening in the scene at the moment but also what happened before and what may happen after the scene. They are also asked to describe what the characters may be thinking and feeling (Bellak, 1993). Although the TAT is considered a global measure of personality by many, its strength may lie in its ability to measure interpersonal relationship tendencies (Ackerman, Fowler, & Clemence, 2008).

Box 10.4 features a simulated TAT card, along with a variety of simulated responses. What inferences would you make about the person telling each of the stories? Compare your interpretations to those of your classmates or friends—how consistent are the interpretations? (Note that the actual interpretation of TAT responses would emphasize recurring themes across multiple stories rather than an interpretation based on a single story.)

The TAT includes a total of 31 cards, but psychologists typically select their own subset of cards—often about 10 or so—to administer to a particular client. As the client tells stories aloud and the psychologist writes them down, the psychologist may ask questions during a client's story to solicit more information and can remind the client of the initial instructions as well. Henry Murray (1943) offered a scoring system for the TAT emphasizing "needs" of the main characters, "press" from the environment, and other variables. Others have offered additional formal scoring systems (e.g., Bellak, 1999; see also Abrams, 1999), but for the most part, formal TAT scoring systems have been "neglected or ignored" (Moretti & Rossini, 2004, p. 357). Currently, the TAT is often analyzed without formal scoring at all: "Most clinicians today seem to rely on their own impressionistic inferences," resulting in "idiosyncratic and inconsistent" use of the TAT (p. 357). Thus, TAT interpretation is frequently more art than science. A client's story may be interpreted one way by one psychologist but very differently by another.

Simulated TAT Card with Simulated Responses

1. "She's really nervous about something. It's only breakfast time, but she's already anxious about something coming up during her day. Maybe she's worrying about a test at school, or some kids who might tease her, or the school bus getting into an accident, or something happening out of the blue that she hasn't even thought about yet. Not sure which, but she's definitely worried about something, and she's only gonna get more worried as the day goes on."

Photo 10.4 Simulated TAT

2. "She is a sad, sad girl. She's looking at that plate and thinking that it's empty, just like her life. Something good may appear on the plate soon, but that will only be temporary. It's just like her life—she wishes she could stay happy, but she just can't. No matter what, she ends up sad again."

3. "She's excited for a family dinner. Soon, her parents and brothers and sisters will be around the table, and there will be eating and laughing and fun. Then, they will all help clean up and have a great evening. As she goes to bed, she'll be looking forward to another great day tomorrow."

4. "She's a guest at this house—her friend invited her to have dinner over. She's thinking about the jewelry she just stole from her friend's mother's bedroom. She snuck in there when no one was looking and grabbed some earrings and a necklace. Some people would be feeling guilty about it, but she doesn't—not at all. She actually gets a rush out of it."

5. "She just finished all of the food on her plate, and now she's thinking about making herself throw up. She definitely doesn't want to get fat. Her mom yells at her older sister all the time about being fat. She doesn't want her mom to criticize her like that, so she's trying hard to stay thin. Sometimes she doesn't eat much at all. When she does, she usually thinks about making herself throw up, and sometimes she actually does it."

Source: Kenney Mencher.

As a result of this nonempirical scoring and interpretation procedure, the TAT is not a preferred test among clinical psychologists who insist on assessment methods supported by strong psychometric data (Holt, 1999). The validity and reliability of the TAT are less well established than those of other personality tests, largely because the scoring, interpretation, or administration is not uniform across psychologists. Henry Murray (1943) himself stated, "The conclusions that are reached by an analysis of TAT stories must be regarded as good 'leads' or working hypotheses to be verified by other methods, rather than as proved facts" (p. 14)—a statement applicable to all assessment methods, especially those with debatable scientific status. Nonetheless, the use of the TAT continues, as well as the use of the related **Children's Apperception Test (CAT)** and **Senior Apperception Test (SAT;** Bellak, 1993; see also Teglasi, 2010), based on the hypothesis that "the stories we tell say something about who we are" (Moretti & Rossini, 2004, p. 357).

A final note on story-telling tests: the Tell-Me-a-Story (TEMAS) apperception test, designed for children and adolescents, is part of a newer generation of TAT-style tests that place greater emphasis on empirical scoring via normative data as well as cultural sensitivity (Malgady & Colon-Malgady, 2008). The TEMAS was developed specifically for Hispanic youth and was later expanded for use with African American and white youth—with images that feature culturally diverse people in scenes more typical of urban settings, rather than the somewhat rural emphasis of the TAT (Teglasi, 2010). The TEMAS is described in more detail in the chapter on clinical child and adolescent psychology.

Sentence Completion Tests

In **sentence completion tests**, the ambiguous stimuli are neither inkblots nor interpersonal scenes; instead, they are the beginnings of sentences. The assumption is that a client's personality is revealed by the endings they add and the sentences they create. Although there are many projective tests using the sentence completion format, the **Rotter Incomplete Sentences Blank (RISB)** tests are by far the most widely known and commonly used (Sherry, Dahlen, & Holaday, 2004). The original RISB was published in 1950, with the most recent revised edition (including high school, college, and adult versions) appearing in 1992. The RISB tests include 40 written sentence "stems" referring to various aspects of the client's life. Each stem is followed by a blank space in which the client completes the sentence. Simulated sentence stems similar to those in the RISB include:

- I enjoy _____.
- It makes me furious _____.
- I feel very nervous _____.
- My proudest moment _____.
- My greatest weakness _____.

Like the TAT, the RISB includes a formal scoring system, but clinical psychologists may not use it regularly, and when they do, scoring is highly dependent on the clinical judgment of the psychologist. Thus, its scientific standing is questionable. However, the RISB can "flesh out" the information obtained through other tests, including objective personality tests (Sherry et al., 2004). For example, a clinical psychologist may conclude that a client is depressed after the client obtains a very high score on the Depression scale (Scale 2) of the MMPI-2. But that scale score alone offers no explanation of the qualitative aspects of the depression or what the depression is "about." If the client answered the simulated RISB items above by stating that "I enjoy . . . very few things now that my spouse is gone," "It makes me furious . . . that life is so unfair," and "I feel very nervous . . . when I think about living alone," the clinical psychologist can hypothesize that the client's depression relates closely to the loss of this significant relationship.

Behavioral Assessment

Most clinical psychologists would consider all the objective and projective measures described so far in this chapter to be **traditional personality assessment** techniques. These traditional techniques share a few basic, implicit assumptions:

- Personality is a stable, internal construct. In other words, behavior is determined primarily by characteristics or dispositions "inside" the person.
- Assessing personality requires a high degree of inference. That is, clinical psychologists use the data provided by personality tests (e.g., MMPI-2 scale scores, Rorschach responses) to deduce or speculate about problem behaviors that clients may actually experience.
- Client behaviors are signs of deep-seated, underlying issues or problems, sometimes taking the form of *DSM* diagnoses.

Behavioral assessment challenges all these assumptions and offers a fundamentally different approach to assessment (Heiby & Haynes, 2004; Ollendick, Alvarez, & Greene, 2004). According to behavioral assessment, client behaviors are not signs of underlying issues or problems; instead, those behaviors *are* the problems. Another way to state this is that the behavior a client demonstrates is a sample of the problem itself, not a sign of some deeper, underlying problem. For example, if Zach, a 9-year-old child, argues with teachers often at school, "arguing with teachers" is the problem. It is unnecessary and unwise, according to behavioral assessors, to understand Zach's arguing as "symptomatic" of a deep-rooted issue, such as oppositional defiant disorder. So to assess the problem, assessment techniques should involve as little inference as possible. Rather than inkblots or questionnaires that may get at the problem indirectly, behavioral assessors would choose the most direct way to measure Zach's problem behavior: observation of Zach in his classroom. By rejecting the idea that Zach "has" some internal disorder or trait that underlies his arguing, behavioral assessors demonstrate their rejection of the more fundamental idea that enduring, internal "personality" characteristics cause all behavior. Instead, behavioral assessors argue that external, situational factors determine our behavior. As such, behavioral assessment is a uniquely empirical approach that capitalizes on "the use of valid, precise, and sensitive measures of well-defined behaviors and contemporaneous events to capture behavior-environment interactions" (Haynes & Kaholokula, 2008, p. 518) in which clinicians diagnose behavior problems rather than the clients who exhibit them.

Methods of Behavioral Assessment

The most essential technique in behavioral assessment is **behavioral observation** or the direct, systematic observation of a client's behavior in the natural environment (Ollendick et al., 2004). Also known as **naturalistic observation,** this practice involves taking a direct sample of the problem at the site where it occurs (home, work, school, public places, etc.). The first step in behavioral observation involves identifying and operationally defining the problem behavior. This takes place via interviews, behavioral checklists, consultation with those who have observed the client (family members, coworkers, teachers, etc.), or self-monitoring by the client. Once the target behavior is identified and defined, systematic observation takes place. This process usually involves tallying the frequency, duration, or intensity of the target behavior across specified time periods—first as a baseline, and then at regular intervals to measure improvement as compared with that baseline. Such direct observation can provide a far more accurate assessment of problem behavior than merely asking the client to recall or summarize it verbally during an interview or on a questionnaire. When observation in the natural environment is not possible, behavioral assessors can arrange an analogue observation, in which they attempt to replicate the real-world setting in the clinic and observe the client's responses there (Haynes & Kaholokula, 2008).

Behavioral observation also typically includes keeping a record of the events that occur immediately before and after the target behavior. Depending on the client, the target behavior, and the setting, the record keeping can be completed by any number of individuals, including a teacher, a parent, a friend or family member, or the client. Documenting these events allows for clinical psychologists to understand the functionality of a particular behavior or how the behavior relates to the environment and contingencies that surround it (Heiby & Haynes, 2004). As an example, let's consider 9-year-old Zach again. If Zach's clinical psychologist, Dr. Davis, was conducting a behavioral observation, Dr. Davis would visit Zach's classroom with an explicit definition of the arguing behavior and would systematically keep track of its occurrence. However, Dr. Davis would also take note of the antecedents and consequences of Zach's behavior. Perhaps Zach's arguments are consistently preceded by a particular stimulus (e.g., a direct question from the teacher or an in-class math assignment) or followed by a particular consequence (e.g., prolonged attention from the teacher or removal from the room). These events surrounding Zach's behavior—the "if . . . , then . . ." contingencies that he has learned regarding the outcomes of his actions—can offer important information regarding the functionality of the target behavior (Cipani & Schock, 2007).

Traditional assessment methods such as interviews and questionnaires are not necessarily foreign to behavioral assessment, but if they are used, they emphasize the instrumental aspect of the behavior in question. That is, rather than the aims of many traditional interviews and questionnaires—diagnostic categorization, for example—the interviews and questionnaires are used by behavioral assessors with the singular goal of identifying the function of the problem behavior. In fact, the terminology they use for these techniques—functional interview and functional questionnaires—illustrates this approach (Haynes & Kaholokula, 2008). If Dr. Davis conducted a functional interview with 9-year-old Zach (or his parents or his teacher), she would ask targeted questions about the antecedents and consequences of Zach's problematic arguing behavior. Of course, asking the client's opinion is no substitute for direct behavioral observation, because the client may lack insight or deliberately mislead the assessor about the sequence of events that typically takes place. However, functional interviews and functional questionnaires can provide important information to guide the behavioral observation. For example, Zach may mention that a consequence of his arguing behavior is that Thomas, the most popular boy in the class, roots him on by subtly smiling and nodding. If Thomas wasn't on Dr. Davis's radar before the functional interview, he will be after Zach mentions him.

Technology in Behavioral Assessment

Especially in recent years, computers and other forms of technology have been used productively by behavioral assessors. In the description above of Dr. Davis's behavioral observation of Zach, Dr. Davis could have used a laptop computer or smartphone to record her observations. Numerous software programs have emerged, allowing for simultaneous recording of multiple variables, instant graphing and statistical analysis of behavior patterns, and other advanced, time-saving features. In fact, clients themselves can benefit from the use of technology in behavioral assessment. For example, clients often conduct **self-monitoring,** either as a way of defining the target behavior or measuring changes in it over time. This self-monitoring has traditionally been done with pencil-and-paper journals, but computers and smartphones offer a method that can be more convenient (for e-mailing, texting, or downloading records) and private (if the device has a password-protection feature). Additionally, most of these devices have timer and alarm features, which can increase clients' compliance with self-monitoring schedules (Richard & Lauterbach, 2003).

CHAPTER SUMMARY

The personality assessment techniques traditionally used by clinical psychologists can generally be divided into objective and projective tests. Objective personality tests are typically pencil-and-paper questionnaires featuring unambiguous stimuli, a limited range of responses, and a self-report format. Some of these tests assess test takers' attitudes as well as clinically relevant variables, which aid in interpretation of test results. Examples of objective personality tests include the MMPI-2, which focuses on various types of psychopathology; the MCMI-III, which focuses on personality disorders; the NEO-PI-R, which focuses on normal personality traits; the CPI-III, which focuses on strengths rather than disorders; and the BDI-II, which is a relatively brief, more targeted test assessing depression only. Projective personality tests involve ambiguous stimuli and an unlimited range of responses and are viewed by many as

less psychometrically sound than objective tests. Examples of projective personality tests include the Rorschach Inkblot Technique; the TAT, in which clients respond to interpersonal scenes rather than inkblots; and sentence completion tests, in which clients fill in the end of unfinished sentence stems. Unlike traditional clinical assessment involving objective or projective testing, behavioral assessment involves a more direct and less inferential approach to client's problems. Behavioral assessors employ techniques such as behavioral observation and client self-monitoring with the belief that problem behavior is the clinical issue, rather than a sign of a deeper underlying issue. Regardless of the techniques they choose when assessing personality or behavior, clinical psychologists should use multiple methods, consider evidence-based assessment methods for particular clinical problems, and strive for cultural competence.

KEY TERMS AND NAMES

CRITICAL THINKING QUESTIONS

1. In your opinion, what are the most important strengths and weaknesses of projective personality tests?

2. In your opinion, what are the most important strengths and weaknesses of objective personality tests?

3. If you were designing an objective personality test, how would you go about creating a measure of test-taking attitudes (such as the validity scales of the MMPI-2)?

4. The NEO-PI-R is founded on the idea that all people share the same five fundamental personality characteristics and that we differ only in the strength of these characteristics. Do you agree that all people share the same personality characteristics, or do you believe that some people have qualitatively different characteristics than others?

5. In your opinion, for what clinical problems is behavioral assessment best suited?

STUDENT STUDY SITE RESOURCES

Visit the study site at www.sagepub.com/pomerantz3eupdate for these additional learning tools:

- Self-quizzes
- eFlashcards
- Culture Expert Interviews

- Full-text SAGE journal articles
- Additional web resources
- Mock Assessment Data

CHAPTER SUMMARY VIDEO

 QR codes at the end of each chapter link to chapter background videos by the author. Visit http://gettag.mobi using your smartphone browser to download the free Microsoft Tag app. Once installed, scan the tags to go directly to these brief videos. In this video, the author expands on the role and function of brief, objective, targeted questionnaires as used by clinical psychologists.

Psychotherapy

CHAPTER 11

General Issues in Psychotherapy

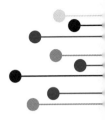

With this chapter, we begin our exploration of **psychotherapy,** the most common professional activity of clinical psychologists (Norcross & Karpiak, 2012). Upcoming chapters offer details on specific approaches to psychotherapy, including psychoanalytic/psychodynamic, humanistic, behavioral, and cognitive techniques. But in this chapter, we consider some important "across-the-board" psychotherapy issues, including how well it works and how it has been practiced by clinical psychologists.

Does Psychotherapy Work?

Questions about the outcome of psychotherapy have been prominent throughout the history of clinical psychology, and studies investigating these questions have taken many forms. Through the mid-1900s, most of the evidence offered in support of psychotherapy came in the form of anecdotes, testimonials, and case studies—essentially, subjective descriptions of individual clients' progress, usually written by the therapists themselves. Controlled, empirical studies of therapy outcome didn't appear regularly until the 1950s (Weissmark & Giacomo, 1998). **Hans Eysenck** (1952) published a historic study during this early period. Its claims were noteworthy and controversial: After reviewing some of the early empirical studies on psychotherapy outcome, Eysenck concluded that most clients got better without therapy and that in general, psychotherapy was of little benefit. His scientific methods have since been criticized and his claims overturned, but Eysenck's allegation that therapy doesn't work inspired thousands of subsequent empirical studies on therapy outcome (Routh, 2011; Wampold, 2010b).

Many of those empirical studies on therapy outcome were conducted in the 1960s and 1970s. By the late 1970s and 1980s, meta-analyses began to appear. A **meta-analysis** statistically combines the results of many separate studies—in some cases, hundreds—to create numerical representations of the effects of psychotherapy as tested across massive numbers of settings, therapists, and clients. As we see in this chapter, these meta-analyses have yielded consistently supportive results about how well psychotherapy works. But before exploring those results, let's consider just some of the methodological issues involved in a simple investigation of psychotherapy outcome.

Whom, When, and How Should Researchers Ask?

Designing and running an empirical study to measure the outcome of psychotherapy can be a complex task for researchers. One of the fundamental questions they must answer involves the fact that different people involved in the therapy may have different vantage points on the results of the therapy. Whose opinion should researchers seek?

Hans Strupp, a legendary and pioneering psychotherapy researcher, identified three parties who have a stake in how well therapy works and who may have different opinions about what constitutes a successful therapy outcome. He and his colleagues have labeled their theory the **tripartite model** (with *tripartite* literally meaning "three parties") (Strupp, 1996; Strupp & Hadley, 1977; Strupp, Hadley, & Gomes-Schwartz, 1977). One party, of course, is the client. After all, clients are the ones whose lives are affected by therapy, and improving their lives in some meaningful way is presumably the focus of the therapy. Clients' opinions about therapy outcome are extremely valuable, but they can also be extremely biased. Some clients may be overly eager to see positive results, especially after investing significant time and money, and therefore overestimate therapy's benefits. Other clients' opinions about psychotherapy may be negatively influenced by the very factors that brought them to therapy in the first place—for example, a depressed client who tends to interpret events in an unrealistically negative way may apply that kind of distorted thinking to his or her therapy. So a researcher may choose to turn to the therapist—the second party—as another source of feedback. The therapist typically has more experience in mental health issues than the client and may therefore have more reasonable expectations. However, therapists' views can be biased as well. Therapists witness only a fraction of clients' lives, and they may feel that negative evaluations reflect poorly on their own therapeutic skills. The third party identified by Strupp and his colleagues, society, can take the form of any outsider to the therapy process who has an interest in how therapy progresses. This can include the general public, the legal system, clients' family and friends, clients' employers, and, especially today, managed-care companies who pay the psychotherapy bill. These third parties tend to bring a perspective that emphasizes the client's ability to perform expected duties in a stable, predictable, unproblematic way. Certainly, the question of who to ask is crucial to the process of measuring therapy outcome. Thankfully, researchers need not choose a single perspective exclusively; they can and often do solicit multiple opinions.

Regardless of *whom* the researchers ask about therapy outcome, *when* should they ask? Perhaps the obvious answer is immediately after therapy ends. At that point, it would be reasonable to expect some improvement from the client's initial level of functioning. But how long should those benefits last? Is it reasonable to expect that therapy's benefits would continue to be evident 1 month, 6 months, 2 years, or 5 years down the road? And what about benefits before therapy ends? Should there be some evidence of improvement at various points in therapy or perhaps even at each session? Again, shrewd researchers may choose multiple answers to the question of *when,* either within or across psychotherapy studies. But it is evident that the time at which the researchers answer this question may influence the results they see (Lambert, 2011).

Finally, researchers have many options regarding *how* they measure the outcome of psychotherapy. If they choose to solicit opinions of an interested party, they can use questionnaires or interviews. Of course, the content and structure of these questionnaires or interviews will have an impact on the data they yield. Researchers may elect to use a more behavioral measure of therapy outcome instead. As an example, consider a researcher who seeks to determine the outcome of psychotherapy for a boy treated for attention-deficit/hyperactivity disorder. Rather than asking the boy, his therapist, his parents, or his teachers, a researcher could directly observe the boy at school or at home to determine if his behavior has changed since therapy began. As with the questions of *who* and *when*, the researcher's decision regarding *how* psychotherapy outcome is measured can shape the results of the investigation.

● ● ● BOX 11.1 ● ● ●

Considering Culture

Culture-Specific Expectations About Psychotherapy

Photo 11.1 Individuals from diverse cultural backgrounds come to psychotherapy with very different expectations about the behaviors of clients and therapists.

Our discussion about psychotherapy outcome, especially from the client's perspective, must take into consideration the fact that clients from diverse cultures often hold widely varying expectations about the psychotherapy process. A culturally competent therapist will be able to attain a more successful psychotherapy outcome by appreciating the presumptions related to each client's cultural background.

As it is traditionally practiced in North America and the Western world, psychotherapy involves verbally discussing one's problems, focusing attention on them, and gaining greater understanding or control over them. These basic processes clash with cultural values common to some non-Western cultures whose members often prefer to "conceal" rather than "reveal" (Fontes, 2008; Toukmanian & Brouwers, 1998). Individuals from Eastern cultures often prefer to avoid, rather than confront, negative thoughts. Thus, the communication styles of clients with psychotherapists—in simplest terms, the extent to which they are comfortable self-disclosing about problematic behaviors, thoughts, and feelings—may depend significantly on their cultural values.

A client's willingness to self-disclose to a psychotherapist may also depend on the individualistic versus collectivistic nature of a client's culture. Western cultures tend to foster an individualistic way of life, emphasizing self-reliance and self-determination. In contrast, Eastern cultures tend to encourage collectivism, whereby the needs of the family/group and the relationships that bind the family/group take priority over individual goals. Thus, whereas a client of European descent may feel slightly uncomfortable discussing a personal problem or shortcoming, a client of Asian descent may feel a much stronger sense of shame about a similar problem or shortcoming because of his or her perception that the problem reflects on family members as well (Sue & Sue, 2008; Toukmanian & Brouwers, 1998).

Training psychotherapists to be culturally competent is the foundation on which they can build an appreciation of clients' expectations about psychotherapy. Like many others, Toukmanian and Brouwers (1998) recommend that training in psychotherapy emphasize the personal development of the therapist's attitude toward diverse cultures.

This training should encompass four levels: self-understanding (of one's own cultural values), listening to clients' cultural values, accepting clients' cultural values, and understanding clients' cultural values.

If you were the client, how important would it be for your psychotherapist to appreciate your expectations about psychotherapy that relate to your cultural background? Specifically, which values would be most important to recognize?

Efficacy Versus Effectiveness of Psychotherapy

Empirical studies of psychotherapy outcome generally fall into two categories. The extent to which psychotherapy works "in the lab" refers to its **efficacy**. Most recent studies of psychotherapy outcome are efficacy studies. They maximize internal validity—that is, the ability to draw conclusions about the cause-effect relationship between therapy and outcome—by controlling as many aspects of therapy as possible. Efficacy studies typically feature well-defined groups of patients, usually meeting diagnostic criteria for a chosen disorder but no others; manualized treatment guidelines to minimize variability between therapists; and random assignment to control and treatment groups (Nathan & Gorman, 2002; Spokas, Rodebaugh, & Heimburg, 2008; Truax & Thomas, 2003).

In contrast, the extent to which psychotherapy works "in the real world" refers to its **effectiveness**. Effectiveness studies tend to include a wider range of clients, including those with complex diagnostic profiles; allow for greater variability between therapists' methods; and may or may not include a control group for comparison to a treatment group.

Effectiveness studies lack the internal validity of efficacy studies, because the researchers control and manipulate fewer variables. However, effectiveness studies typically have greater external validity than efficacy studies because their methods better match therapy that actually takes place in clinics, private practices, hospitals, and other realistic settings (Nathan & Gorman, 2002; Spokas et al., 2008; Truax & Thomas, 2003).

Results of Efficacy Studies

Thousands of efficacy studies of psychotherapy have accumulated in recent decades; in fact, reviews and meta-analyses that serve as summaries of individual studies now number in the hundreds as well. Again and again, these research efforts yield the same affirmative conclusion: Psychotherapy works (Lambert, 2011; Wampold, 2010a). For example, a primary finding of a landmark meta-analysis of 475 psychotherapy efficacy studies (Smith, Glass, & Miller, 1980) was that the average effect size for psychotherapy was .85, indicating that "the average person who receives therapy is better off at the end of it than 80 percent of the persons who do not" (p. 87). More recent reviews and meta-analyses of therapy efficacy studies (e.g., Lambert & Simon, 2008; Shapiro & Shapiro, 1982), including some very large-scale mega-reviews of meta-analyses (e.g., Lipsey & Wilson, 1993; Luborsky et al., 2002) have confirmed these findings. Summarizing their recent comprehensive review of psychotherapy efficacy data, Lambert and Ogles (2004) stated, "The pervasive theme of this large body of psychotherapy research must remain the same—psychotherapy is beneficial. This consistent finding across thousands of studies and hundreds of meta-analyses is seemingly undebatable" (p. 148).

Not only does psychotherapy work, its benefits appear to endure over long periods of time, exceed placebo effects, and represent clinically (not just statistically) significant change in clients' well-being (e.g., Lambert & Ogles, 2004; Smith et al., 1980). It should be noted that psychotherapy is not a panacea—a small minority of therapy clients do appear to worsen during the therapy process (Striano, 1988; Strupp et al., 1977). On a similar note, some clients drop out of therapy prematurely, and others experience only short-lived benefits (Lebow, 2006). However, these negative effects clearly appear to be the exception rather than the rule.

In spite of the overwhelming evidence offered by efficacy studies, their results are not always heeded by those who practice therapy in the real world (Boswell et al., 2011; Safran, Abreu, Ogilvie, & DeMaria, 2011). There is, for lack of a better term, a gap between those who conduct efficacy research on psychotherapy and those who practice it. Depending on which side you ask, the gap is caused either by researchers who conduct studies that are artificial, contrived, and irrelevant to how clinicians really practice in their clinics, hospitals, and offices, or by practitioners who refuse to open their eyes to scientific data regarding the outcome of various therapies and who resist changing their practices accordingly. Regardless of the reason, this gap is problematic for the field of clinical psychology. Fortunately, efforts to recognize and bridge it have increased in recent years (e.g., Dattilio, Edwards, & Fishman, 2010; Littell, 2010).

Results of Effectiveness Studies

Effectiveness studies have not been conducted as frequently as efficacy studies, but those that have been conducted have generated similarly positive results. So, whereas efficacy studies indicate that psychotherapy works when tested in controlled settings, effectiveness studies indicate that psychotherapy works as it is commonly applied in realistic settings.

As an example of an effectiveness study, consider the investigation conducted by *Consumer Reports* magazine in 1995 ("Mental Health," 1995; Seligman, 1995). The popular magazine—the same one that surveys its subscribers about their experiences with cars, DVD players, and laundry detergent—surveyed its many subscribers about their experiences with psychotherapy. The primary finding was that for the vast majority of respondents, psychotherapy had very positive, lasting effects. As stated by Seligman (1995),

There were a number of clear-cut results, among them:

> Treatment by a mental health professional usually worked. Most respondents got a lot better.
>
> Averaged over all mental health professionals, of the 426 people who were feeling *very poor* when they began therapy, 87% were feeling *very good, good,* or at least *so-so* by the time of the survey. Of the 786 people who were feeling *fairly poor* at the outset, 92% were feeling *very good, good,* or at least *so-so* by the time of the survey. These findings converge with meta-analyses of efficacy (Lipsey & Wilson, 1993; Shapiro & Shapiro, 1982; Smith et al., 1980).

Like any effectiveness study, the *Consumer Reports* study is constrained by some troubling methodological questions (Seligman, 1995). For example, was there a sampling bias such that those whose therapy experience was successful were most likely to respond? Of the many clients who improved, how many would have improved without psychotherapy (i.e., in a control group)? How reliable and valid are clients' own self-reports about psychotherapy outcome, especially after months or years have elapsed? Nonetheless, effectiveness studies such as this one complement efficacy studies, and together they strongly support the benefits of psychotherapy.

Alternate Ways to Measure Psychotherapy Outcome

Efficacy and effectiveness studies have been two primary ways of assessing how well therapy has worked, but there are others, both direct and indirect. For example, in recent years, researchers have paid increased attention to the neurobiological effects of psychotherapy. Although this field of study is in the early stages, the initial conclusion is unmistakable: psychotherapy changes the brain (Arden & Linford, 2009; Viamontes & Beitman, 2009). Studies using functional magnetic resonance imaging (fMRI) and positron emission tomography (PET) neuroimaging technologies have repeatedly found that successful therapy for particular disorders produces reliable changes in brain activity and structure. Among other findings, behavioral therapy for obsessive-compulsive disorder has been found to decrease metabolism in the caudate nucleus, behavior activation affects the dorsal striatum of depressed clients, and both cognitive behavioral therapy and interpersonal psychotherapy have been found to decrease activity in dorsal frontal regions and increase activity in ventral frontal and subcortical regions (Dichter et al., 2009; Roffman, Marci, Glick, Dougherty, & Rauch, 2005). (All these therapies are described in more detail in later chapters.) Although medication studies have focused on neurological changes in the brain, such studies are relatively new for psychotherapy studies. As they accumulate, they will provide even further evidence of the effects of psychotherapy.

In an indirect way, medical cost offset is another intriguing way to assess the outcome of psychotherapy. The logic goes like this: Many people with mental or emotional problems will either seek medical (rather than psychological) assistance or will put off treatment for so long that the problem worsens the individual's physical state, necessitating medical treatment. If they seek psychotherapy, will they reduce their medical costs? According to the available data, the answer appears to be a resounding yes (Lambert & Ogles, 2004). A review of more than 90 studies on this issue found that, on average, clients receiving therapy spent fewer days in the hospital and saw their medical costs reduced by 15.7%, while comparable clients in control groups spent more days in the hospital and saw their medical costs increased by 12.3% (Chiles, Lambert, & Hatch, 1999). Additionally, psychotherapy has been found to reduce the need for emergency room visits (Carr, 2008). Whether the medical bills are being paid by a health insurance company or by the clients themselves, the finding that psychotherapy is a good investment in both mental and physical health again points to its positive effects.

Which Type of Psychotherapy Is Best?

Soon after the finding that psychotherapy works started to become an established fact, infighting began among the various orientations and approaches about which had the strongest empirical support (Lambert, 2011). Each claimed superiority over the others, and as the language below implies, the competition was quite fierce.

> Although there were many combatants—Freudians versus cognitivists
> versus humanists—the principals in this war were behaviorists and

nonbehaviorists. These groups have called each other names and traded high sounding insults. But the issue was not over psychotherapy versus no psychotherapy, but brand A psychotherapy versus brand B psychotherapy. . . . Different forms of therapy were viewed as adversaries, competitors, or contestants, and the arena of conflict was the controlled experiment. (Smith et al., 1980, pp. 2–3)

The "Dodo Bird Verdict" and Common Factors

Indeed, many empirical outcome studies throughout the latter half of the 1900s have pitted one form of therapy against another. The collective results of these studies have, again and again, yielded a result that surprised many in the field: a virtual tie. In other words, in the hundreds of empirical studies designed to compare the efficacy of one form of therapy with the efficacy of another, the typical result is that the competing therapies are found to work about equally well (Lambert, 2011; Lambert & Ogles, 2004; Norcross & Newman, 1992; Smith et al., 1980; Wampold, 2001, 2010a, 2010b; Weissmark & Giacomo, 1998). In one of the earliest review articles to reach this conclusion, the authors borrowed a line from the dodo bird in *Alice in Wonderland* who, after judging a race between many competitors, stated that "everybody has won and all must have prizes" (Luborsky, Singer, & Luborsky, 1975, p. 995).

How could the "**dodo bird verdict**" apply to psychotherapy outcome? The various forms of psychotherapy—psychoanalysis, humanism, cognitive, behavioral, and others—are indeed quite discrepant from one another, so how could they consistently produce such similar results? Most researchers explain this finding by pointing to **common factors** across all forms of psychotherapy (e.g., Stricker, 2010; Wampold, 2001). That is, although proponents of each school of therapy tout the unique and distinctive aspects of their own approaches, they all share some fundamental components as well. Actually, the notion that different therapies benefit from the same underlying mechanisms was suggested as early as the 1930s (Rosenzweig, 1936) and has been reiterated numerous times since (e.g., Frank, 1961; Torrey, 1986). The difference in the most recent versions of this argument is that they are supported by extensive empirical data on psychotherapy outcome.

It is important to recognize that these common factors are not merely present; they are therapeutic (Lambert & Ogles, 2004; Wampold, 2010a, 2010b). They function as "active ingredients" in all forms of psychotherapy, which helps explain the comparable results of the various approaches: "All of the specific types of therapy achieve virtually equal— or insignificantly different—benefits because of a common core of curative processes" (Wampold, 2001, p. ix). So what are the common factors that make up this common core of curative processes?

Therapeutic Relationship/Alliance

Of the many common factors for psychotherapy outcome that have been proposed, the leading candidate is a strong relationship between therapist and client (Beitman & Manring, 2009; Crits-Christoph, Gibbons, Hamilton, Ring-Kurtz, & Gallop, 2011; Horvath, Del Re, Fluckiger, & Symonds, 2011; Lebow, 2006; Norcross & Lambert, 2011a, 2011b). This relationship goes by many names: **therapeutic relationship, therapeutic alliance, working alliance.** The word *alliance* is perhaps the most illustrative of the nature of this relationship—a coalition, a partnership between two allies working in a trusting relationship toward a mutual goal. Research unequivocally indicates that whether the clients are adults, children, or families, and whether the therapy format is individual or group, the quality of the therapeutic relationship strongly contributes to psychotherapy outcome (Norcross & Wampold, 2011a, 2011b).

In fact, numerous studies have concluded that the therapeutic relationship is perhaps the most crucial single aspect of therapy. Specifically, researchers have argued that the quality of the therapeutic relationship is the best predictor of therapy outcome and that it accounts for more variability in therapy outcome than do the techniques specific to any given therapy approach (e.g., Beitman & Manring, 2009; Wampold, 2001, 2010b). The strength of the therapeutic relationship is especially important from the client's point of view; after all, the client's perception of this relationship is what facilitates positive change. It is also interesting to note that the quality of the therapeutic relationship is vital to therapy regardless of how much emphasis the therapist places on it. Some therapists (e.g., behaviorists) tend to deemphasize therapy relationships, others tend to pay it moderate attention (e.g., cognitive therapists), and others tend to focus heavily on it (e.g., humanists and psychoanalysts). But through the eyes of the client, the therapeutic relationship remains a consistently vital component of psychotherapy (Norcross & Lambert, 2011a, 2011b).

Having established the centrality of the therapeutic alliance, researchers have begun to investigate how, exactly, it contributes to successful psychotherapy. Kazdin (2007) brings up an interesting point: The connection between a good therapeutic alliance and client improvement is not necessarily a one-way street. In other words, in addition to the likelihood that a good alliance facilitates client improvement, it is also possible that as clients improve, they experience an enhanced relationship with their therapists. (Just imagine how you would rate the alliance with a physician if he or she cured you of a serious disease.) Of course, a reciprocal relationship between the two—an upward spiral of sorts—is also a possibility (Webb et al., 2011). This issue highlights what you may have learned in a statistics course: A correlation between two variables does not necessarily indicate a definitive cause-and-effect relationship.

Researchers have also begun to break down the therapeutic relationship—that is, to look more closely at its specific components to determine exactly what makes a therapeutic relationship beneficial (Horvath et al., 2011; Orlinsky, 2010). Numerous elements have been identified—most emphatically, the therapist's ability to provide empathy and acceptance to the client (Lambert, 2011; Norcross, 2010). (These elements overlap significantly with cornerstones of humanistic therapy, which we will discuss in detail in a later chapter.) Empirical study of the therapeutic relationship remains in the early stages, but as it continues, it promises to guide therapists toward establishing healing interpersonal relationships with their clients, regardless of the clients' presenting problems or the particular techniques chosen by the therapists (Norcross & Wampold, 2011a, 2011b).

So, in addition to empirical data supporting particular techniques that work, clinical psychologists also have data supporting particular kinds of therapeutic relationships that work. Rather than siding with either the techniques or the relationships, clinical psychologists can embrace both. In other words, these two components of therapy can complement each other to create the most beneficial experience for clients. As Castonguay and Beutler (2006) put it,

> One of the most salient controversies in the field of psychotherapy is whether client change is primarily due to the therapist's techniques or the quality of the therapeutic relationship. . . . This controversy reflects, more or less implicitly, an "either/or" assumption that is conceptually flawed and empirically untenable. The complexity of the process of change requires, at least in our view, a consideration of both technical and interpersonal factors. (p. 353)

Other Common Factors

The therapeutic relationship is not the only common factor that psychotherapy researchers have proposed. **Hope** (or positive expectations) has also received support as a common factor (Constantino, Glass, Arnkoff, Ametrano, & Smith, 2011; Prochaska & Norcross, 2010). Simply stated, therapists of all kinds provide hope or an optimism that things will begin to improve. Although the mechanism by which this improvement will take place may differ, the improvement may actually begin before any techniques, per se, have been applied. Anyone who has walked despairingly into a physician's office, or even a car repair shop, and received a confidently delivered message that the problem can be fixed understands the curative power of hope.

Attention may also be a common factor across psychotherapies. Also known as the Hawthorne effect (a name derived from classic organizational psychology studies in

Photo 11.2 The relationship or "alliance" between therapist and client is a common factor for therapeutic success.

which factory workers' performance improved as a result of being observed), the attention the therapist and client direct toward the client's issues may represent a novel approach to the problem. That is, clients may have previously attempted to ignore problems that are ultimately addressed in therapy. Simply by openly acknowledging a problem and focusing on it with the therapist, a client may begin to experience improvement, even before formal intervention begins. In addition to the therapeutic relationship, hope, and attention, other common factors that researchers have proposed include reinforcement of novel behaviors, desensitization to threatening stimuli, confronting a problem, and skill training (Prochaska & Norcross, 2010).

Is it possible that the common factors underlying all forms of psychotherapy occur in a predictable sequence? Lambert and Ogles (2004) put forth a **three-stage sequential model of common factors,** beginning with the "support factors" stage—common factors such as a strong therapist-client relationship, therapist warmth and acceptance, and trust. They label the second stage "learning factors," including such aspects as changing expectations about oneself, changes in thought patterns, corrective emotional experiences, and new insights. The third and final stage consists of "action factors," such as taking risks, facing fears, practicing and mastering new behaviors, and working through problems. In brief, this sequential model suggests that psychotherapists of all kinds help clients by moving them through three common steps: connecting with them and understanding their problems; facilitating change in their beliefs and attitudes about their problems; and, finally, encouraging new and more productive behaviors.

It is interesting to compare this three-step sequence with the more informal process of helping a friend who comes to you with a personal problem. Typically, we begin by communicating understanding and compassion, then move on to help them see their problems in a new light, and ultimately help them develop a strategy and take new action to address it. If we skip any of these steps or do them "out of order," the helping process may be hindered. By the same token, some friends (or clients) may need more time at certain stages and less time at others—perhaps more support and less action or vice versa. And cultural factors can play an important role in the value of each stage to the person seeking help, as members of some groups may tend to favor support, learning, or action.

Metaphorically Speaking

If You Use Toothpaste, Then You Understand Common Factors in Psychotherapy

Toothpaste companies spend a lot of time and money convincing us that, because of some "special" feature, their product is the best. Crest, Colgate, Aim, Gleem, Aquafresh—all make claims that they have something unique that sets their toothpaste apart. You've probably tried a few yourself: toothpastes with baking soda, with mouthwash, with sparkles, in a stand-up tube, in winter-fresh gel, and so on.

Ever read the list of ingredients on one of those tubes of toothpaste? Beneath the full list of ingredients, you'll see a separate, important category: "Active Ingredient." And that category has only one item listed: fluoride. That's true across all the brands, all the varieties. In other words, although the manufacturers and advertisers try to sell us on the unique features—extra ingredients, special flavors—what makes one toothpaste work is the same thing that makes its competitors work: fluoride. (That's why our dentists rarely mention a specific brand when they remind us to brush—as long as it has fluoride, any brand will prevent cavities about as well as the others.)

Decades of outcome studies have suggested that the same type of phenomenon has taken place in the psychotherapy field. Each "brand" of psychotherapy has promoted its unique features, those aspects that distinguish it and supposedly make it better than the other brands. But those claims are contradicted by the consistent result of many controlled, empirical psychotherapy outcome studies: Different forms of psychotherapy work about equally. Consequently, it makes sense to speculate about the underlying common ingredient—the "fluoride" of psychotherapy.

So what is the "fluoride" of psychotherapy? At this point, the therapeutic relationship/alliance has emerged as the leading candidate. That is, a strong relationship between therapist and client has proven beneficial, regardless of whether the therapist in that relationship uses psychoanalytic, humanistic, cognitive, or behavioral techniques. Other common factors have garnered significant attention and support from psychotherapy researchers as well, including

(Continued)

(Continued)

hope/optimism, attention, and insight (Prochaska & Norcross, 2010; Wampold, Imel, Bhati, & Johnson-Jennings, 2007). Perhaps various forms of psychotherapy share not a single ingredient (like toothpastes share fluoride) but a "common core" of ingredients, in which some of the factors described here combine to help a client (Wampold, 2001, p. ix).

The fact that fluoride is the common active ingredient in all toothpastes doesn't make us indifferent about selecting one for ourselves. Just as you wouldn't choose a toothpaste that costs too much or tastes bad to you, you wouldn't choose a therapy that you found unjustifiably expensive or simply not palatable. Instead, with either toothpaste or therapy, your choice reflects your personal values and preferences about the means by which the active ingredients are delivered.

Reconsidering the Dodo Bird Verdict— Specific Treatments for Specific Disorders

🌐 **Web Link 11.1**

Dianne Chambless

The dodo bird verdict has not gone unchallenged. Although it is a widely accepted finding in the field that the various forms of psychotherapy are, in general, equally effective, some researchers have made the case that certain psychotherapies are, in fact, superior to others in the treatment of specific problems (e.g., Antony & Barlow, 2010; Carr, 2008; Chambless & Ollendick, 2001).

Dianne Chambless, a prolific and highly respected psychotherapy researcher, has argued strongly against the idea that all psychotherapy approaches are equally efficacious (e.g., Chambless & Ollendick, 2001; Siev & Chambless, 2007). For instance, in her 2002 article (fittingly titled "Beware the Dodo Bird: Dangers of Overgeneralization"), Chambless points out that although empirical studies have compared many therapies with one another, there are many specific comparisons—certain therapies for certain disorders—that studies have not yet examined. Thus, it would be premature to conclude that all therapies are equal for the treatment of all disorders, even if equal efficacy has been the typical finding in studies so far. Additionally, as described in Chapter 3, Chambless is a champion of the movement toward manualized, evidence-based treatments and has led the task forces that established criteria for efficacious treatments for specific disorders and determined which therapies made that list (Chambless et al., 1996, 1998; Task Force on Promotion and Dissemination of Psychological Procedures, 1995).

The contention made by Chambless and others that the dodo bird verdict is inaccurate— and that, therefore, common factors should take a back seat to specific ingredients in each therapy technique—has itself been countered by other leading psychotherapy researchers (e.g., Norcross, 2002). For example, in their 2002 article (aptly titled "Let's Face Facts: Common Factors Are More Potent Than Specific Therapy Ingredients"), **Stanley Messer** and **Bruce Wampold** (2002) review the literature on therapy efficacy and conclude that "the preponderance of evidence points to the widespread operation of common factors such as therapist-client alliance . . . in determining treatment outcome" (p. 21). They further argue that the **prescriptive approach** to therapy—in which specific therapy techniques are viewed as the treatment of choice for specific disorders (e.g., Antony & Barlow, 2010)—should be replaced by an approach that more broadly emphasizes common factors, especially the therapeutic relationship.

⊕ **Web Link 11.2**
Bruce Wampold

Others are quick to add that the debate over what's best for the client should not overlook what the client wants (Swift & Callahan, 2009; Swift, Callahan, & Vollmer, 2011). In other words, *client preferences* are important to consider for retention (keeping the client from dropping out of therapy), enhancement of the therapy relationship, and, ultimately, outcome. As an example, consider the client's preferred coping style (Beutler, Harwood, Kimpara, Verdirame, & Blau, 2011). Some clients may have an externalizing coping style, so they prefer to deal with problems by presuming that their origins are outside of themselves; as such, they may respond better to a therapy that emphasizes symptoms but deemphasizes their root causes. Other clients may have a more internalizing coping style—presuming that their problems originate from within themselves—and would therefore respond better to a therapy that emphasizes insight into root causes rather than just symptom reduction. Appreciating this client preference could be the key to therapy's success; ignoring it could be the cause of its failure.

⊕ **Web Link 11.3**
Role of science in psychotherapy

● ● ● BOX 11.3 ● ● ●

Considering Culture

Are Evidence-Based Treatments Appropriate for Diverse Clients?

A form of psychotherapy becomes an evidence-based treatment when empirical studies demonstrate that it produces successful results with clients. But what if the clients from the study differ in important ways from clients who might receive the treatment in the real world? Can we expect similarly positive results with all clients?

(Continued)

(Continued)

Empirical studies of psychotherapy have done a poor job of including diverse populations in their clinical trials, according to some recent criticisms. Specifically, a series of entries to an important book titled *Evidence-Based Practices in Mental Health: Debate and Dialogue on the Fundamental Questions* (Norcross, Beutler, & Levant, 2006) argue strongly that studies examining the efficacy of manualized therapies have commonly neglected issues of

Photo 11.3 How should clinical psychologists adapt evidence-based treatments for clients of minority groups—lesbians, for example?

- ethnicity (Sue & Zane, 2006),
- gender (Levant & Silverstein, 2006),
- disability (Olkin & Taliaferro, 2006), and
- lesbian, gay, bisexual, or transgender (LGBT) clients (Brown, 2006).

Regarding ethnicity, Sue and Zane (2006) report that despite the massive number of clinical studies evaluating the efficacy of specific therapies since 1986 (encompassing about 10,000 clients), the number of these studies that measured the efficacy of the treatment according to ethnicity or race is zero. Further, in about half these studies, ethnicity information was not reported at all, and in most of the rest, very few minority clients were included. Regarding people with disabilities, Olkin and Taliaferro (2006) report that they "have been unable to locate any published materials on [evidence-based practices] and people with disabilities," which "fuels our concern that [evidence-based practice] will develop without due consideration of this minority group" (pp. 353–354). Brown (2006) and Levant and Silverstein (2006) offer comparable summaries regarding inattention to LGBT and gender issues, respectively.

Not only are clients from these diverse groups often omitted from clinical trials, but the authors of some clinical studies (and the therapy manuals they test) do not suggest specific adaptations to their treatment to better suit any such clients. Fortunately, very recent research has focused on exactly these kinds of adaptations. That is, there is a current movement among psychotherapy outcome researchers to describe how evidence-based therapies could be adapted to specific cultural populations, and to empirically test these adaptations (Castro, Barrera, & Steiker, 2010; Morales & Norcross, 2010; Smith, Rodríguez, & Bernal, 2011). For example, BigFoot and Schmidt (2010) successfully tested an adaptation of cognitive-behavioral therapy for American Indian and Alaska Native children with posttraumatic symptoms, and Aguilera, Garza, and Muñoz (2010) successfully tested an adaptation of cognitive-behavioral therapy for Spanish-speaking clients with depression.

For a moment, imagine that you are a psychotherapy client. Your clinical psychologist informs you that a particular form of therapy has been shown in a series of studies to successfully treat the disorder with which you have been diagnosed. How important is it to you that the clients on whom the therapy was successfully tested may differ from you in important ways? If most of the clients in the successful clinical trials differed from you in terms of ethnicity, gender, disability status, or sexuality, would you feel confident that the therapy would work equally well for you? If you were the clinical psychologist, how comfortable would you be following a manual empirically supported by research conducted on clients who differ from the client in your office?

The debate over the dodo bird verdict—whether the benefits of psychotherapy are due primarily to ingredients shared across therapies or specific to certain therapies—carries on. In fact, *The Great Psychotherapy Debate,* an important book by Bruce Wampold (2001), suggests that the quarrel is far from over. In the middle ground of this dispute, numerous researchers and clinicians have tried to form a compromise that recognizes the importance of both the specific treatment and more general, common effects (e.g., Norcross, 2005). In fact, some have pointed out that change in therapy can be attributable to *many* factors, including common factors, specific factors, and numerous others. For example, some call attention to the fact that in addition to the specific and common factors cited above, there are client characteristics, therapist characteristics, and problem characteristics (how severe, how chronic, etc.) that can affect the outcome of therapy (Beitman & Manring, 2009; Rosenfeld, 2009). Not to mention, extratherapeutic forces—that is, life events the client experiences while in therapy—can also have a powerful impact on the client's well-being at the end of therapy (Norcross, 2005; Rosenfeld, 2009; Wampold, 2001). Perhaps a wise resolution of this debate is to consider the full range of potential influences on therapy outcome, as suggested by Paul (2007):

> The treatment method, the therapist, the relationship, the client, and principles of change are vital contributors, and all must be studied. Comprehensive evidence-based practices will consider *all* of these determinants and their optimal combinations. "Common and specific effects" and "art and science" appear properly complementary, not as "either/or" dichotomies. (p. 141)

What Types of Psychotherapy Do Clinical Psychologists Practice?

The Past and Present

Seven times since 1960, researchers have surveyed the Division of Clinical Psychology (Division 12) of the American Psychological Association to assess, among other things, the type or orientation of psychotherapy that its members practice. The most recent of these surveys incorporates responses from 549 clinical psychologists and includes a comparative review of the six previous surveys as well (Norcross & Karpiak, 2012). These results are summarized in Table 11.1.

Several observations and trends related to Table 11.1 are noteworthy:

- Eclectic/integrative therapy has been the most commonly endorsed orientation in every survey summarized in the table until 2010, when it fell to second place. That is, over the past half century, more psychologists have described themselves as "mutts" who blend multiple approaches or use an assortment of therapies than as "purebreds" who practice one type exclusively. Additional research (e.g., Cook, Biyanova, Elhai, Schnurr, & Coyne, 2010) has confirmed that combined orientations remain extremely common, not only among clinical psychologists but among psychotherapists more

Table 11.1 Percentage of Clinical Psychologists Endorsing Leading Primary Theoretical Orientations Since 1960

Orientation	1960	1973	1981	1986	1995	2003	2010
Eclectic/Integrative	36	55	31	29	27	29	22
Cognitive	—	2	6	13	24	28	31
Psychodynamic/Psychoanalytic	35	16	30	21	18	15	18
Behavioral	8	10	14	16	13	10	15
Humanistic/Rogerian/Existential/Gestalt	6	7	7	12	4	2	2

Source: Adapted from Norcross, J. C., Karpiak, C. P., & Santoro, S. O. (2005).

broadly. Therapists combine orientations in a wide variety of ways, but surveys suggest that the combination of cognitive and behavioral approaches (each of which is described in detail in a later chapter) is the most common (Hickman, Arnkoff, Glass, & Schottenbauer, 2009).

- Even among those therapists who endorse a singular orientation rather than calling themselves eclectic, the actual techniques they use often fall outside the boundaries of their singular orientation. For example, a therapist who calls herself behavioral may in fact use cognitive techniques from time to time, or another therapist who calls himself humanistic may in fact use psychodynamic techniques occasionally (Thoma & Cecero, 2009).

- The endorsement of psychodynamic/psychoanalytic therapy has declined significantly since 1960, when it far exceeded any other single approach and rivaled the eclectic/integrative approach in terms of popularity. In 2010, only 18% of clinical psychologists endorsed it as their primary orientation—about half the percentage reported in 1960. Nonetheless, psychodynamic/psychoanalytic therapy remains the second most commonly endorsed orientation among the single-school approaches.

- Cognitive therapy has witnessed a remarkable rise in popularity, especially since the 1980s. Prior to the 1980s, the unpopularity of the cognitive approach suggested it was hardly worth including on these surveys, but by 2010, it had become by far the most commonly endorsed single-school approach and had also overtaken the eclectic/integrative approach.

⊕ **Web Link 11.4**

John Norcross discussing stages of change

The same survey (Norcross & Karpiak, 2012) offers a description of the formats, or modalities, most commonly used by clinical psychologists. Table 11.2 presents highlights of these results for clinical psychologists responding to the most recent edition of the survey.

As the table indicates, psychotherapy with individual clients dominates the professional activities of contemporary clinical psychologists (see also Cook et al., 2010). Almost all (98%) conduct some individual therapy. However, the other formats of therapy—couples/marital therapy, family therapy, and group therapy—are also practiced by sizable numbers of clinical psychologists.

Regardless of the type of therapy, it has become increasingly evident that clients enter therapy at various points regarding willingness to change. Simply put, some clients are quite ready to change when they enter therapy, while others are not. Psychotherapy researchers (e.g., Norcross, Krebs, & Prochaska, 2011) have developed and provided empirical support for a **stages of change model** to describe the various points where clients may fall in terms of readiness. Specifically, clients may enter therapy at one of these five stages:

Table 11.2 Involvement of Clinical Psychologists in Various Psychotherapy Formats

Psychotherapy Format	Percentage of Clinical Psychologists Who Practice It
Individual	98
Couples/Marital	48
Family	34
Group	20

Source: Adapted from Norcross, J. C., Karpiak, C. P., & Santoro, S. O. (2005).

- *Precontemplation stage*—no intention to change at all. These clients are largely unaware of their problems, and they may have been pressured to enter therapy by family or friends who are more aware than they are themselves.

- *Contemplation stage*—aware that a problem exists, considering doing something to address it, but not ready to commit to any real effort in that direction. These clients are often ambivalent and are not yet willing to give up the benefits of the behavior they recognize as somewhat problematic.

- *Preparation stage*—intending to take action within a short time (e.g., weeks, a month). These clients may be taking small steps but have not made significant or drastic change.

- *Action stage*—actively changing behavior and making notable efforts to overcome their problems. More than any other stage, this stage requires sustained effort and commitment to the therapeutic goals.

- *Maintenance stage*—preventing relapse and retaining the gains made during the action stage. This stage lasts indefinitely.

It is important for therapists to assess the stage of change clients are in when they seek therapy. It would be a mistake to assume that most are at the action stage; indeed, data suggests that the vast majority are at an earlier stage at the outset of therapy. Thus, initial goals should emphasize increasing clients' readiness to change rather than forcing them to change prematurely (Norcross, Krebs, & Prochaska, 2011; Prochaska & Norcross, 2010).

The Future

The practice of psychotherapy among clinical psychologists has certainly changed in the past half century. How might it change in the near future? Sixty-two psychotherapy experts, including many editors of leading journals in the field, were surveyed about the trends they foresee for the near future (Norcross, Hedges, & Prochaska, 2002). The results included several provocative predictions, including a rise in the use of

- cognitive and behavioral approaches to therapy,
- culturally sensitive therapy,
- eclectic/integrative approaches to therapy, and
- empirically supported or evidence-based forms of therapy.

The survey also suggested that classic psychoanalysis will continue to decline in use soon. Of course, only time will tell if these predictions are accurate.

Eclectic and Integrative Approaches

Eclectic and integrative approaches to psychotherapy hold a unique position among clinical psychologists, as we have seen. Whereas the various single-school forms of therapy have risen and fallen in popularity over the years, eclectic/integrative therapy has remained at or near the top of the list in terms of popularity (Norcross & Karpiak, 2012).

Although the terms are often linked and both involve multiple therapy approaches, an eclectic approach to therapy actually differs in important ways from an integrative approach. **Eclectic** therapy (also known as *technical eclecticism*) involves selecting the best treatment for a given client based on empirical data from studies of the treatment of similar clients (Gold, 1996; Norcross & Newman, 1992; Stricker, 2010). In other words, a truly eclectic therapist turns to the empirical literature as soon as the diagnosis is made and practices whatever technique the literature prescribes for that diagnosis. So if the empirical literature dictates it, an eclectic therapist might practice cognitive therapy with a 9:00 a.m. client with generalized anxiety disorder, behavioral therapy with a 10:00 a.m. client with a phobia, and so on.

An **integrative** approach to therapy, on the other hand, involves blending techniques in order to create an entirely new, hybrid form of therapy (Beitman & Manring, 2009; Norcross, 2005). An integrative therapist may combine elements of psychoanalytic, cognitive, behavioral, humanistic, or other therapies into a personal therapy style applied to a wide range of clients.

Web Link 11.5
John Norcross

In 1977, Paul Wachtel was one of the first to successfully integrate complementary (some might have said incompatible) approaches, namely psychoanalysis and behavior therapy. Soon after, especially in the 1980s, integrative therapy grew into a full-fledged movement. One of the champions of this movement has been **John Norcross,** who explained that the psychotherapy integration movement grew out of "a dissatisfaction with single-school approaches and a concomitant desire to look across and beyond school boundaries to see what can be learned from other ways of thinking about psychotherapy and behavior change" (Norcross & Newman, 1992, p. 4). Norcross and Newman identify a number of factors that have fostered the popularity of integrative forms of psychotherapy, especially since the 1980s. Among the most important of these factors are two that we identify in this chapter: the lack of differential effectiveness among therapies and the recognition that common factors contribute significantly to therapy outcome.

● ● ● BOX 11.4 ● ● ●

Metaphorically Speaking

If You Know the Difference Between a Fruit Salad and a Smoothie, You Understand the Difference Between Eclectic and Integrative Psychotherapists

A fruit salad includes a variety of ingredients, but each bite brings only one flavor: The fork may stab a strawberry first, a blueberry next, and a pineapple chunk third. Each piece is pure, discrete, and easily distinguished from the others. But in a smoothie made of these ingredients, every sip includes the same combination of ingredients, and the taste of every sip reflects that unique blend. Mixed together, the ingredients create a distinct concoction with a taste wholly its own.

An eclectic approach to psychotherapy is a lot like a fruit salad. Eclectic therapists use a pure, discrete approach to therapy with each client, and they choose that approach according to empirical support. They allow empirical studies of psychotherapy efficacy to direct them toward the therapy most likely to succeed for a particular diagnosis. As described in Chapter 3, recent publications have supplied therapists with lists of the most empirically supported treatments for particular disorders (e.g., Chambless et al., 1998). An eclectic therapist would refer to such a list for each client separately. Because such lists prescribe very different forms of therapy for various disorders, eclectic therapists must be versatile enough to practice many techniques competently. Eclectic therapists have no loyalty to any particular approach to therapy; their loyalty is to the empirical data.

Integrative therapy, in contrast, is more like a smoothie—a custom blend of ingredients that forms an original creation. This "hybrid" approach to therapy is often used across clients and across diagnoses. Thus, integrative therapists are less concerned with employing evidence-based, manualized techniques in their pure form; instead, they are concerned with synthesizing the best features of various theories of psychotherapy. Whereas an eclectic therapist's approach might contrast greatly from one client to the next (depending on empirical data for treatments of various disorders), an integrative therapist's approach might remain a bit more constant, just as in a smoothie—the flavor combination doesn't vary much from sip to sip.

As a clinical psychologist, which of these approaches to therapy—eclectic or integrative— would you prefer? If you were the client, which approach might you prefer that your clinical psychologist take? What are the pros and cons of each approach?

Denise: A Fictional Client to Consider From Multiple Perspectives

The next four chapters of this book each feature a specific approach to psychotherapy: psychoanalytic, humanistic, behavioral, and cognitive. To illustrate each fully, we consider a therapy summary of a fictional client named Denise. (As this chapter indicates, if Denise were a real client seen by a real clinical psychologist, she would most likely receive eclectic or integrative treatment, but therapy summaries of the single-school approaches will nonetheless exemplify the elements of the various approaches.) As therapy summaries, these reports appear in the past tense, as if Denise has completed a full course of the featured treatment and the therapist has written a synopsis of the treatment that might be useful if Denise returns later or resumes therapy with another therapist.

As with any client, Denise's cultural background is an important aspect of her therapy. In creating this fictional client, many of her demographic characteristics were selected because they match descriptions of individuals most likely to seek psychotherapy (Vessey & Howard, 1993). Of course, culturally competent clinical psychologists may make adjustments to therapy for clients with similar presenting problems but different cultural characteristics.

A full description of Denise is presented in Box 11.5.

Denise: A Fictional Client to Consider From Multiple Perspectives

Denise is a 30-year-old, single, heterosexual, Caucasian woman who has lived her entire life in a large Midwestern city. She has no history of significant illness or injury and is in generally good health. Denise grew up as the fifth of six children in a middle-class family in which both parents worked full-time. She attended 2 years of college immediately after high school but transferred to culinary school where she graduated near the top of her class. She currently lives alone and maintains an upper-middle-class lifestyle.

Denise has worked as the only chef in a small upscale restaurant for about 5 years. Denise has enjoyed her job very much. One of her favorite aspects of her job had always been coming out of the kitchen to ask customers how they were enjoying their meals, especially because the feedback she received from them was almost exclusively positive. The owner of the restaurant had allowed Denise to do this because he believed it added a personal touch to the dining experience. Another of her favorite aspects of the job had been the creative freedom she enjoyed in the kitchen. The owner had allowed her to create her own unique entrées and change them as frequently as she liked.

Recently, though, Denise's feelings toward her job have changed drastically. A new owner took over the restaurant, and the new owner firmly stated to Denise that her job was to stay in the kitchen preparing food and not talk with customers at all. The new owner has also provided Denise with a strict, predetermined, permanent menu that the owner alone created and that Denise must now follow. She finds this revised job description inconsistent with her own personal style, and she sorely misses both the praise she had become accustomed to receiving from customers and the opportunities to create her own dishes.

Since this change was implemented, Denise has been experiencing mild to moderate depressive symptoms, including sadness, loss of interest in daily activities, low energy, difficulty sleeping, and difficulty concentrating. She has had difficulty getting to work on time and preparing dishes in a timely and conscientious manner, and her exercise routine, which had been very regular, is now sporadic. Sometimes Denise suspects that the new owner may have implemented this new policy specifically to hurt her. She states that she wants to return to the way she felt before this happened, and she is concerned that if she cannot overcome this problem, her performance at work will suffer to the extent that she will lose her job.

CHAPTER SUMMARY

Psychotherapy is the most common professional activity of clinical psychologists. Following some published doubts about its efficacy in the 1950s, researchers in the subsequent decades amassed enormous amounts of empirical outcome data, much of which has been combined in meta-analyses, supporting the conclusion that for the vast majority of clients, psychotherapy works. Recent data suggests that it also reduces medical costs and produces neurological changes in the brain. Outcome studies that have compared the efficacy of various approaches to therapy with one another have consistently resulted in a virtual tie, a finding that has been nicknamed the "dodo bird verdict." The presence of common factors across all forms of therapy, including a strong therapeutic relationship, hope, and attention, may underlie their equal efficacy. More recent and targeted outcome studies focusing on particular manualized therapies for particular disorders have given rise to further debate about the relative contributions of the common factors versus specific therapy techniques. All empirical psychotherapy outcome studies must address numerous methodological issues, including who, when, and how to ask about the outcome of therapy. Additionally, efficacy studies, which assess how well a therapy works "in the lab," should be understood in conjunction with effectiveness studies, which assess how well a therapy works "in the real world." Surveys indicate that since 1960, the eclectic/integrative therapy orientation has generally been most commonly endorsed by clinical psychologists, and among single-school approaches, the psychodynamic/psychoanalytic orientation has been on the decline, whereas the cognitive orientation has been on the rise.

KEY TERMS AND NAMES

CRITICAL THINKING QUESTIONS

1. According to the tripartite model, parties other than the client and the therapist can have a meaningful perspective on the outcome of a client's psychotherapy. Specifically, which third parties might have the most valid perspective? Clients' partners, friends, kids, supervisors, coworkers, managed-care companies, or someone else?

2. What conclusions do you draw from the results of large-scale effectiveness studies such as the 1995 *Consumer Reports* study?

3. When graduate programs train their students in psychotherapy, to what extent should they emphasize common factors (e.g., forming and maintaining strong therapeutic relationships) as opposed to specific therapy techniques?

4. Consider the three-step sequential model of common factors. In your opinion, would men and women tend to move through the sequence identically? What steps might each group tend to emphasize or deemphasize?

5. What are the implications of the finding that the eclectic/integrative orientation has been the most commonly endorsed orientation among clinical psychologists in surveys since 1960?

STUDENT STUDY SITE RESOURCES

Visit the study site at www.sagepub.com/pomerantz3eupdate for these additional learning tools:

- Self-quizzes
- eFlashcards
- Culture Expert Interviews

- Full-text SAGE journal articles
- Additional web resources
- Mock Assessment Data

CHAPTER SUMMARY VIDEO

QR codes at the end of each chapter link to chapter background videos by the author. Visit http://gettag.mobi using your smartphone browser to download the free Microsoft Tag app. Once installed, scan the tags to go directly to these brief videos. In this video, the author elaborates on the metaphor comparing common factors in therapy to fluoride in toothpaste, with an emphasis on choosing what's palatable.

CHAPTER

12

Psychodynamic Psychotherapy

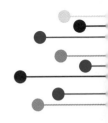

This chapter and the three that follow each focus on a prominent approach to psychotherapy. We begin with the psychodynamic approach for multiple reasons. For one, psychodynamic therapy came first historically. In fact, for much of the first half of the 1900s, the psychodynamic approach was so dominant that it was practically synonymous with psychotherapy itself. Also, many of the therapies that arose in later decades—including humanistic, behavioral, and cognitive therapies—were reactions against the psychodynamic approach. Many of the pioneers of the nonpsychodynamic therapies were actually initially trained in psychodynamic programs but later abandoned that approach to create something different.

But among many clinical psychologists, psychodynamic psychotherapy does not enjoy the reputation or popularity it once held. A leading scholar in psychodynamic therapy recently described its current status quite bluntly:

> There can be little doubt that psychoanalysis and the psychodynamic therapies that arise from it are currently in a beleaguered state. The average educated reader today is likely to be confronted with a series of statements in the popular press that are variations on the following themes: Freud is dead; psychoanalysis is more religion than science; psychodynamic psychotherapy has no research to support its efficacy; cognitive-behavioral therapy has surpassed psychoanalytic therapy as the most accepted form of psychotherapeutic treatment; psychodynamic psychotherapy is too long and too expensive; and the fundamental psychoanalytic concepts are too vague to be rigorously studied. The common wisdom among psychoanalysts these days is that if a patient asks you if you are 'a Freudian,' the correct answer is 'no.' (Gabbard, 2009a, p. vii)

Despite the relative decline of psychodynamic therapy, it remains widely used and quite relevant, especially in certain pockets of the profession. Through adaptations of its traditional methods into novel approaches that better suit contemporary culture, it continues to exert significant influence on clinical psychology. In fact, it is worth emphasizing that the quote above appears in the preface of a full book devoted to evidence-based psychodynamic psychotherapy, the mere existence of which illustrates the continued vitality of psychodynamic psychotherapy in an era that emphasizes empirical efficacy.

Defining Psychodynamic Psychotherapy

⊕ Web Link 12.1
Sigmund Freud

For the sake of simplicity, in this chapter we will use the term **psychodynamic psychotherapy** to cover an extensive range of therapies. Our use of the term refers broadly to the pioneering work of **Sigmund Freud** and all subsequent efforts to revise and expand on it. Thus, it includes Freud's original approach to therapy, which in its classic form is known as psychoanalysis. Of course, Freud had many intellectual descendants, including some who were his contemporaries (such as Carl

Jung, Alfred Adler, and Erik Erikson) and others whose ideas arrived in subsequent generations (such as his daughter Anna Freud, Harry Stack Sullivan, Freida Fromm-Reichmann, Melanie Klein, Karen Horney, D. W. Winnicott, and Hans Kohut). At various points in the evolution of his theory by others, Freud's original term *psychoanalysis* was replaced by terms such as *psychoanalytic psychotherapy*, *neo-Freudian therapy*, and *psychodynamic psychotherapy*, each of which has generated even more specific terms for its offshoots. Rather than trying to make demarcations and distinctions among so many overlapping terms, our purposes in this chapter are best served by choosing a single term—*psychodynamic psychotherapy*—to represent them all.

Goal of Psychodynamic Psychotherapy

The primary goal of psychodynamic psychotherapy is to make the unconscious conscious (Cabaniss, Cherry, Douglas, & Schwartz, 2011; Karon & Widener, 1995). Psychodynamic psychotherapists help their clients become aware of thoughts, feelings, and other mental activities of which the clients are unaware at the start of therapy. The word **insight,** used often by psychodynamic therapists and clients alike, captures this phenomenon—looking inside oneself and noticing something that had previously gone unseen (Gibbons, Crits-Christoph, Barber, & Schamberger, 2007). Once we become aware of unconscious processes, we can make efforts to control them deliberately, rather than them controlling us.

Photo 12.1 Sigmund Freud (1856–1939), the leading figure in psychodynamic psychotherapy.

Of course, the process of making the unconscious conscious presumes that an unconscious part of our mind exists in the first place. This fundamental idea—the existence of the **unconscious**—is one of Freud's most important and enduring contributions to clinical psychology (Kernberg, 2004; Lane & Harris, 2008). Before Freud, there was little acknowledgment among mental health professionals about any mental activity occurring outside our awareness. Freud changed the way we think about ourselves by proposing "mental processes that are outside the awareness of the individual and that have important, powerful influences on conscious experiences" (Karon & Widener, 1995, p. 26). According to Freud and his psychodynamic followers, not only does the unconscious exist, it also exerts a powerful influence on our day-to-day and minute-to-minute lives. In fact, they argue that unconscious processes underlie depression, anxiety, personality disorders, eating disorders, and all other forms of psychopathology that clinical psychologists treat. Thus, gaining access to it is vital (Kris, 2012).

Accessing the Unconscious

Psychodynamic psychotherapists gain an appreciation of their clients' unconscious process in a variety of ways. Of course, these methods are quite **inferential**: Rather than understanding a client's unconscious in an empirical, factual way, psychodynamic psychotherapists understand it through inference, deduction, and conjecture. In more casual language, psychodynamic psychotherapists try to "read" their clients and hypothesize about their unconscious activity using the following processes.

Free Association

Free association is a technique in which psychodynamic psychotherapists simply ask clients to say whatever comes to mind without censoring themselves at all. The client's task is to verbalize any thought that occurs, no matter how nonsensical, inappropriate, illogical, or unimportant it may seem (Kernberg, 2004; Skelton, 2006). It may sound straightforward enough, but free association is no easy task. Consider how rare it is for any of us to speak with complete spontaneity, without editing ourselves in one way or another. Perhaps the only times we hear such speech in daily life are when we listen to very young children or very intoxicated adults. Nonetheless, the words of people in such states of mind can be revealing about their innermost thoughts and feelings, according to the psychodynamic approach. If clients can feel relaxed enough to engage in free association, their unconscious processes can become more evident to the psychodynamic psychotherapist and, ultimately, to themselves.

It is important to distinguish free association from word association, a technique associated with Carl Jung. In word association, the therapist presents the client with a list of words. After hearing each word, the client is to respond with the first word that comes to mind. Jungian therapists have often developed hypotheses about clients based on the content of their associations or the amount of time it takes them to respond to certain words (Hall & Nordby, 1973). In contrast, free association involves no stimulus at all from the therapist.

Freudian "Slips"

According to psychodynamic psychotherapists, all our behavior is determined; there is no such thing as a random mistake, accident, or slip. So if a behavior can't be explained by motivations of which we are aware, unconscious motivations must be the cause. In this way, when we get something wrong or "forget" something, we reveal unconscious wishes. Psychodynamic psychotherapists who witness a client's slips of the tongue during a session or who hear clients' stories of such events may be able to glimpse the clients' underlying intentions. Although most examples of **Freudian slips** are verbal, they can be behavioral as well:

- Ray, a 52-year-old man who lived in New Jersey, was asked by his older sister Tanya to fly home to Ohio. The reason for the meeting was that their 80-year-old father had become quite ill in recent months, and although he currently lived alone, Tanya thought they should discuss assisted-living or nursing home options. Ray agreed to fly home, but a few hours before the flight, he lost his car keys. He found them at the last minute, but on the way to the airport he missed the airport exit off the highway (an exit he had taken dozens of times before). The combination of losing the keys and missing the exit resulted in Ray missing his flight. His "mistakes" uncover that unconsciously, Ray dreaded the meeting and wanted to avoid it. He was fearful of the conflicts that would arise with Tanya as well as the sight of his father as unable to take care of himself.

- Liz and Amy, both 25 years old, have been very close friends since age 18, when they were roommates during their first year of college. At that time, Liz began dating Sean. They continued dating for the next 5 years and got married when Liz was 23. Liz and Sean just had their first baby, a boy named Benjamin. Amy is happy for them, and she is one of many to bring a gift for the new baby. In her card, Amy congratulated the couple on the birth of "Benjamine." Her unique misspelling of the baby's name combines the words "Benjamin" and "mine," revealing Amy's unconscious wish that she, rather than Liz, had dated, married, and had a child with Sean.

- Occasionally, network TV provides a good example of a Freudian slip. On a memorable episode of the sitcom *Friends,* Ross Geller and his fiancée Emily are getting married. During the ceremony, when asked to repeat the words, "I take thee, Emily . . . ," Ross mistakenly replaces "Emily" with "Rachel." He tries in vain to explain it away as a meaningless slip of the tongue, but Emily (and, of course, all the viewers) recognize that although he may not realize it consciously, Ross truly wishes he were marrying his long-time friend Rachel rather than Emily.

Dreams

Although some emphasize **dreams** more than others, psychodynamic psychotherapists generally believe that our dreams communicate unconscious material (Cabaniss et al., 2011). Freud theorized that when we sleep, our minds convert **latent content** (the raw thoughts and feelings of the unconscious) to **manifest content** (the actual plot of the dream as we remember it). This process, called **dream work,** uses symbols to express wishes, which can result in unconscious wishes appearing in a very distorted or disguised form.

In psychodynamic psychotherapy, the therapist analyzes dreams by attempting to uncover the unconscious meaning behind them—essentially, undoing the dream work. Often, the therapist asks the client to help in the dream interpretation process by explaining the personal meaning of the symbols appearing in the dream. As an example, if a client has a dream about, say, a table, the therapist may be unsure about what the table represents. However, if the client explains that the particular table that appeared in the dream was reminiscent of the one she remembers from her childhood in her grandmother's house, the connotations of that symbol may become more apparent. Of course, even with the client's help, dream interpretations (and other attempts to understand the unconscious) remain inferential rather than factual.

Freud (1900) famously called dreams the "royal road" to unconscious material. Although dreams are certainly still valued, the contemporary perspective is more inclusive of other paths as well: "Today the psychoanalytic view is that there are many 'royal roads' to the unconscious" (Kernberg, 2004, p. 18).

Resistance

Sometimes, when certain issues come up during the course of therapy, clients make it clear that they "don't want to go there." They communicate their reluctance in a variety of ways—some obvious, some subtle. They might change the subject, suddenly remembering something new they intended to discuss. They might fill sessions with talk of unessential topics. They might show up late to subsequent appointments or miss them altogether.

Psychodynamic psychotherapists have a name for this client behavior: **resistance** (Dewald, 1964; Gabbard, 2009c; Karon & Widener, 1995; LaFarge, 2012; Lane & Harris, 2008). When clients sense that certain unconscious thoughts and feelings are being laid bare too extensively or too quickly, they feel anxious. That anxiety motivates them to create distractions or obstacles that impede the exploration of those thoughts and feelings. Psychodynamic psychotherapists could be frustrated by clients' resistance, but more often they are intrigued by it and use it to guide future efforts. When they notice resistance, they assume that the therapy has "struck a nerve," and although the client may not be willing to delve into the issue at the moment, the resistance itself may be an important factor in the client's daily life and could become a productive topic of conversation later in therapy.

Photo 12.2 Psychodynamic therapists attempt to help clients access the unconscious in many ways, often including the analysis of dreams. In your opinion, how important is it for clients to uncover and interpret unconscious material during therapy?

As an example, consider Talia, a 24-year-old client who has grown up with a physically abusive father. In therapy, she had no trouble voicing her resentment toward her father; in fact, it was a prominent theme of her sessions. Her psychodynamic psychotherapist, Dr. Harrison, noticed that Talia rarely spoke of her mother, who also lived in the home throughout Talia's childhood. At one point, during a discussion of her father's impact on her life, Dr. Harrison asked Talia whether her mother was aware of her father's abuse toward her. Talia replied, but in a way that sidestepped Dr. Harrison's question: "I just hate him so much for what he did to me." Later in the session, Dr. Harrison asked Talia if anyone knew about the abuse as it was happening to her. Talia abruptly changed the subject, suddenly remembering an unrelated event that had happened the day before. Talia missed her next appointment and was late to the one after that. Dr. Harrison developed the hypothesis that Talia may hold some strong unconscious feelings of resentment toward her mother, who may have known about the abuse but did nothing to stop it. Dr. Harrison also speculated that Talia was uncomfortable acknowledging this buried resentment of her mother, so she found ways to avoid the topic. In future sessions, Dr. Harrison pointed out to Talia her avoidance of this topic, and they discussed the possibility that Talia felt anger toward her mother, as well as Talia's reluctance to discuss that feeling.

Defense Mechanisms

Psychodynamic psychotherapists believe that by identifying clients' unconscious defense mechanisms and bringing them into the clients' awareness, they can improve the quality of their clients' lives. Before we examine the defense mechanisms in detail, however, let's review the personality components that, according to Freud, produce them.

⊕ **Web Link 12.2**

Glossary of Freudian terminology

Freud's structural model of the mind includes three forces, the interaction of which takes place largely outside our awareness: the id, the superego, and the ego. The **id** is the part of the mind that generates all the pleasure-seeking, selfish, indulgent, animalistic impulses. It seeks immediate satisfaction of its wishes, most of which are biological in nature, and is oblivious to any consequences. In contrast, the **superego** is the part of the mind that establishes rules, restrictions, and prohibitions. It tells us what we "should" do, and it often uses guilt to discourage us from overindulging in immediate pleasure. Whereas Freud believed the id was inborn, he theorized that the superego became a part of the mind through experiences with authority figures, especially parents. Essentially, the superego is an internalization of the rules and morals taught to each of us, and it stands in direct opposition to the id (Kernberg, 2004; Moore & Fine, 1990; Skelton, 2006).

So, according to Freud, our unconscious mental processes involve a constant battle between an id demanding instant gratification and a superego demanding constant restraint. How does the mind manage these battles? What does it do with the conflicted impulses? These responsibilities fall to the **ego**, the third component in Freud's structural model of the mind. The ego is a mediator, a compromise maker between the id and the superego. It faces the challenge of partially satisfying both of these opposing forces while also meeting the demands of reality. The ego can be quite creative in the ways it handles id/superego conflict. Over time, it develops a collection of techniques on which it can rely. It is this set of techniques that Freud and his followers call **defense mechanisms** (Gabbard, 2005; Lane & Harris, 2008).

So what are the common defense mechanisms? Although Sigmund Freud offered descriptions of many, his followers, including his daughter Anna Freud, have added to the list (Dewald, 1964; Freud, 1936; Sandler & Freud, 1985). Let's consider some of the most commonly acknowledged defense mechanisms, keeping in mind that all of them occur unconsciously. Examples will follow the series of definitions.

- **Repression.** When the id has an impulse and the superego rejects it, the ego can *repress* conscious awareness of the impulse and id/superego conflict around it. In other words, the ego can take the impulse and the internal conflict it creates and "sweep them under the rug" so that we never even become aware we had them in the first place. *Denial* is a similar defense mechanism, but it usually refers to events that happen to us rather than impulses that come from within us.

- **Projection.** When the id has an impulse and the superego rejects it, the ego can *project* the id impulse onto other people around us. In this way, we try to convince ourselves that the unacceptable impulse belongs to someone else, not to ourselves. Essentially, we attribute our most objectionable qualities to others and, in the process, might cast ourselves as possible recipients of the others' unacceptable behavior rather than the ones with the impulse to carry it out ourselves.

- **Reaction formation.** When the id has an impulse and the superego rejects it, the ego can *form a reaction against* the id impulse—essentially, do the exact opposite. So when the id urges us to do something selfish, we don't simply resist the temptation; we do something selfless, as if overcompensating for the original id impulse.

- **Displacement.** When the id has an impulse and the superego rejects it, the ego can *displace* the id impulse toward a safer target. Rather than aiming the id's desired action at whom or what it wants, we redirect the impulse toward another person or object to minimize the repercussions—this way, the superego is somewhat satisfied as well. The phrase "kicking the dog" has been used to describe displacement, illustrating how the ego can reroute destructive urges.

- **Sublimation.** When the id has an impulse and the superego rejects it, the ego can *sublimate* it—essentially, redirect it in such a way that the resulting behavior actually benefits others. Unlike "kicking the dog," in which no one benefits from the behavior (especially the dog), sublimation allows the id to do what it wants, and in the process, others are helped rather than harmed.

Metaphorically Speaking

If You've Been to a Movie Theater, You Understand Projection

When you're sitting in a theater, where's the movie? The knee-jerk answer is that the movie is on the screen in front of you, but that's actually incorrect. A *projection* of the movie is on the screen; the movie itself is on a reel in the projector behind you.

Projection as a defense mechanism works very similarly to projection in the movie theater, with the ego as the movie projector and the id impulse as the movie. The ego takes an id impulse and "projects" it out of the person and onto others. Thus, the person sees it in others but not in the self. As an example, consider Randy, who frequently has the id impulse, "I want to steal." By projecting this id impulse, Randy sees this impulse on others but not on himself. If Randy literally had a projector on his forehead (pardon the absurd image), his projection of the sentence, "I want to steal," onto everyone around him would be obvious. When Randy sees others walking around with "I want to steal" written across their shirts (while remaining oblivious of the fact that the message actually originates inside himself), he may very well become convinced that he is surrounded by thieves. Randy's case illustrates that when an individual relies heavily on a single defense mechanism, that defense mechanism becomes a prominent feature of the individual's personality. To some extent, a defense mechanism can define a person or at least the kinds of problems they bring to therapy. It would certainly be no surprise to find that Randy suffers from paranoia of one kind or another (perhaps paranoid personality disorder or a paranoid subtype of schizophrenia) because he views others as crooks and himself as a potential victim. Psychodynamic psychotherapists would aim to make Randy more aware of his own unconscious processes, including his tendency to project his own unacceptable unconscious wishes onto others.

To illustrate these five defense mechanisms, let's choose a specific id impulse—physical aggression—and imagine how the ego might manage the internal conflict caused when the superego rejects it. Your ego could repress the impulse, in which case you would never be aware that you had it in the first place. It could project the impulse onto others, such that you became convinced that they—not you—had the impulse to attack. It could form a reaction against the impulse, in which case you would do the opposite of physical aggression—you might be exceedingly gentle and kind with others or dedicate yourself to nonviolent causes. It could displace the impulse to be aggressive onto a safer target; if your id truly wanted to hit your boss, you might instead redirect the aggression toward a friend, family member, partner, pet, or even a punching bag or video-game enemy. Finally, it could sublimate the impulse, in which case you would behave in a physically aggressive way that actually benefited society—perhaps as a police officer subduing criminals or even as a surgeon whose incisions heal rather than harm.

Psychodynamic psychotherapists believe that some of these defense mechanisms are more mature or healthy than others (Dewald, 1964; Freud, 1905; Gabbard, 2005; Karon & Widener, 1995). For example, denial and repression are considered rather immature, largely because they don't effectively satisfy the id, so similar id demands resurface later. At the other end of the spectrum, sublimation is viewed as uniquely mature because it satisfies the individual's id impulses and a societal need simultaneously. Of course, the goal of psychodynamic psychotherapy is to help clients become aware of their unconscious processes, including their defense mechanisms. As clients become enlightened about defense mechanisms they use, they can exert some control over them and, in the process, move toward more mature ways of managing their internal conflicts.

Defense mechanisms may be easier to understand if we consider alternate definitions of some core Freudian terms: id, superego, and ego. Freud wrote in German, and some of his followers have argued that when his terms were translated into English, the translators made the curious choices of *id*, *superego*, and *ego*, which are actually Latin terms uncommon to everyday English. Some have argued that Freud's concept of the id would be better translated as "it": the part of you that is animalistic rather than human (not "he" or "she"). The superego might be better understood as the "over-me": an internalization of the rules and demands that came from authority figures, especially parents. And ego, therefore, refers to "me": the person negotiating between the demands for instant pleasure and the demands to follow rules (Karon & Widener, 1995; Truscott, 2010). This alternate terminology helps personify the ego and highlights the fact that defense mechanisms don't merely characterize some abstract component of the mind (the "ego"); they actually characterize the whole person and, in many cases, the problems he or she brings to a clinical psychologist.

Transference

Of all the ways to access a client's unconscious material, transference may be most essential to the psychodynamic approach. It is "generally regarded as the most important focus" of psychodynamic psychotherapy (Galatzer-Levy, Bachrach, Skolnikoff, & Waldron, 2000, p. 27) and is seen as "the most powerful tool" of those who conduct it (Karon & Widener, 1995, p. 27).

Transference refers to clients' tendency to form relationships with therapists in which they unconsciously and unrealistically expect the therapist to behave like important people from the clients' pasts. In other words, without realizing it, a client "transfers" the feelings, expectations, and assumptions from early relationships—usually parental relationships—onto the relationship with the therapist. Essentially, clients allow powerful previous relationships to distort their view of the therapist, and in subtle ways they "prejudge" the therapist as a person whose responses will echo those of mom, dad, or some other important early figure (Gabbard, 2005; Gabbard, 2009c; Goldberg, 2012b; A. Harris, 2012; Lane & Harris, 2008).

Perhaps the concept of transference is best illustrated through an everyday example. (After all, psychodynamic psychotherapists believe that transference is not exclusive to therapy but present in all kinds of relationships.) Consider Asaan, a 7-year-old boy who has taken piano lessons from Ms. Terrell since age 4. Ms. Terrell is a harsh, demanding teacher. She expects excellence from her students, and when they fall short, she scolds them unsympathetically. She also makes insulting and discouraging comments such as, "That's terrible," "You're wasting your parents' money," and "How many times do I have to teach you this song before you get it right?" As you might expect, Asaan has developed strong feelings toward Ms. Terrell over the years. Specifically, he fears and resents her. When Asaan's family moves to another city, his parents arrange for him to take piano lessons from a new teacher, Ms. Wallace. At his first lesson with Ms. Wallace, Asaan makes a mistake, and—before Ms. Wallace responds at all—strong feelings well up inside Asaan. He anticipates Ms. Wallace's comments—he "knows" that she's thinking, "That's terrible," etc.—and starts to feel fear and resentment toward Ms. Wallace in exactly the same way he did toward Ms. Terrell. In short, Asaan unknowingly *transfers* the feelings and expectations from his early, formative relationship with a piano teacher (Ms. Terrell) onto his subsequent teacher (Ms. Wallace). What he doesn't yet realize is that, in reality, his new teacher is a world apart from his old teacher: Ms. Wallace is extremely supportive, kind, and complimentary toward her students. In time, Asaan may grow to appreciate Ms. Wallace more realistically, but at least at first, his unrealistic, unconscious transference toward her will distort his perception of her and the way they interact with each other.

What happened to Asaan and his piano teachers happens to all of us, according to psychodynamic theory, in a much broader sense. We all experience powerful early relationships in our formative years—especially with parents—and those relationships shape our expectations for future relationships. Thus, when we meet new people and begin to form friendships, romantic partnerships, or work relationships with them, our responses toward them might not be totally objective. Instead, to the extent that our new friends, partners, or coworkers evoke the important people with whom we had our primary, early relationships, we may unconsciously jump to conclusions about them and develop feelings toward them that aren't actually warranted. The role of the psychodynamic psychotherapist is to help clients become aware of their own transference tendencies and the ways these unrealistic perceptions of others affect their relationships and their lives. Once aware of these tendencies, clients can make conscious efforts to manage them.

Rather than learning about clients' transference indirectly through their descriptions of relationships with others, psychodynamic psychotherapists seek to experience that transference firsthand. In other words, psychodynamic psychotherapists presume that clients will bring the same transference issues to the client–therapist relationship that they do to many of the other relationships in their lives. This way, the therapist gets a direct, personal understanding of the expectations and emotions the client unknowingly assigns to new relationships. After the therapist identifies these transference tendencies in the client–therapist relationship, the therapist can call the client's attention to them—in other words, offer **interpretation** of the transference. These comments by the therapist to the client—observations, essentially, of the unconscious tendencies the client shows when he or she forms relationships—are crucial elements of this kind of therapy; in fact, some argue that interpretation "has always been the technique par excellence" of psychoanalysis and psychodynamic psychotherapies (Goldberg, 2012a, p. 292). With any interpretation, it may take clients a long time to fully understand it, accept it, and see its impact on their day-to-day lives. After all, an interpretation can represent a drastically different explanation than the client had ever considered for his or her own behavior. For this reason, psychodynamic therapy often involves a lengthy **working through** process, in which interpretations are reconsidered and reevaluated again and again. Frequently, it takes many sessions for an important interpretation to "sink in" fully and take effect on the client's psychological functioning (Gabbard, 2009c).

The "**blank screen**" **role** of the psychodynamic psychotherapist is essential to the transference process. Psychodynamic psychotherapists typically reveal very little about themselves to their clients through either verbal or nonverbal communication. (In fact, this was a primary reason why Freud had clients lie on a couch while he sat behind them in a chair, out of their line of sight.) Consider the example of Asaan and his new piano teacher, Ms. Wallace, once again. If Ms. Wallace decided that from the beginning, she was going to reveal as little as possible about her own personality—essentially, stay "blank" to Asaan—she could conclude that any feelings Asaan has toward her are based purely on transference from past relationships. If she gives him nothing to respond to—communicates very little verbally and nonverbally, keeps a neutral emotional tone—and Asaan nonetheless expresses resentment and fear toward her, Ms. Wallace can conclude that those feelings are left over from earlier relationships; after all, she couldn't have elicited them herself. For a piano teacher, this would be unusual behavior. But for a psychodynamic psychotherapist, it is quite common and purposeful.

Considering Culture

Culture-Specific Responses to the "Blank Screen" Therapist

Many psychodynamic psychotherapists make great efforts to remain "blank screens" to their clients. They don't self-disclose much at all through their words or their actions, so clients may learn very little about the therapist's personal background. Family, religion, values, hobbies, and the like remain unknown. This blank screen role facilitates transference, which is essential to the psychodynamic process. When a client reacts emotionally to a therapist whose own words and actions couldn't have provoked the reaction, the therapist can be sure that those feelings are the remnants of a previous relationship. The therapist can help the client become more aware of this transference and how it affects relationships in the client's real life.

But how do clients of various cultures respond to a "blank screen" therapist? Are all clients seeking therapists who play this role in their lives? Some have argued that clients outside mainstream U.S. culture might benefit most from therapists whose roles in their lives are at odds with the blank screen role of psychodynamic psychotherapists. For instance, Atkinson, Thompson, and Grant (1993) argued that among diverse clients, there is tremendous cultural variation in the services they want their therapists to perform or the functions they want them to serve. Specifically, these authors have identified eight distinct therapist roles that clients may seek:

- Adviser
- Advocate
- Facilitator of indigenous support systems
- Facilitator of indigenous healing systems
- Consultant
- Change agent
- Counselor
- Psychotherapist

Whereas some of these roles, especially those near the end of the list, may be compatible with the psychodynamic blank screen role, some of the roles near the top of the list may

(Continued)

(Continued)

clash with it. For example, as an adviser or an advocate, it's likely that the therapist would be expected to reveal something personal, such as values and experiences. And certainly, as a facilitator of indigenous support or healing systems, the therapist would at the very least indicate a familiarity and endorsement of these systems and may also make known personal background information in the process.

Atkinson et al. (1993) argue that people less acculturated to mainstream U.S. culture tend to favor the first four roles on the list, whereas people with higher levels of acculturation tend to favor the last four. Indeed, clients with low levels of acculturation may be looking for something very different from what's traditional when they decide to seek help for a psychological or emotional problem. In your opinion, how rigid do psychodynamic psychotherapists have to be regarding the blank screen role? To what extent can it be adapted to accommodate diverse clients?

As a clinical example of transference, consider Felicia, a 27-year-old client seeing Dr. Kirk, a psychodynamic psychotherapist, for depressive symptoms after breaking up with her boyfriend, Dave. At her first appointment, Felicia begins to describe her situation—the relationship with Dave, how they broke up, how she feels about it—but about 10 minutes in, she stops herself and apologizes to Dr. Kirk: "I'm sorry, I know I'm wasting your time. This is really boring, and you're probably thinking, 'I wish I could just tell her to shut up.'" Dr. Kirk encourages Felicia to continue describing her breakup and her depression, and she does, but after 15 more minutes she interrupts herself again: "This is such a stupid problem. I just need to learn how to get over it. I should leave and let you get to the more important things you have to do today." It's important to note that Dr. Kirk was not, in fact, bored with Felicia. He wasn't falling asleep, staring out the window, or glancing at his watch. He had remained attentive and interested, but in spite of this, Felicia was convinced that Dr. Kirk could have no interest in her. In effect, Dr. Kirk had been a blank screen, but when Felicia looked at it, she saw disinterest and impatience.

Why would she have done this? The answer came in time, as Felicia explained to Dr. Kirk that throughout her childhood, her father had shown disinterest and impatience toward her. He had consistently given Felicia the message that she was unworthy of his time and attention. Felicia not only transferred those feelings and expectations onto Dr. Kirk, but as Dr. Kirk learned, she had done something very similar with numerous boyfriends, including Dave. Over and over, without realizing it, she had ended or sabotaged seemingly strong dating relationships by repeatedly insisting to her boyfriends that she couldn't be worth their while.

This wasn't, in reality, what the boyfriends thought, but her experience with her father had left her unconsciously biased toward assuming this response from the men in her life. Unlike Dave or any of her other boyfriends, Dr. Kirk was able to identify this transference—to "catch" Felicia doing it and point it out to her—when she unconsciously directed her expectations for disinterest and impatience toward him. With continued discussion with Dr. Kirk, Felicia gradually became more aware of this tendency in herself. When she started her next dating relationship, she was able to "catch" her own unrealistic transference feelings toward her new boyfriend and replace them with a more realistic, objective appraisal.

As a final note on transference, it's important to remember that therapists are people too, and just as clients can transfer onto therapists, therapists can transfer onto clients. Psychodynamic psychotherapists call this transference by therapists toward clients **countertransference**, and, generally, they strive to minimize it because it involves a reaction to the client that is unconsciously distorted by the therapist's own personal experiences (Brown, 2012; Dewald, 1964; Harris, 2012; Maroda, 2010; Skelton, 2006). One reason that many psychodynamic training programs require trainees to be clients in psychodynamic psychotherapy themselves is to become aware of their own unconscious issues so they won't arise as countertransference toward their own clients (Erwin, 2002; Moore & Fine, 1990).

Psychosexual Stages: Clinical Implications

Freud's psychosexual stages of development—oral, anal, phallic, latency, and genital—are among the most widely known aspects of his theory. Rather than restating the explanations found in introductory psychology textbooks, let's consider the implications most relevant to clinical psychologists and to the psychodynamic psychotherapy approach in particular.

Of the five stages, the first three have generally received the most attention from psychodynamic psychotherapists, especially regarding fixation (Karon & Widener, 1995). **Fixation** refers to the idea that as children move through the developmental stages, they may become emotionally "stuck" at any one of them to some extent and may continue to struggle with issues related to that stage for many years, often well into adulthood. Although fixation can happen for a variety of reasons, most often it occurs when parents either do "too much" or "too little" in response to the child's needs at a certain developmental point.

Oral Stage

Consider the **oral stage**, which takes place during roughly the first year and a half of a child's life. During this time, the child experiences all pleasurable sensations through the mouth, and feeding (breast or bottle) is the focal issue. Of course, kids whose parents mismanage this stage may display blatantly "oral" behaviors later in life: smoking, overeating, drinking, nail biting, etc. Many of the consequences are not so obvious,

Photo 12.3 According to the psychodynamic perspective, the mouth is the focus of pleasurable sensations for children in the oral stage of development.

however. According to psychodynamic theory, a primary issue at this stage is dependency. Babies are, after all, utterly dependent on others for survival and comfort. They cannot feed, clothe, bathe, protect, or otherwise take care of themselves, so they must depend on the adults in their lives. (Perhaps the adult equivalent of this is a hospital patient who is entirely debilitated by illness or injury and whose only option is to call the staff for help.) If parents overindulge children in the oral stage, children may learn that depending on others always works out wonderfully and, in fact, that other people exist solely to anticipate and meet your needs. Such children may develop overly trusting, naive, unrealistically optimistic personalities and, as adults, will form relationships accordingly. On the other hand, if parents are not responsive enough to children during the oral stage, children may learn that depending on others never works out and, in fact, other people have no interest in helping you at all. Such children may develop overly mistrusting, suspicious, and unrealistically pessimistic personalities and, as adults, will form relationships accordingly. These oral issues, especially in extreme form, are often at the root of clients' individual and interpersonal problems and the focus of psychodynamic psychotherapy.

Anal Stage

The **anal stage** follows the oral stage, occurring when the child is about 1.5 to 3 years old. Toilet training is a primary task of this stage, but it is not the only way children are learning to control themselves. Indeed, control is the central issue of this stage. At this age, adults (especially parents) begin to place demands on children regarding their speech and behavior. If parents are too demanding of children at this stage, children can become overly concerned about getting everything just right. In the bathroom, this may mean "no accidents," but, more generally, it means having everything in exactly the right place at the right time. These children often grow to become adults who think obsessively and behave compulsively in order to stay in control: They meticulously organize their desks, they program their daily schedules from start to finish, and they get their cars' oil changed every 3,000 miles exactly. By contrast, if parents are too lenient toward children at this stage, children can become lax about organization, and this trait can continue into adulthood: Their desks are covered in messy piles, their schedules are sloppy and haphazard, and their cars get oil changes "whenever." These "neat freak" or "slob" tendencies can have significant clinical implications, including anxiety disorders such as obsessive-compulsive disorder and relationship problems stemming from incompatible living styles.

Phallic Stage

The **phallic stage,** taking place from about age 3 to about age 6, is one of Freud's most controversial. In fact, many of the ideas originally contained in Freud's description of this stage, especially those closely tied to gender-specific biology, have fallen out of favor and are widely disputed by contemporary psychodynamic psychotherapists (Erwin, 2002; Karon & Widener, 1995). What remains is the fundamental idea implied by the Oedipus and Electra complexes: Children at this age wish to have a special, close relationship with parents. The parents' response to the child's wish is the crucial issue for clinical psychologists, because this parental response powerfully shapes the children's view of themselves. This view of the self—essentially, self-worth—is the key consequence of the phallic stage. Of course, the ideal situation is for parents to respond positively to kids' overtures. But when parents respond too positively, when they reciprocate the child's wishes too strongly, they overinflate the child's sense of self. Such children may grow into adults whose opinions of themselves are so unrealistically high that they strike others as arrogant or egotistical. Conversely, parents who reject their child's wishes for a special, close relationship can wound a child's sense of self-worth. These kids can grow up to become adults who devalue themselves and are overly insecure and self-doubting. (Felicia, the clinical example in the section on transference above, is an example.) As with the other psychosexual stages, the phallic stage often gives rise to issues discussed in psychodynamic psychotherapy, including disorders such as depression, dysthymia, anxiety, relationship problems, and any other issue that can involve questions of self-worth.

More Contemporary Forms of Psychodynamic Psychotherapy

Since its origins with Freud, psychodynamic psychotherapy has been reinvented in countless forms (Orlinsky & Howard, 1995). Most of these revisions have deemphasized the biological and sexual elements of the theory. For example, **ego psychology,** as exemplified by Erik Erikson and his eight-stage theory of development, revised Freud's psychosexual stages to highlight social relationships and emphasized the adaptive tendencies of the ego over the pleasure-based drive of the id. The **object relations** school, led by Melanie Klein, Otto Kernberg, Ronald Fairbairn, and others, deemphasized internal conflict (id vs. superego) and instead emphasized relationships between internalized "objects" (essentially, important people from the client's life; Williams, 2012). The **self-psychology** school of Hans Kohut and others emphasizes parental roles in the child's development of self, with special attention paid to the meaning of narcissism at various points, including in therapy (Karon & Widener, 1995; Skelton, 2006; Terman, 2012).

Other revisions of the Freudian approach have cast doubt on Freud's theories regarding females and their development. Karen Horney was one such critic of Freud, publishing numerous articles and books in the early to mid-1900s that opposed many of Freud's ideas, including his assumptions that females felt inherently inferior and envious toward males. Her commentaries on Freud and her own gender-specific developmental theories represented "a courageous attempt to reform the accepted psychoanalytic ideas on women" (Westkott, 1986, p. 9). Moreover, Horney's writings influenced more recent feminist theorists, including Nancy Chodorow (1978) and Carol Gilligan (1982), who have further advanced theories of female development that account for the experience of girls and women more authentically than do Freud's original theories and do not represent variants of male development.

Throughout its history and in all its many variations, psychodynamic psychotherapy has always been among the longest and most expensive forms of psychotherapy—a mismatch for our current society, which is characterized by a desire for fast results and managed-care companies reluctant to pay for treatment they view as excessive (Galatzer-Levy et al., 2000; Sperling, Sack, & Field, 2000). As a result, most of the recent variations of psychodynamic psychotherapy have emphasized efficiency. Collectively, the many forms of *brief psychodynamic psychotherapy* have become far more common in recent years than the classic, orthodox version of Freudian psychoanalysis from which they derived (Levenson, 2010; Levenson, Butler, & Beitman, 1997; Steenbarger, 2008). The definition of brief in brief psychodynamic psychotherapy varies a bit, but it often refers to therapy lasting fewer than 24 sessions, which amounts to about 6 months of once-a-week sessions. With such a small window of time (by psychoanalytic standards), the therapist and client must quickly form an alliance, develop insights that facilitate new ways of understanding, and translate these insights into real-world changes. Compared with long-term psychodynamic psychotherapy, brief psychodynamic psychotherapy tends to be more successful when the client's problems are mild and narrowly defined, the therapist is active, and the focus includes the present rather than solely the past (Dewan, Weerasekera, & Stormon, 2009). Table 12.1 offers a more extensive comparison of brief and long-term approaches to psychodynamic psychotherapy.

Some particular forms of brief psychodynamic psychotherapy have garnered significant attention in recent years. Let's consider two of them in detail as examples of contemporary variations of psychodynamic psychotherapy.

Interpersonal Therapy

Interpersonal Therapy (IPT), which derives from the interpersonal school of psychodynamic thought of which Harry Stack Sullivan was a leader, was developed in the 1980s by Gerald Klerman, Myrna Weissman, and colleagues. It was originally created to treat depression, but it has since been used to treat numerous other disorders (Blanco & Weissman, 2005; Klerman, Weissman, Rounsaville, & Chevron, 1984; Markowitz

Table 12.1 Comparison of Brief and Long-Term Psychodynamic Psychotherapy

Brief Psychodynamic Psychotherapy	Long-Term Psychodynamic Psychotherapy
Form therapeutic alliance rapidly	Form therapeutic alliance gradually
Focus on specific, narrowly defined problem	Focus on broad range of problems
Therapist's level of activity is relatively high	Therapist's level of activity is relatively low
Client's psychopathology is less severe	Client's psychopathology is more severe
Focus primarily on here and now	Focus on past and present
Client's ability to tolerate separation is high	Client's ability to tolerate separation is variable
Client has good object relationships	Client has poor to good object relationships

Source: Adapted from Dewan, M., Weerasekera, P., & Stormon, L. (2009).

& Weissman, 2012; Weissman, 1995). It is designed to last about 14 to 20 sessions, and, as such, its goals are more focused and limited than structural change of the entire personality. Its methods are outlined in a manual with specific therapeutic guidelines (Klerman et al., 1984).

The fundamental assumption of IPT is that depression happens in the context of interpersonal relationships, so improving the client's relationships with others will facilitate improvement in the client's depressive symptoms. It focuses on current interpersonal relationships and role expectations and tends to deemphasize some of the aspects of more traditional psychodynamic psychotherapy related to intrapsychic structure and childhood fixations (Frank & Levenson, 2011; Levenson et al., 1997; Swartz & Markowitz, 2009; Weissman, 1995). Therapists practicing IPT have found that for most clients, especially those with depression, a few specific interpersonal problem areas tend to contribute to client's problems: *role transitions,* such as becoming a parent or graduating from college; *role disputes,* such as entering a marriage; *interpersonal deficits,* such as a lack of social support; and *grief,* such as the reaction to loss of a loved one (Blanco & Weissman, 2005; Lipsitz, 2009).

IPT proceeds in three stages. The first stage (about 2 sessions in most cases) involves categorizing the client's problems into one of the four categories listed above (role transitions, role disputes, interpersonal deficits, and grief). The intermediate sessions (10–12 sessions) emphasize improving the client's problems as identified in the first stage. Common psychodynamic methods are used, including a focus on current emotions, explorations of transference, and resistance. Also, the intermediate stage often includes an educational component in which the therapist teaches the client about depression and its symptoms. The final stage (2–4 sessions) involves a review of the client's accomplishments, recognition of the client's capacity to succeed over depression without the therapist's continued help, and efforts to prevent relapse (Klerman et al., 1984; Levenson et al., 1997).

IPT is one of the few specific forms of psychodynamic psychotherapy for which researchers have gathered a sizable amount of empirical evidence. In other words, efficacy studies have found that IPT works for depressed individuals, and it appears on published lists of therapies that are known to be successful for particular disorders (e.g., Chambless et al., 1998; Nathan & Gorman, 2002). Most of the evidence of support for IPT comes from studies of depressed clients, but there is also some evidence that it works for clients with eating disorders, anxiety disorders, and some other problems as well (Blanco & Weissman, 2005; Bolton et al., 2003; Frank & Levenson, 2011; Markowitz & Weissman, 2009, 2012; Spinelli & Endicott, 2003). As such, it is a leader among psychodynamic therapies in terms of empirically supported efficacy.

Time-Limited Dynamic Psychotherapy

⊕ Web Link 12.3

Interview with Hanna Levenson, leader in the field of TLDP

Time-Limited Dynamic Psychotherapy (TLDP) is a modern application of the often-referenced "corrective emotional experience" (Alexander & French, 1946): Clients will bring to therapy the same transference issues that they bring to many of their other relationships, and the therapist's task is to make sure that this time, the interaction will end differently. In other words, if the client's relationship with the therapist follows the same unconscious "script" as the client's other relationships, it may end badly, but if the therapist can make the client more aware of this script and offer a chance to enact a healthier, more realistic one, the "emotional experience" will be "corrective" or therapeutic (Binder, Strupp, & Henry, 1995; Steenbarger, 2008).

TLDP is experiential in nature; the here-and-now relationship between therapist and client is the main tool for therapeutic change. Like most newer forms of psychodynamic psychotherapy, it is typically much briefer than classic psychoanalysis (about 20–25 sessions maximum; Levenson, 2010). The therapist's primary task is to identify the "script" that the client appears to be unknowingly following. This script is the byproduct of previous relationships (often with parents), in which the client learned what to expect from others. The TLDP therapist assumes that the client's problems are at least partially due to an application of this script to inappropriate relationships or situations. In other words, a client may get into frequent arguments with a romantic partner because he "knows" what his partner may be thinking and feeling, but this "knowledge" is actually unrealistic and mistaken. When the client tries to enact the same script with the therapist, the therapist recognizes it, refuses to be provoked or prodded into it, and points out this process to the client. In this way, they do not perpetuate the outdated script, and the client is forced to develop a new, more realistic way of relating to others that is not bound by the assumptions of the script that he or she had been unconsciously following (Binder et al., 1995; Steenbarger, 2008).

When therapists conduct TLDP, they often use a visual diagram called the cyclical maladaptive pattern (Levenson, 1995). It is a working model of the client's primary issues organized into four categories: acts of self (how a person actually behaves in public; for example, a client has a job interview); expectations about others' reactions ("I'm sure the interviewer didn't like me"); acts of others toward the self (the interviewer says, "Your application looks great. We'll call you in the next 2 weeks," and the client interprets this as rejection); and acts of the self toward the self (the client tells self, "You are such a failure," and spends next day alone and miserable). By identifying these four components of the cycle, TLDP therapists can help clients become more aware of specific thoughts and behaviors that contribute to the faulty script that they may enact, as well as healthier alternatives to these thoughts and behaviors.

How Well Does It Work?

The nature of psychodynamic psychotherapy makes it especially difficult to gauge its effects. From an empirical researcher's point of view, the challenge of defining and measuring the outcome of psychodynamic psychotherapy—and even the basic psychoanalytic concepts on which therapy rests, such as the unconscious, transference, insight, and defense mechanisms—can be extremely challenging (Gibbons et al., 2007; Luborsky & Barrett, 2006). How, exactly, do we know how well it has worked? Can we measure the extent to which the unconscious has been made conscious? Can we calculate the amount of insight a client has achieved or the extent to which his or her relationships have improved? These questions haunt psychodynamic psychotherapy and elicit criticism from those who prefer therapies of other kinds. Additionally, these questions help us understand why the methodology of many studies of the outcome of psychodynamic therapy are so widely disparaged, and why such a small number of psychodynamic therapies have been manualized, subjected to empirical trials, or included on lists of treatments that work (Sandell, 2012).

In spite of these methodological challenges, there have been many attempts to measure the outcome of psychodynamic psychotherapy. A large-scale review of psychodynamic and psychoanalytic outcome studies that, in total, included almost 2,000 clients treated by about 500 therapists across a wide range of settings suggested that the vast majority of clients improve substantially (Galatzer-Levy et al., 2000). More recent reviews of psychodynamic psychotherapy outcome studies have also touted empirical data supporting its use with a wide range of specific problems, including depression, bulimia, anorexia, panic disorder, and borderline personality disorder—long-standing, complex clinical conditions that may encompass more than one diagnosis (e.g., Gerber et al., 2011; Leichsenring, 2009a; Leichsenring, Rabung, & Leibing, 2004; Sandell, 2012). However, other reviews of the status of psychodynamic therapies have pointed out that the number of empirically sound studies, particularly those that focus on a well-defined, single disorder, is quite small—in fact, for some major disorders, there isn't a single well-done empirical study—suggesting that the evidence that does exist should be interpreted cautiously (Driessen et al., 2010; Gibbons, Crits-Christoph, & Hearon, 2008; Leichsenring, 2009b). Certainly, psychodynamic psychotherapy lags behind some others, especially behavioral and cognitive therapy, in sheer volume of empirical data supporting its use with specific clinical problems. But these reviews indicate that such empirical data has been obtained for some disorders and continues to accumulate.

It is worth noting that some empirical evidence exists for particular components of psychodynamic psychotherapy—namely, interpretation of transference and countertransference reactions. Johansson et al. (2010) conducted a study in which 100 clients with depression, anxiety, personality disorders, or other interpersonal problems received weekly psychodynamic psychotherapy for 1 year. For half of them, therapists offered transference interpretations; for the other half, they did not. Outcome was measured immediately after therapy and also at 1-year and 3-year follow-ups. Results indicated that those whose therapists offered transference interpretations benefited more from the therapy and that this benefit correlated with a greater level of insight. Regarding countertransference, Hayes, Gelso, and Hummel (2011) conducted multiple meta-analyses on countertransference and found that the presence of countertransference reactions by therapists correlated negatively with outcome; that is, the more countertransference, the worse the outcome for the client. They also found a positive correlation between therapist efforts to manage countertransference and therapy outcome; that is, the more therapists tried to keep their own biases toward clients "in check," the better the outcome for clients.

⊕ Web Link 12.4

Allegiance effect

Interestingly, in some meta-analyses, psychodynamic therapies are found to be effective but a bit less so than other forms of therapy. These slight discrepancies disappear, however, when allegiance effects are taken into account. **Allegiance effects** refer to the influence of researchers' own biases and preferences on the outcome of their empirical studies. Typically, the researchers who conduct empirical studies of psychotherapy outcome, including meta-analyses, are not psychodynamic in their own orientation. Instead, they tend to be behavioral or cognitive, which are the two broad categories of therapy to which psychoanalysis was found to be slightly inferior in some meta-analyses (Prochaska & Norcross, 2010).

Allegiance effects can be quite powerful: Luborsky et al. (1999) evaluated many comparative reviews of the psychotherapy literature and comparative studies of psychotherapy and found a surprisingly strong relationship between the way therapies were rated and the orientation of the researcher doing the rating. (Some have since supported this finding, while others have refuted it; e.g., Leykin & DeRubeis, 2009; Stiles, 2009; Wilson, Wilfley, Agras, & Bryson, 2011. See Box 12.3 for more.) This is relevant for all psychotherapy orientations but especially for the psychodynamic approach, because a relatively small number of therapy outcome researchers have been psychodynamic.

● ● ● BOX 12.3 ● ● ●

Metaphorically Speaking

If You've Watched the Olympics, You Understand Allegiance Effects

When we watch Olympic events such as gymnastics or ice skating on TV, we see not only the judges' scores but the judges' nationalities as well. In fact, in the on-screen graphic, each judge's individual score appears in a box just below the flag and abbreviation of the judge's country. Why is the judge's country relevant? Perhaps the assumption is that the judges' allegiance to their home countries limits their objectivity. Even if they try not to, the judges may root for a particular country, and that rooting may influence the way they judge the performances of the athletes. With the athletes' countries known to the judges, who themselves are citizens of certain countries, allegiance effects may be unavoidable in the Olympics.

Allegiance effects may be unavoidable in psychotherapy outcome research, too. The situation is very similar to the Olympics: The researchers who conduct the research and therefore judge the "performance" of various therapies are themselves either supporters or opponents of some of those therapies. Of course, these researchers should be completely objective, and they may believe that they are, but according to Luborsky et al. (1999), most are not. Their own preferences for certain kinds of therapy and against others appear to powerfully influence the results of the studies they conduct. In fact, Luborsky et al. report that allegiance effects can account for about

(Continued)

(Continued)

two thirds of the variance in outcomes of treatment comparisons! Some more recent studies have corroborated the severity of allegiance effects in psychotherapy outcome studies, suggesting that Luborsky et al. may have actually underestimated them (e.g., Stiles, 2009). But others have argued that Luborsky et al. overestimated the severity or importance of their conclusions about therapy outcome (e.g., Leykin & DeRubeis, 2009; Wilson et al., 2011). Just as Olympic judges might feel an underlying favoritism for the athletes from their own countries, so might psychotherapy outcome researchers for the therapies from their own orientations.

The Olympic judge's flag is revealed for all to see, but the psychotherapy outcome researcher's allegiance is often less obvious. When Luborsky et al. (1999) conducted their study on allegiance effects, they had to contact the researchers who had published psychotherapy outcome research, as well as those researchers' colleagues, to determine the researchers' orientations. In your opinion, should psychotherapy outcome researchers be more forthcoming about their own orientations, perhaps including this information in the studies they publish, because these orientations may bring about biases? Should researchers make efforts to conduct studies in collaborative groups that contain members of various orientations so they counterbalance one another's biases? What other measures can psychotherapy outcome researchers take to limit the allegiance effect?

● ● ● BOX 12.4 ● ● ●

Denise in Psychodynamic Psychotherapy

Denise attended 50 sessions over a 1-year period. At my request, she provided background information about her childhood, including the fact that she was the fifth of six children and that her parents both worked full-time. She explained that because of these factors, she received very little attention or praise from her parents throughout childhood. She described her depression stemming from recent changes at work and stated that the most upsetting part of the change was the new restaurant owner's insistence that she stop visiting with diners. She sorely missed their positive feedback about her dishes. In addition to sadness and other common depressive symptoms, Denise also listed a lack of energy that resulted in her being late to work and preparing dishes more slowly than usual. It was also noteworthy that Denise believed that the new owner may have made these changes with the intention of hurting Denise.

Based on this information, my initial conceptualization of Denise included the following hypotheses:

- Denise was dealing with emotional issues from the phallic stage of development, and she may have been partially fixated at that stage. At the points in childhood when Denise sought a special, intimate relationship with a parent, the parent did not provide it. As a result, she lacked self-esteem and sought it from outside sources. The strongest of these sources—the feedback of the diners in her restaurant—had been cut off by the new owner, contributing greatly to her depression.

- Denise was struggling with unacceptable impulses of anger toward the new restaurant owner and was using defense mechanisms—projection, most obviously—to deal with them. Denise stated that she believed the new owner was trying to hurt her by instituting the new policies, but this seems an unlikely motivation for the new owner. Instead, it is probable that Denise is the one with the hurtful intentions toward the new owner, but rather than acknowledge them, she kept them unconscious by projecting them onto the owner, thus portraying the owner as the "bad" person and herself as the innocent victim.

- Denise's unconscious anger toward the new owner also revealed itself through her lateness and slow work. Although she attributed these behaviors to her lack of energy, they may have been unconsciously motivated acts of aggression toward the new owner and the new policies. Several of the specific stories she told—the time she "accidentally" dropped an entrée in the kitchen and the times she "forgot" to set her alarm—appear to fall in the category of Freudian slips.

My relationship with Denise was marked by numerous examples of resistance and transference. Regarding the resistance, Denise often changed the subject in subtle and clever ways when I asked questions regarding the new owner or her feelings toward her parents. Once, after a session ended in the middle of a particularly intense discussion of her work situation, she was 20 minutes late to her next appointment. Another time, she followed a session in which we examined her feelings toward her parents with a session in which she insisted on focusing on a seemingly minor argument with a previously unmentioned friend.

(Continued)

(Continued)

Regarding the transference, Denise often seemed to assume that I didn't think she was worthy of my attention, and, in fact, she said so on many occasions. She also sought my praise on frequent occasions, sometimes directly asking me for feedback after describing something she had accomplished.

The main intention behind my interventions with Denise was to make her more conscious of her unconscious processes. On various occasions, I offered interpretations of her actions. I mentioned that perhaps she had hurtful feelings toward the new owner, rather than vice versa. I asked questions that led her to consider whether her slow and sloppy performance at work may have been motivated by her own wishes. I discussed with her the role that the diners' feedback played in context of the attention and praise her parents did not provide. And, perhaps most important, I pointed out to her the unconscious tendencies (transference) that she brought to the relationship with me, even though our relationship did not realistically merit them: the assumption that I would dismiss her and her need for my praise and admiration. The discussion of transference was especially productive because it shed light on some of Denise's previous relationships as well. Slowly, with continued conversation in all these areas, Denise was able to achieve significant insight into her unconscious processes. By doing so, she was able to view others more realistically and control her motivations more deliberately, and her depressive symptoms eventually lifted.

CHAPTER SUMMARY

Psychodynamic psychotherapy is founded on the theories of Sigmund Freud. It presumes the presence of a powerful unconscious component of the mind, and its primary goal is insight or making unconscious processes conscious. It is a highly inferential approach to psychotherapy in which problems and therapy's impact on them are difficult to assess objectively or empirically. Psychodynamic psychotherapists gain access to clients' unconscious in numerous ways, including free association, Freudian slips, dreams, and resistance clients display during

therapy. The ongoing unconscious conflict between the id and the superego requires the ego to mediate by employing defense mechanisms such as repression, projection, reaction formation, displacement, and sublimation. Reliance on particular defense mechanisms can characterize an individual's personality as well as the clinical issues they bring to therapy. Clients often experience transference toward their psychodynamic therapists, in which they unknowingly and unrealistically expect the therapist to relate to them as important people from the clients' pasts have related to them. Psychodynamic therapists often assume a "blank screen" role to facilitate this transference process and assume that the clients may have transferred similarly onto other people with whom they have formed relationships. Psychodynamic therapists also pay significant attention to clinical issues that may stem from fixation at an early psychosexual stage of development (e.g., oral, anal, or phallic). Psychodynamic psychotherapy has traditionally been relatively long-term, but shorter versions, such as ITP and TLDP, have emerged in recent decades, and evidence has begun to accumulate attesting to their efficacy, especially with depressed clients. Overall, the nature of psychodynamic psychotherapy has hindered the collection of empirical outcome data, but the data that have been collected suggest it is roughly as effective as other forms of psychotherapy.

KEY TERMS AND NAMES

allegiance effects 310

anal stage 304

"blank screen" role 300

brief psychodynamic psychotherapy 306

countertransference 303

defense mechanisms 296

displacement 296

dream work 293

dreams 293

ego 295

ego psychology 305

fixation 303

free association 292

Sigmund Freud 290

Freudian slips 292

id 295

inferential 292

insight 291

Interpersonal Therapy (IPT) 306

interpretation 300

latent content 293

manifest content 293

object relations 305

oral stage 303

phallic stage 305

projection 296

psychodynamic psychotherapy 290

reaction formation 296

repression 296

resistance 294

self-psychology 305

sublimation 296

superego 295

Time-Limited Dynamic Psychotherapy (TLDP) 308

transference 298

unconscious 291

working through 300

CRITICAL THINKING QUESTIONS

1. To what extent do you believe that insight, or making the unconscious conscious, is essential to overcoming psychological problems?

2. To what extent do you believe that Freudian slips accurately reveal unconscious wishes?

3. Box 12.2 lists eight distinct therapist roles that clients may seek. If you were the client, which would you seek? To what extent would a psychodynamic psychotherapist match that role?

4. Many psychodynamic graduate training programs require their trainees to undergo therapy themselves. If you were the client, how would you feel about the fact that your therapist had (or had never) been in therapy?

5. What efforts should psychotherapy outcome researchers make to minimize allegiance effects?

STUDENT STUDY SITE RESOURCES

Visit the study site at www.sagepub.com/pomerantz3eupdate for these additional learning tools:

- Self-quizzes
- eFlashcards
- Culture Expert Interviews

- Full-text SAGE journal articles
- Additional web resources
- Mock Assessment Data

CHAPTER SUMMARY VIDEO

 QR codes at the end of each chapter link to chapter background videos by the author. Visit http://gettag.mobi using your smartphone browser to download the free Microsoft Tag app. Once installed, scan the tags to go directly to these brief videos. In this video, the author raises questions about the reach of the allegiance effect both within and beyond clinical psychology.

CHAPTER 13

Humanistic Psychotherapy

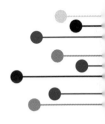

Like most psychologists of his era, **Carl Rogers** was trained psychodynamically. But he didn't stay psychodynamic for long. He came to disagree with many of Freud's presumptions about therapy and, more fundamentally, about people (Cain, 2010). Along with **Abraham Maslow**, Rogers pioneered the humanistic movement in psychology and its clinical application, **humanistic therapy**.

 Web Link 13.1
Carl Rogers

The humanistic approach to understanding people stood in opposition to the biologically based, id-dominated, cynical Freudian view that prevailed at the time. Maslow (1968) summarized its theoretical foundation:

> Inner nature [of people] seems not to be intrinsically or primarily or necessarily evil. . . . Human nature is not nearly as bad as it has been thought to be. . . .

> Since this inner nature is good or neutral rather than bad, it is best to bring it out and encourage it rather than to suppress it. If it is permitted to guide our life, we grow healthy, fruitful, and happy. If this essential core of the person is denied or suppressed, [the person] gets sick sometimes in obvious ways, sometimes in subtle ways, sometimes immediately, sometimes later. (pp. 3–4)

Rogers applied this theory to people with psychological problems and, in doing so, offered an approach to therapy that remains quite influential today. Despite the fact that he shared his most essential ideas about psychotherapy about half a century ago and died in 1987, a recent survey of more than 2,400 psychotherapists found that Carl Rogers was the single most prominent figure in terms of influence on the way they practiced psychotherapy (Cook, Biyanova, & Coyne, 2009).

To simplify our discussion, in this chapter we use the term *humanistic* to cover the family of therapies created by Rogers and his followers. At various times, the terms *nondirective*, *client-centered*, and *person-centered* have been used by Rogers and others to describe these approaches.

Humanistic Concepts: Clinical Implications

Picture a small plant, just sprouting from the soil. We can confidently make several assumptions about this plant. First, we assume that the plant has an innate tendency to grow. In other words, given the proper environment, healthy growth will naturally occur. Second, we assume that the plant's growth utterly depends on sunlight—without it, it simply won't thrive. Third, we assume that if sunlight is available only from certain directions, the plant will bend, twist, or even contort its growth to reach it. Certain branches may blossom while others wither, and the plant may take on an unexpected shape in the process, but the nourishment from the sun is so essential that the plant will alter itself quite drastically to attain it. Of course, if sunlight comes from all directions, the plant need not alter itself at all. It can simply bloom according to its own inherent potential.

There are compelling parallels between this plant and human beings, according to the humanistic approach. Humanists assume that people, like plants, arrive with an inborn tendency to grow. Humanists call this tendency **self-actualization** and presume that if the person's environment fosters it, self-actualization proceeds without interference (Cain, 2002, 2010). Humanists also recognize that people need certain things to live, and just as plants need sunlight, people need positive regard. **Positive regard,** from the humanistic point of view, is essentially the warmth, love, and acceptance of those around us. (Rogers's frequently used term **prizing** may best capture this experience of receiving positive regard from others; e.g., Rogers, 1959.) As children, we bask in the glow of positive regard from our parents; like plants with sunlight, we need it to grow. If we discover that our parents provide positive regard only when we behave in certain ways, we will emphasize certain aspects ("branches") of ourselves and suppress others in order to attain it. The end result may be a version of ourselves that is markedly different from the version that might have blossomed if our parents had provided positive regard no matter what.

Photo 13.1 Carl Rogers (1902– 1987), a leading figure in humanistic psychotherapy

Goal of Humanistic Psychotherapy

The primary goal of humanistic psychotherapy is to foster self-actualization. Humanists believe that psychological problems—depression, anxiety, personality disorders, eating disorders, and most other forms of psychopathology—are the byproducts of a stifled growth process. People who seek professional help for psychological problems have within them the capacity and the will to grow toward health, but, somehow, their growth has been interrupted or distorted. The task of the humanistic therapist is, through the therapeutic relationship, to create a climate in which clients can resume their natural growth toward psychological wellness.

If we are all guided by the self-actualization tendency from the beginning of our lives, how could we find ourselves depressed, anxious, or otherwise struggling with psychological issues? The answer lies in the fact that the need for positive regard can, at times, override the natural tendency to self-actualize. That is, when we face an either/or choice between receiving positive regard from the important people in our lives and following our own natural inclinations, we may, out of necessity, choose the positive regard.

Photo 13.2 Humanists believe that, like plants, people have an inborn tendency to grow and that certain conditions foster their growth.

Problems arise when this positive regard is conditional rather than unconditional. Conditional positive regard communicates that we are prized "only if" we meet certain conditions. If you consider your own family or those of your best childhood friends, you can probably identify some of the **conditions of worth** that parents place on their children. These conditions aren't posted as a list on the refrigerator, but they are clearly communicated nonetheless: We'll love you only if you get good grades, dress how we like, adopt our values, excel in sports, don't gain weight, stay out of trouble, and so on. Usually, kids can keenly sense the conditions their parents place on their acceptance, and because they need their parents' acceptance, they do their best to meet these conditions. In the process, however, they often go astray of their own self-actualization tendency, which may have guided them in another direction. Thus, when they compare the selves they actually are—the **real self**—with the selves they could be if they fulfilled their own potential—the **ideal self**—they perceive a discrepancy. Humanists use the term **incongruence** to describe this discrepancy, and they view it as the root of psychopathology. In contrast, **congruence**—a match between the real self and the ideal self—is achieved when self-actualization is allowed to guide a person's life without interference by any conditions of worth, and, as a result, mental health is optimized. That is, congruence happens when a person experiences unconditional positive regard from others. No "only if" conditions are placed on them for acceptance, so they are free to develop and grow according to their own self-actualization tendency (Cain, 2010).

It is important to note that although conditions of worth originally come from others, they can eventually become incorporated into our own views of ourselves. That is, conditional positive regard from others brings forth conditional positive *self*-regard, whereas unconditional positive regard from others brings forth unconditional positive *self*-regard. The important people in our lives communicate to us what is lovable, acceptable, or "prizeworthy" about ourselves—the whole self or only certain aspects—and, eventually, we adopt those views in our evaluations of ourselves.

As an example of these humanistic principles, consider Mark, a first-year college student. Unlike many of his classmates, who are undecided about a major or career path, Mark long ago decided that he would become a lawyer. During his first month on campus, he declared himself a prelaw major, mapped out a 4-year plan of undergraduate courses designed to enhance his chances of getting into law school, and made a preliminary list of law schools to which he intended to apply. Mark's interest in law was strongly encouraged by his parents. Both of them, as well as Mark's only sibling, are accomplished attorneys themselves. During Mark's childhood, they frequently commented on Mark's potential as a lawyer—"With these good grades, you're on the path to a top-notch law school," "It's wonderful knowing that we'll be able to hand the firm over to you someday," and "Listen to the argument he's putting up about his curfew—he's gonna make a great courtroom attorney someday!" At various points in his childhood, Mark showed interest in other activities, such as acting, sports, and journalism, but his parents never paid much attention to those activities or accomplishments. They were much more interested in his debate club activities, which they viewed as a precursor to his legal career, than in his plays, soccer games, or school newspaper articles.

In his second semester, Mark took an art history course to fulfill an elective requirement. Although he was reluctant to admit it, he found himself fascinated by the subject—much more so than by law. During his free time, he found himself reading ahead in his art history textbook and searching related topics online. He even borrowed some painting materials from his roommate and tried his hand at painting. When his parents arrived for a visit, however, he hid his interest in art from them. He sensed that they would reject it and, more significantly, reject him if they sensed he was passionate about it. They had made it clear that their acceptance of him was contingent on choosing law as a career path, and Mark sensed that they may not support him—emotionally, financially, or in any other way—if he followed his own intrinsic interests. Mark eventually became a lawyer, and although he achieved some success, he was always unhappy that his artistic side was never allowed to grow. In fact, Mark came to realize that whereas the legal "branch" of himself received plenty of "sunlight," numerous other branches had been neglected. When he compared his real life—as a lawyer with no other developed interests, abilities, or skills—with the ideal self he could have been, he noticed an incongruence that left him feeling dissatisfied and unhappy. If Mark were to find himself in a meaningful relationship with someone who prized him "no matter what"—a humanistic therapist, for example—he might be able to view himself more unconditionally, follow his own self-actualization tendencies, and achieve greater congruence between his real and ideal selves.

Elements of Humanistic Psychotherapy

Because self-actualization is a primary, natural tendency in all people, the therapist need only make the conditions right for it to occur. The therapist does not directly heal the client, per se; instead, the therapist fosters the client's self-healing tendencies

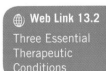

Web Link 13.2

Three Essential Therapeutic Conditions

toward growth. The therapist accomplishes this by creating a therapist–client relationship characterized by **three essential therapeutic conditions** (Cain, 2002, 2010; Rogers, 1957, 1959; Tudor & Worrall, 2006).

Empathy

A therapist experiences **empathy** for a client when the therapist is able to sense the client's emotions, just as the client would, to perceive and understand the events of his or her life in a compassionate way. Empathy involves a deep, nonjudgmental understanding of the client's experiences in which the therapist's own values and point of view are temporarily suspended. The therapist sees life through the client's eyes and adopts the client's frame of reference (Rogers, 1980). Indeed, the term *client-centered therapy*, often used synonymously with humanistic therapy, reflects this emphasis on empathic understanding (Bozarth, 1997).

When a therapist empathizes accurately and communicates that empathy effectively, it can have a profound, positive impact on the client. Empathy can enable clients to clarify their own feelings for themselves and have more confidence in the emotions they experience. It can also make a client feel valued and supported as an individual (Cain, 2002, 2010; Gillon, 2007).

Unconditional Positive Regard

Unconditional positive regard (UPR) is, essentially, full acceptance of another person "no matter what." Rogers (1959) stated that the therapist proving UPR to a client

> prizes the client in a total, rather than a conditional, way. [The therapist] does not accept certain feelings in the client and disapprove of others. . . . It means making no judgments. It involves as much feeling of acceptance for the client's expression of painful, hostile, defensive, or abnormal feelings as for [the client's] expression of good, positive, mature feelings. (pp. 13–14)

Recalling the plant metaphor, sunlight is to plants as positive regard is to people. So a therapist providing UPR is very much like unobstructed sunlight coming from every direction. UPR allows clients to grow in a purely self-directed way, with no need for concern about losing the respect or acceptance of the other person in the relationship. It contributes to a climate in which clients realize they are free to be wholly true to themselves, without modifying, amending, or retooling themselves to meet the standards of another person. When therapists unconditionally prize clients, over time, the clients may come to prize themselves unconditionally, which facilitates higher levels of congruence and self-actualization.

• • • BOX 13.1 • • •

Considering Culture

Empathy Across Cultures

According to the humanistic approach, empathy is fundamental to successful psychotherapy. But does culture place limits on the extent to which a therapist can empathize? To what extent can therapists accurately, genuinely empathize with clients who differ markedly from themselves in terms of ethnicity, gender, age, or other variables?

Consider Stephanie, a 38-year-old woman seeking therapy for depressive symptoms arising after a recent miscarriage. Would a female therapist be more capable of empathizing with Stephanie than would a male therapist? If the female therapist had never had a miscarriage, would that limit her ability to empathize? What if the female therapist had never been pregnant?

Or consider Namrata and Amit, a married couple seeking therapy. Both Namrata and Amit moved from India to the United States as children, and they both speak Hindi and English fluently. They are expecting their first child in about a month, and they are arguing intensely about the language they will speak at home after the baby is born. Namrata believes that they should speak only English at home, in an effort to enhance their child's ability to compete in schools and job markets in which she expects English to be the dominant language. Amit believes that they should speak Hindi at home, in an effort to enhance their child's connection to their heritage and culture. If an Indian, bilingual (Hindi/English) therapist is available, would that therapist have a greater capacity for empathy than a non-Indian therapist or a therapist who spoke only English? If so, would it matter whether that therapist had children?

Finally, consider Faye, a 75-year-old woman struggling with issues of loss and health. Specifically, her spouse and several of her best friends have died in recent years, and her own health has declined significantly as well. Until 10 years ago, she was quite healthy and strong, but she now finds herself in a wheelchair and dependent on caretakers for basic tasks. Can a therapist half her age who has never experienced such loss or decline genuinely empathize with Faye?

In general, can the personal background or experience of the therapist influence the therapist's ability to empathize with clients? Are some clients' problems so specific to their

(Continued)

gender, ethnicity, age, or other variables that only someone with the same background can truly appreciate how the clients may feel? Or are our emotional reactions universal even though the events that evoke them may differ? Little empirical research has been conducted on this topic (e.g., Eisenberg, 2000; Feldstein, 1987; Graham & Ickes, 1997; Lennon & Eisenberg, 1987), and that which has been conducted has been marked by inconsistent results.

As a clinical psychologist, would you feel confident in your capacity for empathy for all clients? As a client, would you seek a clinical psychologist whose cultural background matched yours, with the assumption that it would maximize the psychologist's empathic understanding?

Each of us has experienced relationships in which we were appreciated not for our whole selves but for some specific features of ourselves—personality traits, behaviors, even material things. Although it may not be stated explicitly, the other people in these relationships make it clear that they will continue to accept us as long as we show them the sides of ourselves that they like and hide the sides that they don't. According to humanists, such relationships impede growth and eventually cause us to drift away from our true selves. Therefore, as therapists, humanistic therapists make it a top priority to accept clients entirely and unconditionally. This provides an opportunity for clients to grow naturally into their own potential rather than being pressured by others to grow in various directions (Cain, 2010; Tudor & Worrall, 2006).

Genuineness

Empathy and UPR are worthless if they aren't honest. Humanistic therapists must, therefore, be genuine in their relationships with clients. They don't act empathic toward clients or act as though they unconditionally prize them. Instead, they truly are empathic toward clients and truly do unconditionally prize them. This **genuineness**—which Rogers and his followers have also called therapist congruence, because there is a match between the therapist's real and ideal selves—is the opposite of playing a role or putting up a front. When we sense others (friends, family, or therapists) doing that, we tend not to reveal much of ourselves. On the other hand, when we sense that others authentically care about us and accept us, we tend to open up and engage more fully in the relationship (Gillon, 2007; Rogers, 1959; Tudor & Worrall, 2006).

Being genuine with clients helps humanistic therapists establish therapeutic relationships that feel "real." Such relationships differ strikingly from therapist–client relationships in which the therapist hides behind a facade of professionalism; instead, the therapist's personality plays a more prominent role. As might be expected, Rogers and other humanists encourage a relatively high degree of transparency by the therapist. Unlike the "blank screen" psychodynamic therapist, humanists tend to be more forthcoming and candid about their own thoughts and feelings during sessions. However, they understand that the sessions are for the benefit of the client, not the therapist, and their self-disclosures are guided by this goal (Rogers, 1957).

These three conditions—empathy, UPR, and genuineness—are the essential elements of the relationship between humanistic therapists and their clients, which, in turn, is the cornerstone of the humanistic approach to psychotherapy (Cain, 2010). As Rogers (1961) explained it,

> If I can create a relationship characterized on my part:
>
> - By a genuineness and transparency, in which I am my real feelings;
> - By a warm acceptance of and prizing of the other person as a separate individual;
> - By a sensitive ability to see his world and himself as he sees them;
>
> Then the other individual in the relationship:
>
> - Will experience and understand aspects of himself which previously he has repressed;
> - Will find himself becoming better integrated, more able to function effectively;
> - Will become more similar to the person he would like to be;
> - Will be more self-directing and self-confident;
> - Will become more of a person, more unique and more self-expressive;
> - Will be more understanding, more acceptant of others;
> - Will be able to cope with the problems of life more adequately and more comfortably. (pp. 37–38)

Necessary and Sufficient?

When Rogers described empathy, UPR, and genuineness as the three core conditions for successful psychotherapy, he wasn't merely suggesting that they might be effective for some clients. His claim was much bolder: Those three conditions were both necessary and sufficient for psychotherapy to be successful with any client (Rogers, 1957). In other words, Rogers argued that to facilitate growth and self-actualization in clients with any kinds of problems, the therapist must provide only empathy, UPR, and genuineness. No additional techniques or procedures are necessary.

Rogers's assertion that these three elements are both necessary and sufficient for successful psychotherapy has generated a significant amount of controversy and research. Through the mid-1970s, the research was generally supportive of Rogers's claim, but since that point, results have been more uncertain and inconsistent. More recent research suggests that Rogers's core therapy ingredients are probably necessary but not always sufficient for psychotherapy to succeed. Perhaps they are best understood as a prerequisite for good therapy, a set of conditions that may be enough to facilitate significant improvement in some clients or set the stage for additional therapeutic methods that will cause significant improvement in others. Another interesting way of understanding Rogers's three core conditions—a way supported by empirical research—is to appreciate them as essential parts of the therapeutic relationship, whether the therapist is explicitly humanistic or not. Stated differently, empathy, UPR, and genuineness appear to be common factors, which (as we discuss in more detail in Chapter 11) contribute heavily to the success of all kinds of psychotherapy (Bozarth, Zimring, & Tausch, 2002; Zuroff, Kelly, Leybman, Blatt, & Wampold, 2010).

Therapist Attitudes, Not Behaviors

Whether empathy, UPR, and genuineness are necessary, sufficient, or both, it is important to remember that humanists view them as attitudes, not behaviors (Bozarth, 1997; Tudor & Worrall, 2006). Humanists balk at formulaic, mechanical approaches to therapy, and, as such, they tend not to offer many specific suggestions about *what* therapists should *do* with clients. Rather, they emphasize *how* therapists should *be* with clients:

> Contrary to the opinion of a great many psychotherapists, I have long held that it is not the technical skill or training of the therapist that determines his success—not, for example, his skillful dream interpretations, his sensitive reflections of feeling, his handling of the transference, his subtle use of positive reinforcement. Instead, I believe it is the presence of certain attitudes in the therapist, which are communicated to, and perceived by, the client, that effect success in psychotherapy. (Rogers, 1959, p. 10)

Reflection: An Important Therapist Response

Although they believe that the therapist's attitude is more vital than any particular therapist action, humanists generally agree that one therapist behavior—reflection—can contribute significantly to the success of psychotherapy. It serves as a mechanism by which empathy, UPR, and genuineness can be communicated and as an expression of the attitudes that humanists emphasize.

Reflection takes place when a therapist responds to a client by rephrasing or restating the client's statements in a way that highlights the client's feelings or emotions (Campbell, 2004).

Reflection is not a mere parroting of the client's words to show that they have been heard but a comment by the therapist that shows the therapist's appreciation of the client's emotional experience. (In fact, humanists often use the phrase "reflection of feeling" instead of the shorthand "reflection" to illustrate the emphasis on emotion.) When they reflect, humanistic therapists mirror their clients' affect, even if that affect is not explicitly stated.

As an example, consider Rosa, a single mother of two children (aged 7 and 9 years) who works a full-time job. Rosa tells her humanistic therapist about a typical day: "I get up at 6:00, make the kids' lunches, take them to the bus stop, get myself ready for work, and get there by 8:30. I'm at work until 4:30, fight traffic to pick the kids up from after-school care by 5:00, and then make dinner. After dinner, I help the kids with their homework and get them to bed, at which point I have time to clean the house, pay the bills, and do the other stuff I need to do. The next day, it's the same thing all over again."

Rosa's therapist could assure Rosa that she was paying attention by merely repeating some of the facts: up at 6:00, at work by 8:30, pick up kids by 5:00, and so on. However, an effective reflection of feelings would pick up on the emotional connotations of Rosa's statements, perhaps communicated by her tone of voice or body language more than by the words she chooses: "It's a long, demanding day, and it sounds like you'd be exhausted by the end of it. Seems like you might feel underappreciated and maybe frustrated about your situation. Is that how you feel?" By mirroring the emotions in Rosa's words rather than just the words themselves, her therapist expresses empathy. By doing so nonjudgmentally, she communicates UPR. And by doing so honestly, she communicates genuineness. In combination and over time, these three conditions contribute to a strong therapeutic relationship and facilitate Rosa's growth.

Late in his career, Rogers expressed some regret about the way "reflection of feeling" had been used by many inside and outside the humanistic movement. He was particularly unhappy with the fact that reflection had been mistakenly taught and misunderstood "as a technique, and sometimes a very wooden technique at that" (Rogers, 1986, p. 375). Above all, Rogers believed, reflection should be an attitude rather than a technical skill. And this attitude should include some humility, which can be lost when therapists reflect mechanically. When they reflect, therapists should not be telling clients how they feel but, instead, should be asking clients if their understanding of the clients' feelings is correct. In other words, therapists should not become overconfident in their ability to read clients' emotions and should always defer to the clients' expertise on their own feelings. Rogers went so far as to "suggest that these therapist responses be labeled not 'Reflections of Feeling,' but 'Testing Understandings,' or 'Checking Perceptions.' Such terms would, I believe, be more accurate [in communicating] a questioning desire rather than an intent to 'reflect'" (p. 375). Although the terms *reflection* and *reflection of feeling* have remained, Rogers's reminders about the way they should be understood and used are nonetheless important.

Metaphorically Speaking

If You've Looked in a Magnifying Mirror, Then You Understand Reflection

We look into mirrors all the time—when we try on clothes, brush our hair, put on makeup, shave, and so on. Why? In a pinch, we could probably complete most of these tasks adequately without the mirror. What does the mirror provide? Essentially, it gives us feedback on our appearance. We are able to better appreciate our physical selves when our faces and bodies are mirrored back to us. Without mirrors, we might have a less accurate sense of how we look.

When a humanistic therapist reflects a client's feelings, a similar process takes place. The therapist provides the client with feedback about the client's emotions. Clients are able to better appreciate their emotional selves when their feelings are mirrored back to them. Without such reflection, they might have a less accurate sense of how they feel.

Ordinary mirrors provide some feedback, but magnifying mirrors provide feedback more strongly. Magnifying mirrors amplify the features of our faces, showing us parts of ourselves of which we may not have been fully aware and about which we may not feel entirely comfortable. The emotional mirroring by humanistic therapists can have a comparable effect: It can highlight emotions about which clients may not have been fully aware and about which they may not feel entirely comfortable. For this reason, wise humanistic therapists are always careful to reflect feelings in a cautious, caring way, making sure that clients aren't overly alarmed by what they might see in the emotional mirror.

Likewise, Rogers (1986) always encouraged therapists to take a humble approach to reflection such that any attempt to reflect feelings comes across as more of a question than a statement. After all, a therapist wouldn't want to be like a circus mirror, reflecting a distorted version of the client's feelings back to the client. Just as people who are uncertain about their bodies might be mistakenly convinced by a circus mirror that they are more fat, thin, short, or tall than they really are, clients who are uncertain about their emotions might be mistakenly convinced by an inaccurate therapist reflection that they are more angry, sad, happy, or jealous than they really are.

Alternatives to Humanism

Historical Alternatives

Throughout the history of clinical psychology, numerous forms of psychotherapy have been influenced significantly by humanism. Here, we will discuss two of the most notable of these historical approaches—existential therapy and Gestalt therapy. Although it is accurate to say that their heydays have passed, they nonetheless hold a significant place in the evolution of psychotherapy and continue to influence many therapists today.

Existential psychotherapy is an approach to therapy originally developed by Rollo May, Victor Frankl, and Irvin Yalom. It centers on the premise that each person is essentially alone in the world and that realization of this fact can overwhelm us with anxiety. This anxiety may take a number of forms and is the root of all psychopathology. In addition to the inescapable conclusion of aloneness, existential theory holds that other inevitabilities of human life, especially death, contribute to a powerful sense of meaninglessness in many people. Existential therapists place great emphasis on clients' abilities to overcome meaninglessness by creating their own meaning through the decisions they make. They especially encourage clients to make choices that are true to themselves in the present and future, rather than choices that are determined by restrictive relationships they have had in the past. They empathize with the clients' reactions to the unavoidable facts of existence, but through questioning and discussion, they aid clients in assuming control and assigning significance to their lives (Frankl, 1963; May, 1983; Schneider & Krug, 2010; Yalom, 1980).

Gestalt therapy was founded by Fritz Perls, and it emphasizes a holistic approach to enhancing the client's experience. This experience includes both mental and physical perceptions, and Gestalt therapists attend to both these aspects of client communication. In practice, Gestalt therapists encourage clients to reach their full potential, often through the use of role-play techniques. They deemphasize clients' past experiences and instead focus almost exclusively on the present moment (labeled as "the now"). Integration and awareness of all parts of the self is viewed as a sign of personal growth, and, as such, it is thought to correlate with psychological well-being (Fagan & Shepherd, 1970; Gold & Zahm, 2008; Mackewn, 1997; Perls, 1969).

Motivational Interviewing

In more recent years, new offshoots of humanistic therapy have emerged, many of which emphasize briefer approaches (Tudor, 2008). The prime example—a therapy that has amassed significant empirical evidence and widespread influence on the field—is **motivational interviewing (MI)**, developed by William Miller. Miller describes his MI approach to therapy as a revised application of basic humanistic principles (Hettema, Steele,

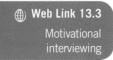
Web Link 13.3
Motivational
interviewing

& Miller, 2005; Miller & Rose, 2009). MI was originally developed to treat addictive behaviors such as substance abuse, but it has been used with a wide range of client problems. MI centers on addressing clients' ambivalence or uncertainty about making major changes to their way of life. Whereas many therapists might label such ambivalence as resistance, denial, or a lack of motivation, MI therapists acknowledge that it is a normal challenge for anyone facing the difficult decision of continuing with an unhealthy familiar lifestyle or committing to live in a more healthy but unfamiliar way. A key to the MI approach is that its practitioners don't pressure clients to change, since such tactics may backfire, resulting in clients arguing against their own improvement. Instead, they help clients see the discrepancy between their behavior and their own values (or as Rogers would call it, their incongruence). By doing so, they *elicit* motivation from within the clients, rather than *imposing* it from without. This enables the clients to activate their own intrinsic values as inspiration to change their behaviors (Rubak, Sandbæk, Lauritzen, & Christensen, 2005). In short, clinicians using MI help clients decide to change for themselves (Miller & Rollnick, 2002; Miller & Rose, 2009; Moyers, 1998).

The central principles of MI reveal its humanistic roots (Arkowitz & Westra, 2009; Miller & Rollnick, 2002; Moyers, 1998):

- *Expressing empathy*. Taking the clients' points of view and honoring their feelings about their experiences are vital to MI.

- *Developing the discrepancy*. MI therapists highlight how a client's behavior is inconsistent with his or her goals or values. This enhances the client's self-motivation to change and puts him or her (rather than the therapist) in the position to argue for a new way of living.

- *Avoiding argumentation*. MI therapists do not directly confront clients, even if clients are engaging in self-destructive behaviors. They recognize that clients must choose to change rather than being strong-armed by a therapist.

- *Rolling with resistance*. When clients express hesitancy to change, MI therapists accept and reflect it rather than battle against it. They respect that clients have mixed feelings about changing. For example, clients may simultaneously want to stop drinking when they recognize that it has become a major problem *and* believe that their drinking is actually under control or that the benefits outweigh the drawbacks.

- *Identifying "sustain talk" and "change talk."* Resistance to change is often communicated by clients as *sustain talk*. Sustain talk takes the form of client statements in favor of continuing the problem behavior: "I've always eaten unhealthy food, and so does my whole family. I wouldn't even know what else to buy at the grocery store or order in a restaurant." *Change talk,* on the other hand, is the statements clients make in favor of changing the problem behavior: "My weight and my cholesterol are getting out of control. I'm so out of shape and unhealthy—I really need to eat healthier." MI therapists acknowledge that both these voices are within the client. They compassionately understand the internal dispute and allow clients to work out a resolution for themselves. Research investigating the specific ingredients within MI that make it successful has started to point toward change talk, which has been found to predict positive behavioral change (Miller & Rose, 2009).

- *Supporting self-efficacy.* MI therapists make efforts to communicate to clients that they have the power to improve themselves. The role of the therapist is facilitative; it is the client who has the most power for change.

Many empirical studies have been conducted on the efficacy of MI, with very impressive results. Meta-analyses of MI outcome studies have indicated that it produces beneficial outcomes for a remarkably wide range of problems, including both psychological and physical symptoms. It has been found to improve substance-related disorders, gambling, smoking, weight-loss efforts, anxiety disorders, depression, violence toward intimate partners, cholesterol levels, and blood pressure—primarily by sparking change in the behaviors that can either worsen or enhance these issues (Arkowitz & Westra, 2009; Burke, Arkowitz, & Menchola, 2003; Jensen et al., 2011; Lundahl & Burke, 2009; Miller & Rose, 2009; Musser & Murphy, 2009; Rubak et al., 2005). Moreover, MI can be integrated into other forms of treatment as well, broadening its potential use (Hettema et al., 2005). On lists of evidence-based treatments that tend to be dominated by behavioral and cognitive therapies, MI is clearly a bright spot for humanistic therapies.

Positive Interventions and Strength-Based Counseling

The positive psychology movement, which emerged in the 1990s under the leadership of Martin Seligman and has expanded rapidly in the 2000s, overlaps with some of the fundamental underpinnings of humanism. **Positive psychology** is a broad-based approach that emphasizes human strengths rather than pathology, and cultivation of happiness in addition to reduction of symptoms in psychotherapy (Duckworth, Steen, & Seligman, 2005; Seligman, 2011). This approach acknowledges the inherent potential of individuals to develop and maintain positive attributes based on such assets as hope, wisdom, creativity, courage, autonomy, optimism, responsibility, and growth. Moreover, it suggests that bolstering these strengths is an often overlooked way of preventing psychological problems such as depression and anxiety or improving the lives of those who already experience them (Seligman, 2003; Seligman & Csikszentmihalyi, 2000; Seligman & Peterson, 2003). Although positive psychology does not claim to derive explicitly from humanism, both positive psychology and humanism share a basic view of people as possessing inborn strengths and capabilities that can guide them throughout their lifetimes and buffer them from unhappiness, and of a corresponding commitment to clinical work designed to enhance those strengths and capabilities.

⊕ **Web Link 13.4**

Positive Psychology Center

Unlike practitioners of most other current forms of psychotherapy who focus more exclusively on a disease-based model, therapists influenced by positive psychology assume a therapeutic role that "embraces both healing what is weak and nurturing what is strong" (Seligman & Peterson, 2003, p. 313; see also Rashid, 2009; Snyder, Lopez, & Pedrotti, 2011). The latter emphasis—nurturing what is strong in clients—is a contemporary echo of Rogers's original theories. In particular, it captures the essence of healthy growth inherent in the self-actualization tendency, a core of the humanistic approach (Joseph & Patterson, 2008).

Therapies that derive from positive psychology go by a variety of names, but they are most often labeled *positive interventions* or *strength-based counseling*. As summarized by Seligman (2011), these therapies look past mere diagnosis-based symptom reduction to the enhancement of a client's overall well-being, particularly such aspects as the client's positive emotion, engagement with life, relationships, meaning, and achievement. Numerous other authors have made similar suggestions to incorporate a more holistic or comprehensive understanding of the client that includes strengths as well as weaknesses. For example, the "four-front approach," developed by Beatrice Wright and others, encourages therapists to consider four areas of each client's life (Wright & Lopez, 2002, as described in Snyder et al., 2011; see also Snyder & Elliott, 2005; Snyder, Ritschel, Rand, & Berg, 2006):

- Weaknesses and undermining characteristics within the person
- Strengths and assets within the person
- Destructive factors and resources that are lacking in the environment
- Resources and opportunities in the environment

Such an approach ensures that a therapist will not only appreciate the positive and the negative elements in a client's life but also delineate which of those elements stem from the client and which stem from the environment in which the client lives.

In addition to being full-fledged forms of therapy themselves, positive interventions and strength-based counseling can be blended into other forms of therapy as well (Kalata & Naugle, 2009; Ward & Reuter, 2011). Although they are relative newcomers to the field of psychotherapy, positive interventions and strength-based counseling strategies have begun to accumulate some empirical data supporting their benefits. For example, Seligman and Steen (2005) found that interventions designed to increase happiness levels in clients did indeed achieve their goal and, at the same time, reduced depressive symptoms. Others have explored the use of positive interventions with individuals who have experienced traumatic events such as active military combat, emphasizing posttraumatic growth and resilience rather than posttraumatic stress and anxiety (e.g., Bonanno, Westphal, & Mancini, 2011; Lee, Luxton, Reger, & Gahm, 2010).

Other Contemporary Alternatives

Another modern adaptation of humanism has been developed by Arthur Bohart and Karen Tallman. The title of the book in which they describe their approach—*How Clients Make Therapy Work: The Process of Active Self-Healing*—illustrates its emphasis (Bohart & Tallman, 1999). Bohart and Tallman argue that therapy is most effective when the therapist recognizes that

> the client is a creative, active being, capable of generating his or her own solutions to personal problems if given the proper learning climate. For us, therapy is the process of trying to create a better problem-solving *climate* rather than one of trying to fix the *person.* (p. xi)

The therapist's role, then, is not of a technician but of a collaborator with clients whose views and opinions are respected. Bohart and Tallman are explicit in their intention of offering a modern therapy that goes against the current movement toward symptom-focused, manualized, technique-dominated approaches to therapy. Such approaches, they believe, place clients in a passive role and underestimate their own abilities to improve their lives. Bohart and Tallman believe that therapists should mobilize clients to help themselves, rather than paternalistically presuming they cannot and applying prescribed techniques to them.

How Well Does It Work?

Despite the empirical challenges inherent to humanistic psychotherapy—how to define and measure self-actualization and how to translate the humanistic attitude into well-defined therapist behaviors—Carl Rogers was a pioneer of psychotherapy outcome research. His approach may not lend itself to empirical tests as much as some other approaches to therapy do (such as behaviorism); nonetheless, he often attempted to present his ideas as testable hypotheses and included with his theoretical writings many ideas for empirical studies (Bozarth et al., 2002; Cain, 2002; Elliott, 2002).

As a professor at Ohio State University in the early 1940s, Rogers was the first to audio-record psychotherapy sessions and play them back on 78 RPM phonographs, and along with training, research was a primary use for this technology (Rogers, 1942). Soon after, he and his colleagues published some of the earliest controlled studies of psychotherapy outcome (Elliott, 2002). By the 1960s and 1970s, however, few humanistic therapists were carrying on Rogers's tradition in empirical research. A resurgence of research interest took place in the 1990s, as represented in some recent meta-analyses of humanistic therapy outcome studies (Elliott, 1996, 2002; Greenberg, Elliott, & Lietaer, 1994). One meta-analysis (Elliott, 2002) was the largest in scope, incorporating 86 separate studies of humanistic therapy that collectively reported on the results of more than 5,000 clients' experiences. The results, after controlling for researcher allegiance effects, indicate that humanistic therapies are generally about as effective as the other major approaches to psychotherapy.

Some recent empirical efforts toward determining how well humanistic therapy works have focused on its specific elements—namely, empathy, positive regard, and genuineness. Results of these studies have repeatedly found that each of these elements plays an important role in the success of therapy—not only for humanistic therapy but for any kind of therapy. In other words, the extent to which empathy, positive regard, and genuineness are present, particularly from the client's point of view, correlates significantly with the success of the therapeutic relationship and, ultimately, with the success of the therapy itself—whether or not the therapist makes a deliberate effort to incorporate or emphasize these three elements. So even if a therapist doesn't identify as a humanist per se, he or she would be wise to consider empathy, positive regard, and genuineness—the elements Rogers always considered essential—as empirically supported components of therapy, along with any technique he or she may also choose to incorporate (Elliott, Bohart, Watson, & Greenberg, 2011; Farber & Doolin, 2011; Kolden, Klein, Wang, & Austin, 2011; Zuroff et al., 2010).

As a final note regarding outcome data of humanistic therapies, it is worth reiterating a point made in the section on motivational interviewing: MI has become, especially in recent years, a bona fide evidence-based psychotherapy for a wide range of psychological and physical problems (Arkowitz & Westra, 2009; Hettema et al., 2005; Jensen et al., 2011; Lundahl & Burke, 2009; Miller & Rose, 2009; Musser & Murphy, 2009; Rubak et al., 2005). In terms of "what works" empirically, it undoubtedly leads the pack of the current generation of therapies derived from humanism.

● ● ● BOX 13.3 ● ● ●

Denise in Humanistic Psychotherapy

In our first sessions, Denise directed our conversations toward two topics—her current dissatisfaction with her job and some personal family history that she saw as relevant. She informed me that, as a kid, she felt loved by her mother and father but only as long as she didn't stray too far from their expectations for her. One of these expectations, Denise explained, involved cooking. During her elementary and middle-school years, she demonstrated a remarkable interest and talent in the kitchen, and with two working parents and five siblings, the family came to rely on Denise to prepare meals. She explained that she felt as though her family came to value her for what she could accomplish in the kitchen. Denise explained to me that, until recently, her job as a chef had given her similar opportunities for appreciation for her cooking but the new owner's policy that she stay in the kitchen and not talk with the customers had put an end to that.

Seeing this experience through Denise's eyes, I could certainly understand why she had been feeling depressed. She had learned early on in her life that the important people prized her only for certain parts of who she was, and, like any of us, she needed that prizing enough to meet their conditions.

Eventually, she came to see herself in very much the same way as her family saw her—in other words, their conditional positive regard had become conditional positive self-regard. I wondered if, in the process of doing what others wanted from her, she had neglected some other aspects of her identity. If so, that must have been a frustrating experience for her. Perhaps there was more to appreciate about Denise than her cooking abilities; in fact, maybe her worth as a person wasn't tied to cooking at all.

In therapy, I did my best to communicate my empathy to Denise—about her experience growing up, as well as the recent changes at work. I remember some of our exchanges vividly. Once, after she had spent about 10 minutes listing the differences the new restaurant owner had imposed—"He makes the menu decisions, he won't let me talk with the customers," and so on—I tried to reflect the feelings I sensed through her words, tone of voice, and facial expressions: "You seem upset about these changes—disappointed and maybe a little angry, too—am I right about that? Do you have other feelings about it?"

Although many of the important people in Denise's life had valued her for certain things—cooking, to be specific—I had a different appreciation of her. I saw Denise (as I see all my clients) as a worthy person no matter what she chose to do, and I suspected that she had the potential to be more multifaceted than her family, her boss, and she herself had allowed her to be. After a number of sessions, as she began to feel more comfortable with me, Denise mentioned, with some hesitancy, that sometimes she didn't even like to cook and that occasionally she found it monotonous and boring. She seemed to expect disapproval from me about this, but I was just as accepting of this feeling as I was of any of Denise's feelings. A bit later, she mentioned that there were other activities she felt more passionate, or at least curious, about but had never allowed herself to think of them as anything more than "dreams" or "fantasies." I pursued this topic with interest, and Denise

(Continued)

(Continued)

had the courage to explain that she had always been fascinated with repairing cars. Her brothers and her father had done a lot of this during her childhood, but Denise was told that it "wasn't for her." I felt that any of Denise's interests were worthwhile, as long as they were true to herself, and I did my best to make this known to her.

Another aspect of Denise's personality that emerged over time was her bitter anger toward her family (about her past) and her new boss (about her current situation). I didn't see this anger at the beginning of therapy, but as time went on, she revealed it first through occasional comments about being "bothered" or "perturbed" and eventually through rants and outbursts that involved shouting and tears. I believed that these moments of anger were important to Denise because they were honest expressions of emotion, and although she seemed to assume originally that such outward anger was unacceptable, I did my best to let her know that I accepted her no matter how she felt.

With time, Denise seemed to internalize my unconditional prizing of her. She seemed to accept herself more fully and completely, allowing herself to recognize a wider range of feelings and interests than she had before. She even explored professional opportunities outside cooking (including a car technician training program). And at her current job, she no longer missed the positive feedback from the diners as sorely as she had before, largely because she wasn't so dependent on it. Instead of seeking positive regard from others based on their conditions, Denise was able to give herself positive regard unconditionally.

CHAPTER SUMMARY

Carl Rogers and his colleagues founded the humanistic approach to psychotherapy on a view of people as inherently striving to grow in a positive, healthy way. This self-actualization tendency at times conflicts with the need for positive self-regard (or "prizing") from others, particularly when others provide positive self-regard conditionally. In these situations, individuals experience incongruence between their real and ideal selves, and psychological problems ensue.

Humanistic therapists foster self-actualization in their clients by establishing a therapeutic relationship in which conditions of worth are absent and congruence is encouraged. More specifically, humanistic therapists provide the three conditions that Rogers identified as necessary and sufficient for therapeutic gain: empathy, UPR, and genuineness. These three conditions are defined more as therapist attitudes than techniques, but one therapist response, reflection of feeling, is a key component of humanistic therapy. The fundamental relationship-based elements of humanistic therapy may constitute common factors across many forms of therapy practiced by therapists who don't identify themselves as humanistic per se. A variety of contemporary approaches, including motivational interviewing and positive interventions/strength-based counseling, are strongly influenced by humanistic principles. Motivational interviewing in particular has achieved high status among psychotherapy practitioners and researchers due in large part to an extensive, growing body of empirical research supporting its benefits for psychological and physical problems. Outside the work on motivational interviewing, empirical research on the benefits of humanistic therapy in general has not been as extensive in recent decades as for some other forms of therapy. Those outcome studies that have been completed suggest that, typically, humanistic psychotherapy is about as beneficial as most other approaches.

KEY TERMS AND NAMES

conditions of worth 320

congruence 320

empathy 322

existential psychotherapy 329

genuineness 324

Gestalt therapy 329

humanistic therapy 317

ideal self 320

incongruence 320

Abraham Maslow 317

motivational interviewing (MI) 329

positive psychology 331

positive regard 319

prizing 319

real self 320

reflection 326

Carl Rogers 317

self-actualization 319

three essential therapeutic conditions 322

unconditional positive regard (UPR) 322

CRITICAL THINKING QUESTIONS

1. To what extent do you agree with the humanistic ideas, as stated by Abraham Maslow (1968), that our "inner nature is good or neutral rather than bad" and that "if it is permitted to guide our life, we grow healthy, fruitful, and happy" (pp. 3–4)?

2. What are some of the most common conditions of worth that you have seen parents place on children? What effects of these conditions of worth have you observed?

3. Rogers argued that empathy, unconditional positive regard, and genuineness were not only necessary but also sufficient for psychotherapeutic benefit. In your opinion, for which clinical problems is this statement most and least valid?

4. In your opinion, which elements of motivational interviewing are most essential to the success it has demonstrated in the treatment of a wide range of psychological and physical problems?

5. Considering the discussion of cross-cultural empathy in Box 13.1, do you believe that a therapist who is culturally similar to a client has a greater capacity for empathy than an equally competent but culturally dissimilar therapist?

STUDENT STUDY SITE RESOURCES

Visit the study site at www.sagepub.com/pomerantz3eupdate for these additional learning tools:

- Self-quizzes
- eFlashcards
- Culture Expert Interviews

- Full-text SAGE journal articles
- Additional web resources
- Mock Assessment Data

CHAPTER SUMMARY VIDEO

QR codes at the end of each chapter link to chapter background videos by the author. Visit http://gettag.mobi using your smartphone browser to download the free Microsoft Tag app. Once installed, scan the tags to go directly to these brief videos. In this video, the author uses his experience with one of his own clients to raise questions about the ability to empathize with diverse clients, particularly from the clients' perspective.

CHAPTER
14

Behavioral Psychotherapy

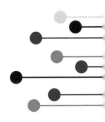

Perhaps the best way to transition from the previous chapters on psychodynamic and humanistic therapy to the current chapter on behavioral therapy is to imagine that your clinical psychology class includes one very empirically oriented (and outspoken) student. When your professor discusses a psychodynamic therapy concept such as, say, defense mechanisms, your classmate raises his hand and asks, "How can you be sure that's what happens in the mind? Can you scientifically test that theory?" When your professor describes the three "necessary and sufficient" conditions for successful therapy according to the humanistic approach, your classmate interrupts to ask, "How, exactly, do you define empathy, unconditional positive regard, and genuineness—what specific therapist behaviors do they consist of? And if those conditions really do help a client self-actualize, how exactly would you be able to observe or measure that outcome?"

Again and again, your professor would have little choice but to respond to your classmate's questions by conceding that the psychodynamic and humanistic approaches to therapy are not entirely empirical. In spite of their intuitive appeal and their clinical successes, they are characterized by speculations about mental processes that can't be precisely defined, directly observed, or scientifically tested. If your classmate insists on a therapy approach grounded in empiricism, he'll need to look elsewhere—to behavioral therapy.

Origins of Behavioral Psychotherapy

🌐 **Web Link 14.1**

Website of journal
Behavior Therapy

🌐 **Web Link 14.2**

Ivan Pavlov

Behavioral psychotherapy is the clinical application of behavioral principles, which have theoretical and experimental roots extending back hundreds of years. A landmark in the history of behaviorism is the work of **Ivan Pavlov,** whose contributions took place in Russia in the late 1800s and early 1900s. Pavlov did not begin his career with aspirations related to psychology at all. In fact, he was a physiologist who studied the digestive systems of dogs. Routinely, Pavlov and his coworkers would present food to dogs and measure the amount of saliva the dogs produced—a natural, automatic response from any canine shown a potential meal. At one point, he noticed that the dogs were salivating before the food was presented. Pavlov first saw this untimely salivating as a problem, and he tried to minimize it so it wouldn't adversely affect the digestion data he was trying to collect. Later, he came to realize that he had inadvertently come across a remarkable phenomenon, which was ultimately labeled "classical conditioning." Through their experience, Pavlov's dogs had learned that food was often preceded by a particular stimulus: the sight of the researcher, the sound of the food being prepared, or similar events. Soon, the dogs were salivating as soon as they perceived a stimulus that, through repeated pairing with food, predicted food. Classical conditioning eventually replaced digestive research as Pavlov's primary interest, and, using a bell as the precursor to food, he conducted many pioneering studies on the topic (Hunt, 1993; Kazdin, 1978). A bit later in this chapter, we examine classical conditioning and its clinical applications in more detail.

The work of Pavlov and other Russian researchers made its way to the United States via **John Watson.** In the early 1900s, Watson fervently argued that the lessons learned from Pavlov's dogs applied to human behavior as well and that, as a result, psychology should refrain from focusing on the inner workings of the mind and should instead examine the ways conditioning shapes behavior. Watson was among the first prominent figures in American psychology to argue that psychology should study only overt, observable responses and the overt, observable stimuli that precede them rather than the inner workings of the mind that may occur in between. Feelings, thoughts, consciousness, and other internal, mental processes were simply not suitable for scientific study, nor were they as powerful as conditioning in determining behavior (Hunt, 1993; Kazdin, 1978; Watson, 1924).

While Pavlov and Watson ushered in classical conditioning to the field of psychology, a second essential type of conditioning—operant conditioning—was heralded by **Edward Lee Thorndike** and **B. F. Skinner.** Actually, Thorndike's (1931) primary contribution, based on his research with cats, was a rather straightforward theory he called the **law of effect.** Essentially, Thorndike's law of effect stated that all organisms pay attention to the consequences (or effects) of their actions. Actions that are followed by pleasurable consequences are more likely to recur, whereas actions that are followed by unpleasant consequences are less likely to recur. Skinner effectively devoted much of his life's work to experimentation on the law of effect, and he made the case that operant conditioning, the mechanism by which the law of effect influenced behavior, was as great an influence on human behavior as classical conditioning. Skinner's research and writings became tremendously influential to the behavioral perspective on the origins of psychological problems and the techniques by which they could be treated (Bjork, 1993; Hunt, 1993; Kazdin, 1978). Thus, through Pavlov, Watson, Thorndike, and Skinner, behaviorism evolved from basic research on animal behavior to an applied form of psychotherapy.

Photo 14.1 B. F. Skinner's studies of operant conditioning play a crucial role in numerous forms of behavioral therapy.

⊕ **Web Link 14.3**
B.F. Skinner Foundation

Goal of Behavioral Psychotherapy

The primary goal of behavioral psychotherapy is observable behavior change. This goal stands in stark contrast to the goals of the psychodynamic and humanistic approaches, each of which emphasizes internal, mental processes—making the unconscious conscious and fostering self-actualization, respectively. In fact, the emergence and rise of the behavioral approach stemmed from strong dissatisfaction with numerous aspects of the psychodynamic approach that dominated through the early and mid-1900s (Craske, 2010). As a reaction against perceived weaknesses of the prominent approaches of the times, early behaviorists forged a new therapy differentiated from the outset by a distinct set of characteristics (Kazdin, 1978, 1980; Spiegler & Guevremont, 2010; Yates, 1970).

Emphasis on Empiricism

Behavioral therapists take the stance that the study of human behavior, whether normal or abnormal, should be scientific (Kazdin, 1978; Yates, 1970). As such, clinical psychologists treating clients should employ methods that can be scientifically evaluated. Theories regarding the treatment of problem behaviors should be stated as **testable hypotheses**; in this way, they can be supported, refuted, modified, and retested. In contrast, if theories of change are not stated as testable hypotheses, they lack scientific rigor and might be best classified as conjecture, inference, or even guesswork. Of course, any scientific process involves data collection, and behavioral therapy is no exception. Behavioral therapists regularly collect **empirical data** on their clients—as a baseline measure at the outset of therapy, at various points during the therapy to evaluate changes from session to session, and at the end of therapy as a final assessment of change (Grant, Young, & DeRubeis, 2005; Spiegler & Guevremont, 2010).

Expanding on the scientific nature of behavioral therapy, Truax (2002) explains that "the endeavor of developing and testing hypotheses in the real clinical setting is much like that of a scientist" (p. 5). Indeed, behavioral therapy is a clinical application of the five steps that are common to the scientific method across all disciplines. Table 14.1 summarizes this association between the scientific method and behavioral therapy.

Defining Problems Behaviorally

According to behavioral therapists, client behaviors are not symptoms of some underlying problem—those behaviors *are* the problem. For example, consider Ryan, who has a habit of excessively checking the front door of his apartment at bedtime to make sure it's locked. According to behavioral therapists, Ryan's door-checking habit is exactly that—a habit. It need not signify that a deeper, diagnosable problem resides within Ryan. Behavior therapists would see little benefit in defining Ryan's problem as obsessive-compulsive disorder, because to do so would suggest that the door checking is part of a cluster of symptoms that share a common source within Ryan's mind. They would prefer not to make unproven (actually, unprovable) inferences about the internal causes of Ryan's behavior and instead focus exclusively on Ryan's door-checking behavior itself as the problem to be addressed.

From the behavioral point of view, a benefit of defining problems in behavioral terms is that such definitions make it easy to identify target behaviors and measure changes in

Table 14.1 Application of the Steps of the Scientific Method by Behavioral Therapists

Steps of the Scientific Method	How Applied by Behavioral Therapists
1. Observing a phenomenon	Assessing client behavior via observation, interview, or testing Defining a target behavior Establishing a baseline level of target behavior
2. Developing hypotheses to explain the phenomenon	Functional analysis of target behavior to determine the factors that cause or influence it Establishing specific behavioral goals for treatment Planning interventions to alter behavior in preferred manner
3. Testing the hypotheses through experimentation	Implementing interventions as planned
4. Observing the outcome of the tests	Collecting data on changes in the target behavior Comparing data collected during or after treatment to baseline data Comparing data to goals
5. Revising the hypotheses	Modifying treatment plan as suggested by observed outcomes Restarting scientific process with revised hypotheses

Source: Adapted from Truax (2002).

therapy (Spiegler & Guevremont, 2010). Such definitions can differ quite drastically from the definitions of their own problems offered by clients. As an example, consider Amber, a 30-year-old client who sought help from Dr. Tyler, a behavioral therapist, because Amber believed she "had depression." Amber entered therapy convinced that the depression was an entity, a "thing" within her mind that couldn't be seen directly but was nonetheless affecting her in numerous adverse ways. She said that the main "symptoms" of her depression were feeling sad and thinking pessimistically. Dr. Tyler redefined Amber's problems in two important ways. First, she asked Amber to describe the observable, measurable *behaviors* she most wanted to change. That is, rather than focusing on feelings and thoughts—none of which can be directly observed or measured—Amber was asked to focus on behaviors she performed too often or too rarely. With some help from Dr. Tyler, Amber was able to list many such behaviors: sleeping too much, missing work too frequently, crying too often, and exercising too little. Because these problems are actions that can be observed and measured, they are ideal targets for behavioral interventions. The second way Dr. Tyler redefined Amber's problem was to explain to Amber that these behaviors weren't symptoms of a deeper problem; instead, they were the problems themselves. After establishing **baselines**—measuring the pretreatment frequencies or durations of Amber's sleep, work attendance, crying, and exercising—Dr. Tyler proceeded by designing and implementing interventions that targeted each of Amber's problem behaviors. As therapy progressed, they measured Amber's behaviors on a regular basis and compared that data with her baseline data to assess her improvement.

Whereas most other types of therapy approaches endorse a **medical model of psychopathology**, the behavioral approach, as exemplified by Dr. Tyler, does not. That is, most other therapy approaches conceptualize psychological problems as medical doctors do physical diseases, especially with regard to the notion of symptoms as manifestations of underlying diseases. Shortness of breath, for example, might be a symptom of asthma; coughing, a symptom of bronchitis; abdominal pain, a symptom of an ulcer. Behavioral therapists don't adopt this medical-model view of psychological problems, largely because the connections between "symptoms" and the underlying "diseases" they indicate are largely speculative in psychology, whereas they are more concrete in medicine. Because we cannot know empirically that a particular behavior is symptomatic of any particular underlying problem, behavioral therapists regard behavioral problems themselves as the most appropriate focus of treatment.

Measuring Change Observably

For behavioral therapists, measuring therapy outcome via **observable changes** goes hand in hand with defining the client's problems behaviorally from the outset. That is, whereas other kinds of therapists may measure change in clients in more inferential ways, behavioral therapists use more unambiguous indications of progress (Grant et al., 2005; Spiegler & Guevremont, 2010).

To illustrate, recall the psychoanalytic and humanistic therapists we studied in the previous chapters. They would have to look in the client's mind for some indication that their therapy has produced an effect. For empiricists such as behavioral therapists, this method of measuring change is unacceptable, primarily because it lacks objectivity. How do we know that the therapist (or the client, or anyone else for that matter) has a reliable, valid, unbiased take on how much insight the client has gained? How can we be certain that the growth a client has experienced is a result of an improved sense of congruence? Behavioral therapists reject **introspection** such as this—that is, they reject the notion that we can simply look inside the mind and attain an objective, accurate assessment of change. Instead, they focus on outward demonstrations of change in clients—overt behavior rather than covert mental processes—as indicators of client change.

Behavior therapists don't simply reject introspection as a means of measuring change in therapy; indeed, they believe that introspection should have no role at all in the clinical process. Therefore, when they consider the contributing factors to clients' problems, they emphasize external, environmental factors over internal personality traits. As an example, consider Jack, a 40-year-old man who is seeking therapy from Dr. Herrera, a clinical psychologist with a behavioral orientation. Jack is 100 pounds overweight and has gained 20 pounds in the past year. He explains to Dr. Herrera that he has tried to lose weight many times but always quits his exercise routine and returns to unhealthy eating habits—chips, cookies, fast food, and so on. At this early point, some therapists would already be speculating about Jack's internal personality characteristics as a cause of his overeating—for example, a psychodynamic therapist may consider an oral fixation. The problem with such a speculation, from a behavioral point of view, is that it cannot be supported or refuted, because it hinges on Jack's mental processes, which are not directly observable. Dr. Herrera makes no such speculations. Instead, the questions he poses to Jack involve observable aspects of the environment in which Jack lives. In other words, what events precede Jack eating a bag of chips or skipping a workout? What consequences follow these actions? In what settings and under what conditions do the unwanted behaviors take place? Questions such as these make it clear that Dr. Herrera, as a behavioral therapist, looks for the causes of Jack's problems not within Jack but in the world around him. In other words, Jack's too-frequent unhealthy eating and too-infrequent exercising are responses to stimuli and consequences from the world around him rather than expressions of some internal flaw in his personality.

Two Types of Conditioning

As discussed above, behavioral therapists contend that our behavior is the byproduct of conditioning (also known as learning). If conditioning explains all behavior, then, by definition, it explains the acquisition of disordered behavior as well as the means by which such behavior can be modified by clinical psychologists (Craske, 2010). Behavioral therapists separate conditioning into two primary types: classical and operant.

Classical Conditioning

Classical conditioning is the type exemplified by Pavlov's dog studies. In those studies, dogs learned through experience that certain stimuli (a bell, for example) predicted that food would be delivered, and, as a result, they began to salivate in response to the stimuli. If we examine this process more closely, its four components can be identified. Let's start before any conditioning takes place, before the dog has had a chance to learn how things work in Pavlov's lab. In fact, let's imagine that the dog has just walked into Pavlov's lab for the first time, so everything it experiences or does is completely "unconditioned." In this situation, the dog will salivate when food is presented. So food is the **unconditioned stimulus,** which evokes salivation, the **unconditioned response.** No dog needs conditioning to learn that association—it's inborn. After spending some time in Pavlov's lab, the dog notices that when a certain bell rings, food comes a few seconds later. In other words, the dog is now becoming conditioned, or learning that the sound of the bell predicts the arrival of food. The dog soon begins to salivate in response to the bell. The sound of the bell, which had originally evoked no response at all in the dog, has become a **conditioned stimulus,** and salivating, when in response to the bell (not the food), is the **conditioned response.**

Several aspects of classical conditioning are worth emphasizing. First, it is important to note that classical conditioning is a rather passive type of learning. Pavlov's dogs didn't need to do much of anything to experience the conditioning, other than remain awake and alert. It's almost as if the classical conditioning happened to them—some combination of sights, sounds, smells, or tastes occurred in rapid succession, and they happened to be there to experience them. Second, a number of variables that can influence behavior surround the classical conditioning process. For example, the extent to which an individual demonstrates behavior that has been classically conditioned will depend on the extent to which generalization or discrimination takes place. **Generalization** occurs when the conditioned response is evoked by stimuli that are similar to, but not an exact match for, the conditioned stimulus. **Discrimination** occurs when the conditioned response is not evoked by such a stimulus (Kazdin, 1978, 1980). For example, if Pavlov conditioned a dog to salivate in response to the sound of a particular bell, would the dog also salivate to the sound of a slightly different bell? What about a very different bell or even a completely different sound, such as a drum? As a clinical version of the same questions, imagine that Wayne, a 16-year-old boy, developed a strong fear response to dogs after being viciously attacked by a golden retriever. To what extent would Wayne generalize his fear? Would he be fearful of all golden retrievers, of dogs of any breed, of all animals of any kind? Conversely, might Wayne discriminate such that he responds fearfully to the one dog that attacked him but no others? The extent to which Wayne generalizes or discriminates his fear response would strongly influence the strategy of a behavior therapist helping Wayne overcome his fear.

Operant Conditioning

Operant conditioning occurs when the organism "operates" on the environment, notices the consequences of the behavior, and incorporates those consequences into decisions regarding future behavior (Sturmey, Ward-Horner, Marroquin, & Doran, 2007). Simply put, "the basic principle of the operant approach is that behavior is a function of its consequences" (Calhoun & Turner, 1981, p. 4). Operant conditioning is a more active style of learning than classical conditioning. For operant conditioning to take place, the organism must take an action of some kind. As a fictional example, imagine that one of Pavlov's dogs had, during a break in the experimenting, started to whine. If the whining brought forth treats, the dog would be more likely to whine again. If the whining brought forth a whack on the nose, the dog would be less likely to whine again. In either case, the point is that the dog experimented with a new behavior, paid attention to the outcome, and will use that outcome as a factor in future decisions about whining.

Skinner and other proponents of operant conditioning proposed that consequences shape all behavior, including behavior labeled as abnormal. In effect, all our actions are governed by **contingencies,** by "if . . . , then . . . " statements, including those labeled as abnormal. By changing the contingencies or revising the "if . . . , then . . . " statements that control a client's behavior, clinical psychologists can induce significant behavioral changes.

Thus, both classical and operant conditioning can be applied clinically to address problematic or unwanted behaviors in clients. Indeed, these two types of conditioning form the foundation for most behavioral therapy techniques. Let's examine some of the most widely known and used techniques deriving from classical and operant conditioning.

Techniques Based on Classical Conditioning

Exposure Therapy

Simply put, **exposure therapy** is the clinical psychologist's version of "facing your fears." Phobias, according to the behavioral therapist, are best understood as the result of classical conditioning: A particular stimulus (spiders, heights, the dark, etc.) becomes paired with an aversive outcome (anxiety, pain, etc.). This pairing can be weakened and ultimately eliminated if the client experiences one without the other. That is, when the client is repeatedly "exposed" to the feared object and the expected aversive outcome does not take place, the client no longer experiences the fear response, which is a more appropriate and rational way to react to such harmless stimuli (Hazlett-Stevens & Craske, 2008).

As a clinical example, let's reconsider Wayne, who was described above as having a fear of dogs as a result of a vicious attack. The essential task for a behavioral therapist conducting exposure therapy is to expose Wayne to dog-related stimuli. Based on his attack, Wayne has associated dogs with fear, but the truth is that for the vast majority of dogs, this is simply an inaccurate expectation. Unfortunately for Wayne, his avoidance of dogs

Photo 14.2 Facing feared stimuli—such as dogs, for someone previously attacked by a dog—is the essential element of exposure therapy.

since the attack has prevented the opportunity for him to "unlearn" the association between dogs and fear. Through exposure therapy, his behavior therapist gives him exactly that opportunity, and the result of the exposure to dog-related stimuli is that Wayne's association between dogs and fear is unlearned.

The behavior therapist has several choices to make when conducting exposure therapy. One of the most important involves the imaginal versus in vivo nature of the stimuli to which the client will be exposed. In other words, the client can be asked to imagine anxiety-provoking objects (without ever being exposed to the real thing) or can be exposed to real-life (in vivo) items or situations that have produced fear (Hazlett-Stevens & Craske, 2008; Spiegler & Guevremont, 2010). In Wayne's case, **imaginal exposure** would involve visualizing dogs and dog-related items, whereas **in vivo exposure** would mean that Wayne would directly see, hear, and touch dogs.

Another important choice regarding exposure therapy involves the extent to which the client will be exposed to fear-inducing stimuli: gradually or all at once. The gradual approach is often called **graded exposure,** and it requires the client and therapist to collaboratively create an **anxiety hierarchy** in which they list about 10 stimuli that might induce fear. These stimuli are typically rated by the client on a scale from 0 to 100 in terms of the amount of subjective distress they produce and are then ranked in ascending order. Exposure begins at the lowest level and then proceeds through the hierarchy until the client reaches the highest level. Table 14.2 illustrates a graded in vivo hierarchy for Wayne's fear of dogs. Exposure that happens all at once rather than gradually is typically called **flooding** or **implosion** (Levis, 2008; Zoellner, Abramowitz, Moore, & Slagle, 2008). Although either of these all-at-once approaches can produce rapid change quickly, they can also be intolerable or even traumatizing for clients and must be used cautiously (Taylor, 2002; Yates, 1970).

⊕ Web Link 14.4

Exposure Plus Response Prevention

Exposure therapies are most commonly used with clients who have phobias and other anxiety disorders. One particular application of exposure therapy, called **exposure plus response prevention,** has received substantial empirical support for the treatment of obsessive-compulsive disorder (Craske, 2010; Franklin & Foa, 2011). It involves graded exposure (as described above) to the obsessive thoughts (e.g., "My hands are filthy—I must wash them") or the situations that elicit such thoughts while simultaneously preventing the client's typical response (e.g., hand washing), which brings temporary relief but has come to interfere with the client's daily life (Rowa, Antony, & Swinson, 2007).

Table 14.2 Example of an Anxiety Hierarchy for Graded In Vivo Exposure for Fear of Dogs

Stimulus	Subjective Distress (0 = No Fear; 100 = Maximum Fear)
1. Hearing a dog bark in another room	5
2. Seeing a dog through a window	15
3. Standing within 20 feet of a dog on a leash	25
4. Standing within 10 feet of a dog on a leash	35
5. Standing within 5 feet of a dog on a leash	45
6. Standing within arm's length of a dog	55
7. Petting a dog for 1 second	65
8. Petting a dog continuously for 10 seconds	75
9. Petting a dog continuously for 1 minute	85
10. Petting a dog continuously for 3 minutes	95

Systematic Desensitization

Systematic desensitization, a treatment also used primarily for phobias and other anxiety disorders, is quite similar to exposure therapy—in fact, exposure to anxiety-provoking stimuli is one of its key components—but rather than simply breaking the association between the feared object and the aversive feeling, systematic desensitization involves re-pairing (or **counterconditioning**) the feared object with a new response that is incompatible with anxiety. When exposure therapy works, the feared object is eventually paired with nothing (rather than the fear response), but when systematic desensitization works, the feared object is paired with a new response that replaces and blocks the fear response (Head & Gross, 2008; McGlynn, 2002; Wolpe, 1958, 1969).

Most often, the new response that replaces and blocks the fear response is relaxation. In fact, the first step of systematic desensitization is **relaxation training,** in which the behavior therapist teaches the client progressive relaxation techniques in which various muscles are systematically tensed and relaxed. Usually, the behavior therapist uses scripted instructions during relaxation training, and these instructions can be shared with the client in a variety of forms (written on paper, recorded on CD, etc.) to facilitate practice at home between sessions. Once clients learn and master the relaxation task (usually about half a dozen sessions), they move through an anxiety hierarchy as described in the section above on exposure therapy. The only difference is that prior to each exposure, the client achieves a relaxed state, such that exposure to the anxiety-producing stimulus becomes paired with relaxation, which inhibits anxiety. Thus, the feared object is no longer paired with anxiety but instead is paired with relaxation, and, gradually, the fear is overcome (Head & Gross, 2008; McGlynn, 2002; Wolpe, 1958, 1969).

In Wayne's case, a behavior therapist using systematic desensitization would construct the anxiety hierarchy and conduct the exposures just as in exposure therapy, but relaxation training would happen first and the relaxation response would be deliberately evoked during the exposure process to facilitate the replacement of anxiety with a new, anxiety-preventing response.

Assertiveness Training

Assertiveness training is a specific application of classical conditioning that targets clients' social anxieties. It is best suited for people whose timid, apprehensive, or ineffectual social behavior has a negative impact on their lives. In practical terms, it can help clients insist on appropriate service (in a restaurant, for example), ask someone out on a date, request a raise at work, communicate effectively with health care providers, or say no to an unreasonable demand from a friend or loved one.

Assertiveness training definitely includes elements of exposure therapy, and it may include elements of systematic desensitization as well (Duckworth, 2008; Gambrill, 2002). The exposure comes in the form of facing interpersonal fears. That is, people who have problems with assertiveness usually avoid situations in which assertiveness might be called for, so by simply exposing themselves to such situations and producing any kind of assertive response, they are taking a significant step forward. The counterconditioning component of systematic desensitization may also come into play, with assertiveness replacing relaxation as the new response that replaces and inhibits anxiety.

Assertiveness training usually begins with direct instructions from the behavior therapist with which the client is taught specifically what to say and do in a particular situation. Next, effective assertive behaviors are modeled for the client. The behavior therapist often does this modeling, but video-recorded models or even live actors can be used as well. Subsequently, the client is given an opportunity to rehearse the assertive behavior in a role-play situation, and the therapist provides specific, constructive feedback. Eventually, clients are given targeted homework assignments in which they are expected to practice their improving assertiveness skills in the "real world" (Gambrill, 2002).

As a clinical example, consider Deborah, a 26-year-old woman who got engaged a few months ago. She described to Dr. Paxton, her behaviorally oriented clinical psychologist, that as she began to make arrangements for her wedding—the guest list, the menu, the flowers, the band, her dress, and so on—she became increasingly frustrated with others "making decisions for her." Specifically, she said that her mother and her sister had been telling her what to do, and she had had a difficult time telling them to "butt out." As an example, she described a recent trip to the wedding dress shop. She had been to the store alone previously and had tentatively chosen a dress for herself. When she went back to the store to try on the dress for her mother and sister, they pressured her to try on other dresses and eventually convinced her to buy a dress she had seen but disliked when she was at the store the first time. Deborah wished she could have taken charge of the situation at the wedding dress shop but told Dr. Paxton that she just couldn't. She added that her day ended by crying about this experience to her fiancé, who, rather than responding with the empathy she sought, told her she needed to stand up to her mother and sister.

Dr. Paxton conducted assertiveness training with Deborah. First, she taught Deborah some specific, appropriately assertive phrases to say, such as, "Thanks for your input, but this is my decision to make" and "I really want you to be a part of this with me, but I need to have the final say." Dr. Paxton also coached Deborah on some specific behaviors involved in assertive responses, such as direct eye contact and appropriate volume and tone in her voice. Next, Dr. Paxton modeled these responses for her. Deborah then rehearsed the assertive responses, with Dr. Paxton playing the role of Deborah's mother or sister. Dr. Paxton offered some helpful feedback, including praise for saying the right things and reminders to make direct eye contact. Together, Deborah and Dr. Paxton came up with some homework assignments that could help Deborah "build up" to the confrontations she anticipated with her mother and sister. These homework assignments involved asserting herself to her mother and sister about less significant upcoming decisions in which they would probably pressure her, such as what she should order at lunch when they went out next Saturday. With time and practice, Deborah's skill in asserting herself increased while her anxiety about asserting herself decreased.

● ● ● **BOX 14.1** ● ● ●

Considering Culture

Assertiveness Training and Collectivist Values

Assertiveness training, as a form of behavioral therapy, is based on the assumption that assertiveness is a good thing: "A value stance . . . is associated with assertion training. It is assumed that people have a right to express their feelings in a way that subjugates neither

(Continued)

(Continued)

others nor themselves, and that well-being includes this expression" (Gambrill, 2002, p. 121). Do all cultures hold this value equally?

Some would argue strongly that they do not. Sue and Sue (2008), for example, point out that "individualism, autonomy, and the ability to become your own person are perceived as healthy and desirable goals" in Western, individualistic cultures, but "not all cultures view individualism as a positive orientation. . . . In many non-Western cultures, identity is not seen apart from the group orientation (collectivism)" (p. 141). A lack of appreciation of this important distinction between individualistic and collectivistic cultures can lead therapists to overpathologize members of some cultures as overly dependent or unable to assert themselves.

In a discussion of cultural issues relevant to psychotherapy with Native American clients, Sutton and Broken Nose (2005) offer two case studies illustrating this concern. In the first, a Native American couple open a restaurant, and all aspects of the new business are successful except for the fact that the couple choose not to charge their family members for food. Moreover, they define family broadly enough to include distant relatives, in-laws, and the like. Because they serve free meals to so many people, the restaurant struggles financially. In the second case study, a Native American college student receives a fellowship to fund his studies but feels compelled to share his money, apartment, and time with siblings and other family members. Their presence causes significant financial and practical obstacles for the student's ability to succeed in school.

Although Native American culture is certainly not the only culture with some degree of collectivist values (many African and Asian cultures, among others, provide more examples), these scenarios highlight some of the sensitivities clinical psychologists should have when considering assertiveness training. In your opinion, in either of the two case studies described above, would assertiveness training be clinically effective? Would it be culturally appropriate? Should it be adjusted in some way to better match the client's cultural values? Should some alternative treatment be considered?

Techniques Based on Operant Conditioning

Contingency Management

Contingencies are the "if . . . , then . . . " statements that, according to behavioral therapists, govern our behavior. So if the goal is to change behavior, a powerful way to do so is to change the contingencies controlling it. Behavioral psychotherapists call this process

contingency management. All behavior occurs because of its consequences, and if those consequences change, the behavior will change correspondingly (Drossel, Garrison-Diehn, & Fisher, 2008; Kearney & Vecchio, 2002; Villamar, Donahue, & Allen, 2008). Behaviorists emphasize that powerful but often overlooked contingencies—for example, "If I behave in a depressed way, I get attention from friends and family and I am excused from responsibilities"—can contribute to the development and maintenance of mental disorders (e.g., Anderson, 2007).

Reinforcement and Punishment

The consequences of a behavior—the words that complete the "then . . ." phrase in our contingencies—can be categorized as either reinforcements or punishments. **Reinforcement** is defined as any consequence that makes a behavior more likely to recur in the future. In contrast, **punishment** is defined as any consequence that makes a behavior less likely to recur in the future. It's important to note the room for individual differences implied by these two definitions. Very few things are either reinforcing or punishing to all people in all situations. That which is punishing to one person may be reinforcing to another and vice versa. Behavior therapists who use contingency management remain aware of this phenomenon and therefore seek client input on all prospective contingencies (Drossel et al., 2008; Spiegler & Guevremont, 2010).

Reinforcement and punishment can each be further divided into two types: positive and negative (Higgins, 1999). In this context, positive refers to adding a consequence, whereas negative refers to removing a consequence. So, simply put, **positive reinforcement** means "getting something good" (such as food), whereas **negative reinforcement** means "losing something bad" (such as pain). Notice that both of these would increase the likelihood of the behavior recurring. **Positive punishment** means "getting something bad," whereas **negative punishment** means "losing something good." Notice that both of these would decrease the likelihood of the behavior recurring (Sturmey, 2007).

Behavior therapists use both reinforcement and punishment during contingency management, but for most clinical situations, reinforcement is generally preferred (e.g., Higgins, 1999). When punishment is used, it must be used ethically, and it is most effective when it occurs immediately and consistently and is accompanied by the reinforcement of an alternate, more desirable response (Poling, Ehrhardt, & Ervin, 2002). **Aversion therapy** represents an example of the clinical use of punishment, in which an unwanted behavior (say, drinking alcohol) brings about an aversive stimulus (nausea or electric shock; Emmelkamp & Kamphuis, 2002; Spiegler & Guevremont, 2010).

As a clinical example of the use of the four varieties of reinforcement (reinforcement and punishment, each in positive and negative forms), consider the work of Dr. Howard, a clinical psychologist engaged in behavioral therapy with Patty, a 15-year-old juvenile detention center inmate. Recently, Patty had been prone to bursts of anger and assault when escorted from her cell to daily classroom sessions. Some of Patty's assaults were so dangerous that they necessitated the use of physical restraints. The consequence for Patty's outbursts was dismissal from the day's schooling; she was returned to her cell, where she spent her time leisurely browsing through magazines approved for inmate possession. Dr. Howard analyzed Patty's outburst behavior and hypothesized that the contingency enacted by the staff was actually reinforcing, not punishing, the outburst response. Dr. Howard discussed with the staff four alternate contingencies, any of which could produce more desirable behavior from Patty:

- Positive reinforcement: If Patty attended her classes without any verbal or physical outbursts, then she received a new magazine of her choice.
- Negative reinforcement: If Patty attended her classes without any outbursts, then her ankle restraints—necessary with the onset of her assaults—would be removed for the next day.
- Positive punishment: If Patty engaged in any type of outburst, then she would receive a 2-hour detention in a cell without magazines.
- Negative punishment: If Patty engaged in any type of outburst, then all her magazines would be confiscated for the next day.

Extinction

When behavior therapists consider the contingencies that have maintained a behavior or new contingencies that may modify it, they often pay close attention to issues involving extinction. In the context of contingency management, **extinction** refers to the removal of an expected reinforcement that results in a decrease in the frequency of a behavior (Kearney & Vecchio, 2002; Poling, Ehrhardt, & Jennings, 2002; Sturmey et al., 2007).

As an example, consider Wendy, an 8-year-old second-grader whose parents brought her to Dr. Evans, a clinical psychologist with a behavioral orientation. Wendy's parents explained that in the past 2 weeks, Wendy had become extremely difficult at meal times: She cried and screamed about the food that had been prepared, saying she didn't like it and it made her stomach hurt. Wendy's parents expressed confusion at her behavior, specifically because it was the same food she had eaten many times before, and they had taken her to her pediatrician, who assured them that Wendy had no stomach ailments. When Dr. Evans asked Wendy's parents what happened after Wendy cried and screamed at meal times, they explained that they typically allowed her to eat something else. When Dr. Evans inquired further, the parents added that they allowed Wendy to choose any food she wanted, and Wendy usually selected her favorite junk food. Dr. Evans developed a contingency management plan based on extinction. His conceptualization was that Wendy's crying and screaming behavior was being positively reinforced by the junk food she received after doing so. He explained this conceptualization to Wendy's parents and recommended that they remove those positive reinforcements—in other words, don't let her replace the family meal with junk food. They did, and although her behavior initially got worse, within a few days, Wendy stopped crying and screaming at meal time and resumed eating with her family as she had previously.

Wendy's case exemplifies an important aspect of extinction-based therapies: the **extinction burst** (Kazdin, 1980; Poling, Ehrhardt, & Jennings, 2002; Spiegler & Guevremont, 2010). Immediately after the reinforcement was removed, Wendy's crying and screaming actually increased—she did it more often and more intensely. Only after her parents "stood their ground" by continuing to withhold the reinforcement did Wendy's crying and screaming dwindle. It is important for behavior therapists and those working with them to anticipate the extinction burst that predictably occurs immediately after the removal of the reinforcement; otherwise, the person controlling the contingency might mistakenly think that the strategy is backfiring and resume the reinforcement again. If Wendy's parents had done this—if they had given in to her especially intense fits on the first days of the extinction process—they would have taught Wendy that if she ups the ante, she can still get what she wants. This would have strengthened, rather than extinguished, her crying and screaming behavior.

● ● ● BOX 14.2 ● ● ●

Metaphorically Speaking

If You've Lost Money in a Soda Machine, You Understand Extinction and the Extinction Burst

Put the dollar in the slot, push the button, get the soda. Put the dollar in the slot, push the button, get the soda. There is no confusion about the contingency of the soda machine, and for many of us, soda-buying behavior is strengthened on a daily basis by the repeated delivery of the cold, bubbly, sweet reinforcement.

But what if the soda machine malfunctions? What if we put the dollar in the slot, push the button, and get nothing? Of course, in the long run, we'll stop putting dollars into that machine. In other words, our soda-buying behavior (at least at that particular machine) will extinguish because the expected reinforcement is no longer forthcoming. In the short run, however, our behavior does not extinguish; in fact, it intensifies. You've seen (or maybe you've been) the person who just lost money in the soda machine demonstrating the extinction burst—pushing every button, trying a different dollar, hitting the machine, kicking

(Continued)

(Continued)

it, tipping it, and so on. It's as if we're responding to the soda machine's refusal to provide the soda with the behavioral statement, "Hey, give me what I'm used to getting!" When the unresponsive soda machine responds with the behavioral statement, "Too bad, you're not getting it," we walk away, but it may take a while for us to become entirely convinced.

Actually, the time it takes for us to become convinced that no soda is forthcoming, and for our soda-buying behavior to therefore extinguish, depends on how consistently the soda machine stiffs us. If it is absolutely consistent, we'll quit pretty quickly. But if we know the machine to be fickle—sometimes the soda comes, sometimes it doesn't, sometimes it requires a good kick—it may take quite a while for our soda-buying behavior to become extinct. Perhaps a better example of such an inconstant, unpredictable machine is a slot machine, from which "you never know" what you might get (Kazdin, 1980). When behavior therapists use extinction methods with clients, which would you expect to be more successful—the consistent or inconsistent approach to denying expected reinforcement? More generally, how might the consistency of a contingency management technique influence its success in changing behavior?

Token Economies

A **token economy** is a setting in which clients earn tokens for participating in predetermined target behaviors (Ghezzi, Wilson, Tarbox, & MacAlesse, 2008). These tokens can be exchanged for a number of reinforcements, including food, games, toys, privileges, time participating in a desired activity, or anything else deemed desirable by the client. In some token economies, clients can also lose tokens for engaging in undesired behaviors (Stuve & Salinas, 2002). Token economies are used most often in settings such as inpatient units, correctional facilities, and other sites where clients' behavior is under ongoing surveillance by supervisory staff. A strength of token economies is their versatility across clients. For example, on a psychiatric inpatient unit, different target behaviors may be identified for each client. One client may earn tokens for making the bed, another for taking a shower, and another for interacting with a group rather than staying alone. Of course, the success of the token economy depends on the perceived value of the reinforcements for which the tokens can be exchanged, so behavioral therapists are careful to select reinforcements that will motivate each client. If you have ever spent any time in Dave and Buster's or Chuck E. Cheese's, you're familiar with the fact that the same "prize" may be valued very differently by different people. When you were 6 years old, you might have spent a lot of time, energy, and money earning enough tokens (tickets) to exchange for stuffed animals, plastic toys, or candy. Today, you might not find those prizes quite as motivating, and your behavior would decrease accordingly. Likewise, a poker chip may not have meant much to you when you were 6, but now, you may have a greater appreciation for its value as a token exchangeable for money (which itself is exchangeable for many reinforcements).

A potential limitation of token economies involves generalization (Spiegler & Guevremont, 2010). As discussed above, generalization refers to the application of a learned contingency to similar behaviors or situations. The goal of any token economy is not only to modify behavior in that environment but to modify it across all settings. For example, the psychiatric inpatients mentioned in the preceding paragraph would ideally apply the lessons learned about bed making, bathing, and socializing to the outside world in addition to the psychiatric unit in which they temporarily live. Behavior therapists can use a number of strategies to maximize generalization, including tapering clients off tokens gradually rather than all at once, using naturally occurring reinforcements (such as social praise) rather than artificial reinforcements, gradually increasing the delay between the behavior and the reinforcement, and providing reinforcement in as wide a variety of settings as possible (Stuve & Salinas, 2002).

Shaping

Contingency management is often based on reinforcing target behaviors in order to increase their frequency. Sometimes, however, the target behavior is so complex, challenging, or novel for a client that, at the outset of treatment, it simply can't be accomplished in its entirety. In these cases, behavioral therapists use **shaping**, which involves reinforcing successive approximations of the target behavior. Put another way, shaping is a technique in which the behavior therapist reinforces "baby steps" toward the desired behavior (Kazdin, 1980; Kearney & Vecchio, 2002; Sturmey et al., 2007).

As an example, consider Dina, a 59-year-old client with serious depressive symptoms. Since she began feeling depressed about 3 months ago, Dina has become increasingly withdrawn. She has neither contacted any of her friends (of which she has many) nor returned their many calls. She has declined when her husband has asked her to go out to dinner, and she has refused invitations from her grown daughter to come to her house for a visit. Dr. Stein, Dina's clinical psychologist, conceptualizes Dina's problem from a behavioral point of view. That is, Dr. Stein has identified social behavior as the area for improvement and has specifically defined the goal as much more frequent social interactions for Dina: during each week, three phone calls with friends, one dinner out with her husband, and one get-together with her daughter. Dr. Stein realizes, however, that Dina is far

Photo 14.3 Shaping is a behavioral treatment used to increase the frequency of complex behaviors. In this case, a single phone call to a friend is a step toward a greater level of social interaction.

from that level of social functioning at the moment. If she waits for Dina to complete all these tasks in a particular week, the wait may be excessive. So Dr. Stein uses a shaping strategy. First, she determines jointly with Dina a personally meaningful reinforcement: renting a DVD. Then she establishes the contingency for the first week: If Dina completes at least one social activity (a call to a friend, dinner out with her husband, or a get-together with her daughter), then she can rent a DVD of her choice. The next week, Dr. Stein raises the bar: at least two social activities, one of which must be in person. Dr. Stein continues to raise the bar each week until Dina is completing the full set of target behaviors for several consecutive weeks.

A key variable in any shaping program is the increment between each successive approximation. Behavior therapists must be careful not to make the steps between each new challenge too difficult for the client. By the same token, the steps should not be so small that therapy takes an unnecessarily long time. Thus, in Dina's case, Dr. Stein should adjust the amount by which she raises the bar if it is evident that Dina finds the tasks either too easy or too hard.

Behavioral Activation

🌐 **Web Link 14.5**

Website of Christopher Martell

Behavioral activation is a form of behavior therapy, designed to treat depression, that has received significant attention and empirical support in recent years (Dimidjian, Barrera, Martell, Muñoz, & Lewinsohn, 2011; Mazzucchelli, Kane, & Rees, 2009). It is based on the simple yet profound notion that in the day-to-day lives of depressed people, there is a shortage of positive reinforcement. So the goal of behavioral activation is to increase the frequency of behaviors that are positively reinforcing to the client. As a result, clients experience more positive emotions and become more fully engaged in their lives. Their tendencies to avoid unpleasant experiences diminish as their depression lifts (Craske, 2010; Dobson & Dobson, 2009; Kanter, Busch, & Rusch, 2009; Martell, 2008).

At the outset of behavioral activation, one of the most important questions the clinical psychologist can ask is, "Are there things you are not doing now that you typically do when you are not depressed?" (Martell, 2009, p. 140). From the client's response to such questions, the client and psychologist can collaborate to form a list of rewarding behaviors and a plan to integrate them into the client's life. Often, clinicians help clients develop a structured routine to guide them through each day's events. Martell highlights that it is important to understand the function of a behavior from the client's point of view. In particular, it is crucial to know whether a client is engaging in a particular behavior because it brings positive reinforcement or enables the client to avoid something unpleasant. For example, a client may choose to go to the movie theater because the movie brings her pleasure or because doing so allows her to avoid an argument with her roommate about the overdue rent. From the point of view of the clinician conducting behavioral activation, the avoidance in the latter scenario is actually part of the problem, so if that is indeed the function of the behavior, an alternative behavior should be used instead.

It is clear that operant conditioning forms the basis of behavioral activation, but classical conditioning may play a role as well. In a manner that resembles the counterconditioning in systematic desensitization (described earlier in this chapter), behavioral activation takes advantage of the fact that depression and reinforcing activities are incompatible. In other words, behaviorists make the argument that it's impossible to feel the reinforcement of a favorite activity and feel depressed at the same time. In this way, behavioral activation is a method of planning and encouraging activities that bring pleasure and preclude depression (Martell, 2008, 2009).

Observational Learning (Modeling)

So far, all the clinical applications of operant conditioning that we have discussed involve clients learning directly from their own experiences. However, much of what we learn comes from contingencies we see applied to other people. This phenomenon is known as **observational learning** but has also been called modeling and social learning. As an example of observational learning, briefly reconsider the broken soda machine scenario described in Box 14.2. If the soda machine stole the dollar of the person in front of you while you were waiting your turn, would you step up and put your dollar in next?

In clinical practice, observational learning is a technique in which the client observes a demonstration of the desired behavior and is given chances to imitate it (Freeman, 2002; Spiegler & Guevremont, 2010). The client typically receives constructive feedback on these imitation efforts as well. The person acting as the model can be the therapist, another live model, or a model who has been video- or audio-recorded. The effects of modeling have been studied extensively by **Albert Bandura** and others (e.g., Bandura, 1977), producing a sizable body of knowledge regarding key variables in the modeling process. Among the findings is that models are most effective when they are similar to the client, an especially relevant point regarding client diversity in terms of cultural and demographic variables. For example, if Ana, a 19-year-old, homosexual, Hispanic, female college sophomore, is struggling with social skills, the success of an observational learning intervention may depend on the degree to which the model matches Ana in terms of age, sexual orientation, ethnicity, gender, and student status.

Observational learning strategies actually afford clients two different ways to learn. The first is **imitation**, in which the client simply mimics the modeled behavior. The second is **vicarious learning**, in which the client observes not only the modeled behavior but also the model receiving consequences for that modeled behavior. In other words, even without imitation, a client can learn to expect reinforcement or punishment for a target behavior by observing what the model receives (Freeman, 2002). In the case of Ana, vicarious learning would take place if Ana observed the model initiating a conversation with an unknown person and receiving obvious feedback—a kind greeting, a snub, or a neutral response—as a consequence. Of course, Ana's behavior therapist would try to ensure to the extent feasible that when the desired response is modeled, it is followed by a reinforcement.

Alternatives to Behavior Therapy

Behavioral Consultation

Behavioral consultation is an indirect way for a behavior therapist to modify a client's behavior. It differs from direct clinical services in that there are always three parties involved: the client, the consultee, and the consultant (therapist). The consultee is a person who spends significant time in the natural setting with the client and who has some control over the contingencies that govern the client's behavior. In many cases, the consultee is an adult who supervises a child in some capacity, such as a parent, teacher, or caretaker (Ehrich & Kratochwill, 2002). However, the consultee can also be seeking help with the behavior of an adult client, such as a corporate manager whose aim is to modify the behavior of an employee (Bailey & Burch, 2006). Some of the examples we consider in this chapter (such as Wendy, the girl who refused to eat the same dinner as her family) have involved a consultation component, but in behavioral consultation, the consultee serves as a true go-between, such that the consultant/therapist and the client may never meet each other.

Behavioral consultation is a flexible process, but it typically involves five stages (Ehrich & Kratochwill, 2002):

- *Initiation of the consulting relationship,* in which the roles and responsibilities of all parties are established.
- *Problem identification,* in which the target behavior is defined, usually through questions involving who, what, where, and when the behavior problem occurs. Baseline and goals are also determined.
- *Problem analysis,* in which the therapist identifies the reinforcement contingency that is maintaining the current behavior.
- *Plan implementation,* in which the consultee carries out the intervention as recommended by the consultant.
- *Plan evaluation,* in which the consultant and consultee measure the client's progress from baseline and toward goals.

As an example of behavioral consultation, consider Kathleen, a managing partner in a private law firm that employs about 20 lawyers. Kathleen seeks the assistance of Dr. Taguchi, a clinical psychologist and behavioral consultant, regarding productivity problems related to a recently hired administrative assistant, Pam. (To clarify, Dr. Taguchi is the consultant, Kathleen is the consultee, and Pam is the client.) Among other things, Kathleen describes one particularly problematic behavior that Pam performs on a regular basis: indulging in long lunches. Specifically, she states that Pam is often out of the office for 2 to 2.5 hours for lunch, always with friends from nearby offices, and that during this time Pam's work piles up. The attorneys in the office grow frustrated with Pam's absence, and they are unable to be as productive as they could be otherwise. Kathleen explains that they had never had such a problem with previous administrative assistants, so she did not present Pam with a clear lunch policy when Pam was initially hired. Dr. Taguchi conceptualized the problem as a contingency in which Pam's long lunches were reinforced by social interaction and were not punished at all. Dr. Taguchi recommended that Kathleen determine a reasonable length to allow Pam for lunch and then either punish her for staying out too long or reinforce her for returning on time. Through discussion with Dr. Taguchi, Kathleen decided to use both the punishment and reinforcement strategies: If Pam stayed at lunch longer than 1 hour, her hourly pay was docked, and if Pam returned on time for an entire week, she was allowed to leave work an hour early on Friday. Kathleen implemented the plan, and Pam's behavior was quickly modified.

Parent Training

Parent training is a specific form of behavioral consultation in which parents seek help with problematic behaviors of their children. The range of problem behaviors for which parent training can be helpful is vast: Sleep-related problems, bedwetting, hyperactivity, oppositional and defiant behaviors, stuttering, fear of the dark, school phobia, and social skills are a subset (Schaefer & Briesmeister, 1989; Spiegler & Guevremont, 2010). Unlike child psychotherapy or family psychotherapy, parent training involves an arrangement in which the consultant (behavior therapist) may never meet the child directly. Parent training typically begins with a definition of the problem behavior, followed by instructions to parents to use reinforcement and punishment effectively. For example, psychologists may educate parents about shaping techniques to teach new complex behaviors or about the use of token economies; likewise, psychologists may educate parents about the use of mild punishment such as time-outs or loss of privileges. The intent is for the child's behavior to improve not only in the setting where the intervention occurs (e.g., home) but to generalize to other settings (e.g., school) as well (Moore & Patterson, 2008).

As an example of parent training, consider Heather, a single mother of a 7-year-old boy, Danny. Heather sought consultation from Dr. Ogden as a result of Danny's problematic bedtime behavior. Heather explained

Photo 14.4
Behavioral therapists use parent training to help parents manage problem behaviors in their children, including problematic bedtime behavior.

that each night, Danny would go through the same bedtime ritual they had gone through for years—put on his pajamas, brush his teeth, read a story with mom, and say goodnight. However, in the past few months, Danny had started calling out, "Mommy, I can't sleep," after being in bed for about 10 to 15 minutes. When Dr. Ogden asked how Heather responded, she said that she often let him come out of his bedroom, thinking that perhaps he genuinely wasn't yet tired. Specifically, Heather explained that she often let Danny join her on the couch, where they watched TV and ate snacks for about an hour. Dr. Ogden saw Heather's behavior as strongly reinforcing to Danny and suggested that Heather no longer provide the reinforcement. Together, they discussed other viable options and decided that the best option would be no longer to allow Danny out of his room after bedtime. Of course, when Heather initially implemented this plan, Danny's behavior actually worsened (he demonstrated an extinction burst), but Dr. Ogden had warned Heather about this and encouraged her to remain consistent. When they evaluated the plan after several weeks, Heather said that Danny's behavior had improved, but she pointed out that a few times, Danny had defiantly come out of his room without permission, and Heather was unsure how to respond. Dr. Ogden recommended that Heather punish this behavior, and they agreed that losing desserts for the next day would be a suitable punishment. After this adjustment, Danny's coming-out-of-bed behavior extinguished.

Teacher Training

Teacher training is quite similar to parent training, but the emphasis is on behaviors that take place at school. Many of these problem behaviors are interpersonal or disruptive in nature, but others are academic and involve refusal to complete assignments and similar task-related behaviors.

Often, when behavioral therapists serve as consultants to teachers, a primary task is to thoroughly analyze the consequences of the child's behavior. That is, the behavioral consultant can often help the teacher see all the reinforcement and punishment that a child receives for particular behaviors. As an example, consider Ms. Palmer, a third-grade teacher who sought behavioral consultation from Dr. Carr. Ms. Palmer explained that one of her students, Brian, was extremely disruptive in class. In particular, Brian frequently called Ms. Palmer "stupid" and "an idiot" during class. Ms. Palmer couldn't understand why this behavior persisted, because each time he did this, she punished him by sending him out of the room and later talking with him one-on-one about his inappropriate behavior. Through additional questioning, Dr. Carr uncovered two important facts: When Brian was sent out of the room, he was able to avoid the work the class was doing at that time, much of which Brian found overwhelming; additionally, the attention Ms. Palmer gave him during the one-on-one talks actually made Brian feel important, not punished. Thus, although Ms. Palmer intended to punish Brian's insulting behavior, she was actually reinforcing it. Ms. Palmer was able to find other means of responding to Brian's insults, including ignoring them, which resulted in a drastic reduction in the target behavior.

How Well Does It Work?

In terms of empirical evidence supporting their benefits, behavioral therapies are unquestionably highly supported. Lists and compilations of "treatments that work" include disproportionately large numbers of behavioral treatments (e.g., Chambless et al., 1998; Nathan & Gorman, 2007), especially in comparison with humanistic and psychodynamic treatments. Behavioral therapies have been found efficacious for an extremely wide range of disorders, but the disorders for which they have garnered the most support include anxiety disorders, depression, and children's behavior disorders (Prochaska & Norcross, 2010; Spiegler & Guevremont, 2010). To a remarkable extent, especially in comparison with many of the other therapy approaches covered in this book, behavior therapy has produced and provided efficacy data for specific interventions for specific problems.

Some have pointed out that behavioral therapies populate lists of empirically supported or evidence-based treatments because, more than any other form of treatment (e.g., psychodynamic, humanistic, cognitive), they lend themselves to empirical testing. In other words, if the worth of a therapy is to be measured solely via quantifiable measures of objective, observable outcomes, it should be no surprise that behavioral therapies are shown to be most successful (e.g., Silverman, 1996). Behavioral therapists have sought from the outset to create such a type of therapy, emphasizing an empirical, scientific approach to therapy as opposed to the more introspective, subjective approach of other methods, such as psychodynamic and humanistic therapies.

● ● ● BOX 14.3 ● ● ●

Denise in Behavioral Psychotherapy

During my initial interview with Denise, she explained that she had been experiencing depression-related difficulties since a new owner introduced new policies at the restaurant where she worked as a chef. Denise spent a lot of time providing background information about her childhood. As a behavior therapist, I found this childhood information rather irrelevant to her current problems. Also, Denise spent a lot of time describing her thoughts and feelings regarding the situation at work, but, through

(Continued)

(Continued)

behaviorally oriented questions, I tried to refocus Denise on overt, observable, measurable behaviors rather than inner mental processes such as thoughts and feelings. Eventually, Denise and I identified three specific behaviors that were suitable for intervention: getting to work on time, preparing dishes accurately, and exercising. We agreed that the aim of therapy would be to modify the frequency of each of these behaviors to more desired levels.

Once we had operationally defined these three behaviors, another important initial step was to establish a baseline for each. In other words, we assessed the frequency with which these behaviors were currently taking place to have a basis for comparison after treatment was implemented. Denise informed me that she was currently arriving to work on time only two times a week (out of 6 work days per week), preparing dishes inaccurately once per work day, and exercising zero times per week. Next, we set specific goals for each of these target behaviors: arriving to work on time 6 days per week, preparing dishes inaccurately only once per week, and exercising four times per week.

I used a contingency management approach incorporating shaping techniques to modify Denise's behaviors in each of these three areas. First, Denise and I explored a variety of options that might be effective reinforcement for her; we decided that time surfing the Internet, one of her favorite leisure activities, was the most reasonable choice. Then we established specific contingencies for each of the three target behaviors. The initial contingencies intentionally fell short of the final goal, because the plan was to shape Denise's behavior by reinforcing behaviors that were "steps in the right direction" and then "raise the bar" after each successful week. The initial contingencies were as follows: If she arrived at work on time on a given day, then she was allowed 20 minutes of Internet surfing; if she prepared all dishes accurately on any given work day, then she was allowed 20 minutes of Internet surfing; if she exercised for at least 30 minutes on any given day, then she was allowed 20 minutes of Internet surfing. Denise was quite successful in meeting these initial goals within 2 weeks, so we gradually began to increase the demands in order to earn the reinforcement. Within a relatively short time (about 8 weeks), Denise was meeting her final behavioral goals in all three areas.

CHAPTER SUMMARY

Behavioral psychotherapy focuses on observable, measurable behavior rather than mental phenomena that can be only indirectly inferred. Problematic or undesirable behavior is viewed as the clinical problem, not as a symptom of some underlying, deeper disorder. The primary goal of behavioral psychotherapy is overt behavioral change, and its methods rely on empirical, testable hypotheses. Behavioral therapists believe that conditioning, either classical or operant, is the primary cause of behavior. As such, their clinical efforts center on altering client's learned contingencies (via such methods as contingency management, behavioral activation, or token economies) or breaking clients' learned associations (via such methods as exposure therapy, systematic desensitization, or assertiveness training). Principles of behavioral psychotherapy have also been used in an indirect, consulting capacity, whereby the behavior therapist helps a consultee (e.g., a parent or teacher) apply behavioral techniques with a client (e.g., a child or student). Empirical outcome studies have offered more empirical support for behavioral psychotherapy than for any other approach, and the disorders for which it has demonstrated empirical efficacy include anxiety disorders, depression, children's behavior disorders, and many others.

KEY TERMS AND NAMES

anxiety hierarchy 348

assertiveness training 350

aversion therapy 353

Albert Bandura 359

baselines 344

behavioral activation 358

behavioral consultation 360

behavioral psychotherapy 340

classical conditioning 345

conditioned response 346

conditioned stimulus 346

contingencies 347

contingency management 352

counterconditioning 349

discrimination 346

empirical data 342

exposure plus response prevention 348

exposure therapy 347

extinction 354

extinction burst 355

flooding 348

generalization 346

graded exposure 348

imaginal exposure 348

imitation 359

implosion 348

in vivo exposure 348

introspection 345

law of effect 341

medical model of psychopathology 344

negative punishment 353

negative reinforcement 353

observable changes 344

observational learning 359

operant conditioning 346

parent training 361

Ivan Pavlov 340

positive punishment 353

positive reinforcement 353

punishment 353

reinforcement 353

relaxation training 349

shaping 357

B. F. Skinner 341

CRITICAL THINKING QUESTIONS

1. Do you believe that the law of effect is equally powerful in humans and animals?

2. To what extent do you agree that the primary goal of psychotherapy should be observable behavior change?

3. To what extent do you agree with the medical model of psychopathology?

4. In your opinion, what can behavioral therapists do to make imaginal exposure as similar to in vivo exposure as possible?

5. For what types of clinical problems does contingency management seem most and least likely to be beneficial?

STUDENT STUDY SITE RESOURCES

Visit the study site at www.sagepub.com/pomerantz3eupdate for these additional learning tools:

-   Self-quizzes
-   eFlashcards
-   Culture Expert Interviews

-   Full-text SAGE journal articles
-   Additional web resources
-   Mock Assessment Data

CHAPTER SUMMARY VIDEO

QR codes at the end of each chapter link to chapter background videos by the author. Visit http://gettag.mobi using your smartphone browser to download the free Microsoft Tag app. Once installed, scan the tags to go directly to these brief videos. In this video, the author tells the story of one of his own clients to illustrate the possible effects of defining problems behaviorally.

CHAPTER 15

Cognitive Psychotherapy

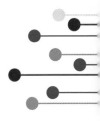

Among today's clinical psychologists, **cognitive therapy** prevails. Surveys indicate a dramatic increase in the popularity of cognitive therapy, especially since the 1980s (e.g., Norcross & Karpiak, 2012). In fact, far more contemporary clinical psychologists endorse cognitive therapy as their primary orientation than any other single-school approach. In short, "cognitive therapy clearly has become the prominent approach to psychotherapy in the early part of the 21st century" (Dobson, 2012, p. 112).

Web Link 15.1

Beck Institute for
Cognitive Therapy
and Research

The attraction to the cognitive approach may stem from a variety of factors. Cognitive therapy strikes a balance between some of the other psychotherapeutic options. Like behavioral therapy, it tends to be brief, structured, and targeted. However, like psychodynamic therapy, it focuses on important mental processes. In some ways, cognitive therapy actually represents a reaction against both the behavioral and psychodynamic approaches. Two important historical developments occurred around the same time, beginning in the 1950s and 1960s, contributing to the development of cognitive therapy:

Photo 15.1 Aaron Beck (left) and Albert Ellis (right) are pioneers of the cognitive approach to psychotherapy, which is now more widely endorsed by clinical psychologists than any other single-school approach.

- Strict applications of behavioral therapy—techniques based on operant and classical conditioning—didn't always work. Gradually, behavioral therapists and researchers began to recognize that cognition played a unique and important role in human behavior. The extreme behavioral view that our actions are determined entirely by external stimuli gave way to the notion that internal mental processes can also exert a strong influence (Goldfried, 1995; O'Donohue, 2009).

- The eventual leaders of the cognitive therapy movement—**Aaron Beck** and **Albert Ellis**—grew disillusioned with the psychoanalytic method in which they and most of their cohorts were trained. They sought a new approach to therapy that addressed clients' symptoms more directly, focused less on the past and more on the present, and produced positive results more efficiently. Eventually, Beck and Ellis each broke from psychoanalytic tradition and forged separate but similar styles of therapy to achieve these goals (Ellis, 1962; Kuehlwein, 1993; Prochaska & Norcross, 2010).

So cognitive therapy began as a revision of behavioral therapy within a context of increasing dissatisfaction with the psychodynamic therapy that dominated at the time (O'Donohue, 2009). Cognitive therapy still overlaps significantly with behavioral therapy: Many cognitive therapists use behavioral techniques also, and a large number of therapists straddle the line by identifying themselves as "cognitive-behavioral." However, cognitive therapy is not just a minor variation of behavioral therapy in which cognitions complement conditioning. Undoubtedly, cognitive therapy has evolved into its own well-established and commonly practiced approach.

Goal of Cognitive Therapy

Simply put, the goal of cognitive therapy is logical thinking. The word *cognition*, after all, is basically synonymous with the word *thought*. Thus, cognitive therapists fundamentally presume that the way we think about events determines the way we respond. In other words, "individuals' interpretations and perceptions of current situations, events, and problems influence how they react" (Beck, 2002, p. 163). Psychological problems arise from illogical cognitions. For example, an illogical (or irrational or unrealistic) interpretation of a life event—a relationship breakup, an F on an exam, a comment from a friend—can cause crippling depression or anxiety. However, psychological wellness stems from logical cognitions. That is, when the cognitions appropriately match the event, they can lead to more adaptive, healthy reactions. Therefore, the role of the cognitive therapist is to fix faulty thinking (Bermudes, Wright, & Casey, 2009; Clark, Hollifield, Leahy, & Beck, 2009; Dobson, 2012; Dobson & Dobson, 2009).

The Importance of Cognition

When they refer to **cognitions**, cognitive therapists use lots of terms interchangeably: *thoughts, beliefs, interpretations,* and *assumptions,* to name a few. Whatever we call them, we often overlook their importance in our day-to-day lives. When someone asks, "Why are you so happy?" or "Why are you so sad?" we typically point to a recent event that made us happy. We portray it as a two-step model in which things happen and those things directly influence our feelings. The truth, according to cognitive therapists, is that such a two-step model is flawed; specifically, it's missing an important step in the middle. The three-step model that cognitive therapists endorse goes like this: Things happen, we *interpret* those things, and *those interpretations* directly influence our feelings. Thus, "it is not a situation in and of itself that determines what people feel but rather the way in which they construe a situation" (Beck, 1995, p. 14). In other words, events don't make us happy or sad. Instead, the way we think about those events does. (See Figure 15.1.)

As an example of the power of our cognitions, consider an unexpected overnight snowfall. At the same time, three neighbors wake up, look out their windows, and see the ground covered in 6 inches of white, with more flakes continuing to fall. In the first house lives a mail carrier who covers her route by foot. For her, the snow causes feelings of dread. It's important to recognize, however, that between seeing the snow and feeling the dread, she has thoughts: "This is going to be a miserable day. I'll be cold and wet, I might slip and fall, and my route will take much longer than usual." Her next-door neighbor owns a snow plow business. He wakes up, sees the same snow, and feels elated. Like his neighbor, somewhere between the sight of the snow and the resulting feeling, the snow-plow driver thinks: "What a great day! I'm going to make a lot of money. Not to mention, I'll be able to help a lot of people." In the next house, a high school student who didn't study for today's biology exam sees the snow and feels tremendous relief. Between the sight and the feeling, he thinks: "Whew! School's going to be cancelled, and I'll have an extra day to study for that exam. What a lucky break." The same snowfall caused very different feelings in these three people, illustrating that it's not the events that happen to us but the meaning we assign to those events that shapes our feelings. Even if that process of assigning meaning happens automatically and within a split second, it nonetheless represents a crucial link to our feelings, including feelings characteristic of psychopathology such as depression or anxiety. Thus, these oft-ignored intermediary cognitions are a focal point in cognitive therapy.

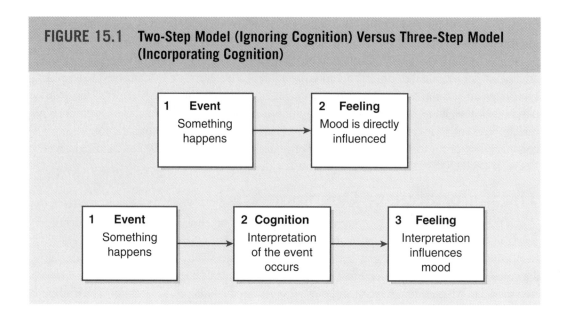

FIGURE 15.1   Two-Step Model (Ignoring Cognition) Versus Three-Step Model (Incorporating Cognition)

| 1   Event
Something happens | → | 2   Feeling
Mood is directly influenced |

| 1   Event
Something happens | → | 2 Cognition
Interpretation of the event occurs | → | 3   Feeling
Interpretation influences mood |

Revising Cognitions

Once we accept the idea that cognitions determine feelings, revising them becomes the foremost task. Specifically, the goal is to ensure that the thoughts a person has about particular events rationally and logically correspond to the event itself. If they don't, they can lead to unnecessary and unpleasant feelings (Dobson & Dobson, 2009; A. Ellis, 2008; Grant, Young, & DeRubeis, 2005). For example, let's reconsider the mail carrier described above. It's reasonable for her to feel some degree of dread about the snow; after all, it will certainly make her day more difficult. But if the thoughts underlying her dread are illogical, they can make the dread excessive. That is, if she thinks, "I'll get fired if my route takes longer than usual today" or "I'll definitely fall on wet pavement and end up with a broken bone or a concussion" or "I may freeze to death on my route," she can cripple herself with anxiety or depression. The goals of the cognitive therapist would not be to make this mail carrier feel unrealistically positive—it would hardly be logical for her to jump for joy about this situation—but to help revise her thoughts so they make realistic sense. At the end of this process, she might be just a bit apprehensive or down, which, in comparison to being devastated by anxiety or depression, represents a significantly improved emotional state.

As we see later in this chapter, there are different methods of revising cognitions. (There are also different terms for it, such as *restructuring* or *modifying* cognitions.) In general, these methods follow a common three-stage sequence: Illogical cognitions are first identified, then challenged, and eventually replaced with more logical cognitions (Beck, 1995; A. Ellis, 2008; Leahy, 2003). The first step—the identification of illogical thoughts—should not be confused with the psychodynamic goal of making the unconscious conscious. Cognitive therapists do not delve into the unconscious depths of the psyche as do psychodynamic therapists. They do, however, acknowledge that some of our cognitions are **automatic thoughts**—that is, they take place in an instant and without any deliberation. (The student with the surprise snow day described above certainly didn't need to pause and ponder, "How do I feel about this snow? Hmm, let me mull it over." The interpretation happened far more immediately.) As such, these cognitions can become so routine and habitual that they are hard to recognize. A primary responsibility of the cognitive therapist, especially early in therapy, is to assist the client in identifying automatic illogical or irrational thoughts.

Photo 15.2 According to the cognitive approach, events—such as an unexpected snowstorm—don't directly influence our feelings. Instead, the way we think about those events does. What are some possible thoughts about, for example, an unexpected snowstorm?

The second step, in which the illogical cognitions are challenged, also takes a variety of forms. As we see later in this chapter, some therapists rely on the power of verbal persuasion to convince clients to abandon illogical beliefs, whereas others encourage clients to test the accuracy of their beliefs by performing assigned behaviors in the real world. The objective of either of these approaches is to cause clients to doubt the truth of their illogical beliefs and to reach the conclusion that these beliefs should be revised. This revising, the third step in this process, is often difficult for clients to do at first—it can feel foreign, since therapists are asking clients to think in ways opposite to the ways they may have been thinking for many years (Roth, Eng, & Heimberg, 2002). The cognitive therapist may, therefore, take the lead in the initial attempts to revise the client's thoughts. Ultimately, however, the goal is for clients to be able to revise their own thoughts without therapist input.

The process of revising cognitions should always take place in a context of cultural sensitivity. There is no such thing as universally or absolutely logical thinking. A belief that is logical, rational, or adaptive for members of one culture may be illogical, irrational, or maladaptive for members of another culture. Culturally competent cognitive therapists are aware of the influence that their own cultural background has on their view of logical thinking and are careful not to impose their own cultural values on clients in the process of revising or restructuring clients' cognitions.

Teaching as a Therapy Tool

Cognitive therapists explicitly include in their duties the education of their clients about the cognitive approach. In other words, cognitive therapists often function as teachers with their clients. For example, they might use a combination of mini-lecture, handouts, and readings to explain to clients the difference between the two-step (events lead directly to feelings) and the preferred three-step (cognitions intervene between events and feelings) models of understanding the sources of our feelings. Moreover, they train clients to recognize illogical thoughts, to assign labels to them, and to track them in a particular written format. And, like any good teacher, cognitive therapists aspire for clients ultimately to be able to use the lessons learned to teach themselves rather than remaining dependent on the teacher (Beck, 1995; Olatunji & Feldman, 2008).

Homework

Another similarity between cognitive therapists and teachers is the assignment of **homework** (Beck, 1995; Kuehlwein, 1993; Olatunji & Feldman, 2008; Robinson, 2008). Cognitive therapists strongly believe that much of the work of therapy is conducted between sessions. Much like the time between class meetings of a college course, the time between therapy sessions is used to explore and confirm the lessons learned during the meetings. In some cases, the homework is written: Clients are asked to keep a record of events, cognitions, feelings, and attempts to revise the cognitions to change the feelings they experience. (Later in this chapter, we examine written formats such as these in more detail.) In other cases, the homework is behavioral: Clients are asked to perform certain behaviors before the next meeting, typically for the purpose of examining the validity of an illogical thought. In either case, discussion of the homework will constitute a significant part of the subsequent session (Kazantzis & Dattilio, 2010).

● ● ● BOX 15.1 ● ● ●

Considering Culture

Cognitive Therapy With Lesbian, Gay, Bisexual, and Transgender Clients

For many, life as a lesbian, gay, bisexual, or transgender (LGBT) person today is quite different from what it was a generation or more ago, as society's attitudes toward members of the LGBT community appear to have become more accepting. However, Purcell, Swann, and Herbert (2003) argue that in spite of these social changes, negative attitudes toward LGBT individuals persist in our society and that these attitudes are reflected even among members of the LGBT community. In fact, these authors make the case that "internalized homophobia"—an aversion to homosexuality applied by gay individuals to themselves—pervades gay and lesbian culture to some extent. That is, gay or lesbian individuals may hold some beliefs that disapprove of their own sexual orientation or lifestyle, such as, "Homosexuality is wrong" or "My family/friends/religion/society will reject me if I come out." These beliefs could hinder self-respect and self-worth and contribute to depression or other clinically significant problems.

Are such beliefs consistent with contemporary societal values? Or expressed in terms of cognitive therapy, are such beliefs logical? To the extent that they are not, could cognitive therapy be helpful in identifying their logical flaws, challenging them, and replacing them with more logical thoughts? These questions illustrate the need for cultural competence and cultural self-awareness in clinical psychologists. It is essential for the clinical psychologist to understand these beliefs from the perspective of the clients—to see their world through their eyes—to appreciate whether such beliefs are sensible or misguided for them. Clinical psychologists should also be well aware of their own personal views on these issues and stop themselves from equating their own views with the "logical" way to think. What seems adaptive from the perspective of the clinical psychologist may be maladaptive from the perspective of the client.

Of course, cognitive therapists' work with LGBT clients often focuses on cognitions that have nothing to do with their sexual orientation. Indeed, LGBT clients bring the same problems to therapy as heterosexual clients do (Martell, Safren, & Prince, 2004), but in addition, they may be struggling with some cognitions related to internalized homophobia, as described by Purcell et al. (2003).

What other cultural groups might experience similar "internalized" self-critical cognitions as a reflection of broader societal views? How might a culturally competent cognitive therapist address the logical or illogical nature of those cognitions?

A Brief, Structured, Focused Approach

Cognitive therapists strive to achieve a positive therapy outcome quite quickly—typically, in fewer than 15 sessions, but significantly longer in complex or severe cases (Beck, 1995, 2002; Roth et al., 2002). For outpatients, sessions typically take place once per week, eventually tapering off in frequency as the client improves. Several factors contribute to the efficiency of cognitive therapy, including its focus on the client's current problems (rather than extensive exploration of the past); a purposeful, goal-oriented focus on clearly identified symptoms; and structured therapy sessions (Grant et al., 2005; Olatunji & Feldman, 2008).

Table 15.1 Typical Sequential Structure of a Cognitive Therapy Session

1. Check on client's mood or emotional status and solicit brief updates on recent events.
2. Set and confirm the agenda for the current session.
3. Establish a link to the previous session, often by reviewing previous homework assignment.
4. Progress through the body of the current session, proceeding step-by-step through the agenda.
5. Develop and assign new homework assignment.
6. Summarize current session; solicit client feedback.

Sources: Beck (1995), Freeman et al. (1990), and Pretzer and Beck (2004).

The structured nature of cognitive therapy sessions differs sharply from the free-flowing, spontaneous style of humanistic therapy (Pretzer & Beck, 2004). Whereas humanistic (or "client-centered") therapists allow clients to determine the topics to be discussed during a session, the amount of time spent on each, and the like, cognitive therapists set an agenda (Beck, 1995; Freeman, Pretzer, Fleming, & Simon, 1990). Typically, each session is sequentially organized into segments (see Table 15.1), and sometimes each segment is allotted a specific amount of time. Of course, the client has input on the content of the agenda for the session, but cognitive therapists usually shun therapy that lacks predetermined, explicit structure.

Two Approaches to Cognitive Therapy

There are two widely recognized pioneers of cognitive therapy: Albert Ellis and Aaron Beck. As described earlier, each developed his own version of cognitive therapy at about the same time, and although each was influenced somewhat by the other, their approaches evolved independently for the most part. The two approaches unquestionably overlap in terms of their emphasis on improving clients' symptoms via correcting illogical thinking, but the terminology and, at times, the techniques they employ distinguish them from each other. Let's consider each separately.

Albert Ellis

Web Link 15.2
Albert Ellis Institute

For many years, Albert Ellis called his approach to therapy Rational Emotive Therapy (RET), but later in his career, he altered the name to **Rational Emotive Behavior Therapy (REBT)**. We'll use the more recent name here, understanding that both refer to Ellis's version of cognitive therapy.

As the first two words of the REBT label indicate, Ellis's therapy approach emphasizes a connection between rationality and emotion (Dryden, 2009; A. Ellis, 2008; Ellis & Ellis, 2011). Ellis (1962) argues that if we can make our beliefs less irrational, we can live happier lives:

> The central theme of [REBT] is that man is a uniquely rational, as well as uniquely irrational animal; that his emotional or psychological disturbances are largely a result of his thinking illogically or irrationally; and that he can rid himself of most of his emotional or mental unhappiness, ineffectuality, and disturbance if he learns to maximize his rational and minimize his irrational thinking. (p. 36)

The ABCDE Model

One of Ellis's most enduring and clinically useful contributions is his **ABCDE model** for understanding and recording the impact of cognitions on emotions (also known as the ABC model) (e.g., Dryden, 1995, 2009; A. Ellis, 2008; Ellis & Ellis, 2011; Ellis & Grieger, 1977; Ellis & Harper, 1975). By creating this model, Ellis was able to frame the essential aspects of cognitive therapy into an accessible acronym that enabled its use by thousands of therapists and clients.

In the ABCDE model, A, B, and C represent the three-step model described near the beginning of this chapter: Events lead to thoughts, which in turn lead to feelings. Ellis's model simply replaces these three terms with more easily remembered terms: **Activating event** (A), **Belief** (B), and **emotional Consequence** (C). According to Ellis, irrational beliefs are toxic because they function as rigid, dogmatic demands that we apply to ourselves—for example, "I must get an A in every class," "I need to be dating someone," or "I can't let my family down." Although these may be strong preferences, they are not, in fact, "musts" or absolute rules. Moreover, we tend to couple these demands with overestimations of the consequences of failure—"If I don't get an A, I'll flunk out of school and end up on the street"; "If I'm not dating anyone, I'm completely worthless"; or "If I let my family down, their disapproval will destroy me." Ellis sees flawed logic in all these self-statements and opportunity for therapeutic benefit in correcting them.

To accomplish this correction, Ellis's model adds two more steps, D and E. In his model, D stands for **Dispute**, and E stands for **Effective new belief**. Specifically, the irrational belief (B) is the target of the dispute. The addition of this step is particularly important within Ellis's model of cognitive therapy. Ellis's model not only helps clients identify irrational beliefs (B) that may intervene with the events in their lives (A) and their subsequent feelings (C); it urges clients to dispute those beliefs as well. This can be an empowering experience for clients who have been stuck in an ABC sequence that leaves them feeling perpetually unhappy, anxious, and so on. When they realize that their experience need not stop at C (the unwanted feeling), that they have the right to challenge the belief that caused C and replace it with something more rational, therapeutic benefit is in the works. In Ellis's model, disputing often takes the form of pointed questions or statements that attack the irrational nature of beliefs or labels that can be assigned to irrational beliefs to discredit them. Regardless of the form of the dispute, if it is effective, it affords the client the opportunity to replace the original, irrational belief with an effective new belief (E) that is more rational and leads to less troubling feelings (Dryden, 2009; A. Ellis, 2008).

As a clinical example, consider Keyon, a 24-year-old man who recently earned a degree in accounting. Keyon sought therapy from Dr. Liu, a clinical psychologist with a cognitive orientation, because he was struggling with excessive anxiety. Specifically, Keyon was scheduled to take the Certified Public Accountant (CPA) exam in about 2 months, but his anxiety about the exam was interfering with his preparation. He intended to study for the exam, but when he tried, he was so anxious that he couldn't concentrate. In fact, just thinking about the CPA exam made Keyon feel panicky. After Dr. Liu educated Keyon about the cognitive model (specifically, Ellis's ABCDE model), they were able to identify steps A and C right away: The activating event was studying for (or thinking about) the CPA exam, and the emotional consequence was anxiety. With Dr. Liu's help, Keyon next identified two beliefs (B) that linked his thoughts of the CPA exam to his feelings of anxiety: "I absolutely have to pass the CPA exam on my first attempt" and "If I don't pass the CPA exam on my first attempt, my career is doomed, and that would destroy me." In the next step, disputing (D), Dr. Liu made efforts to question the logic of Keyon's beliefs:

> Who says you have to pass the CPA exam on your first attempt? I understand that's a preference, but is it a life-or-death necessity? Realistically, don't quite a few accountants fail the CPA exam on their first try? And don't many of them pass it later and go on to have successful careers? And even if you don't end up with the career in accounting that you envisioned, does that mean your life is ruined? There are plenty of ways for you to have a rewarding career that don't involve accounting at all.

In time, Keyon found himself persuaded by the strength of Dr. Liu's arguments and began to disbelieve his own irrational thoughts. Eventually, he was able to replace his original, irrational beliefs with effective new beliefs (E):

> I want to pass the CPA exam on my first attempt, but it's not an absolute necessity. If I pass it on a later attempt, that will probably work out fine also, and in the big picture, my happiness doesn't depend entirely on following the career path I've envisioned.

These new beliefs greatly reduced Keyon's anxiety.

The ABCDE model lends itself quite nicely to written format, and cognitive therapists often take advantage of this. It's likely that Dr. Liu, for example, would have taught Keyon how to view his experiences as ABCDE sequences and chronicle them accordingly. Typically, clients complete forms that are organized into A, B, C, D, and E columns. During sessions or as homework, in retrospect or as an event takes place, clients can sort their experiences into the five-column organizational structure provided by this type of journal form. By doing so, they train themselves to experience life in this sequence. In particular, they become more adept at identifying an irrational belief (B), constructing a dispute (D) in response to the belief, and generating an effective new belief (E). Of course, the goal is not for the clients to depend on this written format for the rest of their lives to feel happier; instead, a five-column ABCDE thought journal can serve as training wheels that stabilize clients while they learn to think more logically, and once they can stabilize themselves, the ABCDE process takes place within the mind, without any outside aids.

Table 15.2 summarizes the full ABCDE acronym, including an applied example from Keyon's therapy with Dr. Liu.

Table 15.2 Albert Ellis's ABCDE Model as Applied to a Clinical Example (Keyon)

A	Activating event	Studying for or thinking about the CPA exam
B	Belief	"I absolutely have to pass the CPA exam on my first attempt." "If I don't pass the CPA exam on my first attempt, my career is doomed, and that would destroy me."
C	Consequence (emotional)	Anxiety
D	Dispute	"Who says you have to pass the CPA exam on your first attempt? I understand that's a preference, but is it a life-or-death necessity? Realistically, don't quite a few accountants fail the CPA exam on their first try? And don't many of them pass it later and go on to have successful careers? And even if you don't end up with the career in accounting that you envisioned, does that mean your life is ruined? There are plenty of ways for you to have a rewarding career that don't involve accounting at all."
E	Effective new belief	"I want to pass the CPA exam on my first attempt, but it's not an absolute necessity. If I pass it on a later attempt, that will probably work out fine also, and in the big picture, my happiness doesn't depend entirely on following the career path I've imagined."

Considering Culture

Are Some Beliefs too Sacred to Dispute?

Cody, a 22-year-old college student, grew up in a family with strict religious beliefs. Among them: Premarital sex is sinful, and anyone who engages in it is an immoral person who will spend the afterlife in hell. Last week, Cody and his girlfriend of 2 years had sex for the first time. And his anxiety is through the roof. He seeks the help of a clinical psychologist, Dr. Talia Brown. Dr. Brown holds different religious beliefs than Cody does, and regarding premarital sex, she does not share Cody's beliefs at all. She believes that premarital sex is not necessarily sinful, and she disagrees that it will result in an eternity in hell. In fact, as she applies a cognitive perspective to Cody's case, Dr. Brown sees Cody's beliefs as irrational and distorted. Her plan to help Cody reduce his anxiety is to replace what's in his B column—"Premarital sex is sinful"—with something she believes to be more logical and less anxiety producing—"Premarital sex is OK in some circumstances."

A fundamental task in cognitive therapy is to dispute irrational beliefs, but who decides what's irrational? Moreover, are some client beliefs—religious, cultural, or otherwise—too sacred to dispute, even if the therapist questions their rationality? Is it appropriate for Dr. Brown to critically examine Cody's beliefs about premarital sex, or should she take a "hands-off" approach in the spirit of cultural sensitivity? In Dr. Brown's situation, many clinical psychologists would choose not to question any of Cody's religious beliefs, with the rationale that respect for Cody's religion is an important part of cultural competence. However, some psychologists disagree. Ridley, Ethington, and Heppner (2008) argue that when the working alliance between therapist and client is strong and the timing is right, *cultural confrontation* is preferable:

> Often [mental health professionals] assume that counselors should accept without question clients' cultural values. In their thinking, uncritical acceptance reflects an unbiased approach to counseling, especially as it pertains to clients whose cultural backgrounds are radically different from their own. . . . We maintain that in some cases, rigid and extreme adherence to cultural values not only is dysfunctional but also creates a great deal of psychological distress. We suggest that examination of clients' cultural impasses and at times cultural confrontation are essential competencies under the larger domains of multicultural counseling competence. (p. 378)

Indeed, cognitive therapists have long recognized the importance of cultural competence as they work with clients of diverse religious, ethnic, and other groups (e.g., Hays & Iwamasa, 2006; Koenig, 2005; Paradis, Cukor, & Friedman, 2006; Pargament, 2007). But the notion of cultural confrontation opposes much of the traditional wisdom about respecting clients' values by declining to challenge them. In your opinion, should Dr. Brown proceed with her plan to challenge Cody's religious beliefs about premarital sex? If she does, will Cody be receptive to her strategy? Will his anxiety decrease? If you were the client, how would you respond? Which beliefs of yours—religious, cultural, political, personal, or otherwise—would you see as too sacred for your psychologist to dispute?

Aaron Beck

Aaron Beck has always used the general term *cognitive therapy* to describe his technique. He originally developed his approach as a way to conceptualize and treat depression (e.g., Beck, 1976; Beck, Rush, Shaw, & Emery, 1979), but it has been very broadly applied since shortly after its inception. (In fact, his daughter, **Judith Beck,** has become a leader of the current generation of cognitive therapists and has spearheaded its application to many new problems.) An important part of Beck's theory of depression is his notion of the **cognitive triad,** in which he argues that three particular cognitions—thoughts about the self, the external world, and the future—all contribute to our mental health. Beck theorized that when all three of these beliefs are negative, they produce depression (Alford & Beck, 1997; Beck, 1995).

⊕ Web Link 15.3
Judith Beck

The essence of Beck's approach to cognitive therapy, like Ellis's, is to increase the extent to which the client thinks logically. And also like Ellis's, Beck's approach incorporates a way of organizing clients' experiences into columns on a written page. In Beck's brand of cognitive therapy, this form is known as a **Dysfunctional Thought Record** (e.g., Beck, 1995, 2002; Freeman et al., 1990; Leahy, 2003), and although its headings differ a bit from Ellis's ABCDE acronym, they function similarly. Typically, the Dysfunctional Thought Record includes columns for

- a brief description of the event/situation,
- automatic thoughts about the event/situation (and the extent to which the client believes these thoughts),
- emotions (and their intensity),
- an adaptive response (identifying the distortion in the automatic thought and challenging it), and
- outcome (emotions after the adaptive response has been identified and the extent to which the client still believes the automatic thoughts).

Conceptually, the columns in Beck's Dysfunctional Thought Record correspond quite closely to the columns of Ellis's ABCDE forms. For example, in the fourth column ("adaptive response") of a Dysfunctional Thought Record, clients perform essentially the same task they would in Column D ("Dispute") of Ellis's form. For this task, Beck created a vocabulary to identify common ways clients' thoughts can be distorted. This vocabulary has become a vital aspect of cognitive therapy. Let's consider it here in more detail.

Common Thought Distortions

An essential step in cognitive therapy is to discredit illogical automatic thoughts by labeling them. To facilitate this labeling, Beck and his followers have identified and defined a list of **common thought distortions** (e.g., Beck, 2002; Beck et al., 1979; Craighead, Craighead, Kazdin, & Mahoney, 1994; Leahy, 2003). Cognitive therapists teach these terms to clients, often using handouts or take-home readings, and train them to use the terms when examining their own thoughts. Examples of these common thought distortions include the following:

- **All-or-nothing thinking:** Irrationally evaluating everything as either wonderful or terrible, with no middle ground or "gray area"
- **Catastrophizing:** Expecting the worst in the future, when, realistically, it's unlikely to occur
- **Magnification/minimization:** For negative events, "making a mountain out of a molehill"; for positive events, playing down their importance
- **Personalization:** Assuming excessive personal responsibility for negative events
- **Overgeneralization:** Applying lessons learned from negative experiences more broadly than is warranted
- **Mental filtering:** Ignoring positive events while focusing excessively on negative events
- **Mind reading:** Presuming to know that others are thinking critically or disapprovingly, when knowing what they think is, in fact, impossible

In Beck's cognitive therapy, when clients assign these thought distortion labels to illogical thoughts, the illogical thoughts grow weaker. Labeling thoughts as illogical enables the client to dismiss them and replace them with more adaptive and logical thoughts, which ultimately decreases the client's psychological distress. As a clinical example, consider Olivia, a 30-year-old woman who was recently divorced after a 3-year marriage and currently lives alone. In her first session with Dr. Zimmerman, a clinical psychologist with a cognitive orientation, Olivia explains that she feels depressed about being without a partner. The comments she made to Dr. Zimmerman could be summed up in these three beliefs: "I'm no good at relationships," "Living alone, even for a short time, is intolerable," and "A lot of my friends are married, but I'm not, so there must be something wrong with me." After educating Olivia about Beck's cognitive approach, including the list of common thought distortions, Dr. Zimmerman and Olivia got to work. Together, they attacked the flawed logic in each of Olivia's beliefs by labeling them as distortions. For example, when Olivia views herself as "no good at relationships," she's overgeneralizing from the recent divorce. Living alone may not be her preference, but to call it "intolerable" constitutes magnification. And to blame the divorce on herself—"there's something wrong with me"—is personalization that is unfounded and unfair. With repeated practice, Olivia developed the ability to identify and oppose her own illogical thoughts and replace them with more logical alternatives. She never became overjoyed about her divorce or the loneliness in her current life—such a reaction would also be illogical—but she was able to lift herself from a state of despair to a state of contentment and mild hopefulness, which made a tremendous difference in her day-to-day life.

Beliefs as Hypotheses

Beck argued that our beliefs are **hypotheses,** even though we may live our lives as if our beliefs are proven facts. Therefore, a potent way to expose a belief as illogical is to "put it to the test" in real life, just as scientists empirically test their hypotheses in the lab. Beck's approach to cognitive therapy often includes such personal "experiments," frequently in the form of homework, designed to bolster or undermine a client's beliefs (Dobson & Hamilton, 2008; Kuehlwein, 1993; Roth et al., 2002).

As a clinical example, consider Frank, a 45-year-old chain-restaurant manager who has held his job for 15 years but has become increasingly unhappy with it. This professional dissatisfaction is the main contributor to the depression for which he seeks therapy. He mentions to Dr. Morris, his cognitively oriented clinical psychologist, that he would like to look for another job, but "I'm sure I wouldn't be able to get one," a belief that leaves Frank feeling dejected about the future. One effective strategy that Dr. Morris might employ would involve challenging the logic of Frank's belief that he is not employable elsewhere. Using Beck's Dysfunctional Thought Record (or Ellis's ABCDE columns), Dr. Morris could try to use words to persuade Frank that his belief is illogical: Perhaps Frank is minimizing his skills and experiences, mind reading when in fact he doesn't know how prospective employers may evaluate him as an applicant, or engaging in some other cognitive distortion. To accompany this argument, Dr. Morris might also assign Frank some homework that will serve to test his belief. For example, Dr. Morris might ask Frank to create a résumé and highlight the parts of it that would be attractive to an employer (training, years of experience, etc.). Or Dr. Morris might ask Frank actually to test the market—respond to some want ads and see what kind of response he gets from employers. If these homework assignments result in some feedback inconsistent with Frank's hypothesis—that is, if his résumé actually looks good or if prospective employers show interest—the experience will force Frank to abandon the belief that he's unemployable. And by replacing that belief with the belief that he is indeed attractive to employers, Frank will be more hopeful and less vulnerable to depressive feelings.

Of course, when cognitive therapists encourage clients to test their hypotheses, they are careful to do so in a way that will effectively refute illogical thoughts (Kuehlwein, 1993). If they assign homework that confirms illogical beliefs, the efforts can backfire.

In practice, the approaches of Ellis and Beck overlap quite a bit. Cognitive therapists often incorporate elements of both styles of therapy into their own techniques. Although the terminology that Beck and Ellis use differs somewhat, their therapeutic goals are essentially the same: to identify and critically evaluate illogical thinking and replace it with more rational alternatives that ultimately alleviate psychological symptoms.

• • • BOX 15.3 • • •

Metaphorically Speaking

If You've Seen Attorneys Argue in Court, Then You Understand How Cognitive Therapists Dispute Thought Distortions

"Objection!" In the courtroom, this is how attorneys protest the unsound tactics of opposing counsel. Usually, the purpose of an objection is to interrupt an illogical argument. In other words, as soon as an attorney notices that the opposition is putting forth a logically flawed argument, the appropriate action is to insist that only logically sound statements be allowed in the argument and that any irrational statement be stricken from the record.

In a way, cognitive therapists teach clients to be their own defense attorneys in the "cognitive courtroom" of the mind. Specifically, cognitive therapists train clients to spot illogical thoughts, object to them, and insist that only logical thoughts be allowed. This process implies that there are two opposing voices in each of our minds, just as there are two opposing attorneys in a courtroom. These two voices are represented by the two columns in the cognitive model in which beliefs are articulated—Columns B (Belief) and E (Effective new belief) in Ellis's ABCDE model. Between them, Column D (Dispute) serves as an objection to the first, illogical voice (B) and an opportunity for the second, logical voice (E) to make a more logical statement.

To illustrate, let's consider an illogical belief held by Shannon, a 20-year-old college student: "If I fail an exam, I'm stupid." Or, stated as an accusation from another person,

"If you fail an exam, you're stupid." If this accusation goes unopposed, as it would in a courtroom with only the prosecuting attorney in attendance, this case may end with the verdict that Shannon is, in fact, stupid. But if Shannon objects to the flawed logic in this belief—in Ellis's terms, if she disputes it effectively—Shannon will exonerate herself of the charge of stupidity. In truth, Shannon may be able to use several different disputes to support her objection—perhaps the test was unfair and many students failed it, or perhaps Shannon wasn't feeling good on the day of the test, or perhaps Shannon has earned As on most of her other tests in college. Any of these objections creates reasonable doubt about the accusation that Shannon is stupid and increases the likelihood that, in her "cognitive courtroom," she will be found innocent of this charge. As a result, she will avoid a "sentence" of depression. A key to this metaphor, and to cognitive therapy more generally, is that when illogical thoughts cross their minds, individuals feel entitled to defend themselves by objecting and correcting the illogical thoughts rather than simply allowing them to continue unchallenged.

Recent Applications of Cognitive Therapy

Although cognitive therapy was originally targeted toward limited types of psychological symptoms, it is now applied almost universally across the range of psychological problems. In fact, it is increasingly used for problems outside the range of traditional mental disorders as well.

The Third Wave:
Mindfulness- and Acceptance-Based Therapies

In recent years, a new brand of therapies based on mindfulness and acceptance have become increasingly popular and empirically supported (Hayes, Villatte, Levin, & Hildebrandt, 2011; Masuda & Wilson, 2009). Collectively, they are often called "third-wave" therapies, referring to the evolution from strict behaviorism (first wave) to cognitive therapy (second wave) to these newer therapies (Follette, Darrow, & Bonow, 2009; Hayes, 2004). As such, they should not necessarily be considered cognitive therapies in the strict sense; although they appear in this chapter on cognitive therapy, they also feature behavioral and other elements. We'll examine three particular forms of these therapies in detail: acceptance and commitment therapy, dialectical behavior therapy, and metacognitive therapy. But first, let's consider some commonalities among therapies of this kind.

Mindfulness lies at the core of the third-wave therapies (Dimidjian & Linehan, 2009; Hayes, Villatte, et al., 2011; Shapiro, 2009). It can be difficult to define in words, but its proponents have made attempts:

- Mindfulness "refers to being able to pay attention in the present moment to whatever arises internally or externally, without becoming entangled or 'hooked' by judging or wishing things were otherwise" (Roemer & Orsillo, 2009, p. 2).

- Mindfulness is "an innate human capacity to deliberately pay full attention to where we are, to our actual experience, and to learn from it. This can be contrasted with living on automatic pilot and going through our day without really being there" (Hick, 2008, p. 5).

- "The short definition of mindfulness . . . is (1) awareness, (2) of present experience, (3) with acceptance" (Germer, 2005, p. 7).

- Mindfulness is "the awareness that arises out of intentionally attending in an open and discerning way to whatever is arising in the present moment" (Shapiro, 2009, p. 555).

As the descriptions above may suggest, mindfulness derives from Buddhist traditions, but it is typically used without any explicit religious ties. (Zen meditation can accompany mindfulness-based therapies, but they are often practiced without any meditation component.) Mindfulness promotes full engagement with one's own internal mental processes in a nonconfrontational way. This is a key difference from the more traditional cognitive therapies of Albert Ellis or Aaron Beck. Whereas Ellis and Beck encouraged people to dispute and revise their thoughts, mindfulness-based therapists prefer to change people's *relationships to* their thoughts rather than the thoughts themselves (Olatunji & Feldman, 2008). So, rather than relating to thoughts as all-powerful determinants of reality or truth, clients can learn to understand their thoughts as fleeting suggestions that may not require much of a reaction at all. Once the relationship with thoughts is changed in this way, individuals may find it easier to face unpleasant thoughts (or feelings or sensations) rather than avoiding them. That is, rather than engaging in **experiential avoidance**, as third-wave therapists call it, the individual can engage in **acceptance**: allowing these internal experiences to run their course without fighting against them. This can facilitate positive change for clients with a wide range of psychological problems (Dimidjian & Linehan, 2008; Farmer & Chapman, 2008; Roemer & Orsillo, 2009).

As a specific illustration of a clinical intervention that relies on mindfulness, consider *urge surfing*. Urge surfing is an approach to the treatment of addictive behaviors such as smoking or drinking, or any other behavior in which clients struggle with unwanted urges, that encourages clients to relate differently to their urges than they have before (Bowen & Marlatt, 2009; Ostafin & Marlatt, 2008). The goal is not to stop, suppress, or fight the urges, as other forms of therapy might encourage; instead, the goal is to experience them, to "ride" or "surf" them like a wave that will rise and then inevitably subside, and to realize that they are temporary and not all-powerful. As described by Lloyd (2009),

> Clients are taught to treat urges as though they were like waves in the ocean. Urges come on, grow in intensity, and eventually subside just like

ocean waves. Moreover, like waves, urges tend to be brief. They do not grow and grow until the client has to do something before they will go away. Urges go away on their own. . . . [In this type of treatment,] clients are taught how to fully experience the urge in a different way—that is, to experience the urge for what it is: brief, nonlethal, of relatively predictable course, and most important, defeatable. (p. 669)

As this description illustrates, the critical element of this treatment is not the urge itself but the way the client responds to the urge. As with all third-wave or mindfulness-based therapies, the emphasis is on helping the client experience the urge (or feeling or thought) that arises in the moment and not overestimate its destructive power or underestimate their own ability to withstand it. It may be unpleasant, but it will pass, and the client can accept and survive it.

Mindfulness and acceptance are valuable new components of their practices whether these concepts form the foundation of the therapy strategy or merely complement other approaches. That is, mindfulness and acceptance don't demand an either/or decision. Therapists can practice forms of therapy for which mindfulness and acceptance are core elements—as in the three therapies described below—or they can enhance other forms of therapy, such as psychodynamic, humanistic, or others, by blending in elements of mindfulness and acceptance (Hick & Bien, 2008).

Acceptance and Commitment Therapy

Steven C. Hayes, a clinical psychologist and professor at the University of Nevada, Reno, is considered a leading figure in **acceptance and commitment therapy (ACT)**. According to Hayes and others, what is "accepted" in ACT is internal psychological experience, such as emotions, thoughts, and sensations (Bach & Moran, 2008; Hayes, 2004; Hayes & Strosahl, 2004). Too often, individuals who struggle with psychological problems have not accepted these private events but have dodged and ducked them via distraction. This kind of experiential avoidance (as described above) can underlie all kinds of psychological problems (Eifert & Forsyth, 2005). It's a bit like a phobia, but the feared object is within rather than outside the individual. And just like phobias of dogs, snakes, or airplanes, avoidance is a common but ultimately unhelpful coping mechanism. So, in this context, acceptance means facing one's *internal* fears.

Web Link 15.4

Website of Steven Hayes

Hayes (2004) presents a couple of metaphors that clarify the basic tenets of acceptance within ACT. For one, he asks us to imagine our thoughts as a parade. In this parade, we are spectators, not participants. As our thoughts march by, we notice them, certainly, but how long can we let the parade flow without reacting to them—without joining the parade or trying to stop it or otherwise getting drawn in? The longer we can acknowledge our thoughts without compulsively reacting to them, according to Hayes, the better our chances of psychological well-being. In a second metaphor, Hayes compares the process of accepting internal experiences to jumping off a step rather than stepping down from it. Stepping down feels safer, he says, because we maintain control the whole time. Jumping down gives all the control to gravity. Clients, according to Hayes, need to "practice jumping" with regard to their thoughts, feelings, and sensations. That is, little by little, they need to stop battling for control with these experiences and simply trust that wherever the experiences drop them, they will be able to land safely and continue on their way.

The *C* in ACT refers to a commitment to one's own personal values. Of course, for many clients, clarification must come before commitment. That is, therapy must first help the client discover exactly what his or her personal values are. Once this happens, the client is poised to make a commitment to remaining true to these values in terms of his or her day-to-day decisions and behaviors. And the *T* in ACT refers to taking action consistent with one's own personal values; here, we see the behavioral emphasis inherent in ACT that connects the client's new way of thinking with new ways of living.

Hayes and others (e.g., Eifert & Forsyth, 2005; Hayes & Strosahl, 2004) describe a pair of acronyms to explain the problematic approach that underlies psychological illness, as well as their strategy for psychological wellness. Essentially, FEAR is replaced by ACT. To explain, FEAR stands for

- *Fusion* with inner experiences such as thoughts, feelings, and sensations that limits flexibility in responding;
- *Evaluation* of self, especially one's own inner experiences;
- *Avoidance* of unpleasant inner experiences via such means as distracting or numbing oneself; and
- *Reason-giving,* or leaning too heavily on rationalizations that sound legitimate but actually perpetuate unhealthy approaches to life.

ACT, on the other hand, stands for

- *Accepting* one's own inner experiences for what they are, and nothing more;
- *Choosing* directions in life based on one's core values, which will enhance life's meaning and purpose; and
- *Taking action* in matters large and small that are consonant with one's own values.

Dialectical Behavior Therapy

Dialectical behavior therapy (DBT) was developed by **Marsha Linehan** specifically for the treatment of borderline personality disorder (BPD) (Koerner, 2012; Koerner & Dimeff,

2007; Linehan, 1993a, 1993b). The treatment has garnered a notable level of empirical support, such that it is now considered a treatment of choice for BPD, and in adapted form it is also used successfully for other disorders (Dimeff & Koerner, 2007; Kliem, Kröger, & Kosfelder, 2010; Lynch, Trost, Salsman, & Linehan, 2007; Paris, 2009).

⊕ **Web Link 15.5**

Website of
Marsha Linehan

DBT is based on a conceptualization of BPD as a problem of emotional regulation. In other words, across most aspects of their lives, individuals with BPD struggle to control the intensity of their feelings (Linehan, 1993a). Emotional dysregulation is thought to stem from two sources: biological predisposition and environment. Specifically, the environmental component is an invalidating interpersonal environment. That is, individuals who develop BPD often come from families who "communicate that the individual's characteristic responses to events (particularly his or her emotional responses) are incorrect, inappropriate, pathological, or not to be taken seriously" (Koerner & Dimeff, 2007, p. 3). Such an environment teaches the individual that only extreme emotional reactions will elicit a response from others, so they often communicate very intense displays of emotion when others might see such displays as excessive or unnecessary. This can explain why individuals with BPD are often very draining to friends and family (not to mention therapists) and why they threaten and attempt suicide at a high rate (Wheelis, 2009).

A few core practices are central to DBT: problem solving, validation, and dialectics. When DBT therapists work with clients on problem solving, they help clients "think through" stressful situations that might otherwise evoke an extreme emotional response. In a pragmatic way, they encourage clients to strategize for the best possible outcome, considering what will happen if they act on emotional impulses versus taking more deliberate actions. Additionally, the problem-solving component of DBT includes some discussion of the factors that might have inhibited effective problem solving in the past and how the client can overcome those factors in the present and the future. The validation component of DBT focuses on the client's feelings, which (as stated earlier) have typically not been validated in the past. Compared with empathy, which is commonplace among many therapies, validation as practiced in DBT is much stronger. It directly, persuasively communicates to BPD clients that their feelings are both important and a sensible reaction to their situation. The dialectics involved in DBT refer to exchanges between client and therapist intended to resolve simultaneous, contradictory feelings held by the client and arrive at the truth of their emotions. For example, clients may express a wish to kill themselves yet not do so. In such a situation, the DBT therapist, with a balance of respect and confrontation, can point out that the client has a wish to live as well as a wish to die and can discuss with the client ways in which the healthier wishes can be strengthened (Dimeff & Koerner, 2007; Koerner, 2012; Koerner & Dimeff, 2007; Wheelis, 2009).

Linehan (1993b) includes four specific modules of skills training within DBT. Collectively, they relate closely to the core components of DBT described above, but they are best described as problem-solving strategies that therapists teach to clients. The skills include:

- emotion regulation, which involves identifying, describing, and accepting rather than avoiding negative emotions;
- distress tolerance, which emphasizes the development of self-soothing techniques and impulse control to help clients with BPD minimize such behaviors as suicide attempts, self-harm, and drug abuse;
- interpersonal effectiveness, which helps clients determine appropriately assertive social skills in order to preserve relationships that might otherwise be damaged by extreme emotional outbursts; and
- mindfulness skills, which encourage clients to engage fully in their present lives, including their internal experiences, such as feelings, thoughts, and sensations, without avoidance or evaluation.

Metacognitive Therapy

In traditional cognitive therapy, as practiced by Albert Ellis, the irrational belief is brought on by an "activating event" (A in the ABCDE model). The primary idea in the relatively new practice of **metacognitive therapy** is that the activating event can be a cognition itself rather than some external occurrence. Simply stated, people can become depressed, anxious, or otherwise psychologically unwell because of reactions to their own thoughts rather than their reactions to the things that happen to them (Fisher & Wells, 2009; Wells, 2009). So the cause of our unhappiness is just as likely to be *thoughts about thoughts* as thoughts about external events.

Metacognitive therapists frequently refer to the cognitive attentional syndrome (CAS), a term that describes a brooding, ruminative, problematic thinking style that can underlie many psychological problems. The CAS can include two types of specific thoughts about worry, positive and negative—and both cause trouble. Positive beliefs about worry may sound like this: "Worrying helps me prepare for the future. If I don't worry, I could get blindsided by something. The last thing I want to do is stop worrying." Negative beliefs about worry may sound like this: "Oh no, I have started worrying. Once I start, I'll never be able to stop. It's gonna be a terrible day now that the worrying is happening. This worry is totally out of control." Whatever the original, external event may have been—a failed exam, upsetting medical news, a relationship breakup, an unexpected financial expense—the client's thoughts about the event may pile up rather quickly, such that not just thoughts about the event but *thoughts about thoughts* about the event can be the most relevant trigger of the anxiety. As such, metacognitive therapists make thinking about thinking the primary focus of their interventions.

Metacognitive therapy has been applied primarily to anxiety disorders, including obsessive-compulsive disorders, posttraumatic stress disorder, and generalized anxiety disorder. Although it is a relatively new treatment, evidence for its effectiveness with these disorders has started to appear (Clark & Beck, 2010; Fisher & Wells, 2008; Wells et al., 2008; Wells & King, 2006).

Cognitive Therapy for Medical Problems

The relationship between mind and body can strongly influence the way an individual deals with a medical problem. Of particular interest to cognitive therapists are the beliefs that medical patients hold regarding their illness, injury, or condition. How will it affect them? How will their family members respond or cope with it? How well will treatment work? What negative effects might treatment have? Irrational answers to these questions could unnecessarily hinder recovery, and, moreover, they could cause excessive worry or despair in the process.

In recent decades, numerous studies have indicated that cognitive therapy can have a significantly beneficial effect on the healing process and the ultimate prognosis of medical patients. For example, Jakes, Hallam, McKenna, and Hinchcliffe (1992) examined the effect of cognitive therapy on patients with tinnitus, an auditory problem involving excessive perception of noises. Some of these patients underwent a brief form of cognitive therapy in which their illogical beliefs about the disease were corrected. Compared with patients who did not receive this cognitive therapy, those who did demonstrated significant improvement regarding their level of distress about tinnitus. Cognitive therapy has been successfully applied to many other medical problems as well, including chronic headache, chronic pain, premenstrual syndrome, sexual disorders, spinal cord injuries, and brain injury (Carter, Forys, & Oswald, 2008; Freeman & Greenwood, 1987; Jay, Elliott, Fitzgibbons, Woody, & Siegel, 1995).

As an example of the potential of cognitive therapy to positively influence the lives of medical patients, consider Jackie, a 45-year-old woman recently diagnosed in the very early stages of breast cancer. Understandably, Jackie is distressed by the diagnosis, but some of her initial beliefs about the disease are in fact illogical, and these thoughts make her more distraught than she needs to be. For example, Jackie firmly believes, "I'm going to die," "I'll need chemotherapy, which will be so painful and miserable that I won't be able to live through it," and "My family and friends will distance themselves from me if they find out." Although these may be possibilities, Jackie may be overestimating their likelihood and, in the process, convincing herself of a worst-case scenario. In cognitive therapy with Dr. Richards, her clinical psychologist, Jackie challenges the validity of these beliefs and learns to identify irrational thoughts and replace them with more rational thoughts. By the end of a brief course of therapy, Jackie remains concerned about her breast cancer but not excessively so. She is realistic rather than pessimistic: "I could die, but the odds are low because it was caught very early and I'm getting good care"; "I may not need chemotherapy, and if I do, it will be very unpleasant but tolerable"; and "I can't be sure how my family and friends will react, but their past behavior leads me to believe that most will be quite supportive." These new beliefs—free of catastrophizing, magnification, mind reading, or other distortions—produce in Jackie a better psychological state and a better medical prognosis as well.

How Well Does It Work?

The efficacy of cognitive therapy is strongly supported by a body of empirical evidence that is enormous and continues to grow. The range of psychological disorders for which cognitive therapy works is expansive, including depression, anxiety disorders, bulimia, posttraumatic stress disorder, hypochondriasis, numerous personality disorders, and others (Beck, 2002; Epp, Dobson, & Cottraux, 2009; Prochaska & Norcross, 2010; Roth et al., 2002). And, as stated earlier, studies support the use of cognitive therapy for some medical problems and some personality disorders as well. Evidence is accumulating for the third-wave, mindfulness-based therapies as well. DBT is particularly well-established as a treatment that works for borderline personality disorder and an increasingly wide range of additional disorders (Dimeff & Koerner, 2007; Kliem et al., 2010; Koerner, 2012; Lynch et al., 2007; Paris, 2009). ACT has also accumulated an impressive amount of empirical evidence in the treatment of various anxiety and mood disorders and some other disorders as well (Davis & Hayes, 2011; Hoffman, Sawyer, Witt, & Oh, 2010; Olatunji & Feldman, 2008; Roemer & Orsillo, 2009). Specific components of cognitive therapy have also received empirical support; for example, numerous studies have found that homework enhances therapy outcome in comparison with similar therapies that do not include homework (e.g., Dozois, 2010; Kazantzis, Whittington, & Dattilio, 2010).

As a result of its roots in the behavioral movement, cognitive therapists typically emphasize aspects of therapy that facilitate empirical evaluation, such as defining problems in terms that can be overtly measured and observed. If these terms are not blatantly behavioral, they may take the form of numerical ratings that clients assign to symptoms' severity (such as depressed mood or anxiety level) both before and after cognitive interventions. So, although a client's anxiety may rate a 90 on a 0 to 100 scale before therapy, it may drop to 60 after a few sessions and to 15 by the time therapy is complete. Such objectivity facilitates empirical outcome research designed to determine how well cognitive therapy works.

● ● ● BOX 15.4 ● ● ●

Denise in Cognitive Psychotherapy

In the first session with Denise, it was evident that her primary symptoms were depressive and that the event that precipitated these depressive symptoms was the change in ownership of the restaurant where she works as a chef. More specifically, the new owner's policies—instituting a menu over which Denise has no control and prohibiting her from visiting with customers in the dining room—seemed to have triggered Denise's depressive symptoms.

I proceeded to treat Denise using a style of cognitive therapy that included aspects of both Ellis's and Beck's techniques. First, I educated Denise about the cognitive model by explaining that although sometimes we experience life as if events directly cause feelings, there are, in fact, automatic thoughts or beliefs that intervene. I used Ellis's ABCDE model to further illustrate how Denise could understand her experience, and I provided her with a list of Beck's cognitive distortions to equip her with the tools she would need to dispute her irrational thoughts in Column D. Denise had no trouble filling in Columns A (activating event) and C (emotional consequence) of this model: The implementation of the new restaurant policies was the activating event, and her depressive symptoms represented the emotional consequence. Our next task was to identify the beliefs (B) that occurred between A and C. This was a bit of a struggle for Denise, but with some exploration and discussion, we identified this powerful thought: "I'm incompetent." Denise explained that she could think of no other reason why her new boss would bar her from determining the menu or from talking with diners. The boss's new policies, Denise believed, were motivated by the boss's desire to prevent Denise's incompetence from ruining the restaurant's business.

The next stage in therapy focused on Stage D (dispute), where I encouraged Denise to think critically about her belief (B) that she was incompetent. I asked a number of questions to facilitate this process, such as, "What evidence do you have that you are incompetent?" "What evidence do you have that you are not incompetent?" and "How else might we be able to interpret your new boss's policies?" At first, the notion of challenging her original (illogical) belief seemed foreign to Denise, and she struggled a bit with this task. But after a few sessions, it became more familiar and comfortable for her. Using homework assignments, I asked Denise to complete a five-column thought journal in which she identified not only activating events, beliefs, and emotional consequences but also disputes and effective new beliefs. These last two columns represented uncharted territory for Denise, but with time she became quite adept at completing the entire table. Specifically, Denise applied the following thought distortion labels:

- Personalization (Maybe the new boss would have implemented these new policies regardless of the chef who held Denise's position; if so, Denise need not take them personally.)
- Mental filtering (Denise had been extremely competent as a chef and in other capacities throughout her life, yet she was focusing exclusively on this presumed slight by her new boss.)
- All-or-nothing thinking (Denise may not share her new boss's preferences, but there were still many things she loved about working as a chef. Just because her job wasn't perfect, she need not think of it as terrible. Instead, it may fall somewhere in between.)

(Continued)

(Continued)

Individually, any of these disputes was effective enough to negate Denise's illogical thoughts of incompetence, and in combination they were especially potent. By the end of therapy, Denise was completing Column E (effective new belief) with ease: "I'm not incompetent at all. My new boss's actions may have little or nothing to do with me personally; I have plenty of evidence that I am a competent person, and even if I don't like my job as much as I used to, it's still enjoyable and fulfilling in some ways." As a result of her disputes and effective new beliefs, Denise's depressive symptoms improved dramatically.

CHAPTER SUMMARY

The primary goal of cognitive therapy, which has become the most commonly practiced approach to psychotherapy among clinical psychologists, is to promote logical thinking. Cognitive therapists accomplish this goal by helping clients recognize and revise cognitions that are illogical or irrational during a course of therapy that is typically brief, structured, and problem focused. Their techniques involve teaching clients about the cognitive model, in which cognitions intervene between events and feelings, and assigning written or behavioral homework to be completed between sessions. Whether using Albert Ellis's ABCDE model (highlighted by disputing irrational beliefs and replacing them with effective new beliefs) or Aaron Beck's list of common thought distortions (e.g., all-or-nothing thinking, personalization, magnification/minimization), cognitive therapists enable clients to overcome psychological and behavioral problems by insisting on a logical response to the events of their lives. Although cognitive therapy originally targeted anxiety and mood disorders, it is now applied to most other psychological disorders, including personality disorders, and to other issues such as medical problems and minor psychological problems that fall short of diagnostic criteria. A large and increasing body of outcome studies suggests that cognitive therapy is highly efficacious for a wide range of psychological disorders, including mood disorders, anxiety disorders, eating disorders, and others.

KEY TERMS AND NAMES

CRITICAL THINKING QUESTIONS

1. To what extent do you agree with the fundamental cognitive assumption that illogical or irrational thinking underlies psychological problems?

2. If you were the client, how would you respond to the assignment of homework by your therapist?

3. If you were a clinical psychologist practicing cognitive therapy, which of Albert Ellis's ABCDE columns would you expect clients to have the most trouble filling in?

4. In your opinion, do any of the common thought distortions that Aaron Beck and his followers defined seem to predispose individuals to particular types of psychological problems (e.g., anxiety, depression, others)?

5. What are the primary differences between traditional cognitive therapy and the more recently developed metacognitive therapy?

STUDENT STUDY SITE RESOURCES

Visit the study site at www.sagepub.com/pomerantz3eupdate for these additional learning tools:

- Self-quizzes
- eFlashcards
- Culture Expert Interviews
- Full-text SAGE journal articles
- Additional web resources
- Mock Assessment Data

CHAPTER SUMMARY VIDEO

 QR codes at the end of each chapter link to chapter background videos by the author. Visit http://gettag.mobi using your smartphone browser to download the free Microsoft Tag app. Once installed, scan the tags to go directly to these brief videos. In this video, the author describes his experience educating his clients about the three-step model, especially the middle step, at the center of the cognitive approach to psychotherapy.

CHAPTER

16

Group and Family Therapy

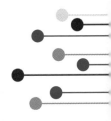

Group therapy and family therapy represent a departure from the individual forms of therapy we've covered so far. Both feature multiple clients in the room together, and both emphasize interpersonal interaction. However, despite the fact that they share a chapter in this book, they differ markedly from each other. Group therapy and family therapy have quite separate histories, and they represent distinct specializations within the mental health field. It would not be unusual to meet a clinical psychologist who practices one regularly but the other rarely or never. Thus, this chapter is divided into separate sections for group and family therapy.

Group Therapy
....

An Interpersonal Emphasis

Group therapy is practiced in a wide variety of forms, including adaptations of many well-known individual therapy approaches such as psychodynamic, behavioral, cognitive, humanistic-existential, and many others (Hopper, Kaklauskas, & Greene, 2008; MacKenzie, 2002; Shaffer & Galinsky, 1989). Most of these group therapies strongly emphasize **interpersonal interaction.** That is, most forms of group therapy take advantage of the fact that the group therapy experience itself is based on interacting with other people. Group therapists' interventions often highlight the way group members feel, communicate, and form relationships with one another. More than any other component, it is this accent on interpersonal interaction that distinguishes group therapy from individual therapy (Burlingame & Baldwin, 2011). Whereas individual therapy is limited to a two-person interaction between client and therapist, group therapy allows for a far more complex network of relationships to develop. In group therapy, a client forms relationships not only with a therapist but also with a room full of other people. Thus, group therapy involves a greater range of interpersonal responses.

⊕ **Web Link 16.1**

American Group
Psychotherapy
Association

⊕ **Web Link 16.2**

Irvin Yalom
demonstrating
group therapy

Irvin Yalom has emerged as a leading figure in the interpersonal approach to group therapy (Brabender, 2002; Burlingame & Baldwin, 2011; Friedman, 1989). In fact, the term *interpersonal* has been used as a label for his approach to group therapy, and his writings (e.g., Yalom, 1983, 2005) have influenced group therapists of all kinds. According to Yalom (2005), although it may be possible to conduct group therapy as a series of one-on-one interactions between therapist and clients, such an approach fails to "reap the full therapeutic harvest" (p. xv) that group therapy can offer. Instead, he encourages group therapists to recognize the unique opportunity that group therapy presents: the display of clients' problematic interpersonal tendencies in the group itself.

Yalom (2005) views these problematic interpersonal tendencies as central to clients' presenting problems, whether or not clients initially recognize it. In fact, he argues that all psychological problems stem from flawed interpersonal relationships, as exemplified by his comments about depression: "Therapists cannot, for example, treat depression per se . . . *it is necessary first to translate the depression into interpersonal terms and then to treat the underlying interpersonal pathology*" (p. 24). This definition of depression differs considerably from traditional medical-model definitions that emphasize intrapersonal or biological roots of disorders. Instead, according to Yalom, an individual's disorder is a byproduct of his or her disturbed way of getting along with other people. If interpersonal relationship problems are the core of all psychopathology, it follows that a primary focus of group therapy would be the strengthening of interpersonal relationship skills.

Therapeutic Factors in Group Therapy

Yalom (2005) describes 11 specific therapeutic factors by which group therapy benefits clients; Table 16.1 outlines the full list. Several of the factors that are especially vital to a fundamental understanding of group therapy are described here in more detail.

Universality

Clients with psychological problems often believe that no one shares their struggles. They may be unaware of the commonality of their problems, symptoms, or diagnoses. To find oneself in a room full of other people who have similar problems can be uplifting in and of itself. Yalom (2005) describes this phenomenon as **universality.**

If the group is organized around a single problem—eating disorders, panic disorder, chemical dependency, and so on—clients may experience this "we're all in the same boat" feeling right away. Universality is built into **homogeneous groups** such as these. In **heterogeneous groups,** however, universality may not be quite as obvious from the outset. With time, however, clients in heterogeneous groups often come to realize that although their symptoms may differ superficially, the fundamental issues that underlie them may in fact be quite similar. Whether homogeneous or heterogeneous, groups provide clients with the sense that they are not alone in a way that individual therapy cannot.

Table 16.1 Yalom's Therapeutic Factors for Group Psychotherapy

1. Instillation of hope
2. Universality
3. Imparting information
4. Altruism
5. Corrective recapitulation of the primary family group
6. Development of socializing techniques
7. Imitative behavior
8. Interpersonal learning
9. Group cohesiveness
10. Catharsis
11. Existential factors

Source: Adapted from Yalom (2005).

Group Cohesiveness

Group cohesiveness refers to feelings of interconnectedness among group members. This interconnectedness is characterized by feelings of warmth, trust, acceptance, belongingness, and value among group members. Participating in an ongoing group of this kind bolsters psychological wellness.

Yalom (2005) and others (e.g., Ormont, 1992) point out that group cohesiveness does not necessarily mean that every group interaction will be polite or courteous. In fact, an ongoing group interaction devoid of negative emotion may actually indicate that the group lacks cohesiveness. Truly cohesive therapy groups—such as cohesive families, work groups, or teams—are strong enough to tolerate anger, sadness, jealousy, disappointment, and the like. They understand that as people become meaningful to one another, they often elicit strong feelings, and they encourage the discussion of those feelings even when doing so is unpleasant or awkward.

Cohesiveness plays the same role in group therapy that the therapeutic relationship/alliance plays in individual therapy. It heals in its own right, and it also sets the stage for other healing factors to take effect (Burlingame, McClendon, & Alonso, 2011; Yalom, 2005). However, whereas a client's perception of the therapeutic alliance in individual therapy involves only one other person, the client's perception of group cohesiveness involves many other people. Thus, for group therapists, it is crucial not only to maintain a trusting, collaborative relationship directly with the client but to foster a group in which clients develop trusting, collaborative relationships with one another as well.

Interpersonal Learning

Learning from the in-group interpersonal experience—**interpersonal learning**—is at the heart of group therapy. Group therapists presume that interpersonal problems contribute to the client's reason for seeking therapy in the first place, that the same interpersonal tendencies will appear within the group, and that the lessons learned via interacting with fellow group members will generalize to clients' lives outside the group. In simple terms, group therapy provides an opportunity for "relationship practice." Much like a group of actors rehearses before a performance or an athletic team scrimmages before a game, members of a therapy group use group meetings as a place to identify problematic relationship tendencies and attempt to revise them. In other words, group members don't just talk about relationships; they form relationships with one another and work to improve them with the assumption that their gains will ultimately benefit their personal relationships outside the group as well.

Social Microcosm   As group therapy progresses, the group becomes a **social microcosm** for each member (Ormont, 1992; Yalom, 2005). In other words, the relationship tendencies that characterize clients' relationships with important people in their personal lives—romantic partners, friends, coworkers, children, siblings, and so on—will predictably characterize the relationships they form with their fellow group members. As Yalom (2005) explains,

> Clients will, over time, automatically and inevitably begin to display their maladaptive interpersonal behavior in the therapy group. There is no need for them to describe or give a detailed history of their pathology: they will sooner or later enact it before the other group members' eyes. (p. 32)

Thus, a client whose unwarranted suspiciousness of his wife is damaging his marriage will probably become overly suspicious of a fellow group member at some point, a client whose passive-aggressive behavior has cost her many friendships may likely behave passive-aggressively toward a fellow group member, and a client whose pessimism has convinced him that searching for a rewarding job is pointless may pessimistically deem the group therapy process as similarly pointless.

The Here and Now   Because the group functions as a social microcosm, an essential task for the group therapist is continually to shine the spotlight on the way members relate to one another within the context of the group. So, rather than encouraging clients to talk about events that have happened in their lives outside the group ("there" and "then"), the group therapist steers clients toward examining the relationships among group members **here and now.**

Photo 16.1 Group therapists encourage clients to discuss the here-and-now relationships they develop with other members of the group.

Specifically, Yalom (2005) promotes two activities among group members to maximize the use of the here and now: interaction (which he calls "experience") and reflection/discussion of that interaction (which he calls "illumination of process"). In other words, through the natural course of their continued interaction, group members communicate directly with one another—perhaps expressing happiness, boredom, dissatisfaction, envy, curiosity, confusion, or rage. The group therapist urges clients to reflect on this process, to talk about the way clients talk to one another, and to enlighten each member about his or her interpersonal tendencies. Once they learn about their tendencies, clients may decide to change them, which could improve the relationships they have within and, ultimately, outside the group.

Group therapy is one of the few social situations in which people are encouraged to talk with others about the way they relate to one another. More often, this is strongly discouraged in social relationships. For example, people who are interpersonally challenging, annoying, or frustrating might see numerous relationships end without receiving any **feedback** about their behavior. They might drive away friends, romantic partners, or employers without hearing directly from them exactly what they did to contribute to the demise of the relationship. For this reason, group therapy represents a unique opportunity for individuals to receive genuine, honest feedback on their behavior and its impact. This feedback often motivates clients to change their behavior, at which point the group becomes a place to try out and practice novel responses in anticipation of incorporating them into clients' lives outside therapy (Ormont, 1992; Yalom, 2005).

As an example, consider a group therapy scenario in which Ron, a very self-centered, narcissistic, and insensitive man, and Michelle, a timid and nervous woman, are among the members. In one session, when Michelle has been discussing her problems for a few minutes, Ron interrupts rudely with comments such as, "How long is this going to go on?" and "Just get over it already—I have some real problems to talk about." Michelle responds to Ron's interruptions by meekly apologizing for taking up so much time. Dr. Hollins, the group therapist, notices this interaction and asks the group, "What do you think about the way Ron and Michelle communicate with each other?" One by one, the group members other than Ron and Michelle offer very similar comments: Ron's behavior is rude and inappropriate, and Michelle's apology was unnecessary. They also add that they find Ron's rudeness unattractive and have a hard time respecting Michelle when she acts so timidly.

Dr. Hollins turns to Michelle and asks questions to explore her tendency to apologize rather than assert herself ("What stops you from confronting Ron about his behavior?" "What options do you have besides apologizing?") and later turns to Ron to explore his tendency to interrupt selfishly ("How does it make you feel to know that others see your behavior as rude and inappropriate?" "How else might you respond to Michelle in that situation?"). These lines of questioning allow Michelle and Ron to see their own behavior in a new light. Specifically, they see how their behavior impacts others and how others' reactions to their behavior subsequently affect their own happiness. Both Michelle and Ron find themselves motivated to change, and the group setting becomes a supportive place for them to practice doing so. The outcome is not only improved interpersonal behavior within the session but also real-life benefits for Michelle and Ron, whose relationships with their respective spouses were on shaky ground largely because of Ron's self-centeredness and Michelle's submissiveness.

Practical Issues in Group Therapy

Group Membership

Groups typically include 5 to 10 clients, and many group therapists find that having 7 to 8 members in a group is ideal (Brabender, 2002; Yalom, 2005). Groups can be either open or closed in terms of enrollment. **Open-enrollment groups** allow individual members to enter or leave the group at any time. A strength of such groups is that at any given point in time, the group includes members at various stages of improvement. Thus, like college freshmen sharing classes with seniors, new group members have experienced models to follow. In **closed-enrollment groups,** all members start and finish therapy together, with no new members added during the process. In this type of group, cohesiveness can be easier to establish and maintain than in open-enrollment groups because of the stability of membership.

Unless a group centers on a particular diagnostic issue, group therapists are typically rather open about clients they might select for a particular group. In fact, greater variability in terms of presenting problems and demographic variables can create a more realistic social microcosm. Typically, characteristics that would cause a group therapist not to select a prospective member include those that would interfere with the client's ability to interact meaningfully with others and reflect on that interaction. Such characteristics often include psychosis, organic brain damage, acute crisis, and pragmatic issues such as travel or transportation that would interfere with regular attendance (Friedman, 1989; Yalom, 2005).

Preparing Clients for Group Therapy

It is clinically wise to make concerted efforts to prepare new clients for the group therapy experience to correct any misconceptions and maximize therapeutic benefit (Brabender, Fallon, & Smolar, 2004). Some clients may mistakenly believe that group therapy is second-rate (in comparison to individual therapy), that they will immediately be forced to disclose intimate personal details to strangers, or that interacting with other people with psychological problems will somehow worsen their own symptoms (MacKenzie, 2002). In pregroup individual meetings, group therapists can assure clients that such notions are false and can provide realistic and encouraging data about how well their therapy works for most clients. In addition, group therapists can orient clients to the kinds of activities that will take place in group therapy and the behaviors that can maximize the benefit they receive, such as active participation and consistent, punctual attendance.

Developmental Stages of Therapy Groups

With time, therapy groups tend to move through a predictable set of stages. These stages have been assigned a variety of different labels (e.g., Brabender et al., 2004; MacKenzie, 2002; Tuckman, 1965; Yalom, 2005), but they have quite similar meanings. In general, clients in the initial stage of group therapy are cautious and concerned about whether they will be accepted into the group. After they overcome these initial concerns, they move onto a second stage in which there is some competition or jockeying for position within the social pecking order. Eventually, this competitive second stage gives way to a third stage in which cohesiveness forms, members feel closely connected and trusting of one another, and the group sessions become more consistently productive as clients learn about and improve on their interpersonal skills.

Cotherapists

In group therapy settings, two therapists often colead a single group. Such an arrangement presents numerous potential advantages and pitfalls. One advantage of a **cotherapist** is the mere presence of a second set of eyes and ears to notice the rich array of verbal and nonverbal communication inevitably produced by a room full of clients. A second advantage involves the cotherapists' ability to model collaborative relationships for group members. Among group members whose previous models of two-person teams (parents, etc.) used destructive or hurtful tactics, the power of two partners working together constructively can be compelling. A third advantage, at least for clients who grew up in two-parent homes, is a **recapitulation of the family group.** With one male and one female cotherapist, for example, a group can evoke the same dynamics as a traditional family, and the way clients from such families respond to each cotherapist—trusting one while fearing the other, for example—can shed light on their interpersonal tendencies with other important people in their lives (Shapiro, 1999; Yalom, 2005).

The potential pitfalls of cotherapy come into play when the cotherapists don't trust each other, compete with each other, or "step on each other's toes" by approaching group therapy with incompatible therapy orientations. Their styles need not be identical—in fact, the group may benefit from somewhat distinct but complementary therapists—but cotherapists do need to be able to work well together both in and out of session. Of course, leading a group as a solo therapist is also a common practice.

Socializing Between Clients

Clients who socialize with one another outside therapy groups constitute a significant problem for group therapists. Often, group therapists educate clients about this potential problem and prohibit it during the pregroup preparation. Nonetheless, it happens with some frequency, as might be expected among clients who find themselves feeling increasingly connected to new people.

The negative consequences of **extra-group socializing** among clients, whether romantic or platonic, are many (Brabender et al., 2004; Yalom, 2005). For example, if Karen and Dena are members of the same therapy group and develop a friendship outside the group, they may become more loyal to their friendship than they are to the group as a whole. They may be reluctant to comment frankly on each other's behavior in front of the group, or they may save their most direct, meaningful exchanges for private moments rather than sharing them during group sessions. In this way, they can become spectators rather than active participants in the group process. Moreover, the exclusiveness of their relationship can adversely affect those members who feel "left out." Group therapists can respond punitively to socializing outside the group, but such behavior can also provide meaningful material for therapy sessions, especially if such defiant or secretive behavior is related to the reasons the client sought treatment in the first place.

Ethical Issues in Group Therapy

Confidentiality

⊕ **Web Link 16.3**
Ethical issues in group psychotherapy

Among the ethical issues especially relevant to group therapy, **confidentiality** is perhaps most concerning. The focus here is not on the group therapist maintaining clients' confidentiality, because this is assured by professional ethics and standards. Instead, the focus is on the possibility that fellow group members might violate a client's confidentiality (Brabender, 2002; Brabender et al., 2004; Lasky & Riva, 2006; Shaffer & Galinsky, 1989). At the outset, group therapists often require clients to agree in writing to hold material from group sessions confidential, but such contracts are "virtually impossible to enforce" (Shaffer & Galinsky, 1989, p. 266).

The consequences of one client violating the confidentiality of another can seriously affect the professional or personal life of the client whose confidentiality has been violated. Moreover, such breaches make the therapy group seem unsafe and untrustworthy, which decreases self-disclosure by other clients. Thus, it is important for the group therapist to do as much as possible to prevent such confidentiality violations. In addition to asking clients to commit to confidentiality during pregroup preparations, therapists' preventive actions can include exemplifying impeccable behavior regarding confidentiality, frequent reminders about confidentiality, and group discussion of any confidentiality violations that do occur (Brabender et al., 2004; Knauss & Knauss, 2012).

How Well Does It Work?

Although the outcome of group therapy has not been studied as extensively as that of individual therapy, the existing empirical research indicates that group therapy works. Specifically, meta-analyses and reviews have consistently found that group therapy is superior to no treatment and generally as effective as individual therapy, although a minority of comparative studies have found individual therapy to be slightly superior (e.g., Burlingame, Fuhriman, & Mosier, 2003; Fuhriman & Burlingame, 1994; McDermut, Miller, & Brown, 2001; McRoberts, Burlingame, & Hoag, 1998; Robinson, Berman, & Neimeyer, 1990; Tillitski, 1990; Vandervoort & Fuhriman, 1991). Moreover, the range of disorders and presenting problems for which group therapy has been found effective is very broad. Also, as described earlier, empirical research indicates that cohesiveness within the group, much like the therapeutic relationship in individual therapy, is a major contributor to successful outcome in group therapy (Burlingame et al., 2011).

It is worth noting that, whereas the outcomes of group and individual therapies are often comparable, group therapy tends to be a less expensive mode of therapy. In this way, group therapy may be a particularly cost-effective approach to therapy (Brabender, 2002; Friedman, 1989).

Denise in Group Therapy

Denise was remarkably quiet during the first five group therapy sessions. Clients often take time to develop trust and feel comfortable in the group, but Denise seemed to take longer than most. Eventually, during the sixth session, Denise spoke about the reasons why she had sought therapy in the first place. Our group—seven clients besides Denise, plus myself and my cotherapist—listened intently as Denise summarized the recent changes at the restaurant where she was the head chef, as well as the depressive symptoms she had experienced as a result.

After Denise had finished the summary and several of the group members had offered sympathy and understanding, my cotherapist posed a question to the group: "How do you feel about Denise's decision to share her story with the group today?" One by one, the group members each mentioned that they were very happy that Denise had become more engaged in the group. Many added that they hoped to hear more from her in upcoming sessions as well. I turned to Denise and asked, "What's your reaction to this consensus from your fellow group members?" Denise responded that she was surprised and relieved to hear it. Several group members seemed perplexed by this, so Denise explained:

> I just haven't felt like it was OK for me to speak up. I never felt like I had the right to take group time away from someone else. No one was directly asking me what was going on with me, so I thought it would be rude just to demand everyone's attention. I thought that would make everyone dislike me. So I just sat quietly, even though I really wanted to share this stuff as soon as I got here.

My cotherapist asked the group if they would have responded the way Denise assumed if she had spoken up earlier, and, of course, they all said no. By the end of that session, Denise seemed to have experienced a meaningful interaction with her fellow group members: She learned that although she assumed they'd dislike her for asserting herself, doing so made them like her more. She genuinely stated she would feel more comfortable speaking up in group in the future, and, in fact, she did so.

The next session, my cotherapist and I planned to pursue this topic with Denise. Our hypothesis was that the lesson Denise learned in the previous session might be applicable to her relationships outside therapy. In fact, we wondered if this issue might play a role in the very problems that caused her to seek therapy in the first place. As the session began, one of Denise's fellow group members got the conversation going by asking Denise a relevant follow-up question: "Have you ever told your new boss how you feel about the new policies at the restaurant?" Denise said no, she never had, and the thought of doing so made her nervous. She assumed that the new boss would dislike her and possibly even fire her for speaking up. Her fellow group members, my cotherapist, and I pointed out the parallels between her assumptions about her new boss and her assumptions about her fellow group members, which had proven completely false.

Over the next few sessions, Denise considered and gradually came to accept the idea that perhaps her tendency to believe that others want her to stay quiet rather than speak up led her to misperceive other people in numerous situations, including the situation with her new boss, and that the result was often sadness and dejection for Denise. Eventually, Denise had a meaningful discussion with her new boss about the new restaurant policies. The new boss was willing to compromise with Denise, allowing her to determine the menu on selected nights but standing firm on his new rule that Denise not visit with diners. Perhaps more important, the new boss had absolutely no hard feelings toward Denise for speaking up about this and, in fact, thanked her for doing so. Denise was quite happy and proud, not so much because she was able to determine the menu some evenings but because she had identified a flawed interpersonal tendency and corrected it both in and out of the group. As group therapy concluded for Denise, she felt especially optimistic about her ability to form healthy relationships and to prevent additional bouts of depression in the future.

Family Therapy

The System as the Problem

When the **family therapy** movement initially arose in the mid-1900s, it was considered revolutionary. Its leaders were seen as mavericks who had formulated an original way of conceptualizing psychological problems and their causes (Nichols, 2010). Specifically, they opposed the widely accepted notion that psychological symptoms originated from solely *within* the mind of the individual. Instead, they believed that psychological symptoms were a byproduct of the dysfunctional families in which the clients lived (Kaslow, 2011). One individual may exhibit the symptoms, but the problem actually belonged to the entire system (Rolland & Walsh, 2009).

With this simple yet profound theory, the pioneers of family therapy opened the door to a fundamentally different mode of treatment in which family members worked together

⊕ **Web Link 16.4**

American Association of Marriage and Family Therapy

Photo 16.2 Family therapists believe that improving relationships between family members will enhance the psychological wellness of individuals within that system. In your opinion, to what extent are psychological disorders due to problems in family relationships?

with a therapist to improve their interactions, which in turn strengthened the mental health of each member. Family therapists actually borrowed this **systems approach,** in which the whole is more than the sum of the parts, from philosophy and the sciences (Becvar & Becvar, 1982; Laszlo, 1972; Rolland & Walsh, 2009). Central to this systems approach is the idea that circular causality explains psychological problems better than does linear causality. **Linear causality,** which tends to be endorsed by individual therapists, suggests that events from the past cause or determine events in the present in a unidirectional or "one-way–street" manner. That is, the way a parent treats a child influences the child's subsequent behavior. **Circular causality,** on the other hand, suggests that events influence one another in a reciprocal way, such that a parent's and a child's behavior each affect the other continuously (more like a "two-way street"). Thus, family therapists tend to believe that regardless of the original cause of a problematic behavior, it is maintained over time by mutually influential, ongoing interaction between family members. See Figure 16.1 for a comparison of linear and circular causality.

Typically, family therapists have pointed to unhealthy **communication patterns** among family members as the type of interaction that most significantly contributes to psychological problems. Early in the history of family therapy, numerous theorists attempted to make connections between particular communication patterns and pathological outcomes in family members. Two well-known examples are the theory of the schizophrenogenic mother (Fromm-Reichmann, 1948)—cold, authoritarian mothers in combination with ineffectual fathers were thought to cause schizophrenic symptoms in their children—and the double-bind theory (Bateson, Jackson, Haley, & Weakland, 1956)—parents who consistently gave their children inescapable mixed-message commands also supposedly caused schizophrenic symptoms. Today, these two particular theories are neither widely held nor empirically supported, especially as findings regarding the biological factors underlying schizophrenia have been strongly established. However, they remain historically relevant as early attempts to link family communication patterns with symptoms of mental illness in individuals.

Another important feature of systems theory as applied to family therapy is its emphasis on **functionalism.** Specifically, family therapists believe that although psychological symptoms may appear maladaptive, they are in fact functional within the individual's family environment. So even though the symptoms may qualify an individual as abnormal according to the *Diagnostic and Statistical Manual of Mental Disorders* (DSM), viewed in the larger context, those symptoms actually benefit the family's overall functioning in some way. For example, consider a family in which the parents' marriage is on shaky ground. Their fighting escalates to the point that their two children sense that a separation or divorce may be imminent. If one of the kids develops an eating disorder, attention-deficit/hyperactivity disorder, or another psychological problem, one effect of his or her symptoms may be that the parents stop arguing and unite in their focus on the child. In this way, the child's symptom actually serves the purpose of reducing the marital

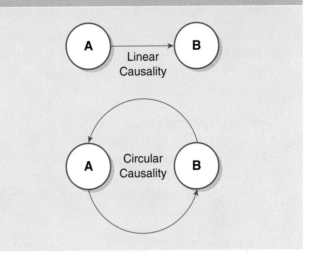

FIGURE 16.1 Unlike individual therapists, who tend to endorse linear causality, family therapists tend to endorse circular causality

conflict and holding the family together. Family therapists do not believe that children consciously or deliberately plan these psychological problems, but they do suggest that family members can perceive tension within their own families and that on some level, this tension can contribute to the development of psychological problems in certain family members (Goldenberg & Goldenberg, 2007; Nichols, 2010).

The idea that family members can perceive tension within families relates closely to another core idea of systems theory: homeostasis. The notion of **homeostasis** suggests that systems have the ability to regulate themselves by returning themselves to a comfort zone or "set point." A thermostat is perhaps the most common example of a homeostatic system. If the thermostat is set at 72 degrees, the system is programmed to detect variations from this temperature and take action—cool or heat the room—to return the temperature back to 72. In much the same way, families have emotional or behavioral comfort zones, and when family members detect that the family is straying from theirs, they may take action to bring the family back. Family therapists often call these actions feedback, and these behaviors may, if viewed in isolation, qualify an individual for a mental disorder: conduct disorder, oppositional defiant disorder, depression, or substance abuse, to name a few. But in the view of family therapists, if the symptoms effectively return the family to a more familiar, comfortable, safe way of interacting, they have served a valuable and often unrecognized function within the context of the family (Hanna, 2007).

Considering Culture

Gender, Abuse, and Family Therapy

Family therapists endorse the notion of circular causality, which contends that problematic behavior within families is part of a complex pattern in which numerous individuals play a role. In other words, although one person may exhibit the symptom, other family members may contribute to the problem in a reciprocal way.

How does this theory apply to abuse within families? Specifically, if one partner (for example, a husband) acts violently toward the other (for example, a wife), does the notion of circular causality suggest that her behavior somehow contributes to his violence? Is violent, abusive behavior indeed a systemic problem that multiple family members maintain, or does the problem belong solely to the abuser? If we conceptualize the problem systemically, are we blaming the victim?

Such critical questions have been raised repeatedly by feminist authors (e.g., Avis, 1992; Goldner, 1985; Hare-Mustin, 1978; Luepnitz, 1992; McGoldrick, Anderson, & Walsh, 1989; Silverstein & Goodrich, 2003). Family therapists are wise to give serious thought to these questions for a variety of reasons. For one, data on the incidence of violence of men toward women in couple relationships suggests that it is quite common: Each year, one in eight husbands engages in physical aggression toward his wife; at least 30% of married couples experience physical aggression at some point in the marriage; and when violence occurs in couple relationships, it tends to continue (Holtzworth-Munroe, Meehan, Rehman, & Marshall, 2002).

In addition to remaining sensitive to the possibility that violence may be occurring, family therapists should also remain sensitive to the messages they communicate to family members about violence. Those who pose the above questions about family therapy generally argue that attributing any responsibility to women being abused by men represents a particularly harmful form of blaming the victim and that the abuser is ultimately responsible for his own behavior. They further warn family therapists not to insensitively or mistakenly apply the notion of circular causality to family situations in which men abuse women.

In your opinion, how does the notion of circular causality apply to families or relationships in which men abuse women? How can family therapists most sensitively and therapeutically understand such problems?

Assessment of Families

As in clinical work with individuals, family therapy usually begins with a thorough assessment of the family's functioning. In fact, the assessment process continues throughout therapy. Assessment practices may vary according to the particular approach to family therapy that the therapist uses, but they typically focus on such issues as defining the presenting problem, understanding family members' beliefs about its causes, and appreciating the relationships within the family (Griffin, 2002).

FIGURE 16.2   Genogram of the Simpsons

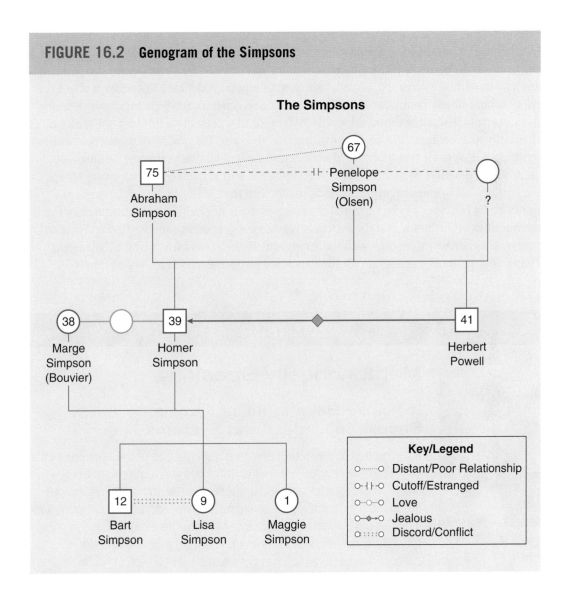

An important initial step in assessing a family is to assess who, exactly, the family includes. The configuration of families can differ greatly across cultures. Some clients may include numerous "aunts," "uncles," "cousins," or other relatives who are not technically related but unquestionably function as family. Others may exclude close relatives who they see as extraneous or outcast from the family. Simple questions such as, "Who do you consider family?" or "Who lives with you?" can go a long way toward helping the clinical psychologist understand the client's perception of family (Fontes, 2008; Grieger, 2008). At times, such questions can yield different answers from members of the same family, and these differences in perception may actually be relevant to the problems for which the family is seeking help.

One helpful technique for understanding the family configuration and relationships within the family is the **genogram** (McGoldrick, Gerson, & Petry, 2008). A genogram is a pencil-and-paper method of creating a family tree that incorporates detailed information about the relationships among family members for at least three generations. It exemplifies the saying that "a picture is worth a thousand words" by graphically presenting not only the structure of the family relationships (marriages, offspring, etc.) but also the quality of those relationships (harmonious, very close, estranged, abusive, etc.). Generally, genograms use a consistent approach to notation: Males are represented by boxes and females by circles, relationships are represented by lines between two individuals, and the quality of these relationships is indicated by the types of lines selected. Not only is the result helpful in understanding the complexities of the family, but the process of creating a genogram can also be a constructive way for the therapist to engage with the family and begin to establish a healthy alliance. Figure 16.2 presents a genogram for the fictional television family from *The Simpsons*.

• • • BOX 16.3 • • •

Metaphorically Speaking

If You've Been to a Car Repair Shop, You Understand Systems Theory

Imagine that there is something wrong with one of the tires on your car. It's showing uneven wear, and it loses air from time to time. Would you consider taking the tire off the car, taking the individual tire to a car repair shop, and asking the mechanic to repair or replace it? Or would you take the entire car in with the expectation that the mechanic would consider both the symptomatic tire and the other parts of the car to which it is connected?

These questions illustrate the role of systems theory in family therapy. In individual therapy, the client is seen in isolation, much like the tire detached from the car. The improved version will ultimately be placed back into the system from which it came. Perhaps the improvements will last, or perhaps the dysfunctional nature of the system will recreate the same problems again. On a car, when the repaired or replaced tire is installed, we might see the same uneven tread or loss of air within a short time. In individual therapy, when the client returns to the family, we might see the same behavioral or emotional problem arise again. In fact, the early applications of systems theory to family therapy were motivated in part by the clinical observation that inpatients who showed great improvement in the psychiatric hospital often deteriorated when they moved back home (Nichols, 2010).

In family therapy, the therapist examines the entire family system in which the symptomatic individual lives, much like the mechanic checking all parts of the car that might influence the performance of the tire, including suspension, joints, axles, and the like. If the car is out of alignment, replacing the tire won't fix the problem but realigning the car will. Similarly, if an individual is displaying psychological symptoms because of a systemic problem within the family, realigning the family may be necessary to address the problem.

Another essential part of the family assessment process is an appreciation of the family's current developmental stage. Just as numerous theorists have put forth sequential, developmental stages for individuals (such as Freud's five psychosexual stages or Erikson's eight psychosocial stages), theorists have also offered sequential, developmental stages for families. Probably the most widely known of these theories is the **family life cycle** created by Betty Carter and Monica McGoldrick (1989, 2004). According to this theory, intact middle-class American families typically proceed through the following seven stages (McGoldrick, Carter, & Garcia-Preto, 2011):

- *Leaving home.* Single young adults become independent and self-sufficient.
- *Joining of families through marriage or union.* A new couple forms a new family system, and the spouse is incorporated into existing family systems.
- *Families with young children.* Taking care of children; adjusting the marriage; and managing child-related, financial, and other responsibilities are among the primary tasks.
- *Families with adolescents.* Parents provide children with increasing amounts of independence and may adopt caretaking roles for their own parents as well.
- *Launching children and moving on in midlife.* Adjusting to the "empty nest," managing relationships with children's partners, and taking on the grandparent role are central.
- *Families in late middle age.* Focus shifts to managing declining health and adapting to new roles in the family and community.

- *Families nearing the end of life.* Accepting the realities and inevitability of death (one's own and those of family members) and, frequently, reversing the caretaker roles between older and younger generations exemplify this stage.

This set of stages may be a helpful way to conceptualize the evolution of a family through the years, but its authors and others emphasize that it must be modified to account for the wide variety of families that a family therapist may see, especially in countries as demographically or culturally diverse as the United States (Barnes, 2004; Carter & McGoldrick, 1989, 2004; McGoldrick et al., 2011). The list of variations to the traditional family on which the family life cycle is based is extensive: Divorced families, step-families, single-parent families, families with gay/lesbian members, families of diverse or blended ethnicities or religions, families with parents in nontraditional gender roles, nonmarried cohabitating couples, couples without children, families that have experienced an unexpected or premature loss, and families with many years between offspring are only some of the ways a family might not match the prototype (Ahrons, 2011; McGoldrick & Carter, 2011; McGoldrick & Walsh, 2011; McGoldrick & Watson, 2011). As an example, Hines (2011) points out that for African American families living in poverty, the life cycle may be a bit accelerated, with family members becoming parents or grandparents sooner than in many other cultural groups. Also, families in these cultures have a relatively high frequency of chronic stress, sudden losses, and households headed by single females—all of which should be taken into account by the family therapist. With appropriate knowledge such as this, along with sensitive adaptation, the life cycle model can provide a useful starting point when working with families, especially during the assessment phase.

It is unfortunate but undeniable that clinical psychologists assessing a family must pay attention to the issue of abuse and violence (Birchler, Simpson, & Fals-Stewart, 2008; Johnson, 2008). Clinical interviews can reveal some information, especially if family members are interviewed separately (Holtzworth-Munroe et al., 2002). The **Conflict Tactics Scales (CTS)** is a more structured and formal way of assessing abuse and violence within families. The CTS is available in versions that assess treatment of partners by each other and treatment of children by parents or caregivers. It is an individually administered, objective, self-report questionnaire that includes about 40 items and takes less than 15 minutes to complete. It includes questions asking the individual about how he or she behaves—speaking calmly, using insults, throwing objects, or hitting others, for example—when family conflicts arise. It has been widely used in clinical and research settings and has established reliability and validity (Straus, 2007; Straus, Hamby, Boney-McCoy, & Sugarman, 1996). Even when abuse or violence is not the presenting problem, it is important for the clinical psychologist to assess for these issues via interviews or other assessment tools such as the CTS.

As the assessment phase leads into the therapy phase, it can be critical for the family therapist to persuade the family that the problem is systemic rather than individual. Often, families enter the therapy process with an **identified patient** or a family member whose symptoms are most obvious or problematic. They may believe that the problem is contained within the identified patient and that the role of other family members is minimal or nonexistent. In fact, they may contact the therapist seeking individual therapy for a son, daughter, or other family member and have no expectation at all for family therapy. In these cases,

> An effort is made to dilute the idea that the presenting problem associated with an individual is encased within that person; instead an attempt is made to modify beliefs so that the problem is perceived to be a byproduct of the situation that characterizes the system. (Griffin, 2002, p. 794)

With family members successfully "onboard," family therapy can commence with positive expectations.

Family Therapy: Essential Concepts

Many varieties of family therapy have been developed and practiced. Most of the widely known approaches to individual therapy have been applied in the family context as well, including psychodynamic, humanistic-existential, behavioral, and cognitive styles (Goldenberg & Goldenberg, 2007; Hanna, 2007; Nichols, 2010; Rolland & Walsh, 2009). Griffin (2002) divides this wide range of styles into three broad categories:

- *Ahistorical styles*, emphasizing current functioning and deemphasizing family history (most common in contemporary clinical psychology)
- *Historical styles*, emphasizing family history and typically longer duration than ahistorical styles (including Bowenian/intergenerational family therapy and psychodynamic approaches)
- *Experiential styles*, emphasizing personal growth and emotional experiencing in and out of sessions (including the approaches of Carl Whitaker and Virginia Satir)

In this section, we review some of the essential "classic" concepts of family therapy, most of which derived from historical approaches, that are still very relevant to contemporary practice. Then we consider two of the more commonly practiced contemporary ahistorical styles (narrative and solution-focused family therapies) in more detail.

Classic Concepts

Family Structure   Every family has rules by which it operates. These rules are rarely explicit, but they nonetheless powerfully govern family members' behavior. Collectively, these rules are known as the **family structure**, and if the family structure is flawed, problems will ensue in the relationships among family members and may manifest as psychological symptoms in some family members (e.g., Minuchin, 1974).

The emphasis of structural family therapy, as practiced by **Salvador Minuchin** and others, is to improve the structure of families as a means of improving the functioning of their members. Structural family therapists emphasize **subsystems** within families (parental subsystems, sibling subsystems, etc.) and **boundaries** between those subsystems. These boundaries should be permeable enough to allow emotional closeness between family members but rigid enough to allow for independence as well. If boundaries are too permeable, family members can become **enmeshed**; if they are too rigid, family members can become **disengaged.** Thus, a primary task of structural therapy is uncovering and correcting and clarifying family rules, often with an emphasis on developing a clear hierarchy of power within the family. Like any organization—a company, the military, and so on—families simply run better when the structure is clear and sensible.

Differentiation of Self According to **Murray Bowen** and his followers (e.g., Bowen, 1978), a primary task for each individual family member is an appropriate degree of self-determination. In other words, healthy families allow each member to become his or her own person without sacrificing emotional closeness with other members of the family. However, families sometimes experience problems in this regard, resulting in family members who remain overly connected with one another in an emotional sense. In other words, rather than achieving **differentiation of self**, the members of these families are **emotionally fused**. Such families have little tolerance for differences in feeling or belief; what one member thinks or feels, all members think or feel. When family therapists encounter a family such as this—often labeled an **undifferentiated ego mass**—the primary goal is to acknowledge the lack of differentiation, explore factors that may have caused or are currently maintaining it, and encourage relationships characterized by less fusion and more independence.

Triangles When two people are in conflict, either one might decide to bring in a third party in an attempt to garner support. In a formal, legal sense, we see this phenomenon take place when attorneys bring in expert witnesses to bolster their cases in court. In families, a similar process occurs, but it can lead to significant problems, especially for the person being coerced into the triangle. A common scenario for **triangles** in families involves parents at odds and a child recruited to side with one parent. Unlike the expert witness in a court case, children are powerless to refuse parental attempts to triangulate and, as a result, can find themselves in a psychologically unhealthy predicament whereby they feel that they must "take sides" with one parent against the other. Although such situations can be obvious in families involving contentious divorce or child custody battles, adverse effects can also occur in intact families in which parents subtly pressure kids to side with them. With families whose triangulation tendencies have become problematic, family therapists often try to bring these tendencies to light and encourage the parties in the conflict to deal more directly with each other rather than involving third parties such as their children (e.g., Bowen, 1978).

Contemporary Approaches

⊕ **Web Link 16.5**

Institute for Solution- Focused Therapy

Solution-Focused Therapy   Families come to therapy because they have specific problems, and, according to solution-focused family therapists, therapy is successful when those problems are solved. **Solution-focused therapy** evolved from the **strategic family therapy** approach of Don Jackson, Jay Haley, and Cloe Madenes and shares its pragmatic emphasis (Goldenberg & Goldenberg, 2007; Nichols, 2010). But where strategic family therapists focused on problems, solution-focused family therapists focus almost exclusively on solutions (Berg, 1994; deShazer, Dolan, & Korman, 2007).

The leaders of the solution-focused therapy approach, including **Steve deShazer** and **Insoo Kim Berg,** emphasize that family therapists should use "solution-talk" rather than "problem-talk" as much as possible. By discussing positive outcomes that the future may hold rather than unpleasant situations that characterize the present, clients begin to adopt a more positive point of view. Similarly, therapists help clients focus on exceptions to their problems. That is, they remind clients that they already have the ability to help themselves, as evidenced by the fact that they have already experienced some moments or days that were better than others. Clients can sometimes assume their problems are ever present when, in fact, they are not. Likewise, improvements are not flukes but the result of efforts by the clients, even if they frequently overlook such successes (Nichols, 2010). So if a family says they argued slightly less in the past week than they had in the previous month, the solution-focused therapist seizes on this improvement and assumes that the family was instrumental in causing it: "What did you do to improve things last week? How can you continue to do more of the same in upcoming weeks?"

Solution-focused therapy uses a list of specific tasks and questions posed to clients to call attention to solutions rather than problems. For example, at the end of the first session, solution-focused therapists often present the **formula first-session task,** in which clients are instructed to take note of aspects of their lives in the upcoming week that they want to continue to happen. This forces clients to focus on the positive rather than the negative facets of their day-to-day lives. They also ask **exception questions** ("When was this not a problem for you? When was it not so bad?"), **miracle questions** ("If the problem disappeared, how would your life be different?"), and **scaling questions** ("On a scale of 1 to 10, how bad has the problem been in the past week? When has the problem been better? How did you make it improve at that time?"). Structured, positive-oriented questions such as these, along with an emphasis on quick resolution of presenting problems, have contributed to the increasing popularity of solution-focused therapy in recent years (Nichols, 2010).

Narrative Therapy   Also very popular among contemporary family therapists, **narrative therapy** highlights clients' tendencies to create meanings about themselves and the events in their lives in particular ways, some of which may cause psychological problems. As the name suggests, narrative therapists believe that the stories we construct about our own lives are powerful influences on the way we experience new events. In a sense, we "edit" our experiences in order to fit the story line we have developed. So if we cast ourselves as failures in our own life stories, we are likely to interpret events in ways that support such a tale. If we can revise our stories and recast ourselves as heroes, however, the same sequence of events might be interpreted in a more flattering way, and our view of ourselves might be enhanced (e.g., White & Epston, 1990).

As an example, consider Phil, a 29-year-old man who has been married for 6 years. Phil and his wife, Jamie, have a 4-year-old daughter and are expecting another child in a few months. The primary reason why Phil and Jamie seek therapy is Phil's depression; specifically, both Phil and Jamie agree that Phil is extremely self-critical and dejected over career-related issues. Phil explains to Dr. Gupta, a narrative family therapist, that immediately after finishing college at age 22, he took an entry-level corporate job. Although he was quite capable and had advanced in the company, Phil found the work very unsatisfying and stifling. After discussing the matter at length with Jamie, at age 27 Phil decided to leave the corporate world and focus on his long-time passion, music. While Jamie continued to work full-time, Phil worked hard to establish himself as a guitarist/singer/songwriter, and he experienced quite a bit of success. He had regular gigs at numerous venues, had recorded several independent CDs that sold well locally, and had recently signed a contract with a record label.

In spite of these successes and the satisfaction he derived from his music, Phil saw his career change as a mistake and an embarrassment. He made less money as a musician than he would in his corporate job, and some of his friends and relatives wondered why he would allow his career to go "off track." Phil also felt that his old job had more stability and prestige and that he wasn't adequately fulfilling his role as a husband and father with his current occupation. Phil's negative feelings about his career decision had a significant impact on his self-image and his relationships with his wife and daughter, both of whom wished to see Phil happier.

Dr. Gupta used the narrative approach to revise Phil's story from one of regret and failure to one of courage, authenticity, and success. If Phil's story had a title when therapy began, it might have been "I'm a Loser," and he found supporting evidence for this tale's theme in his decreased income and second-guessing friends and relatives. But Dr. Gupta offered another title—"A Self-Made Success"—and supported it by pointing out that Phil had made a brave decision early in his career that enabled him to pursue his passion and that he had, in fact, been quite successful in a short time in a difficult business. Dr. Gupta argued that keeping the corporate job might have been the safe or predictable thing to do and may have fit with society's expectations, but Phil's actions showed an independence, self-awareness, and determination that are remarkably admirable. With time, Phil began to see himself more heroically and was able to interpret life events accordingly.

In some ways, narrative therapy is similar to cognitive therapy in its emphasis on altering clients' interpretations of events. In narrative therapy, those interpretations are seen as essential elements of the stories of clients' lives, and the process of changing them resembles editing. Although it is considered a form of family therapy, narrative therapy does emphasize the individual within the family, and it also tends to underscore clients' efforts to resist oppressive cultural or societal forces (Nichols, 2010).

Ethical Issues in Family Therapy

Cultural Competence

Cultural competence is essential in any mode of therapy, but it is especially relevant in family therapy. Family therapists should have a full appreciation and acceptance for the cultural background of the families with whom they work, including such characteristics as ethnicity and religion.

Photo 16.3 An appreciation of the cultural background of a family and each of its members is essential to culturally competent family therapy.

For therapists working with families, an appreciation of some cultural variables can be quite complex yet vital to the therapy process. The members of a family may actually come from or currently live in different cultural worlds. Spouses, for example, might have been raised in different religions or different ethnicities. A three-generation family living in the same house may include three distinct levels of acculturation. For example, the grandparents who immigrated may hold traditional values, the parents may be somewhat more acculturated, and the children may tend toward holding few or no traditional values. A family with adopted children may include parents whose ethnicity is different from that of their adopted children. In any of these cases, family therapists must be capable of considering culture not only as a context for the presenting problem but also as a potentially important aspect of the presenting problem itself.

Confidentiality

Family therapy can present some unique ethical quandaries with regard to confidentiality. Specifically, family therapists often find themselves in the difficult position of having learned information from one family member in a private conversation—perhaps a phone call or a comment made in a brief one-on-one conversation before or after a session. Should the family therapist hold this information confidential from the other family members? Or should any information shared by any family member be shared with all family members? Does the answer depend on how serious or trivial this information may be to the rest of the family?

There are few easy answers to these questions (Knauss & Knauss, 2012; Wilcoxon, Remley, Gladding, & Huber, 2007). In general, it is best to set the ground rules for confidentiality during the initial informed consent process; that way, all family members understand up front that the family therapist will handle private conversations in a particular way. Some family therapists choose never to have private conversations with individual family members, whereas others allow them. To the extent that family therapists hold individual family members' comments confidential, they place a burden on themselves to recall during sessions not only what they know but also how they learned it and how much liberty they have to share that information with the whole family.

Diagnostic Accuracy

Family therapists face a dilemma regarding diagnosis: *DSM* diagnoses apply to disordered individuals, but they work with disordered family systems. The *DSM* contains no diagnostic labels that apply to families, and there is no widely accepted alternate to the *DSM* for categorizing family or relationship problems. Therefore, especially when there is pressure to assign a diagnosis to qualify for payment from managed-care/insurance companies, family therapists may consider assigning a *DSM* diagnosis to one member of the family.

Family therapists often have justified reservations about diagnosing in this manner. For one, to diagnose only the identified patient may reinforce the family's assumption that the problem is individual, not systemic. Also, the identified patient can feel further stigmatized. And, of course, a diagnosis made when *DSM* criteria are not met represents both an ethical violation and insurance fraud (American Psychological Association, 2002). When a family's only means of paying for treatment hinges on a diagnosis, this can be a difficult issue for family therapists. Open and honest discussion with the family during the informed consent process can be helpful in resolving it (Wilcoxon et al., 2007).

How Well Does It Work?

Outcome studies of family therapy involve all the methodological difficulties of outcome studies for individual therapy, with one additional, complicating factor: Various members of the family may have quite different opinions about the result. For example, if family therapy results in previously uninvolved and lenient parents paying more attention to and placing appropriate demands on their children, the parents may view therapy as successful, but some of the children may not.

In spite of this and other methodological challenges, many studies of the efficacy of family therapy have been conducted. Although the amount of research is not as sizable as that for individual therapy, the result is generally the same: Family therapy works. More specifically, family therapy tends to be about as effective as most other modes of therapy, and the differences between various family therapy approaches are typically insignificant (Griffin,

2002; Shadish et al., 1993; Shadish, Ragsdale, Glaser, & Montgomery, 1995). Some specific problems for which family therapy has established success include schizophrenia, couples discord, individual depression related to couples discord, delinquency in adolescents, conduct disorder and other disruptive disorders in children, and numerous others (Glick, Berman, Clarkin, & Rait, 2000; Goldenberg & Goldenberg, 2007; Lebow, 2006). As in individual therapy, a strong therapeutic relationship is a key element to successful family therapy, as demonstrated in an increasing number of empirical studies (e.g., Friedlander, Escudero, Heatherington, & Diamond, 2011).

CHAPTER SUMMARY

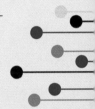

Group therapy is characterized by an emphasis on interpersonal interaction. Irvin Yalom and other leaders in the group therapy field believe that flawed interpersonal styles contribute to clients' presenting problems and that focusing on interpersonal interactions within the group can have positive ramifications for clients outside the group. A number of unique therapeutic factors, including universality, group cohesiveness, and interpersonal learning, distinguish group therapy from individual therapy. Therapy groups can be heterogeneously or homogeneously composed, and they can adopt open- or closed-enrollment policies. Two cotherapists often conduct groups together, allowing both potential benefits and complications. Pitfalls of group therapy include extra-group socializing and breaches of confidentiality by fellow group members. Outcome studies suggest that group therapy is generally as effective as individual therapy.

Family therapy centers on a systems-based approach to psychological problems in which the symptoms of an identified patient are viewed as a byproduct of a pathological pattern of interaction or communication within that person's family. Family therapists often use genograms, a sort of annotated family tree, as an assessment tool and conceptualize their clients developmentally on an adaptation of the family life cycle model of development. Many family therapists continue to be influenced by classic concepts of family therapy such as the subsystems and boundaries of structural family therapy or the differentiation and triangulation issues of Bowenian therapy, but newer approaches such as solution-focused and narrative therapy also exert a powerful influence on contemporary family therapists. As for all clinical psychologists, cultural competence is crucial for those practicing family therapy. Outcome studies of family therapy can be more methodologically complex than those for individual therapy, but those that have been conducted suggest rate of success for its clients is generally comparable with that of individual therapy.

KEY TERMS AND NAMES

CRITICAL THINKING QUESTIONS

1. In your opinion, which clinical problems seem best and least suited to group therapy?

2. In your opinion, which of Yalom's therapeutic factors for group

psychotherapy seem most vital to its success? Why?

3. If you were a clinical psychologist, would you prefer to conduct group therapy alone

or with a cotherapist? What factors might influence your decision?

4. To what extent do you agree with the fundamental assumption of family therapy that the system, rather than the individual, is pathological?

5. To what extent might the contemporary approaches to family therapy (e.g., solution-focused therapy, narrative therapy) also be applicable to individual clients?

STUDENT STUDY SITE RESOURCES

Visit the study site at www.sagepub.com/pomerantz3eupdate for these additional learning tools:

- Self-quizzes
- eFlashcards
- Culture Expert Interviews

- Full-text SAGE journal articles
- Additional web resources
- Mock Assessment Data

CHAPTER SUMMARY VIDEO

 QR codes at the end of each chapter link to chapter background videos by the author. Visit http://gettag.mobi using your smartphone browser to download the free Microsoft Tag app. Once installed, scan the tags to go directly to these brief videos. In this video, the author describes his own clinical experiences with a family who initially sought individual therapy for their child but whose problems proved to be more systemic.

Special Topics

CHAPTER

17

Clinical Child and Adolescent Psychology

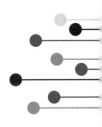

Clinical psychologists have worked with children and adolescents since the inception of the field. In fact, the focus of the very first psychology clinic, created by Lightner Witmer in the late 1800s, was the assessment and treatment of children with learning and behavioral problems (Reisman, 1991; Witmer, 1907). Along with the rest of the profession, **clinical child psychology** has grown tremendously. The membership of the **Society of Clinical Child and Adolescent Psychology** (Division 53 of the

⊕ **Web Link 17.1**
Society of Clinical Child and Adolescent Psychology

American Psychological Association) is currently in the thousands, and a sizeable number of graduate programs train psychologists specifically to work with children and adolescents (American Psychological Association Division 53, 2007).

Clinical child psychologists apply their professional skills in diverse ways. Some specialize in the assessment of problems related to behavioral, emotional, or intellectual functioning. Others are primarily therapists, working with children and their families to bring meaningful improvement to their lives. And, of course, some clinical child psychologists devote their professional lives to research or training. Many clinical child psychologists combine these applied and academic roles. In some cases, the applied work of clinical child psychologists overlaps with that of medical professionals. This cross-disciplinary field, known as **pediatric psychology**, promotes both the mental and physical health of children with medical conditions.

In this chapter, we survey the field of clinical child psychology by exploring three major areas: psychological problems of children, assessment, and psychotherapy.

Psychological Issues of Childhood

Disorders of Childhood

Some disorders are especially common among children, such as attention-deficit/ hyperactivity disorder (ADHD), conduct disorder, oppositional defiant disorder, and separation anxiety disorder. Of course, children and adolescents can also be diagnosed with disorders that are more common in adults. Major depression, posttraumatic stress disorder, anorexia, bulimia, substance use, adjustment disorders, phobias, and generalized anxiety disorder are some of the many problems diagnosed in both adults and children. In some cases, the diagnostic criteria for these disorders are adjusted for children. For example, among the criteria for a major depressive episode, *DSM-5* includes a note that in children and adolescents, irritable mood can replace depressed mood, and failure to gain weight according to growth expectations can replace weight loss. Among the criteria for specific phobia, DSM-5 notes that children may express their fear and anxiety in unique ways, including crying, tantrums, or clinging to caregivers. For posttraumatic stress disorder, the DSM-5 has a distinct set of criteria for children 6 years old and younger, including diminished interest in playing or playing that involves reenactment of the trauma (American Psychiatric Association, 2013).

Some clinical psychologists who work with children have divided children's psychological problems into two broad classes: **externalizing disorders** and **internalizing disorders** (e.g., Kazdin, 2000). Externalizing disorders are those in which the child "acts out" and often becomes a disruption to parents, teachers, or other children. These disorders include ADHD, conduct disorder, and oppositional defiant disorder. Internalizing disorders, on the other hand, are often less noticeable because they involve maladaptive thoughts and feelings more than disruptive outward behavior. Mood disorders and anxiety disorders exemplify internalizing disorders in children.

Resilience and Vulnerability

Why do some children develop psychological disorders whereas other children do not? This is an essential question for clinical child psychologists, especially those who study the topics of **resilience** and **vulnerability**. It is indeed remarkable to notice that children from similar environments—in some cases, the same geographic area, ethnicity, socioeconomic level, school, and family—have very different kinds or degrees of psychological or behavioral problems (Bonanno, Westphal, & Mancini, 2011). Research into factors that contribute to a child's vulnerability to psychological problems has yielded a list of risk factors that encompasses variables both within and around the child (e.g., Lambert, 2006; Laser & Nicotera, 2011; Schroeder & Gordon, 2002; Stormont, 2007):

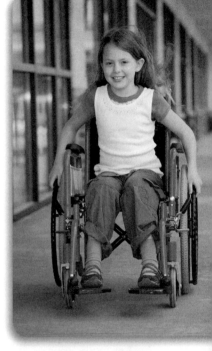

Photo 17.1 Clinical child psychologists are particularly interested in factors that foster resilience rather than vulnerability to psychological or behavioral problems. In your opinion, which factors are most important?

- Environmental factors, such as poverty, serious emotional conflict among parents, single parenthood, an excessive number of children in the home, neighborhood or community factors, and poor schooling

- Parental factors, such as poor parental physical health, poor parent mental health, low parent intelligence quotient (IQ), and hypercritical tendencies in the parent

- Child (internal) factors, such as medical problems, difficult temperament, low IQ, poor academic achievement, and social skills deficits

Fortunately, researchers have also examined the factors that contribute to resilience in children. After reviewing research on children who were somehow able to thrive in risky environments where many of their peers struggled, Grotberg (2003) sorted the differentiating factors into three categories: external supports, inner strengths, and interpersonal problem-solving skills. To these three categories, she assigned kid-friendly labels: "I Have" (external supports), "I Am" (inner strengths), and "I Can" (interpersonal and problem-solving skills). Box 17.1 presents a full description of Grotberg's resilience model. In many cases, interventions by clinical child psychologists can enhance these factors, effectively making the child more resilient to current and future stressors. By combining what researchers have learned about the factors underlying children's resilience and vulnerability, clinical child psychologists can work to prevent and treat children's psychological problems.

● ● ● BOX 17.1 ● ● ●

Factors Fostering Resilience in Children

I Have (external supports)

- People in my family I can trust and who love me
- People outside my family I can trust
- Limits to my behavior
- People who encourage me to be independent
- Good role models
- Access to health, education, and other services I need
- A stable family and community

I Am (inner strengths)

- A person most people like
- Generally a good boy/girl
- An achiever who plans for the future
- A person who respects myself and others
- Caring toward others
- Responsible for my own behavior
- A confident, optimistic, hopeful person

I Can (interpersonal and problem-solving skills)

- Generate new ideas or new ways to do things
- Work hard at something until it is finished
- See the humor in life
- Express my thoughts and feelings
- Solve problems
- Manage my behavior
- Ask for help when I need it

Source: Adapted from Grotberg (2003).

Assessment of Children and Adolescents

The Developmental Perspective

In any competent assessment of a child or adolescent, clinical psychologists adopt a **developmental perspective**. In other words, it is essential to understand the child's behavior within the context of the child's developmental stage (e.g., Drabick & Kendall, 2010; LaGreca, Kuttler, & Stone, 2002). Problems of childhood may take on different meanings and call for different clinical interventions depending on their commonality for children at a given age. For example, imagine that Beth and her parents visit a clinical psychologist because of Beth's defiant, rule-breaking behavior. On several occasions, Beth has ignored her parents' curfews and prohibitions about smoking. A full, accurate understanding of this problem will depend entirely on Beth's age. If Beth is 7, this problem takes on very different connotations than it does if she is 17. Likewise, if Donyell's mother brings him to a clinical psychologist for a bed-wetting problem, whether Donyell is 3, 9, or 15 can make a significant difference in the conceptualization of this problem.

Of course, ethnic or other cultural factors can influence the developmental maturation of children, as parents and other family members from a given culture may expect children to develop relatively quickly or slowly in certain areas (Park-Taylor, Ventura, & Ng, 2010). Clinical psychologists should appreciate these factors to grasp a child's problems more fully. For example, Hines and Boyd-Franklin (2005) describe a pattern common in African American families in which a "parentified" child takes on adult roles in a home with working parents or many younger children. This role "can enhance the parental child's sense of responsibility, competence, and autonomy" (p. 91) but can contribute to behavioral problems later if the child feels overwhelmed or if these parent-like duties conflict with the child's own personal needs.

Considering Culture

Parent–Child Relationships Across Cultures

Culturally competent clinical child psychologists appreciate that the manners in which parents raise their children can differ drastically according to cultural norms. Furthermore, culturally competent clinical child psychologists are knowledgeable about culture-specific norms in child rearing and amend their assessment and treatment accordingly to make them ideally suitable (Park-Taylor et al., 2010).

To illustrate the variety of parent–child relationships across cultural groups, consider the discrepancies among the following descriptions. Each excerpt comes from a separate chapter of the book *Ethnicity and Family Therapy* (McGoldrick, Giordano, & Garcia-Preto, 2005a):

Vietnamese families:

> "Even now, children are regarded as property by their parents, although this belief has loosened gradually since World War II as the culture has become more Westernized. . . . Children are expected to follow their parents' advice in all aspects of life, including matters relating to marriage and career selection." (Leung & Boehnlein, 2005, p. 366)

Jewish families:

> "Jews tend to raise their children through reasoning and explanation of expectations, and Jewish parents have tended to be permissive, overprotective, and concerned about their children's happiness, at times at the expense of their own." (Rosen & Weltman, 2005, p. 675)

Haitian families:

> "In general, parents, who have near absolute power in Haiti, raise children with an understanding that they must be obedient and sometimes administer physical discipline with a belt or switch when they misbehave, which may on occasion be viewed as abuse in this country [the United States]. When child protective services intervene, parents can be stunned." (Menos, 2005, p. 133)

Asian Indian families:

"In general, everyone, including older siblings and extended family, pampers children. A 4- or 5-year-old child is often less independent than children of European background." (Almeida, 2005, p. 387)

Iranian families:

"There is no specific pattern to the punishment; depending on the father's mood, a child may be punished for a trivial act of misbehavior; at other times, a more serious act may be laughed off or overlooked. A child may be slapped if he or she misbehaves in public or in front of a family guest, yet in private the same misbehavior might only merit a scolding. Western methods of disciplining, such as withholding favorite foods or sending children to their rooms, are rarely used." (Jalali, 2005, p. 457)

Arab families:

"Another feature of the Arab family is its style of communication, which is described as . . . hierarchical, creating vertical as opposed to horizontal communication between those in authority and those subservient to that authority. This relationship . . . leads to styles of communication between parents and children in which parents use anger and punishment and the children respond by crying, self-censorship, covering up, or deception." (Abudabbeh, 2005, p. 427)

Photos 17.2 and 17.3 The ways parents raise children can vary greatly across cultural groups. In your opinion, how should clinical child psychologists increase their awareness of these cultural norms?

(Continued)

(Continued)

In addition to knowledge of such divergent cultural norms regarding parent–child interactions, culturally competent clinical child psychologists have abundant knowledge of their own cultural background, especially its influence on their expectations regarding parent–child relationships. With this knowledge, the clinical child psychologist can proficiently and sensitively treat a diverse range of clients.

A Comprehensive Assessment

An extensive amount of background information may be relevant to the psychological problems of a particular child; thus, clinical psychologists should strive to attain as much of it as possible. This background information can help the psychologist appreciate the full set of circumstances in which the child's presenting problems have emerged. Some of this background information relates directly to the presenting problem, whereas some is more contextual but nonetheless important. Among the questions for which a clinical psychologist might seek answers are the following (e.g., Schroeder & Gordon, 2002):

- *The presenting problem:* What, exactly, is the presenting problem? Do all parties (parents, child, teachers, etc.) agree on the definition of the problem? When did the problem arise? For whom is this problem most troubling?

- *Development:* What is the child's current state of physical, cognitive, linguistic, and social development? Have there been any developmental abnormalities during childhood or during the prenatal period? Has the child reached all developmental milestones at the expected points in time?

- *Parents/family:* What are the relevant characteristics of the child's parent or parents? What style of parenting is used? What parent factors (psychological, medical, other) might play a role in the child's problem? How might siblings, grandparents, or other family members influence the child?

- *Environment:* What is the child's larger environment outside the family? What relevant ethnic or cultural factors play a role in the child's behavior? Are there recent major events in the child's life that may factor into the current problems?

The clinical child psychologist may receive different answers to these questions from different people in the child's life. For this reason, it is important to rely on more than one source of information when assessing a child. More generally, a pluralistic approach to assessing children is sound clinical practice. In fact, Merrell (2008) advocates a **multisource, multimethod, multisetting approach** to assessment of children. Multisource assessment involves such parties as parents, relatives, teachers, other school personnel, and, of course, the child as sources of information regarding the child's problems. To rely on only one of these sources is to risk a one-sided or incomplete perspective of the problem. Multimethod assessment involves the use of different methods of data collection by the clinical psychologist such as interviews, pencil-and-paper instruments completed by the child or those who know the child well, direct observation of the child's behavior, and other techniques. Multisetting assessment acknowledges that sometimes children's problems pervade all facets of their lives, but sometimes they are specific to certain situations. Thus, it is wise to solicit data from home, school, the clinician's office, and any other relevant setting.

Photo 17.4 When clinical child psychologists conduct a comprehensive assessment, the child's environment is one of many important areas to consider.

As an example of the value of a multisource, multimethod, multisetting approach to assessing children, consider Ari, a 7-year-old boy whose parents brought him to Dr. Kim, a clinical child psychologist. Ari's parents described Ari as "impossible to manage": He simply won't listen to instructions and refuses to do what he is told. Ari's parents completed a rating scale that confirmed their comments, and they told numerous stories about episodes at home— bedtime, going to school, cleaning up his toys—during which Ari was unruly. To understand the problem more comprehensively, Dr. Kim requested Ari's parents' permission to contact Ari's first-grade teacher and a babysitter who watched Ari several times a week for a few hours at a time, which the parents granted by signing release forms. The information Dr. Kim received from Ari's teacher and babysitter was quite discrepant from the information provided by the parents. Via interview with Dr. Kim and on rating scale forms, the teacher and babysitter both described Ari as very compliant, obedient, and well-behaved. Dr. Kim also visited Ari's school to observe his behavior directly and found him not to be disruptive or disobedient at all. Thus, Dr. Kim was able to conclude that Ari's problem was not pervasive to all aspects of his life; instead, it was situational to his time at home when his parents were present. Dr. Kim was then able to proceed with an intervention specifically designed to improve Ari's parents' ability to communicate and manage contingencies in the home, which proved to be successful.

Assessment Methods

Clinical child psychologists use a vast array of assessment tools and techniques. In general, they can be categorized into six broad categories: clinical interviews, behavioral observation, behavior rating scales, self-report scales, projective/expressive techniques, and intellectual tests (Cashel, 2002; LaGreca et al., 2002; Merrell, 2008; Wodrich, 1997).

Interviews

When a clinical psychologist assesses an adult, very often the client is the only person with whom the psychologist speaks. The process is very different in child assessment, where the clinical psychologist typically interviews not only the child but also other people who, by virtue of their contact with the child, can shed light on the child's problem. Parents and teachers are perhaps most common, but depending on the problem and its circumstances, a number of other people can provide relevant data: siblings, grandparents, other relatives, pediatricians, friends, child-care workers, or tutors, to name a few.

Interviewing those who know the child well—informants, as they are called in this role—is a vital skill for the clinical psychologist. When speaking with parents, it can be helpful to empathize with their experience of the child's problem, which may include frustration or sadness, and correct any misconceptions by reassuring them that the psychologists' role is not to assign blame but to work constructively and collaboratively with the parents to remedy the problem. Regarding interviews with individuals other than parents, it is always essential to obtain permission from parents/guardians prior to contacting them. Once the contact occurs, it is best to be as professional, respectful, and concise as possible. This is especially true when contacting teachers, whose schedules often afford them little time for this important task. Recognizing the value of their time by contacting them during planning periods and thanking them for their efforts afterward can facilitate the process (Kamphaus & Frick, 2005; Villa & Reitman, 2007).

Interviewing children themselves is an obviously crucial yet sometimes challenging component of the clinical child psychologist's job. Children rarely refer themselves to a psychologist; much more often, the referral comes from a parent, teacher, or pediatrician with concerns about the child's behavior (LaGreca et al., 2002). In fact, when children are brought to a clinical psychologist, typically "the focus is on *disturbing* rather than *disturbed* behavior" (Kazdin, 2000, p. 47). So whereas other people may want the child to change, the child may be unmotivated or even resistant. In some cases, the child may be quite anxious about the interview and, depending on age and sophistication, may be under the misconception that the psychologist will do something scary or hurtful, along the lines of a shot at the pediatrician's office.

For this reason, establishing rapport is vital to interviewing children (Kendall, 2012). It can be helpful at the outset to engage in just enough small talk to make the child feel comfortable but not so much that the interview strays from its purpose. Also, the clinical psychologist's speech patterns should match those of the child, and the vocabulary should be comprehensible to the child as well (Kamphaus & Frick, 2005; Villa & Reitman, 2007). Above all, communicating genuine respect for children, concern for their happiness, and a wish to work together to improve their lives can help children feel comfortable in clinical interview situations. This holds true whether conducting structured or unstructured interviews, both of which are used commonly by clinical child psychologists (Nock, Holmberg, Photos, & Michel, 2007; O'Brien & Tabaczynski, 2007).

Behavioral Observations

When the child's problem involves a behavior that can be directly observed, as in most externalizing disorders, clinical child psychologists often do so. **Behavioral observation** may require traveling to the setting where the behavior problem takes place, such as the child's school or home. Once there, the clinical psychologist typically uses a formal, systematic method of observing and coding the child's behavior. There are several published systems available for clinical psychologists to use for this purpose, including the Direct Observation Form developed in conjunction with the Child Behavior Checklist; the Student Observation System, which is a component of the Behavior Assessment System for Children; the Dyadic Parent-Child Interaction Coding System; and the Social Interaction Scoring System (Merrell, 2008; Merrell & Harlacher, 2008).

Behavioral observation systems can be either event or interval based. In an event-based system, the observer simply counts the number of occurrences of a target behavior within a relatively long time frame. For example, the observer may count the number of times an excessively chatty 8-year-old child talks to a classmate during a 30-minute academic period during a school day. In an interval-based system, the observer divides the full time period into smaller intervals and then notes whether or not the target behavior took place during each interval. So the observer may break the 30-minute time period into 30 intervals, each 1 minute in length, and determine the number of minutes out of 30 in which the child talks to a classmate. Either type of system allows for the clinical child psychologist to measure the target behavior empirically. This direct, systematic approach to assessing the problem can prove to be an important complement to indirect data solicited from children, parents, teachers, or others.

One concern regarding direct observation of behavior involves **reactivity.** That is, children's behavior may change simply because of their awareness of the presence of the observer. When reactivity is strong, the observation may be invalid. Thus, clinical child psychologists often wait to begin recording their observations until it seems that the children have become accustomed to the presence of the observer. The reactivity concern can be especially relevant in situations where the observer appears to be of a different cultural background than those in the room where the observation is taking place. Merrell (2008) offers the example of a clinical psychologist observing a child in a classroom in which all the students are of a different ethnicity than the psychologist.

When **naturalistic direct observation**—observation of a behavior in the place where it actually happens—is impractical, clinical child psychologists often conduct **analogue direct observation**. Analogue direct observation typically takes place in the clinic room, where the real-life situation is simulated. By definition, analogue direct observation may not perfectly match the real-world situation in which the problem behavior arises. Nonetheless, it can be an important addition to secondhand descriptions of the problem behavior.

Behavior Rating Scales

Behavior rating scales are standardized pencil-and-paper forms that parents, teachers, or other adults complete regarding a child's presenting problems. They typically consist of a list of behaviors, each of which is followed by a range of responses from which the respondent chooses the one most applicable to the child. For example, a behavior rating scale might include an item such as, "The child pushes other children," and all items on this scale may be followed by a five-point scale consisting of *very frequently*, *frequently*, *sometimes*, *infrequently*, and *very infrequently*. By summing scores across subscales and the full scale, clinical child psychologists can obtain objective data to be compared with published norms for children in the appropriate age range. Among the most commonly used behavior rating scales are parent and teacher versions of the Child Behavior Checklist, for a wide range of problem behaviors; the Behavior Assessment System for Children, also for a wide range of problem behaviors; and Conners' Rating Scale, for attention-related problems (Merrell & Harlacher, 2008).

Advantages of behavior rating scales include their convenience, inexpensiveness, and objectivity. Disadvantages include the fact that they restrict respondents from elaborating on their responses and the possibility that the scale items do not adequately capture the child's problem behaviors.

Self-Report Scales

Just as assessment of adults often involves questionnaires completed directly by the client, assessment of children and adolescents often does as well. Of course, the use of these measures assumes that the client's reading level, attention span, and motivation to complete the test are appropriate. For these reasons, **self-report scales** are more commonly used with adolescents than with younger children (Cashel, 2002).

Self-report scales for children and adolescents are quite similar to self-report scales for adults. In fact, some of the most commonly used adult self-report scales, including the Minnesota Multiphasic Personality Inventory (MMPI) and the Millon Clinical Multiaxial Inventory (MCMI), are available in adolescent versions. These are pencil-and-paper tests in which the adolescents read a series of statements and then mark the response (true/false or one of several choices on a continuum) that best describes them. Scores are derived by comparing the adolescent's patterns of scores to normative data based on age range. The adolescent versions of the MMPI and MCMI are relatively long, broad-based measures of personality, but other self-report scales used with adolescents are more brief and targeted toward particular symptoms such as depression and anxiety.

As with adults, self-report scales to assess children or adolescents must be used in a culturally competent way. For example, the clinical child psychologist should ensure that the client is fluent in the language of the test and that the client's cultural background is represented in normative data with which the client's responses will be compared (Merrell, 2008).

Projective/Expressive Techniques

The projective and expressive techniques used in the assessment of children include some of the same tests used with adults, such as the Rorschach Inkblot Technique, the Thematic Apperception Test (TAT), and sentence-completion techniques (covered in Chapter 10), as well as others that are more exclusive to children. Our discussion in Chapter 10 regarding the projective hypothesis and concerns about the reliability and validity of projective tests applies to their use with children as well.

The Children's Apperception Test is an adaptation of the TAT storytelling test that features animal rather than human characters, about which young clients are asked to tell a story. A more up-to-date and culturally sensitive alternative to this test is the Roberts Apperception Test (2nd edition), in which the characters are children of varied ethnic backgrounds engaged in various common interactions. Also current and culturally relevant is the Tell-Me-A-Story, or TEMAS, technique (Costantino, Dana, & Malgady, 2007; Costantino, Malgady, & Rogler, 1988; Teglasi, 2010). The TEMAS was specifically designed as a culturally sensitive alternative to the TAT. Clinicians can choose between full-color cards that depict either nonminority or Latino/a or African American individuals in a variety of situations, about which children (ages 5–18) are asked to tell a story. The cards of the TEMAS incorporate a lower degree of ambiguity than the TAT, such that each card centers on a particular theme, setting, or issue. Normative data for the TEMAS is culture specific, with norms organized according to age, gender, and specific ethnicities (Flanagan, Costantino, Cardalda, & Costantino, 2008; Malgady & Colon-Malgady, 2008; Teglasi, 2010).

In addition to projective tests such as these in which clients respond with words, this category of children's tests includes some expressive tests in which clients respond with drawings. These drawings, when accurately interpreted, are believed to communicate important information about clients' personalities. In one such test, the Draw-a-Person test, the client is given blank paper and is simply instructed to draw a whole person. Similarly, in the Kinetic Family Drawing technique, the drawing consists of the client's family engaged in some activity, and the House-Tree-Person test requires a drawing of the three items listed in its title. Clinical child psychologists use the drawings produced by tests of this kind to develop hypotheses about the psychological functioning of the client. As in most projective or expressive techniques, drawing techniques tend to rely on inference during the interpretation process. Interpretation of drawing tests should also take culture into account. Drawings that children create can reflect cultural as well as individual issues. For example, Esquivel, Oades-Sese, and Olitzky (2008) point out that Japanese children completing tests in which they draw human figures might be influenced by the popularity of anime and manga animation—which typically features unusually large eyes, among other common characteristics—and the relative infrequency of smiles within Japanese culture, which stems from a cultural norm of restraint rather than open expression of emotion.

Intellectual Tests

⊕ **Web Link 17.2**
Site for WISC-IV

Intellectual tests for children generally consist of IQ tests and achievement tests, and they stand apart from the other methods described above. Whereas the methods described above assess behavioral and emotional functioning, IQ and achievement tests assess intellectual functioning. In a full psychological evaluation, a clinical child psychologist may use methods from all these categories, but in some common types of evaluations such as evaluations for specific learning disorder, the emphasis may be almost exclusively on intellectual tests. Both IQ and achievement tests for children as well as adults are described in detail in Chapter 9.

Among specific intellectual tests, the Spanish version of the Wechsler Intelligence Scale for Children—Fourth Edition (WISC-IV) has been noted as a significant improvement over previous editions of the WISC and a generally strong choice for Spanish-speaking youth (Park-Taylor et al., 2010). It was normed on children whose parents were from a variety of countries where Spanish is spoken predominantly, including Mexico, Cuba, the Dominican Republic, Puerto Rico, and others in Central America and South America. Of course, a drawback of this and many other translated tests is that while items were translated, content did not change. Tests that have culture-specific content or tests that aim to be culture fair by reducing or removing the impact of language—such as the Universal Nonverbal Intelligence Test (UNIT), described in detail in Chapter 9—can also be considered for clients with diverse cultural and linguistic backgrounds.

The Frequency of Use of Specific Assessment Techniques

A 2002 survey of psychologists who specialize in working with children and adolescents measured the frequency with which specific tests were used during assessment procedures

(Cashel, 2002). Respondents were American Psychological Association members who belonged to Division 53 (Clinical Child Psychology) or other divisions that similarly focus on children and assessment issues. Results indicated that interviews were used far more commonly than any specific assessment technique. Among noninterview techniques, clinicians reported using a somewhat different set of instruments with adolescents than with younger children, with greater reliance on self-report measures for adolescents and greater reliance on behavior rating scales (completed by parents or teachers) for younger children. Overall, it appears that some tests (such as the WISC) are relatively common, but a significant amount of variation remains among clinicians. Tables 17.1 and 17.2 summarize the results of this survey.

Table 17.1 Usage of Specific Assessment Techniques in Child Assessment

Assessment Technique	Percentage of Child Clinicians Who Use Technique	Type of Technique
Wechsler Intelligence Scale for Children	75	Intelligence test
Child Behavior Checklist	65	Behavior rating scale
Conners' Parent and Teacher Rating Scale	65	Behavior rating scale
Vineland Adaptive Behavior Scales	63	Semistructured interview and behavior rating scale
Sentence Completion	57	Projective/expressive
Draw-a-Person	56	Projective/expressive
Bender-Gestalt	56	Neuropsychological screen
Beery VMI	56	Neuropsychological screen
Peabody Picture Vocabulary Test	53	Intelligence test
Wechsler Individual Achievement Test	53	Achievement test

Source: Cashel (2002).

Table 17.2 Usage of Specific Assessment Techniques in Adolescent Assessment

Assessment Technique	Percentage of Child Clinicians Who Use Technique	Type of Technique
Wechsler Intelligence Scale for Children	70	Intelligence test
Sentence Completion	60	Projective/expressive
Child Behavior Checklist	53	Behavior rating scale
Rorschach Inkblot Technique	48	Projective/expressive
Conners' Parent and Teacher Rating Scale	48	Behavior rating scale
Beck Depression Inventory	48	Self-report scale
Wechsler Individual Achievement Test	48	Achievement test
Minnesota Multiphasic Personality Inventory-Adolescent	46	Self-report scale
Child Behavior Checklist-Teacher Report Form	44	Behavior rating scale
Thematic Apperception Test	43	Projective/expressive
Youth Self-Report	43	Self-report scale

Source: Cashel (2002).

Psychotherapy With Children and Adolescents

Although therapy with children and adolescents may look or sound quite different than therapy with adults, the techniques used by both types of therapists often originate from the same underlying theories. That is, the major approaches to therapy, including psychodynamic, humanistic, behavioral, and cognitive, have generated applications for children as well as adults.

That being said, children should never be mistaken for miniature adults, so therapy with children necessitates some significant adjustments from the adult model. The assumptions in adult therapy include the client's willingness to be in therapy, motivation to change, and ability to sit relatively calmly and use words to describe experiences or express feelings for prolonged periods of time. When working with children and adolescents, none of these can be taken for granted. Moreover, when working with an adult, the client is typically the only person involved in the sessions. Children, however, don't come to therapy alone. Parents, relatives, teachers, or others may be involved, and it is preferable to keep them involved as allies in treatment. In fact, the therapeutic alliance is just as crucial in therapy with children and adolescents as it is in therapy with adults (Shirk, Karver, & Brown, 2011), but in this case the alliance must include multiple parties—the child *and* the parent(s)—rather than just the client, as in adult therapy.

A full-fledged review of all psychotherapy methods for children and adolescents is beyond the scope of this chapter. In fact, Kazdin (2000) lists 551 distinct psychotherapy techniques for children and adolescents and considers this an underestimate! Instead, we will sample various forms of child therapy being actively practiced today by clinical psychologists. Then we will review the empirical outcome literature on psychotherapy for children and adolescents to gain a current understanding of "what works."

Cognitive-Behavioral Therapies for Children

Cognitive-behavioral therapies for children are undoubtedly on the rise (James & Roberts, 2009; Ollendick & Shirk, 2011). Much more than any other kind of child therapy, they represent the movement toward evidence-based treatment and reliance on empirical data; in other words, they have accumulated evidence that they work (Chorpita et al., 2011). These therapies involve either behavioral or cognitive techniques, and, in many cases, techniques of both types are utilized together.

In most cases, this empirical evidence was obtained in psychotherapy outcome studies in which a particular, manual-based treatment was applied to a specific disorder. Although cognitive-behavioral treatments have been found beneficial for a variety of disorders in children, including depression and ADHD (Curry & Becker, 2008; Hoza, Kaiser, & Hurt, 2008), they are most strongly supported for anxiety disorders. Indeed, there are specific, empirically supported treatments for children with OCD, panic disorder, phobia (including school phobia), and social phobia, among others (Ollendick & Pincus, 2008; Silverman & Pina, 2008; Storch et al., 2008). In general, these child treatments rely on the same principles as their adult counterparts. For example, treatment of phobias in children centers on gradual exposure to the feared object or situation (often augmented by relaxation training); treatment of OCD in children centers on combining exposure with response prevention (prohibiting clients from the compulsive behavior, such as hand washing, that brings them temporary relief from anxiety-causing obsessive thoughts); and treatment of numerous childhood anxiety

⊕ **Web Link 17.3**

Journal of Clinical Child & Adolescent Psychology

problems involves cognitive restructuring in which the child is taught to challenge illogical thoughts and replace them with more logical thoughts (Rapee, Schniering, & Hudson, 2009).

Of course, even if the principles are the same, the way they are delivered to children often differs from the way they are delivered to adults. For example, cognitive-behavioral therapists working with children often adapt their interventions into games of various kinds (Knell & Dasari, 2011). Pincus, Chase, Chow, Weiner, and Pian (2011) describe several such game-based techniques, including "Bravery Bingo," in which a phobic child earns a token, to be placed on a Bingo board, for each successful exposure on the anxiety hierarchy. Pincus et al. also describe "Mr. OCD," in which kids practice cognitive restructuring by refuting a puppet (Mr. OCD) who exhibits flawed logic ("A monster's gonna get you tonight when you're sleeping") by offering more sound logical statements ("A monster has never gotten me before, and it's not gonna happen tonight either! There are no monsters in my room!"). Likewise, when cognitive-behavioral therapists assign homework to their child clients, they often use a much more deliberate reinforcement system to ensure that the homework gets done. Depending on the age and interests of the child (and the preferences of the parent[s]), they may use stickers, candy, privileges, or simply praise to encourage the child to complete assigned between-session tasks.

Self-Instructional Training

Donald Meichenbaum (1977, 1985, 2008) originally developed **self-instructional training** as a method for impulsive and disruptive children to gain greater control over their behavior (see also Meichenbaum & Goodman, 1971). It is still used with that population, but its use has expanded to many other problems of childhood (and adulthood) as well (e.g., Grace, Spirito, Finch, & Ott, 1993). Although it has also been called "guided self-dialogue," *self-instructional training* is the more common term.

Self-instructional training is essentially a form of cognitive therapy in which children are taught to "talk through" situations in which their behavior might be problematic to increase the likelihood of a preferred behavior instead. The process involves a sequence of steps by which children hear instructions aloud and gradually incorporate those instructions into their own thinking. Once a target behavior or situation is identified, the therapist begins the process by modeling the appropriate behavior. The key to the therapist's modeling behavior is that as the child observes, the therapist guides himself or herself through the behavior by talking out loud. Next, the child tries the behavior, with the therapist again saying the instructions aloud. Once this is mastered, the child says the instructions aloud to himself or herself while completing the behavior. Then, the child whispers instructions to himself or herself, and, ultimately, the child completes the behavior silently with only unspoken self-instructions. According to some developmental theorists (e.g., Luria, 1961), this sequence parallels the way children naturally and gradually take instruction from others, such as parents, and incorporate these instructions into their own thinking.

Self-instructional training is "designed to nurture a problem-solving attitude and to engender specific cognitive strategies that clients can use at various phases of their stress response" (Meichenbaum, 1985, p. 69). Rather than changing "cognitions" per se, therapists who use self-instructional training introduce new "self-statements" to their clients. That is, when a child faces a challenge and either lacks problem-solving skills or makes maladaptive self-statements such as, "I can't handle this" or "I have no idea what to do" or "I'm gonna get in trouble," the likelihood of an appropriate behavior is low. If those absent or negative self-statements could be replaced with more constructive, helpful self-statements that steer the child through the necessary steps, preferred behavior is much more likely to occur. Meichenbaum argues that constructive self-statements can be helpful at various points in time: in preparation for the stressor; in the midst of the stressful moment; and afterward, when reflecting on how the stressor was handled. During the training process, the child may need to say self-statements aloud, but with practice, the self-statements need be only thought rather than spoken.

As an example, consider Nicholas, a hyperactive 7-year-old second-grader. Among the many behavioral problems he exhibits at school, his teachers describe transitions from one room to another as one of the most disruptive. When it is time for Nicholas's class to end a classroom activity, get up from their desks, and line up at the door to go to lunch, physical education, an assembly, or recess, Nicholas's tendency is to run excitedly around the room talking to his peers, which creates chaos and prolongs the transition for the whole class. The preferred behavior would be for Nicholas to put away his things and line up quietly at the classroom door, as he has been instructed many times. With Dr. Sanders, a clinical child psychologist, Nicholas works on improving this problem via self-instructional training. They reenact the classroom situation in Dr. Sanders's office, and at first, Dr. Sanders pretends to be the second-grader. When it's time to go to the physical education class, Dr. Sanders says aloud to himself,

> Now, what am I supposed to do? Oh, I know, I'm supposed to put my papers and books and pencils in my desk, quietly walk over to the door, and line up with my friends. I can totally do that. No problem. Here I go—putting away all my stuff. Not running around or making noise. I'm doing good so far. Now I'm getting up, walking over to the door, still staying calm. Now I'm by the door, lined up, waiting quietly 'til the teacher says to go. All right! I knew I could do it!

Next, Nicholas tries the behavior himself, with Dr. Sanders talking him through it. Ultimately, Nicholas is talking himself through it, then whispering himself through it, and then silently instructing himself through it. After repeated practice in Dr. Sanders's office, Nicholas is performing this behavior with regularity in the classroom. Other problem behaviors were similarly addressed, and with each success, Nicholas grew more confident and capable of developing his own helpful self-instructional strategies and behaving in a nondisruptive way.

● ● ● **BOX 17.3** ● ● ●

Metaphorically Speaking

If You've Had Dancing Lessons, You Understand Self-Instructional Training

"Slow, slow, quick-quick; slow, slow, quick-quick." On the first day of dance class, these are the instructions that a dance teacher says aloud to students learning the waltz. Although the rhythm might differ for the samba, the fox trot, the mambo, or the swing, the basic teaching strategy is the same. At the outset of the lessons, the teacher talks the students through the dance by calling the steps out loud and performs the dance as a model. As the dancers begin to develop proficiency, the teacher becomes less vocal, and the dancers talk themselves through the steps. With more practice, their self-talk wanes to a whisper and then fades altogether, unnecessary because the steps have been incorporated into the dancers' thought processes.

Self-instructional training (Meichenbaum, 1977, 1985, 2008; Meichenbaum & Goodman, 1971) is very much like dance lessons. Rather than selecting a particular dance, the therapist and client (with input from parents and teachers) select a particular behavior on which to focus. The therapist then begins the process, much like a dance teacher on the first day of class, by modeling the behavior while saying aloud the steps that must be taken to complete the behavior effectively. Then the child attempts the behavior while the therapist calls out the steps. Next, the child attempts the behavior while making the self-statements aloud, followed by the self-statements being spoken under the client's breath, and, ultimately, only in the client's mind. All the while, the therapist offers feedback and encouragement, much like a dance teacher watching his or her class gradually learn to complete the dance steps less deliberately and more naturally.

Sometimes, a student enters a dance class with the firmly held belief, "I can't dance." Similarly, children often face difficult situations with firmly held self-statements such as, "I can't do this," "I'm gonna get in trouble," and so on. In both cases, the self-directed message is probably inaccurate and definitely maladaptive—in other words, it gets in the way of accomplishing the goal. Just as the dance teacher would work to revise the belief of the self-critical dance student, the therapist in self-instructional training works to replace the child's maladaptive self-statement with a series of constructive, encouraging self-statements that facilitate the successful completion of the target behavior.

Parent Training

Parent training is a form of behavioral therapy in which therapists teach parents to use techniques based on conditioning to modify problematic behavior in their children (Jackson & Leonetti, 2002). The parent training approach to children's behavior problems "utilizes parents as the primary agents of change for their children. It is, after all, the parents who construct and manage the child's environment" (Briesmeister & Schaefer, 1998, p. 1).

Like any form of behavior therapy, parent training begins with a clear, measurable definition of the child's problem behavior. Then, together with the parents, the therapist conducts a functional analysis to try to understand the contingencies that maintain the behavior. Next, again with the parents, the therapist explores different consequences for the behavior. Parents are instructed on contingencies to establish and how to communicate them to the child. Often, the therapist exemplifies the behavior for the parents, providing a model for a behavior that may not have been in their repertoire previously. Parents then apply the new contingency at home and report back to the therapist about the child's behavior using objective, quantifiable outcome measures. Many aspects of conditioning may be discussed as the therapist educates the parents, including reinforcement, punishment, extinction, generalization, discrimination, schedules of reinforcement (e.g., fixed or variable), and other concepts. Parent training programs have been developed for a growing number of childhood problems, including ADHD, conduct disorder, separation anxiety, school refusal, sleep/wake problems, and others. At the end of any such program of treatment, successful parent training yields not only improved behavior in the child but more competent and confident parents as well (Briesmeister & Schaefer, 1998).

As an example, consider Patty, a single mother of 3-year-old Miranda and 6-year-old Joy. Patty seeks the help of Dr. Fisk, a clinical psychologist, because Miranda has developed the habit of physically assaulting her big sister. She hasn't caused any real physical damage yet, but Miranda hits, kicks, and bites Joy on a daily basis. Usually, these actions are unprovoked, and sometimes the girls aren't even interacting before it happens. Dr. Fisk asks Patty what happens after Miranda acts aggressively toward her sister. Patty says that she takes Miranda on her lap and talks with her about the incident, usually for about 5 minutes. Patty says that during these talks, her tone of voice is always kind and concerned rather than punitive and that the 5-minute talks usually end with hugs and kisses and a promise from Miranda that she won't hurt her sister anymore. However, she inevitably does, at which point Patty repeats the same routine. In response to a question from Dr. Fisk, Patty mentioned that one-on-one talks with hugs and kisses happen very rarely other than in these postaggression moments. Dr. Fisk hypothesized that Patty's response to Miranda's behavior was actually reinforcing her aggressive behavior—Miranda's "payoff" was the hugs, kisses, and attention from Mommy. Dr. Fisk taught Patty to introduce new contingencies: A full day without any aggressive behavior earned Miranda a 5-minute snuggle at bedtime, and any aggressive behavior not only cost Miranda the 5-minute bedtime snuggle but also resulted in an immediate 3-minute timeout. If Miranda disobeyed the timeout, additional punishments, such as loss of dessert and TV privileges, were also systematically introduced. Besides offering these instructions to Patty, Dr. Fisk explained the behavioral concepts underlying them, including the likelihood of an extinction burst, in which Miranda's behavior might briefly intensify before it ultimately extinguished. With a full understanding of the reasoning behind it, Patty put the new contingency plan into effect and stuck with it, and within a short time Miranda's aggressive behavior was greatly reduced.

Play Therapy

Play therapy is a form of treatment unique to child clients. Typically used with younger clients (preschool or elementary-school age), it allows children to communicate via actions with objects such as dollhouses, action figures, and toy animals rather than words. Through play, children can reveal to clinical psychologists their emotional concerns and attempts to resolve them. Brems (2008) argues that play therapy has three basic functions: the formation of important relationships (i.e., the therapeutic relationship), disclosure of feelings and thoughts (e.g., expressing emotions, acting out anxieties), and healing (e.g., acquiring coping skills, experimenting with new behaviors). As it is practiced by clinical psychologists, play therapy can be completely unstructured, with the child given free rein in the playroom to determine the course of the session, or structured to varying degrees, with the therapist instructing the child to play with certain objects or inviting the child to play a specific game (Cheung, 2006).

Of course, in any form of play therapy, cultural sensitivity is essential when furnishing the playroom with dolls, toys, and other objects for child clients. Children who find toys representative of and relevant to their own cultural backgrounds are more likely to engage in meaningful play and to find the play therapy experience rewarding. For example, Hinds (2005) encourages play therapists to offer African American children dolls with an array of authentic African American physical features, including variations in skin tone, hair length, and hair style. Similarly, Robles (2006) suggests that for Mexican American children, play therapists should include in the playroom traditional Mexican toys, including such games as *Juego de la Oca* (Game of the Goose) and *Serpientes y Escalaras* (Snakes and Ladders). Drewes (2005a) adds that any set of markers or crayons should include colors that represent multicultural skin tones and that any play kitchen should include multicultural items such as chopsticks or tortilla presses. Especially for children who may be struggling with issues of cultural acceptance, the presence of culture-specific objects in the playroom can itself help strengthen their ethnic and personal identities. In addition, Drewes (2005b) emphasizes that play therapists must be aware of various cultural norms that children may exhibit in the playroom in order to avoid misinterpretation; for example, across cultures, norms may differ in terms of personal space, eye contact, and the meaning of silence.

Play therapy has taken many forms, but two of the most commonly practiced stem from psychodynamic and humanistic theories.

Play Therapy—Psychodynamic

For psychodynamic clinical child psychologists, a child's play symbolically communicates important processes occurring within the child's mind, "revealing aspects of the child's internal life of which he or she may be unaware and unable to verbalize directly" (Marans, Dahl, & Schowalter, 2002, p. 388). So as the child plays, the therapist is both a participant and an observer, interacting with the child but always monitoring the child's choices and actions. As in any form of psychodynamic therapy, the goal is to make the unconscious conscious, but with young children, it is assumed that they lack the verbal skills and attention span to converse directly with the therapist about their issues. Instead, the unconscious is conveyed through play, and the therapist's job is to infer these unconscious issues and, through interpretations, to make the child more consciously aware of them.

In **psychodynamic play therapy**, the playroom usually contains a variety of objects with which the child can choose to play. Psychodynamic play therapists may take note of the objects the child chooses, especially if he or she appears to identify strongly with a particular toy. For example, a child who chooses a damaged doll and uses it as the primary character in make-believe adventures may have a damaged sense of self-esteem; a child who, every session, insists on using only the biggest, strongest truck in the box may be struggling with issues related to power. Of course, once certain objects are chosen, the therapist pays close attention to the way the child uses them, with the actions and themes that manifest in the child's play representing latent unconscious issues. The interpretations the therapist offers the child about his or her actions during play can help make them aware of inner mental processes and increase the child's ability to make deliberate choices about behavior in the future (Marans et al., 2002; O'Connor, 2000).

As an example, consider 5-year-old Cassandra, an only child whose parents separated about 2 months ago. Cassandra currently lives with her mother, Tisha, and sees her father, Marquis, about once a week. Tisha brings Cassandra to Dr. Ball, a psychodynamic play therapist, because she is concerned about how the separation is affecting her. Tisha explains that she hasn't seen any "acting out" behavior, but Cassandra seems more withdrawn, more irritable, and less happy than she usually is. In an early play therapy session, Cassandra builds a small tower with blocks for a few minutes and, seemingly bored with the blocks, wanders over to the dolls. She chooses a doll and returns to the tower she had built. With her free hand, Cassandra slowly begins to knock the top blocks off the tower. At the same time, Cassandra puts the doll near the tower but not quite close enough to stop her free hand from knocking the tower over. She repeats this action in which her free hand destroys the tower while the doll is just unable to prevent it until the tower is completely leveled. All the while, she is narrating in a high-pitched, soft voice: "Oh no . . . save the tower . . . you have to do something . . . don't let the whole thing fall . . . do something." After the tower is destroyed, Cassandra's voice turns harsh and loud as she turns the doll to face her and says, "You are a bad girl! How could you let this happen? It's all your fault that the tower is wrecked!" Dr. Ball makes two inferences from this episode: Cassandra is very concerned about her parents' marriage (as represented by the tower) collapsing, and Cassandra (as represented by the doll) feels responsible yet powerless to safeguard it. The fact that Cassandra re-creates similar scenarios in subsequent sessions confirms Dr. Ball's thoughts. Over time, Dr. Ball talks about the episodes with Cassandra— what the doll is feeling, what her job is, whether it's fair to assign that job to her. Dr. Ball is eventually able to help Cassandra make the conscious connection between the doll's experience and her own, so Cassandra can consciously consider the questions as applied to herself—what Cassandra is feeling, what her job is, and whether that job is fair. Ultimately, Cassandra begins to accept that it's very normal to be sad, angry, or nervous about her parents' relationship but that blaming herself for its demise or expecting herself to protect it are unfair burdens. With this pressure lifted, Cassandra's mood improves despite her difficult situation.

Play Therapy—Humanistic

Humanistic play therapy involves many of the same activities, materials, and assumptions as psychodynamic play therapy does. Children play with objects in the playroom, therapists participate and observe, and the underlying assumption is that the activities and themes in the play express the inner workings of the child's mind. However, there are several key distinctions between humanistic play therapy (sometimes called "child-centered" play therapy) and psychodynamic play therapy (O'Connor, 2000). Although interpretations are a key element of psychoanalytic play therapy, humanistic play therapists rarely offer interpretations, because they do not share the psychodynamic therapists' primary goal of making the unconscious conscious. Rather than interpreting clients' behavior, humanistic play therapists tend to reflect their clients' feelings, which may be expressed indirectly through their play activities. This reflection is an important part of the overall goal of humanistic play therapy, which is the same as humanistic therapy for adults—to facilitate self-actualization. This self-actualization happens in the context of an all-important therapeutic relationship based on true unconditional acceptance and genuine empathy. So as humanistic play therapists observe children and play along with them, they establish relationships in which the children are accepted wholly for who they are. This unconditional positive regard from the therapist is thought to bring about unconditional positive self-regard within the child. When therapists reflect children's feelings in a "real" and nonjudgmental way, children themselves become more accepting of their own emotional experience, which enhances congruence and, ultimately, self-growth (Landreth, 1991; O'Connor, 2000).

If Cassandra, the 5-year-old girl described in the psychodynamic play therapy section above, were seen instead by a humanistic play therapist, the course of therapy might have been somewhat different. Most notably, the act of interpretation would probably be absent; that is, the therapist would not make deliberate efforts to make Cassandra aware of her own unconscious processes. Instead, a humanistic play therapist would focus on Cassandra's emotional experience during the session (expressed directly or through the doll), emphasizing an unqualified acceptance and compassion for any of Cassandra's feelings. With time, a therapeutic relationship characterized by such honest care would have internalizing effects on Cassandra; that is, her own recognition and acceptance of her emotional experience would become enhanced. As a result, she would experience greater congruence between her real and ideal selves, which would in turn facilitate her natural tendency toward growth and self-actualization.

How Well Does Psychotherapy for Children and Adolescents Work?

A significant body of empirical research suggests that, in general, the efficacy of psychotherapy for children and adolescents is quite strong. In fact, the theme of such studies is quite similar to the theme of studies of therapy outcome for adults: Children and adolescents who undergo psychotherapy consistently demonstrate significant improvement in comparison with similar children who receive no treatment. Most often, in meta-analyses and reviews, various approaches to therapy are found to have roughly equal effects; sometimes, behavioral treatments are found to have a slight edge in efficacy over nonbehavioral approaches (Carr, 2008; Evans et al., 2005; Russ & Freedheim, 2002; Weisz, Weiss, Han, Granger, & Morton, 1995).

With the general efficacy of child and adolescent psychotherapy firmly established, researchers have shifted their attention to more specific questions of particular forms of therapy for particular clinical problems (Carr, 2008; Chorpita et al., 2011; Evans et al., 2005). As mentioned above, the broad category of cognitive-behavioral therapies for children has demonstrated strong empirical efficacy with not only anxiety disorders but also a wide range of other presenting problems such as oppositional defiant disorder, depression, hyperactivity, enuresis (bedwetting), and sleep disorders (Ollendick & Shirk, 2011; Powers, 2002). Similarly, the broad category of play therapy has demonstrated efficacy with a wide range of both externalizing and internalizing disorders (Bratton, Ray, Rhine, & Jones, 2005; Ray, 2006). More specifically, a number of particular techniques, mostly behavioral in orientation, have proven successful in treating particular disorders (Curry & Becker, 2008; Hoza, Kaiser, & Hurt, 2008; Kazdin, 2000; Nathan & Gorman, 2002, 2007; Rapee et al., 2009; Silverman & Pina, 2008; Smith, Barkley, & Shapiro, 2006; Storch et al., 2008):

- Systematic desensitization, modeling, and cognitive restructuring for phobia and other anxiety disorders
- Exposure and response prevention for OCD
- Parent-training techniques for oppositional defiant disorder and conduct disorder
- Parent training and classroom contingency management for ADHD
- Cognitive behavioral techniques and interpersonal therapy for childhood depression

Interestingly, some common problems of childhood and adolescence have received significant attention from therapy outcome researchers, whereas other problems have received much less. For example, a review of treatment efficacy for ADHD (Smith et al., 2006) cites an enormous literature consisting of hundreds of relevant studies, whereas a chapter from the same year reviewing anorexia and bulimia in adolescents (Striegel-Moore & Franko, 2006) states that "efficacy studies based on adolescent patients are almost non-existent" (p. 173), leaving clinicians to generalize from outcome studies on adults. The latter situation is certainly less than ideal, as important developmental issues can be overlooked.

CHAPTER SUMMARY

Clinical child and adolescent psychologists work with a wide range of issues, including externalizing disorders (e.g., ADHD, conduct disorder, oppositional defiant disorder) and internalizing disorders (e.g., mood disorders). They also work in a preventive capacity to increase children's resilience and decrease their vulnerability to psychological problems. They incorporate a developmental perspective by remaining aware of clients' ages and developmental stages as a context for clinical issues. Assessments typically involve multiple sources of information, multiple settings, and multiple methods. Particular assessment techniques include interviews, behavioral observations, behavior rating scales, self-report scales, projective/expressive techniques, and intellectual tests. Therapy with children and adolescents takes on a wide variety of forms, most of which derive from the same basic orientations as adult forms of psychotherapy. Cognitive-behavioral therapies for children have accumulated empirical support for numerous disorders, especially anxiety disorders. Self-instructional training teaches children to "talk themselves through" difficult situations, parent training teaches parents to apply behavioral conditioning techniques to their children, and play therapy allows children to communicate and solve their problems via play with toys and other objects. In all aspects of their work, clinical child and adolescent psychologists maintain an appreciation of the cultural backgrounds of their clients and the families in which they live.

KEY TERMS AND NAMES

analogue direct observation   274

behavior rating scales   274

behavioral observation   273

clinical child psychology   263

developmental perspective   267

externalizing disorders   265

humanistic play therapy   286

internalizing disorders   265

Donald Meichenbaum   280

multisource, multimethod, multisetting approach   270

naturalistic direct observation   274

parent training   283

pediatric psychology   264

psychodynamic play therapy   285

reactivity   273

resilience   265

self-instructional training   280

self-report scales   274

Society of Clinical Child and Adolescent Psychology   263

vulnerability   265

CRITICAL THINKING QUESTIONS

1. In your opinion, what are the most important factors in the development of resilience in children?

2. If you were a clinical child psychologist, how would you expect gender to influence the development of internalizing disorders and externalizing disorders?

3. In your opinion, how reliable and valid is the information children provide in clinical interviews? How reliable and valid is the information adults provide about children?

4. If you were a clinical psychologist, for what clinical problems would you expect self-instructional training to be most successful? Does the age of the child make a difference?

5. Under what circumstances would you expect parent training versus direct clinical intervention to be more successful in reducing a child's behavior problems?

STUDENT STUDY SITE RESOURCES

Visit the study site at www.sagepub.com/pomerantz3eupdate for these additional learning tools:

- Self-quizzes
- eFlashcards
- Culture Expert Interviews

- Full-text SAGE journal articles
- Additional web resources
- Mock Assessment Data

CHAPTER SUMMARY VIDEO

 QR codes at the end of each chapter link to chapter background videos by the author. Visit http://gettag.mobi using your smartphone browser to download the free Microsoft Tag app. Once installed, scan the tags to go directly to these brief videos. In this video, the author describes his own clinical experiences with the "multisource" component of assessing children.

CHAPTER 18

Health Psychology

Laura A. Pawlow and Andrew M. Pomerantz

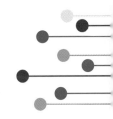

Health psychology is a relatively new subspecialty within clinical psychology. Its emergence corresponds with changes in the types of diseases that pose the greatest threat within our society. A century ago, those diseases were pneumonia, tuberculosis, and influenza, but today, they are diseases such as heart disease, cancer, and stroke. The newer killers have clear-cut behavioral components; they are worsened by smoking, poor eating habits, and lack of exercise. So it should be no surprise that the field of health psychology has surfaced in recent decades and has rapidly become popular among clinicians and researchers (Benjamin, 2005).

The health psychology division of the American Psychological Association (APA Division 38) was founded in 1978, and today there are many journals dedicated to publishing research in this field (e.g., *Health Psychology, Journal of Behavioral Medicine*). Health psychology is primarily concerned with the ways our thoughts, feelings, and behaviors influence our physical health. To become a competent health psychologist, a clinical psychologist needs training beyond the typical doctoral program requirements. This training can take the form of coursework or internships and often involves interaction with professionals from many health professions outside of psychology (Hanson & Kerkhoff, 2012).

Although the term *behavioral medicine* is often used interchangeably with the term *health psychology,* the two terms are not exactly synonymous. Before we explore the area of health psychology, let's start with some basic definitions.

Definitions: Health Psychology Versus Behavioral Medicine

Web Link 18.1

Website of APA Division 38

Health care professionals interested in the ways our minds influence our bodies are likely to be drawn to the broad, interdisciplinary field of **behavioral medicine.** Behavioral medicine involves the integration of knowledge from a wide variety of social sciences, including psychology, sociology, and anthropology, with knowledge from the medical disciplines. **Health psychology** is a subdiscipline of behavioral medicine that deals specifically with how *psychological* processes (e.g., cognitions, moods, social networks) influence health and illness. A primary responsibility of health psychologists is the development, assessment, and application of programs designed to promote wellness; as such, they often work in hospitals or specialized clinics for such issues as weight management, smoking cessation, or pain control (Emery, Anderson, & Andersen, 2011; Lewis, Statt, & Marcus, 2011). They frequently work within primary care teams, alongside physicians, nurses, and other health professionals (Goodheart & Rozensky, 2011). Health psychologists ask questions such as, "Why do students tend to get sick more often around exam week?" and "Will keeping a food diary help my clients lose weight?" Health psychologists might spend their days engaged in research or the application of such activities as promoting healthy behaviors (such as smoking reduction or cessation, abstinence from tanning beds, or the incorporation of more fruits and vegetables into the daily diet) and/or preventing illness through such means as teaching relaxation or coping skills.

Stress

Today's health psychologists have a wide selection of areas in which they can practice, but that was not always the case. The first applications of the field of health psychology dealt solely with the topic of **stress**: the psychological and/or physiological response to difficult or demanding internal or external circumstances (VandenBos, 2007). Although the terms *health psychology* and *behavioral medicine* weren't coined until the 1970s, the idea that stress could negatively impact the body surfaced long ago. In 1932, Walter Cannon described the **fight-or-flight response**: When an organism perceives a threat, the body rapidly mobilizes energy reserves via the sympathetic nervous system and endocrine system to either fight or flee. For primitive humans, the body's behavioral responses were probably actually fighting or fleeing (perhaps from a snarling saber-toothed tiger), but today's "fighting" and "fleeing" look a bit different. Blaring your horn aggressively after being cut off in traffic or withdrawing from anxiety-provoking situations into self-medicating substances such as alcohol are modern variations of fighting and fleeing, respectively.

Photo 18.1 Stress, especially when chronic, can overwhelm our ability to adapt and produce significant psychological and physical symptoms. Can you recall times when this has happened in your own life?

The duration of stressors can vary greatly. **Chronic stress** refers to the all-too-common syndrome defined by stress levels that are consistently high and unremitting, often due to a hectic, fast-paced lifestyle. Many of us have firsthand knowledge of chronic stress: Hamermesh and Lee (2007) found that 55% of adult American women and 43% of adult American men report feeling stressed "always" or "often." Unfortunately, our bodies are not set up to handle this long-term exposure to stress, and given a long enough period of time, we become exhausted and vulnerable to illness. This process was described by **Hans Selye** (1956) in his pioneering work on stress, which culminated in his **general adaptation syndrome** hypothesis: When confronted with a temporary stressor, our fight-or-flight system often works very effectively, but with repeated or prolonged exposure to stress, our bodies eventually wear out and break down.

Stress and Physical Illness

Stress has been linked to myriad symptoms and diseases, including migraine headaches, osteoporosis, chronic back pain, cardiovascular disease, ulcers, diarrhea, acne, and fertility problems (Hafen, Karren, Frandsen, & Smith, 1996; Schneiderman & Siegel, 2007). The same bodily responses that originally provided us with the ability to save ourselves from an immediate danger have, in our society, become maladaptive conditions that lead to illness in many people. In fact, researchers at the American Institute of Stress (1997) estimate that 75% to 90% of all visits to health care providers result from stress-related disorders and that those who are stressed are six times more likely to be hospitalized for a physical ailment than those who are not (Kalia, 2002). Among other health problems, chronic stress can lead to

- increased levels of thyroid hormones, resulting in insomnia and weight loss;
- depleted endorphins, resulting in bodily pain;
- reduced sex hormones, leading to amenorrhea or infertility;
- the shutting down of the digestive system, resulting in nausea, bloating, and dry mouth; and
- an excess of cholesterol release that can contribute to blocked arteries, blood pressure increases of up to 400%, stroke, or aneurism (Hafen et al., 1996).

In addition, one of the most debilitating effects of stress is the weakening of our immune system. Stress activates the **hypothalamic-pituitary-adrenal (HPA) axis,** which controls the release of our body's stress hormone, **cortisol.** Cortisol is beneficial in appropriate amounts; however, chronic stress leads to an increased level of cortisol, which leads to the deterioration of T-cells, essential cells in the immune system. T-cells both attack foreign pathogens and regulate other cells of the immune system. When dysregulated levels of cortisol lead to a decrease in T-cell functioning, the result is a weakened immune system. Or, more simply stated, chronic stress can make you sick. Sheldon Cohen's pioneering work on stress and the common cold found that those participants with the highest amounts of stress were more than five times as likely to become infected with the common cold virus (e.g., Cohen & Williamson, 1991). The study of this phenomenon of emotional stress setting the stage for physical illness is known as **psychoneuroimmunology (PNI).** More specifically, PNI is the scientific field of study concerned with the interactions among behavior, the nervous system, and the immune system (Kropiunigg, 1993).

The deleterious effect of stress on the immune system has opened the door to research and clinical work on the psychology behind two common and deadly diseases: cancer and AIDS. Although it is important to note that there is absolutely no evidence that stress *causes* either of these diseases, there is much evidence to suggest that stress plays a role in the development and maintenance of both. For example, researchers found that being prone to stress was associated with the development of breast cancer (Faragher & Cooper, 1990). In a similar vein, one study of HIV-infected gay men reported that those under considerable stress had a disease progression with a significantly more rapid course (Lesserman et al.,

1999). In partnership with other health professionals, clinical psychologists can play an important role in treatment or prevention of these illnesses.

Stress and Coping

We all know people who seem to be immune to even high levels of stress and others who respond to even minor stressors with psychological or physical ailments. A major difference between these types of people is the way they have learned to cope with their stress. **Coping** has been defined as the process of managing demands that are appraised as exceeding the resources of the person (Lazarus & Folkman, 1984).

What factors determine how well someone copes with stress? Like many questions in psychology, the answer involves both nature and nurture. On the nature side, it appears that our genetic codes can be imprinted with susceptibility for struggling with stress. For example, one study involving 44 identical and 30 fraternal twin pairs suggested that genetic factors accounted for the majority of the variance in 57% of the coping variables studied (Mellins, Gatz, & Baker, 1996). It appears that this biological vulnerability to stress manifests itself in a tendency to overreact or become depressed in response to stress. In fact, researchers have even hypothesized that there is a genotypic inclination toward a **disease-prone personality** that predisposes people to stress-related illnesses such as arthritis, ulcers, and coronary heart disease (Scheier & Bridges, 1995; Smith & MacKenzie, 2006). The personality profile in question is one of marked anxiety, depression, pessimism, and defensive hostility (Guerrero & Palmero, 2010).

Yet studies such as the one described in the paragraph above (Mellins et al., 1996) clearly show that genetics account for only about half the story. What nongenetic factors affect how we cope with stress? One important factor is the individual's *perception* of stress, which may or may not be a realistic appraisal. Indeed, the perception of stress (as opposed to the actual amount or degree of stress) can predict levels of stress-related illness (Hiramoto et al., 1999). In a study of women with breast cancer, the amount of distress—both psychological and physical—resulting from the disease was significantly related to the amount of control the women felt they had. Those who believed they had more control had significantly less distress than did those with perceptions of less control (Barez, Blasco, Fernandez-Castro, & Viladrich, 2009). So whereas health psychologists can do little or nothing about a client's genetics, they commonly work with clients to challenge cognitive misperceptions and replace them with healthier points of view.

A common misperception involves the feeling of being completely devoid of control when faced with stress. However, when clients are challenged to look more carefully at the situation, they will often realize there are some aspects of the situation that are within their control. As an example, consider Max, a 64-year-old military veteran who for many years regularly attended a chronic pain clinic at his local Veterans Affairs hospital. Max benefited greatly from the services he received at the clinic, which had become an integral part of his current pain management plan. On learning that the clinic would be closed due to an abrupt funding cut, Max was devastated. He quickly began to envision a future of miserable, constant back pain. Max's health psychologist, Dr. Phelps, sought to change Max's perception that without the clinic, he had no control over his own back health. She worked with him on compiling a list of the tips and techniques he'd learned from the clinic over the years and ways he could implement them on his own. With input from Max's physician, she also sought out relevant readings, pain management exercise videos, and other resources in the community, including a free weekly pain management support group in a neighboring town. In a relatively brief period of time, Dr. Phelps was able to work with Max to change his perception of being abandoned and helpless to one of having multiple sources of support. It is important to note that this process not only decreased Max's anxiety but his physical pain as well.

Another healthy coping skill that health psychologists can foster is **problem-focused coping**. Problem-focused coping emphasizes proactive, constructive attempts to take action about a stressful situation. This approach is exemplified in the people who, although realizing that the occurrence of a hurricane is completely out of their control, still work to be as optimally prepared as possible by stockpiling emergency supplies and creating evacuation and communication plans. Research has strongly supported the idea that those who believe they can exert some personal control over stressful situations are better off both emotionally and physically than those who view themselves as having little to no control over stressors (Pittner, Houston, & Spiridigliozzi, 1983).

As an example, consider Sandra, a 19-year-old college student who developed ulcers and frequent headaches during her first 2 years in college. Although she had numerous sources of stress, she described her primary stressor as the constant worry that her parents would not be able to continue to support her financially and that without their help she would not be able to continue at her university. With the encouragement of Dr. Yu, a health psychologist who worked in conjunction with the physicians who treated Sandra's ulcers and headaches, Sandra began to search for aspects of this situation that she could control. For example, Dr. Yu helped Sandra identify other colleges that were more affordable, including some in the same city, where she might be able to transfer. Dr. Yu also helped Sandra make a list of other sources of income she could consider, including jobs, loans, and scholarships. Dr. Yu also suggested that Sandra meet with a financial aid specialist at her college, who offered even more resources to Sandra. The result was that by taking control and "doing something" about her problem rather than merely dwelling on it, Sandra's body and mind felt better. Her ulcers and headaches were less severe, and she felt more emotionally stable as well.

Considering Culture

Physical and Psychological Expressions of Depression Across Cultures

According to the *Diagnostic and Statistical Manual of Mental Disorders*—Fifth Edition (*DSM-5*; American Psychiatric Association, 2013), a major depressive episode consists of a combination of at least five of nine possible specific symptoms. Most of these symptoms are psychological in nature (e.g., depressed mood, decreased interest in daily activities, impaired concentration, feeling worthless or guilty, thoughts of death or suicide). The other symptoms are more physical (e.g., appetite/weight changes, sleeping, fatigue, restlessness/slowed movements). But does depression express itself similarly across cultures? Specifically, in members of non-Western cultures, does depression tend to express itself through the body rather than the mind?

Some research suggests that the answer is yes. Specifically, Asian Americans have often been described as exhibiting depression (and some other mental illnesses) through somatic, bodily symptoms to a greater extent than do European Americans (e.g., Sue & Consolacion, 2003; Sue & Sue, 2008). In addition to the physical symptoms listed in the *DSM* definition, headaches, stomach aches, dizziness, aching muscles, and other physical ailments may be included in the experience of depression in many Asian Americans. These physical symptoms may replace the psychological symptoms common to depression in European Americans, such as sad mood and thoughts of death.

There are numerous possible reasons for this relative emphasis on physical symptoms among Asian Americans (Sue & Consolacion, 2003; Sue & Sue, 2008).

- Asian American culture tends to emphasize a holistic view of mind and body. With little or no boundary between these two aspects of life, Asian Americans may present emotional problems as somatic symptoms.

- The importance of collectivism within Asian American culture results in the discouragement of open displays of emotional distress. Such displays could threaten interpersonal harmony or expose personal weakness, neither of which tends to enhance group or family relationships.

- In Asian American cultures, physical illness tends to be less stigmatized than mental illness. Thus, bodily complaints allow clients to maintain a more socially acceptable appearance (i.e., "face") than emotional symptoms.

(Continued)

(Continued)

For those who work with clients whose problems include both physical and psychological symptoms—health psychologists and many other health professionals as well—it is crucial to know that what manifests as physical may have psychological roots. Similarly, it is vital to respect the way clients experience depression and not to pressure clients to think about the problem in a way that is incompatible with their cultural values. So for many Asian American clients, the psychologist would be wise to validate the physical manifestations of depression and to consider a reciprocal interaction between mind and body problems (Sue & Sue, 2008).

Social Support

Friends and family are important weapons against the damaging effects of stress. In fact, some argue that social support is the single most vital resource against stress (e.g., Hafen et al., 1996). **Social support** can be described as the perception that one has relationships with others who can provide support in a time of crisis and can share in good fortune as well. Social support is one of the most documented phenomena in health psychology; its benefits to physical health are ample and undeniable. In the words of Thomas Padus, "The breakdown in the social support structure precipitates a breakdown in the body's immune system" (as quoted in Hafen et al., 1996, p. 262).

House, Kahn, McLeod, and Williams (1985) purport that social resources are composed of three components: social network, social relationships, and social support. One's social network is the broad scope of all social contacts one has. In this large pool is a smaller pool of those with whom one has more meaningful social relationships. And social support refers to the quantity and quality of care and assistance those relationships bring. Thus, someone with a small social network who has a single meaningful social relationship accompanied by a large degree of social support might be better off than a "social butterfly" with a broad social network but no intimate friends. Interestingly, married men report that their main source of social support is their wives, whereas married women rely more heavily on other family members and friends. It is hypothesized that this may account for the fact that men are more likely than women to suffer physically from stress-related ailments after a divorce (Kiecolt-Glaser et al., 1996).

How does social support protect our health? The answer is not yet entirely clear. Some hypothesize that the positive feelings associated with having social support allow us to perceive our stressors in a more manageable light. For example, the social support provided by church attendance was hypothesized to be a primary reason why those who attend religious services regularly are happier and healthier than those who do not (Koenig &

Vaillant, 2009). Another hypothesis, strongly supported by the work of James Pennebaker, is that those who have strong social networks are more likely to confide in others. Pennebaker (1990) has studied the health benefits of confiding and has concluded, "Not disclosing our thoughts and feelings can be unhealthy. Divulging them can be healthy" (p. 82). His work has uncovered benefits to the immune system that are evident after the act of confiding in others. His immune-related findings are mirrored by those of health psychologist Janice Kiecolt-Glaser; one of her studies found clear evidence that those who are more lonely have the most compromised immunities (Kiecolt-Glaser et al., 1985).

Photo 18.2 Social support offers protection from the ill effects of stress.

A third hypothesis regarding how social support protects our health has to do with the sensation of touch. Research in this area was born out of the classic studies of Harry Harlow that compared the development of baby monkeys with and without access to other monkeys and found that monkeys who were touched and cuddled fared significantly better (Harlow & Zimmermann, 1959). Studies on humans have produced similar results. For example, premature babies who were stroked and massaged during their hospital stays were significantly healthier and heavier and had fewer physical problems at an 8-month follow-up period than did those who were not (Weiss, 2005). And another study reported that adults who enjoy regular, loving touch have stronger hearts, lower blood pressures, and report feeling less stress (Engle & Graney, 2000).

Clinical Applications

Today's health psychologists enjoy a wide menu of focus areas, expanding far beyond the original work on stress and health (see Table 18.1). The following sections will review some of the most popular current clinical applications of health psychology. In addition to the following examples of traditional client-based work, it is important to note that health psychologists can also work within a more broad, sociocultural context to craft behavioral health legislation (e.g., mandatory helmet laws, effective public service announcements), school and workplace policies (vending machine and smoking bans), and policymaking regarding health care reform.

⊕ Web Link 18.2

Journal of Health Psychology

Weight Management

In the United States, the prevalence rates for obesity and being overweight are at an all-time high. Currently, 67% of adult Americans are overweight or obese, and the numbers continue to rise each year in both adult and child populations (Centers for Disease

Table 18.1 Common Areas of Clinical Focus in Health Psychology

Alcohol use	Irritable bowel syndrome
Smoking	Weight management
Illicit drug use	Eating disorders
Prescription drug abuse	Stress management
Pain management	Cancer
Chronic fatigue	Coping with medical regimens
HIV/AIDS	Compliance with medical regimens
Cardiovascular disease	Sleep disorders
Diabetes	Sexual disorders

Control, 2008). The risks of carrying excess weight are numerous and well documented; obesity is estimated to cause more than 400,000 deaths annually (16.6% of total deaths) in the United States (Mokdad, Marks, Stroup, & Gerberding, 2004). And health care costs related to obesity are estimated at $117 billion (Jackson et al., 2002), or 6% to 10% of our national health care expenditures (Andreyeva, Sturm, & Ringel, 2004). Health psychologists play a very important role in efforts to stem this national crisis (Fabricatore & Wadden, 2006; Martin, Stewart, Anton, Copeland, & Williamson, 2008). Proper nutrition and physical fitness are no doubt responsible for achieving and maintaining a healthy weight. However, recent research is suggesting that the problem is not that Americans are ignorant of what a healthy diet or exercise regimen is but, rather, that they have a hard time committing to these behaviors in the long term. As such, cognitive-behavioral therapy has become a very necessary and important component of successful weight management.

A common approach health psychologists use in treating people with excess weight is known as the **ABCDS of weight loss**: Activity increase, Behavior change, Cognitive change, Dietary change, and Social support (Blair et al., 1996). Collectively, these components represent a multifaceted, long-term approach to maintaining a healthy weight. To illustrate the use of the ABCDS approach, consider Shannon, a 54-year-old woman who owned and operated a public relations office. Shannon was successful in many ways, but she had been significantly overweight since childhood, and her weight had increased through adulthood. To address her weight problem, Shannon sought the services of Dr. Gold, a health psychologist who worked with a multidisciplinary team of health professionals at a weight management center. Dr. Gold quickly learned that Shannon's many past attempts to lose weight had involved exercise (A) and diets (D) but nothing else (no B, C, or S). Moreover, her exercise and diet efforts had never proven successful, largely because she didn't stick with them.

Regarding her dieting (D) attempts, Shannon explained to Dr. Gold that her diets usually required a complete abstinence from her favorite foods, for which Shannon lacked the willpower over the long haul. Dr. Gold, with help from a dietician colleague, helped Shannon develop a more flexible meal plan (not a diet, per se) that would be more feasible as part of a long-term lifestyle change. Also, in collaboration with a personal trainer, Dr. Gold helped develop an exercise plan (A) that involved five 30-minute workouts per week, some of which involved walking, running, or kayaking with her best friends (S). Also, to address the behavior change (B) aspect of the ABCDS plan, Dr. Gold and Shannon jointly created a list of smart decisions to make at restaurants (e.g., request smaller portions, substitute steamed vegetables for fried side dishes, avoid premeal items such as bread or chips) and grocery stores (reading nutrition labels, limiting purchases of certain high-calorie or high-fat foods).

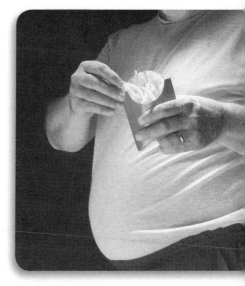

Photo 18.3 Weight-related problems are increasingly prevalent, so weight management has become a common focus of contemporary health psychologists.

To Dr. Gold's surprise, Shannon initially resisted Dr. Gold's suggestions. Shannon explained that they conflicted with some of her beliefs about eating and exercise. Specifically, Shannon believed that "successful weight loss means at least 5 pounds a week," "working out counts only if it lasts at least an hour," and "restaurants don't want to be bothered with special requests." An important aspect of Dr. Gold's job was to challenge these faulty cognitions (C). Dr. Gold persuasively educated Shannon about weight loss goals (1 to 2 pounds per week is more reasonable), exercise duration (any length "counts"), and the fact that most restaurants are very willing to accommodate customer requests. By addressing all the facets of the ABCDS approach, Dr. Gold enabled Shannon's success in maintaining a healthy weight—she lost 35 pounds in the first 6 months and kept that weight off for many years.

An interesting new line of research has focused on the role of **values affirmation** in promoting physical health, including weight management. By writing about the things they value most in life (e.g., relationships, service to others), patients focus their attention on their sense of personal identity and self-worth (Sherman & Cohen,

⊕ Web Link 18.3
Values affirmation

2006). These affirmations bolster self-control, because concentrating on one's most cherished values may lead to a decrease in impulsive behavior that is inconsistent with those values and only rewarding in the short term (Creswell et al., 2005). One notable recent study found that after completing a single session of values affirmation, women weighed significantly less and had significantly smaller waist measurements almost 3 months later than did their peers in a control group that did not complete the values affirmation (Logel & Cohen, 2012).

Smoking

Like obesity, smoking is a massive public health problem in America (Martin et al., 2008). Smoking is currently our single greatest cause of preventable death, accounting for more than 450,000 deaths in the United States each year (Niaura & Abrams, 2002). Smoking has been proven to be a major risk factor in heart disease, cancer, vascular disease, stroke, and major depressive disorder (Haas, Munoz, Humfleet, Reus, & Hall, 2004). Also like obesity, the primary problem is not that people are ignorant of the dangers of smoking; instead, the problem lies in implementing a very difficult behavioral change: quitting.

Unfortunately, once it has become an addiction, smoking exerts very strong control over the physiological, psychological, and social aspects of the smoker's life. Some of the strongest weapons that health psychologists have in the battle against smoking are nicotine replacement, social support, stress management, and relapse prevention.

Nicotine replacement involves the use of over-the-counter or prescription alternatives to cigarettes, including gum or transdermal patches. The mechanism behind this form of therapy is twofold: to break the oral habit of smoking while at the same time slowly weaning the body off nicotine dependence through controlled dosing that decreases over time. A comprehensive review of the efficacy of nicotine replacement therapy has supported it as an agent that produces significant smoking cessation (Cepeda-Benito, 1993). Health psychologists can help educate clients on the research supporting this sort of therapy, how it works, where to obtain it (some can be purchased over the counter, and others need to be prescribed by a physician), and common side effects (e.g., headache, racing heart). In addition, they can help the client work through any potential barriers to compliance with the therapy before they begin (e.g., weighing the affordability and convenience of the various options).

Photo 18.4 The well-established physical risks associated with smoking provide a strong motivation for health psychologists to help smokers quit.

An important aspect of smoking cessation is the availability of a nonsmoking social support network. Having smokers in one's social group has been shown to be both a significant detriment to smoking cessation and a significant predictor of relapse (Mermelstein, Cohen, Lichtenstein, Baer, & Karmarck, 1986). Helping the client create or strengthen a nonsmoking network is often an important first step of smoking cessation treatment. One way this might be accomplished is by first developing problem-solving strategies for limiting, ending, or dealing with relationships with other smokers (e.g., a spouse who smokes). This might include setting such rules as limiting smoking to outside of the house and family vehicles. It is also important to create a list of the number and quality of nonsmoking social contacts across various situations (work, home, recreation). If this list is small, social network building may need to occur. The client would be encouraged to identify and start reaching out to other nonsmoking peers or to seek support through smoking cessation support groups (Smith, Reilly, Houston Miller, DeBusk, & Taylor, 2002). Finally, clients would also be encouraged to identify places where they typically smoke socially and plan alternate locations and activities that would be equally fulfilling. For example, clients who often dine out with friends might consider frequenting only smoke-free restaurants.

Smokers often report that they smoke because they find it relaxing and stress reducing. As such, an important task for the health psychologist is to work with the client to develop and practice alternate replacement strategies for relaxation and stress reduction *before* the smoker begins the quitting process. Relapse prevention goes hand in hand with this concept, as its goal is to predict which factors are likely to trigger a relapse and to prevent those factors from occurring. Given that one of the most common triggers for a relapse is feeling stressed, the use of stress management techniques can play a strong role in relapse prevention. The **ABCs of relapse prevention** (Marlatt & Gordon, 1985) involve an examination by the client and the health psychologists of the events that occur before and after smoking. Specifically, *B* stands for Behavior (smoking), *A* stands for Antecedent, and *C* stands for Consequence. For example, if Julian recognizes that whenever he drinks alcohol at a bar, he's likely to smoke, he has identified drinking in the bar as an antecedent. If he also realizes that smoking a cigarette in the bar provides the consequence of reduced stress, he can identify alternate behaviors for reducing stress (e.g., exercising, watching TV, socializing with friends outside of bars). A health psychologist can be quite helpful in facilitating Julian's efforts by helping him recognize antecedents and consequences and by suggesting alternative behaviors.

Alcohol Use

Drinking alcohol occasionally or in moderation does not in itself constitute an alcohol problem. The use of alcoholic substances becomes pathological when certain criteria are met—for example, when the person can't cut down on alcohol, has strong cravings, or experiences repeated failures at work, school, or home related to alcohol (American Psychiatric Association, 2013). Two other hallmarks of problematic alcohol use are tolerance and withdrawal. **Tolerance** occurs when the body requires increasing amounts of the substance to achieve the desired effect, and **withdrawal** occurs when cessation of the substance produces negative symptoms. Researchers estimate that about 4% of Americans use alcohol in a way that involves tolerance and withdrawal (e.g., Grant et al., 2004), which qualifies alcoholism as a large-scale social health issue along with obesity and smoking.

Very similar to smoking cessation, the successful treatment of alcoholism includes the components of stress management, relapse prevention, and social support. As alcohol is also commonly used to reduce stress, health psychologists would work with clients to identify more healthy alternatives to manage stress, such as working out or calling a friend to talk. Identifying common precursors to drinking (going to a sports event) and developing strategies to avoid them (not carrying enough cash to purchase a drink) uses the same ABCs of relapse prevention that health psychologists use with smoking cessation clients. And also similar to working with smoking cessation clients, health psychologists would help clients who wanted to abstain from drinking identify and, if necessary, expand their social circle of nondrinkers and socializing options that are alcohol free.

The most commonly sought source of help for alcohol-related problems, the self-help support group Alcoholics Anonymous (AA), incorporates many of these strategies in its treatment plan. AA is a network of current and recovered alcoholics who share the goal of helping themselves and other members of AA stay sober. Although this group is not affiliated with health psychology, it uses many of the same principles, especially social support and relapse prevention. One important distinction between AA and health psychology is that AA incorporates a spiritual component to its recovery process.

An important distinction between the treatment for smoking and the treatment for alcohol problems is the fact that alcohol exhibits effects on the brain different from the effects of many other substances, including nicotine, and an addict might experience dangerous side effects as a result of weaning the body off the substance too quickly. As such, a period of medically supervised **detoxification** may be the most appropriate first course of action before proceeding to cognitive-behavioral techniques.

Pain Management and Biofeedback

Chronic pain—pain that lasts 6 months or longer—affects up to 35% of the population (Mantyselka, Turunen, Ahonen, & Kumpusalo, 2003). Although a large component of pain management is medically based (e.g., pain medications, surgery, or physical therapy), the fact that both depression and anxiety worsen the experience of pain (Vowels, Zvolensky, Gross, & Sperry, 2004) suggests that health psychology should also be an integral part of any comprehensive pain management plan.

One unique technique health psychologists employ in pain management is **biofeedback** (Shapiro & Schwartz, 1972). The purpose of biofeedback is to achieve control over the body via educating patients about bodily processes of which they are typically unaware. To bring these processes into the forefront of consciousness, a biofeedback machine converts some aspect of physiological functioning (e.g., heart rate, muscular tension) into a tone for the client to hear or a line on a graph for the client to see. So, for example, as heart rate increases, a tone gets louder, or as shoulder tension declines, a line on a graph dips. The patient is guided through trial-and-error exercises to see what sorts of behaviors (e.g., deep breathing, changing postures, modifying thoughts, imagery) alter the bodily process in question. Once patients have learned the cause–effect relationships between their own behaviors and their bodies' responses, they can use them purposely to achieve the desired level.

As an example, consider Ronald, a 45-year-old client with chronic lumbar-region back pain. Before Ronald saw Dr. Booker, Ronald felt as though there was nothing he could do to control his back pain. As a health psychologist, Dr. Booker allowed Ronald to "see" his own back pain via a graphic biofeedback machine that displayed muscular tension as a visual graph. After trying a number of physical and mental exercises designed to influence the back pain, Ronald and Dr. Booker were pleased to find that two of Ronald's actions—elevating his legs and imagining himself on a quiet, calm beach—caused his back pain to decrease. This decrease in pain was evident both in Ronald's subjective experience and quite undeniably on the monitor he watched. After this discovery, Ronald was able to deliberately elevate his legs and imagine the beach scene in his daily life to reduce the spasms in his lower back.

Photo 18.5 Health psychologists use a variety of techniques to help clients who experience ongoing pain.

● ● ● BOX 18.2 ● ● ●

Metaphorically Speaking

If You've Used Exercise Equipment With a Heart Rate Monitor, You Understand Biofeedback

At the gym, you may have used a treadmill, stationary bike, or elliptical trainer that monitors your pulse via metal sensors in the handles. The machine then converts this pulse

(Continued)

(Continued)

information to a heart rate (usually expressed as beats per minute, or BPM) and displays this information to you in real time throughout your workout. If your goal is to control your heart rate—raise it to a certain level, keep it below a certain level, etc.—you can take note of the cause–effect relationship between your actions and your heart rate. On the stationary bike, for example, you may learn that pedaling at a certain speed against a certain level of resistance brings about a certain heart rate.

Monitoring heart rate may be of secondary importance to many of the people exercising on these machines at the gym, but for clients using biofeedback, it is the primary goal. As the term suggests, a biofeedback machine provides the client with feedback about bodily activities such as heart rate, muscle activity, and the like. With the help of a health psychologist, clients can use biofeedback machines to learn which actions they can choose to take in order to bring about desired changes in the internal systems of their bodies.

This can be an empowering process. Without biofeedback, clients would be unable to know, for example, exactly how fast their hearts are beating. Moreover, it would be impossible for them to make connections between any particular behaviors they perform (e.g., intentionally slow breathing, mental imagery) and subsequent changes in heart rate. But with biofeedback, heart rate is instantly visible and continuously updated as various behaviors are attempted. Thus, a heart rate problem that a client may initially experience as uncontrollable becomes more directly manageable.

Critics of biofeedback training have argued that its benefits are offset by its expense and time-intensiveness. Fortunately, an economical and relatively quick alternative has been found in an intervention originally developed long ago for anxiety disorders (Jacobson, 1938). **Relaxation training** involves teaching clients to consciously shift their bodies into a state of lowered tension and arousal. It can involve a variety of aspects, including guided imagery (e.g., imagining yourself in a gently swinging hammock), deep and controlled "belly breathing," and systematically tensing and then relaxing various large skeletal muscles such as those in the arms and legs. Relaxation training has been found to be successful in alleviating chronic pain, and it may work by increasing the release of endogenous opioids, our bodies' natural analgesics (McGrady et al., 1992). An additional benefit of relaxation training, regarding the stress associated with chronic pain, is that several studies have found beneficial effects of relaxation on immune system functioning (Pawlow & Jones, 2002, 2005).

Pennebaker's work on the therapeutic effects of confiding distressing thoughts to others also included the notion that writing about distressing events could be cathartic and even alter immune system functioning in a positive way (Pennebaker, Kiecolt-Glaser, & Glaser, 1988). A more recent study focusing on chronic pain found similar results: Chronic pain patients who wrote about their angry feelings surrounding their pain experienced improved levels of perceived control and decreased levels of depression (Graham, Lobel, Glass, & Lokshina, 2008). Thus, simply taking the time to journal one's thoughts surrounding one's pain may help alleviate some of the suffering due to that pain.

● ● ● BOX 18.3 ● ● ●

Sample of an Abbreviated Progressive Relaxation Training Script

The following is a small portion of a progressive muscle relaxation script (Bernstein & Borkovec, 1973):

> When I say the word "tense," that is your specific signal to tense the muscles in the group we are working as tightly and as immediately as possible. You will be holding the tension for 7 seconds. Do not begin tensing until you hear this cue. Likewise, when I say the word "release," that is your specific relaxation signal to immediately release the tension. Do not let the tension dissipate gradually, and do not release the tension until I give the cue. I will give you specific instructions on what muscle group to tense, as well as general guidelines on how to tense it. Please do not move unnecessarily; however, feel free to move in any way that helps you to maintain a comfortable position at all times.

> When I say "tense," I want you to tense the muscles in your dominant hand and forearm by making a tight fist. Ready? Tense. (Hold for 7 seconds.) Feel the muscles pull. Notice what it's like to feel tension in these muscles as they pull and remain hard and tight. Release. (Relax for 30 seconds.) Just let the muscles go, notice the difference between tension and relaxation, focus on the feeling in the muscle as it becomes more and more relaxed.

(Continued)

(Continued)

When I say "tense," I want you to tense the muscles in your dominant biceps by pushing your elbow down against the arm of the chair. Ready? Tense. (Hold for 7 seconds.) Feel the muscles pull. Notice what it's like to feel tension in these muscles as they pull and remain hard and tight. Release. (Relax for 30 seconds.) Just let the muscles go, notice the difference between tension and relaxation, focus on the feeling in the muscle as it becomes more and more relaxed.

When I say "tense," I want you to tense the muscles in the upper part of your face by lifting the eyebrows as high as you can and getting tension in the forehead and scalp region. Ready? Tense. (Hold for 7 seconds.) Feel the muscles pull. Notice what it's like to feel tension in these muscles as they pull and remain hard and tight. Release. (Relax for 30 seconds.) Just let the muscles go, notice the difference between tension and relaxation, focus on the feeling in the muscle as it becomes more and more relaxed.

When I say "tense," I want you to tense the muscles in the central part of your face by squinting your eyes very tightly and at the same time wrinkling up your nose to feel the tension in the upper cheeks and the eyes. Ready? Tense. (Hold for 7 seconds.) Feel the muscles pull. Notice what it's like to feel tension in these muscles as they pull and remain hard and tight. Release. (Relax for 30 seconds.) Just let the muscles go, notice the difference between tension and relaxation, focus on the feeling in the muscle as it becomes more and more relaxed.

Source: Bernstein, D., & Borkovec, T. (1973).

Compliance With Medical Regimens

In some cases, health psychologists work with clients whose problems do not stem from psychological contributors of medical illness. Instead, these clients need assistance complying with medical regimens (Goodheart & Rozensky, 2011). Failure to comply with medical regimens can take many forms, including not taking medication, violating dietary restrictions, missing follow-up appointments, and not adhering to activity restrictions. There are many reasons why clients may not adhere to or comply with treatment regimens, including poor provider communication and fears about negative side effects. One study found that patients are less compliant with medication regimens when they are aware of the side effects, even if the side effects are mild and/or very unlikely to occur (Waters,

Weinstein, Colditz, & Emmons, 2009). On average, patient noncompliance is seen in about 26% of all cases, with the highest rates in HIV, arthritis, gastrointestinal disorder, and cancer populations (DiMatteo, Giordani, Lepper, & Croghan, 2002).

Health psychologists can increase compliance with medical regimens in many ways. Sometimes they serve as liaisons between the provider and the patient to communicate the proposed treatment plan more carefully and thoroughly in a comprehensible and compassionate way. In fact, some research has suggested that simply hearing the message in a warm and caring tone leads to greater compliance (e.g., Sherbourne, Hays, Ordway, DiMatteo, & Kravitz, 1992). Another important aspect of reducing noncompliance involves thoroughly educating the patient on the proposed treatment, alternate options (including no treatment), the pros and cons of each, and the current research on the topic. Also, clinicians can aid the patient in securing or bolstering their personal support systems as another mechanism for boosting compliance. In a study of patients with chronic heart failure, those with higher levels of perceived social support demonstrated better medication, behavioral, and dietary adherence to their medical treatment plans (Sayers, Riegel, Pawlowski, Coyne, & Samaha, 2008).

Identifying patient barriers to compliance and working together to suggest time-limited options can also help. For example, a pain patient who doesn't "believe in touchy-feely stuff like relaxation" might be persuaded to give it an honest try for 2 weeks, and if she sees no effect, she can stop with the provider's blessing. And sometimes the health psychologist can adopt a direct problem-solving approach to help clients with problems that seem, to them, quite difficult. For example, Claire, a 78-year-old woman with numerous physical illnesses and conditions, was noncompliant with her medication regimen because she had an abundance of pills to take and was so terrified that she'd take the wrong pills at the wrong time that she chose to forgo all of them. Her health psychologist, Dr. Howard, enlisted Claire's daughter to purchase a cheap, monthly/daily pill case from the local pharmacy and to place her supply of pills in the appropriate boxes once a month. This simple step was sufficient to rectify the situation.

Coping With Medical Procedures

Health psychologists also play a significant role in helping medical patients cope with the stress of facing a medical procedure. These medical procedures may include surgery, therapies with predictable negative side effects (e.g., chemotherapy), painful physical therapy, or more experimental procedures such as deep brain stimulation. A primary duty of health psychologists in this role is to educate the client and demystify the medical procedure, thus increasing the client's sense of control and comfort. Much research has been conducted on the benefits of clear and detailed preintervention communication delivered in an empathic manner. For example, radiation therapy patients who receive this type of information show better postoperative adjustment and healing than those who don't (Johnson, Lauver, & Nail, 1989). Also, the use of prerecorded videos to explain the steps of a complicated procedure such as heart surgery or a sensitive procedure such as a prostate screening has also been shown to be beneficial (e.g., Mahler & Kulik, 1998; Taylor, 2010).

Beyond optimizing communication, health psychologists also use cognitive-behavioral interventions such as relaxation training and learning to think differently about the unpleasantness of the situation (Ludwick-Rosenthal & Neufeld, 1988). As an example, consider Inez, a 50-year-old cancer patient who is about to begin chemotherapy. Inez is distraught about her cancer diagnosis, but she is almost equally distraught about the upcoming chemotherapy. When her health psychologist, Dr. Ricardo, asked Inez to explain her thoughts about chemotherapy, Inez tearfully stated, "It will go on for the rest of my life" and "The side effects will be so horrible—I won't be able to live through it." Dr. Ricardo showed compassion for Inez's concerns, but she also made sure to correct Inez's inaccurate understanding of chemotherapy: It was scheduled to last a few months, not a lifetime, and although most patients experience some unpleasant side effects, they do find that the side effects are ultimately tolerable. Moreover, Dr. Ricardo helped Inez focus on the improved health she could enjoy if the chemotherapy was successful (which, in Inez's case, was likely because her cancer was detected early and was considered very treatable). By correcting Inez's misinformed beliefs and shifting her focus to the possibility of a positive outcome, Dr. Ricardo was able to improve not only Inez's psychological well-being before the chemotherapy but also her chances of benefiting from it physically.

When health psychologists work with hospitalized children, a common goal is the minimization of separation anxiety (anxiety produced by separation from the primary caretaker, generally a parent). Techniques include the assignment of "substitute parents," in which a junior staff member such as a graduate student or student nurse is assigned to be the child's stand-in parent during any hours in which the actual parent is prohibited from visiting. Similarly, health psychologists can arrange for a young child's comfort items, such as a blanket or teddy bear, to be brought from home.

In some cases, a health psychologist may be asked to assess a patient's psychological readiness for a medical procedure before medical personnel decide to conduct it. In this capacity, health psychologists can screen out those patients whose state of mind would be likely to make a medical procedure ineffective or counterproductive. As an example, individuals for whom gastric bypass surgery is being considered routinely undergo a psychological evaluation before the surgery is scheduled. And, according to one study, almost 3% of gastric bypass applicants were deemed psychologically inappropriate to undergo the surgery. Specifically, these individuals, after an assessment including comprehensive clinical interviews, were found to be psychotic or at such a limited level of cognitive functioning that they were unable to fully understand and provide consent for the procedure under consideration (Pawlow, O'Neil, White, & Byrne, 2005).

Another medical procedure for which health psychologists commonly assess psychological appropriateness is organ donation. The medical community wants to be absolutely sure that donors understand the seriousness of their choice, including being able to comprehend all possible negative effects of the donation on both the donor and the recipient. It is also important in these cases to be sure that the donor is making the decision on his or her own and not being pressured by friends or family. Health psychologists are able to use their knowledge of both clinical assessment and the medical and psychological ramifications of organ donation to provide this important service.

A New Trend in Health Psychology: Patient-Centered Medical Homes

Traditionally, patient care in the United States has followed a primary-care model. In recent years, however, our health care system has been facing a crisis brought on by a significant shortage of primary-care physicians as increasing numbers of physicians in training choose to focus their education on specialized, versus general, medical practice. Resulting problems include long delays for patients needing to see their primary-care physicians; shorter office visits, resulting in more confusion among patients; and a lack of coordination between primary-care physicians, specialists, and hospitals.

Patient-centered medical homes (PCMHs) have been proposed as a solution for delivering higher-quality and more cost-effective primary care. PCMHs aim to provide care that is patient centered, highly accessible and affordable, comprehensive, and coordinated. They are more holistic in nature, in that they do not view mental health as separate from physical health, and they are also more focused on prevention of disease than is the traditional primary-care model (Kaslow et al., 2007). In this model, each patient has a personal primary-care doctor responsible for arranging patient care with other professionals on the patient's care team (e.g., nurses, physician assistants, physical therapists, medical specialists, etc.), most of whom are housed in one central location. PCMHs utilize electronic health records for greater communication across providers and promote greater participation in one's own care by the patient and the patient's family. Given that this model views behavioral health as a key aspect of the patient's care, and because clinical health psychologists are uniquely educated to design, implement, and assess strategies that address the prevention and management of

⊕ **Web Link 18.4**

Patient-centered medical homes

various health conditions such as obesity, AIDS, chronic pain, heart disease, diabetes, and cancer, health psychologists are particularly well trained to serve in leadership positions on PCMH care teams and are poised for "unprecedented workforce growth" opportunities even while other mental health employment opportunities are in decline (Beacham, Kinman, Harris, & Masters, 2012, p. 17).

Cultural Factors in Health Psychology

In all aspects of their work, it is crucial for health psychologists to fully appreciate the impact of cultural factors on the health- and illness-related experiences of their clients. In fact, research has indicated that health psychology interventions that have been adapted for particular cultural groups are typically more effective than similar interventions that have not been culturally adapted (Barrera, Castro, Strycker, & Toobert, 2012). As a starting point, it is vital for health psychologists to recognize the disparities that exist in health care between various ethnic groups, as well as the divergent attitudes of members of these groups toward the medical establishment. There are significant differences in the quality of health care and the overall health status of the ethnic groups within the U.S. population, with whites and Asian Americans ranking near the top and African Americans and Native Americans ranking near the bottom in ratings of overall health status (LaVeist, 2005). The historical context of these rankings, including the centuries of oppression suffered by African Americans and Native Americans in the United States, cannot be ignored. A relatively recent example of this oppression is represented by the Tuskegee syphilis study, in which the U.S. Public Health Service intentionally and deceptively withheld adequate treatment from hundreds of African American men with syphilis from 1932 to 1972 in an attempt to learn more about the course of the disease.

These historical factors undoubtedly relate to the perceptions held by members of these cultural groups regarding hospitals and physicians. For example, African American patients appear to demonstrate a greater mistrust of the health care system than do white patients (e.g., LaVeist, 2005). In a survey of medical patients (LaVeist, Nickerson, & Bowie, 2000), a significantly greater percentage of African American patients than white patients agreed with the statements, "Patients have sometimes been deceived or misled at hospitals," "Hospitals often want to know more about your personal affairs or business than they really need to know," "Hospitals have sometimes done harmful experiments on patients without their knowledge," and "Racial discrimination in a doctor's office is common." The same survey found that a significantly lower percentage of African American patients than white patients agreed with the statements, "Doctors treat African American and white people the same" and "In most hospitals, African Americans and whites receive the same kind of care." For health psychologists, appreciation of the discrepancies between cultural groups regarding health care experiences and attitudes is an essential component of cultural competence.

Cultural factors can also play a powerful role in determining the way medically ill people understand the source of their medical problems. According to Huff (1999), the perceived source of a sickness could fall into one of four categories:

- *Within the patient*—an infection, injury, or other biomedical irregularity
- *The natural world*—elements of the environment surrounding an individual, such as toxins or climate-related factors
- *The social world*—interpersonal conflict with others, especially those with whom the individual has close relationships
- *The supernatural world*—sorcery, witchcraft, ancestral spirits, or vengeful gods, for example

Huff (1999) explains that in Western cultures, it is typical for individuals to attribute illness to factors within themselves, and this attribution is quite consistent with mainstream Western medical care, which emphasizes biomedical causes of illness. However, in many non-Western cultures, it is quite common for individuals to attribute illness to one of the other three categories, each of which locates the cause of the illness outside the individual. So it is essential for health psychologists to remember that in a diverse culture, some individuals will maintain an external, rather than internal, locus of control regarding their health problems that may run counter to the assumptions of Western medicine. An appreciation of this difference, along with corresponding adjustments in practice, can ultimately enhance client health.

Culturally competent health psychologists also appreciate that, compared with white clients, members of ethnic minority groups may hold different expectations regarding the type of care they will receive and the types of interactions they will have with their caregivers (Huff, 1999; Kline & Huff, 1999). For example, in many of the largest ethnic minority groups in the United States, including Hispanic Americans, Asian Americans, Native Americans, and African Americans, reliance on culturally traditional healers and healing methods is common. These methods may include medicinal plants and herbs, massage, acupuncture, acupressure, prayer, chants, or other methods. Additionally, these methods often don't involve the type of quick, fact-based, yes/no questioning that characterizes many physician–patient interactions in Western culture. To overcome these discrepancies, health psychologists can play a facilitative role by educating both health care providers and multicultural clients about the expectations of the other party, thereby increasing the effectiveness of the interventions.

Finally, it is important for health psychologists to suspend judgment about how clients from diverse ethnic backgrounds may perceive their illnesses or approach their treatment

(Huff, 1999). The traditional Western way of understanding illness is just one of many, and culturally sensitive health psychologists openly recognize the validity in other ways of understanding as well.

CHAPTER SUMMARY

Health psychology is a burgeoning specialty area for clinical psychologists involving the interaction of psychological processes and physical health. Early efforts in health psychology focused primarily on issues of stress and its health-related consequences, but today health psychologists address a much wider range of issues. For example, they help clients manage their weight, quit smoking, reduce problematic alcohol use, and manage chronic pain. They also work to increase clients' behavioral adherence to medical regimens and their ability to cope with challenging medical procedures. They use a variety of specific therapeutic techniques, but their work often involves an educational component in which they enhance clients' understanding of the connection between their physical health and their psychological or behavioral functioning. In addition, health psychologists conduct psychological evaluations of individuals considering serious medical procedures such as gastric bypass surgery and organ donation. Recently, health psychologists have increasingly practiced via patient-centered medical homes in an attempt to better coordinate care among multiple professionals. Throughout their work, health psychologists maintain an appreciation of the cultural factors that may influence their clients' health-related experiences.

KEY TERMS AND NAMES

ABCDS of weight loss 462

ABCs of relapse prevention 465

behavioral medicine 454

biofeedback 466

chronic pain 466

chronic stress 455

coping 457

cortisol 456

detoxification 466

disease-prone personality 457

fight-or-flight response 455

general adaptation syndrome 455

health psychology 454

hypothalamic-pituitary-adrenal (HPA) axis 456

patient-centered medical 473

homes (PCMHs) 473

problem-focused coping 458

psychoneuroimmunology (PNI) 456

relaxation training 468

Hans Selye 455

social support 462

stress 455

tolerance 465

values affirmation 463

withdrawal 465

CRITICAL THINKING QUESTIONS

1. In general, to what extent do you agree with the notion that psychological factors contribute to physical health problems?

2. If clinical psychologists developed a successful, evidence-based treatment for the disease-prone personality (characterized by marked anxiety, depression, and hostility), what ramifications might this treatment have throughout the health care industry?

3. In your opinion, to what extent should physicians emphasize the creation of a social support network for their patients?

4. In your opinion, to what extent are psychological factors responsible for the large-scale problems with weight and obesity in the United States? To what extent do you think that people who struggle with losing excess body weight recognize these psychological factors?

5. What efforts can clinical psychologists make to increase their cultural competence regarding clients with physical health issues?

STUDENT STUDY SITE RESOURCES

Visit the study site at www.sagepub.com/pomerantz3eupdate for these additional learning tools:

- Self-quizzes
- eFlashcards
- Culture Expert Interviews
- Full-text SAGE journal articles
- Additional web resources
- Mock Assessment Data

CHAPTER SUMMARY VIDEO

QR codes at the end of each chapter link to chapter background videos by the author. Visit http://gettag.mobi using your smartphone browser to download the free Microsoft Tag app. Once installed, scan the tags to go directly to these brief videos. In this video, the author tells the story of one of his own clients to illustrate the importance of professional, multidisciplinary collaboration.

CHAPTER 19

Forensic Psychology

Bryce F. Sullivan and Andrew M. Pomerantz

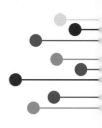

Definition and History

Forensic psychology—the application of psychological methods and principles within the legal system—dates back nearly to the origins of psychology as a recognized science. Psychologists with different academic backgrounds have been drawn to the field due to the interesting and diverse ways psychology and law intersect. Social psychologists are involved in researching and applying psychological science to issues such as jury selection and jury dynamics. Cognitive psychologists bring their expertise to bear on the issues of eyewitness testimony and its accuracy. Clinical psychologists, however, are most qualified for and most often involved in forensic psychology activities due to their extensive training in assessment, treatment, and psychopathology.

With different types of psychologists conducting research and practicing professionally in forensic psychology, it is not surprising that there are disagreements on what the field should be called (Ogloff, 2002). Should it be called law and psychology, psychology and law, criminal psychology, legal psychology, or forensic psychology? For clinical psychologists

⊕ **Web Link 19.1**

American Academy of Forensic Psychology

involved in professional practice, the term *forensic psychology* is most commonly used and most appropriate. Clinical psychologists working in forensic settings evaluate criminal defendants' sanity, assess legal competency to stand trial, assess families in child custody disputes, predict dangerousness, serve as expert witnesses, and engage in other interactions with the legal system that are outlined in this chapter. As this list indicates, the training and expertise of clinical psychologists fulfill many demands of the legal system, especially regarding clinical assessment. Otto and Heilbrun (2002) called forensic psychological assessment "the psychological assessment of persons for the purpose of assisting the legal fact finder" (p. 5), and clinical psychologists are uniquely trained to conduct assessments that are comprehensive, valid, and reliable.

A variety of training opportunities involve the intersection of forensics and psychology, and there is little consensus about exactly what should be included in the training of a forensic psychologist. Within clinical psychology, some doctoral programs offer an elective course or two in forensic issues, others offer a specialized forensic track among other tracks, and still others are entirely devoted to forensic psychology and offer joint graduate degrees in law (JD) and psychology (PhD or PsyD). Additionally, various predoctoral and postdoctoral internships offer various types of forensic training (Burl, Shah, Filone, Foster, & DeMatteo, 2012; Marczyk, Krauss, & Burl, 2012).

Psychologists assisted the courts as early as the beginning of the 1900s, but it wasn't until the latter half of the 1900s that forensic psychology became a major subdiscipline within psychology (Goldstein, 2003). **Hugo Munsterberg** was among the first major promoters of the use of psychology in the legal arena. He wrote a best-selling book in 1908 titled *On the Witness Stand* with chapters on the memory of witnesses, untrue confessions, the detection of crimes, and other topics of interest to modern-day forensic psychologists. Munsterberg's aggressive promotion of psychology in the legal arena went beyond what were then its scientific limits, and his brash writings alienated prominent members of the legal field. Nevertheless, Munsterberg made significant contributions to forensic psychology by showing how psychological science could be applied to the field of law (Bartol & Bartol, 2006). Munsterberg also supported the growth of forensic psychology by mentoring students, such as the psychologist and attorney William Marston. In 1923, Marston presented testimony in a case that created the first standard for expert testimony (*Frye v. United States*, 1923) and paved the way for extensive use of psychological expertise in the courts.

In some ways, the development of forensic psychology mirrors the development of clinical psychology. Like clinical psychology, the field emerged around the end of the 19th century, but significant growth didn't occur until after World War II. Although psychologists in the United States had been expert witnesses for the courts as early as the 1920s, it was not common for psychologists to serve in this role until several decades later. By the middle of the 20th century, psychologists were conducting evaluations to assist the court in matters of mental status, legal competence, and even the sanity of defendants. Psychologists even presented expert evidence and were cited in the Supreme Court's brief in the watershed 1954 school desegregation case *Brown v. Board of Education* (1954). In this case, which led to the desegregation of public schools in the United States, psychologists presented research showing that segregation had a negative effect on the self-esteem of children, and their research was persuasive to the court (A. K. Hess, 2006a). Further signs of the growth of forensic psychology in recent decades include the emergence of professional journals, standards of practice, training programs, professional certifications, and the **American Psychological Association Division 41, the American Psychology-Law Society.** Forensic psychology has grown considerably in the past three decades (DeMatteo, Marczyk, Krauss, & Burl, 2009) and has reached the stage of a maturing discipline (Heilbrun & Brooks, 2010).

Forensic work has evolved into a unique specialty area for clinical psychologists. Unlike most clinical situations, it places the clinical psychologist in the midst of an adversarial relationship between parties in conflict with each other. As a result, "the good feelings and positive relationships common in the psychotherapeutic relationship do not exist in the forensic setting" (Knapp & VandeCreek, 2006, p. 161). Similarly, clinical psychologists working in forensic settings must acknowledge that when they assess an individual, their goal is not necessarily to help that individual but to help the legal system by offering information and recommendations regarding the individual. Thus, when conducting forensic assessments, clinical psychologists must interact with clients in a "detached, neutral, and objective" manner rather than the "supportive, empathic" approach they might take in most other clinical settings (Goldstein, 2003, p. 6). Moreover, the trust that characterizes, and to some extent facilitates, so many other clinical relationships is necessarily lacking in forensic work. This is because the likelihood of clients falsely presenting themselves to appear either more or less disturbed than they really are is simply too great (Goldstein, 2003).

⊕ **Web Link 19.2**
APA Division 41

Forensic Activities of Clinical Psychologists

Assessment Activities

Clinical assessment is a prevalent activity among clinical psychologists who work in forensic settings. The most common assessments are in the areas of child custody, competency, and presentencing evaluations, but assessments are also conducted in some parole decisions, personal injury lawsuits, workers' compensation hearings, preemployment screenings of legal personnel, and Social Security disability evaluations (Wood, Garb, Lilienfeld, & Nezworski, 2002). It is always important to consider ethical issues such as the limits of confidentiality when conducting a psychological examination, especially when conducting forensic evaluations, because the role of the psychologist is not as clear as in more common clinical situations. For

⊕ **Web Link 19.3**
Journal of
Forensic
Psychology
Practice

example, when a psychologist conducts a police officer preemployment screening evaluation, the police department—not the applicant—is considered the client, and the information gained in the evaluation is shared with the police department senior staff. In all forensic evaluations, the question, "Who is the client?"—the person being assessed, an attorney, the court system, or another party—should be clarified by the clinical psychologist from the outset (Goldstein, 2003).

Additionally, in all forensic evaluations the limits of confidentiality should be made clear to the individual being evaluated by way of a written and oral informed consent process (American Psychological Association, 2002). Because the clinical psychologist cannot ensure complete confidentiality of the report once it is shared, care is taken to exclude from the report personal information that is not relevant to the reason the evaluation is being conducted. Although the report and test data are intended to remain confidential, an evaluation conducted for the courts or other legal entities may, unfortunately, become publicly available once it leaves the hands of clinical psychologists. For example, after professional boxer Mike Tyson was denied a license to box in Nevada in 2002 by the Nevada Athletic Commission, a comprehensive psychological evaluation of Tyson was conducted to evaluate anger management problems and other issues. Even though Tyson attempted to have the report kept private, it was made public and posted on various websites. Similarly, in the arena of preemployment testing, it seems that every spring the Wonderlic intelligence quotient (IQ) test results of some low-scoring college football players being evaluated by the National Football League are leaked to the press. In 2012, the problem was so pronounced that the leaking of draft prospect test scores resulted in the NFL commissioner threatening "significant discipline" for anyone leaking these confidential scores (Krawcqynski, 2012).

Although forensic assessment represents a specialized area of clinical practice, many of the techniques used in forensic assessments are the same as those used more generally by clinical psychologists, including the clinical interviews, intelligence tests, and personality tests covered in earlier chapters of this book. A survey of highly credentialed and experienced forensic psychologists examined the use of specific tests for specific forensic purposes (Lally, 2003). The survey indicated that many of the tests receiving the strongest endorsement ("Recommended") were objective personality tests such as the Minnesota Multiphasic Personality Inventory-2 (MMPI-2) and intelligence tests with proven reliability and validity such as the Wechsler Adult Intelligence Scale (WAIS). On the other hand, many of the tests receiving the most negative rating ("Unacceptable") were projective personality tests such as the Rorschach Inkblot Technique, Thematic Apperception Test (TAT), and projective drawing tests. It was also notable that these forensic experts strongly endorsed a multimethod approach to assessment in which numerous tests, rather than any single test, were used. Whatever assessment techniques are used in forensic evaluations, they should be solidly

Table 19.1 Opinions of Forensic Experts Regarding Psychological Tests Used for Various Forensic Purposes

Type of Assessment	Recommended Tests	Unacceptable Tests
Not guilty by reason of insanity (i.e., mental state at time of offense)	MMPI-2; WAIS	Projective drawings; TAT; sentence completion tests
Predicting dangerousness (i.e., risk for violence)	Psychopathy Checklist—Revised	Projective drawings; TAT; Rorschach; sentence completion tests
Competency to stand trial	WAIS; MacArthur Competence Assessment Tool—Criminal Adjudication	Projective drawings; Rorschach; TAT; sentence completion tests; Millon Clinical Multiaxial Inventory

Source: Adapted from Lally, S. J. (2003).

based on the science of psychology and not pseudoscience—the imposter of real science (Lilienfeld & Landfield, 2008). Heilbrun and Brooks (2010) note that there has been progress in the development of special assessment measures for legal capacities. Table 19.1 describes the findings of the survey for several common forensic assessments. We will discuss these assessments and others in the remainder of this section.

While some of the assessment techniques used by forensic psychologists are the same as those used by clinical psychologists more generally, some specialized assessment skills are particularly important for forensic psychologists. Sageman (2003) describes three such skills: knowledge of the legal issues, addressing the demands of the legal system, and skill related to litigation (involvement in court cases). The first skill, knowledge of the legal issues, might involve an understanding of criminal responsibility, the definition of competency, and the definition of insanity. The second skill, addressing the demands of the legal system, often entails striving for neutrality regarding a client, predicting the future as well as possible, and gathering data about the case in a thorough and unbiased way. The third skill applies to litigation (court cases) and involves an understanding of each attorney's strategy, providing appropriate testimony, and deferring to others involved in the case when appropriate.

Predicting Dangerousness

When a legal case centers on the violent or dangerous behavior of an individual, the judge or jury often consider the likelihood that the individual will behave violently or dangerously again in the future. Clinical psychologists are often recruited to assist in **predicting dangerousness**, especially when the individual has a history of mental illness in addition to aggressive behavior. Decisions in these cases, which can include verdicts or sentences, are particularly challenging for the court system.

Photo 19.1 Clinical psychologists who work in forensic settings are often asked to predict the dangerousness of a client. In your opinion, are clinical prediction methods or statistical prediction methods preferable?

Clinical psychologists can assess the potential for future danger in a variety of ways, most of which can be placed into one of two categories: **clinical prediction methods** or **statistical prediction methods** (statistical prediction methods are also known as **actuarial prediction methods**; e.g., Dawes, Faust, & Meehl, 1989). In the clinical method, assessors use psychological tests, clinical interviews, clinical experience, and their personal judgments to make determinations of future dangerousness. In contrast, in the statistical method, assessors predict dangerousness according to a statistical or actuarial formula compiled from a comparison of an individual's characteristics with known correlations to future dangerousness (Grove, Zald, Lebow, Snitz, & Nelson, 2000). Such variables are typically objective rather than subjective and could include

- dispositional variables, such as age, race, sex, social class, and personality variables;
- historical variables, such as history of violence, work history, mental health history, and criminal history;
- contextual variables, such as current social supports, presence or availability of weapons, and current stress level; and
- clinical variables, such as current mental disorders, drug and alcohol abuse, and overall level of functioning (Monahan, 2003).

By its individual and subjective nature, the clinical method differs from clinician to clinician, and these differences between clinicians tend to make the method less reliable. Additionally, the clinical method leaves room for biases and other forms of human errors common in subjective decision making. Statistical methods tend to be less flexible but more empirically sound due to their objectivity. In fact, Grove and his colleagues (2000) conducted a meta-analysis of studies in the area of clinical prediction and found that statistical predictions were about 10% more accurate than clinical predictions.

Experts in the field have debated the use of clinical versus statistical methods of prediction of dangerousness for decades, and some have suggested that the two approaches can be combined. In fact, a clinical prediction of dangerousness, although primarily subjective in nature, may incorporate some objective data about the client. Similarly, a statistical prediction of dangerousness, although primarily objective in nature, may incorporate subjective variables that the evaluator converts into objective ratings (e.g., personality traits, behavioral tendencies). Thus, predicting dangerousness may be seen as existing on a continuum encompassing both clinical and actuarial components (Litwack, Zapf, Groscup, & Hart, 2006; Skeem & Monahan, 2011).

● ● ● BOX 19.1 ● ● ●

Metaphorically Speaking

If You've Bought Car Insurance, You Understand Clinical and Statistical Methods of Predicting Dangerousness

Why does car insurance cost more for some drivers than for others? The reason is that over the years, car insurance companies have compiled statistics indicating that drivers with some characteristics are more likely to get into accidents than are drivers with other characteristics. Using these statistics, the companies can predict with remarkable accuracy the likelihood of accidents for drivers with various combinations of characteristics. If you happen to have characteristics that make you, statistically speaking, a high risk to the insurance company, your premiums will rise to reflect this risk. The characteristics that car insurance companies consider include the driver's gender, age, driving record, and driving education/training, among others. As a specific example, statistics enable car insurance companies reliably to predict that male drivers under 25 with a history of accidents and no driver's education training are especially likely to get into accidents in the future. If any of these driver characteristics were different—above 25, female, no history of accidents, driver's education classes—the prediction would change accordingly.

When clinical psychologists attempt to predict the dangerousness of a forensic client, they can use a similarly statistical (also known as actuarial) method. In other words, they can base their predictions on objective characteristics of the individual that have been empirically tied to specific rates of dangerous behavior, including gender, age, history of dangerous or criminal behavior, history of substance abuse, and presence of psychological symptoms such as psychosis or psychopathy. Just as car insurance companies can create a formula to calculate the odds that drivers with certain characteristics will drive dangerously, clinical psychologists

(Continued)

(Continued)

using the statistical method can create a formula to calculate the odds that forensic clients with certain characteristics will behave dangerously.

Imagine that a car insurance company decided to abandon the statistical approach of predicting accidents and replaced it with a method in which the insurance agents get to know each driver individually and then use their professional judgment to determine how likely the driver is to get into accidents in the future. In other words, each driver would meet with a car insurance agent and undergo an interview and a series of tests. The outcome of the interview and tests, rather than the driver's demographic characteristics or driving history, would determine the individual's insurance rate. This method is essentially similar to the clinical method that clinical psychologists might use when assessing a client for dangerousness. The clinical method involves the clinical psychologist assessing the forensic client as an individual and forming predictions about future dangerousness from the data obtained via the interviews and psychological tests included in this evaluation. Compared with the statistical method, the clinical method involves less reliance on aggregate group data (e.g., young adults, older adults, males, females) and more reliance on the professional judgment of the clinical psychologist. Thus, the clinical method not only allows for more consideration of individual characteristics but also allows for more subjectivity on the part of the assessor, who can be susceptible to bias and error.

If you owned a car insurance company, which method of assessment—a statistical formula based on the groups to which the driver belongs or getting to know each driver individually— would you expect to be more accurate in the prediction of accidents? If you were a clinical psychologist working in forensic settings, which method of assessment—statistical or clinical— would you expect to be more accurate in the prediction of dangerousness?

Whereas clinical psychologists may emphasize clinical or statistical methods in particular cases, research has established some general guidelines for predicting dangerous behavior. Factors associated with dangerousness in the empirical literature include age (with younger people at higher risk), arrest record (with those with more arrests at higher risk), weapon availability (with those who have available weapons at higher risk), social support (with those low in social support at higher risk), and psychological symptoms (with those with active psychosis symptoms at higher risk). The research literature is clear on the fact that although there is a small relationship between the presence of mental illness and violence, the key psychological factors include the presence of substance abuse, psychotic symptoms, or psychopathy (Hemphill & Hart, 2003; Litwack et al., 2006; McNeil et al., 2002; Monahan, 2003).

One of the most significant challenges associated with predicting dangerousness is the **base rate** problem (Grove et al., 2000). Specifically, in predicting dangerousness, base rates constitute a problem because they are so low. To explain, base rates report the incidence of something. For example, about 1% of the population meets the criteria for a diagnosis of schizophrenia; this means that schizophrenia has a base rate of 1%. Making predictions about phenomena with low base rates is very difficult when compared with making predictions about those with higher base rates because the higher the base rate is, the more likely a prediction will be accurate based solely on chance occurrence. Trying to predict whether a person will show the active symptoms of schizophrenia based on genetic and environmental variables would be very difficult—even with full knowledge of all possible predictor variables. The same is true for predicting dangerousness.

When predicting dangerous or violent behavior, the clinical psychologist attempts to accurately identify those who actually will become dangerous (a "true-positive" prediction) and those who will not become dangerous (a "true-negative" prediction). It is impossible to make these identifications correctly in every case, and some mistakes can be far worse than others. In actual practice, to protect society, the clinical psychologists might lean toward identifying someone as more likely to be violent than he or she really is (a "false-positive" prediction). On the other hand, the cost of identifying someone as less violent than he or she really is (a "false-negative" prediction) can be devastating if that person goes on to kill or harm others; so clinical psychologists might be especially cautious about making such a prediction. Imagine, for example, the decision-making process involved in releasing from the court's supervision someone convicted of child abuse. The court and the clinical psychologist hired to assist in the process would try to predict this type of dangerous behavior accurately, but because it is so rare in the population (a low base rate), it is easy to see how false-positive decisions might be made because the risk of making false-negative decisions is so much higher for society. Even though clinical psychologists are far from perfect in predicting dangerousness, research has shown that mental health professionals can make better than chance predictions of violence both in short- and long-range situations (Wood et al., 2002).

Not Guilty by Reason of Insanity (NGRI)

According to the U.S. legal system, people who commit crimes should be punished only when they committed the crime of their own free will. If an individual was unable to control his or her actions due to a mental disorder—even if such actions were criminal in nature—the individual would not be held responsible for the crime but would rather be found **not guilty by reason of insanity (NGRI)**. Thus, a clinical psychologist's assessment of a defendant's mental state at the time of an offense can become a crucial component to legal proceedings. When defendants are found NGRI, they are not imprisoned in the usual sense, because such penalties were created as a means of deterrence and social control (Darley, Fulero, Haney, & Tyler, 2002). Imprisonment would not effectively deter someone who did not commit the crime of his or her own free will. Instead, the institutionalization of individuals found NGRI, which may take place in inpatient psychiatric units or similar facilities, is for their treatment and tailored for the individual's particular constellations of emotional and behavioral problems.

There are many misconceptions of the NGRI defense, some of which stem from highly publicized court cases in which the public perceives that the defendant may have sought an NGRI label solely to avoid punishment. An example is John Hinckley being found NGRI after the 1981 attempted assassination of President Reagan. Melton et al. (2007) identified four common misconceptions regarding the NGRI defense. First, the general public may think this defense is used frequently, and, second, people may think it is often successful. In fact, less than 1% of felony jury trials involve an NGRI defense, and only about 25% of those trials result in an NGRI verdict (Goldstein, Morse, & Shapiro, 2003; Zapf, Golding, & Roesch, 2006). Third, people may think the NGRI defendant is often released without being institutionalized, but this is very uncommon. Typically, the person found NGRI is institutionalized in a mental hospital almost as long as he or she would have been incarcerated if convicted of the crime. Fourth, there is a misperception that individuals found NGRI are more dangerous than they really are. In the case of John Hinckley, more than three decades after the assassination attempt and over the objections of the Justice Department, in June of 2009, a federal judge ordered that Hinckley be allowed extended visits to his mother's home and additional freedoms. He has been living at St. Elizabeth's Hospital in Washington, D.C., since the attempt on President Reagan's life in 1981.

The **M'Naghten test,** the first legal standard for the insanity defense in the history of the American legal system, emerged during the mid-19th century. In the M'Naghten case, the defendant (Daniel M'Naghten) was charged with attempting to kill the prime minister of England. This attempted murder was due to persecutory delusions M'Naghten held about Britain's Tory party and its leader, Prime Minister Sir Robert Peel. Instead of killing the intended target, however, he killed the prime minister's secretary, who was nearby. Although English common law had already recognized that "lunatic idiots" who acted as "wild beasts" due to their mental state were not responsible in the eyes of the law, it was the M'Naghten case that developed the formal test of insanity (Meyer & Weaver, 2006, p. 116). The court ruled,

> To establish a defense on the ground of insanity, it must be clearly proved that, at the time of the committing of the act, the party accused was laboring under such a defect of reason, from disease of mind, as not to know the nature and quality of the act he was doing; or, if he did know it, that he did not know he was doing what was wrong. (Melton et al., 2007, p. 206)

This test focused primarily on the cognitive ability of the defendant, and in the United States the "policeman at the elbow" or "irresistible impulse" test was added to include a volitional component. According to this test, it was argued that a person was legally insane if he or she was unable to control his or her behaviors even when a policeman was at his or her elbow. In 1954, the "product test" was instituted by the District of Columbia Court of Appeals in *Durham v. United States* (1954). The court wrote, "An accused is not criminally responsible if his unlawful act was the product of mental disease or defect" (pp. 874–875). This test was overturned in 1972 due to its definitional ambiguity, and legal experts turned their attention to clarifying criminal responsibility tests.

More recent tests of criminal responsibility were developed by the legal community. One of these legal tests was created by the American Law Institute (1962) and is used by many jurisdictions. The test reads,

> A person is not responsible for criminal conduct if at the time of such conduct as a result of mental disease or defect he lacks substantial capacity either to appreciate the criminality of his conduct or to conform his conduct to the requirements of the law. (Cited in Meyer & Weaver, 2006, p. 119)

By 1972, the American Law Institute rule was embraced by the majority of federal jurisdictions and many states (Meyer & Weaver, 2006). As a reaction to John Hinckley being found NGRI on all counts following his attempt to assassinate President Reagan in 1981, the conformity clause was removed from federal law, and the burden of proof about insanity became the responsibility of the defense, whereas burden of proof previously fell on the prosecution. Currently, legal standards for NGRI vary at the state and federal levels, but they all require that a mental disease or defect be present and operating at the time of the offense (Goldstein et al., 2003).

A recent legal development is the provision by which a defendant can be found **guilty but mentally ill.** According to Roesch, Zapf, and Hart (2009), 13 states have such a provision, and it is intended to provide a middle ground for jurors contemplating whether to assign criminal responsibility (and punishment) to defendants whose mental status is in question.

Child Custody Evaluations

"**Child custody evaluations** may be the most complex, difficult, and challenging of all forensic evaluations" (Otto, Buffington-Vollum, & Edens, 2003, p. 179). Indeed, child custody is an area fraught with challenges due to the importance of the decision and the competing interests of the parents. It is not, however, the parents' interests that are most important in child custody decisions. Instead, custody decisions are made based on a legal principle known as the "best interest of the child doctrine." This has not always been the case. In the 1880s, the father was typically given custody. This later gave way to the "tender years" doctrine (K. D. Hess, 2006) in which the mother was favored in custody disputes, particularly in the case of younger children. Because children, even adolescents, are not considered by the court to be able to make sound judgments (*Parham v. JR*, 1979), parents must make decisions for them. In a divorce situation, when the parents are in a custody dispute, even the parents are often not able to make well-reasoned decisions for the children. In such cases, the courts will sometimes appoint a **guardian ad litem** to make sure the rights of the child are protected. The guardian ad litem is a neutral party, often an attorney unaffiliated with either parent, appointed to avoid decisions being made by individuals who would have conflicts of interest.

After the death of Vickie Lynn Marshall (i.e., Anna Nicole Smith) in 2007, a Miami attorney was appointed by the court to serve as guardian ad litem to her 5-month-old daughter. A guardian ad litem was also appointed for Michael Jackson's children (Prince Michael, Paris, and Blanket) following the King of Pop's death in 2009. In both of these cases, following the death of the celebrity, legal claims were made by individuals claiming to be the parents of the various children. The duty of the guardian ad litem is to represent the interests of the children. Custody and legal cases such as these, in which many parties have interests that might conflict with the best interest of the child, highlight the important role a guardian ad litem plays in child custody disputes.

By the 1990s, child custody evaluations were likely to be conducted only in more complex cases involving psychopathology and parental conflict. Increasingly, these complex cases were handled by highly trained psychologists who based their findings on the scientific literature and solid research rather than on their clinical experiences or hunches (E. Ellis, 2008). Psychologists can participate in the child custody process in a variety of ways: as an evaluator of the parents or children, investigator, expert witness, mediator, research scientist, or treatment provider. To provide guidance to psychologists in these challenging situations, the American Psychological Association (1994) developed 16 standards for conducting child custody evaluations. These standards (see Table 19.2) outline both the purpose of and guidelines for conducting a child custody evaluation.

Even with such guidelines, child custody evaluations can be daunting tasks. Unlike other evaluations, in which only one person or one capacity is in question, child custody cases involve multiple people (and the relationships among them) and multiple capacities of each. Child custody evaluators not only meet with individuals directly involved in the case, such as the parents and children, but often talk with third parties or collateral sources as well, such as extended family members, teachers or day-care staff, mental health professionals, the family physician, and others who may know the family (Symons, 2010).

Table 19.2 American Psychological Association Guidelines for Conducting Child Custody Evaluations

I. Orienting Guidelines: Purpose of a Child Custody Evaluation

  1. The primary purpose of the evaluation is to assess the best psychological interests of the child.

  2. The child's interests and well-being are paramount.

  3. The focus of the evaluation is on parenting capacity, the psychological and developmental needs of the child, and the resulting fit.

II. General Guidelines: Preparing for a Child Custody Evaluation

  4. The role of the psychologist is that of a professional expert who strives to maintain an objective, impartial stance.

  5. The psychologist gains specialized competence.

  6. The psychologist is aware of personal and societal biases and engages in nondiscriminatory practice.

  7. The psychologist avoids multiple relationships.

III. Procedural Guidelines: Conducting a Child Custody Evaluation

  8. The scope of the evaluation is determined by the evaluator, based on the nature of the referral question.

  9. The psychologist obtains informed consent from all adult participants and, as appropriate, informs child participants.

  10. The psychologist informs participants about the limits of confidentiality and the disclosure of information.

  11. The psychologist uses multiple methods of data gathering.

  12. The psychologist neither overinterprets nor inappropriately interprets clinical or assessment data.

  13. The psychologist does not give any opinion regarding the psychological functioning of any individual who has not been personally evaluated.

  14. Recommendations, if any, are based on what is in the best psychological interests of the child.

  15. The psychologist clarifies financial arrangements.

  16. The psychologist maintains written records.

Source: © American Psychological Association.

No two child custody evaluations are exactly alike, but some techniques are commonly used. More than 90% of evaluators conduct each of the following during a typical evaluation: clinical interviews with each parent, a clinical interview with the children, an observation of parent–child interaction, psychological testing with the parents, and a review of relevant documents. Additionally, more than 60% of evaluators conducted psychological testing with the children (Bow & Quinnell, 2001), although the parent interviews, child interview, and parent–child observation are seen as more important than tests by most psychologists surveyed (Bow, 2006). The most common tests for children in custody evaluations include IQ tests and projective personality tests such as the TAT and the Children's Apperception Test, whereas the most common test for adults is the MMPI-2. Some specialized custody-specific tests are also often used (E. Ellis, 2008; Hagen & Castagna, 2001).

Competency to Stand Trial

The U.S. legal system is based on a principle in English common law dating back to the 17th century that holds that a person accused of a crime cannot be tried in court unless that person is mentally fit or **competent to stand trial**. Although the present focus is on the competency to stand trial, there are other important legal competencies such as those concerned with writing wills, entering into a contract, and consenting for medical treatment. All these types of legal competency can be affected by the mental status of the individual. In 1899, a federal appeals court gave competency a constitutional standing. The court ruled that "it is not 'due process of law' to subject an insane person to trial upon an indictment involving liberty or life" (*Youtsey v. United States*; cited in Meyer & Weaver, 2006, p. 94). The two primary reasons for the competency doctrine are that it provides for a dignified criminal process and it supports Sixth Amendment protections, including the right to effective counsel, the right to confront one's accusers, and the right to present evidence. A person with a mental impairment could be sufficiently disturbed so as to be unable to exercise these rights without a change in mental status.

The competency-to-stand-trial standard established in *Dusky v. United States* (1960) is the standard used throughout most of the United States. The Supreme Court stated that to stand trial, a defendant must have "sufficient present ability to consult with his attorney with a reasonable degree of rational understanding and a rational as well as factual understanding of proceedings against him" (cited in Melton et al., 2007, p. 127). This standard covers both the defendant's capacity to understand the criminal process and his or her ability to function within the process. Competency refers to the defendant's present or current ability to understand the criminal process and function within it. The definition of competency does not, however, include the defendant's prior mental status or mental status at the time of the offense; rather, such past mental states would be included in discussions of criminal responsibility. In other words, the time period of concern in assessments of competency is the present, and the time period of concern for criminal responsibility is the point in the past when the offense occurred. For competency, the defendant must have a rational understanding of the proceedings, and this is related to a person's current cognitive ability and mental state. Many psychologists use a clinical interview in which the defendants are assessed regarding their understanding of the legal system to determine whether they can participate in the legal process in their defense. They are evaluated regarding the particular situations and demands of the case. Various psychological instruments are often used in assessing competence, and there are some specialized tests available. The practice of using standard psychological tests instead of specialized competency instruments has been criticized because these tests have not been validated for assessing competency (Zapf, Viljoen, Whittemore, Poythress, & Roesch, 2002).

Currently, between 2% and 8% of all felony defendants undergo competency evaluations—a large number considering the large and increasing number of felony arrests (Zapf & Roesch, 2006). Some experts in the field recommend a **functional evaluation** of competency, based on the idea that competency to stand trial depends on the cognitive and psychological demands of that particular case. Some cases are more complex than others, and some require different competencies than others, so competency should be judged relative to the demands of the case at hand. Thus, a defendant found to have a mental disorder is not necessarily incompetent for a given case, and a defendant found not to have a mental disorder is not necessarily competent for a given case (Zapf & Roesch, 2006).

Some jurisdictions have training programs to increase defendants' understanding of the legal system, because this is crucial to competence. Medications are also commonly used to treat defendants who are not competent to stand trial. While the incompetent defendant is hospitalized or incarcerated, the whole range of treatments available may be used to restore competency. Unless competence is established, the trial remains postponed. A person cannot, however, be held longer than "the reasonable period of time necessary to determine" whether competency will be attained in the near future (*Jackson v. Indiana*, 1972; cited in Melton et al., 2007, p. 137). Nor can a defendant be held longer than he or she would have been held if found guilty of the crime.

Culture can play an important role in competency evaluations. Some of the criteria used to make the determination of competency, including IQ tests and the *Diagnostic and Statistical Manual of Mental Disorders* diagnostic process, can be biased against certain ethnic and racial groups. Moreover, intelligence is defined differently by different cultural groups, so the intelligence reflected by scores on IQ tests derived from European American values does not necessarily capture such attributes as social competence, creativity, musical ability, physical fitness, and others that may be considered relevant to IQ in some cultures. Any competency evaluation should consider culture a factor in the interpretation of assessment data (Tsytsarev & Landes, 2008).

Commitment to Mental Institutions

Civil commitment to a mental institution is a process by which a person is involuntarily hospitalized by civil authorities for the welfare of the person and others. Civil commitments have a lower legal standard than criminal cases, but the standards are much higher now than in the pre-1970s era when individuals were often institutionalized with little more than a family request (Melton et al., 2007). Critics such as Thomas Szasz (1963) have questioned the practice of hospitalizing individuals against their will and have argued that the practice can be abused to remove certain groups of undesirable people from society. In addition to losing their civil rights, the care of individuals who were institutionalized was often very poor. These poor standards of care and limited legal controls on civil commitments led to changes in the 1970s in the criteria, procedures, and outcome of civil commitments.

Decisions about involuntary commitment generally follow a two-step process in which jurisdictions initially grant emergency admission as determined by a clinician or other authority, but judicial approval is required for continued confinement. All states have criteria for involuntary commitment that require the following conditions be met. The fundamental and first criterion for all state statutes is that the individual have a mental disorder. Second, some statutes require that the person be unable to appreciate the need for treatment because of the disorder. Third, the person must be dangerous to self or others due to the mental disorder. Fourth, most states also consider an individual's ability to care for basic needs as part of the commitment criteria. Fifth, some states require that there be a need for treatment. Finally, the commitment must occur in the least restrictive environment (Melton et al., 2007). The evaluation of commitment will focus on these six criteria, along with the person's suicide risk. Clinical psychologists, particularly because of their training in assessment, are well equipped to help determine the extent to which these criteria apply to individuals in question.

Treatment and Other Forensic Activities

Treatment of Forensic Clients

Clinical psychologists are involved in the legal system in many ways, and providing treatment to address problems related to criminal activity or its consequences is vital among them. Treatment in a forensic context can take many forms. For example, as noted above, the primary purpose of hospitalizing individuals found NGRI is the treatment of their psychological and psychiatric symptoms. In the case of individuals found not competent to stand trial, the focus of treatment is typically increasing their knowledge of the judicial system relevant to their case. The treatment of both these classes of individuals is primarily focused on short-term goals leading toward the person's reintroduction into society and community-based services in the first case and leading toward a trial in the second case. Individuals incarcerated in the prison system, on the other hand, typically have more long-range treatment needs.

⊕ **Web Link 19.4**

Journal of Forensic Psychiatry & Psychology

The goals of sentencing criminals to incarceration include retribution, deterrence, incapacitation, and rehabilitation (Melton et al., 2007). Although the clinical psychologist may not be able to "cure" the offender in a global sense, treatment methods can be used to address the emotional and behavioral problems that contribute to unlawful behavior. Efforts in recent years have also been directed toward establishing "practice guidelines" that provide guidance to psychologists on the best treatment options (Heilbrun & Brooks, 2010). When working with criminal offenders, clinical psychologists and other therapists typically focus on four basic therapy tasks, either alone or in combination: crisis management, maintenance, outpatient psychotherapy, and targeted programs (Mobley, 2006). Management treatments are implemented when there is a crisis of some type. This would include someone engaging in self-harming or violent behaviors. Treatments of this type are brief, followed by a referral to long-range treatments. Maintenance treatments are used with incarcerated individuals who have more long-standing problems such as intellectual disability (intellectual developmental disorder, formerly known as mental retardation) and schizophrenia, and they often are held and treated in special housing units. Many types of outpatient psychotherapy are used with prison populations, and successes or failures occur much as they do in more traditional settings. Programs targeting specific problems such as alcohol and drug treatment and sex offender treatment are also often available for incarcerated individuals. Such programs provide some advantages over outpatient treatment, including the ability to have more contact hours with the clients. For example, sex offender programs often last a year or longer and usually involve cognitive-behavioral strategies aimed at a number of treatment targets such as acceptance of responsibility, empathy, social functioning, deviant sexual interests, substance abuse, and relapse prevention (Marshall, 2006). From a rehabilitation perspective, reduced recidivism is a primary goal with all treatment interventions used in a prison population.

The cultural competence that clinical psychologists incorporate into their practices is especially relevant in prison settings. Incarcerated populations include a wide range of ethnic groups, including disproportionately high numbers of some minority groups (e.g., Layde, 2004; Tseng, Matthews, & Elwyn, 2004). Thus, whether serving as a therapist or an assessor, clinical psychologists working with prisoners must be sensitive to the cultural background of each client, as well as the prison culture in which the client currently lives.

Expert Witnesses

Clinical psychologists, along with psychiatrists and social workers, are the professionals who most commonly provide expert testimony to the court about mental health issues, and together they are involved in more than 1 million cases per year (Melton et al., 2007). Dating back to before the days of Hugo Munsterberg's grandiose claims about the benefits of using psychology in the legal system, attorneys and others have expressed cynicism about the role of psychology in the courts. This is partially due to the fundamental philosophical differences between science and law, but it is also rooted in a mistrust that arises from the idea that psychologists and other experts are "selling" their testimony. Although such a practice would be highly unethical, some claim that psychologists and other legal experts sell their opinions to the highest bidder and become "hired guns" (A. K. Hess, 2006b) or "whores of the court" (Hagen, 1997). Subtle or not-so-subtle pressures exist for an **expert witness** to testify in a manner that may be biased to support the case of the attorney who hired him or her. Given these pressures, it is important for psychologists to *be effective advocates for their data*, whether or not that makes them effective advocates for the party that calls them to court" (Melton et al., 2007, p. 578).

• • • BOX 19.2 • • •

Considering Culture

Cultural Competence in Forensic Clinical Psychology

Photo 19.2 Clinical psychologists working with forensic clients must be sensitive to varying abilities, knowledge, and beliefs stemming from diverse cultural backgrounds.

Cultural competence is crucial in all areas of clinical psychology, and forensic work is no exception. Just as the general U.S. population represents a great variety of ethnicities and other cultural variables, the population of forensic clients is similarly diverse. Whether working in prisons or psychiatric institutions, or as independent consultants, conducting assessments, therapy, or other professional duties, clinical psychologists are ethically obligated to interact with clients in a culturally sensitive manner (American Psychological Association, 2002). In recent years, cultural issues within forensic psychology settings have received an increasing amount of attention from professionals in the field (e.g., Layde, 2004; Tseng et al., 2004). Among the primary concerns noted by these authors are the following:

- *Linguistic issues.* Many forensic clients may not be fluent in English. This lack of fluency may interfere with standard assessment procedures (including interviews and both written and oral tests) and therapy efforts. When available, multilingual clinicians or translators can address this problem effectively.

- *Culturally specific definitions of sanity and insanity.* Particular behaviors commonly viewed as symptoms of psychosis within mainstream U.S. culture may be viewed differently by members of various cultural groups. For example, hallucinations based on religious experiences may be understood as normal rather than abnormal in some cultural groups.

- *Cultural limitations of psychological tests.* As discussed in earlier chapters of this book, such issues as readability, language, and cultural representation in normative groups may limit the applicability of certain tests with members of certain forensic clients.

- *Lack of familiarity with the U.S. judicial system.* Some forensic clients, including many who have recently immigrated, may not fully understand the laws and judicial processes of the United States. This is especially relevant in competency-to-stand-trial evaluations but can also be relevant in numerous other aspects of forensic work.

- *Distrust of the legal system.* Forensic clients who are members of oppressed groups may be unwilling to cooperate with the efforts of the clinical psychologist working in a forensic setting. In such cases, the clinical psychologist should attempt to appreciate the historical factors that may play a role in the client's behavior.

Layde (2004) recommends that cultural competency receive heavy emphasis in the training of forensic mental health professionals. Specifically, Layde suggests that such training should include not only seminars, readings, and other didactic experiences but also supervised professional experiences involving direct exposure to forensic clients of diverse cultural backgrounds.

As an example, consider a legal custody dispute in which two parents, Monica and Greg, are battling for custody of their two young children. Monica's attorney learns that 10 years ago, Greg received outpatient psychotherapy for depression. Monica's attorney contacts Dr. Redding, a clinical psychologist with expertise in depression, to serve as an expert witness in the custody trial. Because Monica and her attorney are hiring Dr. Redding to support their side of the argument, Dr. Redding may feel pressured to provide testimony that calls Greg's parenting potential into question and therefore strengthens Monica's case. That is, if Dr. Redding states that depression usually recurs throughout the life span, that it often gets more severe over time, or that children raised by parents who have been depressed have more significant problems than do those raised by nondepressed parents, the court might be persuaded to place the children with Monica. However, Dr. Redding should not make these statements if they do not reflect an accurate, impartial appraisal of the current state of research on depression. Even if Dr. Redding's objectivity and honesty disappoint the attorney paying her to serve as an expert witness, Dr. Redding is obligated as an expert witness to state only that which is supported by valid and reliable findings relevant to the depression and parenting issues involved in this case.

An expert witness is approved for the court through a process called **voir dire.** In the voir dire process, the expert's education, training, and professional experiences are examined. Sometimes both sides stipulate—that is, accept without requiring proof—that a psychologist meets the criteria needed to be an expert witness, and other times the matter is hotly contested by the opposing attorneys. In the process of establishing the expert qualifications of psychologists, attorneys commonly ask many informational questions of the psychologist, such as, "Do you specialize in any particular areas of psychology?" "What has been your experience in these areas of professional practice?" "Are you licensed?" "Are you board certified?" and "Describe your education" (Ewing, 2003).

Photo 19.3 Clinical psychologists serve as expert witnesses in a wide variety of court cases. In your opinion, what are the greatest challenges involved in this responsibility?

An expert witness is allowed to present significantly different kinds of testimony in court than a lay witness, who can testify only to what he or she saw, heard, or otherwise experienced. Experts approved by the court can provide both facts and opinions, can make inferences from facts, can provide information about disputed facts, and can help educate the jury or court about scientific information (Sales & Shuman, 2005). The ability to provide this range of testimony makes the expert witness a powerful contributor to the court's deliberations.

An important concern for clinical psychologists serving as expert witnesses is the admissibility of their testimony. In other words, what are the standards by which their testimony will be allowed or disallowed into the legal proceedings? Prior to 1993, expert scientific testimony was admissible in court if it was generally accepted in the expert's field. This standard was known as the Frye test, named after the 1923 *Frye v. United States* case. A 1993 Supreme Court ruling (*Daubert v. Merrell Dow Pharmaceuticals, Inc.*) supplanted the Frye test with a new set of standards. Under the current standards (known as **Daubert standards,** or Federal Rules of Evidence standards), the admissibility of evidence or testimony in court is based on its reliability and validity rather than its general acceptance in the field. So, according to the current standards, expert testimony can be allowed if it is deemed reliable and valid even if it is outside the boundaries of general acceptance in the field. For example, in psychological assessment, some question the admissibility of projective personality tests such as the Rorschach Inkblot Technique as well as objective personality tests such as the Millon Clinical Multiaxial Inventory-III (Wood et al., 2002). Under the Daubert/Federal Rules of Evidence standards, the judge serves as the gatekeeper in deciding whether the expert evidence passes the threshold of reliability and validity. Since Daubert/Federal Rules of Evidence have been in effect, greater sophistication has been needed by judges who are required to evaluate research methods and experimental inferences (Faigman & Monahan, 2005).

Patient's Rights

Throughout the United States, civil commitment laws exist that allow people to be committed to mental hospitals against their will. These laws are designed to provide mental health care for the individual and are not intended to be punitive. There have been, however, abuses to patients in mental hospitals in which many people were committed based on what today would be trivial reasons. In the first half of the 1900s, people could be committed by various legal mechanisms in different jurisdictions. Depending on the locale, the commitment process might be controlled by a judge, a justice of the peace, a lay jury, an asylum board, or, in some cases, only medical certification (Holstein, 1993). During this same period, medical treatments that were thought to hold great promise were attempted but were found to have significant negative side effects and could even cause patients significant harm. The new psychiatric medications of the 1950s caused long-term side effects such as tardive dyskinesia, with its lifelong symptoms of repetitive and involuntary movements, primarily of the face. Lobotomies were all too commonly conducted in mental hospitals in the mid-20th century. In a lobotomy, the prefrontal cortex of the brain was purposefully damaged in the hope that the patient's maladaptive behaviors would decrease. Although normally reserved for the most disturbed patients, they were also used on patients with serious intellectual limitations, despite lack of scientific evidence that they were effective on any group of patients (Valenstein, 1986).

In the 1960s and 1970s, attitudes and legal opinions grew in support of improving the legal rights of patients. In 1975, the Supreme Court (*O'Connor v. Donaldson*) weighed in on the civil commitment of mental patients by ruling that having a mental illness was not a sufficient criterion for civil commitment. Instead, the Supreme Court made it the law of the land that the person must both have a mental disorder and be considered dangerous. As long as an individual is not dangerous and is capable of surviving with the help of family and friends, involuntary civil commitment is not an option. Thus, the methods described above regarding the ways clinical psychologists assess dangerousness, as well as the way they assess psychopathology more generally, are crucial to cases involving involuntary commitment to a mental institution.

In addition to examining liberties related to civil commitment, the courts have also identified other rights of patients in mental hospitals. In *Youngberg v. Romeo* (1982), the Supreme Court extended the rights of mental patients to include "reasonably safe conditions of confinement, freedom from unreasonable bodily restraints, and such minimally adequate training as reasonably may be required by these interests" (p. 307). The right to refuse medications was also provided by the federal courts in the 1970s. This right to refuse medication can be overridden if the patient has an emergency need for medications, is a danger to self or others, or is unable to make competent decisions (Stafford, 2003).

Consultations With Law Enforcement

Clinical psychologists are increasingly employed by law enforcement agencies to perform a variety of duties (Kitaeff, 2011; Scrivner, 2006). For example, clinical psychologists often conduct preemployment evaluations on candidates for law enforcement jobs or fitness-for-duty evaluations for current officers whose psychological status is under question. Clinical psychologists also work as consultants on a wide range of issues with police departments, and some even work full-time in large police departments. In addition, clinical psychologists often provide direct therapeutic interventions to officers, especially when the stress or trauma of the job is adversely affecting them. Clinical psychologists can be a great benefit to police departments by providing training in areas such as stress reduction, dealing with mentally disturbed people, multicultural training, and other areas of expertise.

Most psychologists who work with police departments do not engage in criminal profiling, despite the portrayal of psychologists in numerous movies and TV shows on this topic. When profiling is used, its purpose is to assist the investigators in providing information on the perpetrator of the crime based on psychological factors. While the results of criminal profiling shown in movies and television shows tend to be dramatic and unrealistic, there have been some advances in this area of forensic science (White, Lester, Gentile, & Rosenbleeth, 2011).

Of all the ways psychologists work with police departments, conducting **preemployment evaluations** is the most common, although such evaluations lack consistency and standardization (Dantzker, 2011). These assessments usually include objective personality tests such as the MMPI-2 to assess psychopathology, a measure of cognitive or problem-solving ability such as the Wonderlic Personnel Test, and a clinical interview. There are also tests specifically designed for preemployment screening of police officers, such as the Inwald Personality Inventory. When psychological tests are used in the selection process, there is always the possibility that the candidates will "fake good" on the test, thus making the results of the test difficult if not impossible to interpret (Rees & Metcalfe, 2003). The goal of the evaluations is to assess the extent to which the candidate has any psychological problems, cognitive limitations, or personality characteristics that might interfere with the duties of a police officer.

Fitness-for-duty evaluations are another type of assessment that clinical psychologists conduct with police personnel (Scrivner, 2006). These evaluations are usually requested after an extremely stressful experience by an officer, such as being shot or witnessing traumatic events in the line of duty. They are also sometimes used to assess whether an officer is able to continue working while he or she is receiving psychotherapy or medications for depression, anxiety, or other psychological problems. These evaluations are often more extensive than the preemployment exams, including more detailed clinical interviews, interviews with significant others, interviews with fellow officers and superiors, and the administration of a variety of psychological tests.

● ● ● BOX 19.3 ● ● ●

From Abu Ghraib to Guantanamo Bay

Psychology and the Nuremberg Ethic

The atrocities of forced sterilization, involuntary experimentation, and medicalized killing that occurred in Germany during World War II under the direction of Nazi medical personnel led to the "Doctors' Trial" after the war. This trial was a part of a series of war crime trials held in Nuremberg, Germany (Annas & Grodin, 1992), and the medical personnel on trial utilized what became known as the "Nuremberg Defense," in which they claimed their actions were the result of "only following orders." This defense was unsuccessful, and the trial led to the formation of the "Nuremberg ethic" (Pope & Gutheil, 2009), in which it is held that acting on the order of a government or a superior is not a sufficient rationale for relieving a person of responsibility for his or her actions.

Psychologists' participation in the interrogations of detainees at Guantanamo Bay Detention Camp and Abu Ghraib prison have brought into question the role of psychologists in these activities and related issues with the American Psychological Association's (APA) ethical standards. While finding verifiable reports about the exact nature of psychologists' participation in interrogations, published reports from various sources describe psychologists' involvement in interrogations ranging from developing and monitoring interrogation plans (Mayer, 2005) to supporting the use of "safe, legal, ethical, and effective interrogation techniques" (Greene & Banks, 2009, p. 29).

Ethical concerns related to psychologists' roles in interrogations were heightened due to changes in the most recent version of APA ethical standards. Section 1.02 of the 2002 APA ethics code states:

(Continued)

(Continued)

> If psychologists' ethical responsibilities conflict with law, regulations, or other governing legal authority, psychologists make known their commitment to the Ethics Code and take steps to resolve the conflict. If the conflict is unresolvable via such means, psychologists may adhere to the requirements of the law, regulations, or other governing legal authority. (p. 1063)

The second sentence of this section was formally adopted in 2002 (although drafted in committee before September 11, 2001) and appears by some to allow psychologists to participate in interrogations that could be characterized as torture as long as the activities occur under the order of some legal authority. The APA (2009a) has unequivocally stated that "there is no defense to torture under the Ethical Principles of Psychologists and Code of Conduct." Further, "any direct or indirect participation in any act of torture or other forms of cruel, degrading or inhuman treatment or punishment by psychologists is strictly prohibited." Acts such as waterboarding and sexual humiliation are violations of APA policy (APA, 2009b).

Some have questioned the involvement of psychologists providing their expertise in interrogations, while the APA and others have pointed out potential and real benefits resulting from the involvement of psychologists. Speaking for the APA, its president wrote "that having psychologists consult with interrogation teams makes an important contribution toward keeping interrogations safe and ethical" (Brehm, 2007). In light of the Nuremberg ethic, Pope and Gutheil (2009) developed three suggested steps for health care professionals working with governmental agencies when dealing with these sorts of challenging and complex issues.

- Teaching and discussing the evolution of various approaches to these ethical issues as part of the basic and continuing education of all health care professionals
- Identifying decision-making patterns and approaches and emphasizing critical thinking about ethical responsibilities in conflict with laws, regulations, and other forms of state authority
- Maintaining active, informed awareness of the full array of relevant legal requirements and ethics codes, and the degree to which they may be in conflict with each other (pp. 163–164)

Clearly, this is a controversial area that demands careful consideration by the profession of psychology, individual psychologists, and psychology trainees.

CHAPTER SUMMARY

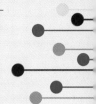

Forensic psychology is a growing specialty area for clinical psychologists. Although mental health professionals have been active in the legal system for about a century, opportunities for clinical psychologists have developed rapidly in recent decades. In particular, the assessment skills of clinical psychologists have been put into practice in forensic psychology for various legal purposes, including the prediction of dangerousness of defendants, the determination of mental status when defendants plead not guilty by reason of insanity, the assessment of family members in child custody cases, the evaluation of defendants' competency to stand trial, and the evaluation of individuals for whom involuntary commitment to a mental institution is being considered. Clinical psychologists also provide treatment to incarcerated individuals and others in forensic settings. Additionally, clinical psychologists serve as expert witnesses in court cases and assist law enforcement agencies via assessment of officers and applicants, direct therapeutic services for officers and their families, and consultation to law enforcement organizations.

KEY TERMS AND NAMES

actuarial prediction methods 484

American Psychological Association Division 41 481

the American Psychology-Law Society 481

base rate 487

child custody evaluations 489

civil commitment 494

clinical prediction methods 484

competent to stand trial 492

Daubert standards 498

expert witness 495

fitness-for-duty evaluations 501

forensic psychology 479

functional evaluation 493

guardian ad litem 490

guilty but mentally ill 489

M'Naghten test 487

Hugo Munsterberg 480

not guilty by reason of insanity (NGRI) 480

On the Witness Stand 480

predicting dangerousness 484

preemployment evaluations 500

statistical prediction methods 484

voir dire 498

CRITICAL THINKING QUESTIONS

1. In your opinion, what is the most fundamental difference between the forensic and therapeutic roles for a clinical psychologist?

2. If you were a clinical psychologist asked to predict the dangerousness of an individual, to what extent would you rely on clinical prediction methods versus statistical (or actuarial) prediction methods?

3. In what ways might an assessment of an individual's competency to stand trial differ from an assessment of an individual pleading NGRI?

4. If you were a clinical psychologist conducting a child custody evaluation, on which sources of data would you rely most heavily when making your recommendations?

5. If you were a clinical psychologist conducting preemployment evaluations for a police department, what assessment data would make you most likely to recommend that the department not hire that individual?

STUDENT STUDY SITE RESOURCES

Visit the study site at www.sagepub.com/pomerantz3eupdate for these additional learning tools:

- Self-quizzes
- eFlashcards
- Culture Expert Interviews

- Full-text SAGE journal articles
- Additional web resources
- Mock Assessment Data

CHAPTER SUMMARY VIDEO

 QR codes at the end of each chapter link to chapter background videos by the author. Visit http://gettag.mobi using your smartphone browser to download the free Microsoft Tag app. Once installed, scan the tags to go directly to these brief videos. In this video, the author elaborates on the specialized nature of forensic psychology.

GLOSSARY

ABAB design: A particular type of research design for case studies in which a treatment is alternately applied and removed

ABCDE model: In cognitive therapy, a model for understanding and recording the impact of cognitions on emotions

ABCDS of weight loss: A common approach used by health psychologists in treating people with excess weight, including *A*ctivity increase, *B*ehavior change, *C*ognitive change, *D*ietary change, and *S*ocial support

ABCs of relapse prevention: A component of substance abuse relapse prevention involving an examination by the client and the health psychologist of the events that occur before (*A*ntecedents) and after (*C*onsequences) consuming the substance (*B*ehavior)

abnormality: Forms of behavior that are outside the normal range; often labeled mental disorders, psychiatric diagnoses, or psychopathology

Academy of Psychological Clinical Science: An organization of graduate programs subscribing to the clinical scientist model of graduate training in clinical psychology

acceptance: In acceptance and commitment therapy, allowing unpleasant thoughts, feelings, and other internal sensations to run their course without fighting against them

acceptance and commitment therapy (ACT): An increasingly popular form of psychotherapy emphasizing the acceptance rather than avoidance of an unpleasant internal psychological experience

acculturation: Response or adaptation to a new cultural environment, particularly with regard to adopting elements of the new culture or retaining elements of the original culture

achievement: In contrast to intelligence (what a person *can* accomplish intellectually), what a person *has* accomplished, especially in academic subjects

achievement tests: Type of standardized tests used to measure how much students have learned in specific, clearly defined content areas, including but not limited to reading, mathematics, science, and social studies

activating event: The *A* in the ABCDE model of cognitive therapy; the occurrence that initiates the sequence of mental events that may prompt illogical cognitions or beliefs

actuarial prediction methods: An approach to predicting dangerousness in which assessors predict dangerousness according to a statistical or actuarial formula compiled from a comparison of an individual's characteristics with known correlations to future dangerousness; also known as statistical prediction methods

allegiance effects: In psychotherapy outcome research, the influence of researchers' own biases and preferences on the outcome of their empirical studies

all-or-nothing thinking: In cognitive psychotherapy, a common thought distortion in which the individual irrationally evaluates everything as either wonderful or terrible, with no middle ground or "gray area"

American Psychological Association (APA): Prominent professional organization for psychologists of which many clinical psychologists are members

American Psychological Association Division 41, the American Psychology-Law Society: A division of the American Psychological Association devoted to issues related to forensic psychology

American Society for the Advancement of Pharmacotherapy (American Psychological Association, Division 55): A division of the American Psychological Association devoted to issues related to prescription privileges for psychologists

anal stage: In psychodynamic psychotherapy, the second of the psychosexual developmental stages, and the stage from which issues of control may emerge

analogue design: A research design that involves an approximation of the target client or situation as a substitute for the actual clients or situations

analogue direct observation: In contrast to naturalistic direct observation, a type of behavioral observation that typically takes place in the clinic room, where the real-life situation is simulated

anxiety hierarchy: In exposure therapy, a rank-ordered list of anxiety-provoking stimuli to which the client will be gradually exposed

aspirational: In contrast to enforceable, an approach to psychology ethics that emphasizes aspirational ideals describing how psychologists should strive to conduct themselves

assertiveness training: A form of behavioral therapy based on classical conditioning in which clients improve on timid, apprehensive, or ineffectual social behaviors

assessment: A common professional activity of clinical psychologists in which clients are evaluated or appraised via clinical interviews, testing, observation, or other means

attending behaviors: Fundamental aspects of listening, including eye contact, body language, vocal qualities, and verbal tracking

attention: In the context of psychotherapy outcome research, the interest a therapist takes in the client that may constitute a common factor across therapies

automatic thoughts: In cognitive psychotherapy, cognitions that take place instantly and without any deliberation

aversion therapy: A form of contingency management therapy that emphasizes the use of punishment as a consequence for an unwanted behavior

Albert Bandura: A leading researcher in the area of observational learning, modeling, and social learning

base rate: In forensic psychology (and more broadly in all psychology), the rate at which a behavior

occurs, whereby phenomena with a low base rate (low frequency) are more difficult to predict (e.g., dangerous behaviors)

Aaron Beck: A leader in the field of cognitive psychotherapy and the developer of the concepts of the cognitive triad and common thought distortions, among others

Judith Beck: A leading figure in contemporary cognitive psychotherapy and the daughter of Aaron Beck

baselines: In behavioral therapy, pretreatment data on a problem behavior used as a basis for later comparisons

Beck Depression Inventory-II (BDI-II): The current edition of a brief objective test that assesses depression

behavior rating scales: In clinical child psychology, standardized forms that parents, teachers, or other adults complete regarding a child's presenting problems

behavioral: An approach to clinical psychology emphasizing empiricism, observable and quantifiable problems and progress, and a lack of speculation about internal mental processes

behavioral activation: A form of behavior therapy for depression, the goal of which is to increase the frequency of behaviors that are positively reinforcing to the client

behavioral assessment: In contrast to traditional personality assessment, an approach to assessment that assumes that client behaviors are not signs of underlying issues; instead, those behaviors *are* the problems

behavioral consultation: An indirect alternative to behavioral therapy whereby the therapist serves as a consultant to an individual such as a parent, teacher, or supervisor who ultimately implements the behavioral interventions with the client in the natural setting

behavioral medicine: An area of specialization for clinical psychologists and other health professionals focused on the impact of behavior on wellness and involving the integration of knowledge from a wide variety of social sciences, including psychology, sociology, and anthropology, with knowledge from the medical disciplines

behavioral observation: The direct, systematic observation of a client's behavior in the natural environment; also known as naturalistic observation

behavioral psychotherapy: An approach to psychotherapy emphasizing empiricism, observable and quantifiable problems and progress, and a lack of speculation about internal mental processes

being self-aware: A general skill for clinical interviewers involving the ability to know how the interviewer might affect others interpersonally and how others tend to relate to him or her

belief: The *B* in the ABCDE model of cognitive therapy; the illogical cognition linking the activating event to the emotional consequence

Bender Visual-Motor Gestalt Test—Second Edition (Bender-Gestalt-II): The current edition of a brief neuropsychological screen in which clients are asked to copy simple geometric designs

Insoo Kim Berg: A leading figure in solution-focused family therapy

between-group design: A research design in which participants in different conditions, one of which is often a control group, receive different treatments

Alfred Binet: A pioneer in the assessment of intelligence who co-created the Binet-Simon scale in the early 1900s, which evolved into the Stanford-Binet Intelligence Scales

biofeedback: A type of treatment used by health psychologists for pain management clients designed to achieve control over the body via educating patients about bodily processes of which they are typically unaware

"blank screen" role: In psychodynamic psychotherapy, the therapist role in which little personal information is revealed to facilitate transference

body language: In the context of the clinical interview, a behavior that can communicate strong nonverbal messages

Boulder conference: A historic 1949 conference in Boulder, Colorado, of directors of graduate training in clinical psychology from which the Boulder model of graduate training emerged

Boulder model: Alternate name for the scientist-practitioner model of graduate training stemming from the historic 1949 conference of directors of training in Boulder, Colorado

boundaries: An essential concept in structural family therapy; the divisions between family subsystems

boundaries of competence: The limits of competence that a clinical psychologist has an ethical obligation not to overstep

Murray Bowen: A leading figure in family therapy who is closely associated with the concept of differentiation of self

brief psychodynamic psychotherapy: A more efficient and increasingly common version of psychodynamic psychotherapy, typically lasting about 6 months or less

burnout: A state of exhaustion that relates to engaging continually in emotionally demanding work

California Psychological Inventory-III (CPI-III): The current edition of an objective personality test that emphasizes positive attributes of personality

John Carroll: A contemporary leader in the study of intelligence who has proposed the three-stratum theory of intelligence

case studies: Research methods that involve a thorough and detailed examination of one person or situation

catastrophizing: In cognitive psychotherapy, a common thought distortion in which the individual unrealistically expects catastrophic consequences

categorical approach: In contrast to the dimensional approach, an approach to diagnosis based on the notion that an individual either has or does not have a particular disorder

James Cattell: A leading figure in the study of intelligence who proposed separate fluid and crystallized intelligences

Dianne Chambless: A leading contemporary psychotherapy researcher who has argued strongly against the idea that all psychotherapy approaches are equally efficacious and in favor of a prescriptive approach to treatment

child abuse: In the context of clinical psychology, a condition that mandates the clinical psychologist to break confidentiality (per state laws) in an attempt to protect the welfare of the child at risk

child custody evaluations: Evaluations conducted by forensic psychologists for the purpose of providing recommendations for child custody

Children's Apperception Test (CAT): A projective test similar to the Thematic Apperception Test, created specifically for children

chronic pain: Pain that lasts 6 months or longer

chronic stress: Stress levels that are consistently high and unremitting

circular causality: In contrast to linear causality, a theory typically endorsed by family therapists whereby events influence one another in a reciprocal way

civil commitment: A process by which a person is involuntarily hospitalized by civil authorities for the welfare of the person and others

clarification: A clinical interview technique designed to make sure the interviewer has an accurate understanding of the client's comments

classical conditioning: Conditioning in which an unconditioned stimulus that produces an unconditioned response is paired with a conditioned stimulus such that the conditioned stimulus elicits a similar response (labeled as the conditioned response)

clinical child psychology: An area of specialization within clinical psychology focusing on issues of children

clinical interview: A common assessment technique used by clinical psychologists involving a purposeful conversation with clients characterized by questions and answers

clinical prediction methods: An approach to predicting dangerousness in which assessors utilize psychological tests, clinical interviews, clinical experience, and their personal judgments

clinical psychology: Rigorous study and applied practice directed toward understanding and improving the psychological facets of the human experience, including but not limited to issues or problems of behavior, emotions, or intellect

clinical scale: One of 10 scales on the MMPI and MMPI-2 indicating the extent to which an individual endorses symptoms of a particular category

clinical scientist model: A model of graduate training in clinical psychology that emphasizes empirical research over practice

clinical utility: In psychological assessment, the extent to which a technique benefits the clinician and ultimately the client in a meaningful way

closed-ended question: In contrast to open-ended question, an interview question that allows for far less elaboration and self-expression by the client but yields a quick and precise answer

closed-enrollment groups: In contrast to open-enrollment groups, therapy groups in which all members start and finish therapy together, with no new members added during the process

code of ethics: Ethical guidelines for psychologists, originally published by the American Psychological Association in 1953 and most recently updated in 2002

cognitions: The focus of cognitive psychotherapy, the way individuals interpret the events that happen to them and determine their resulting emotions; also known as beliefs, interpretations, assumptions, or thoughts

cognitive: An approach to clinical psychology emphasizing illogical thought as the foundation of psychopathology and logical thought as the foundation of psychological wellness

cognitive therapy: An approach to psychotherapy emphasizing illogical thought as the foundation of psychopathology and logical thought as the foundation of psychological wellness

cognitive triad: A component of Aaron Beck's theory of depression whereby negative thoughts about the self, the external world, and the future contribute to depression

common factors: Factors common to all forms of psychotherapy that play an active role in client improvement and may explain the dodo bird verdict in psychotherapy outcome research

common thought distortions: In cognitive psychotherapy, particular ways in which a thought, cognition, or belief can be illogical

communication patterns: An area commonly targeted by family therapists as the source of psychological symptoms and an area for improvement in family therapy

competence: Sufficient capability, skill, experience, and expertise to complete particular professional tasks adequately

competent to stand trial: A required condition of the defendant in the U.S. legal system for which forensic psychologists often conduct assessments

Comprehensive System: The leading scoring system for the Rorschach Inkblot Test, created by John Exner

conclusion: A clinical interview technique that may involve summarization, an initial conceptualization, a diagnosis, or recommendations

conditioned response: In classical conditioning, the response elicited by the conditioned stimulus after the conditioned stimulus has been paired with the unconditioned stimulus

conditioned stimulus: In classical conditioning, the stimulus paired with the unconditioned stimulus that ultimately elicits the conditioned response

conditions of worth: In humanistic psychotherapy, the stipulations that individuals may place on their positive regard of others

confidentiality: As mandated by the code of ethics of the American Psychological Association, upholding the privacy of clinical information

Conflict Tactics Scales (CTS): A questionnaire designed to assess how individuals behave when family conflicts arise, often used to explore interpersonal abuse or violence

confrontation: A clinical interview technique used when the interviewer notices discrepancies or inconsistencies in the client's comments

congruence: In humanistic psychotherapy, consistency between the real self and the ideal self; the source of mental health

content scales: In addition to the clinical scales, scales of the MMPI and MMPI-2 that provide relevant clinical information

contingencies: The "if … , then… " statements connecting actions to outcomes that organisms learn through operant conditioning

contingency management: A form of behavior therapy based on operant conditioning in which the consequences following selected behaviors are changed to produce more desirable behavior

continuing education: Learning experiences by which clinical psychologists maintain their competence throughout their careers; often required by state licensing boards for license renewal

continuing education units (CEUs): Educational credits earned by licensed clinical psychologists by attending workshops, taking courses, reading selected material, or similar means; often required by states for license renewal

control group: The condition or group in a between-subject design that receives no treatment

coping: The process of managing the demands of stress

correlational methods: Research methods that examine the relationship that exists between two or more variables and in which causality is not implied

cortisol: The human body's stress hormone, the release of which is controlled by the hypothalamic-pituitary-adrenal axis

Paul Costa: With Robert McCrae, an author of the NEO Personality Inventory-Revised

cotherapist: A therapist who coleads group therapy sessions with another therapist

counseling psychologists: Professionals with some similarities to clinical psychologists but whose work tends to emphasize less seriously disturbed clients, vocational testing, and career counseling

counterconditioning: Re-pairing a conditioned stimulus with a response that is incompatible with the previously conditioned response; an essential component of systematic desensitization

countertransference: In psychodynamic psychotherapy, transference by the therapist toward the client

crisis interview: A type of clinical interview designed not only to assess a problem demanding urgent attention (most often, clients actively considering suicide or another act of harm toward self or others) but also to provide immediate and effective intervention for that problem

cross-sectional designs: In contrast to longitudinal designs, research designs that assess or compare a participant or group of participants at one particular point in time

crystallized intelligence: The body of knowledge one has accumulated as a result of life experiences

cultural competence: For clinical psychologists, the ability to work sensitively and expertly with culturally diverse members of a heterogeneous society

cultural concepts of distress: As listed in *DSM-5*, psychological problems observed in cultural groups from various parts of the world

cultural diversity: Heterogeneity in the cultural background of members of a society

cultural fairness: The extent to which an intelligence test is based on universal rather than culture-specific concepts or methods

cultural self-awareness: An important component of cultural competence by which the clinical psychologist recognizes the uniqueness of his or her own cultural perspective

cybertherapy: The use of technology, including the Internet, videoconferencing, smartphones, and text-based services, in the application of clinical psychology

Daubert standards: In forensic psychology, current standards for admissibility of the testimony of expert witnesses

defense mechanisms: In psychodynamic psychotherapy, techniques used by the ego to manage conflict between the id and superego

Patrick H. DeLeon: A prominent proponent of prescription privileges for clinical psychologists and a former president of the American Psychological Association

dementia praecox: Emil Kraepelin's term for a cluster of psychological symptoms similar to what is currently known as schizophrenia

dependent variables: Variables in an experiment that are expected to change as a result of changes in the independent variables

Steve deShazer: A leading figure in solution-focused family therapy

detoxification: A common and important component of the treatment of substance abuse problems designed to prevent any dangerous side effects that may result from weaning the body off the substance too quickly

developing positive working relationships: A general skill for clinical interviewers often facilitated by attentive listening, appropriate empathy, genuine respect, and cultural sensitivity

developmental perspective: An essential aspect of clinical child psychology whereby clinicians understand the child's behavior within the context of the child's developmental stage

Diagnostic and Statistical Manual of Mental Disorders (DSM): The prevailing diagnostic guide for mental health professionals, containing the definitions of all mental disorders, published by the American Psychiatric Association

diagnostic criteria: Specific lists of symptoms used to define mental disorders

diagnostic interview: A type of clinical interview in which the primary purpose is to diagnose the client's problems

dialectical behavior therapy (DBT): A form of cognitive psychotherapy—and an example of an evidence-based treatment—developed by Marsha Linehan that has been found to be effective in the treatment of borderline personality disorder

differentiation of self: In family therapy, the healthy process whereby families allow each member to become his or her own person without sacrificing emotional closeness with other members of the family

dimensional approach: In contrast to the categorical approach, an approach to diagnosis based on the issue of severity of an individual's symptoms on a continuum or dimension, rather than the presence or absence of disorder

directive: In the context of the clinical interview, an approach by which interviewers obtain the information they need by asking clients specifically for it

discrimination: In classical conditioning, a process by which the conditioned response is not evoked by stimuli that are similar to, but not an exact match for, the conditioned stimulus

disease-prone personality: A personality characterized by marked anxiety, depression, and hostility that predisposes people to stress-related illnesses such as arthritis, ulcers, and coronary heart disease

disengaged: In structural family therapy, an unhealthy type of relationship between family members resulting from overly rigid boundaries between subsystems

displacement: In psychodynamic psychotherapy, a defense mechanism in which the ego displaces an id impulse toward a safer target

dispute: The *D* in the ABCDE model of cognitive therapy; challenging the illogical belief by labeling it as a particular type of thought distortion

Division of Clinical Psychology (Division 12): Division of the American Psychological Association devoted to clinical psychology

Dorothea Dix: A pioneer of reform in the treatment of the mentally ill in the United States and elsewhere in the 1800s

dodo bird verdict: A nickname for the common research finding that different forms of psychotherapy are roughly equally effective; derived from the line in *Alice in Wonderland,* "Everybody has won and all must have prizes"

dream work: In psychodynamic psychotherapy, the process of converting the latent content of a dream to its manifest content

dreams: In psychodynamic psychotherapy, an important means by which the client's unconscious material is communicated, and a common focus of interpretation

DSM-I: The first edition of the *Diagnostic and Statistical Manual of Mental Disorders* (*DSM*), published in 1952

DSM-II: The second edition of the *Diagnostic and Statistical Manual of Mental Disorders* (*DSM*), published in 1968

DSM-III: The third edition of the *Diagnostic and Statistical Manual of Mental Disorders* (*DSM*), published in 1980

DSM-III-R: A revision of the third edition of the *Diagnostic and Statistical Manual of Mental Disorders* (*DSM*), published in 1987

DSM-IV: The fourth edition of the *Diagnostic and Statistical Manual of Mental Disorders* (*DSM*), published in 1994

DSM-IV-TR: A text revision of the fourth edition of the *Diagnostic and Statistical Manual of Mental Disorders* (*DSM*), published in 2000

DSM-5: The fifth and current edition of the *Diagnostic and Statistical Manual of Mental Disorders* (*DSM*), published in May 2013

duty to warn: Stemming from the *Tarasoff* case, the obligation of clinical psychologists to alert people toward whom their clients have made credible, serious threats

Dysfunctional Thought Record: A form used in cognitive psychotherapy that organizes clients' experiences into columns on a written page

eclectic: A psychotherapy orientation that involves selecting the best treatment for a given client based on empirical data from studies of the treatment of similar clients

effective new belief: The *E* in the ABCDE model of cognitive therapy; the logical belief or cognition that replaces the original illogical belief

effectiveness: In contrast to efficacy, the success of a therapy in actual clinical settings in which client problems span a wider range and are not chosen as a result of meeting certain diagnostic criteria

efficacy: In contrast to effectiveness, the success of a particular therapy in a controlled study conducted with clients who were chosen according to particular study criteria

ego: In psychodynamic psychotherapy, the part of the mind that manages conflict between id and the superego and also meets the demands of reality; the part of the mind that generates defense mechanisms

ego psychology: A variation of psychodynamic psychotherapy emphasizing the adaptive tendencies of the ego over the pleasure-based drive of the id

Albert Ellis: A leader in the field of cognitive psychotherapy and the developer of Rational Emotive Behavior Therapy and the ABCDE model

emic: In contrast to *etic*, a perspective held by some psychologists emphasizing culture-specific norms and the appreciation of clients within the context of their own culture

emotional consequence: The *C* in the ABCDE model of cognitive therapy; the feeling that results from the illogical belief about the activating event

emotionally fused: In family therapy, a type of family relationship resulting from incomplete differentiation of self whereby family members remain overly emotionally connected with one another

empathy: In humanistic psychotherapy, one of the three essential therapeutic conditions; the therapist's ability to sense the client's emotions just as the client would, to perceive and understand the events of the client's life in a compassionate way

empirical criterion keying: The method of test construction used in the creation of the MMPI, which involves identifying distinct groups of people, asking all of them to respond to the same test items, and selecting items that yield different patterns of responses between groups

empirical data: An essential feature of behavioral therapy that can take the form of frequencies of problem behavior at various points in therapy

endogenous disorders: Emil Kraepelin's term for disorders caused by internal factors

enforceable: In contrast to aspirational, an approach to psychology ethics that emphasizes specific rules of conduct that can be violated

enmeshed: In structural family therapy, an unhealthy type of relationship between family members resulting from overly permeable boundaries between subsystems

ethical decision making: A process by which psychologists make decisions in ethically challenging situations

Ethical Standards: The section of the code of ethics of the American Psychological Association based on enforceable rules of conduct

etic: In contrast to *emic*, a perspective held by some psychologists emphasizing the similarities between all people and deemphasizing differences between cultural groups

evidence-based assessment: An approach to assessment emphasizing those methods that have strong psychometrics, clinical utility, and normative data and are sensitive to issues of diversity such as age, gender, race, and ethnicity

evidence-based practice: The practice of clinical psychology based on empirical research evidence in combination with clinical expertise and client characteristics, culture, and preferences

Examination for Professional Practice in Psychology (EPPP): A standardized exam used by states and provinces as a criterion for licensure

exception questions: In solution-focused family therapy, a technique whereby therapists ask families to recall situations when the problem was absent or less severe

existential psychotherapy: An approach to psychotherapy, related to the humanistic approach, that centers on the premise that each person is essentially alone in the world, and that realization of this fact can cause overwhelming anxiety

John Exner: Creator of the Comprehensive System of scoring for the Rorschach Inkblot Test

exogenous disorders: Emil Kraepelin's term for disorders caused by external factors

experiential avoidance: A tendency to circumvent rather than experience unpleasant thoughts (or feelings or other internal sensations) that may contribute to a variety of forms of psychopathology

experimental condition: The condition or group in a between-subject design that receives the treatment being examined

experimental method: A research process that follows a number of discrete, sequential steps including observation of events, hypothesis development, definition of independent and dependent variables, empirical testing of the hypothesis, and altering the hypothesis according to results obtained

expert witness: In forensic psychology, a clinical psychologist or other mental health professional who provides expert testimony to the court about mental health issues

exposure plus response prevention: A particular form of exposure therapy—and an example of an evidence-based practice—that has received substantial empirical support for the treatment of obsessive-compulsive disorder

exposure therapy: A form of behavioral therapy based on classical conditioning in which clients gradually face a feared object or situation

external validity: The generalizability of research results, or the extent to which a particular finding is valid for different settings and populations

externalizing disorders: In clinical child psychology, disorders in which the child "acts out" and often becomes a disruption to parents, teachers, or other children

extinction: In behavior therapy, the removal of an expected reinforcement that results in a decrease in the frequency of a behavior

extinction burst: In behavior therapy, the initial increase in intensity of the unwanted behavior immediately after the expected reinforcement is removed

extra-group socializing: A problematic and discouraged behavior among group therapy members; interacting as friends, romantic partners, and so on outside the group sessions

Hans Eysenck: An important figure in the history of psychotherapy outcome research whose negative review of psychotherapy outcome in 1952 inspired many subsequent empirical studies on psychotherapy outcome

family life cycle: A six-stage theory of family development that can be modified to account for the wide variety of families that a family therapist may see

family structure: In family therapy, the implicit rules that govern family members' behavior

family therapy: A form of psychotherapy in which family members attend sessions together and a primary goal is the improvement of dysfunctional characteristics of the family system

feedback: In family therapy, action taken by a family member to return the family to a state of homeostasis

fight-or-flight response: The response that takes place when an organism perceives a threat and the body rapidly mobilizes energy reserves via the sympathetic nervous system and endocrine system to either fight or flee

Celia Fisher: A leading figure in psychology ethics who served as chair of the committee responsible for creating the 2002 revision of the code of ethics of the American Psychological Association

fitness-for-duty evaluations: Psychological evaluations conducted by forensic psychologists, often for law enforcement agencies, to assess the extent to which current employees remain fit for duty after extremely stressful or traumatic experiences or in the midst of psychological problems

five-factor model of personality: A theory of personality thought by many to identify the fundamental, shared traits of human personality on which a dimensional approach to diagnosis may be based; also the basis of the NEO-PI-R personality test

fixation: In psychodynamic psychotherapy, unsuccessful resolution of the psychological tasks of a particular developmental stage

flooding: In exposure therapy, all-at-once in vivo exposure to feared objects or situations (in contrast to graded exposure)

fluid intelligence: The ability to reason when faced with novel problems

fluid reasoning: The ability to solve novel problems; also one of five factor scores of the Stanford-Binet Intelligence Scales—Fifth Edition

forensic psychology: The application of psychological methods and principles within the legal system

formula first-session task: In solution-focused family therapy, a technique whereby clients are instructed to take note in the upcoming week of aspects of their lives they want to continue

free association: A therapy technique in which psychodynamic psychotherapists simply ask clients to say whatever comes to mind without censoring themselves at all

Sigmund Freud: The pioneer of the psychodynamic approach to clinical psychology

Freudian slips: Verbal or behavioral mistakes determined, according to psychodynamic psychotherapists, by unconscious motivations

full-scale intelligence score: A feature of most contemporary tests of intelligence indicating overall or general level of intelligence

functional evaluation: An approach to competency-to-stand-trial evaluations based on the idea that competency to stand trial depends on the cognitive and psychological demands of that particular case

functionalism: In family therapy, the belief that although psychological symptoms may appear maladaptive, they are in fact functional within the family environment of the individual

"g": An abbreviation for general intelligence, as posited to exist by Charles Spearman and others (in contrast to "s," or specific intelligences)

general adaptation syndrome: The hypothesis developed by Hans Selye stating that when confronted with a temporary stressor, the fight-or-flight system works effectively to provide energy for immediate fight-or-flight needs, but when faced with repeated or prolonged exposure to stress, the body eventually fails to adapt and becomes vulnerable to illness

General Principles: The section of the code of ethics of the American Psychological Association based on aspirational ideals describing how psychologists should strive to conduct themselves

generalization: In classical conditioning, a process by which the conditioned response is evoked by stimuli that are similar to, but not an exact match for, the conditioned stimulus

genogram: A pencil-and-paper assessment technique in family therapy involving the creation of a family tree that incorporates detailed information about the relationships among family members

genuineness: In humanistic psychotherapy, the quality in the therapist of truthfulness, realness, or congruence, in contrast to playing the therapist role falsely

Gestalt therapy: An approach to psychotherapy, related to the humanistic approach, emphasizing a holistic approach to enhancing the client's current experience and often relying on the use of role-play techniques during therapy

graded exposure: In exposure therapy, a gradual approach to exposing clients to feared objects or situations

group cohesiveness: A therapeutic factor in group therapy; feelings of interconnectedness among group members and the equivalent of the therapist–client relationship in individual therapy

group level: One of three levels of the tripartite model of personal identity emphasizing the perspective that each individual is like some others

group therapy: A form of psychotherapy in which multiple clients participate in sessions together and interpersonal interaction is typically emphasized

guardian ad litem: In child custody evaluations, a neutral party (often an attorney unaffiliated with either parent) appointed to protect the rights of the child

guilty but mentally ill: In the U.S. legal system, a relatively new trial outcome in some states that constitutes a middle ground between full criminal responsibility and a finding of not guilty by reason of insanity

Halstead-Reitan Neuropsychological Battery (HRB): A relatively popular, comprehensive battery of eight standardized neuropsychological tests

harmful dysfunction theory: A theory of abnormality stating that the definition of disorder should include aspects of harmfulness (which is more socially determined) and dysfunction (which is more scientifically determined)

Starke Hathaway: With J. C. McKinley, one of the creators of the Minnesota Multiphasic Personality Inventory

health insurance/managed care: A method of payment for psychological services involving a third-party payer, in contrast to client self-pay

health psychology: A subdiscipline of behavioral medicine that deals specifically with how psychological processes (e.g., cognitions, moods, social networks) influence health and illness

here and now: A focus in group therapy on the present interpersonal interactions with fellow group members rather than events that have happened in clients' lives outside the group

heterogeneity: In the context of cultural diversity, the variety of cultural backgrounds among members of a society, both between and within particular cultural groups

heterogeneous groups: Therapy groups in which no single common characteristic (such as a diagnosis) is shared by all members

hierarchical model of intelligence: A model of intelligence in which specific abilities ("s") play an important role but are all at least somewhat related to one another and to a global, overall, general intelligence ("g")

homeostasis: In family therapy, the notion that systems have the ability to regulate themselves by returning themselves to a comfort zone or "set point"

homework: An important aspect of cognitive psychotherapy whereby therapists assign clients behavioral or written tasks

homogeneous groups: Therapy groups in which all members share a common characteristic, such as a diagnosis

hope: In the context of psychotherapy outcome research, the positive expectations that may constitute a common factor across therapies

humanistic: An approach to clinical psychology deriving primarily from the theories of Carl Rogers and Abraham Maslow, emphasizing the tendency toward healthy growth within each individual

humanistic play therapy: A form of psychotherapy with children emphasizing reflection of feelings in the context of a genuinely empathic and unconditionally accepting therapeutic relationship to facilitate self-actualization

humanistic therapy: An approach to psychotherapy deriving primarily from the theories of Carl Rogers and Abraham Maslow, emphasizing the tendency toward healthy growth within each individual

hypothalamic-pituitary-adrenal (HPA) axis: A system of structures (i.e., hypothalamus, pituitary gland, adrenal gland) that is activated by stress and controls the release of cortisol

hypotheses: In cognitive psychotherapy, according to Aaron Beck, the category of unproven theories in which thoughts, beliefs, and cognitions belong (in contrast to proven facts)

id: In psychodynamic psychotherapy, the part of the mind that generates and seeks immediate satisfaction for all the pleasure-seeking, selfish, indulgent, animalistic impulses

ideal self: In humanistic psychotherapy, the self that an individual could experience if he or she fulfilled his or her own potential, in contrast to the real self

identified patient: In family therapy, the family member whose symptoms are most obvious or problematic to other members

idiographic approach: In contrast to nomothetic approach, an approach to research emphasizing or revealing the unique qualities of each person

imaginal exposure: In exposure therapy, exposure to anxiety-provoking objects via imagination, in contrast to in vivo exposure

imitation: In behavioral therapy, a way in which clients can benefit from observational learning simply by mimicking the modeled behavior

implosion: In exposure therapy, all-at-once imaginal exposure to feared objects or situations (in contrast to graded exposure)

in vivo exposure: In exposure therapy, exposure to anxiety-provoking objects in real life, in contrast to imaginal exposure

incongruence: In humanistic psychotherapy, a discrepancy between the real self and the ideal self; the source of psychopathology

independent variables: Variables in an experiment that are manipulated by the experimenter and are typically hypothesized to influence dependent variables

index scores: A feature of most contemporary tests of intelligence indicating intellectual ability in one of a small number of broad areas

individual level: One of three levels of the tripartite model of personal identity emphasizing the perspective that each individual is like no other

inferential: A characteristic of psychodynamic psychotherapy referring to the clinician's reliance on deduction or conjecture rather than empirical or directly observable information

informed consent: The ethically mandated process of informing an individual about proposed activities (e.g., as a therapy client or research participant) and obtaining the individual's voluntary consent before proceeding with the activities

insight: A primary goal of psychodynamic psychotherapy; making the unconscious conscious

intake interview: A type of clinical interview in which the primary purpose is essentially to determine whether to "intake" the client to the setting where the interview is taking place

integrative: A psychotherapy orientation that involves blending techniques to create an entirely new, hybrid form of therapy

intelligence: Aptitude or intellect; the exact definition has long been a subject of debate among psychologists and may or may not include speed of mental processing, sensory capacity, abstract thinking, imagination, adaptability, capacity to learn through experience, memory, reasoning, or inhibition of instinct

intelligence tests: Psychological tests that measure a client's intellectual abilities

internal validity: The extent to which the change in the dependent variable is due solely to the change in the independent variable

internalizing disorders: In clinical child psychology, disorders that involve maladaptive thoughts and feelings more than disruptive outward behavior

interpersonal interaction: An emphasis of most forms of group therapy whereby therapists attempt to improve clients' abilities to relate to others in healthy ways

interpersonal learning: A therapeutic factor in group therapy; learning from the in-group interpersonal experience

Interpersonal Therapy (IPT): A specific, manualized, contemporary form of psychodynamic psychotherapy that emphasizes interpersonal relationships and has received empirical support for the treatment of depression

interpretation: In psychodynamic psychotherapy, the therapist's attempt to formulate and discuss with the client a hypothesized connection between unconscious material and client behavior

introspection: The process of looking inside the mind for evidence of mental processes or therapeutic change, rejected by behaviorists for its lack of objectivity

knowledge: General information accumulated over time via personal experiences, including education, home, and environment; also one of five factor scores of the Stanford-Binet Intelligence Scales—Fifth Edition

Emil Kraepelin: A pioneer of diagnostic categorization in mental health who was one of the first to assign formal labels to particular clusters of symptoms

latent content: In psychodynamic psychotherapy, the raw, unconscious thoughts and feelings represented by a dream

law of effect: The behavioral principle that actions followed by pleasurable consequences are more likely to recur, whereas actions followed by unpleasant consequences are less likely to recur

licensure: Status granted to clinical psychologists by states on meeting educational, experiential, and exam-related requirements that allows the individual to identify self as a member of the profession and to practice independently

linear causality: In contrast to circular causality, a theory typically endorsed by individual therapists whereby events from the past cause or determine events in the present in a unidirectional manner

Marsha Linehan: The developer of dialectical behavior therapy, which has been found effective in the treatment of borderline personality disorder

listening: A simple yet vital task for the clinical psychologist, especially in the context of the clinical interview

longitudinal designs: In contrast to cross-sectional designs, research designs that emphasize changes across time, often making within-group comparisons from one point in time to another

Luria-Nebraska Neuropsychological Battery (LNNB): A relatively popular, comprehensive battery of 12 standardized neuropsychological scales

magnification/minimization: In cognitive psychotherapy, a common thought distortion in which the individual overemphasizes the importance of negative events and underemphasizes the importance of positive events

manifest content: In psychodynamic psychotherapy, the actual plot of the dream as remembered by the dreamer, which represents the latent content

manualized therapy: Forms of psychotherapy that follow a therapy manual, which provides detailed instructions for all phases of the treatment of a specific disorder; typically used in outcome studies supporting evidence-based treatments

Abraham Maslow: A pioneer of the humanistic approach to clinical psychology

Robert McCrae: With Paul Costa, an author of the NEO Personality Inventory-Revised

Richard McFall: Author of the "manifesto" that served as the foundation for the clinical scientist model of graduate training in clinical psychology

Robert McGrath: A prominent proponent of prescription privileges for clinical psychologists and president of the American Society for the Advancement of Pharmacology (Division 55 of the American Psychological Association)

J. C. McKinley: With Starke Hathaway, one of the creators of the Minnesota Multiphasic Personality Inventory

medical model of psychopathology: A method of defining mental disorders in which each disorder is an entity defined categorically and features a list of specific symptoms

Donald Meichenbaum: The creator of self-instructional training, a treatment method intended to help impulsive and disruptive children gain greater control over their behavior

mental filtering: In cognitive psychotherapy, a common thought distortion in which the individual ignores positive events while focusing excessively on negative events

mental status exam: A type of clinical interview often used in medical settings, the primary purpose of which is to assess quickly how the client is functioning at the time of the evaluation

Stanley Messer: A leading contemporary psychotherapy researcher who has argued strongly in favor of the dodo bird verdict and against a prescriptive approach to treatment

meta-analysis: A statistical method of combining results of separate studies (translated into effect sizes) to create a summation (or, statistically, an overall effect size) of the findings

metacognitive therapy: A relatively new form of cognitive therapy emphasizing thoughts about one's own thoughts, rather than thoughts about external events, as causal factors in psychopathology

microaggressions: Comments or actions made in a cross-cultural context that convey prejudicial, negative, or stereotypical beliefs and may suggest dominance or superiority of one group over another

Theodore Millon: A widely recognized scholar on personality disorders and the creator of the MCMI personality tests

Millon Clinical Multiaxial Inventory-III (MCMI-III): Current version of a comprehensive objective personality test that emphasizes personality disorders

mind reading: In cognitive psychotherapy, a common thought distortion in which the individual presumes to know that others are thinking critically or disapprovingly, when knowing what they think is, in fact, impossible

mindfulness: A key component of many recent forms of cognitive therapy promoting full engagement with one's own internal mental processes in a nonconfrontational way

Minnesota Multiphasic Personality Inventory (MMPI): A popular and empirically sound objective personality test for adults, originally published in 1943

Minnesota Multiphasic Personality Inventory-Adolescent (MMPI-A): Revision of the MMPI for adolescent clients published in 1992

Minnesota Multiphasic Personality Inventory-2 (MMPI-2): Current version of the most widely used comprehensive objective personality test, published in 1989

Salvador Minuchin: A leading figure in structural family therapy

miracle questions: In solution-focused family therapy, a technique whereby therapists ask families to imagine life without the problem

mixed-group design: A research design that combines aspects of between-group and within-group designs

MMPI-2 Restructured Form (MMPI-2-RF): A relatively brief 2008 revision of the MMPI-2 in which the clinical scales include fewer items due to the omission of overlapping items

M'Naghten test: The first legal standard for the insanity defense in the history of the American legal system; based on a legal standard from England

Christiana Morgan: One of the creators of the Thematic Apperception Test, a popular projective personality test

motivational interviewing (MI): A contemporary variation of the humanistic approach to psychotherapy in which therapists empathically help clients see the discrepancy between their behavior and their own values when they experience ambivalence about making major changes

multiaxial assessment: An approach to assessment introduced in *DSM-III* by which mental health professionals can provide diagnostic information on each of five distinct axes or domains

multiaxial system: An assessment system used by recent editions of the *DSM* that allows mental health professionals to provide diagnostic information on each of five distinct axes or domains

multiculturalism: An approach in clinical psychology emphasizing the appreciation of cultural diversity and awareness of how techniques can be best applied to individuals of various cultural backgrounds

multimethod assessment: An approach to assessment incorporating multiple methods, including tests of different types, interview data, observations, or other sources

multiple relationships: A circumstance in which a clinical psychologist has a professional relationship with an individual and also has another type of relationship with the same person or has a relationship with someone closely associated with the person

multisource, multimethod, multisetting approach: An approach to the assessment involving multiple sources of information, multiple methods of obtaining information, and multiple settings in which information is solicited

Hugo Munsterberg: An important figure in the history of forensic psychology; an early promoter of the use of psychology in the legal arena and the author of *On the Witness Stand*

Henry Murray: One of the creators of the Thematic Apperception Test, a popular projective personality test

narrative therapy: A contemporary form of family therapy that emphasizes the revision of the stories that family members use to explain and

interpret the events in their lives such that the stories describe the members more positively

naturalistic direct observation: In contrast to analogue direct observation, a type of behavioral observation in which a behavior is observed in the place where it actually happens

naturalistic observation: The direct, systematic observation of a client's behavior in the natural environment; also known as behavioral observation

negative punishment: A form of punishment in which the individual "loses something good"

negative reinforcement: A form of reinforcement in which the individual "loses something bad"

NEO Five Factor Inventory (NEO-FFI): A short form of the NEO Personality Inventory-Revised that produces a less detailed personality profile

NEO Personality Inventory-Revised (NEO-PI-R): The current edition of an objective personality test that emphasizes normal personality characteristics rather than forms of abnormality

neuropsychological tests: Psychological tests that focus on issues of cognitive or brain dysfunction, including the effects of brain injuries and illnesses

neurosis: Along with psychosis, one of the two broad categories of mental illness used in Europe in the 1800s; refers to disorders such as anxiety and depression in which the individual maintains an intact grasp on reality

nomothetic approach: In contrast to idiographic approach, an approach to research emphasizing the determination of similarities or common qualities among people

nondirective: In the context of the clinical interview, an approach by which interviewers allow clients to determine the course of the interview

nonsexual multiple relationships: A type of multiple relationship in which a clinical psychologist has a professional relationship with an individual and also has another nonsexual relationship (e.g., friendship, business relationship) with the same person

John Norcross: A leading contemporary psychotherapy researcher and a champion of the integrative orientation to psychotherapy

normative data: A sample of test-result data gathered by creators of a psychological test and typically designed to accompany the test that constitutes a basis for comparison for individuals who take the test in clinical settings

not guilty by reason of insanity (NGRI): In the U.S. legal system, a possible finding whereby an individual was unable to control his or her criminal actions due to a mental disorder at the time of the offense and is therefore not held responsible for the crime

object relations: A variation of psychodynamic psychotherapy deemphasizing internal conflict (id vs. superego), and instead emphasizing relationships between internalized "objects" (essentially, important people from the client's life)

objective personality tests: Personality tests characterized by unambiguous test items, a limited range of client responses, and objective scoring

observable changes: An essential feature of behavioral therapy; therapeutic changes that are directly observable rather than inferred

observational learning: In behavioral therapy, conditioning that takes place when the individual observes contingencies applied to others rather than the self; also known as modeling and social learning

On the Witness Stand: A popular early book on forensic psychology authored by Hugo Munsterberg

open-ended question: In contrast to closed-ended question, an interview question that allows for individualized and spontaneous responses from clients

open-enrollment groups: In contrast to closed-enrollment groups, therapy groups in which individual members are allowed to enter or leave the group at any time

operant conditioning: Conditioning in which the organism "operates" on the environment, notices the consequences of the behavior, and incorporates those consequences into decisions regarding future behavior

oral stage: In psychodynamic psychotherapy, the first of the psychosexual developmental stages, and the stage from which issues of dependency may emerge

overgeneralization: In cognitive psychotherapy, a common thought distortion in which the individual applies lessons learned from negative experiences more broadly than is warranted

overpathologizing: Viewing as abnormal that which is actually normal; can be reduced by increasing cultural competence

paraphrasing: A clinical interview technique used simply to assure clients that they are being accurately heard

parent training: A form of behavioral consultation in which the therapist serves as a consultant to a parent, who ultimately implements the behavioral interventions with the child in the home

patient-centered medical homes (PCMHs): A relatively new model of care, often involving health psychologists, that emphasizes primary care that is high quality, cost-effective, comprehensive, holistic, and coordinated

Ivan Pavlov: An important figure in the history of behavioral psychotherapy; a researcher whose classical conditioning studies provided a foundation for many behavioral techniques

Philippe Pinel: A pioneer of reform in the treatment of the mentally ill in France in the late 1700s and early 1800s

pediatric psychology: A specialty area within clinical child psychology focusing on the mental and physical health of children with medical conditions

Perceptual Reasoning Index: A measure of fluid reasoning, spatial processing, and visual-motor integration; also one of four index scores yielded by the Wechsler intelligence tests

personalization: In cognitive psychotherapy, a common thought distortion in which the individual assumes excessive personal responsibility for negative events

phallic stage: In psychodynamic psychotherapy, the third of the psychosexual developmental stages, and the stage from which issues of self-worth may emerge

positive psychology: A recent, growing movement within the mental health field that accentuates the strong and healthy rather than the pathological aspects of human behavior

positive punishment: A form of punishment in which the individual "gets something bad"

positive regard: In humanistic psychotherapy, the warmth, love, and acceptance of those closest to us; also known as prizing

positive reinforcement: A form of reinforcement in which the individual "gets something good"

postdoctoral internship: A 1- or 2-year internship occurring after the doctoral degree in clinical psychology is granted that consists of supervised clinical experience in an applied setting, often with a specialized focus

practitioner-scholar model: A model of graduate training in clinical psychology that emphasizes practice over empirical research

predicting dangerousness: The practice whereby a forensic psychologist assesses the likelihood that an individual will behave violently or dangerously in the future

predoctoral internship: A year-long internship occurring near the end of graduate training in clinical psychology that consists primarily of supervised clinical experience in an applied setting

preemployment evaluations: A psychological evaluation conducted by forensic psychologists, often for law enforcement agencies, to assess the extent to which the candidate has any psychological problems, cognitive limitations, or personality characteristics that might interfere with the duties of the job

premenstrual dysphoric disorder (PMDD): A provisional or proposed mental disorder characterized by severe premenstrual symptoms, possibly including depressed mood, anxiety, affective lability, and decreased interest in activities

prescription privileges: The ability to prescribe medication to clients, which constitutes a controversy among contemporary clinical psychologists

prescriptive approach: An approach to psychotherapy in which specific therapy techniques with the most empirical evidence are viewed as the treatment of choice for specific disorders

prizing: In humanistic psychotherapy, the warmth, love, and acceptance of those closest to us; also known as positive regard

problem-focused coping: An approach to coping with stress that emphasizes proactive, constructive attempts to take action about a stressful situation

Processing Speed Index: A measure of the ability to process simple or rote information rapidly and accurately; also one of four index scores yielded by the Wechsler intelligence tests

professional counselors: Professionals with some similarities to clinical psychologists but who attend master's programs in professional counseling that typically have relatively high admissions rates, and whose activities emphasize counseling and deemphasize assessment and research

projection: In psychodynamic psychotherapy, a defense mechanism in which the ego projects an id impulse onto other people

projective personality test: A personality test in which individuals are assumed to project their personality characteristics via responses to ambiguous or vague stimuli

proposed criteria set: A set of symptoms described in Section III of *DSM-5* and under consideration for inclusion as an official disorder in a future edition of the *DSM*

psychiatrists: Professionals with some similarities to clinical psychologists but who are medically trained, able to prescribe medication, and emphasize the biological aspects of clients' problems

psychodynamic: An approach to clinical psychology deriving from the theories of Sigmund Freud and emphasizing the goal of making the unconscious conscious

psychodynamic play therapy: A form of psychotherapy with children in which a child's play symbolically communicates important unconscious processes occurring within the child's mind

psychodynamic psychotherapy: An approach to psychotherapy deriving from the theories of Sigmund Freud, the primary goal of which is to make the unconscious conscious

The Psychological Clinic: The first scholarly journal in the field of clinical psychology, founded by Lightner Witmer in 1907

psychoneuroimmunology (PNI): The field of study concerned with the interactions among behavior, the nervous system, and the immune system

psychosis: Along with neurosis, one of the two broad categories of mental illness used in Europe in the 1800s; refers to disorders in which the individual demonstrates a break from reality in the form of hallucinations, delusions, or grossly disorganized thinking

psychotherapy: Techniques and approaches used by clinical psychologists and other mental health professionals to alleviate psychological symptoms or improve some aspect of emotional, cognitive, or behavioral functioning

PsyD: A doctoral degree obtained by clinical psychologists who graduate from practitioner-scholar programs that has become an increasingly common alternative to the more traditional PhD degree

punishment: In behavior therapy, any consequence that makes a behavior less likely to recur in the future

quality of life therapy: a recent application of cognitive therapy principles to individuals who are experiencing psychological distress that doesn't meet the criteria for a mental disorder

quantitative reasoning: The ability to solve numerical problems; also one of five factor scores of the Stanford-Binet Intelligence Scales—Fifth Edition

quasi-experimental design: A type of research design used when truly experimental design is not feasible

quieting yourself: A general skill for clinical interviewers involving the minimization of internal, self-directed thoughts that can preoccupy or distract the interviewer

rapport: A positive, comfortable relationship between clinician and client, especially important in the context of the clinical interview

Rational Emotive Behavior Therapy (REBT): Formerly known as Rational Emotive Therapy, the form of cognitive therapy developed by Albert Ellis and incorporating the ABCDE model

reaction formation: In psychodynamic psychotherapy, a defense mechanism in which the ego forms a reaction against the id impulse, resulting in a behavior opposite of the original id impulse

reactivity: In the context of behavioral observation, a problem whereby the client's behavior may change simply because of his or her awareness of the presence of the observer

real self: In humanistic psychotherapy, the self that an individual actually experiences, in contrast to the ideal self

recapitulation of the family group: A phenomenon in group therapy whereby a group evokes the same dynamics as a client's family of origin

reflection: In humanistic psychotherapy, a therapist response to a client involving a rephrase or restatement of the client's statements in a way that highlights the client's feelings or emotions

reflection of feeling: A clinical interview technique intended to make clients feel that their emotions are recognized, even if their comments did not explicitly include labels of their feelings

reinforcement: In behavior therapy, any consequence that makes a behavior more likely to recur in the future

relaxation training: The first step of systematic desensitization in which the behavior therapist teaches the client progressive relaxation techniques that induce a relaxation response incompatible with anxiety

reliability: In psychological assessment, the extent to which a technique yields consistent, repeatable results

Repeatable Battery for the Assessment of Neuropsychological Status (RBANS): A neuropsychological screen that focuses on a range of abilities, including visuomotor abilities, verbal skills, attention, and visual memory

repression: In psychodynamic psychotherapy, a defense mechanism in which the ego represses conscious awareness of conflict between id and superego

resilience: In contrast to vulnerability, the tendency to remain psychologically healthy in spite of the presence of risk factors that contribute to psychological problems in others

resistance: In psychodynamic psychotherapy, client behavior that impedes discussion or conscious awareness of selected topics or emotions

The Retreat: A residential treatment center in Connecticut founded by Eli Todd in which the mentally ill were treated in a humane and dignified way

Rey-Osterrieth Complex Figure Test: A neuropsychological screen involving the reproduction of a single, complex geometric figure

Carl Rogers: A pioneer of the humanistic approach to clinical psychology

Hermann Rorschach: Swiss psychiatrist who created the Rorschach Inkblot Method, a popular projective personality test

Rorschach Inkblot Method: The projective personality test created by Hermann Rorschach involving 10 ambiguous inkblots

Rotter Incomplete Sentences Blank (RISB): The most commonly used sentence completion test

"s": An abbreviation for specific intelligences that may not correlate with one another (in contrast to "g," or general intelligence)

Morgan T. Sammons: A prominent proponent of prescription privileges for clinical psychologists and a widely recognized expert on psychopharmacology

scaling questions: In solution-focused family therapy, a technique whereby therapists ask families to rate the severity of a problem over time and emphasize strategies the families have used to cause the reductions in severity

school psychologists: Professionals with some similarities to clinical psychologists but who work primarily in schools and often perform psychological and educational testing and conduct interventions with students

scientist-practitioner model: The traditional model of graduate training in clinical psychology with a dual emphasis on empirical research and practice resulting in the PhD degree

self-actualization: In humanistic psychotherapy, the inborn tendency to grow in a healthy way

self-instructional training: A treatment method intended to help impulsive and disruptive children gain greater control over their behavior

self-monitoring: In behavioral assessment, techniques in which clients observe and keep a record of their own target behaviors

self-psychology: A variation of psychodynamic psychotherapy emphasizing parental roles in the child's development of self, with special attention paid to the meaning of narcissism at various points, including in therapy

self-report scales: Assessment techniques that are completed directly by the client

Hans Selye: A pioneer in stress research who developed the general adaptation syndrome hypothesis

semistructured interview: Also known as a partially structured interview, a clinical interview that has some characteristics of structured interviews as well as some characteristics of unstructured interviews

Senior Apperception Test (SAT): A projective test similar to the Thematic Apperception Test created specifically for older adults

sentence completion tests: Projective personality tests in which the individual is asked to complete sentence stems

sexual multiple relationships: A type of multiple relationship in which a clinical psychologist has a professional relationship with an individual and also has a sexual relationship with the same person

shaping: In behavioral therapy, reinforcing successive approximations of the target behavior

B. F. Skinner: A pioneer of behaviorism whose experimentation on the law of effect and operant conditioning formed the foundation for many forms of behavioral therapy

Charles Spearman: A pioneer in the study of intelligence who argued for the existence of "g," a general intelligence thought to overlap with many particular abilities

social microcosm: A phenomenon in group therapy whereby the relationship tendencies that characterize clients' relationships with important people in their personal lives predictably characterize the relationships they form with their fellow group members

social support: Relationships with others who can provide support in a time of crisis and who can share in good fortune as well

social workers: Professionals with some similarities to clinical psychologists but who typically obtain a master's degree and whose work emphasizes the social and environmental factors that contribute to an individual's problems

Society of Clinical Child and Adolescent Psychology: Division 53 of the American Psychological Association, focusing on issues related to clinical psychology applied to children and adolescents

solution-focused therapy: A contemporary approach to family therapy that relies on solution-talk and similar techniques in attempting to solve families' problems

solution-talk: An essential aspect of solution-focused family therapy whereby therapists emphasize positive outcomes that the future may hold rather than unpleasant situations that characterize the present to help clients begin to adopt a more positive point of view

specific learning disorder: A diagnosis based primarily on the level of academic achievement falling significantly below expected levels of achievement for people of the same age

stages of change model: A theory of readiness to change asserting that psychotherapy clients may enter therapy in one of five stages: precontemplation, contemplation, preparation, action, or maintenance

Stanford-Binet Intelligence Scales: A widely accepted test of intelligence originally developed by Alfred Binet and Theodore Simon

Stanford-Binet Intelligence Scales—Fifth Edition (SB5): The current edition of a prominent test of intelligence for individuals across the life span

statistical prediction methods: An approach to predicting dangerousness in which dangerousness is predicted according to a statistical or actuarial formula compiled by comparing an individual's characteristics with known relationships to future dangerousness; also known as actuarial prediction methods

strategic family therapy: A pragmatic, problem-focused approach to family therapy from which solution-focused therapy evolved

stress: The psychological and/or physiological response to difficult or demanding internal or external circumstances

Structured Clinical Interview for *DSM-IV* Disorders (SCID): A prominent structured interview technique appropriate for a wide range of *DSM-IV* disorders

structured interview: In contrast to an unstructured interview, an interview with a predetermined, planned sequence of questions that an interviewer asks a client

Hans Strupp: A pioneering psychotherapy researcher who developed the tripartite model of assessing psychotherapy outcome

subcultures: Relatively small groups within a society that may not fully constitute cultural groups but whose members may nonetheless possess typical and culturally meaningful characteristics for the clinical psychologist

sublimation: In psychodynamic psychotherapy, a defense mechanism in which the ego redirects the id impulse in such a way that the resulting behavior actually benefits others

subsystems: An essential concept in structural family therapy; subgroups of family members separated by boundaries

subtest scores: A feature of most contemporary tests of intelligence indicating intellectual ability in one of many specifically defined areas

summarizing: A clinical interview technique that usually involves tying together various topics that may have been discussed, connecting statements that may have been made at different points, and identifying themes that have recurred during the interview

superego: In psychodynamic psychotherapy, the part of the mind that establishes rules, restrictions, and prohibitions

supplemental scales: In addition to the clinical scales, scales of the MMPI and MMPI-2 that provide relevant clinical information

systematic desensitization: A form of behavior therapy based on classical conditioning involving re-pairing (or counterconditioning) the feared object with a new response, such as relaxation, that is incompatible with anxiety

systems approach: A foundation of family therapy whereby clinical problems originate in the family system rather than in an individual family member

***Tarasoff* case:** A landmark legal case resulting in clinical psychologists' duty to warn potential victims of dangerous or harmful acts whose identity is revealed by clients during psychological services

teacher training: A form of behavioral consultation in which the therapist serves as a consultant to a teacher, who ultimately implements the behavioral interventions with the student in the school

technique: In the context of the clinical interview, the procedures and methods (e.g., types of questions) used by the interviewer

test data: The raw data provided by clients during an assessment

test security: Protection of the integrity of psychological test materials by preventing them from entering the public domain

test selection: For a clinical psychologist conducting an assessment, the selection of tests that are appropriate in terms of the psychologist's competence; the client's culture, language, and age; and the test's reliability and validity, among other factors

testable hypotheses: In behavioral therapy, an essential feature of theories underlying problem behaviors whereby theories can be empirically supported, refuted, modified, and retested

test-taking attitudes: The manner in which the test taker approaches a test, as measured by the validity scales of the MMPI and MMPI-2

Thematic Apperception Test (TAT): A projective personality test in which individuals create stories in response to ambiguous interpersonal scenes

therapeutic alliance: Also known as the therapeutic relationship or working alliance, and an established common factor in psychotherapy outcome research; a coalition or partnership between two allies (client and therapist) working in a trusting relationship toward a mutual goal

therapeutic relationship: Also known as the therapeutic alliance or working alliance, and an established common factor in psychotherapy outcome research; a coalition or partnership between two allies (client and therapist) working in a trusting relationship toward a mutual goal

therapy manual: A manual that provides detailed instructions for all phases of the treatment of a specific disorder; typically used in treatment outcome studies

third-party payer: Typically, health insurance or managed-care companies that pay some or all of a client's mental health expenses

Edward Lee Thorndike: A pioneer in the study of intelligence who promoted the idea that each person possesses separate, independent intelligences; also, a leading researcher in the area of operant conditioning and the law of effect

three essential therapeutic conditions: In humanistic psychotherapy, the three necessary and sufficient conditions that a therapist must provide for therapeutic benefit: empathy, unconditional positive regard, and genuineness

three-stage sequential model of common factors: A model explaining the order in which common factors contribute to psychotherapeutic change, beginning with support factors, moving on to learning factors, and concluding with action factors

three-stratum theory of intelligence: A contemporary theory that intelligence operates at three levels: a single "g" at the top, 8 broad factors immediately beneath "g," and more than 60 highly specific abilities beneath these broad factors

Louis Thurstone: A pioneer in the study of intelligence who argued that intelligence should not be understood as a single, unified ability but as numerous distinct abilities that have little relationship to one another

Time-Limited Dynamic Psychotherapy (TLDP): A specific, contemporary form of psychodynamic psychotherapy in which the therapist makes efforts to form a "corrective" relationship with the client that does not follow the same unconscious "script" as the client's previous problematic relationships

Eli Todd: A pioneer of reform in the treatment of the mentally ill in the United States in the late 1700s and early 1800s

token economy: A form of behavior therapy based on operant conditioning in which clients earn tokens, exchangeable for reinforcements, for performing predetermined target behaviors

tolerance: A phenomenon whereby the body requires increasing amounts of a substance to achieve the desired effect

traditional personality assessment: In contrast to behavioral assessment, an approach to assessment that assumes that personality is a stable, internal construct; assessing personality requires a high degree of inference; and client behaviors are signs of underlying problems

transference: In psychodynamic psychotherapy, the tendency of clients to form relationships with therapists in which they unconsciously and unrealistically expect the therapist to behave like important people from the clients' past

treatment outcome: A common area of research for clinical psychologists focusing on the assessment of the benefits of psychological treatments

triangle: In family therapy, a phenomenon in which one or both of two family members in conflict attempt to bring a third member into the conflict to garner support

tripartite model: A model of assessing psychotherapy outcome developed by Hans Strupp and his colleagues that acknowledges the viewpoints of three parties (the client, the therapist, and third parties such as society, family, or managed-care companies)

tripartite model of personal identity: A three-level model of personal identity in which each individual is recognized as being entirely unique, similar to some other individuals, and similar to all other individuals

William Tuke: A pioneer of reform in the treatment of the mentally ill in England in the late 1700s and early 1800s

unconditional positive regard (UPR): In humanistic psychotherapy, one of the three essential therapeutic conditions; the full acceptance of another person without any conditions or stipulations

unconditioned response: In classical conditioning, the response elicited by the unconditioned stimulus before any conditioning has taken place

unconditioned stimulus: In classical conditioning, the stimulus that elicits the unconditioned response before any conditioning has taken place

unconscious: Mental activity occurring outside our awareness; a cornerstone of the psychodynamic approach

undifferentiated ego mass: In family therapy, a term used to describe an emotionally fused family

universal level: One of three levels of the tripartite model of personal identity emphasizing the perspective that each individual is like all others

Universal Nonverbal Intelligence Test (UNIT): A recently published intelligence test that was designed as entirely language-free in an attempt to maximize cultural fairness

universality: A therapeutic factor in group therapy; the experience that one's problems are not unique but are common to others

unstructured interview: In contrast to a structured interview, an interview that involves no predetermined or planned questions and in which interviewers determine the course of the interview as it takes place

Vail model: Alternate name for the practitioner-scholar model of graduate training stemming from a 1973 professional conference in Vail, Colorado

validity: In psychological assessment, the extent to which a technique measures what it claims to measure

validity scales: Scales of the MMPI and MMPI-2 that inform the psychologist about the client's approach to the test and allow the psychologist to determine whether the test is valid and what kinds of adjustments might be appropriate to make during the process of interpreting the clinical scales

values affirmation: A relatively new clinical approach in health psychology in which clients are encouraged to clarify and affirm, often in writing, their own personal values, which often contrast with their unhealthy behaviors

Verbal Comprehension Index: A measure of verbal concept formation and verbal reasoning; also one of four index scores yielded by the Wechsler intelligence tests

verbal tracking: In the context of the clinical interview, the ability to repeat key words and phrases back to clients to assure the clients that they have been accurately heard

vicarious learning: In behavioral therapy, a way in which clients can benefit from observational learning whereby the client observes not only the modeled behavior but also the model receiving consequences for that modeled behavior

visual-spatial processing: The ability to analyze visually presented information, including relationships between objects, spatial orientation, assembling pieces to make a whole, and detecting visual patterns; also one of five factor scores of the Stanford-Binet Intelligence Scales—Fifth Edition

vocal qualities: In the context of the clinical interview, pitch, tone, volume, and fluctuation of voice that are important to appreciate and use effectively

voir dire: In forensic psychology, a process by which an expert witness is approved for the court via examination of the expert's education, training, and professional experience

vulnerability: In contrast to resilience, the tendency to experience psychological problems in the presence of risk factors

Jerome Wakefield: A scholar in the field of abnormal psychology and the author of the harmful dysfunction theory of mental disorders

Bruce Wampold: A leading contemporary psychotherapy researcher who has argued strongly in favor of the dodo bird verdict and against a prescriptive approach to treatment

John Watson: An important figure in the history of behavioral psychotherapy and early promoter of behaviorism in the United States

David Wechsler: A pioneer in the assessment of intelligence for various age groups, including adults, children, and preschoolers

Wechsler-Bellevue: The first intelligence scale created by David Wechsler in 1939, designed for adults

Wechsler Adult Intelligence Scale (WAIS): A prominent scale of intelligence for adults

Wechsler Adult Intelligence Scale—Fourth Edition (WAIS-IV): The current edition of a prominent intelligence test for adults

Wechsler Individual Achievement Test—Third Edition (WIAT-III): The current edition of a comprehensive achievement test for clients aged 4 to 50

Wechsler Intelligence Scale for Children (WISC): A prominent scale of intelligence for children

Wechsler Intelligence Scale for Children—Fourth Edition (WISC-IV): The current edition of a prominent intelligence test for children

Wechsler Memory Scale—Fourth Edition (WMS-IV): A scale of visual and auditory memory involving both immediate and delayed recall; often used for neuropsychological purposes

Wechsler Preschool and Primary Scale of Intelligence (WPPSI): A prominent scale of intelligence for preschoolers

Wechsler Preschool and Primary Scale of Intelligence—Third Edition (WPPSI-III): The current edition of a prominent intelligence test for preschoolers

withdrawal: A phenomenon whereby cessation of a substance produces negative symptoms

within-group design: A research design that involves comparisons of participants in a single condition to themselves at various points in time

Lightner Witmer: The founder of the field of clinical psychology, the first psychological clinic, and the first journal devoted to clinical psychology

working alliance: Also known as the therapeutic alliance or therapeutic relationship, and an established common factor in psychotherapy outcome research; a coalition or partnership between two allies (client and therapist) working in a trusting relationship toward a mutual goal

working memory: The ability to hold and transform information in short-term memory; also one of five factor scores of the Stanford-Binet Intelligence Scales—Fifth Edition

Working Memory Index: A measure of the capacity to store, transform, and recall incoming information and data in short-term memory; also one of four index scores yielded by the Wechsler intelligence tests

working through: An often lengthy component of psychodynamic therapy in which interpretations are reconsidered and reevaluated again and again

Irvin Yalom: A leading figure in contemporary group therapy, especially the interpersonal approach

York Retreat: A residential treatment center in England founded by William Tuke in which the mentally ill were treated with kindness, dignity, and decency

REFERENCES

Abrams, D. M. (1999). Six decades of the Bellak scoring system, among others. In L. Gieser & M. I. Stein (Eds.), *Evocative images: The Thematic Apperception Test and the art of projection* (pp. 143–159). Washington, DC: American Psychological Association.

Abudabbeh, N. (2005). Arab families: An overview. In M. McGoldrick, J. Giordano, & N. Garcia-Preto (Eds.), *Ethnicity and family therapy* (3rd ed., pp. 423–436). New York: Guilford Press.

Academy of Psychological Clinical Science. (2009). Origins and background. Retrieved from http://acadpsychclinicalscience.org/index.php?page=origins

Achenbach, T. M. (2009). Some needed changes in *DSM-V*: But what about children? *Clinical Psychology: Science and Practice, 16,* 50–53.

Ackerley, G. D., Burnell, J., Holder, D. C., & Kurdek, L. A. (1988). Burnout among licensed psychologists. *Professional Psychology: Research and Practice, 19,* 624–631.

Ackerman, S. J., Fowler, J. C., & Clemence, A. J. (2008). TAT and other performance-based assessment techniques. In R. P. Archer & S. R. Smith (Eds.), *Personality assessment* (pp. 337–378). New York: Routledge.

Ackley, D. C. (1997). *Breaking free of managed care.* New York: Guilford Press.

Acosta, F. X., Yamamoto, J., & Evans, L. A. (1982). *Effective psychotherapy for low-income and minority patients.* New York: Plenum Press.

Acuff, C., Bennett, B. E., Bricklin, P. M., Canter, M. B., Knapp, S. J., Moldawsky, S., et al. (1999). Considerations for ethical practice in managed care. *Professional Psychology: Research and Practice, 30,* 563–575.

Aguilera, A., Garza, M. J., & Muñoz, R. F. (2010). Group cognitive-behavioral therapy for depression in Spanish: Culture-sensitive manualized treatment in practice. *Journal of Clinical Psychology, 66,* 857–867.

Ahmed, S., & Amer, M. M. (Eds.). (2012). *Counseling Muslims: Handbook of mental health issues and interventions.* New York: Routledge.

Ahrons, C. R. (2011). Divorce: An unscheduled family transition. In M. McGoldrick, B. Carter, & N. Garcia-Preto (Eds.), *The expanded family life cycle: Individual, family, and social perspectives* (4th ed., pp. 292–306). Boston: Pearson.

Alcaron, R. D. (2000). Culture and ethics of managed care in the United States. In A. Okasha, J. Arboleda-Florez, & N. Sartorius (Eds.), *Ethics, culture, and psychiatry: International perspectives* (pp. 83–101). Washington, DC: American Psychiatric Press.

Alexander, F., & French, T. M. (1946). *Psychoanalytic therapy.* New York: Ronald Press.

Alford, B. A., & Beck, A. T. (1997). *The integrative power of cognitive therapy.* New York: Guilford Press.

Almeida, R. (2005). Asian Indian families: An overview. In M. McGoldrick, J. Giordano, & N. Garcia-Preto (Eds.), *Ethnicity and family therapy* (3rd ed., pp. 377–394). New York: Guilford Press.

American Institute of Stress. (1997). *America's No. 1 health problem.* Retrieved from http://www.stress.org/americas.htm?AIS=b4b07d6a4fee6c7f4b4a39edb464066f

American Law Institute. (1962). *Model penal code 4.01.* Philadelphia: Author.

American Psychiatric Association. (1952). *Diagnostic and statistical manual of mental disorders.* Washington, DC: Author.

American Psychiatric Association. (1968). *Diagnostic and statistical manual of mental disorders* (2nd ed.). Washington, DC: Author.

American Psychiatric Association. (1980). *Diagnostic and statistical manual of mental disorders* (3rd ed.). Washington, DC: Author.

American Psychiatric Association. (1987). *Diagnostic*

and statistical manual of mental disorders (3rd ed., rev.). Washington, DC: Author.

American Psychiatric Association. (1994). *Diagnostic and statistical manual of mental disorders* (4th ed.). Washington, DC: Author.

American Psychiatric Association. (2000). *Diagnostic and statistical manual of mental disorders* (4th ed., text rev.). Washington, DC: Author.

American Psychiatric Association. (2011). *DSM-5 revisions for personality disorders reflect major change* [Press release]. Retrieved from http://www.dsm5.org/Newsroom/Documents/DSM-5-Revisions-for-Personality-Disorders-Reflect-Major-Change-.pdf

American Psychiatric Association (2013). Diagnostic and Statistical Manual of Mental Disorders (Fifth Edition) (DSM-5). Washington, DC: American Psychiatric Publishing.

American Psychological Association. (1953). *Ethical standards of psychologists.* Washington, DC: Author.

American Psychological Association. (1993). Guidelines for providers of psychological services to ethnic, linguistic, and culturally diverse populations. *American Psychologist, 48,* 45–48.

American Psychological Association. (1994). Guidelines for child custody evaluations in divorce proceedings. *American Psychologist, 49,* 677–680.

American Psychological Association. (1996a). *Model legislation for prescription privileges.* Washington, DC: Author.

American Psychological Association. (1996b). *Recommended postdoctoral training in psychopharmacology for prescription privileges.* Washington, DC: Author.

American Psychological Association. (2002). Ethical principles of psychologists and code of conduct. *American Psychologist, 57,* 1060–1073.

American Psychological Association. (2005). *Guidelines and principles for accreditation of programs in professional psychology.* Retrieved June 8, 2006, from www.apa.org/ed/G&P052.pdf

American Psychological Association. (2007). *Getting in: A step-by-step plan for gaining admission to graduate school in psychology* (2nd ed.). Washington, DC: American Psychological Association.

American Psychological Association. (2009a). *APA Ethics Committee statement: No defense to torture under the APA Ethics Code.* Retrieved from http://www.apa.org/ethics/programs/statement/torture-code.aspx

American Psychological Association. (2009b). Position on ethics and interrogations. Retrieved http://www.apa.org/ethics/programs/position/index.aspx

American Psychological Association. (2012a). *About clinical psychology.* Retrieved from http://www.apa.org/divisions/div12/aboutcp .html

American Psychological Association. (2012b). *Graduate study in psychology.* Washington, DC: Author.

American Psychological Association Division 53. (2007). *Society of Clinical Child and Adolescent Psychology.* Retrieved from www.clinical childpsychology.org

Anderson, C. M. (2007). Functional assessment with clinical populations: Current status and future directions. In P. Sturmey (Ed.), *Functional analysis in clinical treatment* (pp. 455–472). Burlington, MA: Elsevier.

Anderson, S. K., & Kitchener, K. S. (1996). Nonromantic, nonsexual posttherapy relationships between psychologists and former clients: An exploratory study of critical incidents. *Professional Psychology: Research and Practice, 27,* 59–66.

Andreyeva, T., Sturm, R., & Ringel, J. S. (2004). Moderate and severe obesity have large differences in health care costs. *Obesity Research, 12,* 1936–1943.

Angold, A., Costello, E. J., & Erkanli, A. (1999). Comorbidity. *Journal of Child Psychology and Psychiatry, 40*(1), 57–87.

Annas, G. J., & Grodin, M. A. (1992). *The Nazi doctors and the Nuremberg Code: Human rights in human experimentation.* New York: Oxford University Press.

Antony, M. M., & Barlow, D. H. (Eds.). (2010). *Handbook of assessment and treatment planning for psychological disorders* (2nd ed.). New York: Guilford Press.

APA Presidential Task Force on Evidence-Based Practice. (2006). Evidence-based practice in psychology. *American Psychologist, 61,* 271–285.

Archer, R. P. (1997). *MMPI-A: Assessing adolescent psychopathology* (2nd ed.). Mahwah, NJ: Lawrence Erlbaum.

Arden, J. B., & Linford, L. (2009). *Brain-based therapy with adults: Evidence-based treatment for everyday practice.* Hoboken, NJ: Wiley.

Arean, P. A., & Alvidrez, J. (2002). Ethical considerations in psychotherapy effectiveness research: Choosing the comparison group. *Ethics & Behavior, 12,* 63–73.

Arkowitz, H., & Westra, H. A. (2009). Introduction to the special series on motivational interviewing and psychotherapy. *Journal of Clinical Psychology, 65,* 1149–1155.

Arredondo, P., Toporek, R., Brown, S. P., Jones, J., Locke, D. C., Sanchez, J., et al. (1996). Operationalization of the multicultural counseling competencies. *Journal of Multicultural Counseling and Development, 24,* 42–78.

Artman, L. K., & Daniels, J. A. (2010). Disability and psychotherapy practice: Cultural competence and practical tips.

Professional Psychology: Research and Practice, 41, 442–448.

Atkinson, D. R., & Hackett, G. (Eds.). (2003). *Counseling diverse populations* (3rd ed.). Boston: McGraw-Hill.

Atkinson, D. R., Thompson, C. E., & Grant, S. K. (1993). A three-dimensional model for counseling racial-ethnic minorities. *The Counseling Psychologist, 21,* 257–277.

Avis, J. M. (1992). Where are all the family therapists? Abuse and violence within families and family therapy's response. *Journal of Marital and Family Therapy, 18,* 225–232.

Bach, P. A., & Moran, D. J. (2008). *ACT in practice: Case conceptualization in acceptance and commitment therapy.* Oakland, CA: New Harbinger.

Baer, R. A., & Rinaldo, J. C. (2004). The Minnesota Multiphasic Personality Inventory-Adolescent (MMPI-A). In M. J. Hilsenroth & D. L. Segal (Eds.), *Comprehensive handbook of psychological assessment: Personality assessment* (Vol. 2, pp. 213–223). Hoboken, NJ: Wiley.

Bailey, J., & Burch, M. (2006). *How to think like a behavior analyst.* Mahwah, NJ: Lawrence Erlbaum.

Baker, D. C., & Bufka, L. F. (2011). Preparing for the telehealth world: Navigating legal, regulatory, reimbursement, and ethical issues in an electronic age. *Professional Psychology: Research and Practice, 42,* 405–411.

Baker, K. D., & Ray, M. (2011). Online counseling: The good, the bad, and the possibilities. *Counselling Psychology Quarterly, 24*(4), 341–346.

Baker, R. R., & Pickren, W. E. (2011). Training systems and sites: Department of Veterans Affairs. In J. C. Norcross, G. R. Vandenbos, & D. K. Freedheim (Eds.), *History of psychotherapy: Continuity and change* (2nd ed., pp. 673–683). Washington, DC: American Psychological Association.

Balon, R., Martini, S., & Singareddy, R. K. (2004). Patient perspective on collaborative treatment. *Psychiatric Services, 55,* 945–946.

Bandura, A. (1977). *Social learning theory.* New York: Prentice Hall.

Barber, C. (2008). *Comfortably numb: How psychiatry is medicating a nation.* New York: Vintage Books.

Barez, M., Blasco, T., Fernandez-Castro, J., & Viladrich, C. (2009). Perceived control and psychological distress in women with breast cancer: A longitudinal study. *Journal of Behavioral Medicine, 32,* 187–196.

Barlow, D. H., & Carl, J. R. (2011). The future of clinical psychology: Promises, perspectives, and predictions. In D. H. Barlow (Ed.), *The Oxford handbook of clinical psychology* (pp. 891–911). New York: Oxford University Press.

Barlow, D. H., Craske, M. G., Cerny, J. A., & Klosko, J. S.

(1989). Behavioral treatment of panic disorder. *Behavior Therapy, 20,* 261–282.

Barlow, D. H., & Durand, V. M. (2005). *Abnormal psychology* (4th ed.). Belmont, CA: Wadsworth.

Barnes, G. G. (2004). *Family therapy in changing times* (2nd ed.). Hampshire, UK: Palgrave.

Barnett, J. E. (2008). Impaired professionals: Distress, professional impairment, self-care, and psychological wellness. In M. Hersen & A. M. Gross (Eds.), *Handbook of clinical psychology* (Vol. 1, pp. 857–884). Hoboken, NJ: Wiley.

Barnett, J. E. (2011). Utilizing technological innovations to enhance psychotherapy supervision, training, and outcomes. *Psychotherapy, 48,* 103–108.

Barnett, J. E., & Campbell, L. F. (2012). Ethics issues in scholarship. In S. J. Knapp (Ed.), *APA handbook of ethics in psychology, Vol. 2: Practice, teaching, and research* (pp. 309–333). Washington, DC: American Psychological Association.

Barnett, J. E., & Cooper, N. (2009). Creating a culture of self-care. *Clinical Psychology: Science and Practice, 16,* 16–20.

Barnett, J. E., & Scheetz, K. (2003). Technological advances and telehealth: Ethical, law, and the practice of psychotherapy. *Psychotherapy: Theory, Research, Practice, Training, 40,* 86–93.

Barrera, M., Jr., & Castro, F. G. (2006). A heuristic framework for the cultural adaptation of interventions. *Clinical Psychology: Science and Practice, 13,* 311–316.

Barrera, M., Jr., Castro, F. G., Strycker, L. A., & Toobert, D. J. (2012, January 30). Cultural adaptations of behavioral health interventions: A progress report. *Journal of Consulting and Clinical Psychology.* Retrieved from http://www.ncbi.nlm.nih.gov/pubmed/22289132

Bartol, C. R., & Bartol, A. M. (2006). History of forensic psychology. In I. B. Weiner & A. K. Hess (Eds.), *The handbook of forensic psychology* (3rd ed., pp. 3–27). Hoboken, NJ: Wiley.

Bateson, G., Jackson, D. D., Haley, J., & Weakland, J. H. (1956). Toward a theory of schizophrenia. *Behavioral Science, 1,* 251–264.

Beacham, A. O., Kinman, C., Harris, J. G., & Masters, K. S. (2012). The patient-centered medical home: Unprecedented workforce growth potential for professional psychology. *Professional Psychology: Research and Practice, 43,* 17–23.

Beck, A. T. (1976). *Cognitive therapy and the emotional disorders.* New York: International Universities Press.

Beck, A. T., Rush, A. J., Shaw, B. F., & Emery, G. (1979). *Cognitive therapy of depression.* New York: Guilford Press.

Beck, A. T., & Steer, R. A. (1993). *Beck Anxiety Inventory manual.* San Antonio, TX: Psychological Corporation.

Beck, A. T., Steer, R. A., & Brown, G. K. (1996). *BDI-II manual.* San Antonio, TX: Psychological Corporation.

Beck, J. S. (1995). *Cognitive therapy: Basics and beyond.* New York: Guilford Press.

Beck, J. S. (2002). Beck therapy approach. In M. Hersen & W. Sledge (Eds.), *Encyclopedia of psychotherapy* (Vol. 1, pp. 155–163). San Diego, CA: Academic Press.

Becker, A. E., Burwell, R. A., Gilman, S. E., Herzog, D. B., & Hamburg, P. (2002). Eating behaviours and attitudes following prolonged exposure to television among ethnic Fijian adolescent girls. *British Journal of Psychiatry, 180,* 509–514.

Becker, D., & Lamb, S. (1994). Sex bias in the diagnosis of borderline personality disorder and posttraumatic stress disorder. *Professional Psychology: Research and Practice, 25,* 55–61.

Becvar, R. J., & Becvar, D. S. (1982). *Systems theory and family therapy: A primer.* Lanham, MA: University Press of America.

Behnke, S. H., & Jones, S. E. (2012). Ethics and ethics codes for psychologists. In S. J. Knapp (Ed.), *APA handbook of ethics in psychology, Vol. 1: Moral foundations and common themes* (pp. 43–74). Washington, DC: American Psychological Association.

Beidas, R. S., & Kendall, P. C. (2010). Training therapists in evidence-based practice: A critical review of studies from a systems-contextual perspective.

Clinical Psychology: Science and Practice, 17, 1–30.

Beitman, B. D., & Manring, J. (2009). Theory and practice of psychotherapy integration. In G. O. Gabbard (Ed.), *Textbook of psychotherapeutic treatments* (pp. 705–726). Washington, DC: American Psychiatric Publishing.

Bellak, L. (1993). *The TAT, CAT, and SAT in clinical use* (5th ed.). Needham Heights, MA: Allyn & Bacon.

Bellak, L. (1999). My perceptions of the Thematic Apperception Test in psychodiagnosis and psychotherapy. In L. Gieser & M. I. Stein (Eds.), *Evocative images: The Thematic Apperception Test and the art of projection* (pp. 133–141). Washington, DC: American Psychological Association.

Benjamin, L. T., Jr. (1996). Introduction: Lightner Witmer's legacy to American psychology. *American Psychologist, 51*, 235–236.

Benjamin, L. T., Jr. (2005). A history of clinical psychology as a profession in America (and a glimpse at its future). *Annual Review of Clinical Psychology, 1*, 1–30.

Benjamin, L. T., Jr. (2007). *A brief history of modern psychology*. Malden, MA: Blackwell.

Ben-Porath, Y. S., & Archer, R. P. (2008). The MMPI-2 and MMPI-A. In R. P. Archer & S. R. Smith (Eds.), *Personality assessment* (pp. 81–131). New York: Routledge.

Ben-Porath, Y. S., & Tellegen, A. (2008). *Minnesota Multiphasic Personality Inventory-2 Restructured Form manual*. Minneapolis, MN: Pearson Assessments.

Berg, I. K. (1994). *Family based services: A solution-focused approach*. New York: W. W. Norton.

Bermudes, R. A., Wright, J. H., & Casey, D. (2009). Techniques of cognitive-behavioral therapy. In G. O. Gabbard (Ed.), *Textbook of psychotherapeutic treatments* (pp. 201–237). Washington, DC: American Psychiatric Publishing.

Bernal, G., Jiménez-Chafey, M. I., & Rodríguez, M. M. D. (2009). Cultural adaptation of treatments: A resource for considering culture in evidence-based practice. *Professional Psychology: Research and Practice, 40*, 361–368.

Bernal, G., & Scharro-del-Rio, M. R. (2001). Are empirically supported treatments valid for ethnic minorities? Toward an alternative approach for treatment research. *Cultural Diversity and Ethnic Minority Psychology, 7*, 328–342.

Bernstein, D., & Borkovec, T. (1973). *Progressive relaxation training*. Champagne, IL: Research Press.

Berry, J. W. (2003). Conceptual approaches to acculturation. In K. M. Chun, P. B. Organista, & G. Marin (Eds.), *Acculturation: Advances in theory, measurement, and applied research* (pp. 17–37). Washington, DC: American Psychological Association.

Bersoff, D. N. (1976). Therapists as protectors and policemen: New roles as a result of Tarasoff? *Professional Psychology, 7*, 267–273.

Bersoff, D. N., Dematteo, D., & Foster, E. E. (2012). Assessment and testing. In S. J. Knapp (Ed.), *APA handbook of ethics in psychology, Vol. 2: Practice, teaching, and research* (pp. 45–74). Washington, DC: American Psychological Association.

Beutler, L. E., Harwood, T. M., Kimpara, S., Verdirame, D., & Blau, K. (2011). Coping style. *Journal of Clinical Psychology, 67*, 176–183.

Beutler, L. E., Kim, E. J., Davison, E., & Karno, M. (1996). Research contributions to improving managed health care outcomes. *Psychotherapy: Theory, Research, Practice, Training, 33*, 197–206.

Bieschke, K. J., Perez, R. M., & DeBord, K. A. (Eds.). (2007). *Handbook of counseling and psychotherapy with lesbian, gay, bisexual, and transgender clients* (2nd ed.). Washington, DC: American Psychological Association.

BigFoot, D. S., & Schmidt, S. R. (2010). Honoring children, mending the circle: Cultural adaptation of trauma-focused cognitive-behavioral therapy for American Indian and Alaska Native children. *Journal of Clinical Psychology, 66*, 847–856.

Binder, J. L., Strupp, H. H., & Henry, W. P. (1995). Psychodynamic therapies in practice: Time-limited dynamic psychotherapy. In B. Bongar & L. E. Beutler (Eds.), *Comprehensive textbook of psychotherapy: Theory and practice* (pp. 48–63). New York: Oxford University Press.

Birchler, G. R., Simpson, L. E., & Fals-Stewart, W. (2008). Marital therapy. In M. Hersen & A. M. Gross (Eds.), *Handbook of clinical psychology* (Vol. 1, pp. 617–646). Hoboken, NJ: Wiley.

Bjork, D. W. (1993). *B. F. Skinner: A life.* New York: Basic Books.

Bjornsson, A. S. (2011). Beyond the "psychological placebo": Specifying the nonspecific in psychotherapy. *Clinical Psychology: Science and Practice, 18,* 113–118.

Black, D. W. (2013). DSM-5 is approved, but personality disorders criteria have not changed. *Annals of Clinical Psychiatry, 25*(1), 1.

Blair, S., O'Neil, P., Brownell, K., Rhodes, S., Hager, D., St. Jeor, S., et al. (1996). *The lifestyle counselor's guide for weight control.* Dallas, TX: American Health.

Blais, M. A., & Smith, S. R. (2008). Improving the integrative process in psychological assessment: Data organization and report writing. In R. P. Archer & S. R. Smith (Eds.), *Personality assessment* (pp. 405–439). New York: Routledge.

Blanco, C., & Weissman, M. M. (2005). Interpersonal psychotherapy. In G. O. Gabbard, J. S. Beck, & J. Holmes (Eds.), *Oxford textbook of psychotherapy* (pp. 27–34). New York: Oxford University Press.

Blashfield, R. K. (1991). Models of psychiatric classification. In M. Hersen & S. M. Turner (Eds.), *Adult psychopathology and diagnosis* (2nd ed., pp. 3–22). New York: Wiley.

Blashfield, R. K., & Burgess, D. R. (2007). Classification provides an essential basis for organizing mental disorders. In S. O. Lilienfeld & W. T. O'Donohue (Eds.), *The great ideas of clinical science: 17 principles that every mental health professional should understand* (pp. 93–117). New York: Routledge.

Blashfield, R. K., Flanagan, E., & Raley, K. (2010). Themes in the evolution of the 20th-century *DSMs.* In T. Millon, R. F. Krueger, & E. Simonsen (Eds.), *Contemporary directions in psychopathology: Scientific foundations of the DSM-V and ICD-11* (pp. 53–71). New York: Guilford Press.

Blazer, D. (2013). Neurocognitive Disorders in DSM-5. *American Journal of Psychiatry, 170*(6), 585-587.

Boake, C. (2002). From the Binet-Simon to the Wechsler-Bellevue: Tracing the history of intelligence testing. *Journal of Clinical Experimental Neuropsychology, 24,* 383–405.

Bohart, A. C., & Tallman, K. (1999). *How clients make therapy work: The process of active self-healing.* Washington, DC: American Psychological Association.

Bolton, P., Bass, J., Neugebauer, R., Verdeli, H., Clougherty, K. F., Wickramaratne, P., et al.

(2003). Group interpersonal psychotherapy for depression in rural Uganda: A randomized controlled trial. *Journal of the American Medical Association, 289,* 3117–3124.

Bonanno, G. A., Westphal, M., & Mancini, A. D. (2011). Resilience to loss and potential trauma. *Annual Review of Clinical Psychology, 7,* 511–535.

Boneau, C. A., & Cuca, J. M. (1974). An overview of psychology's human resources: Characteristics and salaries from the 1972 APA survey. *American Psychologist, 29,* 821–839.

Borys, D. S., & Pope, K. S. (1989). Dual relationships between therapist and client: A national study of psychologists, psychiatrists, and social workers. *Professional Psychology: Research and Practice, 20,* 283–293.

Boswell, J. F., Sharpless, B. A., Greenberg, L. S., Heatherington, L., Huppert, J. D., Barber, J. P., et al. (2011). Schools of psychotherapy and the beginnings of a scientific approach. In D. H. Barlow (Ed.), *The Oxford handbook of clinical psychology* (pp. 98–127). New York: Oxford University Press.

Bow, J. N. (2006). Review of empirical research on child custody practice. *Journal of Child Custody, 3,* 23–50.

Bow, J. N., & Quinnell, F. A. (2001). Psychologists' current practices and procedures in child custody evaluations: Five years after American Psychological Association Guidelines.

Professional Psychology: Research and Practice, 32, 261–268.

Bowen, M. (1978). *Family therapy in clinical practice.* New York: Aronson.

Bowen, S., & Marlatt, G. A. (2009). Surfing the urge: Brief mindfulness-based intervention for college student smokers. *Psychology of Addictive Behaviors, 23,* 666–671.

Boyd-Franklin, N. (1989). *Black families in therapy.* New York: Guilford Press.

Bozarth, J. D. (1997). Empathy from the framework of client-centered theory and the Rogerian hypothesis. In A. C. Bohart & L. S. Greenberg (Eds.), *Empathy reconsidered: New directions in psychotherapy* (pp. 81–102). Washington, DC: American Psychological Association.

Bozarth, J. D., Zimring, F. M., & Tausch, R. (2002). Client-centered therapy: The evolution of a revolution. In D. J. Cain & J. Seeman (Eds.), *Humanistic psychotherapies: Handbook of research and practice* (pp. 147–188). Washington, DC: American Psychological Association.

Brabender, V. A. (2002). *Introduction to group therapy.* New York: Wiley.

Brabender, V. A., Fallon, A. E., & Smolar, A. I. (2004). *Essentials of group therapy.* Hoboken, NJ: Wiley.

Bracken, B. A., & McCallum, S. (2009). Universal Nonverbal Intelligence Test (UNIT). In J. A.

Naglieri & S. Goldstein (Eds.), *Practitioner's guide to assessing intelligence and achievement* (pp. 291–313). Hoboken, NJ: Wiley.

Brantley, P. J., Dutton, G. R., & Wood, K. B. (2004). The Beck Depression Inventory-II (BDI-II) and the Beck Depression Inventory-Primary Care (BDI-PC). In M. W. Maruish (Ed.), *The use of psychological testing for treatment planning and outcomes assessment* (3rd ed., Vol. 3, pp. 313–326). Mahwah, NJ: Erlbaum.

Bratton, S., Ray, D., Rhine, T., & Jones, L. (2005). The efficacy of play therapy with children: A meta-analytic review of treatment outcomes. *Professional Psychology: Research and Practice, 36,* 376–390.

Brehm, S. (2007, January 9). American Psychological Association news release of letter from the APA president to the editor of *Washington Monthly.* Retrieved June 5, 2008, http://www.apa.org/releases/washingtonmonthly.pdf

Brems, C. (2008). *A comprehensive guide to child psychotherapy and counseling.* Long Grove, IL: Waveland Press.

Briesmeister, J. M., & Schaefer, C. E. (Eds.). (1998). *Handbook of parent training: Parents as co-therapists for children's behavior problems.* New York: Wiley.

Brody, N. (2000). History of theories and measurements of intelligence. In R. J. Sternberg (Ed.), *Handbook of intelligence* (pp. 16–33). Cambridge, UK: Cambridge University Press.

Broshek, D. K., & Barth, J. T. (2000). The Halstead-Reitan Neuropsychological Battery. In G. Groth-Marnat (Ed.), *Neuropsychological assessment in clinical practice* (pp. 223–262). New York: Wiley.

Broverman, I., Broverman, D., Clarkson, F., Rosenkrantz, P., & Vogel, S. (1970). Sex-role stereotypes and clinical judgments of mental health. *Journal of Consulting and Clinical Psychology, 34,* 1–7.

Brown, A. W. (1935). Report of committee of clinical section of American Psychological Association: I. The definition of clinical psychology and standards of training for clinical psychologists. II. Guide to psychological clinics in the United States. *Psychological Clinic, 23,* 1–140.

Brown, D. L., & Pomerantz, A. M. (2011). Multicultural incompetence and other unethical behaviors: Perceptions of therapist practices. *Ethics & Behavior, 21,* 498–508.

Brown, L. J. (2012). Countertransference: An instrument of the analysis. In G. O. Gabbard, B. E. Litowitz, & P. Williams (Eds.), *Textbook of psychoanalysis* (2nd ed., pp. 79–92). Washington, DC: American Psychiatric Publishing.

Brown, L. S. (2006). The neglect of lesbian, gay, bisexual, and transgendered clients. In J. C. Norcross, L. E. Beutler, & R. F. Levant (Eds.), *Evidence-based practices in mental health: Debate and dialogue on the fundamental questions* (pp. 346–353). Washington, DC: American Psychological Association.

Brown, L. S. (2011). Psychotherapy patients: Client diversity in psychotherapy. In J. C. Norcross, G. R. Vandenbos, & D. K. Freedheim (Eds.), *History of psychotherapy: Continuity and change* (2nd ed., pp. 475–483). Washington, DC: American Psychological Association.

Brown v. Board of Education, 347 U.S. 483 (1954).

Bryant, R. A., Harvey, A. G., Dang, S. T., & Sackville, T. (1998). Assessing acute stress disorder: Psychometric properties of a structured clinical interview. *Psychological Assessment, 10,* 215–220.

Buchanan, T. (2002). Online assessment: Desirable or dangerous? *Professional Psychology: Research and Practice, 33,* 148–154.

Bugental, J. F. (1964). The third force in psychology. *Journal of Humanistic Psychology, 4,* 19–25.

Burke, B. L., Arkowitz, H., & Menchola, M. (2003). The efficacy of motivational interviewing: A meta-analysis of controlled clinical trials. *Journal of Consulting and Clinical Psychology, 71,* 843–861.

Burl, J., Shah, S., Filone, S., Foster, E., & DeMatteo, D. (2012). A survey of graduate training programs and coursework in forensic psychology. *Teaching of Psychology, 39,* 48–53.

Burlingame, G. M., & Baldwin, S. (2011). Treatment modalities: Group therapy. In J. C. Norcross, G. R. Vandenbos, & D. K. Freedheim (Eds.), *History of psychotherapy: Continuity and change* (2nd ed., pp. 505–515). Washington, DC: American Psychological Association.

Burlingame, G. M., Fuhriman, A., & Mosier, A. (2003). The differential effectiveness of group psychotherapy: A meta-analytic perspective. *Group Dynamics: Theory, Research, and Practice, 7,* 2–13.

Burlingame, G. M., McClendon, D. T., & Alonso, J. (2011). Cohesion in group therapy. In J. C. Norcross (Ed.), *Psychotherapy relationships that work: Evidence-based responsiveness* (2nd ed., pp. 110–131). New York: Oxford University Press.

Burns, W. J., Rey, J., & Burns, K. A. (2008). Psychopharmacology as practiced by psychologists. In M. Hersen & A. M. Gross (Eds.), *Handbook of clinical psychology* (Vol. 1, pp. 663–692). Hoboken, NJ: Wiley.

Burr, V., & Butt, T. W. (2000). Psychological distress and post-modern thought. In D. Fee (Ed.), *Pathology and the post-modern: Mental illness, discourse, and experience.* London: Sage.

Butcher, J. N. (2010). Personality assessment from the nineteenth to the early twenty-first century: Past achievements and contemporary challenges. *Annual Review of Clinical Psychology, 6,* 1–20.

Butcher, J. N. (2011). *A beginner's guide to the MMPI-2* (3rd ed.).

Washington, DC: American Psychological Association.

Butcher, J. N., & Beutler, L. E. (2003). The MMPI-2. In L. E. Beutler & G. Groth-Marnat (Eds.), *Integrative assessment of adult personality* (2nd ed., pp. 157–191). New York: Guilford Press.

Butcher, J. N., Cheung, F. M., & Lim, J. (2003). Use of the MMPI-2 with Asian populations. *Psychological Assessment, 15,* 248–256.

Butcher, J. N., Mineka, S., & Hooley, J. M. (2007). *Abnormal psychology* (13th ed.). Boston: Pearson.

Butcher, J. N., Mosch, S. C., Tsai, J., & Nezami, E. (2006). Cross-cultural applications of the MMPI-2. In J. N. Butcher (Ed.), *MMPI-2: A practitioner's guide* (pp. 505–537). Washington, DC: American Psychological Association.

Butcher, J. N., & Williams, C. L. (2009). Personality assessment with the MMPI-2: Historical roots, international adaptations, and current challenges. *Applied Psychology: Health and Well-Being, 1,* 105–135.

Cabaniss, D. L., Cherry, S., Douglas, C. J., & Schwartz, A. R. (2011). *Psychodynamic psychotherapy: A clinical manual.* New York: Wiley.

Caccavale, J. (2013, July). Mental healthcare professionals need to boycott the DSM-5. *The Clinical Practitioner, 8* (4), 1–3.

Cain, D. J. (2002). Defining characteristics, history, and evolution of humanistic psychotherapies. In D. J. Cain & J. Seeman (Eds.), *Humanistic psychotherapies: Handbook of research and practice* (pp. 3–54). Washington, DC: American Psychological Association.

Cain, D. J. (2010). *Person-centered psychotherapies.* Washington, DC: American Psychological Association.

Calhoun, K. S., & Turner, S. M. (1981). Historical perspectives and current issues in behavior therapy. In S. M. Turner, K. S. Calhoun, & H. E. Adams (Eds.), *Handbook of clinical behavior therapy* (pp. 1–11). New York: Wiley.

Camara, W. J., Nathan, J. S., & Puente, A. E. (2000). Psychological test usage: Implications in professional psychology. *Professional Psychology: Research and Practice, 31*, 141–154.

Campbell, R. J. (2004). *Campbell's psychiatric dictionary* (8th ed.). New York: Oxford University Press.

Canivez, G. L., & Watkins, M. W. (2010). Investigation of the factor structure of the Wechsler Adult Intelligence Scale—Fourth Edition (WAIS–IV): Exploratory and higher order factor analyses. *Psychological Assessment, 22*, 827–836.

Cannon, W. (1932). *The wisdom of the body.* New York: W. W. Norton.

Caplan, P. J. (1992). Gender issues in the diagnosis of mental disorder. *Women & Therapy, 12*, 71–82.

Caplan, P. J. (1995). *They say you're crazy.* New York: Perseus.

Caplan, P. J. (2012, April 27). Psychiatry's bible, the DSM, is doing more harm than good. Washington Post.

Caplan, P. J., & Cosgrove, L. (Eds.). (2004). *Bias in psychiatric diagnosis.* Lanham, MD: Rowman & Littlefield

Carey, B. & Harris, G. (2008, July 12). Psychiatric group faces scrutiny over drug industry ties. New York Times. Retrieved July 26, 2013 from http://www.nytimes.com/2008/07/12/washington/12psych.html?pagewanted=all&_r=0

Carr, A. (2008). *What works with children, adolescents, and adults? A review of research on the effectiveness of psychotherapy.* New York: Routledge.

Carroll, J. B. (2005). The three-stratum theory of cognitive abilities. In D. P. Flanagan & P. L. Harrison (Eds.), *Contemporary intellectual assessment: Theories, tests, and issues* (2nd ed., pp. 69–76). New York: Guilford Press.

Carter, B., & McGoldrick, M. (1989). Overview: The changing family life cycle: A framework for family therapy. In B. Carter & M. McGoldrick (Eds.), *The changing family life cycle* (2nd ed., pp. 3–28). Boston: Allyn & Bacon.

Carter, B., & McGoldrick, M. (Eds.). (2004). *The expanded family life cycle: Individual, family, and social perspectives* (3rd ed.). Boston: Allyn & Bacon.

Carter, M. M., Forys, K. L., & Oswald, J. C. (2008). The cognitive-behavioral model. In M. Hersen & A. M. Gross (Eds.), *Handbook of clinical psychology* (Vol. 1, pp. 171–201). Hoboken, NJ: Wiley.

Cashel, M. L. (2002). Child and adolescent psychological assessment: Current clinical practice and the impact of managed care. *Professional Psychology: Research and Practice, 33*, 446–453.

Castelnuovo, G., & Simpson, S. (2011). Ebesity—E-health for obesity: New technologies for the treatment of obesity in clinical psychology and medicine. *Clinical Practice and Epidemiology in Mental Health, 7*, 5–8.

Castonguay, L. G., & Beutler, L. E. (2006). Common and unique principles of therapeutic change: What do we know and what do we need to know? In L. G. Castonguay & L. E. Beutler (Eds.), *Principles of therapeutic change that work* (pp. 353–369). New York: Oxford University Press.

Castro, F. G., Barrera, M., Jr., & Steiker, L. K. H. (2010). Issues and challenges in the design of culturally adapted evidence-based interventions. *Annual Review of Clinical Psychology, 6*, 213–239.

Caterino, L. C., Gómez-Benito, J., Balluerka, N., Amador-Campos, J. A., & Stock, W. A. (2009). Development and validation of a scale to assess the symptoms of attention-deficit/hyperactivity disorder in young adults. *Psychological Assessment, 21*, 152–161.

Cattell, J. M. (1890). Mental tests and measurements. *Mind, 15,* 373–381.

Cautin, R. L. (2011). A century of psychotherapy, 1860–1960. In J. C. Norcross, G. R. Vandenbos, & D. K. Freedheim (Eds.), *History of psychotherapy: Continuity and change* (2nd ed., pp. 3–38). Washington, DC: American Psychological Association.

Center for Multicultural Human Services. (2006). Cross-cultural training. Retrieved July 9, 2006, from www.cmhsweb.org/programs/training.html

Centers for Disease Control. (2008). *State-specific prevalence of obesity among adults.* Retrieved from http://www.cdc.gov/nchs/fastats/overwt.htm

Cepeda-Benito, A. (1993). Meta-analytical review of the efficacy of nicotine chewing gum in smoking treatment programs. *Journal of Consulting and Clinical Psychology, 61,* 822–830.

Chambless, D. L. (2002). Beware the dodo bird: The dangers of overgeneralization. *Clinical Psychology: Science and Practice, 9,* 13–16.

Chambless, D. L., Baker, M. J., Baucom, D. H., Beutler, L. E., Calhoun, K. S., Crits-Christoph, P., et al. (1998). Update on empirically validated therapies, II. *Clinical Psychologist, 51,* 3–13.

Chambless, D. L., & Ollendick, T. H. (2001). Empirically supported psychological interventions:

Controversies and evidence. *Annual Review of Psychology, 52,* 685–716.

Chambless, D. L., Sanderson, W. C., Shoham, V., Johnson, S. B., Pope, K. S., Crits-Christoph, P., et al. (1996). An update on empirically validated therapies. *Clinical Psychologist, 49,* 5–18.

Chambliss, C. H. (2000). *Psychotherapy and managed care.* Needham Heights, MA: Allyn & Bacon.

Chenneville, T. (2000). HIV, confidentiality, and duty to protect: A decision-making model. *Professional Psychology: Research and Practice, 31,* 661–670.

Chentsova-Dutton, Y. E., & Tsai, J. L. (2007). Cultural factors influence the expression of psychopathology. In S. O. Lilienfeld & W. T. O'Donohue (Eds.), *The great ideas of clinical science: 17 principles that every mental health professional should understand* (pp. 375–396). New York: Routledge.

Cheung, M. (2006). *Therapeutic games and guided imagery: Tools for mental health and school professionals working with children, adolescents, and their families.* Chicago: Lyceum.

Chiles, J. A., Lambert, M. J., & Hatch, A. L. (1999). The impact of psychological interventions on medical cost offset: A meta-analytic review. *Clinical Psychology: Science and Practice, 6,* 204–220.

Chodorow, N. (1978). *The reproduction of mothering: Psychoanalysis and the sociology*

of gender. Berkeley: University of California Press.

Chorpita, B. F., Daleiden, E. L., Ebesutani, C., Young, J., Becker, K. D., Nakamura, B. J., et al. (2011). Evidence-based treatments for children and adolescents: An updated review of indicators of efficacy and effectiveness. *Clinical Psychology: Science and Practice, 18,* 154–172.

Chu, B. C., & Kendall, P. C. (2009). Therapist responsiveness to child engagement: Flexibility within manual-based CBT for anxious youth. *Journal of Clinical Psychology, 65,* 736–754.

Cipani, E., & Schock, K. M. (2007). *Functional behavioral assessment, diagnosis, and treatment.* New York: Springer.

Clark, D. A., & Beck, A. T. (2010). *Cognitive therapy of anxiety disorders: Science and practice.* New York: Guilford Press.

Clark, D. A., Hollifield, M., Leahy, R., & Beck, J. (2009). Theory of cognitive therapy. In G. O. Gabbard (Ed.), *Textbook of psychotherapeutic treatments* (pp. 165–200). Washington, DC: American Psychiatric Publishing.

Clark, D. M., Salkovskis, P. M., Hackman, A., Middelton, H., Anastasiades, P., & Gelder, M. (1994). A comparison of cognitive therapy, applied relaxation and imipramine in the treatment of panic disorder. *British Journal of Psychiatry, 164,* 759–769.

Clarke, D. E., Narrow, W. E., Regier, D. A., Kuramoto, S. J.,

Kupfer, D. J., Kuhl, E. A., ... & Kraemer, H. C. (2013). DSM-5 Field Trials in the United States and Canada, part I: Study design, sampling strategy, implementation, and analytic approaches. *American Journal of Psychiatry, 170*(1), 43-58.

Coalson, D. L., Raiford, S. E., Saklofske, D. H., & Weiss, L. G. (2010). The WAIS-IV: Advanced in the assessment of intelligence. In L. G. Weiss, D. H. Saklofske, D. Coalson, & S. E. Raiford (Eds.), *WAIS-IV clinical use and interpretation: Scientist-practitioner perspectives* (pp. 3–24). London: Elsevier.

Cohen, J., Marecek, J., & Gillham, J. (2006). Is three a crowd? Clients, clinicians, and managed care. *American Journal of Orthopsychiatry, 76,* 251–259.

Cohen, S., & Williamson, G. (1991). Stress and infectious disease in humans. *Psychological Bulletin, 109,* 5–24.

Comas-Díaz, L. (2011). Multicultural approaches to psychotherapy. In J. C. Norcross, G. R. Vandenbos, & D. K. Freedheim (Eds.), *History of psychotherapy: Continuity and change* (2nd ed., pp. 243–268). Washington, DC: American Psychological Association.

Comas-Díaz, L. (2012). *Multicultural care: A clinician's guide to cultural comptence.* Washington, DC: American Psychological Association.

Compton, W. M., Dawson, D. A., Goldstein, R. B., & Grant, B. F. (in press). Crosswalk between DSM-IV dependence and DSM-5 substance use disorders for opioids, cannabis, cocaine and alcohol. *Drug and alcohol dependence.*

Conner, B. T. (2010). When is the difference significant? Estimates of meaningfulness in clinical research. *Clinical Psychology: Science and Practice, 17,* 52–57.

Constantine, M. G., Redington, R. M., & Graham, S. V. (2009). Counseling and psychotherapy with African Americans. In H. A. Neville, B. M. Tynes, & S. O. Utsey (Eds.), *Handbook of African American psychology* (pp. 431–444). Thousand Oaks, CA: Sage.

Constantino, M. J., Glass, C. R., Arnkoff, D. B., Ametrano, R. M., & Smith, J. Z. (2011). Expectations. In J. C. Norcross (Ed.), *Psychotherapy relationships that work: Evidence-based responsiveness* (2nd ed., pp. 354–376). New York: Oxford University Press.

Cook, J. M., Biyanova, T., & Coyne, J. C. (2009). Influential psychotherapy figures, authors, and books: An Internet survey of over 2,000 psychotherapists. *Psychotherapy: Theory, Research, Practice, Training, 46,* 42–51.

Cook, J. M., Biyanova, T., Elhai, J., Schnurr, P. P., & Coyne, J. C. (2010). What do psychotherapists really do in practice? An Internet study of over 2,000 practitioners. *Psychotherapy: Theory, Research, Practice, Training, 47,* 260–267.

Cooper, G. (2013). Will DSM Survive? Psychotherapy Networker, July/August, p. 10-11.

Copeland, W. E., Angold, A., Costello, E. J., & Egger, H. (2013). Prevalence, comorbidity, and correlates of DSM-5 proposed disruptive mood dysregulation disorder. *American Journal of Psychiatry, 170*(2), 173-179.

Corey, G. (2009). *Theory and practice of counseling and psychotherapy* (8th ed.). Belmont, CA: Thomson.

Cosgrove, L., & Krimsky, S. (2012). A comparison of *DSM-IV* and *DSM-5* panel members' financial associations with industry: A pernicious problem persists. *Public Library of Science Medicine, 9* (3).

Cosgrove, L., Krimsky, S., Vijayaraghavan, M., & Schneider, L. (2006). Financial ties between *DSM-IV* panel members and the pharmaceutical industry. *Psychotherapy and Psychosomatics, 75,* 154–160.

Cosgrove, L., & Riddle, B. (2004). Gender bias and sex distribution of mental disorders in *DSM-IV-TR*. In P. J. Caplan & L. Cosgrove (Eds.), *Bias in psychiatric diagnosis* (pp. 127–140). Lanham, MD: Aronson.

Cosgrove, L., & Wheeler, E. E. (2013). Industry's colonization of psychiatry: Ethical and practical implications of financial conflicts of interest in the DSM-5. *Feminism & Psychology, 23*(1), 93-106.

Costa, P. T., & McCrae, R. R. (1985). *The NEO Personality*

Inventory manual. Odessa, FL: Psychological Assessment Resources.

Costa, P. T., & McCrae, R. R. (1992). Revised NEO Personality Inventory and NEO Five-Factor Inventory professional manual. Odessa, FL: Psychological Assessment Resources.

Costa, P. T., Jr., & McCrae, R. R. (2008). The NEO inventories. In R. P. Archer & S. R. Smith (Eds.), Personality assessment (pp. 213–246). New York: Routledge.

Costa, P. T., & Widiger, T. A. (Eds.). (2001). Personality disorders and the five-factor model of personality (2nd ed.). Washington, DC: American Psychological Association.

Costantino, G., & Malgady, R. G. (1999). The Tell-Me-A-Story Test: A multicultural offspring of the Thematic Apperception Test. In L. Gieser & M. I. Stein (Eds.), Evocative images: The Thematic Apperception Test and the art of projection (pp. 191–206). Washington, DC: American Psychological Association.

Costantino, G., Dana, R., & Malgady, R. G. (2007). The TEMAS test: Research and applications. Mahwah, NJ: Erlbaum.

Costantino, G., Malgady, R. G., Rogler, L. H. (1988). Technical manual: The TEMAS Thematic Apperception Test. Lost Angeles: Western Psychological Services.

Cottone, R. R. (2012). Ethical decision making in mental health contexts: Representative models and an organizational

framework. In S. J. Knapp (Ed.), APA handbook of ethics in psychology, Vol. 1: Moral foundations and common themes (pp. 99–121). Washington, DC: American Psychological Association.

Craig, R. J. (2008). Millon Clinical Multiaxial Inventory-III. In R. P. Archer & S. R. Smith (Eds.), Personality assessment (pp. 133–165). New York: Routledge.

Craighead, L. W., Craighead, W. E., Kazdin, A. E., & Mahoney, M. J. (1994). Cognitive and behavioral interventions. Needham Heights, MA: Allyn & Bacon.

Craske, M. G. (2010). Cognitive-behavioral therapy. Washington, DC: American Psychological Association.

Creswell, J. D., Welch, W. T., Taylor, S. D., Sherman, D. K., Gruenewald, T. L., & Mann, T. (2005). Affirmation of personal values buffers neuroendocrine and psychological stress responses. Psychological Science, 16, 846–851.

Crits-Christoph, P., Gibbons, M. B. C., Hamilton, J., Ring-Kurtz, S., & Gallop, R. (2011). The dependability of alliance assessments: The alliance–outcome correlation is larger than you might think. Journal of Consulting and Clinical Psychology, 79, 267–278.

Cummings, N. A. (2007). Treatment and assessment take place in an economic context, always. In S. O. Lilienfeld & W. T. O'Donohue (Eds.), The great ideas of clinical science: 17

principles that every mental health professional should understand (pp. 163–184). New York: Routledge.

Curry, J. F. (2009). Research psychotherapy: Aspirin or music? Clinical Psychology: Science and Practice, 16, 318–322.

Curry, J. F., & Becker, S. J. (2008). Empirically supported psychotherapies for adolescent depression and mood disorders. In R. G. Steele, T. D. Elkin, & M. C. Roberts (Eds.), Handbook of evidence-based therapies for children and adolescents: Bridging science and practice (pp. 161–176). New York: Springer.

Curry, K. T., & Hanson, W. E. (2010). National survey of psychologists' test feedback training, supervision, and practice: A mixed methods study. Journal of Personality Assessment, 92, 327–336.

Curtin, L., & Hargrove, D. S. (2010). Opportunities and challenges of rural practice: Managing self amid ambiguity. Journal of Clinical Psychology, 66, 549–561.

Dana, R. H. (1993). Multicultural assessment perspectives for professional psychology. Boston: Allyn & Bacon.

Dana, R. H. (1995). Culturally competent MMPI assessment of Hispanic populations. Hispanic Journal of Behavioral Sciences, 17, 305–319.

Dana, R. H. (2005). Multicultural assessment: Principles, applications, *and examples.* Mahwah, NJ: Erlbaum.

Dantzker, M. L. (2011). Psychological preemployment screening for police candidates: Seeking consistency if not standardization. *Professional Psychology: Research and Practice, 42,* 276–283.

Darley, J., Fulero, S., Haney, C., & Tyler, T. (2002). Psychological jurisprudence: Taking psychology and law into the twenty-first century. In J. R. P. Ogloff (Ed.), *Taking psychology and law into the twenty-first century* (pp. 37–59). New York: Kluwer Academic/Plenum Press.

Dattilio, F. M., Edwards, D. J. A., & Fishman, D. B. (2010). Case studies within a mixed methods paradigm: Toward a resolution of the alienation between researcher and practitioner in psychotherapy research. *Psychotherapy: Theory, Research, Practice, Training, 47,* 427–441.

Daubert v. Merrell Dow Pharmaceuticals, Inc. 509 U.S. 579 (1993).

Davidson, J. E., & Downing, C. L. (2000). Contemporary models of intelligence. In R. J. Sternberg (Ed.), *Handbook of intelligence* (pp. 34–49). Cambridge, UK: Cambridge University Press.

Davis, D. M., & Hayes, J. A. (2011). What are the benefits of mindfulness? A practice review of psychotherapy-related research. *Psychotherapy, 48,* 198–208.

Davison, G. C., & Lazarus, A. A. (2007). Clinical case studies are important in the science and practice of psychotherapy. In S. O. Lilienfeld & W. T. O'Donohue (Eds.), *The great ideas of clinical science: 17 principles that every mental health professional should understand* (pp. 149–162). New York: Routledge.

Dawes, R. M., Faust, D., & Meehl, P. E. (1989). Clinical versus actuarial judgment. *Science, 243,* 1668–1674.

De Fruyt, F., De Clercq, B., De Bolle, M., Wille, B., Markon, K., & Krueger, R. F. (2013). General and maladaptive traits in a five-factor framework for DSM-5 in a university student sample. *Assessment, 20*(3), 295–307.

Decker, H. S. (2013). The Making of DSM-III: A Diagnostic Manual's Conquest of American Psychiatry. New York: Oxford University Press.

DeLeon, P. H., Dunivin, D. L., & Newman, R. (2002). The tide rises. *Clinical Psychology: Science and Practice, 9,* 249–255.

DeLeon, P. H., Kenkel, M. B., Garcia-Shelton, L., & Vandenbos, G. R. (2011). Psychotherapy, 1960 to the present. In J. C. Norcross, G. R. Vandenbos, & D. K. Freedheim (Eds.), *History of psychotherapy: Continuity and change* (2nd ed., pp. 39–62). Washington, DC: American Psychological Association.

DeLeon, P. H., Kenkel, M. B., Gray, J. M. O., & Sammons, M. T. (2011). Emerging policy issues for psychology: A key to the future of the profession. In D. H. Barlow (Ed.), *The Oxford handbook of clinical psychology* (pp. 34–51). New York: Oxford University Press.

DeLeon, P. H., & Wiggins, J. G., Jr. (1996). Prescription privileges for psychologists. *American Psychologist, 51,* 225–229.

DeMatteo, D., Marczyk, G., Krauss, D. A., & Burl, J. (2009). Educational and training models in forensic psychology. *Training and Education in Professional Psychology, 3,* 184–201.

deShazer, S., Dolan, Y. M., & Korman, H. (2007). *More than miracles: The state of the art of solution-focused brief therapy.* Binghamton, NY: Haworth.

Devlin, A. S., & Nasar, J. L. (2012). Impressions of psychotherapists' offices: Do therapists and clients agree? *Professional Psychology: Research and Practice, 43,* 118–122.

Dewald, P. A. (1964). *Psychotherapy: A dynamic approach.* New York: Basic Books.

Dewan, M., Weerasekera, P., & Stormon, L. (2009). Techniques of brief psychodynamic psychotherapy. In G. O. Gabbard (Ed.), *Textbook of psychotherapeutic treatments* (pp. 69–96). Washington, DC: American Psychiatric Publishing.

Diamond, L. M., Butterworth, M. R., & Savin-Williams, R. C. (2011). Working with sexual-minority individuals. In D. H. Barlow (Ed.), *The Oxford* handbook of clinical psychology (pp. 837–867). New York: Oxford University Press.

Dichter, G. S., Felder, J. N., Petty, C., Bizzell, J., Eronnst, M., & Smoski, M. J. (2009). The effects of psychotherapy on neural responses to rewards in major depression. *Biological Psychiatry, 66*, 886–897.

DiMatteo, M., Giordani, P., Lepper, H., & Croghan, T. (2002). Patient adherence and medical treatment outcomes: A meta-analysis. *Medical Care, 40*, 794–811.

Dimeff, L. A., & Koerner, K. (Eds.). (2007). *Dialectical behavior therapy in clinical practice: Applications across disorders and settings.* New York: Guilford Press.

Dimeff, L. A., Paves, A. P., Skutch, J. M., & Woodcock, E. A. (2011). Shifting paradigms in clinical psychology: How innovative technologies are shaping treatment delivery. In D. H. Barlow (Ed.), *The Oxford handbook of clinical psychology* (pp. 618–648). New York: Oxford University Press.

Dimidjian, S., Barrera, M., Jr., Martell, C., Muñoz, R. F., & Lewinsohn, P. M. (2011). The origins and current status of behavioral activation treatments for depression. *Annual Review of Clinical Psychology, 7*, 1–38.

Dimidjian, S., & Linehan, M. M. (2008). Mindfulness practice. In W. T. O'Donohue & J. E. Fisher (Eds.), *Cognitive behavior therapy: Applying empirically supported techniques in your practice* (2nd

ed., pp. 327–336). Hoboken, NJ: Wiley.

Dimidjian, S., & Linehan, M. M. (2009). Mindfulness practice. In W. T. O'Donohue & J. E. Fisher (Eds.), *General principles and empirically supported techniques of cognitive behavior therapy* (pp. 425–434). Hoboken, NJ: Wiley.

Dingfelder, S. (2012, April). The internship match imbalance worsens, but there are signs of hope in otherwise grim numbers. *Monitor on Psychology, 43*, 10.

Di Nardo, P. A., & Barlow, D. H. (1988). *Anxiety Disorders Interview Schedule-Revised (ADIS-R).* Albany, NY: Graywind.

Dittman, M. (2003). Psychology's first prescribers. *APA Monitor on Psychology, 34*, 36.

Division 44/Committee on Lesbian, Gay, and Bisexual Concerns Joint Task Force on Guidelines for Psychotherapy With Lesbian, Gay, and Bisexual Clients. (2000). Guidelines for psychotherapy with lesbian, gay, and bisexual clients. *American Psychologist, 55*, 1440–1451.

Dobbs, D. (2013). Psychiatry: A very sad story. *Nature, 497*(7447), 36-37.

Dobson, D., & Dobson, K. S. (2009). *Evidence-based practice of cognitive-behavioral therapy.* New York: Guilford Press.

Dobson, K. S. (2012). *Cognitive therapy.* Washington, DC: American Psychological Association.

Dobson, K. S., & Hamilton, K. E. (2008). Cognitive restructuring: Behavioral tests of negative cognitions. In W. T. O'Donohue & J. E. Fisher (Eds.), *Cognitive behavior therapy: Applying empirically supported techniques in your practice* (2nd ed., pp. 96–100). Hoboken, NJ: Wiley.

Donnay, D. A. C., & Elliott, T. R. (2003). The California Psychological Inventory. In L. E. Beutler & G. Groth-Marnat (Eds.), *Integrative assessment of adult personality* (2nd ed., pp. 227–261). New York: Guilford Press.

Dozois, D. J. A. (2010). Understanding and enhancing the effects of homework in cognitive-behavioral therapy. *Clinical Psychology: Science and Practice, 17*, 157–161.

Drabick, D. A. G., & Kendall, P. C. (2010). Developmental psychopathology and the diagnosis of mental health problems among youth. *Clinical Psychology: Science and Practice, 17*, 272–280.

Drewes, A. A. (2005a). Appendix: Multicultural play therapy resources. In E. Gil & A. A. Drewes (Eds.), *Cultural issues in play therapy* (pp. 195–205). New York: Guilford Press.

Drewes, A. A. (2005b). Play in selected cultures: Diversity and universality. In E. Gil & A. A. Drewes (Eds.), *Cultural issues in play therapy* (pp. 26–71). New York: Guilford Press.

Driessen, E., Cuijpers, P., de Maat, S., Abaass, A. A., de

Jonghe, F., & Dekker, J. J. M. (2010). The efficacy of short-term psychodynamic psychotherapy for depression: A meta-analysis. *Clinical Psychology Review, 30,* 25–36.

Drossel, C., Garrison-Diehn, C. G., & Fisher, J. E. (2008). Contingency management interventions. In W. T. O'Donohue & J. E. Fisher (Eds.), *Cognitive behavior therapy: Applying empirically supported techniques in your practice* (2nd ed., pp. 116–122). Hoboken, NJ: Wiley.

Drozdick, L. W., Holdnack, J. A., & Hilsabeck, R. C. (2011). *Essentials of WMS-IV assessment.* Hoboken, NJ: Wiley.

Dryden, W. (1995). *Brief rational emotive behaviour therapy.* Chichester, UK: Wiley.

Dryden, W. (2009). *Understanding emotional problems: The REBT perspective.* New York: Routledge.

Duckworth, A. L., Steen, T. A., & Seligman, M. E. P. (2005). Positive psychology in clinical practice. *Annual Review of Clinical Psychology, 1,* 629–651.

Duckworth, M. P. (2008). Assertiveness skills and the management of related factors. In W. T. O'Donohue & J. E. Fisher (Eds.), *Cognitive behavior therapy: Applying empirically supported techniques in your practice* (2nd ed., pp. 26–34). Hoboken, NJ: Wiley.

Durand, V. M., & Wang, M. (2011). Clinical trials. In J. C. Thomas & M. Hersen (Eds.),

Understanding research in clinical and counseling psychology (2nd ed., pp. 201–227). New York: Taylor & Francis.

Durbin, C. E., & Klein, D. N. (2006). Ten-year stability of personality disorders among outpatients with mood disorders. *Journal of Abnormal Psychology, 115,* 75–84.

Durham v. United States, 214 F.2d 862, D.C. Cir. (1954).

Durlak, J. A. (2003). Basic principles of meta-analysis. In M. C. Roberts & S. S. Ilardi (Eds.), *Handbook of research methods in clinical psychology* (pp. 196–209). Malden, MA: Blackwell.

Dusky v. United States, 362 U.S. 402 (1960).

Edens, J. F., Marcus, D. K., & Morey, L. C. (2009). Paranoid personality has a dimensional latent structure: Taxometric analyses of community and clinical samples. *Journal of Abnormal Psychology, 118,* 545–553.

Ehrenwald, J. (Ed.). (1991). *The history of psychotherapy.* Northvale, NJ: Aronson.

Ehrich, M. E., & Kratochwill, T. R. (2002). Behavioral consultation and therapy. In M. Hersen & W. Sledge (Eds.), *Encyclopedia of psychotherapy* (Vol. 1, pp. 191–205). San Diego, CA: Academic Press.

Eifert, G. H., & Forsyth, J. P. (2005). *Acceptance and commitment therapy for anxiety disorders.* Oakland, CA: New Harbinger.

Eisenberg, N. (2000). Empathy and sympathy. In M. Lewis & J. M. Haviland-Jones (Eds.), *Handbook of emotions* (2nd ed., pp. 677–691). New York: Guilford Press.

Elliott, R. (1996). Are client-centered/experiential therapies effective? A meta-analysis of outcome research. In U. Esser, H. Pabst, & W. W. Speierer (Eds.), *The power of the person-centered approach: New challenges, perspectives, answers* (pp. 125–138). Koln, Germany: GWG Verlag.

Elliott, R. (2002). The effectiveness of humanistic therapies: A meta-analysis. In D. J. Cain & J. Seeman (Eds.), *Humanistic psychotherapies: Handbook of research and practice* (pp. 57–81). Washington, DC: American Psychological Association.

Elliott, R., Bohart, A. C., Watson, J. C., & Greenberg, L. S. (2011). Empathy. In J. C. Norcross (Ed.), *Psychotherapy relationships that work: Evidence-based responsiveness* (2nd ed., pp. 132–152). New York: Oxford University Press.

Ellis, A. (1962). *Reason and emotion in psychotherapy.* New York: Lyle Stuart.

Ellis, A. (2008). Cognitive restructuring of the disputing of irrational beliefs. In W. T. O'Donohue & J. E. Fisher (Eds.), *Cognitive behavior therapy: Applying empirically supported techniques in your practice* (2nd ed., pp. 91–95). Hoboken, NJ: Wiley.

Ellis, A., & Ellis, D. J. (2011). *Rational emotive behavior therapy*. Washington, DC: American Psychological Association.

Ellis, A., & Grieger, R. (1977). *Handbook of rational-emotive therapy*. New York: Springer.

Ellis, A., & Harper, R. A. (1975). *A new guide to rational living*. North Hollywood, CA: Wilshire.

Ellis, E. (2008). Child custody evaluations. In R. L. Jackson (Ed.), *Learning forensic assessment* (pp. 417–448). New York: Taylor & Francis.

Emery, C. F., Anderson, D. R., & Andersen, B. L. (2011). Psychological interventions in health-care settings. In D. H. Barlow (Ed.), *The Oxford handbook of clinical psychology* (pp. 701–716). New York: Oxford University Press.

Emmelkamp, P. M. (2011). Effectiveness of cybertherapy in mental health: A critical appraisal. *Studies in Health Technology and Informatics, 167*, 3–8.

Emmelkamp, P. M. G., & Kamphuis, J. H. (2002). Aversion relief. In M. Hersen & W. Sledge (Eds.), *Encyclopedia of psychotherapy* (Vol. 1, pp. 139–143). San Diego, CA: Academic Press.

Engel, J. (2008). *American therapy: The rise of psychotherapy in the United States*. New York: Gotham.

Engle, V., & Graney, M. (2000). Biobehavioral effects of therapeutic touch. *Journal of Nursing Scholarship, 32*, 287–293.

Eonta, A. M., Christon, L. M., Hourigan, S. E., Ravindran, N., Vrana, S. R., & Southam-Gerow, M. A. (2011). Using everyday technology to enhance evidence-based treatments. *Professional Psychology: Research and Practice, 42*, 513–520.

Epp, A. M., Dobson, K. S., & Cottraux, J. (2009). Applications of individual cognitive-behavioral therapy to specific disorders. In G. O. Gabbard (Ed.), *Textbook of psychotherapeutic treatments* (pp. 239–262). Washington, DC: American Psychiatric Publishing.

Eriksen, K. (2005). *Beyond the DSM story*. Thousand Oaks, CA: Sage.

Eriksen, K., & Kress, V. E. (2005). *Beyond the DSM story: Ethical quandaries, challenges, and best practices*. Thousand Oaks, CA: Sage.

Erwin, E. (Ed.). (2002). *The Freud encyclopedia: Theory, therapy, and culture*. New York: Routledge.

Esquivel, G. B., Oades-Sese, G. V., & Olitzky, S. L. (2008). Multicultural issues in projective assessment. In L. A. Suzuki & J. G. Ponterotto (Eds.), *Handbook of multicultural assessment: Clinical, psychological, and educational applications* (3rd ed., pp. 346–374). Hoboken, NJ: Wiley.

Evans, D. L., Foa, E. B., Gur, R. E., Hendin, H., O'Brien, C. P., Seligman, M. E. P., et al. (Eds.). (2005). *Treating and preventing adolescent mental health disorders: What we know and what we don't know*. New York: Oxford University Press.

Ewing, C. P. (2003). Expert testimony: Law and practice. In A. M. Goldstein (Ed.), *Handbook of psychology, Vol. 11: Forensic psychology* (pp. 55–66). Hoboken, NJ: Wiley.

Exner, J. E., Jr. (1986). *The Rorschach: A comprehensive system* (2nd ed.). New York: Wiley.

Eysenck, H. J. (1952). The effects of psychotherapy: An evaluation. *Journal of Consulting Psychology, 16*, 319–324.

Fabricatore, A. N., & Wadden. T. A. (2006). Obesity. *Annual Review of Clinical Psychology, 2*, 357–377.

Fagan, J., & Shepherd, I. L. (1970). *Gestalt therapy now*. Palo Alto, CA: Science and Behavior Books.

Faigman, D. L., & Monahan, J. (2005). Psychological evidence at the dawn of the law's scientific age. *Annual Review of Psychology, 56*, 631–659.

Faragher, E., & Cooper, C. (1990). Type A stress prone behavior and breast cancer. *Psychological Medicine, 20*, 663–670.

Farber, B. A., & Doolin, E. M. (2011). Positive regard and affirmation. In J. C. Norcross (Ed.), *Psychotherapy relationships that work: Evidence-based responsiveness* (2nd ed., pp. 168–186). New York: Oxford University Press.

Farmer, R. F., & Chapman, A. L. (2008). *Behavioral interventions in cognitive behavior therapy*. Washington, DC: American Psychological Association.

Feldstein, J. (1987). Relationship of counselor and client sex and sex role to counselor empathy and client self-disclosure. In G. A. Gladstein (Ed.), *Empathy and counseling: Explorations in theory and research* (pp. 109–119). New York: Springer-Verlag.

Finn, S. E., & Kamphus, J. H. (2006). Therapeutic Assessment with the MMPI-2. In J. N. Butcher (Ed.), *MMPI-2: A practitioner's guide* (pp. 165–191). Washington, DC: American Psychological Association.

Finn, S. E., & Tonsager, M. (1992). Therapeutic effects of providing MMPI-2 test feedback to college students awaiting therapy. *Psychological Assessment, 4*, 278–287.

First, M. B., Gibbon, M., Spitzer, R. L., Williams, J. B. W., & Benjamin, L. S. (1997). *User's guide for the structured clinical interview for* DSM-IV *Axis II personality disorders*. Washington, DC: American Psychiatric Press.

First, M. B., Spitzer, R. L., Gibbon, M., & Williams, J. B. W. (1997a). *Structured clinical interview for* DSM-IV *Axis I disorders: Clinician version*. Washington, DC: American Psychiatric Press.

First, M. B., Spitzer, R. L., Gibbon, M., & Williams, J. B. W. (1997b). *Structured clinical interview for* DSM-IV *Axis I disorders: Clinician version: Administration Booklet*. Washington, DC: American Psychiatric Press.

First, M. B., Spitzer, R. L., Gibbon, M., & Williams, J. B. W. (1997c). *User's guide for the structured clinical interview for* DSM-IV *Axis I disorders: Clinician version*. Washington, DC: American Psychiatric Press.

Fisher, C. B. (2012). *Decoding the ethics code: A practical guide for psychologists* (Updated 2nd ed.). Thousand Oaks, CA: Sage.

Fisher, C. B., & Fried, A. A. (2003). Internet-mediated psychological services and the American Psychological Association ethics code. *Psychotherapy: Theory, Research, Practice, Training, 40*, 103–111.

Fisher, C. B., & Vacanti-Shova, K. (2012). The responsible conduct of psychological research: An overview of ethical principles, APA ethics code standards, and federal regulations. In S. J. Knapp (Ed.), *APA handbook of ethics in psychology, Vol. 2: Practice, teaching, and research* (pp. 335–369). Washington, DC: American Psychological Association.

Fisher, M. A. (2012). Confidentiality and record keeping. In S. J. Knapp (Ed.), *APA handbook of ethics in psychology, Vol. 1: Moral foundations and common themes* (pp. 333–375). Washington, DC: American Psychological Association.

Fisher, P. L., & Wells, A. (2008). Metacognitive therapy for obsessive-compulsive disorder: A case series. *Journal of Behavior Therapy and Experimental Psychiatry, 39*, 117–132.

Fisher, P., & Wells, A. (2009). *Metacognitive therapy*. New York: Routledge.

Flanagan, D. P., & Kaufman, A. S. (2009). *Essentials of WISC-IV assessment* (2nd ed.). Hoboken, NJ: Wiley.

Flanagan, R., Costantino, G., Cardalda, E., & Costantino, E. (2008). TEMAS: A multicultural test and its place in an assessment battery. In L. A. Suzuki & J. G. Ponterotto (Eds.), *Handbook of multicultural assessment: Clinical, psychological, and educational applications* (3rd ed., pp. 323–345). Hoboken, NJ: Wiley.

Follette, W. C., Darrow, S. M., & Bonow, J. T. (2009). Cognitive behavior therapy: A current appraisal. In W. T. O'Donohue & J. E. Fisher (Eds.), *General principles and empirically supported techniques of cognitive behavior therapy* (pp. 42–62). Hoboken, NJ: Wiley.

Fontes, L. A. (2008). *Interviewing clients across cultures: A practitioner's guide*. New York: Guilford Press.

Forehand, R., Dorsey, S., Jones, D. J., Long, N., & McMahon, R. J. (2010). Adherence and flexibility: They can (and do) coexist! *Clinical Psychology: Science and Practice, 17*, 258–264.

Fouad, N. A. (2006). Multicultural guidelines: Implementation in an urban counseling psychology program. *Professional Psychology: Research and Practice, 37*, 6–13.

Fouad, N. A., & Arredondo, P. (2007). *Becoming culturally oriented: Practical advice for psychologists and educators.* Washington, DC: American Psychological Association.

Fowler, J. C., & Groat, M. D. (2008). Personality assessment using implicit (projective) methods. In M. Hersen & A. M. Gross (Eds.), *Handbook of clinical psychology* (Vol. 1, pp. 475–494). Hoboken, NJ: Wiley.

Fox, J. and Jones, K. D. (2013), *DSM-5* and Bereavement: The Loss of Normal Grief?. Journal of Counseling & Development, 91: 113–119. doi: 10.1002/j.1556-6676.2013.00079.x

Frances, A. (2012a, May 2). Wonderful News: DSM-5 Finally Begins Its Belated and Necessary Retreat. Retreived from http://www.psychologytoday.com/blog/dsm5-in-distress/201205/wonderful-news-dsm-5-finally-begins-its-belated-and-necessary-retreat

Frances, A. (2012b, December 2). DSM-5 Is Guide Not Bible—Ignore Its Ten Worst Changes. Retrieved from http://www.psychologytoday.com/blog/dsm5-in-distress/201212/dsm-5-is-guide-not-bible-ignore-its-ten-worst-changes.

Frances, A. (2012c, July 11). Two Who Resigned from DSM-5 Explain Why. Retrieved from http://www.psychologytoday.com/blog/dsm5-in-distress/201207/two-who-resigned-dsm-5-explain-why

Frances, A. (2012d, November 11). You Can't Turn a Sow's Ear Into a Silk Purse. Retrieved from http://www.psychologytoday.com/blog/dsm5-in-distress/201211/you-cant-turn-sows-ear-silk-purse

Frances, A. (2012e, June 15). Top 10 Indicators of DSM-5 Openness. Retrieved from http://www.psychologytoday.com/blog/dsm5-in-distress/201206/top-10-indicators-dsm-5-openness

Frances, A. (2012f, January 3). Is DSM-5 a Public Trust or an APA Cash Cow? Retrieved from http://www.psychologytoday.com/blog/dsm5-in-distress/201201/is-dsm-5-public-trust-or-apa-cash-cow

Frances, A. (2013a). Saving Normal: An Insider's Revolt against Out-of-Control Psychiatric Diagnosis, DSM-5, Big Pharma, and the Medicalization of Ordinary Life. New York: HarperCollins.

Frances, A. (2013b). The past, present and future of psychiatric diagnosis. *World Psychiatry,* 12(2), 111–112.

Frances, A. (2013c). DSM in Philosophyland: Curiouser and Curiouser. In J. Paris & J. Phillips (Eds.), Making the DSM-5: Concepts and Controversies, pp. 95-103. New York: Springer.

Frances, A. (2013d). The new somatic symptom disorder in DSM-5 risks mislabeling many people as mentally ill. *BMJ: British Medical Journal, 346.*

Frances, A. (2013e, April 25). The International Reaction to DSM-5. Retrieved from http://www.psychologytoday.com/blog/saving-normal/201304/the-international-reaction-dsm-5

Frances, A. (2013f, April 16). Does DSM-5 Have a Captive Audience? Retrieved from http://www.psychologytoday.com/blog/saving-normal/201304/does-dsm-5-have-captive-audience

Frances, A. (2013g, February 8). DSM-5 Boycotts and Petitions. Retrieved from http://www.psychologytoday.com/blog/saving-normal/201302/dsm-5-boycotts-and-petitions.

Frances, A. (2013h, January 23). Price Gouging: Why Will DSM-5 Cost $199 a Copy? Retrieved from http://www.psychologytoday.com/blog/dsm5-in-distress/201301/price-gouging-why-will-dsm-5-cost-199-copy.

Frances, A. (2013i). The New Crisis in Confidence in Psychiatric Diagnosis. *Annals of Internal Medicine, May17,* doi:10.7326/0003-4819-159-3-201308060-00655

Frances, A., & Batstra, L. (2013). Why so many epidemics of childhood mental disorder? *Journal of Developmental & Behavioral Pediatrics, 34*(4), 291-292.

Frances, A., & Chapman, S. (2013). DSM-5 somatic symptom disorder mislabels medical illness as mental disorder. *Australian and New Zealand Journal of Psychiatry, 47*(5), 483-484.

Frances, A. J., & Nardo, J. M. (2013). ICD-11 should not repeat the mistakes made by DSM-5. *The British Journal of Psychiatry, 203*(1), 1-2.

Frances, A., First, M. B., & Pincus, H. A. (1995). *DSM-IV guidebook*. Washington, DC: American Psychiatric Press.

Frank, E., & Levenson, J. C. (2011). *Interpersonal Psychotherapy*. Washington, DC: American Psychological Association.

Frank, J. D. (1961). *Persuasion and healing*. Baltimore: Johns Hopkins University Press.

Frankl, V. E. (1963). *Man's search for meaning*. New York: Pocket Books.

Franklin, A. J. (2007). Gender, race, and invisibility in psychotherapy with African American men. In J. C. Muran (Ed.), *Dialogues on difference: Studies of diversity in the therapeutic relationship* (pp. 117–131). Washington, DC: American Psychological Association.

Franklin, M. E., & Foa, E. B. (2011). Treatment of obsessive compulsive disorder. *Annual Review of Clinical Psychology, 7,* 229–243.

Frauenhoffer, D., Ross, M. J., Gfeller, J., Searight, H. R., & Piotrowski, C. (1998). Psychological test usage among licensed mental health

practitioners: A multidisciplinary survey. *Journal of Psychological Practice, 4,* 28–33.

Freeman, A., & Greenwood, V. B. (Eds.). (1987). *Cognitive therapy: Applications in psychiatric and medical settings*. New York: Human Sciences Press.

Freeman, A., Pretzer, J., Fleming, B., & Simon, K. M. (1990). *Clinical applications of cognitive therapy*. New York: Plenum Press.

Freeman, K. A. (2002). Modeling. In M. Hersen & W. Sledge (Eds.), *Encyclopedia of psychotherapy* (Vol. 2, pp. 147–154). San Diego, CA: Academic Press.

Freeman, K. A., & Eagle, R. F. (2011). Single-subject research designs. In J. C. Thomas & M. Hersen (Eds.), *Understanding research in clinical and counseling psychology* (2nd ed., pp. 129–154). New York: Taylor & Francis.

Freud, A. (1936). *The ego and the mechanisms of defense*. New York: International Universities Press.

Freud, S. (1900). *The interpretation of dreams*. London: Hogarth Press.

Freud, S. (1905). *Three essays on the theory of sexuality*. London: Hogarth Press.

Friedlander, M. L., Escudero, V., Heatherington, L., & Diamond, G. M. (2011). Alliance in couple and family therapy. *Psychotherapy, 48,* 25–33.

Friedman, W. H. (1989). *Practical group therapy: A guide*

for clinicians. San Francisco: Jossey-Bass.

Fromm-Reichmann, F. (1948). Notes on the development of treatment of schizophrenics by psychoanalytic psychotherapy. *Psychiatry, 11,* 263–274.

Frye v. United States, 293 F. 1013, D.C. Cir. (1923).

Fuhriman, A., & Burlingame, G. M. (1994). Group psychotherapy: Research and practice. In A. Fuhriman & G. M. Burlingame (Eds.), *Handbook of group psychotherapy: An empirical and clinical synthesis* (pp. 3–40). New York: Wiley.

Gabbard, G. O. (2005). Major modalities: Psychoanalytic/ psychodynamic. In G. O. Gabbard, J. S. Beck, & J. Holmes (Eds.), *Oxford textbook of psychotherapy* (pp. 3–14). New York: Oxford University Press.

Gabbard, G. O. (2009a). Foreword. In R. A. Levy & J. S. Ablon (Eds.), *Handbook of evidence-based psychodynamic psychotherapy: Bridging the gap between science and practice* (pp. vii–ix). New York: Humana.

Gabbard, G. O. (2009b). Professional boundaries in psychotherapy. In G. O. Gabbard (Ed.), *Textbook of psychotherapeutic treatments* (pp. 809–827). Washington, DC: American Psychiatric Publishing.

Gabbard, G. O. (2009c). Techniques of psychodynamic psychotherapy. In G. O. Gabbard (Ed.), *Textbook of psychotherapeutic treatments* (pp. 43–67). Washington, DC: American Psychiatric Publishing.

Gaddy, C. D., Charlot-Swilley, D., Nelson, P. D., & Reich, J. N. (1995). Selected outcomes of accredited programs. *Professional Psychology: Research and Practice, 26,* 507–513.

Galatzer-Levy, R. M., Bachrach, H., Skolnikoff, A., & Waldron, S. (2000). *Does psychoanalysis work?* New Haven, CT: Yale University Press.

Gallant, S. J., & Hamilton, J. A. (1988). On a premenstrual psychiatric diagnosis: What's in a name? *Professional Psychology: Research and Practice, 19,* 271–278.

Gallardo, M. E., Johnson, J., Parham, T. A., & Carter, J. A. (2009). Ethics and multiculturalism: Advancing cultural and clinical responsiveness. *Professional Psychology: Research and Practice, 40,* 425–435.

Gambrill, E. (2002). Assertion training. In M. Hersen & W. Sledge (Eds.), *Encyclopedia of psychotherapy* (Vol. 1, pp. 117–124). San Diego, CA: Academic Press.

Garb, H. N. (2005). Clinical judgment and decision making. *Annual Review of Clinical Psychology, 1,* 67–89.

Garfield, S. L. (1996). Some problems associated with "validated" forms of psychotherapy. *Clinical Psychology: Science and Practice, 3,* 218–229.

Garrido, M., & Velasquez, R. (2006). Interpretation of Latino/Latina MMPI-2 profiles: Review and application of empirical findings and cultural-linguistic considerations. In J. N. Butcher (Ed.), *MMPI-2: A practitioner's guide* (pp. 477–504). Washington, DC: American Psychological Association.

Garske, J. P., & Anderson, T. (2003). Toward a science of psychotherapy research: Present status and evaluation. In S. O. Lilienfeld, S. J. Lynn, & J. M. Lohr (Eds.), *Science and pseudoscience in clinical psychology* (pp. 145–175). New York: Guilford Press.

Gately, L., & Stabb, S. D. (2005). Psychology students' training in the management of potentially violent clients. *Professional Psychology: Research and Practice, 36,* 681–687.

Gay, P. (Ed.). (1995). *The Freud reader.* New York: W. W. Norton.

Gelso, C. J. (2010). The diversity status of the psychotherapist: Editorial introduction. *Psychotherapy: Theory, Research, Practice, Training, 47,* 143.

Gelso, C. J. (2011). Emerging and continuing trends in psychotherapy: Views from an editor's eye. *Psychotherapy, 48,* 182–187.

Gerber, A. J., Kocsis, J. H., Milrod, B. L., Roose, S. P., Barber, J. P., Thase, M. E., et al. (2011). A quality-based review of randomized controlled trials of psychodynamic psychotherapy.

American Journal of Psychiatry, 168, 19–28.

Germer, C. K. (2005). Mindfulness: What is it? What does it matter? In C. K. Germer, R. D. Siegel, & P. R. Fulton (Eds.), *Mindfulness and psychotherapy* (pp. 3–27). New York: Guilford Press.

Ghezzi, P. M., Wilson, G. R., Tarbox, R. S. F., & MacAlesse, K. R. (2008). Guidelines for developing and managing a token economy. In W. T. O'Donohue & J. E. Fisher (Eds.), *Cognitive behavior therapy: Applying empirically supported techniques in your practice* (2nd ed., pp. 565–570). Hoboken, NJ: Wiley.

Gibbons, M. B. C., Crits-Christoph, P., Barber, J. P., & Schamberger, M. (2007). Insight in psychotherapy: A review of empirical literature. In L. G. Castonguay & C. E. Hill (Eds.), *Insight in psychotherapy* (pp. 143–165). Washington, DC: American Psychological Association.

Gibbons, M. B. C., Crits-Christoph, P., & Hearon, B. (2008). The empirical status of psychodynamic therapies. *Annual Review of Clinical Psychology, 4,* 93–108.

Gieser, L., & Stein, M. I. (1999). An overview of the Thematic Apperception Test. In L. Gieser & M. I. Stein (Eds.), *Evocative images: The Thematic Apperception Test and the art of projection* (pp. 3–11). Washington, DC: American Psychological Association.

Gillberg, C., Gillberg, C., Rastam, M., & Wentz, E. (2001). The Asperger Syndrome (and high-functioning autism) Diagnostic Interview (ASDI): A preliminary study of a new structured clinical interview. *Autism, 5,* 57–66.

Gilligan, C. (1982). *In a different voice: Psychological theory and women's development.* Cambridge, MA: Harvard University Press.

Gillon, W. (2007). *Person-centred counseling psychology: An introduction.* Thousand Oaks, CA: Sage.

Glick, I. D., Berman, E. M., Clarkin, J. F., & Rait, D. S. (2000). *Marital and family therapy* (4th ed.). Washington, DC: American Psychiatric Press.

Godley, S. H., Garner, B. R., Smith, J. E., Meyers, R. J., & Godley, M. D. (2011). A large-scale dissemination and implementation model for evidence-based treatment and continuing care. *Clinical Psychology: Science and Practice, 18,* 67–83.

Gold, E. K., & Zahm, S. G. (2008). Gestalt therapy. In M. Hersen & A. M. Gross (Eds.), *Handbook of clinical psychology* (Vol. 1, pp. 585–616). Hoboken, NJ: Wiley.

Gold, J. R. (1996). *Key concepts in psychotherapy integration.* New York: Plenum Press.

Goldberg, P. (2012a). Process, resistance, and interpretation. In G. O. Gabbard, B. E. Litowitz, & P. Williams (Eds.), *Textbook of psychoanalysis* (2nd ed., pp. 283–302). Washington, DC: American Psychiatric Publishing.

Goldberg, S. H. (2012b). Transference. In G. O. Gabbard, B. E. Litowitz, & P. Williams (Eds.), *Textbook of psychoanalysis* (2nd ed., pp. 65–78). Washington, DC: American Psychiatric Publishing.

Golden, C. J. (2004). The adult Luria-Nebraska neuropsychological battery. In M. Hersen (Ed.), *Comprehensive handbook of psychological assessment* (Vol. 1, pp. 133–146). New York: Wiley.

Golden, C. J. (2008). Neuropsychological assessment. In M. Hersen & A. M. Gross (Eds.), *Handbook of clinical psychology* (Vol. 1, pp. 422–450). Hoboken, NJ: Wiley.

Golden, C. J., Freshwater, S. M., & Vayalakkara, J. (2000). The Luria-Nebraska neuropsychological battery. In G. Groth Marnat (Ed.), *Neuropsychological assessment in clinical practice* (pp. 263–289). New York: Wiley.

Goldenberg, H., & Goldenberg, I. (2007). *Family therapy: An overview* (7th ed.). Pacific Grove, CA: Brooks/Cole.

Goldfinger, K., & Pomerantz, A. M. (2010). *Psychological assessment and report writing.* Thousand Oaks, CA: Sage.

Goldfried, M. R. (1995). *From cognitive-behavior therapy to psychotherapy integration: An evolving view.* New York: Springer.

Goldfried, M. R., Glass, C. R., & Arnkoff, D. B. (2011). Integrative approaches to psychotherapy. In J. C. Norcross, G. R. Vandenbos, & D. K. Freedheim (Eds.), *History of psychotherapy: Continuity and change* (2nd ed., pp. 269–296). Washington, DC: American Psychological Association.

Goldner, V. (1985). Feminism and family therapy. *Family Process, 24,* 31–47.

Goldstein, A. M. (2003). Overview of forensic psychology. In A. M. Goldstein (Ed.), *Handbook of psychology, Vol. 11: Forensic psychology* (pp. 3–20). Hoboken, NJ: Wiley.

Goldstein, A. M., Morse, S. J., & Shapiro, D. L. (2003). Evaluation of criminal responsibility. In A. M. Goldstein (Ed.), *Handbook of psychology, Vol. 11: Forensic psychology* (pp. 381–406). Hoboken, NJ: Wiley.

Goldstein, G. (2008). Intellectual evaluation. In M. Hersen & A. M. Gross (Eds.), *Handbook of clinical psychology* (Vol. 1, pp. 395–421). Hoboken, NJ: Wiley.

Goldstein, G. (2011). Correlational methods. In J. C. Thomas & M. Hersen (Eds.), *Understanding research in clinical and counseling psychology* (2nd ed., pp. 181–199). New York: Taylor & Francis.

Goldstein, G., & Sanders, R. D. (2004). Sensory-perceptual and motor function. In M. Hersen (Ed.), *Comprehensive handbook of psychological assessment* (Vol. 1, pp. 309–319). New York: Wiley.

Good, G. E., Khairallah, T., & Mintz, L. B. (2009). Wellness and impairment: Moving beyond noble us and troubled them. *Clinical Psychology: Science and Practice, 16*, 21–23.

Goodheart, C. D., & Rozensky, R. H. (2011). Psychotherapy patients: Health and medical conditions. In J. C. Norcross, G. R. Vandenbos, & D. K. Freedheim (Eds.), *History of psychotherapy: Continuity and change* (2nd ed., pp. 467–474). Washington, DC: American Psychological Association.

Gore, W. L., & Widiger, T. A. (2013). The DSM-5 Dimensional Trait Model and Five-Factor Models of General Personality.

Gottlieb, M. C., & Younggren, J. N. (2009). Is there a slippery slope? Considerations regarding multiple relationships and risk management. *Professional Psychology: Research and Practice, 40*(6), 564–571.

Grace, N., Spirito, A., Finch, A. J., & Ott, E. S. (1993). Coping skills for anxiety control in children. In A. J. Finch, W. M. Nelson, & E. S. Ott (Eds.), *Cognitive-behavioral procedures with children and adolescents* (pp. 257–288). Boston: Allyn & Bacon.

Graham, J. D., Lobel, M., Glass, P., & Lokshina, I. (2008). Effects of written anger expression in chronic pain patients: Making meaning from pain. *Journal of Behavioral Medicine, 31*, 201–212.

Graham, J. M., & Kim, Y.-H. (2011). Predictors of doctoral student success in professional psychology: Characteristics of students, programs, and universities. *Journal of Clinical Psychology, 67*, 340–354.

Graham, J. R. (2012). *MMPI-2: Assessing personality and psychopathology* (5th ed.). New York: Oxford University Press.

Graham, T., & Ickes, W. (1997). When women's intuition isn't greater than men's. In W. Ickes (Ed.), *Empathic accuracy* (pp. 117–143). New York: Guilford Press.

Grant, B. F., Dawson, D. A., Stinson, F. S., Chou, P. S., Dufour, M. C., & Pickering, R. P. (2004). The 12-month prevalence and trends in *DSM-IV* alcohol abuse and dependence: United States, 1991–1992 and 2001–2002. *Drug and Alcohol Dependence, 74*, 223–234.

Grant, P., Young, P. R., & DeRubeis, R. J. (2005). Cognitive and behavioral therapies. In G. O. Gabbard, J. S. Beck, & J. Holmes (Eds.), *Oxford textbook of psychotherapy* (pp. 15–25). New York: Oxford University Press.

Green, D., Callands, T. A., Radcliffe, A. M., Luebbe, A. M., & Klonoff, E. A. (2009). Clinical psychology students' perceptions of diversity training: A study of exposure and satisfaction. *Journal of Clinical Psychology, 65*, 1056–1070.

Greenberg, G. (2013). *The book of woe: The DSM and the unmaking of psychiatry*. New York: Penguin Group.

Greenberg, L. S., Elliott, R., & Lietaer, G. (1994). Research on humanistic and experiential psychotherapies. In A. E. Bergin & S. L. Garfield (Eds.), *Handbook of psychotherapy and behavior change* (4th ed., pp. 509–539). New York: Wiley.

Greene, B. (2007). How difference makes a difference. In J. C. Muran (Ed.), *Dialogues on difference: Studies of diversity in the therapeutic relationship* (pp. 47–63). Washington, DC: American Psychological Association.

Greene, C. H., & Banks, L. M. (2009). Ethical guideline evolution in psychological support of interrogation operations. *Consulting Psychology Journal: Practice and Research, 61*, 25–32.

Greene, R. L., & Clopton, J. R. (2004). Minnesota Multiphasic Personality Inventory-2 (MMPI-2). In M. W. Maruish (Ed.), *The use of psychological testing for treatment planning and outcomes assessment* (3rd ed., Vol. 3, pp. 449–477). Mahwah, NJ: Erlbaum.

Greenhoot, A. F. (2003). Design and analysis of experimental and quasi-experimental investigations. In M. C. Roberts & S. S. Ilardi (Eds.), *Handbook of research methods in clinical psychology* (pp. 92–114). Malden, MA: Blackwell.

Greenson, R. R., & Jaffe, L. (2004). Do you take notes during the initial interview? In L. Jaffe (Ed.), *The technique and practice of psychoanalysis: Vol. 3. The training seminars of Ralph R. Greenson, M.D.: Transcripts of the Greenson seminars on assessment and the* initial interviews (pp. 21–28). Madison, CT: International Universities Press.

Grieger, I. (2008). A cultural assessment framework and interview protocol. In L. A. Suzuki & J. G. Ponterotto (Eds.), *Handbook of multicultural assessment: Clinical, psychological, and educational applications* (3rd ed., pp. 132–161). Hoboken, NJ: Wiley.

Griffin, W. A. (2002). Family therapy. In M. Hersen & W. Sledge (Eds.), *Encyclopedia of psychotherapy* (Vol. 1, pp. 793–800). San Diego, CA: Academic Press.

Griffiths, B. (2001). Have you paxiled lately? *Annals of the American Psychotherapy Association, 4,* 9.

Grosch, W. N., & Olsen, D. C. (1995). Prevention: Avoiding burnout. In M. B. Sussman (Ed.), *A perilous calling: The hazards of psychotherapy practice* (pp. 275–287). New York: Wiley.

Grotberg, E. H. (2003). What is resilience? How do you promote it? How do you use it? In E. H. Grotberg (Ed.), *Resilience for today: Gaining strength from adversity* (pp. 1–29). Westport, CT: Praeger.

Groth-Marnat, G. (2009). *Handbook of psychological assessment* (5th ed.). Hoboken, NJ: Wiley.

Grove, W. M., Zald, D. H., Lebow, B. S., Snitz, B. E., & Nelson, C. (2000). Clinical versus mechanical prediction:

A meta-analysis. *Psychological Assessment, 12,* 19–30.

Grus, C. L. (2011). Training, credentialing, and new roles in clinical psychology: Emerging trends. In D. H. Barlow (Ed.), *The Oxford handbook of clinical psychology* (pp. 150–168). New York: Oxford University Press.

Guedj, M., Sastre, M. T., Mullet, E., & Sorum, P. C. (2009). Is it acceptable for a psychiatrist to break confidentiality to prevent spousal violence? *International Journal of Law and Psychiatry, 32,* 108–114.

Guerrero, C., & Palmero, F. (2010). Impact of defensive hostility in cardiovascular disease. *Behavioral Medicine, 36,* 77–84.

Guilmette, T. J., & Faust, D. (1991). Characteristics of neuropsychologists who prefer the Halstead-Reitan or the Luria-Nebraska neuropsychological battery. *Professional Psychology: Research and Practice, 22,* 80–83.

Gutheil, T. G., & Brodsky, A. (2008). *Preventing boundary violations in clinical practice.* New York: Guilford Press.

Haas, A. L., Munoz, R. F., Humfleet, G. L., Reus, V. I., & Hall, S. M. (2004). Influences of mood, depression history, and treatment modality on outcomes in smoking cessation. *Journal of Consulting and Clinical Psychology, 72,* 563–570.

Haas, L. J., & Cummings, N. A. (1991). Managed outpatient mental health plans: Clinical, ethical, and practical guidelines

for participation. *Professional Psychology: Research and Practice, 22,* 45–51.

Hafen, B., Karren, K., Frandsen, K., & Smith, L. (1996). *Mind/body health: The effects of attitudes, emotions, and relationships.* Boston: Allyn & Bacon.

Hagen, M. A. (1997). *Whores of the court: The fraud of psychiatric testimony and the rape of American justice.* New York: Regan Books/HarperCollins.

Hagen, M. A., & Castagna, N. (2001). The real numbers: Psychological testing in custody evaluations. *Professional Psychology: Research and Practice, 32,* 269–271.

Hahn, J. (2005). Faking bad and faking good by college students on the Korean MMPI-II. *Journal of Personality Assessment, 85,* 65–73.

Hall, C. S., & Nordby, V. J. (1973). *A primer of Jungian psychology.* New York: Taplinger.

Hall, G. C. N., Hong, J. J., Zane, N. W. S., & Meyer, O. L. (2011). Culturally competent treatments for Asian Americans: The relevance of mindfulness and acceptance-based psychotherapies. *Clinical Psychology: Science and Practice, 18,* 215–231.

Hamermesh, D. S., & Lee, J. (2007). Stressed out on four continents: Time crunch or yuppie kvetch? *The Review of Economics and Statistics, 89,* 374–383.

Hanna, S. M. (2007). *The practice of family therapy: Key elements* across models (4th ed.). Pacific Grove, CA: Brooks/Cole.

Hansen, N. D., Randazzo, K. V., Schwartz, A., Marshall, M., Kalis, D., Frazier, R., et al. (2006). Do we practice what we preach? An exploratory survey of multicultural psychotherapy competencies. *Professional Psychology: Research and Practice, 37,* 66–74.

Hanson, S. L., & Kerkhoff, T. R. (2012). The health care setting: Implications for ethical psychology practice. In S. J. Knapp (Ed.), *APA Handbook of Ethics in Psychology, Vol. 2: Practice, teaching, and research* (pp. 75–90). Washington, DC: American Psychological Association.

Hanson, W. E., & Poston, J. M. (2011). Building confidence in psychological assessment as a therapeutic intervention: An empirically based reply to Lilienfeld, Garb, and Wood (2011). *Psychological Assessment, 23,* 1056–1062.

Hardy, K. V., & Laszloffy, T. A. (1992). Training racially sensitive family therapists: Context, content, and contact. *Families in Society, 73,* 364–370.

Hare-Mustin, R. (1978). A feminist approach to family therapy. *Family Process, 17,* 181–194.

Hargrove, D. S. (1986). Ethical issues in rural mental health practice. *Professional Psychology: Research and Practice, 17,* 20–23.

Harlow, H., & Zimmermann, R. (1959). Affectional responses in the infant monkey. *Science, 130,* 421–432.

Harper, K. V. (1996). Culturally relevant health care service delivery for Appalachia. In M. C. Julia (Ed.), *Multicultural awareness in the health care professions* (pp. 42–59). Boston: Allyn & Bacon.

Harris, A. (2012). Transference, countertransference, and the real relationship. In G. O. Gabbard, B. E. Litowitz, & P. Williams (Eds.), *Textbook of psychoanalysis* (2nd ed., pp. 255–268). Washington, DC: American Psychiatric Publishing.

Harris, G. (2011, March 5). Talk doesn't pay, so psychiatry turns instead to drug therapy. *New York Times.* Retrieved from http://www .nytimes.com/2011/03/06/health/policy/06 doctors.html?_r=1&pagewanted=all

Harris, J. E. (2012). Multicultural counseling in a multitheoretical context: New applications for practice. In M. E. Gallardo, C. J. Yeh, J. E. Trimble, & T. A. Parham (Eds.), *Culturally adaptive counseling skills: Demonstrations of evidence-based practices* (pp. 287–312). Thousand Oaks, CA: Sage.

Hasin, D. S., Auriacombe, M., Borges, G., Bucholz, K., Budney, A., Crowley, T., ... & Wall, M. M. (2013). The DSM-5 Field Trials and Reliability of Alcohol Use Disorder. *American Journal of Psychiatry, 170*(4), 442-443.

Hathaway, S. R., & McKinley, J. C. (1943). *The Minnesota Multiphasic Personality Inventory.* New York: Psychological Corporation.

Hayes, J. A., Gelso, C. J., & Hummel, A. M. (2011). Managing countertransference. *Psychotherapy, 48,* 88–97.

Hayes, S. C. (2004). Acceptance and commitment therapy and the new behavior therapies: Mindfulness, acceptance, and relationship. In S. C. Hayes, V. M. Follette, & M. M. Linehan (Eds.), *Mindfulness and acceptance: Expanding the cognitive-behavioral tradition* (pp. 1–29). New York: Guilford Press.

Hayes, S. C., & Strosahl, K. D. (Eds.). (2004). *A practical guide to acceptance and commitment therapy.* New York: Springer.

Hayes, S. C., Villatte, M., Levin, M., & Hildebrandt, M. (2011). Open, aware, and active: Contextual approaches as an emerging trend in the behavioral and cognitive therapies. *Annual Review of Clinical Psychology, 7,* 141–168.

Haynes, S. N., & Kaholokula, J. K. (2008). Behavioral assessment. In M. Hersen & A. M. Gross (Eds.), *Handbook of clinical psychology* (Vol. 1, pp. 495–522). Hoboken, NJ: Wiley.

Hays, P. A., & Iwamasa, G. Y. (Eds.). (2006). *Culturally responsive cognitive-behavioral therapy: Assessment, practice, and supervision.* Washington, DC: American Psychological Association.

Hazlett-Stevens, H., & Craske, M. G. (2008). Live (in vivo) exposure. In W. T. O'Donohue

& J. E. Fisher (Eds.), *Cognitive behavior therapy: Applying empirically supported techniques in your practice* (2nd ed., pp. 309–316). Hoboken, NJ: Wiley.

Head, L. S., & Gross, A. M. (2008). Systematic desensitization. In W. T. O'Donohue & J. E. Fisher (Eds.), *Cognitive behavior therapy: Applying empirically supported techniques in your practice* (2nd ed., pp. 542–549). Hoboken, NJ: Wiley.

Healy, D. (2004). *Let them eat Prozac: The unhealthy relationship between the pharmaceutical industry and depression*. New York: New York University.

Hebben, N., & Milberg, W. (2009). *Essentials of neuropsychological assessment* (2nd ed.). Hoboken, NJ: Wiley.

Hebert, R. (2002). We'd like to thank the academy: APCS creates fusion of science and clinical training. *APS Observer, 15*. Retrieved from http://www.psychologicalscience.org/index.php/uncategorized/wed-like-to-thank-the-academy-apcs-creates-fusion-of-science-and-clinical-training.html

Heiby, E. M. (2002). It is time for a moratorium on legislation enabling prescription privileges for psychologists. *Clinical Psychology: Science and Practice, 9,* 256–258.

Heiby, E. M. (2010). Concerns about substandard training for prescription privileges for psychologists. *Journal of Clinical Psychology, 66,* 104–111.

Heiby, E. M., & Haynes, S. N. (2004). Introduction to behavioral assessment. In S. N. Haynes & E. M. Heiby (Eds.), *Comprehensive handbook of psychological assessment: Behavioral assessment* (Vol. 3, pp. 3–18). Hoboken, NJ: Wiley.

Heilbrun, K., & Brooks, S. (2010). Forensic psychology and forensic science: A proposed agenda for the next decade. *Psychology and Public Policy, 16,* 210–253.

Helbok, C. M., Marinelli, R. P., & Walls, R. T. (2006). National survey of ethical practices across rural and urban communities. *Professional Psychology: Research and Practice, 37,* 36–44.

Helmes, E. (2000). Learning and memory. In G. Groth Marnat (Ed.), *Neuropsychological assessment in clinical practice* (pp. 293–334). New York: Wiley.

Hemphill, J. F., & Hart, S. D. (2003). Forensic and clinical issues in the assessment of psychopathy. In A. M. Goldstein (Ed.), *Handbook of psychology, Vol. 11: Forensic psychology* (pp. 87–107). Hoboken, NJ: Wiley.

Hess, A. K. (2006a). Defining forensic psychology. In I. B. Weiner & A. K. Hess (Eds.), *The handbook of forensic psychology* (3rd ed., pp. 28–58). Hoboken, NJ: Wiley.

Hess, A. K. (2006b). Serving as an expert witness. In I. B. Weiner & A. K. Hess (Eds.), *The handbook of forensic psychology* (3rd ed., pp. 652–697). Hoboken, NJ: Wiley.

Hess, K. D. (2006). Understanding child domestic law issues: Custody, adoption, and abuse. In I. B. Weiner & A. K. Hess (Eds.), *The handbook of forensic psychology* (3rd ed., pp. 98–123). Hoboken, NJ: Wiley.

Hettema, J., Steele, J., & Miller, W. R. (2005). Motivational interviewing. *Annual Review of Clinical Psychology, 1,* 91–111.

Hick, S. F. (2008). Cultivating therapeutic relationships: The role of mindfulness. In S. F. Hick & T. Bien (Eds.), *Mindfulness and the therapeutic relationship* (pp. 3–18). New York: Guilford Press.

Hick, S. F., & Bien, T. (Eds.). (2008). *Mindfulness and the therapeutic relationship*. New York: Guilford Press.

Hickman, E. E., Arnkoff, D. B., Glass, C. R., & Schottenbauer, M. A. (2009). Psychotherapy integration as practiced by experts. *Psychotherapy: Theory, Research, Practice, Training, 46*(4), 486–491.

Hickling, L. P., Hickling, E. J., Sison, G. F., & Radetsky, S. (1984). The effect of note-taking on a simulated clinical interview. *Journal of Psychology: Interdisciplinary and Applied, 116,* 235–240.

Higgins, S. T. (1999). Introduction. In S. T. Higgins & K. Silverman (Eds.), *Motivating behavior change among illicit-drug abusers* (pp. 3–13). Washington, DC: American Psychological Association.

Hinds, S. (2005). Play therapy in the African American "village."

In E. Gil & A. A. Drewes (Eds.), *Cultural issues in play therapy* (pp. 115–147). New York: Guilford Press.

Hines, P. M. (2011). The life cycle of African American families living in poverty. In M. McGoldrick, B. Carter, & N. Garcia-Preto (Eds.), *The expanded family life cycle: Individual, family, and social perspectives* (4th ed., pp. 89–102). Boston: Pearson.

Hines, P. M., & Boyd-Franklin, N. (2005). African American families. In M. McGoldrick, J. Giordano, & N. Garcia-Preto (Eds.), *Ethnicity and family therapy* (3rd ed., pp. 87–100). New York: Guilford Press.

Hinshaw, S. P., & Stier, A. (2008). Stigma as related to mental disorders. *Annual Review of Clinical Psychology, 4*, 367–393.

Hiramoto, R., Solvason, H., Hsueh, C., Rogers, C., Demissie, S., Hiramoto, N., et al. (1999). Psychoneuroendocrine immunology: Perception of stress can alter body temperature and natural killer cell activity. *International Journal of Neuroscience, 98*, 95–129.

Hoffman, S. G., Sawyer, A. T., Witt, A. A., & Oh, D. (2010). The effect of mindfulness-based therapy on anxiety and depression: A meta-analytic review. *Journal of Consulting and Clinical Psychology, 78*, 169–183.

Holdnack, J. A., & Drozdick, L. W. (2010). Using WAIS-IV with WMS-IV. In L. G. Weiss, D. H. Saklofske, D. Coalson, & S. E. Raiford (Eds.), *WAIS-IV clinical use and interpretation: Scientist-practitioner perspectives* (pp. 237–283). London: Elsevier.

Hollon, S. D., & DiGiuseppe, R. (2011). Cognitive theories of psychotherapy. In J. C. Norcross, G. R. Vandenbos, & D. K. Freedheim (Eds.), *History of psychotherapy: Continuity and change* (2nd ed., pp. 203–242). Washington, DC: American Psychological Association.

Holstein, J. A. (1993). *Court-ordered insanity: Interpretive practice and involuntary commitment.* New York: Aldine de Gruyter.

Holt, R. R. (1999). Empiricism and the Thematic Apperception Test: Validity is the payoff. In L. Gieser & M. I. Stein (Eds.), *Evocative images: The Thematic Apperception Test and the art of projection* (pp. 99–105). Washington, DC: American Psychological Association.

Holtzworth-Munroe, A., Meehan, J. C., Rehman, U., & Marshall, A. D. (2002). Intimate partner violence: An introduction for couple therapists. In A. S. Gurman & N. S. Jacobson (Eds.), *Clinical handbook of couple therapy* (3rd ed., pp. 441–465). New York: Guilford Press.

Hopper, S., Kaklauskas, F., & Greene, L. R. (2008). Group psychotherapy. In M. Hersen & A. M. Gross (Eds.), *Handbook of clinical psychology* (Vol. 1, pp. 647–662). Hoboken, NJ: Wiley.

Hopwood, C. J., Schade, N., Krueger, R. F., Wright, A. G., & Markon, K. E. (2013). Connecting DSM-5 personality traits and pathological beliefs: Toward a unifying model. *Journal of Psychopathology and Behavioral Assessment, 35*, 162–172.

Horvath, A. O., Del Re, A. C., Fluckiger, C., & Symonds, D. (2011). Alliance in individual psychotherapy. In J. C. Norcross (Ed.), *Psychotherapy relationships that work: Evidence-based responsiveness* (2nd ed., pp. 25–69). New York: Oxford University Press.

Horton, A. M., Jr. (2008). Neuropsychological assessment in a multicultural context: Past, present, and future. In L. A. Suzuki & J. G. Ponterotto (Eds.), *Handbook of multicultural assessment: Clinical, psychological, and educational applications* (3rd ed., pp. 542–564). Hoboken, NJ: Wiley.

Horwitz, A. V. & Wakefield, J. C. (2007). The loss of sadness: How psychiatry transformed normal sorrow into depressive disorder. New York: Oxford University Press.

Horwitz, A. V., & Wakefield, J. C. (2012). *All we have to fear: Psychiatry's transformation of natural anxieties into mental disorders.* New York: Oxford University Press.

House, J., Kahn, R., McLeod, J., & Williams, D. (1985). Measures and concepts of social support. In S. Cohen & L. Syme (Eds.), *Social support and health* (pp.

83–108). San Diego, CA: Academic Press.

Houts, A. C. (2002). Discovery, invention, and the expansion of the modern diagnostic and statistical manuals of mental disorders. In L. E. Beutler & M. L. Malik (Eds.), *Rethinking the DSM: A psychological perspective* (pp. 17–65). Washington, DC: American Psychological Association.

Hoza, B., Kaiser, N., & Hurt, E. (2008). Evidence-based treatments for attention-deficit/hyperactivity disorder (ADHD). In R. G. Steele, T. D. Elkin, & M. C. Roberts (Eds.), *Handbook of evidence-based therapies for children and adolescents: Bridging science and practice* (pp. 197–220). New York: Springer.

Hsiung, R. C. (Ed.). (2002). *E-therapy: Case studies, guiding principles, and the clinical potential of the Internet.* New York: W. W. Norton.

Huber, C. H. (1997). Time-limited counseling, invisible rationing, and informed consent. *Family Journal: Counseling and Therapy for Couples and Families, 5,* 325–327.

Huff, R. M. (1999). Cross-cultural concepts of health and disease. In R. M. Huff & M. V. Kline (Eds.), *Promoting health in multicultural populations: A handbook for practitioners* (pp. 23–39). Thousand Oaks, CA: Sage.

Humphreys, K. (1996). Clinical psychologists as psychotherapists: History, future,

and alternatives. *American Psychologist, 51,* 190–197.

Hunsley, J., Lee, C. M., & Wood, J. M. (2003). Controversial and questionable assessment techniques. In S. O. Lilienfeld, S. J. Lynn, & J. M. Lohr (Eds.), *Science and pseudoscience in clinical psychology* (pp. 39–76). New York: Guilford Press.

Hunsley, J., & Mash, E. J. (2008a). Developing criteria for evidence-based assessment: An introduction to assessments that work. In J. Hunsley & E. J. Mash (Eds.), *A guide to assessments that work* (pp. 3–14). New York: Oxford University Press.

Hunsley, J., & Mash, E. J. (Eds.). (2008b). Preface. In J. Hunsley & E. J. Mash (Eds.), *A guide to assessments that work* (pp. xiii–xvi). New York: Oxford University Press.

Hunt, M. G., & Rosenheck, R. A. (2011). Psychotherapy in mental health clinics of the Department of Veterans Affairs. *Journal of Clinical Psychology, 67,* 561–573.

Hunt, M. H. (1993). *The story of psychology.* New York: Doubleday.

Hwang, W.-C. (2011). Cultural adaptations: A complex interplay between clinical and cultural issues. *Clinical Psychology: Science and Practice, 18,* 238–241.

Imber, S. D., Glanz, L. M., Elkin, E., Sotsky, S. M., Boyer, J. L., & Leber, W. R. (1986). Ethical issues in psychotherapy research. *American Psychologist, 41,* 137–146.

Insel, T. (2013, April 29). Director's Blog: Transforming Diagnosis. Retrieved from http://www.nimh.nih.gov/about/director/2013/transforming-diagnosis.shtml.

Ivey, A. E., Ivey, M. B., & Zalaquett, C. P. (2010). *Intentional interviewing and counseling: Facilitating client development in a multicultural society* (7th ed.). Belmont, CA: Brooks/Cole.

Jackson v. Indiana, 406 U.S. 715 (1972).

Jackson, R. H., & Leonetti, J. (2002). Parenting: The child in the context of the family. In C. E. Walker & M. C. Roberts (Eds.), *Handbook of child clinical psychology* (3rd ed., pp. 807–824). New York: Wiley.

Jackson, Y., Dietz, W. H., Sanders, C., Kolbe, L. J., Whyte, J. J., Wechsler, H., et al. (2002). Summary of the 2000 Surgeon General's listening session: Towards a national action plan on overweight and obesity. *Obesity Research, 10,* 1299–1305.

Jacobson, E. (1938). *Progressive relaxation.* Chicago: University of Chicago Press.

Jakes, S. C., Hallam, R. S., McKenna, L., & Hinchcliffe, R. (1992). Group cognitive therapy for medical patients: An application to tinnitus. *Cognitive Therapy and Research, 16,* 67–82.

Jalali, B. (2005). Iranian families. In M. McGoldrick, J. Giordano, & N. Garcia-Preto (Eds.), *Ethnicity and family therapy* (3rd ed., pp. 451–467). New York: Guilford Press.

James, R. L., & Roberts, M. C. (2009). Future directions in clinical child and adolescent psychology: A delphi survey. *Journal of Clinical Psychology, 65,* 1009–1020.

Jay, S., Elliott, C. H., Fitzgibbons, I., Woody, P., & Siegel, S. (1995). A comparative study of cognitive behavior therapy versus general anesthesia for painful medical procedures in children. *Pain, 62,* 3–9.

Jensen, C. D., Cushing, C. C., Aylward, B. S., Craig, J. T., Sorell, D. M., & Steele, R. G. (2011). Effectiveness of motivational interviewing interventions for adolescent substance use behavior change: A meta-analytic review. *Journal of Consulting and Clinical Psychology, 79,* 433–440.

Jensen-Doss, A., Hawley, K. M., Lopez, M., & Osterberg, L. D. (2009). Using evidence-based treatments: The experiences of youth providers working under a mandate. *Professional Psychology: Research and Practice, 40,* 417–424.

Jeste, D. V., Lieberman, J. A., Scully, J. H. Jr., & Kupfer, D. J. (2012, December 21). DSM crosses the finish line. Psychiatric News, DOI: 10.1176/appi.pn.2012.12a14.

Johansson, P., Høglend, P., Ulberg, R., Amlo, S., Marble, A., Bøgwald, K., et al. (2010). The mediating role of insight for long-term improvements in psychodynamic therapy. *Journal of Consulting and Clinical Psychology, 78,* 438–448.

Johnson, J., Lauver, D., & Nail, L. (1989). Process of coping with radiation therapy. *Journal of Consulting and Clinical Psychology, 57,* 358–364.

Johnson, M. P. (2008). *A typology of domestic violence: Intimate terrorism, violent resistance, and situational couple violence.* Lebanon, NH: Northeastern University Press.

Joseph, S., & Patterson, T. G. (2008). The actualizing tendency: A meta-theoretical perspective for positive psychology. In B. E. Levitt (Ed.), *Reflections on human potential: Bridging the person-centered approach and positive psychology* (pp. 1–15). Herefordshire, UK: PCCS Books.

Julien, R. M. (2011). Psychopharmacology training in clinical psychology: A renewed call for action. *Journal of Clinical Psychology, 67,* 446–449.

Kafka, M. P. (2013). The development and evolution of the criteria for a newly proposed diagnosis for DSM-5: Hypersexual Disorder. *Sexual Addiction & Compulsivity, 20*(1-2), 19–26.

Kalata, A. H., & Naugle, A. E. (2009). Positive psychology: A behavioral conceptualization and application to contemporary behavior therapy. In W. T. O'Donohue & J. E. Fisher (Eds.), *General principles and empirically supported techniques of cognitive behavior therapy* (pp. 445–454). Hoboken, NJ: Wiley.

Kalia, M. (2002). Assessing the economic impact of stress: The modern day hidden epidemic. *Metabolism, 51,* 49–53.

Kamen, C., Cosgrove, V., McKellar, J., Cronkite, R., & Moos, R. (2011). Family support and depressive symptoms: A 23-year follow-up. *Journal of Clinical Psychology, 67,* 215–223.

Kamphaus, R. W., & Frick, P. J. (2005). *Clinical assessment of child and adolescent personality and behavior* (2nd ed.). New York: Springer.

Kamphaus, R. W., & Kroncke, A. P. (2004). "Back to the future" of the Stanford-Binet Intelligence Scales. In M. Hersen (Ed.), *Comprehensive handbook of psychological assessment* (Vol. 1, pp. 77–86). New York: Wiley.

Kanter, J. W., Busch, A. M., & Rusch, L. C. (2009). *Behavioral activation: Distinctive features.* New York: Routledge.

Karon, B. P., & Widener, A. J. (1995). Psychodynamic therapies in historical perspective: "Nothing human do I consider alien to me." In B. Bongar & L. E. Beutler (Eds.), *Comprehensive textbook of psychotherapy: Theory and practice* (pp. 24–47). New York: Oxford University Press.

Kaslow, F. W. (2011). Treatment modalities: Family therapy. In J. C. Norcross, G. R. Vandenbos, & D. K. Freedheim (Eds.), *History of psychotherapy: Continuity and change* (2nd ed., pp. 497–504). Washington, DC: American Psychological Association.

Kaslow, N. J., Bollini, A. M., Druss, B., Glueckauf, R. L., Goldfrank, L. R., Kelleher, K. J., et al. (2007). Health care for the whole person: Research update. *Professional Psychology: Research and Practice, 38,* 278–289.

Kaslow, N. J., & Webb, C. (2011). Training systems and sites: Internship and postdoctoral residency. In J. C. Norcross, G. R. Vandenbos, & D. K. Freedheim (Eds.), *History of psychotherapy: Continuity and change* (2nd ed., pp. 640–650). Washington, DC: American Psychological Association.

Kastrup, M. (2000). Scandinavian approaches. In A. Okasha, J. Arboleda-Florez, & N. Sartorius (Eds.), *Ethics, culture, and psychiatry: International perspectives* (pp. 65–82). Washington, DC: American Psychiatric Press.

Kazantzis, N., & Dattilio, F. M. (2010). Definitions of homework, types of homework, and ratings of the importance of homework among psychologists with cognitive behavior therapy and psychoanalytic theoretical orientations. *Journal of Clinical Psychology, 66,* 758–773.

Kazantzis, N., Whittington, C., & Dattilio, F. (2010). Meta-analysis of homework effects in cognitive and behavioral therapy: A replication and extension. *Clinical Psychology: Science and Practice, 17,* 144–156.

Kazdin, A. E. (1978). *History of behavior modification: Experimental foundations of contemporary research.* Baltimore: University Park Press.

Kazdin, A. E. (1980). *Behavior modification in applied settings* (Rev. ed.). Homewood, IL: Dorsey Press.

Kazdin, A. E. (2000). *Psychotherapy for children and adolescents: Directions for research and practice.* New York: Oxford University Press.

Kazdin, A. E. (2007). Mediators and mechanisms of change in psychotherapy research. *Annual Review of Clinical Psychology, 3,* 1–27.

Kazdin, A. E. (2011). *Single-case research designs: Methods for clinical and applied settings* (2nd ed.). New York: Oxford University Press.

Kazdin, A. E., & Weisz, J. R. (Eds.). (2003). *Evidence-based psychotherapies for children and adolescents.* New York: Guilford Press.

Kearney, C. A., & Vecchio, J. (2002). Contingency management. In M. Hersen & W. Sledge (Eds.), *Encyclopedia of psychotherapy* (Vol. 1, pp. 525–532). San Diego, CA: Academic Press.

Keel, P. K., & Klump, K. L. (2003). Are eating disorders culture-bound syndromes? Implications for conceptualizing their etiology. *Psychological Bulletin, 129,* 747–769.

Keilin, W. G. (2000). Internship selection in 1999: Was the association of psychology postdoctoral and internship centers' match a success? *Professional Psychology: Research and Practice, 31,* 281–287.

Keilin, W. G., & Constantine, M. G. (2001). Applying to professional psychology internship programs. In S. Walfish & A. K. Hess (Eds.), *Succeeding in graduate school: The career guide for psychology students* (pp. 319–333). Mahwah, NJ: Lawrence Erlbaum.

Keilin, W. G., Thorn, B. E., Rodolfa, E. R., Constantine, M. G., & Kaslow, N. J. (2000). Examining the balance of internship supply and demand: 1999 Association of Psychology postdoctoral and internship centers' match implications. *Professional Psychology: Research and Practice, 31,* 288–294.

Kendall, P. C. (2012). Guiding theory for therapy with children and adolescents. In P. C. Kendall (Ed.), *Child and adolescent therapy: Cognitive-behavioral procedures* (4th ed., pp. 3–24). New York: Guilford Press.

Kendall, P. C., & Drabick, D. A. G. (2010). Problems for the book of problems? Diagnosing mental health disorders among youth. *Clinical Psychology: Science and Practice, 17,* 265–271.

Kendler, K. S. (in press). A history of the DSM-5 scientific review committee. *Psychological Medicine.*

Kent, R. G., Carrington, S.J., Couteur, A., Gould, J., Wing, L.,

Maljaars, J., Noens, I., van Berckelaer-Onnes, I, & Leekam, S. R. (2013). Diagnosing Autism Spectrum Disorder: who will get a DSM-5 diagnosis?. *Journal of Child Psychology and Psychiatry*.

Kernberg, O. F. (2004). *Contemporary controversies in psychoanalytic theories, techniques, and their applications.* New Haven, CT: Yale University Press.

Kessler, R. C. (1994). The national comorbidity survey of the United States. *International Review of Psychiatry, 6,* 365–376.

Kiecolt-Glaser, J., Glaser, R., Williger, D., Stout, J., Messick, G., & Sheppard, S. (1985). Psychosocial enhancement of immunocompetence in a geriatric population. *Health Psychology, 4,* 25–41.

Kiecolt-Glaser, J., Newton, T., Cacioppo, J., MacCallum, R., Glaser, R., & Malarkey, W. (1996). Marital conflict and endocrine function: Are men really more psychologically affected than women? *Journal of Consulting and Clinical Psychology, 64,* 324–332.

Kielbasa, A. M., Pomerantz, A. M., Krohn, E. J., & Sullivan, B. F. (2004). How does clients' method of payment influence psychologists' diagnostic decisions? *Ethics & Behavior, 14,* 187–195.

Kilgore, H., Sideman, L., Amin, K., Baca, L., & Bohanske, B. (2005). Psychologists' attitudes and therapeutic approaches toward gay, lesbian, and bisexual issues

continue to improve: An update. *Psychotherapy: Theory, Research, Practice, Training, 42,* 395–400.

King, D. L., & Delfabbro, P. H. (2013). Issues for DSM-5: Video-gaming disorder? *Australian and New Zealand Journal of Psychiatry, 47*(1), 20-22.

Kinghorn, W. (2013). The biopolitics of defining "mental disorder." In J. Paris & J. Phillips (Eds.), Making the DSM-5: Concepts and Controversies, pp. 47-61. New York: Springer.

Kirmayer, L. J., & Minas, H. (2000). The future of cultural psychiatry: An international perspective. *Canadian Journal of Psychiatry, 45,* 438–446.

Kitaeff, J. (2011). History of police psychology. In J. Kitaeff (Ed.), *Handbook of police psychology* (pp. 1–62). New York: Taylor & Francis.

Klerman, G. (1984). The advantages of *DSM-III. American Journal of Psychiatry, 141,* 539–542.

Klerman, G. L., Weissman, M. M., Rounsaville, B. J., & Chevron, E. S. (1984). *Interpersonal psychotherapy of depression.* New York: Basic Books.

Kliem, S., Kröger, C., & Kosfelder, J. (2010). Dialectical behavior therapy for borderline personality disorder: A meta-analysis using mixed-effects modeling. *Journal of Consulting and Clinical Psychology, 78,* 936–951.

Kline, M. V., & Huff, R. M. (1999). Tips for the practitioner. In R. M. Huff & M. V. Kline

(Eds.), *Promoting health in multicultural populations: A handbook for practitioners* (pp. 103–111). Thousand Oaks, CA: Sage.

Klonoff, E. A. (2011). Training systems and sites: PhD programs. In J. C. Norcross, G. R. Vandenbos, & D. K. Freedheim (Eds.), *History of psychotherapy: Continuity and change* (2nd ed., pp. 615–629). Washington, DC: American Psychological Association.

Knabb, J. J., Vogt, R. G., & Newgren, K. P. (2011). MMPI-2 characteristics of the Old Order Amish: A comparison of clinical, nonclinical, and United States normative samples. *Psychological Assessment, 23,* 865–875.

Knapp, S. J., & VandeCreek, L. D. (2006). *Practical ethics for psychologists: A positive approach.* Washington, DC: American Psychological Association.

Knauss, L. K., & Knauss, J. W. (2012). Ethical issues in multiperson therapy. In S. J. Knapp (Ed.), *APA handbook of ethics in psychology, Vol. 2: Practice, teaching, and research* (pp. 29–43). Washington, DC: American Psychological Association.

Knell, S. M., & Dasari, M. (2011). Cognitive-behavioral play therapy. In S. W. Russ & L. N. Niec (Eds.), *Play in clinical practice: Evidence-based approaches* (pp. 236–263). New York: Guilford Press.

Koenig, H. G. (2005). *Faith and mental health: Religious resources for healing.* Philadelphia: Templeton Foundation Press.

Koenig, L. B., & Vaillant, G. E. (2009). A prospective study of church attendance and health over the lifespan. *Health Psychology, 28,* 354–363.

Koerner, K. (2012). *Doing dialectical behavior therapy: A practical guide.* New York: Guilford Press.

Koerner, K., & Dimeff, L. A. (2007). Overview of dialectical behavior therapy. In L. A. Dimeff & K. Koerner (Eds.), *Dialectical behavior therapy in clinical practice: Applications across disorders and settings* (pp. 1–18). New York: Guilford Press.

Kolden, G. G., Klein, M. H., Wang, C., & Austin, S. B. (2011). Congruence/genuineness. In J. C. Norcross (Ed.), *Psychotherapy relationships that work: Evidence-based responsiveness* (2nd ed., pp. 187–202). New York: Oxford University Press.

Koocher, G. P. (2009). Any minute now but far far away: Electronically mediated mental health. *Clinical Psychology: Science and Practice, 16,* 339–342.

Koocher, G. P., & Daniel, J. H. (2012). Treating children and adolescents. In S. J. Knapp (Ed.), *APA handbook of ethics in psychology, Vol. 2: Practice, teaching, and research* (pp. 3–14). Washington, DC: American Psychological Association.

Koocher, G. P., & Keith-Spiegel, P. (2008). *Ethics in psychology and the mental health professions* (3rd ed.). New York: Oxford University Press.

Kosciulek, J. F. (2003). Counseling and psychotherapy with clients with disabilities. In D. R. Atkinson & G. Hackett (Eds.), *Counseling diverse populations* (3rd ed., pp. 194–216). Boston: McGraw-Hill.

Kraemer, H. C. (2013). An idea worth researching: DSM diagnosis of mental disorders as a living document. *International Journal of Eating Disorders, 46*(5), 412-415.

Kraus, R. (2004). Ethical and legal considerations for providers of mental health services online. In R. Kraus, J. Zack, & G. Stricker (Eds.), *Online counseling: A handbook for mental health professionals* (pp. 123–144). San Diego, CA: Elsevier.

Kraus, R. (2011). Online counseling: Does it work? Research findings to date. In R. Kraus, G. Stricker, & C. Speyer (Eds.), *Online counseling: A handbook for mental health professionals* (2nd ed., pp. 55–63). Burlington, MA: Elsevier.

Kraus, R., Zack, J., & Stricker, G. (Eds.). (2004). *Online counseling: A handbook for mental health professionals.* San Diego, CA: Elsevier.

Krawcqynski, J. (2012, April 5). Goodell warns NFL about leaking Wonderlic scores. Retrieved from http://news.yahoo.com/goodell-warns-nfl-leaking-wonderlic-scores-164752308--spt.html

Kris, A. O. (2012). Unconscious processes. In G. O. Gabbard, B. E. Litowitz, & P. Williams (Eds.), *Textbook of psychoanalysis* (2nd ed., pp. 53–64). Washington, DC: American Psychiatric Publishing.

Kropiunigg, U. (1993). Basics in psychoneuroimmunology. *Annals of Medicine, 25,* 473–479.

Kuehlwein, K. T. (1993). A survey and update of cognitive therapy systems. In K. T. Kuehlwein & H. Rosen (Eds.), *Cognitive therapies in action* (pp. 1–32). San Francisco: Jossey-Bass.

Kupfer, D. J., Kuhl, E. A., & Regier, D. A. (2013). DSM-5—The Future Arrived. *JAMA, 309*(16), 1691–1692.

Kutchins, K., & Kirk, S. A. (1997). *Making us crazy: DSM: The psychiatric bible and the creation of mental disorders.* New York: Free Press.

Kwan, K. K., & Maestas, M. L. (2008). MMPI-2 and MCMI-III performances of non-white people in the United States: What we (don't) know and where we go from here. In L. A. Suzuki & J. G. Ponterotto (Eds.), *Handbook of multicultural assessment: Clinical, psychological, and educational applications* (3rd ed., pp. 425–446). Hoboken, NJ: Wiley.

La Roche, M. J., Batista, C., & D'Angelo, E. (2011). A content analysis of guided imagery scripts: A strategy for the development of cultural adaptations. *Journal of Clinical Psychology, 67,* 45–57.

La Roche, M. J., & Christopher, M. S. (2009). Changing paradigms from empirically supported treatment to evidence-based practice: A cultural perspective. *Professional Psychology: Research and Practice, 40*, 396–402.

Lacks, P. (1999). *Bender-Gestalt screening for brain dysfunction* (2nd ed.). New York: Wiley.

Lacks, P. (2000). Visuoconstructive abilities. In G. Groth Marnat (Ed.), *Neuropsychological assessment in clinical practice* (pp. 401–436). New York: Wiley.

LaFarge, L. (2012). Defense and resistance. In G. O. Gabbard, B. E. Litowitz, & P. Williams (Eds.), *Textbook of psychoanalysis* (2nd ed., pp. 93–104). Washington, DC: American Psychiatric Publishing.

LaGreca, A. M., Kuttler, A. F., & Stone, W. L. (2002). Assessing children through interviews and behavioral observations. In C. E. Walker & M. C. Roberts (Eds.), *Handbook of child clinical psychology* (3rd ed., pp. 90–110). New York: Wiley.

Lally, S. J. (2003). What tests are acceptable for use in forensic evaluations? A survey of experts. *Professional Psychology: Research and Practice, 34*, 491–498.

Lambert, M. C. (2006). Normal and abnormal development: What the child clinician should know. In C. A. Essau (Ed.), *Child and adolescent psychopathology: Theoretical and clinical*

implications (pp. 1–25). New York: Routledge.

Lambert, M. J. (2011). Psychotherapy research and its achievements. In J. C. Norcross, G. R. Vandenbos, & D. K. Freedheim (Eds.), *History of psychotherapy: Continuity and change* (2nd ed., pp. 299–332). Washington, DC: American Psychological Association.

Lambert, M. J., & Ogles, B. M. (2004). The efficacy and effectiveness of psychotherapy. In M. J. Lambert (Ed.), *Bergin and Garfield's handbook of psychotherapy and behavior change* (5th ed., pp. 139–193). New York: Wiley.

Lambert, M. J., & Simon, W. (2008). The therapeutic relationship: Central and essential in psychotherapy outcome. In S. F. Hick & T. Bien (Eds.), *Mindfulness and the therapeutic relationship* (pp. 19–33). New York: Guilford Press.

Landreth, G. (1991). *Play therapy: The art of the relationship.* Muncie, IN: Accelerated Development.

Lane, C. (2007). *Shyness: How normal behavior became a sickness.* New Haven, CT: Yale University Press.

Lane, R. C., & Harris, M. (2008). Psychodynamic psychotherapy. In M. Hersen & A. M. Gross (Eds.), *Handbook of clinical psychology* (Vol. 1, pp. 525–550). Hoboken, NJ: Wiley.

Langenbucher, J., & Nathan, P. E. (2006). Diagnosis and classification. In M. Hersen &

J. C. Thomas (Eds.), *Comprehensive handbook of personality and psychopathology* (Vol. 2, pp. 3–20). Hoboken, NJ: Wiley.

Laser, J. A., & Nicotera, N. (2011). *Working with adolescents: A guide for practitioners.* New York: Guilford Press.

Lasky, G. B., & Riva, M. T. (2006). Confidentiality and privileged communication in group psychotherapy. *International Journal of Group Psychotherapy, 56*, 455–476.

Laszlo, E. (1972). *The systems view of the world.* New York: Braziller.

Lau, A. S. (2006). Making the case for selective and directed cultural adaptations of evidence-based treatments: Examples from parent training. *Clinical Psychology: Science and Practice, 13*, 295–310.

LaVeist, T. A. (2005). *Minority populations and health: An introduction to health disparities in the United States.* San Francisco: Jossey-Bass.

LaVeist, T. A., Nickerson, K., & Bowie, J. (2000). Attitudes about racism, medical mistrust, and satisfaction with care among African American and White cardiac patients. *Medical Care Research and Review, 57*, 146–161.

Layde, J. B. (2004). Cross-cultural issues in forensic psychiatry training. *Academic Psychiatry, 28*, 34–39.

Lazarus, R., & Folkman, S. (1984). Coping and adaptation.

In W. D. Gentry (Ed.), *The handbook of behavioral medicine* (pp. 282–325). New York: Guilford Press.

Leahy, R. L. (2003). *Cognitive therapy techniques: A practitioner's guide*. New York: Guilford Press.

Lebow, J. (2006). *Research for the psychotherapist: From science to practice*. New York: Routledge.

Lee, E. (Ed.). (1997). *Working with Asian Americans: A guide for clinicians*. New York: Guilford Press.

Lee, E., & Mock, M. R. (2005). Asian families: An overview. In M. McGoldrick, J. Giordano, & N. Garcia-Preto (Eds.), *Ethnicity and family therapy* (3rd ed., pp. 269–289). New York: Guilford Press.

Lee, J., Lim, N., Yang, E., & Lee, S. M. (2011). Antecedents and consequences of three dimensions of burnout in psychotherapists: A meta-analysis. *Professional Psychology: Research and Practice, 42,* 252–258.

Lee, J. A., Luxton, D. D., Reger, G. M., & Gahm, G. A. (2010). Confirmatory factor analysis of the posttraumatic growth inventory with a sample of soldiers previously deployed in support of the Iraq and Afghanistan wars. *Journal of Clinical Psychology, 66,* 813–819.

Leichsenring, F. (2009a). Applications of psychodynamic psychotherapy to specific disorders: Efficacy and indications. In G. O. Gabbard (Ed.), *Textbook of psychotherapeutic treatments* (pp. 97–132). Washington, DC: American Psychiatric Publishing.

Leichsenring, F. (2009b). Psychodynamic psychotherapy: A review of efficacy and effectiveness studies. In R. A. Levy & J. S. Ablon (Eds.), *Handbook of evidence-based psychodynamic psychotherapy: Bridging the gap between science and practice* (pp. 3–27). New York: Humana.

Leichsenring, F., Rabung, S., & Leibing, E. (2004). The efficacy of short-term psychodynamic therapy in specific psychiatric disorders: A meta-analysis. *Archives of General Psychiatry, 61,* 1208–1216.

Lennon, R., & Eisenberg, N. (1987). Gender and age differences in empathy and sympathy. In N. Eisenberg & J. Strayer (Eds.), *Empathy and its development* (pp. 195–217). Cambridge, UK: Cambridge University Press.

Lesserman, J., Jackson, E., Petitto, J., Golden, R., Silva, S., & Perkins, D. (1999). Progression to AIDS: The effects of stress, depressive symptoms, and social support. *Psychosomatic Medicine, 61,* 397–406.

Leung, P. K., & Boehnlein, J. K. (2005). Vietnamese families. In M. McGoldrick, J. Giordano, & N. Garcia-Preto (Eds.), *Ethnicity and family therapy* (3rd ed., pp. 363–373). New York: Guilford Press.

Levant, R. F., & Silverstein, L. B. (2006). Gender is neglected by both evidence-based practices and treatment as usual. In J. C. Norcross, L. E. Beutler, & R. F. Levant (Eds.), *Evidence-based practices in mental health: Debate and dialogue on the fundamental questions* (pp. 338–345). Washington, DC: American Psychological Association.

Levenson, H. (1995). *Time-limited dynamic psychotherapy: A guide to clinical practice*. New York: Basic Books.

Levenson, H. (2010). *Brief dynamic therapy*. Washington, DC: American Psychological Association.

Levenson, H., Butler, S. F., & Beitman, B. D. (1997). *Concise guide to brief dynamic psychotherapy*. Washington, DC: American Psychiatric Association.

Levis, D. J. (2008). The prolonged exposure techniques of implosive (flooding) therapy. In W. T. O'Donohue & J. E. Fisher (Eds.), *Cognitive behavior therapy: Applying empirically supported techniques in your practice* (2nd ed., pp. 272–282). Hoboken, NJ: Wiley.

Lewis, B. A., Statt, E., & Marcus, B. H. (2011). Behavioral interventions in public health settings: Physical activity, weight loss, and smoking. In D. H. Barlow (Ed.), *The Oxford handbook of clinical psychology* (pp. 717–738). New York: Oxford University Press.

Lewis-Fernandez, R., & Kleinman, A. (1994). Culture, personality, and psychopathology. *Journal of Abnormal Psychology, 103,* 67–71.

Leykin, Y., & DeRubeis, R. J. (2009). Allegiance in psychotherapy outcome research: Separating association from bias. *Clinical Psychology: Science and Practice, 16,* 54–65.

Lichtenberger, E. O., & Breaux, K. C. (2010). *Essentials of WIAT-III and KTEA-II assessment.* Hoboken, NJ: Wiley.

Lichtenberger, E. O., & Kaufman, A. S. (2004). *Essentials of WPPSI-III assessment.* New York: Wiley.

Lichtenberger, E. O., & Kaufman, A. S. (2009). *Essentials of WAIS-IV assessment.* Hoboken, NJ: Wiley.

Lilenfeld, L. R. R., Wonderlich, S., Riso, L. P., Crosby, R., & Mitchell, J. (2006). Eating disorders and personality: A methodological and empirical review. *Clinical Psychology Review, 26,* 299–320.

Lilienfeld, S. O., & Landfield, K. (2008). Science and psuedoscience in law enforcement: A user-friendly primer. *Criminal Justice and Behavior, 35,* 1215–1230.

Lilienfeld, S. O., Lynn, S. J., Ruscio, J., & Beyerstein, B. L. (2010). *50 great myths of popular psychology.* Malden, MA: Wiley-Blackwell.

Lilienfeld, S. O., & Landfield, K. (2008). Issues in diagnosis: Categorical vs. dimensional. In W. E. Craighead, D. J. Milkowitz, & L. W. Craighead (Eds.), *Psychopathology: History, diagnosis, and empirical foundations* (pp. 1–33). Hoboken, NJ: Wiley.

Lilienfeld, S. O., & Marino, L. (1999). Essentialism revisited: Evolutionary theory and the concept of mental disorder. *Journal of Abnormal Psychology, 108,* 400–411.

Lilienfeld, S. O., Wood, J. M., & Garb, H. N. (2000). The scientific status of projective techniques. *Psychological Science in the Public Interest, 1,* 27–66.

Lindsey, R. T. (1984). Informed consent and deception in psychotherapy research: An ethical analysis. *The Counseling Psychologist, 12*(3), 79–86.

Linehan, M. M. (1993a). *Cognitive-behavioral treatment of borderline personality disorder.* New York: Guilford Press.

Linehan, M. M. (1993b). *Skills training manual for treating borderline personality disorder.* New York: Guilford Press.

Linscott, R. J., & van Os, J. (2010). Systematic reviews of categorical versus continuum models in psychosis: Evidence for discontinuous subpopulations underlying a psychometric continuum. Implications for DSM-V, DSM-VI, and DSM-VII. *Annual Review of Clinical Psychology, 6,* 391–419.

Lipsey, M. W., & Wilson, D. B. (1993). The efficacy of psychological, educational, and behavioral treatment: Confirmation from meta-analysis. *American Psychologist, 48,* 1181–1209.

Lipsitz, J. D. (2009). Theory of interpersonal psychotherapy. In G. O. Gabbard (Ed.), *Textbook of psychotherapeutic treatments* (pp. 289–307). Washington, DC: American Psychiatric Publishing.

Litwack, T. R., Zapf, P. A., Groscup, J. L., & Hart, S. D. (2006). Violence risk assessment: Research, legal, and clinical considerations. In I. B. Weiner & A. K. Hess (Eds.), *Handbook of forensic psychology* (3rd ed., pp. 487–533). Hoboken, NJ: Wiley.

Littell, J. H. (2010). Evidence-based practice: Evidence or orthodoxy? In B. L. Duncan, S. D. Miller, B. E. Wampold, & M. A. Hubble (Eds.), *The heart and soul of change: Delivering what works in therapy* (2nd ed., pp. 167–198). Washington, DC: American Psychological Association.

Lloyd, A. (2009). Urge surfing. In W. T. O'Donohue & J. E. Fisher (Eds.), *General principles and empirically supported techniques of cognitive behavior therapy* (pp. 669–673). Hoboken, NJ: Wiley.

Logel, C., & Cohen, G. L. (2012). The role of the self in physical health: Testing the effect of a values-affirmation intervention on weight loss. *Psychological Science, 23,* 53–55.

Lohr, J. M., Fowler, K. A., & Lilienfeld, S. O. (2002). The dissemination and promotion of pseudoscience in clinical psychology: The challenge to legitimate clinical science. *Clinical Psychologist, 55,* 4–10.

Long, J. E., Jr. (2005). Power to prescribe: The debate over prescription privileges for psychologists and the legal issues implicated. *Law and Psychology Review, 29,* 243–260.

Lönnqvist, J.-E., Verkasalo, M., Mäkinen, S., & Henriksson, M. (2009). High neuroticism at age 20 predicts history of mental disorders and low self-esteem at age 35. *Journal of Clinical Psychology, 65,* 781–790.

Lorber, W., & Garcia, H. A. (2010). Not supposed to feel this: Traditional masculinity in psychotherapy with male veterans returning from Afghanistan and Iraq. *Psychotherapy: Theory, Research, Practice, Training, 47,* 296–305.

Lowe, J., Pomerantz, A. M., & Pettibone, J. C. (2007). The influence of payment method on psychologists' diagnostic decisions: Expanding the range of presenting problems. *Ethics & Behavior, 17,* 83–93.

Luborsky, L., & Barrett, M. S. (2006). The history and empirical status of key psychoanalytic concepts. *Annual Review of Clinical Psychology, 2,* 1–19.

Luborsky, L., Diguer, L., Seligman, D. A., Rosenthal, R., Krause, E. D., Johnson, S., et al. (1999). The researcher's own therapy allegiances: A "wild card" in comparisons of treatment efficacy. *Clinical Psychology: Science and Practice, 6,* 95–106.

Luborsky, L., Rosenthal, R., Diguer, L., Andrusyna, T. P., Berman, J. S., Levitt, J. T., et al.

(2002). The dodo bird verdict is alive and well—mostly. *Clinical Psychology: Science and Practice, 9,* 2–12.

Luborsky, L., Singer, J., & Luborsky, L. (1975). Comparative studies of psychotherapy. *Archives of General Psychiatry, 32,* 995–1008.

Ludwick-Rosenthal, R., & Neufeld, R. (1988). Stress management during noxious medical procedures: An evaluative review of outcome studies. *Psychological Bulletin, 104,* 326–342.

Luepnitz, D. (1992). *The family interpreted.* New York: Basic Books.

Lukas, S. (1993). *Where to start and what to ask: An assessment handbook.* New York: W. W. Norton.

Lundahl, B., & Burke, B. L. (2009). The effectiveness and applicability of motivational interviewing: A practice-friendly review of four meta-analyses. *Journal of Clinical Psychology, 65,* 1232–1245.

Luria, A. (1961). *The role of speech in the regulation of normal and abnormal behaviors.* New York: Liveright.

Lyddon, W. J., & Chatkoff, D. K. (2001). Empirically supported treatments: Recent trends, current limitations, and future promise. In W. J. Lyddon (Ed.), *Empirically supported cognitive therapies: Current and future applications* (pp. 235–246). New York: Springer.

Lynch, T. R., Trost, W. T., Salsman, N., & Linehan, M. M. (2007). Dialectical behavior therapy for borderline personality disorder. *Annual Review of Clinical Psychology, 3,* 181–205.

Lyons, H. Z., Bieschke, K. J., Dendy, A. K., Worthington, R. L., & Georgemiller, R. (2010). Psychologists' competence to treat lesbian, gay and bisexual clients: State of the field and strategies for improvement. *Professional Psychology: Research and Practice, 41,* 424–434.

MacKenzie, K. R. (2002). Group psychotherapy. In M. Hersen & W. Sledge (Eds.), *Encyclopedia of psychotherapy* (Vol. 1, pp. 891–906). San Diego, CA: Academic Press.

Mackewn, J. (1997). *Developing Gestalt counseling.* London: Sage.

Maguen, S., Cohen, G., Cohen, B. E., Lawhon, G. D., Marmar, C. R., & Seal, K. H. (2010). The role of psychologists in the care of Iraq and Afghanistan veterans in primary care settings. *Professional Psychology: Research and Practice, 41,* 135–142.

Magyar-Moe, J. L., Pedrotti, J. T., Edwards, L. M., Ford, A. I., Petersen, S. E., Rasmussen, H. N., et al. (2005). Perceptions of multicultural training in predoctoral internships: A survey of interns and training directors. *Professional Psychology: Research and Practice, 36,* 446–450.

Maheu, M. M., Pulier, M. L., Wilhelm, F. H., McMenamin, J. P., & Brown-Connolly, N. E.

(2005). *The mental health professional and the new technologies: A handbook for practice today*. Mahwah, NJ: Erlbaum.

Mahler, H., & Kulik, J. (1998). Effects of preparatory videotapes on self-efficacy beliefs and recovery from coronary bypass surgery. *Annals of Behavioral Medicine, 20,* 39–46.

Malgady, R. G., & Colon-Malgady, G. (2008). Building community test norms: Considerations for ethnic minority populations. In L. A. Suzuki & J. G. Ponterotto (Eds.), *Handbook of multicultural assessment: Clinical, psychological, and educational applications* (3rd ed., pp. 34–51). Hoboken, NJ: Wiley.

Malik, M. L., & Beutler, L. E. (2002). The emergence of dissatisfaction with the DSM. In L. E. Beutler & M. L. Malik (Eds.), *Rethinking the DSM: A psychological perspective* (pp. 3–15). Washington, DC: American Psychological Association.

Manninen, B. A. (2006). Medicating the mind: A Kantian analysis of overprescribing psychoactive drugs. *Journal of Medical Ethics, 32,* 100–105.

Manring, J., Greenberg, R. P., Gregory, R., & Gallinger, L. (2011). Learning psychotherapy in the digital age. *Psychotherapy, 48,* 119–126.

Mantyselka, P. T., Turunen, J. H., Ahonen, R. S., & Kumpusalo, E. A. (2003). Chronic pain and poor self-rated health. *Journal of the American Medical Association, 290,* 2435–2442.

Marans, S., Dahl, K., & Schowalter, J. (2002). Child and adolescent psychotherapy: Psychoanalytic principles. In M. Hersen & W. Sledge (Eds.), *Encyclopedia of psychotherapy* (Vol. 1, pp. 381–400). San Diego, CA: Academic Press.

Marczyk, G., Krauss, D. A., & Burl, J. (2012). Educational and training models in forensic psychology. In C. R. Bartol & A. M. Bartol (Eds.), *Current perspectives in forensic psychology and criminal behavior* (pp. 2–10). Thousand Oaks, CA: Sage.

Markowitz, J. C., & Weissman, M. M. (2009). Applications of individual interpersonal psychotherapy to specific disorders: Efficacy and indications. In G. O. Gabbard (Ed.), *Textbook of psychotherapeutic treatments* (pp. 339–364). Washington, DC: American Psychiatric Publishing.

Markowitz, J. C., & Weissman, M. M. (2012). Interpersonal Psychotherapy: Past, present and future. *Clinical Psychology and Psychotherapy, 19,* 99–105.

Marks, I., & Cavanagh, K. (2009). Computer-aided psychological treatments: Evolving issues. *Annual Review of Clinical Psychology, 5,* 121–141.

Markus, H., & Kitayama, S. (1991). Culture and the self: Implications for cognition, emotion, and motivation. *Psychological Review, 98,* 224–253.

Marlatt, G., & Gordon, J. (1985). *Relapse preventions: Maintenance strategies in the treatment of addictive behaviors*. New York: Guilford Press.

Maroda, K. J. (2010). *Psychodynamic techniques: Working with emotion in the therapeutic relationship*. New York: Guilford Press.

Marshall, W. L. (2006). Diagnosis and treatment of sexual offenders. In I. B. Weiner & A. K. Hess (Eds.), *The handbook of forensic psychology* (3rd ed., pp. 751–789). Hoboken, NJ: Wiley.

Martell, C. R. (2008). Behavioral activation for depression. In W. T. O'Donohue & J. E. Fisher (Eds.), *Cognitive behavior therapy: Applying empirically supported techniques in your practice* (2nd ed., pp. 40–45). Hoboken, NJ: Wiley.

Martell, C. R. (2009). Behavioral activation treatment for depression. In W. T. O'Donohue & J. E. Fisher (Eds.), *General principles and empirically supported techniques of cognitive behavior therapy* (pp. 138–143). Hoboken, NJ: Wiley.

Martell, C. R., Safren, S. A., & Prince, S. S. (2004). *Cognitive-behavioral therapies with lesbian, gay, and bisexual clients*. New York: Guilford Press.

Martin, C. K., Stewart, T. M., Anton, S. D., Copeland, A. L., & Williamson, D. A. (2008). Health psychology. In M. Hersen & A. M. Gross (Eds.), *Handbook of clinical psychology* (Vol. 1, pp. 693–723). Hoboken, NJ: Wiley.

Martinez, R. (2004). *The new Americans*. New York: New Press.

Maruish, M. E. (2008). The clinical interview. In R. P. Archer & S. R. Smith (Eds.), *Personality assessment* (pp. 37–80). New York: Routledge.

Maser, J. D., Norman, S. B., Zisook, S., Everall, I. P., Stein, M. B., Schettler, P. J., et al. (2009). Psychiatric nosology is ready for a paradigm shift in *DSM-V*. *Clinical Psychology: Science and Practice, 16*, 24–40.

Maslow, A. H. (1968). *Toward a psychology of being* (2nd ed.). Princeton, NJ: Van Nostrand.

Masuda, A., & Wilson, K. (2009). Mindfulness: Being mindful in psychotherapy. In W. O'Donohue & S. R. Graybar (Eds.), *Handbook of contemporary psychotherapy: Toward an improved understanding of effective psychotherapy* (pp. 249–268). Thousand Oaks, CA: Sage.

Matarazzo, J. D. (1983). The reliability of psychiatric and psychological diagnosis. *Clinical Psychology Review, 3*, 103–145.

Maultsby, M. C. (1982). A historical view of blacks' distrust of psychiatry. In S. M. Turner & R. T. Jones (Eds.), *Behavior modification in black populations* (pp. 39–56). New York: Plenum Press.

Maxie, A. C., Arnold, D. H., & Stephenson, M. (2006). Do therapists address ethnic and racial differences in cross-cultural psychotherapy? *Psychotherapy: Theory, Research, Practice, Training, 43*, 85–98.

May, R. (1983). *The discovery of being: Writings in existential psychology*. New York: W. W. Norton.

Mayer, J. (2005, July). The experiment. *New Yorker*. Retrieved from http://www.newyorker.com/archive/2005/07/11/050711fa_fact4

Mayes, S. D., Black, A., & Tierney, C. D. (2013). DSM-5 under-identifies PDDNOS: Diagnostic agreement between the DSM-5, DSM-IV, and Checklist for Autism Spectrum Disorder. *Research in Autism Spectrum Disorders, 7*(2), 298–306.

Mayne, T. J., Norcross, J. C., & Sayette, M. A. (1994). Admission requirements, acceptance rates, and financial assistance in clinical psychology programs: Diversity across the practice-research continuum. *American Psychologist, 49*, 806–811.

Mazzucchelli, T., Kane, R., & Rees, C. (2009). Behavioral activation treatments for depression in adults: A meta-analysis and review. *Clinical Psychology: Science and Practice, 16*, 383–411.

McCaffrey, R. J., Lynch, J. K., & Westervelt, H. J. (2011). Clinical neuropsychology. In D. H. Barlow (Ed.), *The Oxford handbook of clinical psychology* (pp. 680–700). New York: Oxford University Press.

McCallum, R. S., & Bracken, B. A. (2005). The Universal Nonverbal Intelligence Test: A multidimensional measure of intelligence. In D. P. Flanagan &

P. L. Harrison (Eds.), *Contemporary intellectual assessment: Theories, tests, and issues* (2nd ed., pp. 425–440). New York: Guilford Press.

McCloskey, M. S. (2011). Training in empirically supported treatments using alternative learning modalities. *Clinical Psychology: Science and Practice, 18*, 84–88.

McConnell, S. C. (1984). Doctor of psychology degree: From hibernation to reality. *Professional Psychology: Research and Practice, 15*, 362–370.

McDermut, W., Miller, I. W., & Brown, R. A. (2001). The efficacy of group psychotherapy for depression: A meta-analysis and review of the empirical research. *Clinical Psychology: Science and Practice, 8*, 98–116.

McFall, R. M. (1991). Manifesto for a science of clinical psychology. *Clinical Psychologist, 44*, 75–88.

McFall, R. M. (2006). Doctoral training in clinical psychology. *Annual Review of Clinical Psychology, 2*, 21–49.

McGlynn, F. D. (2002). Systematic desensitization. In M. Hersen & W. Sledge (Eds.), *Encyclopedia of psychotherapy* (Vol. 2, pp. 755–764). San Diego, CA: Academic Press.

McGoldrick, M., Anderson, C., & Walsh, F. (Eds.). (1989). *Women in families*. New York: W. W. Norton.

McGoldrick, M., & Carter, B. (2011). Families transformed

by the divorce cycle: Reconstituted, multinuclear, recoupled, and remarried families. In M. McGoldrick, B. Carter, & N. Garcia-Preto (Eds.), *The expanded family life cycle: Individual, family, and social perspectives* (4th ed., pp. 317–335). Boston: Pearson.

McGoldrick, M., Carter, B., & Garcia-Preto, N. (2011). Overview: The life cycle in its changing context: Individual, family, and social perspectives. In M. McGoldrick, B. Carter, & N. Garcia-Preto (Eds.), *The expanded family life cycle: Individual, family, and social perspectives* (4th ed., pp. 1–19). Boston: Pearson.

McGoldrick, M., Gerson, R., & Petry, S. (2008). *Genograms: Assessment and intervention* (3rd ed.). New York: W. W. Norton.

McGoldrick, M., Giordano, J., & Garcia-Preto, N. (Eds.). (2005a). *Ethnicity and family therapy* (3rd ed.). New York: Guilford Press.

McGoldrick, M., Giordano, J., & Garcia-Preto, N. (2005b). Overview: Ethnicity and family therapy. In M. McGoldrick, J. Giordano, & N. Garcia-Preto (Eds.), *Ethnicity and family therapy* (3rd ed., pp. 1–40). New York: Guilford Press.

McGoldrick, M., & Walsh, F. (2011). Death, loss, and the family life cycle. In M. McGoldrick, B. Carter, & N. Garcia-Preto (Eds.), *The expanded family life cycle: Individual, family, and social perspectives* (4th ed., pp. 278–291). Boston: Pearson.

McGoldrick, M., & Watson, M. (2011). Siblings and the life cycle. In M. McGoldrick, B. Carter, & N. Garcia-Preto (Eds.), *The expanded family life cycle: Individual, family, and social perspectives* (4th ed., pp. 149–162). Boston: Pearson.

McGrady, A., Conron, P., Dickey, D., Garman, D., Farris, E., & Schumann-Brzezinski, C. (1992). The effects of biofeedback-assisted relaxation on cell-mediated immunity, cortisol, and white blood cell count in healthy adult subjects. *Journal of Behavioral Medicine, 13,* 343–354.

McGrath, R. (2004). Saving our psychosocial souls. *American Psychologist, 59,* 644–645.

McGrath, R. E. (2010). Prescriptive authority for psychologists. *Annual Review of Clinical Psychology, 6,* 21–47.

McGrath, R. E., Wiggins, J. G., Sammons, M. T., Levant, R. F., Brown, A., & Stock, W. (2004). Professional issues in pharmacotherapy for psychologists. *Professional Psychology: Research and Practice, 35,* 158–163.

McGuire, F. (1994). Army alpha and beta tests of intelligence. In R. J. Sternberg (Ed.), *Encyclopedia of intelligence* (Vol. 1, pp. 125–129.). New York: Macmillan.

McKitrick, D. S., & Li, S. T. (2008). Multicultural treatment. In M. Hersen & A. M. Gross (Eds.), *Handbook of clinical psychology* (Vol. 1, pp. 724–751). Hoboken, NJ: Wiley.

McMinn, M. R., Bearse, J., Heyne, L. K., Smithberger, A., & Erb, A. L. (2011). Technology and independent practice: Survey findings and implications. *Professional Psychology: Research and Practice, 42,* 176–184.

McNeil, D. E., Borum, R., Douglas, K. S., Hart, S. D., Lyon, D. R., Sullivan, L. E., et al. (2002). Risk assessment. In J. R. P. Ogloff (Ed.), *Taking psychology and law into the twenty-first century* (pp. 148–170). New York: Kluwer Academic/Plenum Press.

McNulty, J. L., Graham, J. R., Ben-Porath, Y. S., & Stein, L. A. R. (1997). Comparative validity of MMPI-2 scores of African American and Caucasian mental health center clients. *Psychological Assessment, 9,* 464–470.

McReynolds, P. (1997). *Lightner Witmer: His life and times.* Washington, DC: American Psychological Association.

McRoberts, C., Burlingame, G. M., & Hoag, M. J. (1998). Comparative efficacy of individual and group psychotherapy: A meta-analytic perspective. *Group Dynamics: Theory, Research, and Practice, 2,* 101–117.

Meagher, S. E., Grossman, S. D., & Millon, T. (2004). Treatment planning and outcome assessment in adults: The Millon Clinical Multiaxial Inventory-III (MCMI-III). In M. W. Maruish (Ed.), *The use of psychological testing for treatment planning and outcomes assessment* (3rd ed.,

Vol. 3, pp. 479–508). Mahwah, NJ: Erlbaum.

Meichenbaum, D. (1977). *Cognitive-behavior modification: An integrative approach.* New York: Plenum Press.

Meichenbaum, D. (1985). *Stress inoculation training.* New York: Pergamon Press.

Meichenbaum, D. (2008). Stress inoculation training. In W. T. O'Donohue & J. E. Fisher (Eds.), *Cognitive behavior therapy: Applying empirically supported techniques in your practice* (2nd ed., p. 529). Hoboken, NJ: Wiley.

Meichenbaum, D., & Goodman, J. (1971). Training impulsive children to talk to themselves: A means of developing self-control. *Journal of Abnormal Psychology, 77,* 115–126.

Mellins, C., Gatz, M., & Baker, L. (1996). Children's methods of coping with stress: A twin study of genetic and environmental influences. *Journal of Childhood Psychology and Psychiatry, 37,* 721–730.

Melton, G. B., Petrila, J., Poythress, N. G., Slobogin, C., Lyons, P. M., & Otto, R. K. (2007). *Psychological evaluations for the courts: A handbook for mental health professionals and lawyers* (3rd ed.). New York: Guilford Press.

Menos, J. (2005). Haitian families. In M. McGoldrick, J. Giordano, & N. Garcia-Preto (Eds.), *Ethnicity and family therapy* (3rd ed., pp. 127–137). New York: Guilford Press.

Mental health: Does therapy help? (1995, November). *Consumer Reports,* pp. 734–739.

Mermelstein, R., Cohen, S., Lichtenstein, E., Baer, J., & Karmarck, T. (1986). Social support and smoking cessation and maintenance. *Journal of Consulting and Clinical Psychology, 54,* 447–453.

Merrell, K. W. (2008). *Behavioral, social, and emotional assessment of children and adolescents* (3rd ed.). New York: Lawrence Erlbaum.

Merrell, K. W., & Harlacher, J. E. (2008). Behavior rating scales. In R. P. Archer & S. R. Smith (Eds.), *Personality assessment* (pp. 247–280). New York: Routledge.

Messer, S. B. (2004). Evidence-based practice: Beyond empirically supported treatments. *Professional Psychology: Research and Practice, 35,* 580–588.

Messer, S. B., & Wampold, B. E. (2002). Let's face facts: Common factors are more potent than specific therapy ingredients. *Clinical Psychology: Science and Practice, 9,* 21–25.

Meyer, G. J. (2004). The reliability and validity of the Rorschach and Thematic Apperception Test (TAT) compared to other psychological and medical procedures: An analysis of systematically gathered evidence. In M. J. Hilsenroth & D. L. Segal (Eds.), *Comprehensive handbook of psychological assessment: Personality assessment* (Vol. 2, pp. 315–342). Hoboken, NJ: Wiley.

Meyer, G. J., & Viglione, D. J. (2008). An introduction to Rorschach assessment. In R. P. Archer & S. R. Smith (Eds.), *Personality assessment* (pp. 281–336). New York: Routledge.

Meyer, R. G., & Weaver, C. M. (2006). *Law and mental health: A case-based approach.* New York: Guilford Press.

Mezzich, J. E., Kleinman, A., Fabrega, H., Jr., & Parron, D. L. (Eds.). (1996). *Culture and psychiatric diagnosis: A DSM-IV perspective.* Washington, DC: American Psychiatric Association.

Miller, C., & Williams, A. (2011). Ethical guidelines in research. In J. C. Thomas & M. Hersen (Eds.), *Understanding research in clinical and counseling psychology* (2nd ed., pp. 245–268). New York: Taylor & Francis.

Miller, D. J., & Thelen, M. H. (1986). Knowledge and beliefs about confidentiality in psychotherapy. *Professional Psychology: Research and Practice, 17,* 15–19.

Miller, J. G. (1946). Clinical psychology in the Veterans Administration. *American Psychologist, 1,* 181–189.

Miller, W. R., & Rollnick, S. (2002). *Motivational interviewing: Preparing people for change* (2nd ed.). New York: Guilford Press.

Miller, W. R., & Rose, G. R. (2009). Toward a theory of motivational interviewing. *American Psychologist, 64,* 527–537.

Millon, T., & Simonsen, E. (2010). A précis of psychopathological history. In T. Millon, R. F. Krueger, & E. Simonsen (Eds.), *Contemporary directions in psychopathology: Scientific foundations of the DSM-V and ICD-11* (pp. 3–52). New York: Guilford Press.

Minuchin, S. (1974). *Families and family therapy.* Cambridge, MA: Harvard University Press.

Mio, J. S., Barker-Hackett, L., & Tumambing, J. (2006). *Multicultural psychology: Understanding our diverse communities.* New York: McGraw-Hill.

Mio, J. S., Barker-Hackett, L., & Tumambing, J. S. (2009). *Multicultural psychology: Understanding our diverse communities* (2nd ed.). New York: McGraw-Hill.

Miranda, J., Azocar, F., Organista, K. C., Munoz, R. F., & Lieberman, A. (1996). Recruiting and retaining low-income Latinos in psychotherapy research. *Journal of Consulting and Clinical Psychology, 64,* 868–874.

Miranda, J., Bernal, G., Lau, A., Kohn, L., Hwang, W., & LaFromboise, T. (2005). State of the science on psychosocial interventions for ethnic minorities. *Annual Review of Clinical Psychology, 1,* 113–142.

Miranda, R., Jr., & Marx, B. P. (2003). Fees and financial arrangements. In W. O'Donohue & K. Ferguson (Eds.), *Handbook of professional ethics for psychologists: Issues, questions, and controversies* (pp. 135–145). Thousand Oaks, CA: Sage.

Mirkin, M. P., & Okun, B. F. (2005). Orthodox Jewish families. In M. McGoldrick, J. Giordano, & N. Garcia-Preto (Eds.), *Ethnicity and family therapy* (3rd ed., pp. 689–700). New York: Guilford Press.

Mirkin, M. P., Suyemoto, K. L., & Okun, B. F. (2005). *Psychotherapy with women: Exploring diverse contexts and identities.* New York: Guilford Press.

Mirsalimi, H. (2010). Perspectives of an Iranian psychologist practicing in America. *Psychotherapy: Theory, Research, Practice, Training, 47,* 151–161.

Mishara, A. L. & Schwartz, M. A. (2013). What does phenomenology contribute to the debate about DSM-5? In J. Paris & J. Phillips (Eds.), Making the DSM-5: Concepts and Controversies, pp. 125-142. New York: Springer.

Mobley, M. J. (2006). Psychotherapy with criminal offenders. In I. B. Weiner & A. K. Hess (Eds.), *The handbook of forensic psychology* (3rd ed., pp. 751–789). Hoboken, NJ: Wiley.

Mohr, D. C. (2009). Telemental health: Reflections on how to move the field forward. *Clinical Psychology: Science and Practice, 16,* 343–347.

Mojtabai, R., & Olfson, M. (2011). Proportion of antidepressants prescribed without a psychiatric diagnosis is growing. *Health Affairs, 30*(8), 1434-1442.

Mokdad, A. H., Marks, J. S., Stroup, D. F., & Gerberding, J. L. (2004). Actual causes of death in the United States, 2000. *Journal of the American Medical Association, 291,* 1238–1245.

Monahan, J. (2003). Violence risk assessment. In A. M. Goldstein (Ed.), *Handbook of psychology, Vol. 11: Forensic psychology* (pp. 527–540). Hoboken, NJ: Wiley.

Moore, B. E., & Fine, B. D. (Eds.). (1990). *Psychoanalytic terms and concepts.* New Haven, CT: American Psychoanalytic Association.

Moore, K. J., & Patterson, G. R. (2008). Parent training. In W. T. O'Donohue & J. E. Fisher (Eds.), *Cognitive behavior therapy: Applying empirically supported techniques in your practice* (2nd ed., pp. 383–389). Hoboken, NJ: Wiley.

Morales, E., & Norcross, J. C. (2010). Evidence-based practices with ethnic minorities: Strange bedfellows no more. *Journal of Clinical Psychology, 66,* 821–829.

Moran, M. (2013). Eating, sleep disorder criteria revised in DSM-5. *Psychiatric News, 48*(6), 14-15.

Moran, M. (2013, May 17). Section III of new manual looks to future. Jeste, D. V., Lieberman, J. A., Scully, J. H. Jr., & Kupfer, D. J. (2012, December 21). DSM crosses the finish line. Psychiatric News, DOI: 10.1176/appi.pn.2013.5b8

Moretti, R. J., & Rossini, E. D. (2004). The Thematic Apperception Test (TAT). In M. J. Hilsenroth & D. L. Segal (Eds.), *Comprehensive handbook of psychological assessment: Personality assessment* (Vol. 2, pp. 356–371). Hoboken, NJ: Wiley.

Morey, L. C., & Hopwood, C. J. (2008). Objective personality evaluation. In M. Hersen & A. M. Gross (Eds.), *Handbook of clinical psychology* (Vol. 1, pp. 451–474). Hoboken, NJ: Wiley.

Morgan, C. D., & Murray, H. A. (1935). A method for investigating fantasies: The Thematic Apperception Test. *Archives of Neurology and Psychiatry, 34,* 289–306.

Morgan, W. G. (1999). The 1943 images: Their origin and history. In L. Gieser & M. I. Stein (Eds.), *Evocative images: The Thematic Apperception Test and the art of projection* (pp. 65–83). Washington, DC: American Psychological Association.

Morrison, J. (2008). *The first interview* (3rd ed.). New York: Guilford Press.

Morrissette, P. J. (2004). The pain of helping: Psychological injury of helping professionals. New York: Brunner-Routledge.

Moyer, K. H., & Gross, A. (2011). Group designs. In J. C. Thomas & M. Hersen (Eds.), *Understanding research in clinical and counseling psychology* (2nd ed., pp. 155–179). New York: Taylor & Francis.

Moyers, T. B. (1998). Motivational interviewing. In G. P. Koocher, J. C. Norcross, & S. S. Hill, III (Eds.), *Psychologists' desk reference.* New York: Guilford Press.

Mulvaney-Day, N. E., Earl, T. R., Diaz-Linhart, Y., & Alegría, M. (2011). Preferences for relational style with mental health clinicians: A qualitative comparison of African American, Latino and non-Latino white patients. *Journal of Clinical Psychology, 67,* 31–44.

Munoz, R. F., & Mendelson, T. (2005). Toward evidence-based interventions for diverse populations: The San Francisco General Hospital prevention and treatment manuals. *Journal of Consulting and Clinical Psychology, 73,* 790–799.

Munsterberg, H. (1908). *On the witness stand.* New York: Doubleday.

Munsterberg, H. (1909). *Psychotherapy.* New York: Moffat, Yard.

Murphy, M. J., DeBernardo, C. R., & Shoemaker, W. E. (1998). Impact of managed care on independent practice and professional ethics: A survey of independent practitioners. *Professional Psychology: Research and Practice, 29,* 43–51.

Murray, H. A. (1943). *Thematic Apperception Test: Manual.* Cambridge, MA: Harvard University Press.

Muse, M., & McGrath, R. E. (2010). Training comparison among three professions prescribing psychoactive medications: Psychiatric nurse practitioners, physicians, and pharmacologically trained psychologists. *Journal of Clinical Psychology, 66,* 96–103.

Musser, P. H., & Murphy, C. M. (2009). Motivational interviewing with perpetrators of intimate partner abuse. *Journal of Clinical Psychology, 65,* 1218–1231.

Myers, D. G. (2013). *Psychology* (10th ed.). New York: Worth.

Naglieri, J. A., Drasgow, F., Schmit, M., Handler, L., Prifitera, A., Margolis, A., et al. (2004). Psychological testing on the Internet: New problems, old issues. *American Psychologist, 59,* 150–162.

Nagy, T. F. (2012). Competence. In S. J. Knapp (Ed.), *APA handbook of ethics in psychology, Vol. 1: Moral foundations and common themes* (pp. 147–174). Washington, DC: American Psychological Association.

Narrow, W. E., & Kuhl, E. A. (2011). Clinical significance and disorder thresholds in *DSM-5.* In D. A. Regier, W. E. Narrow, E. A. Kuhl, & D. J. Kupfer (Eds.), *The conceptual evolution of DSM-5* (pp. 147–162). Washington, DC: American Psychiatric Publishing.

Nasar, J. L., & Devlin, A. S. (2011). Impressions of psychotherapists' offices. *Journal of Counseling Psychology, 58,* 310–320.

Nathan, P. E. (2008). Foreword. In J. Hunsley & E. J. Mash (Eds.), *A guide to assessments that work* (pp. xvii–xix). New York: Oxford University Press.

Nathan, P. E., & Gorman, J. M. (Eds.). (1998). *A guide to treatments that work.* New York: Oxford University Press.

Nathan, P. E., & Gorman, J. M. (2002). Efficacy, effectiveness, and the clinical utility of psychotherapy research. In P. E. Nathan & J. M. Gorman (Eds.), *A guide to treatments that work* (2nd ed., pp. 643–654). New York: Oxford University Press.

Nathan, P. E., & Gorman, J. M. (Eds.). (2007). *A guide to treatments that work* (3rd ed.). New York: Oxford University Press.

Neimeyer, G. J., Rice, K. G., & Keilin, W. (2009). Internship placements: Similarities and differences between clinical and counseling psychology programs. *Training and Education in Professional Psychology, 3,* 47–52.

Neimeyer, G. J., & Taylor, J. M. (2011). Training systems and sites: Continuing education in psychology. In J. C. Norcross, G. R. Vandenbos, & D. K. Freedheim (Eds.), *History of psychotherapy: Continuity and change* (2nd ed., pp. 663–672). Washington, DC: American Psychological Association.

Nelson, E. L., & Bui, T. (2010). Rural telepsychology services for children and adolescents. *Journal of Clinical Psychology, 66,* 490–501.

Nelson, T. D., & Nelson, J. M. (2010). Evidence-based practice and the culture of adolescence. *Professional Psychology: Research and Practice, 41,* 305–311.

Newman, M. L., & Greenway, P. (1997). Therapeutic effects of providing MMPI-2 feedback to clients at a university counseling service: A collaborative approach. *Psychological Assessment, 9,* 122–131.

Nezu, A. M. (2010). Cultural influences on the process of conducting psychotherapy: Personal reflections of an ethnic minority psychologist. *Psychotherapy: Theory, Research, Practice, Training, 47,* 169–176.

Niaura, R., & Abrams, D. B. (2002). Smoking cessation progress, priorities and prospectus. *Journal of Consulting and Clinical Psychology, 70,* 494–509.

Nisbett, R. E., Aronson, J., Blair, C., Dickens, W., Flynn, J., Halpern, D. F., et al. (2012). Intelligence: New findings and theoretical developments. *American Psychologist, 67,* 130–159.

Nichols, D. S. (2001). *Essentials of MMPI-2 assessment.* New York: Wiley.

Nichols, M. P. (2010). *Family therapy: Concepts and methods* (9th ed.). Boston: Allyn & Bacon.

Nock, M. K., Holmberg, E. B., Photos, V. I., & Michel, B. D. (2007). Structured and semistructured diagnostic interviews. In M. Hersen & J. C. Thomas (Eds.), *Handbook of clinical interviewing with children* (pp. 30–49). Thousand Oaks, CA: Sage.

Norcross, J. C. (2000). Clinical versus counseling psychology: What's the diff? *Eye on Psi Chi, 5*(1), 20–22.

Norcross, J. C. (Ed.). (2002). *Psychotherapy relationships that work: Therapist contributions and responsiveness to patients.* New York: Oxford University Press.

Norcross, J. C. (2005). A primer on psychotherapy integration. In J. C. Norcross & M. R. Goldfried (Eds.), *Handbook of psychotherapy integration* (2nd ed., pp. 3–24). New York: Oxford University Press.

Norcross, J. C. (2010). The therapeutic relationship. In B. L. Duncan, S. D. Miller, B. E. Wampold, & M. A. Hubble (Eds.), *The heart and soul of change: Delivering what works in therapy* (2nd ed., pp. 113–142). Washington, DC: American Psychological Association.

Norcross, J. C., Beutler, L. E., & Levant, R. F. (2006). Prologue. In J. C. Norcross, L. E. Beutler, & R. F. Levant (Eds.), *Evidence-based practices in mental health: Debate and dialogue on the fundamental questions* (pp. 3–12). Washington, DC: American Psychological Association.

Norcross, J. C., & Castle, P. H. (2002). Appreciating the PsyD: The facts. *Eye on Psi Chi, 7,* 22–26.

Norcross, J. C., Freedheim, D. K., & Vandenbos, G. R. (2011). Into the future: Retrospect and prospect in psychotherapy. In J. C. Norcross, G. R. Vandenbos, & D. K. Freedheim (Eds.), *History of psychotherapy: Continuity and change* (2nd ed., pp. 743–760). Washington, DC: American Psychological Association.

Norcross, J. C., Hanych, J. M., & Terranova, R. D. (1996). Graduate study in psychology: 1992–1993. *American Psychologist, 51,* 631–643.

Norcross, J. C., Hedges, M., & Castle, P. H. (2002). Psychologists conducting psychotherapy in 2001: A study of the Division 29 membership. *Psychotherapy: Theory, Research, Practice, Training, 39,* 97–102.

Norcross, J. C., Hedges, M., & Prochaska, J. O. (2002). The face of 2010: A Delphi poll on the future of psychotherapy. *Professional Psychology, Research and Practice, 33,* 316–322.

Norcross, J. C., & Karpiak, C. P. (2012). Clinical psychologists in the 2010s: 50 years of the APA Division of Clinical Psychology. *Clinical Psychology: Science and Practice, 19,* 1–12.

Norcross, J. C., Karpiak, C. P., & Santoro, S. O. (2005). Clinical psychologists across the years: The division of clinical psychology from 1960 to 2003. *Journal of Clinical Psychology, 61,* 1467–1483.

Norcross, J. C., Kohout, J. L., & Wicherski, M. (2005). Graduate study in psychology: 1971–2004. *American Psychologist, 60,* 959–975.

Norcross, J. C., Krebs, P. M., & Prochaska, J. O. (2011). Stages of change. *Journal of Clinical Psychology, 67,* 143–154.

Norcross, J. C., & Lambert, M. J. (2011a). Evidence-based therapy relationships. In J. C. Norcross (Ed.), *Psychotherapy relationships that work: Evidence-based responsiveness* (2nd ed., pp. 3–21). New York: Oxford University Press.

Norcross, J. C., & Lambert, M. J. (2011b). Psychotherapy relationships that work II. *Psychotherapy, 48,* 4–8.

Norcross, J. C., & Newman, C. F. (1992). Psychotherapy integration: Setting the context. In J. C. Norcross & M. R. Goldfried (Eds.), *Handbook of psychotherapy integration* (pp. 3–45). New York: Basic Books.

Norcross, J. C., & Sayette, M. A. (2012). *Insider's guide to graduate programs in clinical and counseling psychology.* New York: Guilford Press.

Norcross, J. C., Sayette, M. A., Mayne, T. J., Karg, R. S., & Turkson, M. A. (1998). Selecting a doctoral program in professional psychology: Some comparisons among PhD counseling, PhD clinical, and PsyD clinical psychology programs. *Professional Psychology: Research and Practice, 29,* 609–614.

Norcross, J. C., & Wampold, B. E. (2011a). Evidence-based therapy relationships: Research conclusions and clinical practices. In J. C. Norcross (Ed.), *Psychotherapy relationships that work: Evidence-based responsiveness* (2nd ed., pp. 423–430). New York: Oxford University Press.

Norcross, J. C., & Wampold, B. E. (2011b). What works for whom: Tailoring psychotherapy to the person. *Journal of Clinical Psychology, 67,* 127–132.

O'Brien, W. H., & Tabaczynski, T. (2007). Unstructured interviewing. In M. Hersen & J. C. Thomas (Eds.), *Handbook of clinical interviewing with children* (pp. 16–29). Thousand Oaks, CA: Sage.

O'Connor, K. J. (2000). *The play therapy primer* (2nd ed.). New York: Wiley.

O'Connor v. Donaldson, 422 U.S. 563 (1975).

O'Donohue, W. (2009). A brief history of cognitive behavior therapy: Are there troubles ahead? In W. T. O'Donohue & J. E. Fisher (Eds.), *General principles and empirically supported techniques of cognitive behavior therapy* (pp. 1–14). Hoboken, NJ: Wiley.

Office of the Surgeon General, Army Service Forces. (1946). Nomenclature of psychiatric disorders and reactions. *Journal of Clinical Psychology, 2,* 289–296.

Ogloff, J. R. P. (Ed.). (2002). *Taking psychology and law into the twenty-first century.* New York: Kluwer Academic/Plenum Press.

Okagaki, L., & Sternberg, R. J. (1993). Parental beliefs and children's early school performance. *Child Development, 64*(1), 36–56.

Okasha, A. (2000). The impact of Arab culture on psychiatric ethics. In A. Okasha, J. Arboleda-Florez, & N. Sartorius (Eds.), *Ethics, culture, and psychiatry: International* perspectives (pp. 15–28). Washington, DC: American Psychiatric Press.

Okasha, A., Arboleda-Florez, J., & Sartorius, N. (Eds.). (2000). *Ethics, culture, and psychiatry: International perspectives.* Washington, DC: American Psychiatric Press.

Olatunji, B. O., & Feldman, G. (2008). Cognitive-behavioral therapy. In M. Hersen & A. M. Gross (Eds.), *Handbook of clinical psychology* (Vol. 1, pp. 551–584). Hoboken, NJ: Wiley.

Olkin, R., & Taliaferro, G. (2006). Evidence-based practices have ignored people with disabilities. In J. C. Norcross, L. E. Beutler, & R. F. Levant (Eds.), *Evidence-based practices in mental health: Debate and dialogue on the fundamental questions* (pp. 353–359). Washington, DC: American Psychological Association.

Ollendick, T. H., Alvarez, H. K., & Greene, R. W. (2004). Behavioral assessment: History of underlying concepts and methods. In S. N. Haynes & E. M. Heiby (Eds.), *Comprehensive handbook of psychological assessment: Behavioral assessment* (Vol. 3, pp. 19–34). Hoboken, NJ: Wiley.

Ollendick, T. H., & King, N. J. (2012). Evidence-based treatments for children and adolescents: Issues and commentary. In P. C. Kendall (Ed.), *Child and adolescent therapy: Cognitive-behavioral procedures* (4th ed., pp. 499–519). New York: Guilford Press.

Ollendick, T. H., & Pincus, D. (2008). Panic disorder in adolescents. In R. G. Steele, T. D. Elkin, & M. C. Roberts (Eds.), *Handbook of evidence-based therapies for children and adolescents: Bridging science and practice* (pp. 83–102). New York: Springer.

Ollendick, T. H., & Shirk, S. R. (2011). Clinical interventions with children and adolescents: Current status, future directions. In D. H. Barlow (Ed.), *The Oxford handbook of clinical psychology* (pp. 762–788). New York: Oxford University Press.

Organista, P. B., Marin, G., & Chun, K. M. (2010). *The psychology of ethnic groups in the United States.* Thousand Oaks, CA: Sage.

Orlinsky, D. E. (2010). Foreword. In B. L. Duncan, S. D. Miller, B. E. Wampold, & M. A. Hubble (Eds.), *The heart and soul of change: Delivering what works in therapy* (2nd ed., pp. xix–xxv). Washington, DC: American Psychological Association.

Orlinsky, D. E., & Howard, K. I. (1995). Unity and diversity among psychotherapies: A comparative perspective. In B. Bongar & L. E. Beutler (Eds.), *Comprehensive textbook of psychotherapy: Theory and practice* (pp. 3–23). New York: Oxford University Press.

Ormont, L. R. (1992). *The group therapy experience: From theory to practice.* New York: St. Martin's Press.

Ornstein, R. M., Rosen, D. S., Mammel, K. A., Callahan, S. T.,

Forman, S., Jay, M. S., ... & Walsh, B. T. (2013). Distribution of Eating Disorders in Children and Adolescents Using the Proposed DSM-5 Criteria for Feeding and Eating Disorders. *Journal of Adolescent Health.*

Ortiz, S. O., & Dynda, A. M. (2005). Use of intelligence tests with culturally and linguistically diverse populations. In D. P. Flanagan & P. L. Harrison (Eds.), *Contemporary intellectual assessment: Theories, tests, and issues* (2nd ed., pp. 545–556). New York: Guilford Press.

Ostafin, B. D., & Marlatt, G. A. (2008). Surfing the urge: Experiential acceptance moderates the relation between automatic alcohol motivation and hazardous drinking. *Journal of Social and Clinical Psychology, 27,* 426–440.

Othmer, E. O., & Othmer, S. C. (1994). *The clinical interview using DSM-IV: Vol. 1. Fundamentals.* Washington, DC: American Psychiatric Press.

Otto, R. K., Buffington-Vollum, J. K., & Edens, J. F. (2003). Child custody evaluation. In A. M. Goldstein (Ed.), *Handbook of psychology, Vol. 11: Forensic psychology* (pp. 179–208). Hoboken, NJ: Wiley.

Otto, R. K., & Heilbrun, K. (2002). The practice of forensic psychology: A look toward the future in light of the past. *American Psychologist, 57,* 5–18.

Owen, J. J., Tao, K., Leach, M. M., & Rodolfa, E.

(2011). Clients' perceptions of their psychotherapists' multicultural orientation. *Psychotherapy, 48*, 274–282.

Paradis, C. M., Cukor, D., & Friedman, S. (2006). Cognitive-behavioral therapy with Orthodox Jews. In P. A. Hays & G. Y. Iwamasa (Eds.), *Culturally responsive cognitive-behavioral therapy: Assessment, practice, and supervision* (pp. 161–175). Washington, DC: American Psychological Association.

Pargament, K. I. (2007). *Spiritually integrated psychotherapy: Understanding and addressing the sacred.* New York: Guilford Press.

Parham v. JR, 99 S. Ct. 2493 (1979).

Paris, J. (2009). The treatment of borderline personality disorder: Implications of research on diagnosis, etiology, and outcome. *Annual Review of Clinical Psychology, 5*, 277–290.

Paris, J. (2013a). The ideology behind DSM-5. In J. Paris & J. Phillips (Eds.), Making the DSM-5: Concepts and Controversies, pp. 39-44. New York: Springer.

Paris, J. (2013b). Preface. In J. Paris & J. Phillips (Eds.), Making the DSM-5: Concepts and Controversies, pp. v-vi. New York: Springer.

Paris, J. (2013c). The Intelligent Clinician's Guide to DSM-5. New York: Oxford University Press.

Park-Taylor, J., Ventura, A. B., & Ng, V. (2010). Multicultural counseling and assessment with children. In J. G. Ponterotto, J. M. Casas, L. A. Suzuki, & C. M. Alexander (Eds.), *Handbook of multicultural counseling* (3rd ed., pp. 621–635). Thousand Oaks, CA: Sage.

Parker, G. (2013), Opening Pandora's box: How DSM-5 is coming to grief. *Acta Psychiatrica Scandinavica*, 128: 88–91. doi: 10.1111/acps.12110

Parry, P., Furber, G., & Allison, S. (2009). The paediatric bipolar hypothesis: The view from Australia and New Zealand. *Child and Adolescent Mental Health, 14*, 140–147.

Paul, G. L. (2007). Psychotherapy outcome can be studied scientifically. In S. O. Lilienfeld & W. T. O'Donohue (Eds.), *The great ideas of clinical science: 17 principles that every mental health professional should understand* (pp. 119–147). New York: Routledge.

Pawlow, L., & Jones, G. (2002). The impact of abbreviated progressive muscle relaxation on salivary cortisol. *Biological Psychology, 60*, 1–16.

Pawlow, L., & Jones, G. (2005). The impact of abbreviated progressive muscle relaxation on salivary cortisol and salivary immunoglobulin A. *Applied Psychophysiology and Biofeedback, 30*, 375–387.

Pawlow, L., O'Neil, P., White, M., & Byrne, T. (2005). Findings and outcomes of psychological evaluations of gastric bypass applicants. *Surgery for Obesity and Related Diseases, 1*, 523–529.

Pedersen, P. (1990). The multicultural perspective as a fourth force in counseling. *Journal of Mental Health Counseling, 12,* 93–95.

Pedersen, P. (1999). *Multiculturalism as a fourth force.* Philadelphia: Brunner/Mazel.

Pedersen, P. B. (2008). Ethics, competence, and professional issues in cross-cultural counseling. In P. B. Pedersen, J. G. Draguns, W. J. Lonner, & J. E. Trimble (Eds.), *Counseling across cultures* (6th ed., pp. 5–20). Thousand Oaks, CA: Sage.

Pelco, L. E., Ward, S. B., Coleman, L., & Young, J. (2009). Teacher ratings of three psychological report styles. *Training and Education in Professional Psychology, 3*, 19–27.

Pennebaker, J. (1990). *Opening up: The healing power of confiding in others.* New York: William Morrow.

Pennebaker, J. W., Kiecolt-Glaser, J., & Glaser, R. (1988). Disclosure of traumas and immune function: Health implications for psychotherapy. *Journal of Consulting and Clinical Psychology, 56*, 239–245.

Perls, F. S. (1969). *Gestalt therapy verbatim.* Moab, UT: Real People Press.

Perry, K. M., & Boccaccini, M. T. (2009). Specialized training in APA-accredited clinical psychology doctoral programs: Findings from a review of program websites. *Clinical Psychology: Science and Practice, 16*, 348–359.

Persons, J. B., & Fresco, D. M. (2008). Adult depression. In J. Hunsley & E. J. Mash (Eds.), *A guide to assessments that work* (pp. 96–120). New York: Oxford University Press.

Peter, M. I. (1998). Psychology, AIDS, and ethics: A discussion of selected practice issues. In R. M. Anderson, Jr., T. L. Needles, & H. V. Hall (Eds.), *Avoiding ethical misconduct in psychology specialty areas* (pp. 159–165). Springfield, IL: Charles C. Thomas.

Peterson, C., & Seligman, M. E. P. (2004). *Character strengths and virtues: A handbook and classification*. Washington, DC: American Psychological Association.

Peterson, R. L., Peterson, D. R., Abrams, J. C., Stricker, G., & Ducheny, K. (2010). The National Council of Schools and Programs of Professional Psychology: Educational model 2009. In M. B. Kenkel & R. L. Peterson (Eds.), *Competency-based education for professional psychology* (pp. 13–42). Washington, DC: American Psychological Association.

Petry, N. M., & O'Brien, C. P. (2013). Internet gaming disorder and the DSM-5. *Addiction, 108,* 1186-1187.

Phillips, J. (2013). The conceptual status of DSM-5 diagnoses. In J. Paris & J. Phillips (Eds.), Making the DSM-5: Concepts and Controversies, pp. 159-175. New York: Springer.

Photos, V. I., Michel, B. D., & Nock, M. K. (2008). Single-case research. In M. Hersen & A. M. Gross (Eds.), *Handbook of clinical psychology* (Vol. 1, pp. 224–245). Hoboken, NJ: Wiley.

Pierre, J. M. (2013). Overdiagnosis, underdiagnosis, synthesis: A dialectic for psychiatry and the DSM. In J. Paris & J. Phillips (Eds.), Making the DSM-5: Concepts and Controversies, pp. 105-124. New York: Springer.

Pieterse, A. L., & Miller, M. J. (2010). Current considerations in the assessment of adults. In J. G. Ponterotto, J. M. Casas, L. A. Suzuki, & C. M. Alexander (Eds.), *Handbook of multicultural counseling* (3rd ed., pp. 649–666). Thousand Oaks, CA: Sage.

Pike, K. L. (1967). *Language in relation to a unified theory of structure of human behavior* (2nd ed.). The Hague, Netherlands: Mouton.

Pilgrim, D., & Bentall, R. (1999). The medicalisation of misery: A critical realist analysis of the concept of depression. *Journal of Mental Health, 8,* 261–274.

Pina-Camacho, L., Villero, S., Boada, L., Fraguas, D., Janssen, J., Mayoral, M., ... & Parellada, M. (2013). Structural magnetic resonance imaging data do not help support DSM-5 autism spectrum disorder category. *Research in Autism Spectrum Disorders, 7*(2), 333–343.

Pincus, D. B., Chase, R. M., Chow, C., Weiner, C. L., & Pian, J. (2011). Integrating play into cognitive-behavioral therapy for child anxiety disorders. In S. W. Russ & L. N. Niec (Eds.), *Play in clinical practice: Evidence-based approaches* (pp. 218–235). New York: Guilford Press.

Pines, A., & Aronson, E. (1988). *Career burnout: Causes and cures* (2nd ed.). New York: Free Press.

Pittner, M., Houston, B., & Spiridigliozzi, G. (1983). Control over stress, type A behavior pattern, and response to stress. *Journal of Personality and Social Psychology, 44,* 627–637.

Poling, A., Ehrhardt, K. E., & Ervin, R. A. (2002). Positive punishment. In M. Hersen & W. Sledge (Eds.), *Encyclopedia of psychotherapy* (Vol. 2, pp. 359–366). San Diego, CA: Academic Press.

Poling, A., Ehrhardt, K. E., & Jennings, R. L. (2002). Extinction. In M. Hersen & W. Sledge (Eds.), *Encyclopedia of psychotherapy* (Vol. 1, pp. 769–775). San Diego, CA: Academic Press.

Pomerantz, A. M. (2000). What if prospective clients knew how managed care impacts psychologists' practice and ethics? An exploratory study. *Ethics & Behavior, 10,* 159–171.

Pomerantz, A. M. (2005). Increasingly informed consent: Discussing distinct aspects of psychotherapy at different points in time. *Ethics & Behavior, 15,* 351–360.

Pomerantz, A. M. (2012a). Ethical? Toward whom? *American Psychologist, 67*(4), 324–325.

Pomerantz, A. M. (2012b). Informed consent to

psychotherapy (empowered collaboration). In S. J. Knapp (Ed.), *APA handbook of ethics in psychology, Vol. 1: Moral foundations and common themes* (pp. 311–332). Washington, DC: American Psychological Association.

Pomerantz, A. M., & Handelsman, M. M. (2004). Informed consent revisited: An updated written question format. *Professional Psychology: Research and Practice, 35,* 201–205.

Pomerantz, A. M., & Pettibone, J. C. (2005). The influence of client characteristics on psychologists' ethical beliefs: An empirical investigation. *Journal of Clinical Psychology, 61,* 517–528.

Pomerantz, A. M., & Segrist, D. J. (2006). The influence of payment method on psychologists' diagnostic decisions regarding minimally impaired clients. *Ethics & Behavior, 16,* 253–263.

Pomerantz, A. M., & Sullivan, B. F. (2006). Ethical issues in testing. In N. J. Salkind (Ed.), *Encyclopedia of measurement and statistics* (Vol. 1, pp. 318–321). Thousand Oaks, CA: Sage.

Pope, K. S. (1994). *Sexual involvement with therapists: Patient assessment, subsequent therapy, forensics.* Washington, DC: American Psychological Association.

Pope, K. S. (2011). Ethical issues in clinical psychology. In D. H. Barlow (Ed.), *The Oxford handbook of clinical psychology* (pp. 184–209). New York: Oxford University Press.

Pope, K. S., & Gutheil, T. G. (2009). Psychologists abandon the Nuremberg ethic: Concerns for detainee interrogations. *International Journal of Law and Psychiatry, 32,* 161–166.

Pope, K. S., Tabachnick, B. G., & Keith-Spiegel, P. (1987). Ethics of practice: The beliefs and behaviors of psychologists as therapists. *American Psychologist, 42,* 993–1006.

Pope, K. S., & Vasquez, M. J. T. (2011). *Ethics in psychotherapy and counseling: A practical guide* (4th ed.). Hoboken, NJ: Wiley.

Porter, D. (2013). Establishing normative validity for scientific psychiatric nosology: The significance of integrating patient perspectives. In J. Paris & J. Phillips (Eds.), *Making the DSM-5: Concepts and Controversies,* (pp. 63-74). New York: Springer.

Porter, R., Mulder, R., & Lacey, C. (2013). DSM-5 and the elimination of the major depression bereavement exclusion. *Australian and New Zealand Journal of Psychiatry, 47*(4), 391-393.

Poston, J. M., & Hanson, W. E. (2010). Meta-analysis of psychological assessment as a therapeutic intervention. *Psychological Assessment, 22,* 203–212.

Powers, S. W. (2002). Behavior therapy with children. In C. E. Walker & M. C. Roberts (Eds.), *Handbook of child clinical psychology* (3rd ed., pp. 825–839). New York: Wiley.

Pretzer, J., & Beck, J. S. (2004). Cognitive therapy of personality disorders: Twenty years of progress. In R. L. Leahy (Ed.), *Contemporary cognitive therapy: Theory, research, and practice* (pp. 299–318). New York: Guilford Press.

Prochaska, J. O., & Norcross, J. C. (2010). *Systems of psychotherapy: A transtheoretical analysis* (7th ed.). Belmont, CA: Brooks/Cole.

Pull, C. B. (2013). Too few or too many? Reactions to removing versus retaining specific personality disorders in DSM-5. *Current opinion in psychiatry, 26*(1), 73-78.

Purcell, D. W., Swann, S., & Herbert, S. E. (2003). Sexual orientation and professional ethics. In W. O'Donohue & K. Ferguson (Eds.), *Handbook of professional ethics for psychologists: Issues, questions, and controversies* (pp. 319–342). Thousand Oaks, CA: Sage.

Qualls, S. H. (2003). Psychotherapy with older clients. In D. R. Atkinson & G. Hackett (Eds.), *Counseling diverse populations* (3rd ed., pp. 240–254). Boston: McGraw-Hill.

Quilty, L. C., Zhang, K. A., & Bagby, R. M. (2010). The latent symptom structure of the Beck Depression Inventory-II in outpatients with major depression. *Psychological Assessment, 22,* 603–608.

Ragusea, A. S. (2012). The more things change, the more they stay the same: Ethical issues in the provision of telehealth. In S. J. Knapp (Ed.), *APA handbook of ethics in psychology, Vol. 2: Practice, teaching, and research* (pp. 183–198). Washington, DC: American Psychological Association.

Ragusea, A. S., & VandeCreek, L. (2003). Suggestions for the ethical practice of online psychotherapy. *Psychotherapy: Theory, Research, Practice, Training, 40,* 94–102.

Raiford, S. E., Coalson, D. L., Saklofske, D. H., & Weiss, L. G. (2010). Practical issues in WAIS-IV administration and scoring. In L. G. Weiss, D. H. Saklofske, D. Coalson, & S. E. Raiford (Eds.), *WAIS-IV clinical use and interpretation: Scientist-practitioner perspectives* (pp. 25–60). London: Elsevier.

Rainer, J. P. (2010). The road much less travelled: Treating rural and isolated clients. *Journal of Clinical Psychology, 66,* 475–478.

Randolph, C. (1998). *Repeatable Battery for the Assessment of Neuropsychological Status manual.* San Antonio, TX: Psychological Corporation.

Rapee, R. M., Schniering, C. A., & Hudson, J. L. (2009). Anxiety disorders during childhood and adolescence: Origins and treatment. *Annual Review of Clinical Psychology, 5,* 311–341.

Rashid, T. (2009). Positive interventions in clinical practice. *Journal of Clinical Psychology, 65,* 461–466.

Rashid, T., & Ostermann, R. F. (2009). Strength-based assessment in clinical practice. *Journal of Clinical Psychology, 65,* 488–498.

Ray, D. C. (2006). Evidence-based play therapy. In C. E. Shaefer & H. G. Kaduson (Eds.), *Contemporary play therapy* (pp. 136–157). New York: Guilford Press.

Rees, C. J., & Metcalfe, B. (2003). The faking of personality questionnaire results: Who's kidding whom? *Journal of Managerial Psychology, 18,* 156–165.

Reger, M. A., & Gahm, G. A. (2009). A meta-analysis of the effects of Internet- and computer-based cognitive-behavioral treatments for anxiety. *Journal of Clinical Psychology, 65,* 53–75.

Regier, D. A., Narrow, W. E., Clarke, D. E., Kraemer, H. C., Kuramoto, S. J., Kuhl, E. A., & Kupfer, D. J. (2013). DSM-5 Field Trials in the United States and Canada, part II: test-retest reliability of selected categorical diagnoses. *American Journal of Psychiatry, 170*(1), 59–70.

Regier, D. A., Kuhl, E. A., & Kupfer, D. J. (2013). The DSM-5: Classification and criteria changes. *World Psychiatry, 12*(2), 92-98.

Rehm, L. P., & Lipkins, R. H. (2006). The examination for professional practice in psychology. In T. J. Vaughn (Ed.), *Psychology licensure and certification* (pp. 39–53). Washington, DC: American Psychological Association.

Reich, L., & Kolbasovsky, A. (2006). *Mental health provider's guide to managed care.* New York: W. W. Norton.

Reisman, J. M. (1991). *A history of clinical psychology* (2nd ed.). New York: Hemisphere.

Reitan, R. M., & Wolfson, D. (2004). Theoretical, methodological, and validational bases of the Halstead-Reitan Neuropsychological Test Battery. In M. Hersen (Ed.), *Comprehensive handbook of psychological assessment* (Vol. 1, pp. 105–132). New York: Wiley.

Resnick, R. J., & Norcross, J. C. (2002). Prescription privileges for psychologists: Scared to death? *Clinical Psychology: Science and Practice, 9,* 270–274.

Retzlaff, P. D., & Dunn, T. (2003). The Millon Clinical Multiaxial Inventory-III. In L. E. Beutler & G. Groth-Marnat (Eds.), *Integrative assessment of adult personality* (2nd ed., pp. 192–226). New York: Guilford Press.

Richard, D. C. S., & Lauterbach, D. (2003). Computers in the training and practice of behavioral assessment. In S. N. Haynes & E. M. Heiby (Eds.), *Comprehensive handbook of psychological assessment: Behavioral assessment* (Vol. 3, pp. 222–245). Hoboken, NJ: Wiley.

Richards, D. F. (2003). The central role of informed consent in ethical treatment and research with children. In W. O'Donohue & K. Ferguson (Eds.), *Handbook of professional ethics for* psychologists: Issues, questions, and controversies (pp. 377–389). Thousand Oaks, CA: Sage.

Richardson, L. K., Frueh, B. C., Grubaugh, A. L., Egede, L., & Elhai, J. D. (2009). Current directions in videoconferencing tele-mental health research. *Clinical Psychology: Science and Practice, 16*, 323–338.

Ridley, C. R., Ethington, L. L., & Heppner, P. P. (2008). Cultural confrontation: A skill of advanced cultural empathy. In P. B. Pedersen, J. G. Draguns, W. J. Lonner, & J. E. Trimble (Eds.), *Counseling across cultures* (6th ed., pp. 377–393). Thousand Oaks, CA: Sage.

Ridley, C. R., Tracy, M. L., Pruitt-Stephens, L., Wimsatt, M. K., & Beard, J. (2008). Multicultural assessment validity: The preeminent ethical issue in psychological assessment. In L. A. Suzuki & J. G. Ponterotto (Eds.), *Handbook of multicultural assessment: Clinical, psychological, and educational applications* (3rd ed., pp. 22–33). Hoboken, NJ: Wiley.

Ritchie, M. H. (1994). Cultural and gender biases in definitions of mental and emotional health and illness. *Counselor Education and Supervision, 33,* 344–348.

Rivera, L. M. (2008). Acculturation and multicultural assessment: Issues, trends, and practice. In L. A. Suzuki & J. G. Ponterotto (Eds.), *Handbook of multicultural assessment: Clinical, psychological, and educational applications* (3rd ed., pp. 73–91). Hoboken, NJ: Wiley.

Rivera, L. M. (2010). Acculturation. In J. G. Ponterotto, J. M. Casas, L. A. Suzuki, & C. M. Alexander (Eds.), *Handbook of multicultural counseling* (3rd ed., pp. 331–341). Thousand Oaks, CA: Sage.

Roberts, S. (2004). *Who we are now: The changing face of America in the 21st century.* New York: Times Books.

Robiner, W. N., Bearman, D. L., Berman, M., Grove, W. M., Colon, E., Armstrong, J., et al. (2002). Prescriptive authority for psychologists: A looming health hazard? *Clinical Psychology: Science and Practice, 9,* 231–248.

Robinson, L., Berman, J., & Neimeyer, R. (1990). Psychotherapy for the treatment of depression: A comprehensive review of controlled outcome research. *Psychological Bulletin, 108,* 30–49.

Robinson, P. (2008). Putting it on the street: Homework in cognitive behavioral therapy. In W. T. O'Donohue & J. E. Fisher (Eds.), *Cognitive behavior therapy: Applying empirically supported techniques in your practice* (2nd ed., pp. 260–271). Hoboken, NJ: Wiley.

Robinson-Wood, T. L. (2009). Extending cultural understanding beyond race and ethnicity. In C. C. Lee, D. A. Burnhill, A. L. Butler, C. P. Hipolito-Delgado, M. Humphrey, O. Munoz, et al. (Eds.), *Elements of culture in counseling* (pp. 31–41). Upper Saddle River, NJ: Pearson.

Robles, R. (2006). Culturally competent play therapy with the Mexican American child and family. In C. E. Shaefer & H. G. Kaduson (Eds.), *Contemporary play therapy* (pp. 238–269). New York: Guilford Press.

Roemer, L., & Orsillo, S. M. (2009). *Mindfulness- and acceptance-based behavioral therapies in practice.* New York: Guilford Press.

Roesch, R., Zapf, P. A., & Hart, S. D. (2009). *Forensic psychology and law.* Hoboken, NJ: Wiley.

Roffman, J. L., Marci, C. D., Glick, D. M., Dougherty, D. D., & Rauch, S. L. (2005). Neuroimaging and the functional neuroanatomy of psychotherapy. *Psychological Medicine, 35,* 1385–1398.

Rogers, C. R. (1942). The use of electrically recorded interviews in improving psychotherapeutic techniques. *American Journal of Orthopsychiatry, 12,* 429–434.

Rogers, C. R. (1957). The necessary and sufficient conditions of therapeutic personality change. *Journal of Consulting Psychology, 21,* 95–103.

Rogers, C. R. (1959). Client-centered therapy. In S. Arieti (Ed.), *American handbook of psychiatry* (Vol. 3). New York: Basic Books.

Rogers, C. R. (1961). *On becoming a person.* Boston: Houghton-Mifflin.

Rogers, C. R. (1980). *A way of being.* Boston: Houghton-Mifflin.

Rogers, C. R. (1986). Reflection of feelings and transference. *Person-Centered Review, 1,* 375–377.

Rolland, J. S., & Walsh, F. (2009). Family systems theory and practice. In G. O. Gabbard (Ed.), *Textbook of psychotherapeutic treatments* (pp. 499–531). Washington, DC: American Psychiatric Publishing.

Rorschach, H. (1921). *Psychodiagnostik.* Bern, Switzerland: Huber.

Rose, T., Kaser-Boyd, N., & Maloney, M. P. (2001). *Essentials of Rorschach assessment.* New York: Wiley.

Rosen, E. J., & Weltman, S. F. (2005). Jewish families: An overview. In M. McGoldrick, J. Giordano, & N. Garcia-Preto (Eds.), *Ethnicity and family therapy* (3rd ed., pp. 667–679). New York: Guilford Press.

Rosenfeld, G. W. (2009). *Beyond evidence-based psychotherapy: Fostering the eight sources of change in child and adolescent treatment.* New York: Routledge.

Rosenzweig, S. (1936). Some implicit common factors in diverse methods of psychotherapy. *American Journal of Orthopsychiatry, 6,* 422–425.

Rosqvist, J., Thomas, J. C., & Truax, P. (2011). Effectiveness versus efficacy studies. In J. C. Thomas & M. Hersen (Eds.), Understanding research in clinical and counseling psychology (2nd ed., pp. 319–354). New York: Taylor & Francis.

Roth, A., & Fonagy, P. (2005). *What works for whom? A critical review of psychotherapy research* (2nd ed.). New York: Guilford Press.

Roth, D. A., Eng, W., & Heimberg, R. G. (2002). Cognitive behavior therapy. In M. Hersen & W. Sledge (Eds.), *Encyclopedia of psychotherapy* (Vol. 1, pp. 451–458). San Diego: Academic Press.

Rothbaum, P. A., Bernstein, D. M., Haller, O., Phelps, R., & Kohout, J. (1998). New Jersey psychologists' report on managed mental health care. *Professional Psychology: Research and Practice, 29,* 37–42.

Rothstein, H. R., Haller, O. L., & Bernstein, D. (2000). Remarks and reflections on managed care: Analysis of comments by New Jersey psychologists. *Journal of Psychotherapy in Independent Practice, 1,* 73–82.

Rotter, J. B., & Rafferty, J. E. (1950). *The Rotter incomplete sentences blank manual: College form.* New York: Psychological Corporation.

Routh, D. K. (1996). Lightner Witmer and the first 100 years of clinical psychology. *American Psychologist, 51,* 244–247.

Routh, D. K. (2011). A history of clinical psychology. In D. H. Barlow (Ed.), *The Oxford handbook of clinical psychology* (pp. 23–33). New York: Oxford University Press.

Rowa, K., Antony, M. M., & Swinson, R. P. (2007). Exposure and response prevention. In M. M. Antony, C. Purdon, & L. J. Summerfeldt (Eds.), *Psychological treatment of obsessive compulsive disorders: Fundamentals and beyond* (pp. 79–109). Washington, DC: American Psychological Association.

Rubak, S., Sandbæk, A., Lauritzen, T., & Christensen, B. (2005). Motivational interviewing: A systematic review and meta-analysis. *British Journal of General Practice, 55,* 305–312.

Rummell, C. M., & Joyce, N. R. (2010). "So wat do u want to wrk on 2day?": The ethical implications of online counseling. *Ethics & Behavior, 20,* 482–496.

Russ, S. W., & Freedheim, D. K. (2002). Psychotherapy with children. In C. E. Walker & M. C. Roberts (Eds.), *Handbook of child clinical psychology* (3rd ed., pp. 840–859). New York: Wiley.

Sadler, J. Z. (2013). Considering the economy of DSM alternatives. In J. Paris & J. Phillips (Eds.), *Making the DSM-5: Concepts and Controversies,* (pp. 21-38). New York: Springer.

Safran, J. D., Abreu, I., Ogilvie, J., & DeMaria, A. (2011). Does psychotherapy research influence the clinical practice of researcher–clinicians? *Clinical Psychology: Science and Practice, 18,* 357–371.

Sageman, M. (2003). Three types of skills for effective forensic psychological assessments. *Assessment, 10,* 321–328.

Saks, E. R., Jeste, D. V., Granholm, B. W., Palmer, B. W., & Schneiderman, L. (2002). Ethical issues in psychosocial interventions research involving controls. *Ethics & Behavior, 12,* 87–101.

Sales, B. D., & Shuman, D. W. (2005). *Experts in court: Reconciling law, science, and professional knowledge.* Washington, DC: American Psychological Association.

Salter, D. S., & Salter, B. R. (2012). Competence with diverse populations. In S. J. Knapp (Ed.), *APA handbook of ethics in psychology, Vol. 1: Moral foundations and common themes* (pp. 217–240). Washington, DC: American Psychological Association.

Sammons, M. T. (2011). Treatment modalities: Pharmacotherapy. In J. C. Norcross, G. R. Vandenbos, & D. K. Freedheim (Eds.), *History of psychotherapy: Continuity and change* (2nd ed., pp. 516–532). Washington, DC: American Psychological Association.

Sammons, M. T., Sexton, J. L., & Meredith, J. M. (1996). Basic science training in psychopharmacology: How much is enough? *American Psychologist, 51,* 230–234.

Sandell, R. (2012). Research on outcomes of psychoanalysis and psychoanalysis-derived psychotherapies. In G. O. Gabbard, B. E. Litowitz, & P. Williams (Eds.), *Textbook of psychoanalysis* (2nd ed., pp. 385–404). Washington,

DC: American Psychiatric Publishing.

Sanderson, W. C. (2003). Why empirically supported psychological treatments are important. *Behavior Modification, 27,* 290–299.

Sandler, J., & Freud, A. (1985). *The analysis of defense: The ego and the mechanisms of defense revisited.* New York: International Universities Press.

Sayers, S. T., Riegel, B., Pawlowski, S., Coyne, J. C., & Samaha, F. F. (2008). Social support and self-care of patients with heart failure. *Annals of Behavioral Medicine, 35,* 70–79.

Schaefer, C. E., & Briesmeister, J. M. (Eds.). (1989). *Handbook of parent training: Parents as co-therapists for children's behavior problems.* New York: Wiley.

Schaffer, J. B., DeMers, S. T., & Rodolfa, E. (2011). Training systems and sites: Licensing and credentialing. In J. C. Norcross, G. R. Vandenbos, & D. K. Freedheim (Eds.), *History of psychotherapy: Continuity and change* (2nd ed., pp. 651–662). Washington, DC: American Psychological Association.

Schank, J. A., Helbok, C. M., Haldeman, D. C., & Gallardo, M. E. (2010). Challenges and benefits of ethical small-community practice. *Professional Psychology: Research and Practice, 41,* 502–510.

Schank, J. A., & Skovholt, T. M. (1997). Dual-relationship dilemmas of rural and small-community psychologists.

Professional Psychology: Research and Practice, 28, 44–49.

Schank, J. A., & Skovholt, T. M. (2006). *Ethical practice in small communities: Challenges and rewards for psychologists.* Washington, DC: American Psychological Association.

Schank, J., Slater, R., Banerjee-Stevens, D., & Skovholt, T. M. (2003). Ethics of multiple and overlapping relationships. In W. O'Donohue & K. Ferguson (Eds.), *Handbook of professional ethics for psychologists: Issues, questions, and controversies* (pp. 181–193). Thousand Oaks, CA: Sage.

Scheier, M., & Bridges, M. (1995). Person variables and health: Personality predispositions and acute psychological states as shared determinants for disease. *Psychosomatic Medicine, 57,* 255–268.

Schneider, K. J., & Krug, O. T. (2010). *Existential-humanistic therapy.* Washington, DC: American Psychological Association.

Schneiderman, N., & Siegel, S. D. (2007). Mental and physical health influence each other. In S. O. Lilienfeld & W. T. O'Donohue (Eds.), *The great ideas of clinical science: 17 principles that every mental health professional should understand* (pp. 329–346). New York: Routledge.

Schroeder, C. S., & Gordon, B. N. (2002). *Assessment and treatment of childhood problems: A clinician's guide* (2nd ed.). New York: Guilford Press.

Schultz, D. P., & Schultz, S. E. (2011). *A history of modern psychology* (10th ed.). Belmont, CA: Wadsworth.

Scotti, J. R., Morris, T. L., Stacom, E. E., & Cohen, S. H. (2011). Validity: Controlling and balancing interrelated threats. In J. C. Thomas & M. Hersen (Eds.), *Understanding research in clinical and counseling psychology* (2nd ed., pp. 87–125). New York: Taylor & Francis.

Scrivner, E. (2006). Psychology and law enforcement. In I. B. Weiner & A. K. Hess (Eds.), *Handbook of forensic psychology* (3rd ed., pp. 534–551). Hoboken, NJ: Wiley.

Seligman, M. E. P. (1995). The effectiveness of psychotherapy: The *Consumer Reports* survey. *American Psychologist, 50,* 965–974.

Seligman, M. E. P. (2003). Foreword: The past and future of positive psychology. In C. L. M. Keyes & J. Haidt (Eds.), *Flourishing: Positive psychology and the life well-lived* (pp. xi–xx). Washington, DC: American Psychological Association.

Seligman, M. E. P. (2011). *Flourish: A visionary new understanding of happiness and well-being.* New York: Free Press.

Seligman, M. E. P., & Csikszentmihalyi, M. (2000). Positive psychology: An introduction. *American Psychologist, 55,* 5–14.

Seligman, M. E. P., & Levant, R. F. (1998). Managed care policies rely on inadequate science. *Professional Psychology: Research and Practice, 29,* 211–212.

Seligman, M. E. P., & Peterson, C. (2003). Positive clinical psychology. In L. G. Aspinwall & U. M. Staudinger (Eds.), *A psychology of human strengths: Fundamental questions and future directions for a positive psychology* (pp. 305–317). Washington, DC: American Psychological Association.

Seligman, M. E. P., & Steen, T. A. (2005). Positive psychology progress: Empirical validation of interventions. *American Psychologist, 60,* 410–421.

Selye, H. (1956). *The stress of life.* New York: McGraw-Hill.

Sewell, H. (2009). *Working with ethnicity, race, and culture in mental health: A handbook for practitioners.* London: Jessica Kingsley.

Shadish, W. R., Montgomery, L. M., Wilson, P., Wilson, M. R., Bright, I., & Okwumabua, T. (1993). The effects of family and marital therapies: A meta-analysis. *Journal of Consulting and Clinical Psychology, 59,* 883–893.

Shadish, W. R., Ragsdale, K., Glaser, R. R., & Montgomery, L. M. (1995). The efficacy and effectiveness of marital and family therapy: A perspective from meta-analysis. *Journal of Marital and Family Therapy, 21,* 345–360.

Shaffer, J., & Galinsky, M. D. (1989). *Models of group therapy* (2nd ed.). Englewood Cliffs, NJ: Prentice Hall.

Shapiro, D., & Schwartz, G. (1972). Biofeedback and visceral learning: Clinical applications. *Seminars in Psychiatry, 4,* 171–184.

Shapiro, D. A., & Shapiro, D. (1982). Meta-analysis of comparative therapy outcome studies: A replication and refinement. *Psychological Bulletin, 92,* 581–604.

Shapiro, D. E., & Schulman, C. E. (1996). Ethical and legal issues in e-mail therapy. *Ethics & Behavior, 6,* 107–124.

Shapiro, E. (1999). Cotherapy. In J. R. Price, D. R. Hescheles, & A. R. Price (Eds.), *A guide to starting psychotherapy groups* (pp. 53–61). San Diego, CA: Academic Press.

Shapiro, S. L. (2009). The integration of mindfulness and psychology. *Journal of Clinical Psychology, 65,* 555–560.

Sherbourne, C., Hays, R., Ordway, L., DiMatteo, M., & Kravitz, R. (1992). Antecedents of adherence to medical recommendations: Results from the medical outcomes study. *Journal of Behavioral Medicine, 15,* 447–468.

Sherman, D. K., & Cohen, G. L. (2006). The psychology of self-defense: Self-affirmation theory. In M. P. Zanna (Ed.), *Advances in experimental social psychology* (Vol. 38, pp. 183–242). San Diego, CA: Academic Press.

Sherman, J. A. (1980). Therapist attitudes and sex-role stereotyping. In A. M. Brodsky &

R. T. Hare-Mustin (Eds.), *Women and psychotherapy: An assessment of research and practice*. New York: Guilford Press.

Sherry, A., Dahlen, E., & Holaday, M. (2004). The use of sentence completion tests with adults. In M. J. Hilsenroth & D. L. Segal (Eds.), *Comprehensive handbook of psychological assessment: Personality assessment* (Vol. 2, pp. 372–386). Hoboken, NJ: Wiley.

Shibusawa, T. (2005). Japanese families. In M. McGoldrick, J. Giordano, & N. Garcia-Preto (Eds.), *Ethnicity and family therapy* (3rd ed., pp. 339–348). New York: Guilford Press.

Shin, H., & Munoz, O. (2009). Acculturation: Context, dynamics, and conceptualization. In C. C. Lee, D. A. Burnhill, A. L. Butler, C. P. Hipolito-Delgado, M. Humphrey, O. Munoz, et al. (Eds.), *Elements of culture in counseling* (pp. 57–76). Upper Saddle River, NJ: Pearson.

Shirk, S. R., Karver, M. S., & Brown, R. (2011). The alliance in child and adolescent psychotherapy. *Psychotherapy, 48*(1), 17–24.

Shorter, E. (2013). The history of DSM. In J. Paris & J. Phillips (Eds.), *Making the DSM-5: Concepts and Controversies*, (pp. 3-19). New York: Springer.

Shorter-Gooden, K. (2009). Therapy with African American men and women. In H. A. Neville, B. M. Tynes, & S. O. Utsey (Eds.), *Handbook of African American psychology* (pp. 445–458). Thousand Oaks, CA: Sage.

Siev, J., & Chambless, D. L. (2007). Specificity of treatment effects: Cognitive therapy and relaxation for generalized anxiety and panic disorders. *Journal of Consulting and Clinical Psychology, 75*, 513–522.

Silverman, W. H. (1996). Cookbooks, manuals, and paint-by-numbers: Psychotherapy in the 90s. *Psychotherapy: Theory, Research, Practice, Training, 33*, 207–215.

Silverman, W. K., & Pina, A. A. (2008). Psychosocial treatments for phobic and anxiety disorders in youth. In R. G. Steele, T. D. Elkin, & M. C. Roberts (Eds.), *Handbook of evidence-based therapies for children and adolescents: Bridging science and practice* (pp. 65–82). New York: Springer.

Silverstein, L. B., & Goodrich, T. J. (Eds.). (2003). *Feminist family therapy: Empowerment in social context*. Washington, DC: American Psychological Association.

Simonsen, E. (2010). The integration of categorical and dimensional approaches to psychopathology. In T. Millon, R. F. Krueger, & E. Simonsen (Eds.), *Contemporary directions in psychopathology: Scientific foundations of the DSM-V and ICD-11* (pp. 350–361). New York: Guilford Press.

Skeem, J. L., & Monahan, J. (2011). Current directions in violence risk assessment. *Current Directions in Psychological Science, 20*, 38–42.

Skelton, R. M. (Ed.). (2006). *The Edinburgh international encyclopaedia of psychoanalysis*. Edinburgh, UK: Edinburgh University Press.

Skodol, A. E. (2010). Dimensionalizing existing personality disorder categories. In T. Millon, R. F. Krueger, & E. Simonsen (Eds.), *Contemporary directions in psychopathology: Scientific foundations of the DSM-V and ICD-11* (pp. 362–373). New York: Guilford Press.

Skodol, A. E., Krueger, R. F., Bender, D. S., Morey, L. C., Clark, L. A., Bell, C. C., ... & Oldham, J. M. (2013). Personality Disorders in DSM-5 Section III.*FOCUS: The Journal of Lifelong Learning in Psychiatry, 11*(2), 187-188.

Smalley, K. B., Yancey, C. T., Warren, J. C., Naufel, K., Ryan, R., & Pugh, J. L. (2010). Rural mental health and psychological treatment: A review for practitioners. *Journal of Clinical Psychology, 66*, 479–489.

Smith, B. H., Barkley, R. A., & Shapiro, C. J. (2006). Attention-deficit/hyperactivity disorder. In E. J. Mash & R. A. Barkley (Eds.), *Treatment of childhood disorders* (3rd ed., pp. 65–136). New York: Guilford Press.

Smith, M. L., & Glass, G. V. (1977). Meta-analysis of psychotherapy outcome studies. *American Psychologist, 32*, 752–760.

Smith, M. L., Glass, G. V., & Miller, T. I. (1980). *The benefits of psychotherapy*. Baltimore: Johns Hopkins University Press.

Smith, P. L., & Moss, S. B. (2009). Psychologist impairment: What is it, how can it be prevented, and what can be done to address it? *Clinical Psychology: Science and Practice, 16*, 1–15.

Smith, P. M., Reilly, K. R., Houston Miller, N., DeBusk, R. F., & Taylor, C. B. (2002). Application of a nurse-managed inpatient smoking cessation program. *Nicotine Tobacco Research, 4*, 211–222.

Smith, R. E., Fagan, C., Wilson, N. L., Chen, J., Corona, M., Nguyen, H., et al. (2011). Internet-based approaches to collaborative therapeutic assessment: New opportunities for professional psychologists. *Professional Psychology: Research and Practice, 42*, 494–504.

Smith, S. R., & Archer, R. P. (2008). Introducing personality assessment. In R. P. Archer & S. R. Smith (Eds.), *Personality assessment* (pp. 1–35). New York: Routledge.

Smith, S. R., Wiggins, C. M., & Gorske, T. T. (2007). Survey of psychological assessment feedback practices. *Assessment, 14*, 310–319.

Smith, T. B., Rodríguez, M. M. D., & Bernal, G. (2011). Culture. In J. C. Norcross (Ed.), *Psychotherapy relationships that work: Evidence-based responsiveness* (2nd ed., pp.

316–335). New York: Oxford University Press.

Smith, T. W., & MacKenzie, J. (2006). Personality and risk of physical illness. *Annual Review of Clinical Psychology, 2*, 435–467.

Snowden, L. R., & Yamada, A. (2005). Cultural differences in access to care. *Annual Review of Clinical Psychology, 1*, 143–166.

Snyder, C. R., & Elliott, T. R. (2005). 21st-century graduate education in clinical psychology: A four-level matrix model. *Journal of Clinical Psychology, 61*, 1033–1054.

Snyder, C. R., Lopez, S. J., & Pedrotti, J. T. (2011). *Positive psychology: The scientific and practical explorations of human strengths* (2nd ed.). Thousand Oaks, CA: Sage.

Snyder, C. R., Ritschel, L. A., Rand, K. L., & Berg, C. J. (2006). Balancing psychological assessments: Including strengths and hope in client reports. *Journal of Clinical Psychology, 62*, 33–46.

Sommers-Flanagan, J., & Sommers-Flanagan, R. (2009). *Clinical interviewing* (4th ed.). Hoboken, NJ: Wiley.

Sommers-Flanagan, R. (2012). Boundaries, multiple roles, and the professional relationship. In S. J. Knapp (Ed.), *APA handbook of ethics in psychology, Vol. 1: Moral foundations and common themes* (pp. 241–277). Washington, DC: American Psychological Association.

Sonne, J. L. (2012). Sexualized relationships. In S. J. Knapp

(Ed.), *APA handbook of ethics in psychology, Vol. 1: Moral foundations and common themes* (pp. 295–310). Washington, DC: American Psychological Association.

Spence, S. H., Donovan, C. L., March, S., Gamble, A., Anderson, R. E., Prosser, S., et al. (2011). A randomized controlled trial of online versus clinic-based CBT for adolescent anxiety. *Journal of Consulting and Clinical Psychology, 79*, 629–642.

Sperling, M. B., Sack, A., & Field, C. L. (2000). *Psychodynamic practice in a managed care environment: A strategic guide for clinicians*. New York: Guilford Press.

Spiegler, M. D., & Guevremont, D. C. (2010). *Contemporary behavior therapy* (5th ed.). Belmont, CA: Wadsworth.

Spinelli, M. G., & Endicott, J. (2003). Controlled clinical trial of interpersonal psychotherapy versus parenting education program for depressed pregnant women. *American Journal of Psychiatry, 160*, 555–562.

Spitzer, R. L. (1999). Harmful dysfunction and the *DSM* definition of mental disorder. *Journal of Abnormal Psychology, 108*, 430–432.

Spitzer, R. L., & Wakefield, J. C. (1999). *DSM-IV* diagnostic criterion for clinical significance: Does it help to solve the false positives problem? *American Journal of Psychiatry, 156*, 1856–1864.

Spokas, M. E., Rodebaugh, T. L., & Heimburg, R. G. (2008). Treatment research. In M. Hersen & A. M. Gross (Eds.), *Handbook of clinical psychology* (Vol. 1, pp. 300–338). Hoboken, NJ: Wiley.

Spring, B., & Neville, K. (2011). Evidence-based practice in clinical psychology. In D. H. Barlow (Ed.), *The Oxford handbook of clinical psychology* (pp. 128–149). New York: Oxford University Press.

Stafford, K. P. (2003). Assessment of competence to stand trial. In A. M. Goldstein (Ed.), *Handbook of psychology, Volume 11: Forensic psychology* (p. 359–380). Hoboken, NJ: Wiley.

Steenbarger, B. N. (2008). Brief therapy. In M. Hersen & A. M. Gross (Eds.), *Handbook of clinical psychology* (Vol. 1, pp. 752–775). Hoboken, NJ: Wiley.

Steenhuis, M., Serra, M., Minderaa, R. B., & Hartman, C. A. (2009). An Internet version of the Diagnostic Interview Schedule for Children (DISC-IV): Correspondence of the ADHD section with the paper-and-pencil version. *Psychological Assessment, 21*(2), 231–234.

Sternberg, R. J. (2000). The concept of intelligence. In R. J. Sternberg (Ed.), *Handbook of intelligence* (pp. 3–15). Cambridge, UK: Cambridge University Press.

Sternberg, R. J., & Grigorenko, E. L. (2008). Ability testing across cultures. In L. A. Suzuki & J. G. Ponterotto (Eds.), *Handbook of multicultural assessment: Clinical, psychological, and educational applications* (3rd ed., pp. 449–470). Hoboken, NJ: Wiley.

Stevanovic, P., & Rupert, P. A. (2009). Work-family spillover and life satisfaction among professional psychologists. *Professional Psychology: Research and Practice, 40,* 62–68.

Stewart, R. E., & Chambless, D. L. (2010). Interesting practitioners in training in empirically supported treatments: Research reviews versus case studies. *Journal of Clinical Psychology, 66,* 73–95.

Stewart, R. E., Chambless, D. L., & Baron, J. (2012). Theoretical and practical barriers to practitioners' willingness to seek training in empirically supported treatments. *Journal of Clinical Psychology, 68,* 8–23.

Stice, E., Marti, C. N., & Rohde, P. (2013). Prevalence, incidence, impairment, and course of the proposed DSM-5 eating disorder diagnoses in an 8-year prospective community study of young women. *Journal of abnormal psychology, 122*(2), 445.

Stiles, W. B. (2009). Responsiveness as an obstacle for psychotherapy outcome research: It's worse than you think. *Clinical Psychology: Science and Practice, 16,* 86–91.

Storch, E. A., Larson, M., Adkins, J., Geffken, G. R., Murphy, T. K., & Goodman, W. K. (2008). Evidence-based treatment of pediatric obsessive-compulsive disorder. In R. G. Steele, T. D. Elkin, & M. C. Roberts (Eds.), *Handbook of evidence-based therapies for children and adolescents: Bridging science and practice* (pp. 103–120). New York: Springer.

Stormont, M. (2007). *Fostering resilience in young children at risk for failure.* Upper Saddle River, NJ: Pearson.

Straus, M. A. (2007). Conflict Tactics Scales. In N. A. Jackson (Ed.), *Encyclopedia of domestic violence* (pp. 190–197). New York: Routledge.

Straus, M. A., Hamby, S. L., Boney-McCoy, S., & Sugarman, D. B. (1996). The Revised Conflict Tactics Scales (CTS2): Development and preliminary psychometric data. *Journal of Family Issues, 17,* 283–316.

Street, L. L., & Luoma, J. B. (2002). Control groups in psychosocial intervention research: Ethical and methodological issues. *Ethics & Behavior, 12,* 1–30.

Striano, J. (1988). *Can psychotherapists hurt you?* Santa Barbara, CA: Professional Press.

Stricker, G. (2010). *Psychotherapy integration.* Washington, DC: American Psychological Association.

Stricker, G. (2011). Training systems and sites: PsyD programs. In J. C. Norcross, G. R. Vandenbos, & D. K. Freedheim (Eds.), *History of psychotherapy: Continuity and change* (2nd ed., pp. 630–639). Washington, DC: American Psychological Association.

Striegel-Moore, R. H., & Franko, D. L. (2006). Adolescent eating disorders. In C. A. Essau (Ed.), *Child and adolescent psychopathology: Theoretical and clinical implications* (pp. 160–183). New York: Routledge.

Striegel-Moore, R. H., & Franko, D. L. (2008). Should binge eating disorder be included in the *DSM-V*? A critical review of the state of the evidence. *Annual Review of Clinical Psychology, 4,* 305–324.

Stringaris, A. (2013), Editorial: The new DSM is coming – it needs tough love .... Journal of Child Psychology and Psychiatry, 54: 501–502. doi: 10.1111/jcpp.12078

Strub, R. L., & Black, F. W. (1977). *The mental status examination in neurology.* Philadelphia: Davis.

Strupp, H. H. (1996). The tripartite model and the Consumer Reports study. *American Psychologist, 51,* 1017–1024.

Strupp, H. H., & Hadley, S. W. (1977). A tripartite model of mental health and therapeutic outcomes: With special reference to negative effects in psychotherapy. *American Psychologist, 32,* 187–196.

Strupp, H. H., Hadley, S. W., & Gomes-Schwartz, B. (1977). *Psychotherapy for better or worse: The problem of negative effects.* New York: Aronson.

Sturmey, P. (Ed.). (2007). *Functional analysis in clinical treatment.* Burlington, MA: Elsevier.

Sturmey, P., Ward-Horner, J., Marroquin, M., & Doran, E. (2007). Operant and respondent behavior. In P. Sturmey (Ed.), *Functional analysis in clinical treatment* (pp. 23–50). Burlington, MA: Elsevier.

Stuve, P., & Salinas, J. A. (2002). Token economy. In M. Hersen & W. Sledge (Eds.), *Encyclopedia of psychotherapy* (Vol. 2, pp. 821–827). San Diego, CA: Academic Press.

Sue, D. W. (2010). *Microaggressions in everyday life: Race, gender, and sexual orientation.* Hoboken, NJ: Wiley.

Sue, D. W., Capodilupo, C. M., & Holder, A. M. B. (2008). Racial microaggressions in the life experience of black Americans. *Professional Psychology: Research and Practice, 39,* 329–336.

Sue, D., Capodilupo, C. M., Torino, G. C., Bucceri, J. M., Holder, A. M. B., Nadal, K. L., et al. (2007). Racial microaggressions in everyday life: Implications for clinical practice. *American Psychologist, 62,* 271–286.

Sue, D. W., Ivey, A. E., & Pedersen, P. B. (1996). *A theory of multicultural counseling and therapy.* Pacific Grove, CA: Brooks/Cole.

Sue, D. W., & Sue, D. (2003). *Counseling the culturally diverse* (4th ed.). New York: Wiley.

Sue, D. W., & Sue, D. (2008). *Counseling the culturally diverse* (5th ed.). New York: Wiley.

Sue, S., Cheng, J. K. Y., & Sue, L. (2011). Problems in generalizing research to other cultures. In J. C. Thomas & M. Hersen (Eds.), *Understanding research in clinical and counseling psychology* (2nd ed., pp. 355–376). New York: Taylor & Francis.

Sue, S., & Consolacion, T. B. (2003). Clinical psychology issues among Asian/Pacific Islander Americans. In J. S. Mio & G. Y. Iwamasa (Eds.), *Culturally diverse mental health: The challenges of research and resistance* (pp. 173–189). New York: Brunner-Routledge.

Sue, S., & Zane, N. (2006). Ethnic minority populations have been neglected by evidence-based practices. In J. C. Norcross, L. E. Beutler, & R. F. Levant (Eds.), *Evidence-based practices in mental health: Debate and dialogue on the fundamental questions* (pp. 329–337). Washington, DC: American Psychological Association.

Sutton, C. T., & Broken Nose, M. A. (2005). American Indian families: An overview. In M. McGoldrick, J. Giordano, & N. Garcia-Preto (Eds.), *Ethnicity and family therapy* (3rd ed., pp. 43–54). New York: Guilford Press.

Swartz, H. A., & Markowitz, J. C. (2009). Techniques of individual interpersonal psychotherapy. In G. O. Gabbard (Ed.), *Textbook of psychotherapeutic treatments* (pp. 309–338). Washington, DC: American Psychiatric Publishing.

Swift, J. K., & Callahan, J. L. (2009). The impact of client treatment preferences on outcome: A meta-analysis. *Journal of Clinical Psychology, 65*, 368–381.

Swift, J. K., Callahan, J. L., & Vollmer, B. M. (2011). Preferences. *Journal of Clinical Psychology, 67*, 155–165.

Symons, D. K. (2010). A review of the practice and science of child custody and access assessment in the United States and Canada. *Professional Psychology: Research and Practice, 41*, 267–273.

Szasz, T. S. (1961). *The myth of mental illness*. New York: Delta.

Szasz, T. S. (1963). *Law, liberty, and psychiatry: An inquiry into the social uses of mental health practices*. New York: Macmillan.

Szasz, T. S. (1970). *The manufacture of madness*. New York: Harper & Row.

Tamura, L. J. (2012). Emotional competence and well-being. In S. J. Knapp (Ed.), *APA handbook of ethics in psychology, Vol. 1: Moral foundations and common themes* (pp. 175–216). Washington, DC: American Psychological Association.

Tarasoff v. The Regents of the University of California, 529 P.2d 533 (Cal. 1974).

Task Force on Promotion and Dissemination of Psychological Procedures. (1995). Training in and dissemination of empirically validated psychological treatments: Report and recommendations. *Clinical Psychologist, 48*, 3–23.

Taylor, K. (2010). Use and evaluation of a CD-rom-based decision aid for prostate cancer treatment decisions. *Behavioral Medicine, 36*, 130–140.

Taylor, S. (2002). Exposure. In M. Hersen & W. Sledge (Eds.), *Encyclopedia of psychotherapy* (Vol. 1, pp. 755–759). San Diego, CA: Academic Press.

Teglasi, H. (2010). *Essentials of TAT and other storytelling assessments* (2nd ed.). Hoboken, NJ: Wiley.

Terman, D. M. (2012). Self psychology. In G. O. Gabbard, B. E. Litowitz, & P. Williams (Eds.), *Textbook of psychoanalysis* (2nd ed., pp. 199–210). Washington, DC: American Psychiatric Publishing.

Terman, L. M. (1916). *The measurement of intelligence*. Boston: Houghton Mifflin.

Terrell, F., Taylor, J., Menzise, J., & Barett, R. K. (2009). Cultural mistrust: A core component of African American consciousness. In H. A. Neville, B. M. Tynes, & S. O. Utsey (Eds.), *Handbook of African American psychology* (pp. 299–309). Thousand Oaks, CA: Sage.

Thoma, N. C., & Cecero, J. J. (2009). Is integrative use of techniques in psychotherapy the exception or the rule? Results of a national survey of doctoral-level practitioners. *Psychotherapy: Theory, Research, Practice, Training, 46*, 405–417.

Thomas, J. C., & Michael, P. G. (2011). Meta-analysis. In J. C. Thomas & M. Hersen (Eds.), *Understanding research in clinical and counseling psychology* (2nd ed., pp. 229–242). New York: Taylor & Francis.

Thorndike, E. L. (1931). *Human learning*. New York: Century.

Tillitski, L. (1990). A meta-analysis of estimated effect sizes for group versus individual versus control treatments. *International Journal of Group Psychotherapy, 40*, 215–224.

Tjeltveit, A. C., & Gottlieb, M. C. (2010). Avoiding the road to ethical disaster: Overcoming vulnerabilities and developing resilience. *Psychotherapy: Theory, Research, Practice, Training, 47*, 98–110.

Toporek, R. L. (2012). So what should I actually do? Developing skills for greater multicultural competence. In M. E. Gallardo, C. J. Yeh, J. E. Trimble, & T. A. Parham (Eds.), *Culturally adaptive counseling skills: Demonstrations of evidence-based practices* (pp. 267–285). Thousand Oaks, CA: Sage.

Torrey, E. F. (1986). *Witchdoctors and psychiatrists: The common roots of psychotherapy and its future*. New York: Perennial Library.

Toukmanian, S. G., & Brouwers, M. C. (1998). Cultural aspects of self-disclosure and psychotherapy. In S. S. Kazarian & D. R. Evans (Eds.), *Cultural clinical psychology* (pp. 106–124). New York: Oxford University Press.

Treppa, J. A. (1998). A practitioner's guide to ethical decision-making. In R. M. Anderson, Jr., T. L. Needles, & H. V. Hall (Eds.), *Avoiding ethical misconduct in psychology specialty areas* (pp. 26–41). Springfield, IL: Charles C. Thomas.

Tribbensee, N. E., & Claiborn, C. D. (2003). Confidentiality in psychotherapy and related contexts. In W. O'Donohue & K. Ferguson (Eds.), *Handbook of professional ethics for psychologists: Issues, questions, and controversies* (pp. 287–300). Thousand Oaks, CA: Sage.

Truax, P. (2002). Behavioral case conceptualization for adults. In M. Hersen (Ed.), *Clinical behavior therapy: Adults and children* (pp. 3–36). New York: Wiley.

Truax, P., & Thomas, J. C. (2003). Effectiveness versus efficacy studies: Issues, designs, and methodologies. In J. C. Thomas & M. Hersen (Eds.), *Understanding research in clinical and counseling psychology* (pp. 342–378). Mahwah, NJ: Lawrence Erlbaum.

Trull, T. J., & Durrett, C. A. (2005). Categorical and dimensional models of personality disorder. *Annual Review of Clinical Psychology, 1,* 355–380.

Truscott, D. (2010). *Becoming an effective psychotherapist: Adopting a theory of psychotherapy that's right for you and your client.* Washington, DC: American Psychological Association.

Tryon, W. W. (2008). History and theoretical foundations. In M. Hersen & A. M. Gross (Eds.), *Handbook of clinical psychology* (Vol. 1, pp. 3–37). Hoboken, NJ: Wiley.

Tseng, W., Matthews, D., & Elwyn, T. S. (Eds.). (2004). *Cultural competence in forensic mental health: A guide for psychiatrists, psychologists, and attorneys.* New York: Brunner-Routledge.

Tsuang, M. T., Van Os, J., Tandon, R., Barch, D. M., Bustillo, J., Gaebel, W., ... & Carpenter, W. (in press). Attenuated psychosis syndrome in DSM-5.*Schizophrenia research.*

Tsytsarev, S. V., & Landes, A. (2008). Competency to stand trial: A multicultural perspective. In L. A. Suzuki & J. G. Ponterotto (Eds.), *Handbook of multicultural assessment: Clinical, psychological, and educational applications* (3rd ed., pp. 651–665). Hoboken, NJ: Wiley.

Tubbs, P., & Pomerantz, A. M. (2001). Ethical behaviors of psychologists: Changes since 1987. *Journal of Clinical Psychology, 57,* 395–399.

Tuckman, B. (1965). Developmental stages in small groups. *Psychological Bulletin, 63,* 384–399.

Tudor, K. (Ed.). (2008). *Brief person-centered therapies.* Thousand Oaks, CA: Sage.

Tudor, K., & Worrall, M. (2006). *Person-centered therapy: A clinical philosophy.* New York: Routledge.

U.S. Census Bureau. (2001). *Population profile of the United States.* Washington, DC: Government Printing Office.

U.S. Census Bureau. (2003). *Language use and English-speaking ability: 2000.* Retrieved from www.census.gov/prod/2003pubs/c2kbr-29.pdf

U.S. Census Bureau. (2006a). *State and county QuickFacts: Detroit (city), Michigan.* Retrieved from http://quickfacts.census. gov/qfd/states/26/2622000.html

U.S. Census Bureau. (2006b). *State and county QuickFacts: District of Columbia.* Retrieved from http://quickfacts.census. gov/qfd/states/11000.html

U.S. Census Bureau. (2006c). *State and county QuickFacts: Miami (city), Florida.* Retrieved from http://quickfacts.census. gov/qfd/states/12/1245000.html

U.S. Census Bureau. (2006d). *State and county QuickFacts: San Francisco (city), California.* Retrieved from http:// quickfacts.census.gov/qfd/ states/06/0667000.html

U.S. Census Bureau. (2008). *Percent of the projected population by race and Hispanic origin for the United States: 2010 to 2050* (NP2008-T6). Retrieved May 1, 2009, from www.census.gov/ipc/ www/usinterimproj/

Valenstein, E. S. (1986). *Great and desperate cures: The rise and decline of psychosurgery and other radical treatments for mental illness.* New York: Basic Books.

VandenBos, G. R. (2007). *APA dictionary of psychology.*

Washington, DC: American Psychological Association.

Vandervoort, D., & Fuhriman, A. (1991). The efficacy of group therapy for depression. *Small Group Research, 22,* 320–338.

Vasquez, M. J. T. (2010). Ethics in multicultural counseling practice. In J. G. Ponterotto, J. M. Casas, L. A. Suzuki, & C. M. Alexander (Eds.), *Handbook of multicultural counseling* (3rd ed., pp. 127–145). Thousand Oaks, CA: Sage.

Vaughn, T. J. (2006). Overview of licensure requirements to meet "high standard" in the United States and Canada. In T. J. Vaughn (Ed.), *Psychology licensure and certification* (pp. 7–15). Washington, DC: American Psychological Association.

Velasquez, R. J., Garrido, M., Castellanos, J., & Burton, M. P. (2004). Culturally competent assessment of Chicana/os with the Minnesota Multiphasic Personality Inventory-2. In R. J. Velasquez, L. M. Arellano, & B. W. McNeill (Eds.), *The handbook of Chicana/o psychology and mental health* (pp. 153–174). Mahwah, NJ: Lawrence Erlbaum.

Velasquez, R. J., Johnson, R., & Brown-Cheatham, M. (1993). Teaching counselors to use the *DSM-III-R* with ethnic minority clients: A paradigm. *Counselor Education and Supervision, 32,* 323–331.

Vessey, J. T., & Howard, K. I. (1993). Who seeks psychotherapy? *Psychotherapy:*

Theory, Research, Practice, Training, 30, 546–553.

Viamontes, G. I., & Beitman, B. D. (2009). Brain processes informing psychotherapy. In G. O. Gabbard (Ed.), *Textbook of psychotherapeutic treatments* (pp. 781–808). Washington, DC: American Psychiatric Publishing.

Villa, M., & Reitman, D. (2007). Overview of interviewing strategies with children, parents, and teachers. In M. Hersen & J. C. Thomas (Eds.), *Handbook of clinical interviewing with children* (pp. 2–15). Thousand Oaks, CA: Sage.

Villamar, A. J., Donohue, B. C., & Allen, D. N. (2008). Applied behavior analysis. In M. Hersen & A. M. Gross (Eds.), *Handbook of clinical psychology* (Vol. 1, pp. 161–170). Hoboken, NJ: Wiley.

Vowels, K., Zvolensky, M., Gross, R., & Sperry, J. (2004). Pain-related anxiety in the prediction of chronic low-back pain distress. *Journal of Behavioral Medicine, 27,* 77–89.

Vrieze, S. I., & Grove, W. M. (2009). Survey on the use of clinical and mechanical prediction methods in clinical psychology. *Professional Psychology: Research and Practice, 40,* 525–531.

Wachtel, P. L. (1977). *Psychoanalysis and behavior therapy: Toward an integration.* New York: Basic Books.

Wakefield, J. C. (1992). The concept of mental disorder: On the boundary between biological

facts and social values. *American Psychologist, 47,* 373–388.

Wakefield, J. C. (1999). Evolutionary versus prototype analyses of the concept of disorder. *Journal of Abnormal Psychology, 108,* 374–399.

Wakefield, J. C. (2010). Taking disorder seriously: A critique of psychiatric criteria for mental disorders from the harmful-dysfunction perspective. In T. Millon, R. F. Krueger, & E. Simonsen (Eds.), *Contemporary directions in psychopathology: Scientific foundations of the DSM-V and ICD-11* (pp. 275–300). New York: Guilford Press.

Wakefield, J. C. (in press). The DSM-5 debate over the bereavement exclusion: Psychiatric diagnosis and the future of empirically supported treatment. *Clinical psychology review.*

Wakefield, J. C. (2013a). DSM-5: An overview of changes and controversies. *Clinical Social Work Journal,* 1-16.

Wakefield, J. C. (2013b). DSM-5 grief scorecard: Assessment and outcomes of proposals to pathologize grief. *World Psychiatry, 12*(2), 171-173.

Wampold, B. E. (2001). *The great psychotherapy debate: Models, methods, and findings.* Mahwah, NJ: Lawrence Erlbaum.

Wampold, B. E. (2009). Series editor's foreword. In G. W. Rosenfeld (Ed.), *Beyond evidence-based psychotherapy: Fostering the eight sources of change in child and* adolescent treatment (p. ix). New York: Routledge.

Wampold, B. E. (2010a). *The basics of psychotherapy: An introduction to theory and practice.* Washington, DC: American Psychological Association.

Wampold, B. E. (2010b). The research evidence for the common factors model: A historically situated perspective. In B. L. Duncan, S. D. Miller, B. E. Wampold, & M. A. Hubble (Eds.), *The heart and soul of change: Delivering what works in therapy* (2nd ed., pp. 49–81). Washington, DC: American Psychological Association.

Wampold, B. E., Imel, Z. E., Bhati, K. S., & Johnson-Jennings, M. D. (2007). Insight as a common factor. In L. G. Castonguay & C. E. Hill (Eds.), *Insight in psychotherapy* (pp. 119–139). Washington, DC: American Psychological Association.

Wampold, B. E., Mondin, G. W., Moody, M., Stich, I., Benson, K., & Ahn, H. (1997). A meta-analysis of outcome studies comparing bona fide psychotherapies: Empirically "all must have prizes." *Psychological Bulletin, 122,* 203–215.

Ward, C. C., & Reuter, T. (2011). *Strength-centered counseling: Integrating postmodern approaches and skills with practice.* Thousand Oaks, CA: Sage.

Waschbusch, D. A., & King, S. (2006). Should sex-specific norms be used to assess attention-deficit/hyperactivity disorder or oppositional defiant disorder? *Journal of Consulting and Clinical Psychology, 74,* 179–185.

Wasserman, J. D., & Tulsky, D. S. (2005). A history of intelligence assessment. In D. P. Flanagan & P. L. Harrison (Eds.), *Contemporary intellectual assessment: Theories, tests, and issues* (2nd ed., pp. 3–22). New York: Guilford Press.

Waters, E. A., Weinstein, N. D., Colditz, G. A., & Emmons, K. (2009). Explanations for side effect aversion in preventive medical treatment decisions. *Health Psychology, 28,* 201–209.

Watkins, C. E., Campbell, V. L., Nieberding, R., & Hallmark, R. (1995). Contemporary practice of psychological assessment by clinical psychologists. *Professional Psychology: Research and Practice, 26,* 54–60.

Watson, J. B. (1924). *Behaviorism.* Chicago: People's Institute.

Watson, J. B., & Rayner, R. (1920). Conditioned emotional reactions. *Journal of Experimental Psychology, 3,* 1–14.

Webb, C. A., DeRubeis, R. J., Amsterdam, J. D., Shelton, R. C., Hollon, S. D., & Dimidjian, S. (2011). Two aspects of the therapeutic alliance: Differential relations with depressive symptom change. *Journal of Consulting and Clinical Psychology, 79,* 279–283.

Wechsler, D. (1939). *The measurement of adult intelligence.* Baltimore: Williams & Wilkins.

Wechsler, D. (1949). *WISC manual.* New York: Psychological Corporation.

Wechsler, D. (1967). *Manual for the Wechsler Preschool and Preliminary Scale of Intelligence.* New York: Psychological Corporation.

Wechsler, D. (2008). *Wechsler Adult Intelligence Scale* (4th ed.). San Antonio, TX: NCS Pearson.

Wechsler, D. (2009a). *Wechsler Memory Scale—Fourth Edition administration and scoring manual.* San Antonio, TX: Pearson.

Wechsler, D. (2009b). *Wechsler Memory Scale—Fourth Edition technical and interpretive manual.* San Antonio, TX: Pearson.

Weiner, I. B. (2004). Rorschach Inkblot Method. In M. W. Maruish (Ed.), *The use of psychological testing for treatment planning and outcomes assessment* (3rd ed., Vol. 3, pp. 553–587). Mahwah, NJ: Erlbaum.

Weiss, L. G., Saklofske, D. H., Coalson, D. L., & Raiford, S. E. (2010). Theoretical, empirical, and clinical foundations of the WAIS-IV index scores. In L. G. Weiss, D. H. Saklofske, D. Coalson, & S. E. Raiford (Eds.), *WAIS-IV clinical use and interpretation: Scientist-practitioner perspectives* (pp. 61–94). London: Elsevier.

Weiss, S. (2005). Haptic perception and the psychosocial functioning of preterm, low birth weight infants. *Infant Behavior and Development, 28,* 329–359.

Weissman, M. M. (1995). *Mastering depression: A patient's guide to interpersonal psychotherapy*. Albany, NY: Graywind.

Weissmark, M. S., & Giacomo, D. A. (1998). *Doing psychotherapy effectively*. Chicago: University of Chicago Press.

Weisz, J. R., Weiss, B., Han, S. S., Granger, D. A., & Morton, T. (1995). Effects of psychotherapy with children and adolescents revisited: A meta-analysis of treatment outcome studies. *Psychological Bulletin, 117,* 450–468.

Welfel, E. R., Werth, J. L., Jr., & Benjamin, G. A. H. (2012). Treating clients who threaten others or themselves. In S. J. Knapp (Ed.), *APA handbook of ethics in psychology, Vol. 1: Moral foundations and common themes* (pp. 377–400). Washington, DC: American Psychological Association.

Wells, A. (2009). *Metacognitive therapy for anxiety and depression*. New York: Guilford Press.

Wells, A., & King, P. (2006). Metacognitive therapy for generalized anxiety disorder: An open trial. *Journal of Behavior Therapy and Experimental Psychiatry, 37,* 206–212.

Wells, A., Welford, M., Fraser, J., King, P., Mendel, E., Wisely, J., et al. (2008). Chronic PTSD treated with metacognitive therapy: An open trial. *Cognitive and Behavioral Practice, 15,* 85–92.

Werth, J. L., Hastings, S. L., & Riding-Malon, R. (2010). Ethical challenges of practicing in rural areas. *Journal of Clinical Psychology, 66,* 537–548.

Wertheimer, M. (2000). *A brief history of psychology* (4th ed.). Fort Worth, TX: Harcourt Brace.

Westkott, M. (1986). *The feminist legacy of Karen Horney*. New Haven, CT: Yale University Press.

Wheelis, J. (2009). Theory and practice of dialectical behavioral therapy. In G. O. Gabbard (Ed.), *Textbook of psychotherapeutic treatments* (pp. 727–756). Washington, DC: American Psychiatric Publishing.

White, J. H., Lester, D., Gentile, M., & Rosenbleeth, J. (2011). The utilization of forensic science and criminal profiling for capturing serial killers. *Forensic Science International, 209,* 160–165.

White, M., & Epston, D. (1990). *Narrative means to therapeutic ends*. New York: W. W. Norton.

Whooley, O. & Horwitz, A. V. (2013). The paradox of professional success: Grand ambition, furious resistance, and the derailment of the DSM-5 revision process. In J. Paris & J. Phillips (Eds.), Making the DSM-5: Concepts and Controversies, pp. 75-92. New York: Springer.

Widiger, T. A., & Mullins-Sweatt, S. N. (2008). Classification. In M. Hersen & A. M. Gross (Eds.), *Handbook of clinical psychology* (Vol. 1, pp. 341–370). Hoboken, NJ: Wiley.

Widiger, T. A., & Mullins-Sweatt, S. N. (2009). Five-factor model of personality disorder: A proposal for *DSM-V. Annual Review of Clinical Psychology, 5,* 197–220.

Widiger, T. A., & Trull, T. J. (2007). Plate tectonics in the classification of personality disorder: Shifting to a dimensional model. *American Psychologist, 62,* 71–83.

Wiebe, J. S., & Penley, J. A. (2005). A psychometric comparison of the Beck Depression Inventory-II in English and Spanish. *Psychological Assessment, 17,* 481–485.

Wilcoxon, S. A., Remley, T. P., Jr., Gladding, S. T., & Huber, C. H. (2007). *Ethical, legal, and professional issues in the practice of marriage and family therapy* (4th ed.). Upper Saddle River, NJ: Pearson.

Williams, B. E., Pomerantz, A. M., Pettibone, J. C., & Segrist, D. J. (2010). How impaired is too impaired? Ratings of psychologist impairment by psychologists in independent practice. *Ethics & Behavior, 20,* 149–160.

Williams, P. (2012). Object relations. In G. O. Gabbard, B. E. Litowitz, & P. Williams (Eds.), *Textbook of psychoanalysis* (2nd ed., pp. 171–184). Washington, DC: American Psychiatric Publishing.

Wilson, G. T., Wilfley, D. E., Agras, W. S., & Bryson, S. W. (2011). Allegiance bias and therapist effects: Results of a randomized controlled trial of binge eating disorder. *Clinical Psychology: Science and Practice,*

18, 119–125.

Wilson, M. (1993). *DSM-III and the transformation of American psychiatry: A history. American Journal of Psychiatry, 150,* 399–410.

Witmer, L. (1897). The organization of practical work in psychology. *Psychological Review, 4,* 116–117.

Witmer, L. (1907). Clinical psychology. *Psychological Clinic, 1,* 1–9.

Wittenberg, R. (1997). *Opportunities in social work careers.* Lincolnwood, IL: VGM Career Horizons.

Wodrich, D. L. (1997). *Children's psychological testing: A guide for nonpsychologists* (3rd ed.). Baltimore, MD: Paul H. Brookes.

Wolf, A. W. (2011). Internet and video technology in psychotherapy supervision and training. *Psychotherapy, 48,* 179–181.

Wolpe, J. (1958). *Psychotherapy by reciprocal inhibition.* Stanford, CA: Stanford University Press.

Wolpe, J. (1969). *The practice of behavior therapy.* New York: Pergamon Press.

Woo, S. M., & Keatinge, C. (2008). *Diagnosis and treatment of mental disorders across the lifespan.* Hoboken, NJ: Wiley.

Wood, J. (1994). *Gendered lives: Communication, gender, and culture.* Belmont, CA: Wadsworth.

Wood, J. (1999). Gender, communication, and culture. In L. A. Somovar & R. E. Porter (Eds.), *Intercultural communication: A reader* (8th ed., pp. 164–174). Belmont, CA: Wadsworth.

Wood, J. M., Garb, H. N., Lilienfeld, S. O., & Nezworski, M. T. (2002). Clinical assessment. *Annual Review of Psychology, 53,* 519–543.

Wood, J. M., Garb, H. N., & Nezworski, M. T. (2007). Psychometrics: Better measurement makes better clinicians. In S. O. Lilienfeld & W. T. O'Donohue (Eds.), *The great ideas of clinical science: 17 principles that every mental health professional should understand* (pp. 77–92). New York: Routledge.

Wood, J. M., Lilienfeld, S. O., Nezworski, M. T., Garb, H. N., Allen, K. H., & Wildermuth, J. L. (2010). Validity of Rorschach Inkblot scores for discriminating psychopaths from nonpsychopaths in forensic populations: A meta-analysis. *Psychological Assessment, 22,* 336–349.

Wood, J. M., Nezworski, M. T., Lilienfeld, S. O., & Garb, H. N. (2003). *What's wrong with the Rorschach?* San Francisco: Jossey-Bass.

Woody, S. R., & Sanderson, W. C. (1998). Manuals for empirically supported treatments: 1998 update. *Clinical Psychologist, 51*(1), 17–21.

Wright, B. A., & Lopez, S. J. (2002). Widening the diagnostic focus: A case for including human strengths and environmental resources. In C. R. Snyder & S. J. Lopez (Eds.), *The handbook of positive psychology* (pp. 71–87). New York: Oxford University Press.

Yalom, I. D. (1980). *Existential therapy.* New York: Basic Books.

Yalom, I. D. (1983). *Inpatient group psychotherapy.* New York: Basic Books.

Yalom, I. D. (2005). *The theory and practice of group psychotherapy* (5th ed.). New York: Basic Books.

Yates, A. J. (1970). *Behavior therapy.* New York: Wiley.

Yonkers, K. A., & Clarke, D. E. (2011). Gender and gender-related issues in *DSM-5*. In D. A. Regier, W. E. Narrow, E. A. Kuhl, & D. J. Kupfer (Eds.), *The conceptual evolution of DSM-5* (pp. 287–301). Washington, DC: American Psychiatric Publishing.

Youngberg v. Romeo, 457 U.S. 307 (1982).

Yuen, E. K., Goetter, E. M., Herbert, J. D., & Forman, E. M. (2012). Challenges and opportunities in Internet-mediated telemental health. *Professional Psychology: Research and Practice, 43,* 1–8.

Zapf, P. A., Golding, S. L., & Roesch, R. (2006). Criminal responsibility and the insanity defense. In I. B. Weiner & A. K. Hess (Eds.), *Handbook of forensic psychology* (3rd ed., pp. 332–363). Hoboken, NJ: Wiley.

Zapf, P. A., & Roesch, R. (2006). Competency to stand trial: A guide for evaluators. In I. B. Weiner & A. K. Hess (Eds.), *Handbook of forensic psychology* (3rd ed., pp. 305–331). Hoboken, NJ: Wiley.

Zapf, P. A., Viljoen, J. L., Whittemore, K. E., Poythress, N. G., & Roesch, R. (2002). Competency: Past, present, and future. In J. R. P. Ogloff (Ed.), *Taking psychology and law into the twenty-first century* (pp. 172–198). New York: Kluwer Academic/Plenum Press.

Zedlow, P. B. (2009). In defense of clinical judgment, credentialed clinicians, and reflective practice. *Psychotherapy: Theory, Research, Practice, Training, 46,* 1–10.

Zhu, J., & Weiss, L. (2005). The Wechsler scales. In D. P. Flanagan & P. L. Harrison (Eds.), *Contemporary intellectual assessment: Theories, tests, and issues* (2nd ed., pp. 297–324). New York: Guilford Press.

Zoellner, L. A., Abramowitz, J. S., Moore, S. A., & Slagle, D. M. (2008). Flooding. In W. T. O'Donohue & J. E. Fisher (Eds.), *Cognitive behavior therapy: Applying empirically supported techniques in your practice* (2nd ed., pp. 202–210). Hoboken, NJ: Wiley.

Zur, O. (2007). *Boundaries in psychotherapy: Ethical and clinical explorations.* Washington, DC: American Psychological Association.

Zur, O. (2009). Therapeutic boundaries and effective therapy: Exploring the relationships. In W. O'Donohue & S. R. Graybar (Eds.), *Handbook of contemporary psychotherapy: Toward an improved understanding of effective psychotherapy* (pp. 341–357). Thousand Oaks, CA: Sage.

Zuroff, D. C., Kelly, A. C., Leybman, M. J., Blatt, S. J., & Wampold, B. E. (2010). Between-therapist and within-therapist differences in the quality of the therapeutic relationship: Effects on maladjustment and self-critical perfectionism. *Journal of Clinical Psychology, 66,* 681–697.

Photo Credits

Name Index

BigFoot, D. S., 278 (box)
Binder, J. L., 308, 309
Binet, A., 36, 46
Birchler, G. R., 412
Biyanova, T., 280, 318
Bjork, D. W., 341
Bjornsson, A. S., 122
Black, D. W., 162
Black, F. W., 202
Blair, S., 462
Blais, M. A., 223
Blanco, C., 306, 307, 308
Blasco, T., 457
Blashfield, R. K., 156, 157, 158, 175, 176, 177
Blatt, S. J., 326
Blau, K., 277
Blazer, D., 165
Boake, C., 39 (box)
Boccaccini, M. T., 5
Boehniein, J. K., 430 (box)
Bohanske, B., 138
Bohart, A. C., 333, 334
Bolton, P., 308
Bonanno, G. A., 332, 427
Boneau, C. A., 6
Boney-McCoy, S., 412
Bonow, J. T., 383
Borkovec, T., 469 (box), 470 (box)
Borys, D. S., 115
Boswell, J. F., 268
Bow, J. N., 492
Bowen, M., 414
Bowen, S., 384
Bowie, J., 474
Boyd-Franklin, N., 235, 429
Bozarth, J. D., 322, 326, 333
Brabender, V. A., 400, 401, 402, 403
Bracken, B. A., 219
Brantley, P. J., 248
Bratton, S., 450
Breaux, K. C., 223
Brehm, S., 502 (box)
Brems, C., 446
Bridges, M., 457
Briesmeister, J. M., 361, 445
Brodsky, A., 117, 118

Brody, N., 210, 211
Broken Nose, M. A., 352 (box)
Brooks, S., 481, 483, 495
Broshek, D. K., 224, 225
Brouwers, M. C., 266 (box), 267 (box)
Broverman, D., 173
Broverman, I., 173
Brown, A. W., 31
Brown, D. L., 119
Brown, G. K., 38
Brown, L. J., 303
Brown, L. S., 96, 278 (box)
Brown, R., 441
Brown, R. A., 403
Brown-Cheatham, M., 172
Brown-Connolly, N. E., 69
Bryant, R. A., 201
Bryson, S. W., 311
Buchanan, T., 124
Buffington-Vollum, J. K., 489
Bufka, L. E., 70
Bugental, J. F., 77
Bui, T., 69
Burgess, D. R., 177
Burke, B. L., 334
Burl, J., 480, 481
Burlingame, G. M., 396, 398, 403
Burnell, J., 120
Burns, K. A., 50
Burns, W. J., 50, 52
Burr, V., 171
Burton, M. P., 237 (box)
Burwell, R. A., 170 (box)
Busch, A. M., 358
Butcher, J. N., 37, 38, 156, 237, 237 (box), 241 (table), 242
Butler, S. F., 306
Butt, T. W., 171
Butterworth, M. R., 95
Byrne, T., 473

Cabaniss, D. L., 291, 293
Cain, D. J., 317, 319, 320, 322, 324, 325, 333
Calhoun, K. S., 347
Callahan, J. L., 277

Callands, T. A., 96
Camara, W. J., 237
Campbell, R. J., 326
Campbell, V. L., 185, 225, 250
Canivez, G. L., 217
Cannon, W., 455
Caplan, P. J., 34, 64, 171, 173, 174 (box), 175
Capodilupo, T. B., 92, 188
Cardalda, E., 437
Carey**, 65
Carl, J. R., 10
Carr, A., 56, 270, 276, 449
Carroll, J., 211
Carter, B., 411, 412
Carter, J. A., 119
Carter, M. M., 389
Casey, D., 369
Cashel, M. L., 433, 436, 439, 440 (table)
Castagna, N., 492
Castellanos, J., 237 (box)
Castelnuovo, G., 69
Castle, P. H., 185
Castonguay, L. G., 273
Castro, F. G., 92, 99, 278 (box), 474
Caterino, L. C., 135
Cattell, J. M., 30, 211
Cautin, R. L., 29, 42
Cavanagh, K., 68, 69, 71
Cecero, J. J., 281
Cepeda-Benito, A., 464
Cerny, J. A., 132
Chambless, D. L., 56, 61, 62, 67, 132, 276, 284 (box), 308, 363
Chambliss, C. H., 123
Chapman, A. L., 384
Chapman, S., 165
Charlot-Swilley, D., 8 (box)
Chase, R. M., 442
Chatkoff, D. K., 59
Cheng, J.K.Y., 134 (box)
Chenneville, T., 109
Chentsova-Dutton, Y. E., 81
Cherry, S., 291
Cheung, F. M., 237 (box)
Cheung, M., 446

Chevron, E. S., 306
Chiles, J. A., 270
Chodorow, N., 306
Chorpita, B. F., 441, 449
Chow, C., 442
Christensen, B., 330
Christopher, M. S., 56
Chu, B. C., 61
Chun, K. M., 89
Cipani, E., 257
Claiborn, C. D., 109, 110, 113
Clark, D. A., 369, 388
Clark, D. M., 132
Clarke, D. E., 161, 173
Clarkin, J. F., 419
Clarkson, F., 173
Clarkson, K., 239 (box)
Clemence, A. J., 252
Clopton, J. R., 242
Coalson, D. L., 213, 214, 215
Cohen, G. L., 463, 464
Cohen, J., 115
Cohen, S., 456, 465
Cohen, S. H., 133
Colditz, G. A., 471
Coleman, L., 138
Colon-Malgady, G., 254, 437
Comas-Díaz, L., 41, 76, 77, 91
Conner, B. T., 133
Consolacion, T. B., 459 (box)
Constantine, M. G., 17, 89, 273
Cook, J. M., 280, 281, 318
Cooper, E. M., 456
Cooper, G., 166
Cooper, N., 120
Copeland, A. L., 462
Copeland, W. E., 164
Corey, G., 41
Cosgrove, L., 65, 168, 173,
    174 (box), 175
Cosgrove, V., 145
Costa, P. T., 38, 176, 177, 178,
    179 (box), 245, 246, 247
Costantino, E., 437
Costantino, G., 437
Costello, E. J., 60
Cottone, R. R., 107
Cottraux, J., 390
Coyne, J. C., 280, 318, 471

Craig, R. J., 245
Craighead, L. W., 380
Craighead, W., 380
Craske, M. G., 132, 342, 345,
    347, 348, 358
Creswell, J. D., 464
Crits-Christoph, P., 272,
    291, 310
Croghan, T., 471
Cronkite, R., 145
Crosby, R., 137
Csikszentmihalyi, M., 247, 331
Cuca, J. M., 6
Cukor, D., 379 (box)
Cummings, N. A., 51, 52,
    53, 123
Curry, J. F., 61, 441, 450
Curry, K. T., 184
Curtin, L., 125

Dahl, K., 447
Dahlen, E., 254
Dana, R., 437
Dana, R. H., 91 (box), 93, 234,
    237 (box)
Dang, S. T., 201
D'Angelo, E., 92
Daniel, J. H., 110, 113
Daniels, J. A., 94
Dantzker, M. L., 500
Darley, J., 487
Darrow, S. M., 383
Dasari, M., 442
Dattilio, F. M., 269, 372, 390
Davis, D. M., 390
Davison, E., 60
Davison, G. C., 142
Davison, J. E., 211
Dawes, R. M., 59, 484
DeBernardo, C. R., 52
DeBord, K. A., 88 (box)
DeBusk, R. F., 465
Decker, H. S., 33, 158
DeFruyt, F., 162
Del Re, A. C., 272
DeLeon, P. H., 42, 50, 52
Delfabbro, P. H., 163
DeMaria, A., 62, 268
DeMatteo, D., 121, 480, 481

DeMers, S. T., 18
Dendy, A. K., 94
DeRubeis, R. J., 311, 312 (box),
    342, 370
deShazer, S., 415
Devlin, A. S., 198
Dewald, P. A., 294, 296,
    298, 303
Dewan, M., 306
Diamond, G. M., 419
Diamond, L. M., 95
Diaz-Linhart, Y., 92
Dichter, G. S., 270
DiGiuseppe, R., 41
DiMatteo, M., 471
Dimeff, L. A., 68, 69, 386,
    387, 390
Dimidjian, S., 358, 383, 384
Dingfelder, S., 17
Dittman, M., 50
Dix, D., 29–30, 32, 46
Dobbs, D., 63, 168
Dobson, K. S., 358, 369, 370,
    381, 390
Dodson, D., 358, 369, 370
Dodson, K. S., 367, 369, 370
Dolan, Y. M., 415
Donahue, B. C., 353
Donnay, D.A.C., 247
Doolin, E. M., 334
Doran, E., 346
Dorsey, S., 61
Dougherty, D. D., 270
Douglas, C. J., 291
Downing, C. L., 211
Dozois, D.J.A., 390
Drabick, D.A.G., 171, 429
Drewes, A. A., 447
Driessen, E., 310
Drossel, C., 353
Drozdick, L. W., 227
Dryden, W., 375, 376
Ducheny, K., 10
Duckworth, A. L., 331, 350
Dunivin, D. L., 50
Dunn, T., 245
Durand, V. M., 132, 171
Durbin, C. E., 137
Durlak, J. A., 143

Durrett, C. A., 176
Dutton, G. R., 248
Dynda, A. M., 220

Eagle, R. F., 143
Earl, T. R., 92
Edens, J. F., 136, 489
Edwards, D.J.A., 269
Egede, L., 69
Ehrenwald, J., 27, 29
Ehrhardt, K. E., 353, 354, 355
Ehrich, M. E., 360
Eifert, G. H., 385, 386
Eisenberg, N., 324, 324 (box)
Elhai, J. D., 69, 280
Elliott, C. H., 389
Elliott, R., 333, 334
Elliott, T. R., 247, 332
Ellis, A., 370, 374, 375, 376, 380, 382 (box), 383 (box), 384, 388, 391 (box)
Ellis, D. J., 375
Ellis, E., 490, 492
Elwyn, T. S., 495
Emery, C. F., 454
Emery, G., 379
Emmelkamp, P.M.G., 70, 353
Emmons, K., 471
Endicott, J., 308
Eng, W., 371
Engel, J., 41
Engle, V., 461
Eonta, A. M., 68
Epp, A. M., 390
Epston, D., 416
Erb, A. L., 71
Eriksen, K., 34, 156, 172, 174 (box)
Erikson, E., 291
Erkanli, A., 60
Ervin, R. A., 353
Erwin, E., 303, 305
Escudero, V., 419
Esquivel, G. B., 438
Ethington, L. L., 378 (box)
Evans, D. L., 449
Evans, L. A., 95
Ewing, C. P., 498

Exner, J., 250
Eysenck, H. J., 42, 54, 130, 264

Fabrega, H., Jr., 172
Fabricatore, A. N., 462
Fagan, J., 329
Faigman, D. L., 499
Fairbairn, R., 305
Fallon, A. E., 401
Fals-Stewart, W., 412
Faragher, E., 456
Farber, B. A., 334
Farmer, R. F., 384
Faust, D., 59, 225, 484
Feldman, G., 372, 373, 384, 390
Feldstein, J., 324
Fernandez-Castro, J., 457
Field, C. L., 306
Filone, S., 480
Finch, A. J., 442
Fine, B. D., 295, 303
Finn, S. E., 244
First, M. B., 176, 201
Fisher, C. B., 71, 104, 106, 121, 122, 123, 124
Fisher, J. E., 353
Fisher, M. A., 108
Fisher, P., 388
Fishman, D. B., 269
Fitzgibbons, I., 389
Flanagan, D. P., 82, 157
Flanagan, R., 437
Fleming, B., 374
Fluckiger, C., 272
Foa, E. B., 348
Folkman, S., 457
Follette, W. C., 383
Fonagy, P., 56
Fontes, L. A., 188, 197, 205, 206 (box), 266 (box), 410
Forehand, R., 61
Forman, E. M., 68
Forsyth, J. P., 385, 386
Forys, K. L., 389
Foster, E., 480
Foster, E. E., 121
Fouad, N. A., 83, 86 (box), 91, 97, 98
Fowler, J. C., 249, 252

Fowler, K. A., 58
Fox, J., 165, 168
Frances, A., 29, 62, 63, 64, 65, 163, 165, 166, 167, 168, 169, 176
Frances, A. J., 161
Frandsen, K., 456
Frank, E., 307, 308
Frank, J. D., 271
Frankl, V., 329
Franklin, A. J., 92
Franklin, M. E., 348
Franko, D. L., 450
Frauenhoffer, D., 237
Freedheim, D. K., 56, 449
Freeman, A., 374 (table), 379, 389
Freeman, K. A., 143, 359
French, T. M., 308
Fresco, D. M., 233
Freshwater, S. M., 225
Freud, A., 291, 296
Freud, S., 40 (box), 290, 293, 294, 295, 298, 305, 306, 317, 411
Frick, P. J., 434
Fried, A. A., 71, 124
Friedlander, M. L., 419
Friedman, S., 379 (box)
Friedman, W. H., 396, 401, 403
Fromm-Reichmann, F., 291, 406
Frueh, B. C., 69
Fuhriman, A., 403
Fulero, S., 487
Furber, G., 123

Gabbard, G. O., 117, 118, 290, 294, 296, 298, 299, 300
Gaddy, C. D., 8 (box), 20
Gahm, G. A., 69, 332
Galatzer-Levy, R. M., 298, 306, 310
Galinsky, M. D., 396, 403
Gallant, S. J., 174 (box)
Gallardo, M. E., 119, 124
Gallinger, L., 10
Gallop, R., 272
Gambrill, E., 350, 352 (box)

Neufeld, R., 472
Neville, K., 56
Newgren, K. P., 237 (box)
Newman, C. F., 271, 283, 284
Newman, M. L., 244
Newman, R., 50
Nezami, E., 237
Nezu, A. M., 83
Nezworski, M. T., 184,
    185 (table), 209, 236 (box),
    250, 481
Ng, V., 429
Niaura, R., 464
Nichols, D. S., 82
Nichols, M. P., 405, 407,
    411 (box), 413, 415, 417
Nickerson, K., 474
Nicotera, N., 427
Nieberding, R., 185, 225, 250
Nisbett, R. E., 211
Nock, M. K., 143, 202, 435
Norcross, J. C., 5, 6, 7, 8 (box),
    10, 13 (table),
    14, 16 (box), 19, 20, 21,
    41, 53, 54, 56,
    60, 61, 185, 264, 271, 272,
    273, 274, 276 (box), 277,
    278 (box), 279, 280 (table),
    281, 282 (table), 283, 284,
    310, 363, 367, 390
Nordby, V. J., 292

Oades-Sese, G. V., 438
O'Brien, C. P., 163
O'Brien, W. H., 200, 435
O'Connor, K. J., 447, 448, 449
O'Donohue, W., 41, 368
Ogilvie, J., 62, 268
Ogles, B. M., 268, 270, 271, 274
Ogloff, J.R.P., 479
Oh, D., 390
Okagaki, L., 222 (box)
Okasha, A., 111 (box)
Okun, B. F., 78, 95
Olatunji, B. O., 372, 373,
    384, 390
Olfson, M., 64
Olitzky, S. L., 438
Olkin, R., 278 (box)

Ollendick, T. H., 54, 255, 276,
    441, 450
Olsen, D. C., 120
O'Neil, P., 473
Ordway, L., 471
Organista, P. B., 89, 134 (box)
Orlinsky, D. E., 273, 305
Ormont, L. R., 398, 400
Ornstein, R. M., 164, 166
Orsillo, S. M., 384, 390
Ortiz, S. O., 220
Osterberg, L. D., 62
Ostermann, R. F., 247
Oswald, J. C., 389
Othmer, E. O., 189, 190, 193
Othmer, S. C., 189, 190, 193
Ott, E. S., 442
Otto, R. K., 480, 489
Owen, J. J., 82

Palmer, B. W., 122, 146
Palmero, F., 457
Paradis, C. M., 379 (box)
Parham, T. A., 119
Paris, J., 62, 63, 64, 65, 160,
    161, 162, 163,
    164, 166, 167, 390
Park-Taylor, J., 429,
    430 (box), 438
Parker, G., 165, 168
Parron, D. L., 172
Parry, P., 123
Patterson, G. R., 361
Patterson, T. G., 332
Paul, G. L., 279
Paves, A. P., 68
Pavlov, I., 340, 341,
    345, 346, 347
Pawlow, L., 468, 473
Pawlowski, S., 471
Pedersen, P. B., 76, 94
Pedrotti, J. T., 332
Peel, Sir R., 488
Pelco, L. E., 138
Penley, J. A., 136
Pennebaker, J., 461, 469
Perez, R. M., 88 (box)
Perls, F. S., 329
Perry, K. M., 5

Persons, J. B., 233
Peter, M. I., 109
Peterson, C., 248, 331, 332
Peterson, D. R., 10
Peterson, R. L., 10
Petry, N. M., 163
Petry, S., 410
Pettibone, J. C., 68,
    108, 120
Phillips, J., 162
Photos, V. I., 202, 435
Pian, J., 442
Pickren, W. E., 16, 39 (box),
    40 (box)
Pierre, J. M., 62, 63, 65, 162,
    164
Pieterse, A. L., 221
Pike, K. L., 93
Pilgrim, D., 171
Pina, A. A., 441, 450
Pina-Camacho, L., 166
Pincus, D. B., 442
Pincus, H. A., 176, 441
Pinel, P., 28–29, 30, 32,
    46, 157
Pines, A., 120
Piotrowski, C., 237
Pittner, M., 458
Poling, A., 353, 354, 355
Pomerantz, A. M., 67, 68, 107,
    108, 115, 119,
    120, 121, 123, 223
Pope, K. S., 104, 106, 107, 115,
    116, 117, 501 (box),
    502 (box)
Porter, D., 161, 165
Poston, J. M., 244
Powers, S. W., 450
Poythress, N. G., 493
Pretzer, J., 374 (table)
Prince, S. S., 373
Prochaska, J. O., 41, 273,
    274, 276 (box), 281, 283,
    310, 363, 390
Pruitt-Stephens, L., 206
Puente, A. E., 237
Pulier, M. L., 69
Pull, C. B., 162
Purcell, D. W., 372 (box)

Subject Index

ABAB design, 143
ABCDE model
  as applied to clinical example, 377 (table)
  to understand impact of cognitions on emotions, 375–377
ABCDS of weight loss, 462–463
ABCs of relapse prevention, 465
Abnormality
  clinical research and practice on, 151
  considering cultural context to define, 152 (box)–153 (box)
  family therapy focus on family's overall functioning vs., 407
  importance of definition for professionals and clients, 155–156
  medical model of psychopathology to identify symptoms of, 154
  what defines, 152
  who defines, 153–154
Abu Ghraib prison, 501 (box)–502 (box)
Academy of Psychological Clinical Science, 9
Acceptance, 383
Acceptance and commitment therapy (ACT), 385–386
Acculturation
  description and process of, 89
  different strategies for, 89
Achievement
  definition of, 10
  intelligence versus, 221, 222–223
  testing for, 214 (table), 223
Achievement tests
  Gray Oral Reading, 223
  KeyMath, 223

Wechsler Individual Achievement Test (WIAT), 214 (table)
Wechsler Individual Achievement Test–Third Edition (WIAT-III), 223
ACT (accepting, choosing, taking action), 386
Actions feedback, 407
Activating event, 375
Actuarial prediction methods, 484
Addictive behaviors
  Substance use disorder, 166
  urge surfing approach to treating, 384–385
ADHD (attention-deficit/hyperactivity disorder)
  assessment methods used for, 135
  cognitive-behavioral therapies for, 441
  DSM-V criteria for diagnosis of, 166
  research on diagnostic issues of, 136
  treatment efficacy for, 450
Adolescent assessment
  comprehensive, 432–433
  developmental perspective and cultural context of, 429–432 (box)
  Millon Clinical Multiaxial Inventory-III (MCMI-III) for, 245, 436–437
  Minnesota Multiphasic Personality Inventory-Adolescent (MMPI-A) for, 38, 243, 436–437
  multisource, multimethod, multisetting assessment approach to, 432–433
Adolescent assessment techniques

behavior rating scales, 436
behavioral observations, 435–436
frequency of use of specific, 438–440 (table)
intellectual tests, 438
interviews, 434–435
projective/expressive, 437–438
self-report scales, 436–437
Adolescents
  confidentiality when it concerns child client, 110–111, 113 (photo)
  family conflict triangles and "taking sides" by, 414
  psychotherapy with children and, 440–451
  See also Children; Clinical child psychology; Parent-client relationships
African Americans
  communication style of, 191 (box)
  cultural competence with clients among, 86 (box)
  cultural sensitivity as essential for child play therapy, 446–447
  how history impacts the health psychology of, 474–475
  "parentified" child taking adult role among, 429
  population identification as, 76
Ahistorical style of family therapy, 413
Alcohol use/abuse, 462 (table), 465–466
Alcoholics Anonymous (AA), 466
All-or-nothing thinking, 380

Arab parent-child relationships, 431 (photo)
Argosy University graduate program, 13 (table)
Army Alpha intelligence test, 39 (box)
Army Beta intelligence test, 39 (box)
Asian Americans/Pacific Islanders
  communication style of, 190 (box)–191 (box)
  cultural competence with clients among, 85 (box)
  cultural concepts of distress among, 81
  cultural context of health psychology and, 475
  culture-specific expectations about psychotherapy by, 266 (box)–267 (box)
  increasing population percentage of, 76
  major depressive episode symptoms of, 459 (box)
Asians
  Asian Indian parent-child relationships, 431 (box)
  cultural competence with clients among, 85 (box)
  interpretation of child drawing tests and influence of anime on, 438
Aspirational ethics, 104, 105 (table)
Assertiveness training
  considering culture and collectivist values in, 351 (box)–352 (box)
  description and process of, 350–351
Assessment
  achievement tests, 214 (table), 223
  of ADHD, 135
  APA's "Ethical Principles of Psychologists and Code of Conduct" (APA) on interpreting, 80 (table)

behavioral, 255–257
of children and adolescents, 429–440 (table)
clinical research on, 135–136
Conflict Tactics Scales (CTS), 412
cultural competence, 234–235
diagnostic issues of, 32–35 (box)
DSM multiaxial assessment system, 33, 158, 163–164
DSM-V revisions of methods for, 82
ethics in clinical, 121
evidence-based, 232–234
families, 409 (figure)–413
feedback element of all kinds of, 184
forensic psychology, 481–483 (table)
intelligence tests, 35–37, 213–221
multimethod, 232
neuropsychological tests, 210, 214 (table), 224–227
personality tests, 37–38, 136, 237–248
strength-based, 247
Therapeutic Assessment (TA), 244
validity, reliability, and utility of clinical, 184, 185 (table)
See also Clinical interviews
Attending behaviors, 187
Attention (or Hawthrone effect), 273–274
Attenuated psychosis symptoms, 35 (box)
Attenuated psychosis syndrome, 155, 163
Autism spectrum disorder, 165–166
Automatic thoughts, 371

Bandura, Albert, 359
Base rate, 487
Baselines, 344

Beck, Aaron, 248, 368 (photo), 379–380
Beck Depression Inventory, 233
Beck Depression Inventory-II (BDI-II), 136, 248
Beck, Judith, 379
Behavior Assessment System for Children, 435, 436
Behavior change
  ABCDS of weight loss, 462–463
  behavioral consultation for, 360–361
  "change talk" used for, 330–331
  classical conditioning and techniques for, 345–346, 347–352 (box)
  as goal of behavioral psychotherapy, 341–345
  observable, 344–345
  operant conditioning and techniques for, 346–347, 352–360
  parent training for, 361 (photo)–632
  teacher training for, 362
  See also Behaviors
Behavior rating scales, 436
Behavioral activation, 358–359
Behavioral assessment
  behavioral or naturalistic observation, 256–257
  description of, 255–256
  technology for self-monitoring by clients, 257
  traditional methods for, 257
Behavioral consultation, 360–361
Behavioral medicine, 454
Behavioral observation
  child and adolescent assessment using, 435–436
  description of, 256–257
  reactivity to, 435
Behavioral psychotherapy
  alternatives to, 360–362

professional self-views of, 21 (figure)

psychiatrists compared to, 21–22

school psychologists compared to, 23

social workers compared to, 22

See also Psychologists

Clinical psychology

cultural issues to consider in, 76–101

education and training in, 5–6, 40 (box)

more recent definitions of, 4–5

original definition of, 4

origins and historic evolution of, 28–46

See also Psychology

Clinical psychology controversies

cybertherapy and influence of technology, 68–72

evidence-based practice and manualized therapy, 54–62 (box)

overexpansion of mental disorders, 62–66, 167–168

payment methods, 66–68

prescription privileges, 50–54 (box)

Clinical psychology graduate programs

clinical research on training and, 138–139

comparing general PhD to PsyD, 7 (box)–8 (box)

comparison of PsyD and PhD programs, 8 (table)

information on specific graduate programs, 11 (table)–13 (table)

interview questions to anticipate, 16 (box)

predoctoral and postdoctoral internships associated with, 16–17, 139

suggestions for getting into a, 10, 14–16

training in cultural issues included in, 80–81, 97–99

Clinical psychology historic development

of assessment procedures, 32–38

development of the profession, 41–43

early pioneers of, 28–30

influence of war on, 39 (box)–40 (box)

Lightner Witmer's significant role in, 30–32

of psychotherapy, 39–41

timeline of key events in the, 43 (box)–45 (box)

Clinical psychology models

clinical scientist, 9–10

practitioner-scholar (or Vail) model, 6–7

scientists-practitioner (or Boulder) model, 6, 9, 40 (box)

Clinical psychology practice

places and settings of, 18 (photo)–19

professional activities associated with, 19 (photo)–20

Clinical psychology training

APA's accreditation standards on multiculturalism program, 80–81

clinical research on teaching and, 138–139

in cultural issues, 97–99

emphasis on specific competencies during, 10

getting licensed, 17–18

graduate programs for, 7 (box)–16 (box)

improved evidence-based practice/manualized therapy, 59

predoctoral and postdoctoral internships, 16–17

prescription privileges and issue of, 52–53

Veterans Administration's request for APA to formalize, 40 (box)

Clinical research

allegiance effects in, 311 (box)–312 (box)

on assessment methods, 135–136

considering culture in, 133 (box)–135 (box)

on diagnostic issues, 136–137

on efficacy versus effectiveness, 132–133

ethical issues in, 121–122, 146 (box)

internal versus external validity issue of, 133

on professional issues, 137 (photo)–138

on psychotherapy outcomes, 264–266

on resilience and vulnerability in children, 427–429 (box)

on teaching and training issues, 138–139

on treatment outcome, 130–131 (box)

Clinical research design

analogue designs, 141

between-group versus within-group designs, 140–141

case studies, 142–143

correlational methods, 141–142

cross-sectional versus longitudinal designs, 145

experimental method, 139

meta-analysis, 143–145 (box)

quasi-experiments, 139–140

Clinical scale, 240

Clinical scientist model, 9–10

Clinical utility, 184, 185 (table)

Closed-ended questions, 193–194 (box)

Closed-enrollment groups, 401

China's *Chinese Classification of Mental Disorders*
  alternative to, 161
  compared to *DSM-II,* 159 (table)–160 (table)
  compared to other *DSM* editions, 158
  consideration of culture in, 169 (box)–170 (box), 172–173
  controversial cutoffs, 171–172
  controversy surrounding the, 166–169
  criticisms of the, 170–176
  development of NIMH's Research Domain Criteria (RDoC) alternative of, 168
  gender bias in, 173
  International Classification of Diseases (ICD) alternative to, 161
  limitations on objectivity, 176
  major depressive episode, 165, 459 (box)
  new disorders included in, 164–165
  new features in, 163–164
  nonempirical influences, 175
  overview of the development of, 160–161
  premenstrual dysphoric disorder (PMDD), 173 (box)–175 (box)
  revised disorders in, 165–166
DSM-V (Diagnostic and Statistical Manual of Mental Disorders) [2013]
  anxiety neurosis/generalized anxiety disorder as defined in, 159 (table)–176
  broad definition of mental disorder in the, 153–154
  controversy surrounding the, 166–169
  Cultural Formulation Interview included in the, 172
  decisions regarding what to include or exclude in, 34 (box)–35 (box)
  description of, 33
  efforts toward multiculturalism, 81
  Glossary of Cultural Concepts of Distress in the, 169 (box)–170 (box)
  health insurance and managed-care requirements related to, 67–68, 123, 175
  Outline for Cultural Formulation included in the, 172
  overexpansion of mental disorders response by, 62–65, 167–168
  "proposed criteria sets" considered but rejected for the, 34 (box)–35 (box)
  revisions of prominent assessment methods in, 82
  See also Mental disorders
Durham v. United States, 489
Dusky v. United States, 492
Duty to warn
  rationale behind the, 109
  Tarasoff decision on, 108–109
Dyadic Parent-Child Interaction Coding System, 435
Dysfunctional Thought Record therapy
  attorneys arguing in court metaphor of, 382 (box)–383 (box)
  on beliefs as hypotheses, 381–382
  on common thought distortions, 380–381
  description of, 379–380

Eating disorders
  anorexia, 169 (box)–170 (box)
  binge eating disorder (BED), 164
  bulimia nervosa, 166, 169 (box)–170 (box)
  cultural context of, 169 (box)–170 (box)
  research on relationship between personality disorders and, 137
Eclectic psychotherapy
  description of, 283
  percentage of psychologists endorsing, 280 (table), 281
  understanding difference between integrative and, 284 (box)–285 (box)
Effective new belief, 393
Effectiveness of therapy, 132–133, 267, 269
Efficacy of therapy
  for ADHD, 450
  considering issue of culture, 133 (box)–135 (box)
  description and research on, 132, 267–269
  motivational interviewing (MI), 331
  play therapy, 449–450
  See also Psychotherapy outcomes; Treatment outcomes
Ego, 295–296, 297, 298
Ego psychology, 305
Electra complex, 305
Ellis, Albert, 368 (photo), 374–377 (table)
Emic perspective, 93
Emotional consequence, 375
Emotionally fused family members, 414
Emotions
  ABCDE model to understand impact of cognitions on, 375–377
  assertiveness training and value stance on expressing, 351 (box)–352 (box)

psychoneuroimmunology (PNI) on physical illness and, 456
reflection of feelings and, 195, 326–328 (box)
See also Fears

Empathy
cultural context of, 323 (box)–324 (box)
as essential therapeutic condition, 322

Empirical criterion keying
Amazon.com as example of, 239 (box)–240 (box)
description of, 238

Empirical data, 342

Empirical evidence, evidence-based practice/manualized therapy and debatable, 61–62

Endogenous disorders
dementia praecox (schizophrenia), 32
description of, 32

Enforceable rules of conduct
APA Code of Ethics' Ethical Standards on, 104–106
description of, 104

Enmeshed family membership, 414

Erikson's eight-stage theory of development, 305

Essay questions, 193 (box)–194 (box)

Ethical issues
APA guidelines when working with governmental agencies, 501 (box)–502 (box)
in clinical assessment, 121
in clinical research, 121–122, 146 (box)
cybertherapy and technology and related, 70–71, 123–124
ethical decision making by psychologists, 106–107
in family therapy, 417–418
group therapy, 403

informed consent, 70, 113–115, 482
managed care and, 122–123
multiple or dual relationships, 115–118, 124–126 (box)
Nuremberg ethic, Abu Ghrabi, and Guantanamo Bay, 501 (box)–502 (box)
payment method and related, 67
special issues when living in small communities, 124–125
test security, 121
See also American Psychological Association Code of Ethics; Confidentiality; Professional issues

"Ethical Principles of Psychologists and Code of Conduct" (APA), 79 (table)–80 (table)

Ethical Standards (APA Code of Ethics), 104–106

Ethnicity
APA's "Ethical Principles of Psychologists and Code of Conduct" relating to, 79 (table)–80 (table)
confidentiality in context of, 111 (box)–112 (box)
training psychologists in issues of, 97–99
See also Cultures; Multiculturalism

Ethnicity and Family Therapy (McGoldrick, Giordano, & Garcia-Preto), 78, 86 (box), 430 (box)

Etic perspective, 93

European Americans. *See* Whites

Evidence-based assessment, 232–234

Evidence-based practice/manualized therapy
advantages of, 58–59
client preference regarding, 62 (box)

culture as consideration for using, 277 (box)–279 (box)
definition of, 56
dialectical behavior therapy, 55–56
exposure plus response prevention, 55–56
professional debate over, 54–56
therapy manuals for, 55, 56 (box)–58 (box)

Evidence-Based Practices in Mental Health: Debate and Dialogue on the Fundamental Questions (Norcross, Beutler, & Levant), 278 (box)

Examination for Professional Practice in Psychology (EPPP), 18

Exception questions, 415

Existential psychotherapy, 329

Exner, John, 250

Exogenous disorders, 32

Experiential avoidance, 384

Experiential style of family therapy, 413

Experimental condition, 140

Experimental method, 139

Expert witnesses, 495–499

Exposure therapy
description of, 347–348
exposure plus response prevention form of, 55, 348
to overcome fear of dogs, 348, 349 (table)

External validity, 133

Externalizing disorders, 427

Extinction
description and process of, 354–355
extinction burst aspect of, 355
soda machine coin loss as metaphor for, 355 (box)–356 (box)

Extinction burse, 355

Informed consent
    APA Code of Ethics on,
        114–115
    cybertherapy and, 70
    description and issues related
        to, 113
    forensic psychology
        issue of, 482
Insanity defense, 483 (table),
    487–489
*Insider's Guide to Graduate
    Programs in Clinical and
    Counseling Psychology,* 10
Intake interviews, 199–200
Integrative psychotherapy
    description of, 283
    percentage of psychologists
        endorsing,
        280 (table), 281
    understanding difference
        between eclectic and,
        284 (box)–285 (box)
Intellectual disability (intellectual
    development disorder), 166
Intelligence
    achievement versus, 221,
        222–223
    assessment of, 35–37,
        210–221
    contemporary theories of, 211
    crystallized, 211
    cultural context of, 221
        (box)–222 (box)
    definition of, 210
    fluid, 211
    "g" (general intelligence)
        measure of, 210
    hierarchical model of, 211
    Michael Jordan as example of
        complexity
        of defining, 212 (box)–
        213 (box)
    Spearman's intelligence is one
        thing theory
        of, 210
    three-stratum theory of, 211
    Thurstone's intelligence is
        many things theory
        of, 211

Intelligence tests
    addressing cultural fairness of,
        219–221
    Army Alpha and Beta,
        39 (box)
    at-a-glance chart on the,
        214 (table)
    definition of, 210
    full-scale intelligence score,
        index scores, and subtest
        scores of, 213
    the Stanford-Binet Intelligence
        Scales, 36, 214 (table),
        218–219
    Universal Nonverbal
        Intelligence Test
        (UNIT), 214 (table),
        219–221, 438
    Wodnerlic intelligence
        quotient (IQ) test, 482
    See also Wechsler intelligence
        tests
Internal validity, 133
Internalizing, 427
*International Classification of
    Diseases* (ICD), 161
Internet gaming disorder,
    35 (box), 163
Internships
    clinical research on, 139
    predoctoral and postdoctoral,
        16–17
Interpersonal learning
    as heart of group
        therapy, 398
    here-and-now relationship in
        group therapy
        and, 399–400
    social microcosm of group
        therapy contributing to,
        398–399
Interpersonal therapy (IPT),
    306–308
Interpretation of the
    transference, 300
Interview rooms, 197–198 (box)
Interviews
    child and adolescent
        assessment, 434–435

child custody evaluation use
    of, 492
Cultural Formulation
    Interview (*DSM*-V), 172
Diagnostic Interview Schedule
    for Children-Version
    4 (DISC-IV), 135
motivational interviewing
    (MI), 329–331
See also Clinical interviews
Introspection, 345
Involuntary commitment, 494
Inwald Personality
    Inventory, 500
Iranian parent-child
    relationships,
    431 (box)
Irish American clients, 86 (box)

Jackson v. Indiana, 493
Jewish American clients, cultural
    competence with,
    87 (box)–88 (box)
Jewish parent-child
    relationships, 430 (box)
Jordan, Michael,
    212 (box)–213 (box)

KeyMath achievement
    test, 223
Kinetic Family Drawing
    technique, 437–438
Knowledge
    description of, 219
    Stanford-Binet scale on,
        218–219
Kraepelin, Emil, 32

Language issues
    forensic psychology and,
        496 (box)
    research on English and
        Spanish versions of
        assessment tests, 136
    vocal qualities, 188
Latent content, 293
Latinos/Latinas/Hispanics
    communication style
    of, 191 (box)

triangles formed during conflict in the, 414
See also Adolescents; Clients; Families; Relationships
"Parentified" child, 429
Patient-centered medical homes (PCMHs), 473–474
Patient's rights, 499–500
Pavlov, Ivan, 340–341
Pavlov's dog studies, 340, 345–346
Payment methods
    effect on diagnosis by, 67–68
    effect on therapy by, 66–67
    managed care requirement for *DSM* diagnosis for, 67–68, 123, 175
    third-party vs. self-payment, 66
Pediatric psychology, 426
Perceptual Reasoning Index (Wechsler tests), 215
Persistent complex bereavement, 35 (box)
Personality
    assessment of, 37–38
    disease-pron, 457
    five-factor model of, 177, 178 (box)
Personality disorders
    DSM-V inclusion of, 162
    research on diagnostic issues of, 137
    research on relationship between eating disorders and, 137
Personality tests
    Beck Depression Inventory-II (BDI-II), 136, 248
    California Psychological Inventory-III (CPI-III), 247–248
    Children's Apperception Test (CAT), 254
    considering culture-specific norms for, 235 (box)–237 (box)
    Draw-a-Person test, 37, 437

Incomplete Sentence Blank, 37
Inwald Personality Inventory, 500
Millon Clinical Multiaxial Inventory-III (MCMI-III), 245, 436–437
Minnesota Multiphasic Personality Inventory (MMPI), 38, 82, 239 (box)–240 (box), 241 (table), 242–245
Minnesota Multiphasic Personality Inventory-2 (MMPI-2), 38, 82, 136, 235 (box)–237 (box), 235 (box)–238 (box), 241 (table), 243–245, 482, 483 (table)
Minnesota Multiphasic Personality Inventory-2 Restructured Form (MMPI-2-RF), 243–244
Minnesota Multiphasic Personality Inventory-Adolescent (MMPI-A), 38, 243, 436–437
NEO Five Factor Inventory (NEO-FFI), 247
NEO Personality Inventory (NEO-PI), 38
NEO Personality Inventory-Revised (NEO-PI-R), 245–247
    objective, 237–248
    projective, 249–255
Rorschach Inkblot Method and Comprehensive System, 37, 250–252, 437, 482, 483 (table)
Rotter Incomplete Sentences Blank (RISB), 254–255
Senior Apperception Test (SAT), 254
Tell-Me-a-Story (TEMAS), 254, 537

Thematic Apperception Test (TAT), 37, 252–254, 437, 482, 483 (table)
    as traditional personality assessment, 255
Personalization, 380
Pharmaceutical industry
    influence on overexpansion of mental health disgnoses by the, 64–65
    prescription privileges and potential influence of, 54
Phobia treatment, 441–442
Physicial illness
    disease-pron personality that predisposes, 457
    focus of clinical health psychology on, 462 (table)
    psychoneuroimmunology (PNI) on emotions triggering, 456
    stress and relationship to, 455–457
Pinel, Philippe, 28–29, 30, 46
Play therapy
    cultural sensitivity as essential for, 446–447
    description of, 446
    humanistic, 448–449
    psychodynamic, 447–448
Positive psychology, 247, 331–332
Positive punishment, 353–354
Positive regard, 319
Positive reinforcement, 353–354
Postdoctoral internships, 17
Posttraumatic stress disorder, 40 (box)
Practitioner-scholar (or Vail) model, 6–7, 9
Predicting dangerousness, 483 (table), 484–487
Predoctoral internship, 16–17
Preemployment evaluations, 500
Premenstrual dysphoric disorder (PMDD), 164, 173 (box)–175 (box)
Prescription privileges

influence of war on, 39 (box)–40 (box)

involvement in different formats of, 282 (table)

prediction of future trends in, 283

prescription privileges perceived as threat to, 53

research on outcomes of, 264–266

stages of change model on client process during, 281–283

tripartite model of, 264–265

See also Denise (fictional client); Therapies; Therapists

Psychotherapy approaches
humanistic, 41, 317–337
psychodynamic, 280 (table), 281, 289–315

Psychotherapy formats
couples/marital, 282 (table)
family, 41, 282 (table)
group, 282 (table)
individual, 282 (table)

Psychotherapy orientations
behavioral, 280 (table)
cognitive therapy, 280 (table), 281
eclectic/integrative, 280 (table), 281, 283–285 (box)
humanistic/Rogerian/ existential/gestalt, 280 (table)
psychodynamic/ psychoanalytic, 280 (table), 281

Psychotherapy outcomes
alternative ways to measure, 269–270
behavioral psychotherapy, 363
for children and adolescents, 449–450
cognitive therapy, 390
efficacy versus effectiveness of, 132–135 (box), 267–269
family therapy, 418–419

group therapy, 403

how the "dodo bird verdict" applies to, 271, 276–277, 279

humanistic psychotherapy, 333–334

which types of psychotherapy has the best, 270–279 (box)

See also Efficacy of therapy; Treatment outcomes

Psychotherapy relationships
boundaries of multiple relationships and, 115–118, 124–126 (box)
as common factor in psychotherapy, 271–273, 274 (photo)
cultural competence that may impact the, 82–112 (box)
developing positive working, 187
evidence-based practice/ manualized therapy threat to, 59–60
informed consent as establishing collaborative, 115
payment method as factor in, 66–68
therapeutic or working alliance aspect of, 272–273

See also Clients; Competence; Relationships

Psychotherapy with Women (Mirkin, Suyemoto, & Okun), 78

PsyD programs
comparing general PhD to, 7 (box)–8 (box)
comparison of clinical psychology PhD and, 8 (table)

Punishment, 353–354

Quantitative reasoning, 219

Quasi-experiments, 139–140

Questions. *See* Clinical interview questions

Quieting yourself, 189

Rapport
child and adolescent interviews and importance of, 434–435
description of, 189
established between clinical interviewer and client, 189–190

Rational Emotive Behavior Therapy (REBT), 374–375

Re-pairing (or counterconditioning), 349

Reaction formation, 296

Reactivity to observation, 435

Real self, 320

Recapitulation of the family group, 402

Reflection
of feelings, 195, 327
humanistic therapist and, 326
magnifying mirror metaphor for, 328 (box)

The Regents of the University of California, Tarasoff v., 108–109, 113

Reinforcement
description of, 353
four varieties of, 353–354

Relationships
group therapy social microcosm impact on clients' other, 398–399
group therapy's here-and-now, 399 (photo)–400
multiple or dual, 115–118, 124–126 (box)
parent-client, 99–100
social support benefit of, 460–461

See also Families; Parent-client relationships; Psychotherapy relationships

Working alliance,
272–273
Working with Asian Americans
(Lee), 78
Working memory
description
of, 219

Working Memory Index
(Wechsler tests)
measure of, 215
Working through
process, 300
World Health Organization
(WHO), 161

Yale University graduate
program, 11 (table)
Yalom, Irvin, 396
Yao Ming, 90 (box)–91 (box)
York Retreat, 28
Youngberg v. Romeo, 499–500
Youtsey v. United States, 492

⑤SAGE researchmethods

The essential online tool for researchers from the world's leading methods publisher

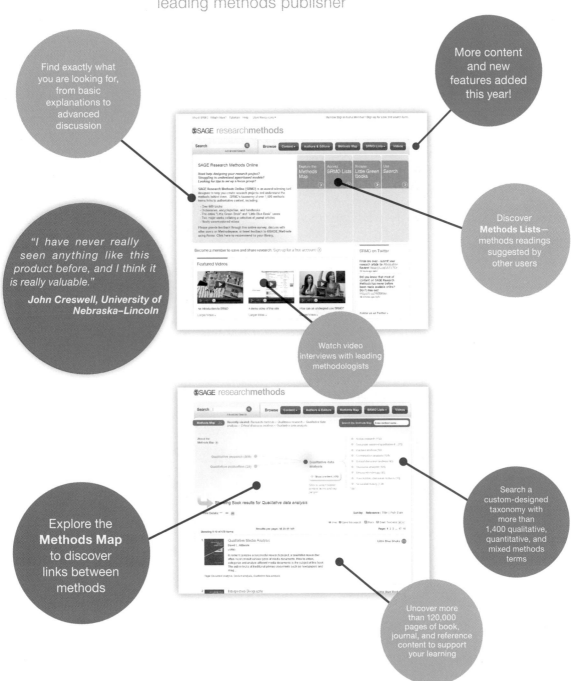

Find exactly what you are looking for, from basic explanations to advanced discussion

More content and new features added this year!

"I have never really seen anything like this product before, and I think it is really valuable."

John Creswell, University of Nebraska–Lincoln

Discover **Methods Lists**— methods readings suggested by other users

Watch video interviews with leading methodologists

Explore the **Methods Map** to discover links between methods

Search a custom-designed taxonomy with more than 1,400 qualitative, quantitative, and mixed methods terms

Uncover more than 120,000 pages of book, journal, and reference content to support your learning

Find out more at
www.sageresearchmethods.com